H. IGOR ANSOFF

# H. IGOR ANSOFF

Critical Evaluations in Business and Management

*Edited by John C. Wood and Michael C. Wood*

**Volume II**

LONDON AND NEW YORK

First published 2007
by Routledge
2 Park Square, Milton Park, Abingdon, Oxon, OX14 4RN, UK

Simultaneously published in the USA and Canada
by Routledge
270 Madison Avenue, New York, NY 10016

*Routledge is an imprint of the Taylor & Francis Group, an informa business*



Typeset in 10/12pt Times by Graphicraft Limited, Hong Kong
Printed and bound in Great Britain by
MPG Books Ltd., Bodmin, Cornwall



*British Library Cataloguing in Publication Data*
A catalogue record for this book is available from the British Library

*Library of Congress Cataloging in Publication Data*
A catalog record for this book has been requested

ISBN10: 0-415-32557-9 (Set)
ISBN10: 0-415-32559-5 (Volume II)

ISBN13: 978-0-415-32557-8 (Set)
ISBN13: 978-0-415-32559-2 (Volume II)

**Publisher's Note**

References within each chapter are as they appear in the original complete work.

# CONTENTS

# ACKNOWLEDGEMENTS

The Publishers would like to thank the following for permission to reprint their material:

Reprinted by permission, Mintzberg, H., 'Managerial work: analysis from observation', *Management Science*, 18, 2, Application series: B97–B110 (1971) © the Institute for Operations Research and the Management Sciences (INFORMS), 7240 Parkway Drive, Suite 310, Hanover, MD 21076, USA.

Reprinted by permission, Mintzberg, H., 'Patterns in strategy formation', *Management Science*, 24, 9: 934–948 (1978) © the Institute for Operations Research and the Management Sciences (INFORMS), 7240 Parkway Drive, Suite 310, Hanover, MD 21076, USA.

Harvard Business School Publications for permission to reprint Mintzberg, H. (1987) 'Crafting strategy', *Harvard Business Review*, 65, 4: 66–75.

Elsevier for permission to reprint Mintzberg, H. (1993) 'Twenty-five years later . . . the illusive strategy', in A. G. Bedeian (ed.) *Management Laureates: Collection of Autobiographical Essays* (vol. 2), pp. 321–374, Stamford, CT: JAI Press.

Harvard Business School Publications for permission to reprint Mintzberg, H. (1994) 'The fall and rise of strategic planning', *Harvard Business Review*, 72, 1: 107–114.

Reprinted by permission, Meising, P. and Wolfe, J., 'The art and science of planning at the business unit level', *Management Science*, 31, 6: 773–781 (1985) © the Institute for Operations Research and Management Sciences (INFORMS), 7240 Parkway Drive, Suite 310, Hanover, MD 21076, USA.

Elsevier for permission to reprint Camillus, J. C. and Datta, D. K. (1991) 'Managing strategic issues in a turbulent environment', *Long Range Planning*, 24, 2: 67–74.

John Wiley & Sons, Ltd for permission to reprint Barnett, W. B. and Burgelman, R. A. (1996) 'Evolutionary perspectives on strategy', *Strategic Management Journal*, 17: 5–19. Reproduced by permission of John Wiley & Sons Limited.

John Wiley & Sons, Ltd for permission to reprint Dutton, J. E. and Duncan, R. B. (1987) 'The creation of momentum for change through the process of strategic issue diagnosis', *Strategic Management Journal*, 8, 3: 279–295. Reproduced by permission of John Wiley & Sons Limited.

John Wiley & Sons, Ltd for permission to reprint Wissema, J. G., van der Pol, H. W. and Messer, H. M. (1980) 'Strategic management archetypes', *Strategic Management Journal*, 1, 1: 37–47. Reproduced by permission of John Wiley & Sons Limited.

MIT *Sloan Management Review* for permission to reprint Williamson, P. J. (1999) 'Strategy as options on the future', *Sloan Management Review*: 117–126. © by Massachusetts Institute of Technology.

Reprinted by permission, Ackoff, R. L., 'Management misinformation systems', *Management Science*, 14, 4: B147–B156 (1967) © the Institute for Operations Research and the Management Sciences (INFORMS), 7240 Parkway Drive, Suite 310, Hanover, MD 21076, USA.

John Wiley & Sons, Ltd for permission to reprint Christensen, H. K. and Montogomery, C. A. (1981) 'Corporate economic performance: diversification strategy versus market structure', *Strategic Management Journal*, 2, 4: 327–343. Reproduced by permission of John Wiley & Sons Limited.

John Wiley & Sons, Ltd for permission to reprint Fahey, L. (1981) 'On strategic management decision processes', *Strategic Management Journal*, 2, 1: 43–60. Reproduced by permission of John Wiley & Sons Limited.

Reprinted by permission, Jemison, D. B., 'Risk and the relationship among strategy, organizational processes, and performance', *Management Science*, 33, 9: 1087–1101 (1987) © the Institute for Operations Research and the Management Sciences (INFORMS), 7240 Parkway Drive, Suite 310, Hanover, MD 21076, USA.

Reprinted by permission, Segev, E., 'Strategy, strategy making and performance: an empirican investigation', *Management Science*, 33, 2: 258–269 (1987) © the Institute for Operations Research and the Management Sciences (INFORMS), 7240 Parkway Drive, Suite 310, Hanover, MD 21076, USA.

Harvard Business School Publications for permission to reprint Hamel, G. and Prahalad, C. K. (1989) 'Strategic intent', *Harvard Business Review*, 67, 3: 63–76.

John Wiley & Sons, Ltd for permission to reprint Goold, M. (1992) 'Design, learning and planning: a further observation on the design school debate', *Strategic Management Journal*, 13, 2: 169–170. Reproduced by permission of John Wiley & Sons Limited.

Harvard Business School Publications for permission to reprint Stalk, G., Evans, P. and Schulman, L. E. (1992) 'Competing on capabilitites: the new rules of corporate strategy', *Harvard Business Review*, 70, 2.

Emerald Group Publishing Limited for permission to reprint Nwankwo, S. and Richardson, B. (1996) 'Quality management through visionary leadership', *Managing Service Quality*, 6, 4: 44–47.

Elsevier for permission to reprint Kaufman, B. E. (2001) 'The theory and practice of strategic HRM and participative management: antecedents in early industrial relations', *Human Resource Management Review*, 11, 4: 505–533.

John Wiley & Sons, Ltd for permission to reprint Arcelus, F. J. and Schaefer, N. V. (1982) 'Social demands as strategic issues: some conceptual problems', *Strategic Management Journal*, 3, 4: 347–357. Reproduced by permission of John Wiley & Sons Limited.

John Wiley & Sons, Ltd for permission to reprint Reed, R. and Luffman, G. A. (1986) 'Diversification: the growing confusion', *Strategic Management Journal*, 7, 1: 29–35. Reproduced by permission of John Wiley & Sons Limited.

John Wiley & Sons, Ltd for permission to reprint Ginsberg, A. (1988) 'Measuring and modelling changes in strategy: theoretical foundations and empirical directions', *Strategic Management Journal*, 9, 6: 559–575. Reproduced by permission of John Wiley & Sons Limited.

John Wiley & Sons, Ltd for permission to reprint Singer, A. E. (1994) 'Strategy as moral philosophy', *Strategic Management Journal*, 15, 3: 191–213. Reproduced by permission of John Wiley & Sons Limited.

Harvard Business School Publications for permission to reprint Hamel, G. (1996) 'Strategy as revolution', *Harvard Business Review*, 74, 4: 69–71, 74–82.

Harvard Business School Publications for permission to reprint Mintzberg, H. (1996) 'Musings on management', *Harvard Business Review*, 74, 4: 61–67.

Sage Publications for permission to reprint Caldwell, R. (2005) 'Things fall apart? Discourses on agency and change in organizations', *Human Relations*, 58, 1: 83–114.

## Disclaimer

# Part 2

# STRATEGIC MANAGEMENT, continued

23

# MANAGERIAL WORK

## Analysis from observation

*Henry Mintzberg*

Source: *Management Science* 18(2), Application series (1971): B97–B110.

The progress of management science is dependent on our understanding of the manager's working processes. A review of the literature indicates that this understanding is superficial at best. Empirical study of the work of five managers (supported by those research findings that are available) led to the following description: Managers perform ten basic roles which fall into three groupings. The interpersonal roles describe the manager as figurehead, external liaison, and leader; the information processing roles describe the manager as the nerve center of his organization's information system; and the decision-making roles suggest that the manager is at the heart of the system by which organizational resource allocation, improvement, and disturbance decisions are made. Because of the huge burden of responsibility for the operation of these systems, the manager is called upon to perform his work at an unrelenting pace, work that is characterized by variety, discontinuity and brevity. Managers come to prefer issues that are current, specific, and ad hoc, and that are presented in verbal form. As a result, there is virtually no science in managerial work .The management scientist has done little to change this. He has been unable to understand work which has never been adequately described, and he has poor access to the manager's information, most of which is never documented. We must describe managerial work more precisely, and we must model the manager as a programmed system. Only then shall we be able to make a science of management.

What do managers do? Ask this question and you will likely be told that managers plan, organize, coordinate, and control. Since Henri Fayol [9] first proposed these words in 1916, they have dominated the vocabulary of management. (See, for example, [8], [12], [17].) How valuable are they in describing managerial work? Consider one morning's work of the president of a large organization:

> As he enters his office at 8:23, the manager's secretary motions for him to pick up the telephone. "Jerry, there was a bad fire in the plant last night, about $30,000 damage. We should be back in operation by Wednesday. Thought you should know."
>
> At 8:45, a Mr. Jamison is ushered into the manager's office. They discuss Mr. Jamison's retirement plans and his cottage in New Hampshire. Then the manager presents a plaque to him commemorating his thirty-two years with the organization.
>
> Mail processing follows: An innocent-looking letter, signed by a Detroit lawyer, reads: "A group of us in Detroit has decided not to buy any of your products because you used that anti-flag, anti-American pinko, Bill Lindell, upon your Thursday night TV show." The manager dictates a restrained reply.
>
> The 10:00 meeting is scheduled by a professional staffer. He claims that his superior, a high-ranking vice-president of the organization, mistreats his staff, and that if the man is not fired, they will all walk out. As soon as the meeting ends, the manager rearranges his schedule to investigate the claim and to react to this crisis.

Which of these activities may be called planning, and which may be called organizing, coordinating, and controlling? Indeed, what do words such as "coordinating" and "planning" mean in the context of real activity? In fact, these four words do not describe the actual work of managers at all; they describe certain vague objectives of managerial work. ". . . they are just ways of indicating what we need to explain." [1, p. 537]

Other approaches to the study of managerial work have developed, one dealing with managerial decision-making and policy-making processes, another with the manager's interpersonal activities. (See, for example, [2] and [10].) And some empirical researchers, using the "diary" method, have studied, what might be called, managerial "media"—by what means, with whom, how long, and where managers spend their time.[1] But in no part of this literature is the actual content of managerial work systematically and meaningfully described.[2] Thus, the question posed at the start—what do managers do?—remains essentially unanswered in the literature of management.

This is indeed an odd situation. We claim to teach management in schools of both business and public administration; we undertake major research programs in management; we find a growing segment of the management science community concerned with the problems of senior management.

Most of these people—the planners, information and control theorists, systems analysts, etc.—are attempting to analyze and change working habits that they themselves do not understand. Thus, at a conference called at M.I.T. to assess the impact of the computer on the manager, and attended by a number of America's foremost management scientists, a participant found it necessary to comment after lengthy discussion [20, p. 198]:

> I'd like to return to an earlier point. It seems to me that until we get into the question of what the top manager does or what the functions are that define the top management job, we're not going to get out of the kind of difficulty that keeps cropping up. What I'm really doing is leading up to my earlier question which no one really answered. And that is: Is it possible to arrive at a specification of what constitutes the job of a top manager?

His question was not answered.

## Research study on managerial work

In late 1966, I began research on this question, seeking to replace Fayol's words by a set that would more accurately describe what managers do. In essence, I sought to develop by the process of induction a statement of managerial work that would have empirical validity. Using a method called "structured observation", I observed for one-week periods the chief executives of five medium to large organizations (a consulting firm, a school system, a technology firm, a consumer goods manufacturer, and a hospital).

Structured as well as unstructured (i.e., anecdotal) data were collected in three "records". In the *chronology record*, activity patterns throughout the working day were recorded. In the *mail record*, for each of 890 pieces of mail processed during the five weeks, were recorded its purpose, format and sender, the attention it received and the action it elicited. And, recorded in the *contact record*, for each of 368 verbal interactions, were the purpose, the medium (telephone call, scheduled or unscheduled meeting, tour), the participants, the form of initiation, and the location. It should be noted that all categorizing was done during and after observation so as to ensure that the categories reflected only the work under observation. [19] contains a fuller description of this methodology and a tabulation of the results of the study.

Two sets of conclusions are presented below. The first deals with certain characteristics of managerial work, as they appeared from analysis of the numerical data (e.g., How much time is spent with peers? What is the average duration of meetings? What proportion of contacts are initiated by the manager himself?). The second describes the basic content of managerial work in terms of ten roles. This description derives from an analysis of the data on the recorded *purpose* of each contact and piece of mail.

The liberty is taken of referring to these findings as descriptive of managerial, as opposed to chief executive, work. This is done because many of the findings are supported by studies of other types of managers. Specifically, most of the conclusions on work characteristics are to be found in the combined results of a group of studies of foremen [11], [16], middle managers [4], [5], [15], [25], and chief executives [6]. And although there is little useful material on managerial roles, three studies do provide some evidence of the applicability of the role set. Most important, Sayles' empirical study of production managers [24] suggests that at least five of the ten roles are performed at the lower end of the managerial hierarchy. And some further evidence is provided by comments in Whyte's study of leadership in a street gang [26] and Neustadt's study of three U.S. presidents [21]. (Reference is made to these findings where appropriate.) Thus, although most of the illustrations are drawn from my study of chief executives, there is some justification in asking the reader to consider when he sees the terms "manager" and his "organization" not only "presidents" and their "companies", but also "foremen" and their "shops", "directors" and their "branches", "vice-presidents" and their "divisions". The term *manager* shall be used with reference to all those people in charge of formal organizations or their subunits.

## Some characteristics of managerial work

Six sets of characteristics of managerial work derive from analysis of the data of this study. Each has a significant bearing on the manager's ability to administer a complex organization.

### *Characteristic 1. The manager performs a great quantity of work at an unrelenting pace*

Despite a semblance of normal working hours, in truth managerial work appears to be very taxing. The five men in this study processed an average of thirty-six pieces of mail each day, participated in eight meetings (half of which were scheduled), engaged in five telephone calls, and took one tour. In his study of foremen, Guest [11] found that the number of activities per day averaged 583, with no real break in the pace.

Free time appears to be very rare. If by chance a manager has caught up with the mail, satisfied the callers, dealt with all the disturbances, and avoided scheduled meetings, a subordinate will likely show up to usurp the available time. It seems that the manager cannot expect to have much time for leisurely reflection during office hours. During "off" hours, our chief executives spent much time on work-related reading. High-level managers appear to be able to escape neither from an environment which recognizes the power and status of their positions nor from their own minds which have been trained to search continually for new information.

### *Characteristic 2. Managerial activity is characterized by variety, fragmentation, and brevity*

There seems to be no pattern to managerial activity. Rather, variety and fragmentation appear to be characteristic, as successive activities deal with issues that differ greatly both in type and in content. In effect the manager must be prepared to shift moods quickly and frequently.

A typical chief executive day may begin with a telephone call from a director who asks a favor (a "status request"); then a subordinate calls to tell of a strike at one of the facilities (fast movement of information, termed "instant communication"); this is followed by a relaxed scheduled event at which the manager speaks to a group of visiting dignitaries (ceremony); the manager returns to find a message from a major customer who is demanding the renegotiation of a contract (pressure); and so on. Throughout the day, the managers of our study encountered this great variety of activity. Most surprisingly, the significant activities were interspersed with the trivial in no particular pattern.

Furthermore, these managerial activities were characterized by their brevity. Half of all the activities studied lasted less than nine minutes and only ten percent exceeded one hour's duration. Guest's foremen averaged 48 seconds per activity, and Carlson [6] stressed that his chief executives were unable to work without frequent interruption.

In my own study of chief executives, I felt that the managers demonstrated a preference for tasks of short duration and encouraged interruption. Perhaps the manager becomes accustomed to variety, or perhaps the flow of "instant communication" cannot be delayed. A more plausible explanation might be that the manager becomes conditioned by his workload. He develops a sensitive appreciation for the opportunity cost of his own time. Also, he is aware of the ever present assortment of obligations associated with his job—accumulations of mail that cannot be delayed, the callers that must be attended to, the meetings that require his participation. In other words, no matter what he is doing, the manager is plagued by what he must do and what he might do. Thus, the manager is forced to treat issues in an abrupt and superficial way.

### *Characteristic 3. Managers prefer issues that are current, specific, and ad hoc*

Ad hoc operating reports received more attention than did routine ones; current, uncertain information—gossip, speculation, hearsay—which flows quickly was preferred to historical, certain information; "instant communication" received first consideration; few contacts were held on a routine or "clocked" basis; almost all contacts concerned well-defined issues. The managerial environment is clearly one of stimulus-response.

It breeds, not reflective planners, but adaptable information manipulators who prefer the live, concrete situation, men who demonstrate a marked action-orientation.

### *Characteristic 4. The manager sits between his organization and a network of contacts*

In virtually every empirical study of managerial time allocation, it was reported that managers spent a surprisingly large amount of time in horizontal or lateral (nonline) communication. It is clear from this study and from that of Sayles [24] that the manager is surrounded by a diverse and complex web of contacts which serves as his self-designed external information system. Included in this web can be clients, associates and suppliers, outside staff experts, peers (managers of related or similar organizations), trade organizations, government officials, independents (those with no relevant organizational affiliation), and directors or superiors. (Among these, directors in this study and superiors in other studies did *not* stand out as particularly active individuals.)

The managers in this study received far more information than they emitted, much of it coming from contacts, and more from subordinates who acted as filters. Figuratively, the manager appears as the neck of an hourglass, sifting information into his own organization from its environment.

### *Characteristic 5. The manager demonstrates a strong preference for the verbal media*

The manager has five media at his command—mail (documented), telephone (purely verbal), unscheduled meeting (informal face-to-face), scheduled meeting (formal face-to-face), and tour (observational). Along with all the other empirical studies of work characteristics, I found a strong predominance of verbal forms of communication.

#### *Mail*

By all indications, managers dislike the documented form of communication. In this study, they gave cursory attention to such items as operating reports and periodicals. It was estimated that only thirteen percent of the input mail was of specific and immediate use to the managers. Much of the rest dealt with formalities and provided general reference data. The managers studied initiated very little mail, only twenty-five pieces in the five weeks. The rest of the outgoing mail was sent in reaction to mail received—a reply to a request, an acknowledgment, some information forwarded to a part of the organization. The managers appeared to dislike this form of communication, perhaps because the mail is a relatively slow and tedious medium to use.

### *Telephone and unscheduled meetings*

The less formal means of verbal communication—the telephone, a purely verbal form, and the unscheduled meeting, a face-to-face form—were used frequently (two-thirds of the contacts in the study) but for brief encounters (average duration of six and twelve minutes respectively). They were used primarily to deliver requests and to transmit pressing information to those outsiders and subordinates who had informal relationships with the manager.

### *Scheduled meetings*

These tended to be of long duration, averaging sixty-eight minutes in this study, and absorbing over half the managers' time. Such meetings provided the managers with their main opportunities to interact with large groups and to leave the confines of their own offices. Scheduled meetings were used when the participants were unfamiliar to the manager (e.g., students who request that he speak at a university), when a large quantity of information had to be transmitted (e.g., presentation of a report), when ceremony had to take place, and when complex strategy-making or negotiation had to be undertaken. An important feature of the scheduled meeting was the incidental, but by no means irrelevant, information that flowed at the start and end of such meetings.

### *Tours*

Although the walking tour would appear to be a powerful tool for gaining information in an informal way, in this study tours accounted for only three percent of the managers' time.

In general, it can be concluded that the manager uses each medium for particular purposes. Nevertheless, where possible, he appears to gravitate to verbal media since these provide greater flexibility, require less effort, and bring faster response. It should be noted here that the manager does not leave the telephone or the meeting to get back to work. Rather, communication is his work, and these media are his tools. The operating work of the organization—producing a product, doing research, purchasing a part—appears to be undertaken infrequently by the senior manager. The manager's productive output must be measured in terms of information, a great part of which is transmitted verbally.

## ***Characteristic 6. Despite the preponderance of obligations, the manager appears to be able to control his own affairs***

Carlson suggested in his study of Swedish chief executives that these men were puppets, with little control over their own affairs. A cursory examination of our data indicates that this is true. Our managers were responsible for the initiation of only thirty-two percent of their verbal contacts and a smaller proportion of their mail. Activities were also classified as to the nature of the managers' participation, and the active ones were outnumbered by the passive ones (e.g., making requests vs. receiving requests). On the surface, the manager is indeed a puppet, answering requests in the mail, returning telephone calls, attending meetings initiated by others, yielding to subordinates' requests for time, reacting to crises.

However, such a view is misleading. There is evidence that the senior manager can exert control over his own affairs in two significant ways: (1) It is he who defines many of his own long-term commitments, by developing appropriate information channels which later feed him information, by initiating projects which later demand his time, by joining committees or outside boards which provide contacts in return for his services, and so on. (2) The manager can exploit situations that appear as obligations. He can lobby at ceremonial speeches; he can impose his values on his organization when his authorization is requested; he can motivate his subordinates whenever he interacts with them; he can use the crisis situation as an opportunity to innovate.

Perhaps these are two points that help distinguish successful and unsuccessful managers. All managers appear to be puppets. Some decide who will pull the strings and how, and they then take advantage of each move that they are forced to make. Others, unable to exploit this high-tension environment, are swallowed up by this most demanding of jobs.

## The manager's work roles

In describing the essential content of managerial work, one should aim to model managerial activity, that is, to describe it as a set of programs. But an undertaking as complex as this must be preceded by the development of a useful typological description of managerial work. In other words, we must first understand the distinct components of managerial work. At the present time we do not.

In this study, 890 pieces of mail and 368 verbal contacts were categorized as to purpose. The incoming mail was found to carry acknowledgements, requests and solicitations of various kinds, reference data, news, analytical reports, reports on events and on operations, advice on various situations, and statements of problems, pressures, and ideas. In reacting to mail, the managers acknowledged some, replied to the requests (e.g., by sending information), and forwarded much to subordinates (usually for their information). Verbal contacts involved a variety of purposes. In 15% of them activities were scheduled, in 6% ceremonial events took place, and a few involved external board work. About 34% involved requests of various kinds, some insignificant, some for information, some for authorization of proposed actions. Another 36% essentially involved the flow of information to and from the manager, while the remainder dealt specifically with issues of strategy and with negotiations. (For details, see [19].)

In this study, each piece of mail and verbal contact categorized in this way was subjected to one question: Why did the manager do this? The answers were collected and grouped and regrouped in various ways (over the course of three years) until a typology emerged that was felt to be satisfactory. While an example, presented below, will partially explain this process to the reader, it must be remembered that (in the words of Bronowski [3, p. 62]): "Every induction is a speculation and it guesses at a unity which the facts present but do not strictly imply."

Consider the following sequence of two episodes: A chief executive attends a meeting of an external board on which he sits. Upon his return to his organization, he immediately goes to the office of a subordinate, tells of a conversation he had with a fellow board member, and concludes with the statement: "It looks like we shall get the contract."

The purposes of these two contacts are clear—to attend an external board meeting, and to give current information (instant communication) to a subordinate. But why did the manager attend the meeting? Indeed, why does he belong to the board? And why did he give this particular information to his subordinate?

Basing analysis on this incident, one can argue as follows: The manager belongs to the board in part so that he can be exposed to special information which is of use to his organization. The subordinate needs the information but has not the status which would give him access to it. The chief executive does. Board memberships bring chief executives in contact with one another for the purpose of trading information.

Two aspects of managerial work emerge from this brief analysis. The manager serves in a "liaison" capacity because of the status of his office, and what he learns here enables him to act as "disseminator" of information into his organization. We refer to these as *roles*—organized sets of behaviors belonging to identifiable offices or positions [23]. Ten roles were chosen to capture all the activities observed during this study.

All activities were found to involve one or more of three basic behaviors—interpersonal contact, the processing of information, and the making of decisions. As a result, our ten roles are divided into three corresponding groups. Three roles—labelled *figurehead, liaison*, and *leader*—deal with behavior that is essentially interpersonal in nature. Three others—*nerve center, disseminator*, and *spokesman*—deal with information-processing activities performed by the manager. And the remaining four—*entrepreneur, disturbance handler, resource allocator*, and *negotiator*—cover the decision-making activities of the manager. We describe each of these roles in turn, asking the reader to note that they form a *gestalt*, a unified whole whose parts cannot be considered in isolation.

### *The interpersonal roles*

Three roles relate to the manager's behavior that focuses on interpersonal contact. These roles derive directly from the authority and status associated with holding managerial office.

#### *Figurehead*

As legal authority in his organization, the manager is a symbol, obliged to perform a number of duties. He must preside at ceremonial events, sign legal documents, receive visitors, make himself available to many of those who feel, in the words of one of the men studied, "that the only way to get something done is to get to the top." There is evidence that this role applies at other levels as well. Davis [7, pp. 43–44] cites the case of the field sales manager who must deal with those customers who believe that their accounts deserve his attention.

#### *Leader*

Leadership is the most widely recognized of managerial roles. It describes the manager's relationship with his subordinates—his attempts to motivate them and his development of the milieu in which they work. Leadership actions pervade all activity—in contrast to most roles, it is possible to designate only a few activities as dealing exclusively with leadership (these mostly related to staffing duties). Each time a manager encourages a subordinate, or meddles in his affairs, or replies to one of his requests, he is playing the *leader* role. Subordinates seek out and react to these leadership clues, and, as a result, they impart significant power to the manager.

#### *Liaison*

As noted earlier, the empirical studies have emphasized the importance of lateral or horizontal communication in the work of managers at all levels. It is clear from our study that this is explained largely in terms of the *liaison* role. The manager establishes his network of contacts essentially to bring information and favors to his organization. As Sayles notes in his study of production supervisors [24, p. 258], "The one enduring objective [of the manager] is the effort to build and maintain a predictable, reciprocating system of relationships. . . ."

Making use of his status, the manager interacts with a variety of peers and other people outside his organization. He provides time, information, and favors in return for the same from others. Foremen deal with staff groups and other foremen; chief executives join boards of directors, and maintain extensive networks of individual relationships. Neustadt notes this behavior in analyzing the work of President Roosevelt [21, p. 150]:

> His personal sources were the product of a sociability and curiosity that reached back to the other Roosevelt's time. He had an enormous acquaintance in various phases of national life and at various levels of government; he also had his wife and her variety of contacts. He extended his acquaintanceships abroad; in the war years Winston Churchill, among others, became a "personal source". Roosevelt quite deliberately exploited these relationships and mixed them up to widen his own range of information. He changed his sources as his interests changed, but no one who had ever interested him was quite forgotten or immune to sudden use.

### *The informational roles*

A second set of managerial activities relate primarily to the processing of information. Together they suggest three significant managerial roles, one describing the manager as a focal point for a certain kind of organizational information, the other two describing relatively simple transmission of this information.

#### *Nerve center*

There is indication, both from this study and from those by Neustadt and Whyte, that the manager serves as the focal point in his organization for the movement of nonroutine information. Homans, who analyzed Whyte's study, draws the following conclusions [26, p. 187]:

> Since interaction flowed toward [the leaders], they were better informed about the problems and desires of group members than were any of the followers and therefore better able to decide on an appropriate course of action. Since they were in close touch with other gang leaders, they were also better informed than their followers about conditions in Cornerville at large. Moreover, in their positions at the focus of the chains of interaction, they were better able than any follower to pass on to the group decisions that had been reached.

The term *nerve center* is chosen to encompass those many activities in which the manager receives information.

Within his own organization, the manager has legal authority that formally connects him—and only him—to *every* member. Hence, the manager emerges as *nerve center* of internal information. He may not know as much about any one function as the subordinate who specializes in it, but he comes to know more about his total organization than any other member. He is the information generalist. Furthermore, because of the manager's status and its manifestation in the *liaison* role, the manager gains unique access to a variety of knowledgeable outsiders including peers who are themselves *nerve centers* of their own organizations. Hence, the manager emerges as his organization's *nerve center* of external information as well.

As noted earlier, the manager's nerve center information is of a special kind. He appears to find it most important to get his information quickly and informally. As a result, he will not hesitate to bypass formal information channels to get it, and he is prepared to deal with a large amount of gossip, hearsay, and opinion which has not yet become substantiated fact.

#### *Disseminator*

Much of the manager's information must be transmitted to subordinates. Some of this is of a *factual* nature, received from outside the organization or from other subordinates. And some is of a *value* nature. Here, the manager acts as the mechanism by which organizational influencers (owners, governments, employee groups, the general public, etc., or simply the "boss") make their preferences known to the organization. It is the manager's duty to integrate these value positions, and to express general organizational preferences as a guide to decisions made by subordinates. One of the men studied commented: "One of the principal functions of this position is to integrate the hospital interests with the public interests." Papandreou describes this duty in a paper published in 1952, referring to management as the "peak coordinator" [22].

#### *Spokesman*

In his *spokesman* role, the manager is obliged to transmit his information to outsiders. He informs influencers and other interested parties about his organization's performance, its policies, and its plans. Furthermore, he is expected to serve outside his organization as an expert in its industry. Hospital administrators are expected to spend some time serving outside as public experts on health, and corporation presidents, perhaps as chamber of commerce executives.

### ***The decisional roles***

The manager's legal authority requires that he assume responsibility for all of his organization's important actions. The *nerve center* role suggests that only he can fully understand complex decisions, particularly those involving difficult value tradeoffs. As a result, the manager emerges as the key figure in the making and interrelating of all significant decisions in his organization, a process that can be referred to as *strategy-making*. Four roles describe the manager's control over the strategy-making system in his organization.

### *Entrepreneur*

The *entrepreneur* role describes the manager as initiator and designer of much of the controlled change in his organization. The manager looks for opportunities and potential problems which may cause him to initiate action. Action takes the from of *improvement projects*—the marketing of a new product, the strengthening of a weak department, the purchasing of new equipment, the reorganization of formal structure, and so on.

The manager can involve himself in each improvement project in one of three ways:

(1) He may *delegate* all responsibility for its design and approval, implicitly retaining the right to replace that subordinate who takes charge of it.
(2) He may delegate the design work to a subordinate, but retain the right to *approve* it before implementation.
(3) He may actively *supervise* the design work himself.

Improvement projects exhibit a number of interesting characteristics. They appear to involve a number of subdecisions, consciously sequenced over long periods of time and separated by delays of various kinds. Furthermore, the manager appears to supervise a great many of these at any one time—perhaps fifty to one hundred in the case of chief executives. In fact, in his handling of improvement projects, the manager may be likened to a juggler. At any one point, he maintains a number of balls in the air. Periodically, one comes down, receives a short burst of energy, and goes up again. Meanwhile, an inventory of new balls waits on the sidelines and, at random intervals, old balls are discarded and new ones added. Both Lindblom [2] and Marples [18] touch on these aspects of strategy-making, the former stressing the disjointed and incremental nature of the decisions, and the latter depicting the sequential episodes in terms of a stranded rope made up of fibres of different lengths each of which surfaces periodically.

### *Disturbance handler*

While the *entrepreneur* role focuses on voluntary change, the *disturbance handler* role deals with corrections which the manager is forced to make. We may describe this role as follows: The organization consists basically of specialist operating programs. From time to time, it experiences a stimulus that cannot be handled routinely, either because an operating program has broken down or because the stimulus is new and it is not clear which operating program should handle it. These situations constitute disturbances. As generalist, the manager is obliged to assume responsibility for dealing with the stimulus. Thus, the handling of disturbances is an essential duty of the manager.

There is clear evidence for this role both in our study of chief executives and in Sayles' study of production supervisors [24, p. 162]:

> The achievement of this stability, which is the manager's objective, is a never-to-be-attained ideal. He is like a symphony orchestra conductor, endeavoring to maintain a melodious performance in which contributions of the various instruments are coordinated and sequenced, patterned and paced, while the orchestra members are having various personal difficulties, stage hands are moving music stands, alternating excessive heat and cold are creating audience and instrument problems, and the sponsor of the concert is insisting on irrational changes in the program.

Sayles goes further to point out the very important balance that the manager must maintain between change and stability. To Sayles, the manager seeks "a dynamic type of stability" (p. 162). Most disturbances elicit short-term adjustments which bring back equilibrium; persistent ones require the introduction of long-term structural change.

### *Resource allocator*

The manager maintains ultimate authority over his organization's strategy-making system by controlling the allocation of its resources. By deciding who will get what (and who will do what), the manager directs the course of his organization. He does this in three ways:

(1) *In scheduling his own time*, the manager allocates his most precious resource and thereby determines organizational priorities. Issues that receive low priority do not reach the *never center* of the organization and are blocked for want of resources.
(2) In designing the organizational structure and in carrying out many improvement projects, the manager *programs the work of his subordinates*. In other words, he allocates their time by deciding what will be done and who will do it.
(3) Most significantly, the manager maintains control over resource allocation by the requirement that he *authorize all significant decisions* before they are implemented. By retaining this power, the manager ensures that different decisions are interrelated—that conflicts are avoided, that resource constraints are respected, and that decisions complement one another.

Decisions appear to be authorized in one of two ways. Where the costs and benefits of a proposal can be quantified, where it is competing for specified resources with other known proposals, and where it can wait for a certain time of year, approval for a proposal is sought in the context of a formal *budgeting* procedure. But these conditions are most often not met—timing may be crucial, nonmonetary costs may predominate, and so on. In these cases, approval is sought in terms of an *ad hoc request for authorization.* Subordinate and manager meet (perhaps informally) to discuss one proposal alone.

Authorization choices are enormously complex ones for the manager. A myriad of factors must be considered (resource constraints, influences preferences, consistency with other decisions, feasibility, payoff, timing, subordinate feelings, etc.). But the fact that the manager is authorizing the decision rather than supervising its design suggests that he has little time to give to it. To alleviate this difficulty, it appears that managers use special kinds of *models* and *plans* in their decision-making. These exist only in their minds and are loose, but they serve to guide behavior. Models may answer questions such as, "Does this proposal make sense in terms of the trends that I see in tariff legislation?" or "Will the EDP department be able to get along with marketing on this?" Plans exist in the sense that, on questioning, managers reveal images (in terms of proposed improvement projects) of where they would like their organizations to go: "Well, once I get these foreign operations fully developed, I would like to begin to look into a reorganization," said one subject of this study.

### *Negotiator*

The final role describes the manager as participant in negotiation activity. To some students of the management process [8, p. 343], this is not truly part of the job of managing. But such distinctions are arbitrary. Negotiation is an integral part of managerial work, as this study notes for chief executives and as that of Sayles made very clear for production supervisors [24, p. 131]: "Sophisticated managers place great stress on negotiations as a way of life. They negotiate with groups who are setting standards for their work, who are performing support activity for them, and to whom they wish to 'sell' their services."

The manager must participate in important negotiation sessions because he is his organization's legal authority, its *spokesman* and its *resource allocator*. Negotiation is resource trading in real time. If the resource commitments are to be large, the legal authority must be present.

These ten roles suggest that the manager of an organization bears a great burden of responsibility. He must oversee his organization's status system; he must serve as a crucial informational link between it and its environment; he must interpret and reflect its basic values; he must maintain the stability of its operations; and he must adapt it in a controlled and balanced way to a changing environment.

## Management as a profession and as a science

Is management a profession? To the extent that different managers perform one set of basic roles, management satisfies one criterion for becoming a profession. But a profession must require, in the words of the Random House Dictionary, "knowledge of some department of learning or science." Which of the ten roles now requires specialized learning? Indeed, what school of business or public administration teaches its students how to disseminate information, allocate resources, perform as figurehead, make contacts, or handle disturbances? We simply know very little about teaching these things. The reason is that we have never tried to document and describe in a meaningful way the procedures (or programs) that managers use.

The evidence of this research suggests that there is as yet no science in managerial work—that managers do not work according to procedures that have been prescribed by scientific analysis. Indeed, except for his use of the telephone, the airplane, and the dictating machine, it would appear that the manager of today is indistinguishable from his predecessors. He may seek different information, but he gets much of it in the same way—from word-of-mouth. He may make decisions dealing with modern technology but he uses the same intuitive (that is, nonexplicit) procedures in making them. Even the computer, which has had such a great impact on other kinds of organizational work, has apparently done little to alter the working methods of the general manager.

How do we develop a scientific base to understand the work of the manager? The description of roles is a first and necessary step. But tighter forms of research are necessary. Specifically, we must attempt to model managerial work—to describe it as a system of programs. First, it will be necessary to decide what programs managers actually use. Among a great number of programs in the manager's repertoire, we might expect to find a time scheduling program, an information disseminating program, and a disturbance-handling program. Then, researchers will have to devote a considerable amount of effort to studying and accurately describing the content of each of these programs—the information and heuristics used. Finally, it will be necessary to describe the interrelationships among all of these programs so that they may be combined into an integrated descriptive model of managerial work.

When the management scientist begins to understand the programs that managers use, he can begin to design meaningful systems and provide help for the manager. He may ask: Which managerial activities can be fully reprogrammed (i.e., automated)? Which cannot be reprogrammed because they require human responses? Which can be partially reprogrammed to operate in a man-machine system? Perhaps scheduling, information collecting, and resource allocating activities lend themselves to varying degrees of reprogramming. Management will emerge as a science to the extent that such efforts are successful.

## Improving the manager's effectiveness

Fayol's fifty year old description of managerial work is no longer of use to us. And we shall not disentangle the complexity of managerial work if we insist on viewing the manager simply as a decision-maker or simply as a motivator of subordinates. In fact, we are unlikely to overestimate the complexity of the manager's work, and we shall make little headway if we take overly simple or narrow points of view in our research.

A major problem faces today's manager. Despite the growing size of modern organizations and the growing complexity of their problems (particularly those in the public sector), the manager can expect little help. He must design his own information system, and he must take full charge of his organization's strategy-making system. Furthermore, the manager faces what might be called the *dilemma of delegation*. He has unique access to much important information but he lacks a formal means of disseminating it. As much of it is verbal, he cannot spread it around in an efficient manner. How can he delegate a task with confidence when he has neither the time nor the means to send the necessary information along with it?

Thus, the manager is usually forced to carry a great burden of responsibility in his organization. As organizations become increasingly large and complex, this burden increases. Unfortunately, the man cannot significantly increase his available time or significantly improve his abilities to manage. Hence, in the large, complex bureaucracy, the top manager's time assumes an enormous opportunity cost and he faces the real danger of becoming a major obstruction in the flow of decisions and information.

Because of this, as we have seen, managerial work assumes a number of distinctive characteristics. The quantity of work is great; the pace is unrelenting; there is great variety, fragmentation, and brevity in the work activities; the manager must concentrate on issues that are current, specific, and ad hoc, and to do so, he finds that he must rely on verbal forms of communications. Yet it is on this man that the burden lies for designing and operating strategy-making and information processing systems that are to solve his organization's (and society's) problems.

The manager can do something to alleviate these problems. He can learn more about his own roles in his organization, and he can use this information to schedule his time in a more efficient manner. He can recognize that only he has much of the information needed by his organization. Then, he can seek to find better means of disseminating it into the organization. Finally, he can turn to the skills of his management scientists to help reduce his workload and to improve his ability to make decisions.

The management scientist can learn to help the manager to the extent he can develop an understanding of the manager's work and the manager's information. To date, strategic planners, operations researchers, and information system designers have provided little help for the senior manager.

They simply have had no framework available by which to understand the work of the men who employed them, and they have had poor access to the information which has never been documented. It is folly to believe that a man with poor access to the organization's true *nerve center* can design a formal management information system. Similarly, how can the long-range planner, a man usually uninformed about many of the *current* events that take place in and around his organization, design meaningful strategic plans? For good reason, the literature documents many manager complaints of naive planning and many planner complaints of disinterested managers. In my view, our lack of understanding of managerial work has been the greatest block to the progress of management science.

The ultimate solution to the problem—to the overburdened manager seeking meaningful help—must derive from research. We must observe, describe, and understand the real work of managing; then and only then shall we significantly improve it.

## Notes

This report is based on the author's doctoral dissertation, carried out at the Sloan School of Management, M.I.T. The author wishes to thank for their help the three thesis committee members, Donald Carroll, Jim Hekimian, and Charles Myers, and Bill Litwack as well.

1 Carlson [6] carried out the classic study just after World War II. He asked nine Swedish managing directors to record on diary pads details of each activity in which they engaged. His method was used by a group of other researchers, many of them working in the U.K. (See [4], [5], [15], [25].)

2 One major project, involving numerous publications, took place at Ohio State University and spanned three decades. Some of the vocabulary used followed Fayol. The results have generated little interest in this area. (See, for example, [13].)

## References

1 Braybrooke, David, "The Mystery of Executive Success Re-examined," *Administrative Science Quarterly*, Vol. 8 (1964), pp. 533–560.

2 —— and Lindblom, Charles E., *A Strategy of Decision*, Free Press, New York, 1963.

3 Bronowski, J., "The Creative Process," *Scientific American*, Vol. 199 (September 1958), pp. 59–65.

4 Burns, Tom, "The Directions of Activity and Communications in a Departmental Executive Group," *Human Relations*, Vol. 7 (1954), pp. 73–97.

5 ——, "Management in Action," *Operational Research Quarterly*, Vol. 8 (1957), pp. 45–60.

6 Carlson, Sune, *Executive Behaviour*, Strömbergs, Stockholm, 1951.

7 Davis, Robert T., *Performance and Development of Field Sales Managers*, Division of Research, Graduate School of Business Administration, Harvard University, Boston, 1957.

8 DRUCKER, PETER F., *The Practice of Management*, Harper and Row, New York, 1954.

9 FAYOL, HENRI, *Administration industrielle et générale*, Dunods, Paris, 1950 (first published 1916).

10 GIBB, CECIL A., "Leadership," Chapter 31 in Gardner Lindzey and Elliot A. Aronson (editors), *The Handbook of Social Psychology*, Vol. 4, Second edition, Addison-Wesley, Reading, Mass., 1969.

11 GUEST, ROBERT H., "Of Time and the Foreman," *Personnel*, Vol. 32 (1955–56) pp. 478–486.

12 GULICK, LUTHER H., "Notes on the Theory of Organization," in Luther Gulick and Lyndall Urwick (editors), *Papers on the Science of Administration*, Columbia University Press, New York, 1937.

13 HEMPHILL, JOHN K., *Dimensions of Executive Positions*, Bureau of Business Research Monograph Number 98, The Ohio State University, Columbus, 1960.

14 HOMANS, GEORGE C., *The Human Group*, Harcourt, Brace, New York, 1950.

15 HORNE, J. H. AND LUPTON, TOM, "The Work Activities of Middle Managers—An Exploratory Study," *The Journal of Management Studies*, Vol. 2 (February 1965), pp. 14–33.

16 KELLY, JOE, "The Study of Executive Behavior by Activity Sampling," *Human Relations*, Vol. 17 (August 1964), pp. 277–287.

17 MACKENZIE, R. ALEX, "The Management Process in 3D," *Harvard Business Review* (November–December 1969), pp. 80–87.

18 MARPLES, D. L., "Studies of Managers—A Fresh Start?," *The Journal of Management Studies*, Vol. 4 (October 1967), pp. 282–299.

19 MINTZBERG, HENRY "Structured Observation as a Method to Study Managerial Work," *The Journal of Management Studies*, Vol. 7 (February 1970), pp. 87–104.

20 MYERS, CHARLES A. (EDITOE), *The Impact of Computers on Management*, The M.I.T. Press, Cambridge, Mass., 1967.

21 NEUSTADT, RICHARD E., *Presidential Power: The Politics of Leadership*, The New American Library, New York, 1964.

22 PAPANDREOU, ANDREAS G., "Some Basic Problems in the Theory of the Firm," in Bernard F. Haley (editor), *A Survey of Contemporary Economics*, Vol. II, Irwin, Homewood, Illinois, 1952, pp. 183–219.

23 SARBIN, T. R. AND ALLEN, V. L., "Role Theory," in Gardner Lindzey and Elliot A. Aronson (editors), *The Handbook of Social Psychology*, Vol. I, Second edition, Addison-Wesley, Reading, Mass., 1968, pp. 488–567.

24 SAYLES, LEONARD R., *Managerial Behavior: Administration in Complex Enterprises*, McGraw-Hill, New York, 1964.

25 STEWART, ROSEMARY, *Managers and Their Jobs*, Macmillan, London, 1967.

26 WHYTE, WILLIAM F., *Street Corner Society*, 2nd edition, University of Chicago Press, Chicago, 1955.

# 24

# PATTERNS IN STRATEGY FORMATION

*Henry Mintzberg*

Source: *Management Science* 24(9) (1978): 934–48.

The literature on strategy formation is in large part theoretical but not empirical, and the usual definition of "strategy" encourages the notion that strategies, as we recognize them ex post facto, are deliberate plans conceived in advance of the making of specific decisions. By defining a strategy as "a pattern in a stream of decisions", we are able to research strategy formation in a broad descriptive context. Specifically, we can study both strategies that were intended and those that were realized despite intentions. A research program suggested by this definition is outlined, and two of the completed studies are then reviewed—the strategies of Volkswagenwerk from 1934 to 1974 and of the United States government in Vietnam from 1950 to 1973. Some general conclusions suggested by these studies are then presented in terms of three central themes: that strategy formation can fruitfully be viewed as the interplay between a dynamic environment and bureaucratic momentum, with leadership mediating between the two forces; that strategy formation over time appears to follow some important patterns in organizations, notably life cycles and distinct change-continuity cycles within these; and that the study of the interplay between intended and realized strategies may lead us to the heart of this complex organizational process.

What are strategies and how are they formed in organizations? A large body of literature, under the title of strategy formulation in the private sector, and policy making in the public sector, addresses the question of how organizations make and interrelate their significant (that is, strategic) decisions. A brief review [14] has suggested that a good deal of this literature falls distinctly into one of three theoretical groupings, or "modes", The *planning mode*, comprising the largest body of published materials and in the tradition of both management science and bureaucratic theory, depicts the process as a highly ordered, neatly integrated one, with strategies explicated on schedule by a purposeful organization [2], [17]. In sharp contrast, the *adaptive mode*, popularized by writers such as Lindblom [4], [12], [13] in the public sector and Cyert and March [8] in the context of business, depicts the process as one in which many decision-makers with conflicting goals bargain among themselves to produce a stream of incremental, disjointed decisions. And in some of the literature of classical economics and contemporary management, the process is described in the *entrepreneurial mode*, where a powerful leader takes bold, risky decisions toward his vision of the organization's future [6], [9].

Some interesting research has been undertaken to put the theory into empirical context, for example, Allison's development of three models to explain policy making perceptions during the Cuban Missle Crises [1], Collins and Moore's description of the entrepreneurial personality [7], and Bowman's investigation into strategic effectiveness [3]. But most of the literature remains theoretical without being empirical, and the contradictions among these three modes remains to be investigated.

This paper presents the results of the first stage of a research project begun in 1971, and continuing, to study patterns in the process of strategy formation. The first section describes the term "strategy", and shows how the definition leads naturally to the choice of a research methodology. This methodology is described in the second section. A third section then describes briefly the results of the formation of strategies in two organizations, and a final section presents some theoretical conclusions about strategy formation that arise from these results.

## Definition of strategy

The term *strategy* has been defined in a variety of ways, but almost always with a common theme, that of a deliberate conscious set of guidelines that determines decisions into the future. In Game Theory, strategy represents the set of rules that is to govern the moves of the players. In military theory, strategy is "the utilization during both peace and war, of all of the nation's forces, through large-scale, long-range planning and development, to ensure security and victory" (Random House Dictionary). And in management theory, the Chandler definition is typical: ". . . the determination of the basic long-term goals and objectives of an enterprise, and the adoption of courses of action and the allocation of resources necessary for carrying out these goals" [5, p. 13]. All these definitions treat strategy as (a) explicit, (b) developed consciously and purposefully, and (c) made in advance of the specific decisions to which it applies. In common terminology, a strategy is a "plan".

The position taken here is that this definition is incomplete for the organization and nonoperational for the researcher. It conceals one important side of the decisional behavior of organizations that all of the above theorists would likely consider strategic (that is, important). And by restricting strategy to explicit, a priori guidelines, it forces the researcher to study strategy formation as a perceptual phenomenon, all too often reducing his conclusions to abstract normative generalizations.

In this paper, the concept defined above will be referred to as *intended* strategy. Strategy in general, and *realized* strategy in particular, will be defined as a *pattern in a stream of decisions*.[1] In other words, when a sequence of decisions in some area exhibits a consistency over time, a strategy will be considered to have formed. A few examples will clarify this definition. When Richard Nixon, early in his first term of office, made a number of decisions to favor Southern voters (appointment of Supreme Court justices from the South, interference with school integration plans, etc.), the press quickly coined the phrase "Southern strategy". Their action corresponded exactly to ours as researchers: despite no explicit statement of intent, the press perceived a consistency in a stream of decisions and labeled it a strategy. To take a very different illustration, art critics seek to delineate distinct periods during which the works of great artists (and, by imputation, their decisions about those works) exhibited certain consistencies in their use of form, color and so on. Again, the procedure corresponds to ours: Picasso's "Blue Period" would be our "Blue Strategy"!

Defining strategy as we do enables us to consider both sides of the strategy formation coin: strategies as intended, a priori guidelines as well as strategies as evolved, a posteriori consistencies in decisional behavior. In other words, the strategy-maker may *formulate* a strategy through a conscious process before the makes specific decisions, or a strategy may *form* gradually, perhaps unintentionally, as he makes his decisions one by one. This definition operationalizes the concept of strategy for the researcher. Research on strategy formation (not necessarily formulation) focusses on a tangible phenomenon—the decision stream—and strategies become observed patterns in such streams.

## The research methodology

This definition of strategy necessitated the study of decision streams in organizations over time periods long enough to detect the development and breakdown of patterns. Furthermore, because there was little precedent for such research, wherein the basic parameters were defined and operationalized, and because the process of strategy formation appeared to be an extremely complex one, it was evident at the outset that our research would have to be exploratory and as purely inductive as possible. Thus it was decided to concentrate on intensive historical studies of single organizations over periods of decades. These studies proceeded in four steps.

### *Step 1: Collection of basic data*

All studies began with the development of two chronological listings over the whole period, one of important decisions and actions by the organization, the other of important events and trends in the environment. The choices of what decisions and events to study, as well as the sources of the data, varied considerably from one study to another. Our task was to uncover whatever traces were left of decisions and events that had taken place as many as fifty years earlier. In one case, back issues of a magazine served as the trace of its decisions on content; in another case, newspaper reports served in part to reveal military decisions of a government. Other sources included product catalogs, minutes of executive meetings, interviews, and so on.

### *Step 2: Inference of strategies and periods of change*

From the chronology of decisions, divided into distinct strategic areas (in the case of the magazine, for example, content, format, and administration), various strategies were inferred as patterns in streams of decisions. These strategies were then compared with each other, as well as with other data such as sales, budgets, and staff levels, in order to identify distinct periods of change in the formation of strategy. Some periods of change were *incremental*, during which new strategies formed gradually; others were *piecemeal*, during which some strategies changed while others remained constant; and still others were *global*, during which many strategies changed quickly and in unison. In addition, we identified periods of *continuity*, during which established patterns remain unchanged; periods of *limbo*, during which the organization hesitated to make decisions; periods of *flux*, during which no important patterns seemed evident in the decision streams, and so on.

### *Step 3: Intensive analysis of periods of change*

At this point the study shifted from the broad perception of overall patterns to the intensive investigation of specific periods of change. Here we relied on in-depth reports and, where possible, interviews with the original strategy-makers.

### *Step 4: Theoretical analysis*

At this point a report was written and a group then met in a series of brainstorming sessions to generate hypotheses to explain the findings. These sessions were guided by a list of open-ended questions designed to focus attention and stimulate the flow of ideas, for example: When is a strategy made explicitly that controls subsequent decisions, and when does a strategy evolve implicitly as a convergence in a stream of ad hoc decisions? When do intended strategies differ from realized ones? What is the role of planning, leadership, shared goals, and bargaining in integrating different strategies? Under what conditions are formal analysis and planning used? (Indeed, what does the term "planning" mean in the context of strategy formation?) What are the relative influences of external forces, organizational forces, and leadership in strategy formation? When and why are organizations proactive and reactive? How do organizations balance change with stability? What overall patterns does the process of strategy formation follow? These questions stimulated debate and discussion, which in turn led to the generation of hypotheses. These in turn are on their way to being woven into theories, the skeletons of which are reported here.

## Patterns in two studies

Four major studies, each involving some significant portion of one man-year of funded research, have been completed, involving a large automobile company, a government military strategy, a magazine, and a national film agency. In addition, over twenty smaller studies have been carried out as graduate student term papers and theses, ranging from an expansion period in a hockey league to the development of a university's strategy across a century and a half. The major periods of two of the intensive studies are reviewed briefly below, using the terminology of the research.

## The strategies of Volkswagenwerk, 1920 to 1974

This study divides into seven distinct periods, as follows:

*Before 1948: flux*

Ferdinand Porsche conceived the idea of a "people's car" in the 1920s; in 1934, the German Nazi government decided to support the project, and in 1937, with the problems worked out of the design, construction was begun on a large automobile manufacturing plant at Wolfsburg. Just as the plant was to go into full operation war was declared, and it was immediately converted to production of war vehicles. By 1945 the plant was largely destroyed.[2] The British occupation forces used it to service their vehicles. Later there began some primitive production of Porsche's "Volkswagen", using in large part East German refugees as the labor force, with many of the raw materials procured by barter. The plant was offered to various Allied interests (including Henry Ford), but all declined, seeing no value in the Volkswagen. In 1948 the British selected Heinrich Nordhoff, a former division chief of Opel, to run the operations.

*1948: global change*

Nordhoff inherited half an intended strategy—Porsche's design and his concept of the market (an inexpensive automobile for the common man). To this he added the other components of an intended strategy—an emphasis on quality and technical excellence, aggressive exporting, and rigorous service standards, all integrated around the dominant element of the "people's car".

*1949 to 1958: continuity*

This intended strategy was ideally suited to the environment of post-war Germany as well as to world-wide export markets. For the next ten years, Nordhoff realized his intended strategy, building up the central organization and expanding manufacturing capacity and distribution channels very rapidly. Two new models were introduced (work on both having begun in 1949), but these were really modifications of the basic Volkswagen. (In 1954 Nordhoff ordered work halted on the design of a completely new model.)

*1959: minor change*

Increasing competition and changing consumer tastes in Germany and abroad spurred Volkswagen to make some minor modifications in its strategies around 1959. Advertising was introduced in the United States in anticipation of the compacts; design of the first really new model, the medium-priced 1500, was pursued; the firm was about to go public and investment was increased sharply in anticipation of a dividend load. But all essential aspects of the original strategy remained unchanged; only some new, essentially peripheral elements, were grafted on to the old strategy.

*1960 to 1964: continuity*

The Volkswagen strategy remained essentially the same in almost all respects, although profits were being squeezed by competitive pressures and increasing costs despite increasing sales. The larger 1500 model was introduced, but it again emphasized durability, economy, and unexcelled appearance.

*1965 to 1970: groping*

Facing ever more severe pressures, the firm finally reacted in the form of an anxious and disjointed search for new models. Many were introduced in this period, some in contrast to Volkswagen's economy-car image. Some the firm designed itself; others were acquired. Nordhoff died in 1968, and Kurt Lotz became managing director. By 1970, profits were down for the third straight year. The old strategy had clearly disintegrated, but a clear new one had yet to emerge.[3]

*1971 to 1974: global change*

An experienced Volkswagen executive, Rudolf Leiding, replaced Lotz in 1971 and immediately began a period of consolidation of the new acquisitions and the development of a new integrated turnaround strategy. The new product strategy was modeled around the successful Audi—stylish, front-wheel drive, water cooled. Accordingly, a host of existing lines were dropped, a few new ones being concentrated on to avoid direct competition between models. Complementarity was stressed in their design to assure reliable, economic assembly, and attempts were made to rationalize production on a world-wide basis and to build plants abroad, in low wage areas where possible. Marketing strategy emphasized performance, reliability, and service. Capital expenditures were very large throughout the period. (These strategies were pursued in what proved to be a period of continuity after 1974, despite Leiding's resignation, with the new products selling well. After large losses in 1974, Volkswagenwerk became profitable again in the second half of 1975.)

## U.S. strategy in Vietnam, 1950 to 1973

It is impossible, in a few lines, to review comprehensively a situation as complex as the U.S. experience in Vietnam from 1950 to 1973. (Our chronology record alone numbers 101 pages.) Nevertheless, the central themes can be reviewed briefly, in ten distinct periods, to show the main patterns of change and continuity.

*1950: global change*

Until 1950, the United States government refused requests by France to aid its forces fighting in Indochina. Shortly after Communist forces took over the Chinese government, however, the U.S. changed its strategy and began a program of direct monetary aid to the French.

*1950 to 1953: continuity*

For three and a half years, the U.S. followed a more or less uninterrupted strategy of steadily increasing aid to the French in Indochina. This was accompanied, particularly at the outset, by a strategy of encouraging the French to reduce their colonial ties to the so-called "Associated States". Neither strategy accomplished its purpose. By the end of 1953, despite a massive infusion of U.S. aid, the French military position was weaker than in 1950.

*1954: flux, then global change*

Late in 1953 the French military position began to disintegrate. Before and during the multination Geneva conference in April, Secretary of State John Foster Dulles negotiated with the allies of the U.S. in order to reach agreement, but his efforts were not successful. The day before the Indochina phase of the conference opened on May 8, the French garrison at Dien Bien Phu fell. At a press conference on June 8, Dulles claimed there was no plan to ask Congress for authorization of American aid to Indochina, a position confirmed two days later by President Eisenhower. Shortly thereafter the French government fell, and Pierre Mendès-France became Premier on a platform of ending the war by July 20. At Geneva a settlement was reached, among other points dividing Vietnam in two. In the aftermath of Geneva, the French left Vietnam and the U.S. began a program of direct aid to the South Vietnamese, with the intended strategy of democratizing the government of Premier Diem.

*1955 to 1961: continuity*

To the end of the Eisenhower administration, the U.S. pursued an uninterrupted strategy of direct aid to the South Vietnamese, while the intended strategy of democratization was neither realized nor vigorously pursued.

*1961: global change*

The change in strategy in 1961 was the first time the U.S. government acted in a purely proactive manner, without tangible external stimulus. The new Kennedy team in Washington chose to change the intended strategy from passive aid to active support. On May 11, 1961, a contingent of Special Forces was dispatched to Vietnam to advise and train the Vietnamese. Kennedy also approved the initiation of a covert warfare campaign against North Vietnam. At the end of the year, under pressure from Diem, Kennedy agreed to a build-up of support troops.

*1962 to 1965: incremental change leading to global change*

The number of U.S. advisors increased from 948 at the end of November, 1961, to 2,646 by January, 1962, to 5,576 by June 30, and to 11,000 by the end of 1962. In 1963, public manifestations began against the Diem government, and the U.S. strategy of support for Diem gradually changed (apparently in contradiction of intentions). First, Washington brought economic pressures to bear on the Diem government, by the deferring of decisions on aid, and eventually, it tacitly supported the coup that overthrew him (after considerable confusion between Washington, the military, and the CIA). With the assassination of Kennedy less than a month later, Lyndon Johnson became president. From the early days of his administration, the debate within the U.S. government over the intended strategy for Vietnam (bombing, escalation, etc.) grew more intense. As the debate went on, the realized strategy began to change to one of escalation of the U.S. war effort. For example, in February 1964, clandestine American attacks began, including patrols and air operations in Laos against the North Vietnamese. Then in August 1964 the first spate of bombings was carried out against the North in reprisal for the attack on U.S. destroyers in the

Gulf of Tonkin. And in October 1964 the covert air war in Laos was intensified. Meanwhile the debate over the official (intended) strategy continued, with various options debated in meeting, memo and report. Throughout the period, Johnson seemed uncertain how to proceed and reluctant about approving large-scale bombings. But events were dragging him along. Opinion within the government was more and more favoring bombing and escalation; the government crisis in Saigon was worsening; the Viet Cong was stepping up its harassment. On February 6, 1965, after the Viet Cong had attacked American personnel at Plei Ku, Johnson ordered a major retaliatory strike on the North. On February 11, another similarly justified attack was launched. And on February 13 Johnson ordered sustained bombing on a non-retaliatory basis. Thereafter, with the bombing seeming to prove relatively ineffective, the debate over troop deployment began in earnest. Under pressure from the Pentagon, Johnson approved in April 1964 the first major troop increases and "a change of mission for all Marine battalions deployed in Vietnam to permit their more active use . . ." By June the "search and destroy" strategy had begun to replace the "enclave" strategy, and in July Johnson approved General Westmoreland's request for 44 battalions.

*1965 to 1967: continuity*

Three strategies were pursued in parallel during this period. First, the land war was escalated until the U.S. troop level in Vietnam reached a peak of over half a million in 1967. Second, the bombing campaign was intensified sporadically throughout the period. And third, Johnson put pressure on the North Vietnamese, through periodic variations in the bombing campaign, to come to the negotiating table. Meanwhile, pressures began to build in Washington, notably from McNamara, for a reassessment of the whole strategy. Although this may have constrained the escalation decisions Johnson made, it did not change the basic course of the strategy. By the end of 1967, the ground war was being fought extensively, the air war was being widened slowly, and diplomatic activity went on at a furious pace.

*1968: global change*

A series of factors apparently stunned Johnson into a major reassessment of the strategy. One was the Tet offensive, begun on January 31, 1968, which for the first time provided tangible evidence of the military reality (a stalemate) in Vietnam. Second was the military request, on February 28, for 206, 756 more troops, which according to the *Pentagon Papers* would have meant the call-up of reserve forces. Third, a new Secretary of Defense, Clark Clifford, was working behind the scenes for a bombing halt. And fourth, the New Hampshire presidential primary, and other manifestations of public sentiment, made clear the great resistance to the war effort that was growing among the U.S. population. On March 13, 1968, Johnson decided to deploy 30,000 more troops, but then a few days later a massive change in the strategy was signaled. On March 22, General Westmoreland was recalled to Washington and on March 31 Johnson announced a partial bombing halt, a reduction of the latest deployment to 13,500 troops, and his intention not to seek re-election. Three days later he announced North Vietnam's readiness to meet with American negotiators.

*1968 to 1969: limbo, then global change*

After a brief period of limbo to the end of 1968, ending the term of the lame-duck president, Richard Nixon took over the presidency and initiated global change in strategy. In effect, Johnson's global change was to halt an old strategy; Nixon's was to replace it with a new one. His was a proactive, integrated strategy—he referred to its goal as "peace with honor"—consisting of the following elements: "Vietnamization", which meant the withdrawal of U.S. troops and the equiping of the South Vietnamese to take over the fighting; active peace initiatives to negotiate a settlement, alternated with military pressure (based on air and naval power, to replace the withdrawn land power) to encourage the North Vietnamese to undertake serious negotiations; and "linkage", the bringing of pressure on the Russians—by threatening a withdrawal of cooperation on other East-West negotiations—to influence the North Vietnamese to reach a settlement.

*1970 to 1973: continuity*

That strategy remained intact into 1973, with only the emphasis of its various components changed from time to time to gain advantage. U.S. troop withdrawals continued rather steadily throughout the period. So did U.S. military pressure, which consisted primarily of periodic bombing offensives, but also included a ground excursion into Cambodia in mid 1970 and air support for a South Vietnamese one into Laos in early 1971, as well as the mining of North Vietnamese ports in mid 1972. Political pressure was maintained on the Soviet Union during the entire period. And negotiation also continued throughout, although sporadically. An agreement was finally reached in January 1973, at which time the U.S. halted all offensive military activity. (The heaviest bombing of the war took place in North Vietnam just three weeks prior, after an earlier agreement fell apart.) By March 29, 1973, all American combat and support forces had left Vietnam, and effective August 15, all funding for American military activity in or over Indochina was ended. (Fighting, however, continued, the South Vietnamese army and government finally collapsing in April, 1975.)

## Some general conclusions about strategy formation

Three themes will be pursued in this section. The first is that strategy formation can fruitfully be viewed as the interplay between a dynamic environment and bureaucratic momentum, with leadership mediating between the two.

Second, strategy formation over periods of time appears to follow distinct regularities which may prove vital to understanding the process. And third, the study of the interplay between intended and realized strategies may lead us to the heart of this complex organizational process.

## Strategy formation as the interplay of environment, leadership and bureaucracy

In general terms, strategy formation in most organizations can be thought of as revolving around the interplay of three basic forces: (a) an *environment* that changes continuously but irregularly, with frequent discontinuities and wide swings in its rate of change, (b) an organizational operating system, or *bureaucracy*, that above all seeks to stabilize its actions, despite the characteristics of the environment it serves, and (c) a *leadership* whose role is to mediate between these two forces, to maintain the stability of the organization's operating system while at the same time insuring its adaptation to environmental change. Strategy can then be viewed as the set of consistent behaviors by which the organization establishes for a time its place in its environment, and strategic change can be viewed as the organization's response to environmental change, constrained by the momentum of the bureaucracy and accelerated or dampened by the leadership.

Both Volkswagen and Vietnam are above all stories of how bureaucratic momentum constrains and conditions strategic change, at least after the initial strategic direction has been set. Any large automobile company is mightily constrained by its technical system. Retooling is enormously expensive. This helps to explain Volkswagen's slow response to the environmental changes of the 1960s. But this explanation is not sufficient. Volkswagen was clearly constrained by momentum of a psychological nature as well. The very success of its unique and integrated strategy seemed to reinforce its psychological commitment to it, and to act as a great barrier to the consideration of strategic change.

Even leadership was absent when needed in the 1960s. Nordhoff's period of great leadership began in 1948, when there was little to lose by acting boldly and when little bureaucratic momentum was present. That leadership lasted for the next ten years. But by the early 1960s, when bold action was needed in the face of an increasingly changed environment, the central leadership was not forthcoming. Quite the contrary, instead of pushing the bureaucracy to change, Nordhoff became a force for continuity. When change did come, it was late and it lacked a conceptual focus. The organization groped awkwardly in its new environment, until a new, dynamic leader came on the scene with a fresh strategy in 1971.

Bureaucratic momentum played a major role in the U.S. strategy in Vietnam as well. Earlier in our discussion, the periods 1954, 1961, and 1965 were labeled as global change because various strategies changed quickly and in unison. But in a broader perspective, all of these changes were incremental. The precedent of resisting Communist expansion in Southeast Asia—the "metastrategy" (a strategy of strategies)—was set in 1950. After that, the changes of 1954, 1961, and 1965, while substituting one means for another, simply reinforced the basic direction; they did not change it. Each escalation step seemed to be a natural outgrowth of the last one, one commitment leading to the next. (A management scientist might be tempted to describe this as exponential smoothing, in which the current strategy was always some exponentially weighted sum of past ones.) Only in 1968, when the organization was faced with a massive failure, was there a truly global change in strategy.

At no time was bureaucratic momentum more evident than during the great debate of 1963–1965. The pressures on Johnson to do more of the same—to escalate—became enormous. One could even argue that the creation of the Special Forces by Kennedy became a self-confirming contingency plan. In effect a guerilla fighting force, created in case it might be needed, found a way to make itself needed. It came to be used because it was there. This suggests that strategies can be evoked by available resources (as in the case of the employees, factory, and people's car of Volkswagenwerk of 1948 looking for something to do),[4] and that contingency plans, a favorite prescriptive tool of planning theorists in times of environmental turbulence, may have a habit of making themselves self-confirming, whether they are needed or not.

Of course the environment played a major role in Vietnam too. The U.S. altered its strategy in 1954 and 1965, albeit within the metastrategy, because the changed environment was proving inhospitable to its existing strategy. And the global changes of 1950 and 1968 were certainly evoked by environmental change, in these two cases rather specific events—the fall of the Chinese government and the Tet offensive.

What of leadership? The real tragedy of Vietnam is that, up until 1968, the leadership never seemed to mediate appropriately between the bureaucracy and the environment. In 1961, for example, leadership acted proactively in the absence of either significant environmental change or bureaucratic momentum. Kennedy voluntarily escalated the war in a way that made the 1965 escalation all but inevitable. "All but" because sufficiently strong leadership in 1965 might have been able to resist the environmental and bureaucratic pressures. But the cards were stacked against Johnson. Both the environmental change and the bureaucratic momentum were pulling him in the same direction, each suggesting more of the same (escalation) as the natural next step. It would have taken very powerful leadership indeed to resist these forces, and Johnson did not exhibit it. Only in 1968, facing the most dramatic failure of all and a markedly changed domestic environment, did Johnson finally exert the leadership initiative that reversed the eighteen-year course of the meta-strategy.

Thereafter, Nixon exhibited strong leadership too, introducing proactive change in 1969 and pursuing it vigorously to the end. But again, admittedly in retrospect, that proactivity served only to prolong what was inevitably a lost cause. And bureaucratic momentum seemed to play a minor role in the Nixon years, his strong chief advisor Kissinger, standing in place of the policy-making machinery of government. But those two men also fell prey to psychological momentum, pursuing their costly and ultimately futile strategy against public and congressional resistance.

## Patterns of strategic change

There is no need to dwell on the point that strategy formation is not a regular, nicely sequenced process running on a standard five-year schedule or whatever. An organization may find itself in a stable environment for years, sometimes for decades, with no need to reassess an appropriate strategy. Then, suddenly, the environment can become so turbulent that even the very best planning techniques are of no use because of the impossibility of predicting the kind of stability that will eventually emerge. (What kind of strategic plan was John Foster Dulles to carry in his briefcase to Geneva in 1954?) In response to this kind of inconsistency in the environment, patterns of strategic change are never steady, but rather irregular and ad hoc, with a complex intermingling or periods of continuity, change, flux, limbo, and so on.

But that should not lead to the conclusion that patterns in strategy formation do not exist. Indeed, if we are to make any normative headway in this area, we must find consistencies that will enable organizations to understand better their strategic situations. Thus the prime thrust of our research has been to identify patterns of strategic change.

Most of our studies show evidence of two main patterns, one superimposed on the other. The first is the life cycle of an overall strategy—its conception, elaboration, decay, and death. The second is the presence of periodic waves of change and continuity within the life cycle. (Longer cycles of this kind could be identified as well, from one life cycle to the next.) What this second pattern suggests is that strategies do not commonly change in continuous incremental fashion; rather, change—even incremental change—takes place in spurts, each followed by a period of continuity. Nowhere is this better demonstrated than in the stepwise escalation of the Vietnam metastrategy in 1950, 1954, 1961, and 1965.

Why do organizations undergo distinct periods of change and continuity? For one thing, such a pattern seems to be consistent with human cognition. We do not react to phenomena continuously, but rather in discreet steps, in response to changes large enough for us to perceive. Likewise, strategic decision processes in organizations are not continuous, but irregular [15]. They must be specifically evoked; they proceed for a time; and then they terminate. Furthermore, consistent with the Cyert and March notion of sequential attention to goals [8], the leadership of an organization may choose to deal with the conflicting pressures for change from the environment and continuity from the bureaucracy by first acceding to one and then the other. To most bureaucracies—for example, the automobile assembly line—change is disturbing. So the leadership tries to concentrate that disturbance into a specific period of time, and then to leave the bureaucracy alone for a while to consolidate the change. But of course, while the bureaucracy is being left alone, the environment continues to change, so that no matter how well chosen the strategy, eventually a new cycle of change must be initiated.

With these two patterns in mind, we can now consider the patterns of strategic change in both studies. Volkswagen began its life (or at least left the incubation stage) in 1948 with what we call a *gestalt* strategy, defined as one that is (a) unique and (b) tightly integrated (in the sense that its elements are mutually complementary, or *synergistic*, in Volkswagen's case fusing around the dominant element of the people's car). The first feature, uniqueness, means that the gestalt strategy deposits the organization in a *niche*, a corner of the environment reserved for itself. If well chosen, therefore, that strategy can protect the organization from attack for a period of time. That is exactly what happened in the case of Volkswagen. But the second feature, tight integration, makes a gestalt strategy difficult to change. The changing of a single dimension may cause *dis*integration of the whole strategy. That also became clear when Volkswagen had to change, when competitors moved into its niche and the market moved away from it. Volkswagenwerk's initial response to the changes in environment was two-fold. Before 1959, and after 1959 until 1965, it essentially ignored the changes. And in the 1959 period it resorted to a *grafting* procedure, adding a new piece to its existing gestalt strategy, but avoiding any fundamental change in it. When Volkswagen finally did begin to respond seriously in 1965, that response was an awkward one, a *groping* procedure with no clear focus. After seventeen years with one gestalt strategy, the organization was not accustomed to making major changes in strategy. It was only in the 1970s that Volkswagen was able to develop a clear new strategy, in part, we shall soon argue, a result of its groping procedure.

A few words on gestalt strategies are in order, since they appear frequently in organizations. First, they seem to develop at one point in time, most frequently when the organization is founded. That is when bureaucratic momentum is weakest, leadership typically strong (entrepreneurial), and environments rather tolerant. In contrast, achieving a gestalt strategy is difficult in an ongoing organization, which has a great deal more bureaucratic momentum. Yet both the Volkswagenwerk of 1971 and the United States Government of 1969 seemed able to, no doubt because both faced environments beginning to settle down after periods of great turbulence that had severely disrupted their bureaucratic momentum.

Second, gestalt strategies seem to be associated with single, powerful leaders. This is especially true of the two periods mentioned above, as well as that of Volkswagenwerk of 1948. Perhaps the sophisticated integration called for by such strategies can be effected only in one mind. The development of a gestalt strategy requires innovative thinking, rooted in synthesis rather than analysis, based on the "intuitive" or inexplicit processes that have been associated with the brain's right hemisphere [16]. Thus we are led to hypothesize that gestalt strategies are the products of single individuals, and only appear in organizations with strong leadership, in effect, those that use the entrepreneurial mode. It is difficult to imagine one coming out of a decentralized organization, unless all the decision-makers follow the conceptual lead of one creative individual. Nor can one be imagined resulting from a formal management science or planning process per se, these being essentially analytic rather than synthetic. (That is not to say, of course, that a synthesizer cannot parade under the title of planner or management scientist, or for that matter, advisor, as in the case of Kissinger.) We hypothesize then that the planning mode will normally lead to what can be called *main-line* strategies, typical and obvious ones for the organization to adopt (for example, because the competitors are using them).

Vietnam represents the classic strategic life cycle, although the pattern differs somewhat from that of Volkswagen. The Vietnam metastrategy had a clearly identifiable birthdate, 1950, and unlike that of Volkswagen, which grew rapidly from the outset, this one grew slowly, receiving three distinct boosts, in 1954, 1961 and 1965. It was only after this third boost, however, fifteen years after its birth, that the metastrategy really underwent rapid expansion. Its demise also differed from that of Volkswagen. Whereas the Volkswagen strategy experienced a long, agonizing death, like a developing cancer, the U.S. metastrategy in Vietnam experienced one major setback, like a massive stroke, in 1968, and thereafter remained in a coma until 1973, when it finally expired. (The new gestalt strategy that arose in 1969 served only to bury it. In Volkswagen, of course, only the strategy expired; out of its ashes a new one emerged, and the automobile operations carried on. The Vietnam operations did not.)

The change-continuity cycles were also very marked in the case of Vietnam. Except for the period of 1962 to 1965, when the change was gradual, and largely out of control of the central leadership, periods of change and continuity were always evident. And in the broad perspective, as noted earlier, up to 1968 that change was always incremental. Vietnam in fact represents a classic case of incrementalism, and exhibits profoundly its dangers. Each escalation step was taken without an assessment of what the next step might have entailed, with the result that Lyndon Johnson in 1968 found himself in a situation that Harry Truman, the President under whom the first step was taken in 1950, as well as all the Presidents in between (including the Lyndon Johnson of 1965), would have considered inconceivable.

Strategy-makers seem prepared to assume positions in incremental steps that they would never begin to entertain in global ones. On the other hand, some of our other studies, notably of the magazine, show that even in simple situations global change is very difficult to conceive and execute successfully. This, perhaps, is the strategy-maker's greatest dilemma—the danger of incremental change versus the difficulty of global change.

## Deliberate versus emergent strategies

Earlier it was claimed that the definition of strategy used in this research opens up the other side of the strategy formation question, strategies as ex post facto results of decisional behavior as well as strategies as a priori guidelines to decision-making. Two kinds of strategies were identified: intended and realized. These two, at least in theory, can now be combined in three ways, as shown in Figure I and listed below:

(1) Intended strategies that get realized; these may be called *deliberate* strategies.
(2) Intended strategies that do not get realized, perhaps because of unrealistic expectations, misjudgments about the environment, or changes in either during implementation; these may be called *unrealized* strategies.
(3) Realized strategies that were never intended, perhaps because no strategy was intended at the outset or perhaps because, as in (2), those that were got displaced along the way; these may be called *emergent* strategies.

The Volkswagen strategy of 1948 to 1958 is perhaps the best illustration of a deliberate strategy, both intended and realized. Kennedy's intended strategy of 1961 of advising the Vietnamese is probably the best example of an unrealized strategy. And the subsequent United States strategy of finding itself in a fighting instead of advising role is probably the best example of an emergent strategy, realized despite intentions. (Note the association of these last two with Kennedy's proactive strategy making.)

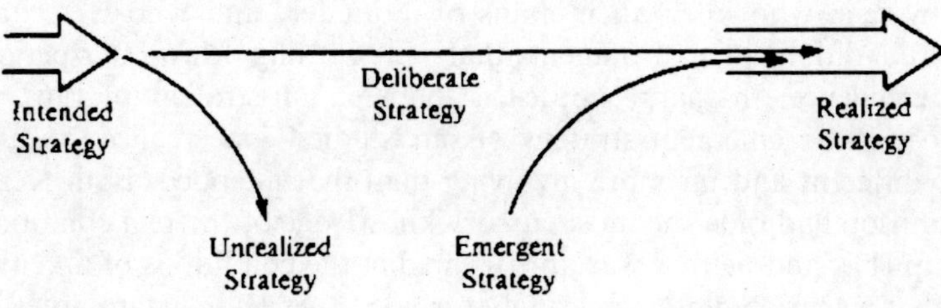


*Figure 1* Types of Strategies.

But practice is always more complicated—and more interesting—than theory, and despite our neat trichotomy, we found a number of other relationships between intended and realized strategies. These include intended strategies that, as they get realized, change their form and become, in part at least, emergent; emergent strategies that get formalized as deliberate ones; and intended strategies that get overrealized.

Planning theory postulates that the strategy-maker "formulates" from on high while the subordinates "implement" lower down. Unfortunately, however, this neat dichotomy is based on two assumptions which often prove false: that the formulator is fully informed, or at least as well informed as the implementor, and that the environment is sufficiently stable, or at least predictable, to ensure that there will be no need for *re*formulation during implementation. The absence of either condition should lead to a collapse of the formulation-implementation dichotomy, and the use of the adaptive mode instead of the planning one. Strategy formation then becomes a learning process, whereby so-called implementation feeds back to formulation and intentions get modified en route, resulting in an emergent strategy.

The failure to so adapt is dramatically illustrated in a paper by Feld [10]. He describes the problems that arise in military organizations that hold rigidly to this dichotomy, "The command function of planning and coordination [being] considered to require a sheltered position" despite the fact that "The conditions of combat are fluid and haphazard in the extreme" (p. 17). Thus, in the infamous battle of World War I, where the British casualties numbered 300,000:

> No senior officer from the Operations Branch of the General Headquarters, it was claimed, ever set foot (or eyes) on the Passchendaele battlefield during the four months the battle was in progress. Daily reports on the condition of the battle-field were first ignored, then ordered discontinued. Only after the battle did the Army chief of staff learn that he had been directing men to advance through a sea of mud. (p. 21)

The most successful deliberate strategies of our two studies—the gestalt ones of Nordhoff and later Leiding in Volkswagenwerk—were both formulated by men who knew their industry intimately and who were able to predict conditions in environments that were settling down after periods of great turbulence. In sharp contrast is the Vietnam strategy of 1962–1965, the most costly emergent strategy of our studies—one realized in a form totally different and far more involving than that intended. Both Kennedy and Johnson had only the most cursory knowledge of the real conditions in Vietnam [11], and neither was able to predict the conditions of an environment that was becoming increasingly turbulent. As Halberstam notes in his detailed study of the U.S. experience in Vietnam:

> . . . it was something they slipped into more than they chose; they thought they were going to have time for clear, well-planned choices, to decide how many men and what type of strategy they would follow, but events got ahead of them. The pressures from Saigon for more and more men would exceed Washington's capacity to slow it down and think coolly, and so the decisions evolved rather than were made, and Washington slipped into a ground combat war.
>
> [11, p. 544]

What can we say then about Johnson's decisions to escalate the war in 1965? Here we have a situation, apparently a common one if our other studies can be used as a guide, where an emergent strategy became a deliberate one. Johnson's decisions of 1965, unlike those of 1968, did not break any pattern. Quite the contrary, they formalized one that was becoming increasingly evident since 1962. The U.S. was fighting a war in 1965, no longer advising an ally. In other words, the strategy-maker perceived an unintended pattern in a stream of decisions and made that pattern the intended one for the future. An emergent strategy, once recognized, became a deliberate strategy. (Thus not only we, but also the leaders we studied, were perceivers of patterns in decision streams.) A similar phenomenon—although less pronounced—seemed to be at play in Volkswagen in the 1970s. Out of the grouping of the 1960s, Leiding perceived an emergent pattern, which we might call the Audi strategy. One car—stylish, front-wheel drive, water cooled—seemed to be most successful in the new environment. And so he built the new gestalt around it. The general conclusion seems to be that new strategies sometimes have incubation periods. While the old strategy is decaying, one or more emergent strategies are developing peripherally in the organization. Eventually one is selected and formalized as the new, intended strategy. Decisional behavior in effect coalesces around what seems to have worked for the organization—and perhaps also what lends coherence to the frustrating years of failing to realize intentions.

But the formalization of an emergent strategy is hardly incidental to the organization. As the Vietnam period of 1965 to 1968 shows so clearly, the very act of explicating an implicit strategy—of stating clearly and officially that it is to be the intended strategy—changes profoundly the attitude of the bureaucracy and of the environment to it. Johnson's decisions of 1965 opened the flood-gates of escalation. Had he remained in limbo, refusing to make a decision (all the while, the decisions in fact being made for him on the battlefield), it is doubtful that the military bureaucracy could have pursued escalation so vigorously. In effect, the very fact of making a strategy explicit—even an implicit one that is evident to all—provides a clear and formal invitation to the bureaucracy to run with it. (One could of course make the reverse point, that the very fact of his having remained in limbo for two years built up a charge in the military establishment that went off with that much more explosive force when the detonator was finally released.)

To overstate the bureaucracy's position, it says to its top management: "Our business is running the operations; your's is formulating the strategy. But we need a clearly defined, intended strategy to do our job—to buy our machines, hire our workers, standardize our procedures. So please give us such a strategy—any strategy—so long as it is precise and stable [and lets us grow]." The danger in this innocent statement, of course, is that the bureaucracy runs like an elephant. The strategy that gets it moving may be no more consequential than a mouse, but once underway there is no stopping it. As Halberstam notes about Kennedy in 1963 and Johnson after 1965: ". . . the capacity to control a policy involving the military is greatest before the policy is initiated, but once started, no matter how small the initial step, a policy has a life and a thrust of its own, it is an organic thing" [11, p. 209]. Bureaucratic momentum takes over, happy to have a clear strategy, never stopping to question it. The strategy-maker may awake one day—as did Lyndon Johnson in 1968—to find that his intended strategy has somehow been implemented beyond his wildest intentions. It has been *overrealized.* Thus, "make your strategy explicit" may be a popular prescription of the management consultant [18], but in the light of this research it can sometimes be seen to constitute questionable advice indeed.

## Conclusion

This article has been written with the intention of bringing a new kind of description to the much misunderstood process of strategy formation in organizations. A few descriptive studies—two of which are reported here—constitute a limited data base, but they do call into question a number of assumptions about the process, at least in certain contexts. A strategy is not a fixed plan, nor does it change systematically at pre-arranged times solely at the will of management. The dichotomy between strategy formulation and strategy implementation is a false one under certain common conditions, because it ignores the learning that must often follow the conception of an intended strategy. Indeed the very word "form*ul*ation" is misleading since we commonly refer to as "strategies" many patterns in organizational decisions that form without conscious or deliberate thought. Even Chandler's well known edict of structure follows strategy [5] must be called into question because of the influence of bureaucratic momentum on strategy formation. The aggressive, proactive strategymaker—the hero of the literature on entrepreneurship—can under some conditions do more harm than the hesitant, reactive one. Contingency planning, a popular prescription in times of environmental turbulence, can be risky because the plans may tend to become actualized, whether needed or not. And so too can it sometimes be risky to make strategy explicit, notably in an uncertain environment with an aggressive bureaucracy. In general, the contemporary prescriptions and normative techniques of analysis and planning—and the debate that accompanies them—seem unable to address the complex reality of strategy formation. To tell management to state its goals precisely, assess its strengths and weaknesses, plan systematically on schedule, and make the resulting strategies explicit are at best overly general guide-lines, at worst demonstrably misleading precepts to organizations that face a confusing reality.

There is perhaps no process in organizations that is more demanding of human cognition than strategy formation. Every strategy-maker faces an impossible overload of information (much of it soft); as a result he can have no optimal process to follow. The researcher or management scientist who seeks to understand strategy formation is up against the same cognitive constraints, but with poorer access to the necessary information. Thus he faces no easy task. But proceed he must, for the old prescriptions are not working and new ones are badly needed. These will only grow out of a sophisticated understanding of the rich reality of strategy formation, and that will require an open mind, a recognition of how little we really know, and intensive, painstaking research.[5]

## Notes

1 Where a decision is defined as a commitment to action, usually a commitment of resources [15].

2 The war production period could also have been viewed as one of continuity in strategy.

3 This is called a period of flux in the sense that Volkswagenwerk was looking haphazardly for a replacement for its beetle. It could also be called a period of continuity in the sense that the firm pursued a strategy of model diversification.

4 Chandler [5] makes the same point to explain the expansion of the DuPont company after World War I, when it found itself with excess capacity.

5 The author wishes to acknowledge the contributions of Ron Wilson, Danny Miller, Bill Litwack, and Bob Woolard, who carried out the studies associated with this research; the Canada Council, which funded them; André Théorêt and later Roger Gosselin, who joined the group for the hypotheses-generating sessions; and Jim Waters who commented on an earlier draft of the paper.

## References

1 Allison, G. T., *Essence of Decision*, Little Brown, Boston, Mass., 1971.

2 Ansoff, H. I., *Corporate Strategy*, McGraw-Hill, New York, 1965.

3 Bowman, E. H., "Strategy and the Weather," *Sloan Management Review*, (Winter, 1976), pp. 49–58.

4 Braybrooke, D. and Lindblom, C. E., *A Strategy of Decision*, Free Press, New York, 1963.

5 Chandler, A. D., *Strategy and Structure*, MIT Press, Cambridge, Mass., 1962.

6 Cole, A. H., *Business Enterprise in a Social Setting*, Harvard Univ. Press, Cambridge, Mass., 1959.

7 Collins, O. and Moore, D. G., *The Organization Makers*, Appleton-Century-Crofts, New York, 1970.

8 Cyert, R. M. and March, J. G., *A Behavioral Theory of the Firm*, Prentice-Hall, Englewood Cliffs, N. J., 1963.

9 Drucker, P. F., "Entrepreneurship in the Business Enterprise," *Journal of Business Policy*, Vol. 1, No. 1 (1970), pp. 3–12.

10 Feld, M. O., "Information and Authority: The Structure of Military Organization," *American Sociological Review*, Vol. 24 (1959), pp. 15–22.

11 Halberstam, D., *The Best and the Brightest*, Random House, New York, 1972.

12 Lindblom, C. E., "The Science of 'Muddling Through'," *Public Administration Review*, Vol. 19 (1959), pp. 79–88.

13 ——, *The Policy-Making Process*, Prentice-Hall, Englewood Cliffs, N.J., 1968.

14 Mintzberg, H., "Strategy-Making in Three Modes," *California Management Review*, Vol. 16, No. 2 (1973), pp. 44–53.

15 ——, Raisinghani, D. and Théorêt, A., "The Structure of 'Unstructured' Decision Processes," *Administrative Science Quarterly*, Vol. 21, No. 2 (1976), pp. 246–275.

16 Ornstein, R. E., *The Psychology of Consciousness*, Freeman, San Francisco, Calif., 1972.

17 Steiner, G. A., *Top Management Planning*, Macmillan, New York, 1969.

18 Tilles, S., "How to Evaluate Corporate Strategy," *Harvard Business Review*, Vol. 41 (July–August, 1963), pp. 111–121.

# 25

# CRAFTING STRATEGY

*Henry Mintzberg*

Source: *Harvard Business Review* 65(4) (1987): 66–75.

Imagine someone planning strategy. What likely springs to mind is an image of orderly thinking: a senior manager, or a group of them, sitting in an office formulating courses of action that everyone else will implement on schedule. The keynote is reason – rational control, the systematic analysis of competitors and markets, of company strengths and weaknesses, the combination of these analyses producing clear, explicit, full-blown strategies.

Now imagine someone *crafting* strategy. A wholly different image likely results, as different from planning as craft is from mechanization. Craft evokes traditional skill, dedication, perfection through the mastery of detail. What springs to mind is not so much thinking and reason as involvement, a feeling of intimacy and harmony with the materials at hand, developed through long experience and commitment. Formulation and implementation merge into a fluid process of learning through which creative strategies evolve.

My thesis is simple: the crafting image better captures the process by which effective strategies come to be. The planning image, long popular in the literature, distorts these processes and thereby misguides organizations that embrace it unreservedly.

In developing this thesis, I shall draw on the experiences of a single craftsman, a potter, and compare them with the results of a research project that tracked the strategies of a number of corporations across several decades. Because the two contexts are so obviously different, my metaphor, like my assertion, may seem farfetched at first. Yet if we think of a craftsman as an organization of one, we can see that he or she must also resolve one of the great challenges the corporate strategist faces: knowing the organization's capabilities well enough to think deeply enough about its strategic direction. By considering strategy making from the perspective of one person, free of all the paraphernalia of what has been called the strategy industry, we can learn something about the formation of strategy in the corporation. For much as our potter has to manage her craft, so too managers have to craft their strategy.

At work, the potter sits before a lump of clay on the wheel. Her mind is on the clay, but she is also aware of sitting between her past experiences and her future prospects. She knows exactly what has and has not worked for her in the past. She has an intimate knowledge of her work, her capabilities, and her markets. As a craftsman, she senses rather than analyzes these things; her knowledge is "tacit." All these things are working in her mind as her hands are working the clay. The product that emerges on the wheel is likely to be in the tradition of her past work, but she may break away and embark on a new direction. Even so, the past is no less present, projecting itself into the future.

In my metaphor, managers are craftsmen and strategy is their clay. Like the potter, they sit between a past of corporate capabilities and a future of market opportunities. And if they are truly craftsmen, they bring to their work an equally intimate knowledge of the materials at hand. That is the essence of crafting strategy.

In the pages that follow, we will explore this metaphor by looking at how strategies get made as opposed to how they are supposed to get made. Throughout, I will be drawing on the two sets of experiences I've mentioned. One, described in the insert, is a research project on patterns in strategy formation that has been going on at McGill University under my direction since 1971. The second is the stream of work of a successful potter, my wife, who began her craft in 1967.

## Strategies are both plans for the future and patterns from the past

Ask almost anyone what strategy is, and they will define it as a plan of some sort, an explicit guide to future behavior. Then ask them what strategy a competitor or a government or even they themselves have actually pursued. Chances are they will describe consistency in *past* behavior – a pattern in action over time. Strategy, it turns out, is one of those words that people define in one way and often use in another, without realizing the difference.

The reason for this is simple. Strategy's formal definition and its Greek military origins not-withstanding, we need the word as much to explain past actions as to describe intended behavior. After all, if strategies can be planned and intended, they can also be pursued and realized (or not realized, as the case may be). And pattern in action, or what we call realized strategy, explains that pursuit. Moreover, just as a plan need not produce a pattern (some strategies that are intended are simply not realized), so too a pattern need not result from a plan. An organization can have a pattern (or realized strategy) without knowing it, let alone making it explicit.

Patterns, like beauty, are in the mind of the beholder, of course. But anyone reviewing a chronological lineup of our craftsman's work would have little trouble discerning clear patterns, at least in certain periods. Until 1974, for example, she made small, decorative ceramic animals and objects of various kinds. Then this "knickknack strategy" stopped abruptly, and eventually new patterns formed around waferlike sculptures and ceramic bowls, highly textured and unglazed.

Finding equivalent patterns in action for organizations isn't that much more difficult. Indeed, for such large companies as Volkswagenwerk and Air Canada, in our research, it proved simpler! (As well it should. A craftsman, after all, can change what she does in a studio a lot more easily than a Volkswagenwerk can retool its assembly lines.) Mapping the product models at Volkswagenwerk from the late 1940s to the late 1970s, for example, uncovers a clear pattern of concentration on the Beetle, followed in the late 1960s by a frantic search for replacements through acquisitions and internally developed new models, to a strategic reorientation around more stylish, water-cooled, front-wheel-drive vehicles in the mid-1970s.

But what about intended strategies, those formal plans and pronouncements we think of when we use the term *strategy*? Ironically, here we run into all kinds of problems. Even with a single craftsman, how can we know what her intended strategies really were? If we could go back, would we find expressions of intention? And if we could, would we be able to trust them? We often fool ourselves, as well as others, by denying our subconscious motives. And remember that intentions are cheap, at least when compared with realizations.

### *Reading the organization's mind*

If you believe all this has more to do with the Freudian recesses of a craftsman's mind than with the practical realities of producing automobiles, then think again. For who knows what the intended strategies of a Volkswagenwerk really mean, let alone what they are? Can we simply assume in this collective context that the company's intended strategies are represented by its formal plans or by other statements emanating from the executive suite? Might these be just vain hopes or rationalizations or ploys to fool the competition? And even if expressed intentions exist, to what extent do others in the organization share them? How do we read the collective mind? Who is the strategist anyway?

The traditional view of strategic management resolves these problems quite simply, by what organizational theorists call attribution. You see it all the time in the business press. When General Motors acts, it's because Roger Smith has made a strategy. Given realization, there must have been intention, and that is automatically attributed to the chief.

In a short magazine article, this assumption is understandable. Journalists don't have a lot of time to uncover the origins of strategy, and GM is a large, complicated organization. But just consider all the complexity and confusion that gets tucked under this assumption – all the meetings and debates, the many people, the dead ends, the folding and unfolding of ideas. Now imagine trying to build a formal strategy-making system around that assumption. Is it any wonder that formal strategic planning is often such a resounding failure?

To unravel some of the confusion – and move away from the artificial complexity we have piled around the strategy-making process – we need to get back to some basic concepts. The most basic of all is the intimate connection between thought and action. That is the key to craft, and so also to the crafting of strategy.

## Strategies need not be deliberate – they can also emerge

Virtually everything that has been written about strategy making depicts it as a deliberate process. First we think, then we act. We formulate, then we implement. The progression seems so perfectly sensible. Why would anybody want to proceed differently?

Our potter is in the studio, rolling the clay to make a waferlike sculpture. The clay sticks to the rolling pin, and a round form appears. Why not make a cylindrical vase? One idea leads to another, until a new pattern forms. Action has driven thinking: a strategy has emerged.

Out in the field, a salesman visits a customer. The product isn't quite right, and together they work out some modifications. The salesman returns to his company and puts the changes through; after two or three more rounds, they finally get it right. A new product emerges, which eventually opens up a new market. The company has changed strategic course.

In fact, most salespeople are less fortunate than this one or than our craftsman. In an organization of one, the implementor is the formulator, so innovations can be incorporated into strategy quickly and easily. In a large organization, the innovator may be ten levels removed from the leader who is supposed to dictate strategy and may also have to sell the idea to dozens of peers doing the same job.

Some salespeople, of course, can proceed on their own, modifying products to suit their customers and convincing skunkworks in the factory to produce them. In effect, they pursue their own strategies. Maybe no one else notices or cares. Sometimes, however, their innovations do get noticed, perhaps years later, when the company's prevalent strategies have broken down and its leaders are groping for something new. Then the salesperson's strategy may be allowed to pervade the system, to become organizational.

Is this story farfetched? Certainly not. We've all heard stories like it. But since we tend to see only what we believe, if we believe that strategies have to be planned, we're unlikely to see the real meaning such stories hold.

Consider how the National Film Board of Canada (NFB) came to adopt a feature-film strategy. The NFB is a federal government agency, famous for its creativity and expert in the production of short documentaries. Some years back, it funded a filmmaker on a project that unexpectedly ran long. To distribute his film, the NFB turned to theaters and so inadvertently gained experience in marketing feature-length films. Other filmmakers caught onto the idea, and eventually the NFB found itself pursuing a feature-film strategy – a pattern of producing such films.

My point is simple, deceptively simple: strategies can *form* as well as be *formulated.* A realized strategy can emerge in response to an evolving situation, or it can be brought about deliberately, through a process of formulation followed by implementation. But when these planned intentions do not produce the desired actions, organizations are left with unrealized strategies.

Today we hear a great deal about unrealized strategies, almost always in concert with the claim that implementation has failed. Management has been lax, controls have been loose, people haven't been committed. Excuses abound. At times, indeed, they may be valid. But often these explanations prove too easy. So some people look beyond implementation to formulation. The strategists haven't been smart enough.

While it is certainly true that many intended strategies are ill conceived, I believe that the problem often lies one step beyond, in the distinction we make between formulation and implementation, the common assumption that thought must be independent of (and precede) action. Sure, people could be smarter – but not only by conceiving more clever strategies. Sometimes they can be smarter by allowing their strategies to develop gradually, through the organization's actions and experiences. Smart strategists appreciate that they cannot always be smart enough to think through everything in advance.

### *Hands & minds*

No craftsman thinks some days and works others. The craftsman's mind is going constantly, in tandem with her hands. Yet large organizations try to separate the work of minds and hands. In so doing, they often sever the vital feedback link between the two. The salesperson who finds a customer with an unmet need may possess the most strategic bit of information in the entire organization. But that information is useless if he or she cannot create a strategy in response to it or else convey the information to someone who can – because the channels are blocked or because the formulators have simply finished formulating. The notion that strategy is something that should happen way up there, far removed from the details of running an organization on a daily basis, is one of the great fallacies of conventional strategic management. And it explains a good many of the most dramatic failures in business and public policy today.

We at McGill call strategies like the NFB's that appear without clear intentions – or in spite of them – emergent strategies. Actions simply converge into patterns. They may become deliberate, of course, if the pattern is recognized and then legitimated by senior management. But that's after the fact.

All this may sound rather strange, I know. Strategies that emerge? Managers who acknowledge strategies already formed? Over the years, our research group at McGill has met with a good deal of resistance from people upset by what they perceive to be our passive definition of a word so bound up with proactive behavior and free will. After all, strategy means control – the ancient Greeks used it to describe the art of the army general.

### *Strategic learning*

But we have persisted in this usage for one reason: learning. Purely deliberate strategy precludes learning once the strategy is formulated, emergent strategy fosters it. People take actions one by one and respond to them, so that patterns eventually form.

Our craftsman tries to make a freestanding sculptural form. It doesn't work, so she rounds it a bit here, flattens it a bit there. The result looks better, but still isn't quite right. She makes another and another and another. Eventually, after days or months or years, she finally has what she wants. She is off on a new strategy.

In practice, of course, all strategy making walks on two feet, one deliberate, the other emergent. For just as purely deliberate strategy making precludes learning, so purely emergent strategy making precludes control. Pushed to the limit, neither approach makes much sense. Learning must be coupled with control. That is why the McGill research group uses the word *strategy* for both emergent and deliberate behavior.

Likewise, there is no such thing as a purely deliberate strategy or a purely emergent one. No organization – not even the ones commanded by those ancient Greek generals – knows enough to work everything out in advance, to ignore learning en route. And no one – not even a solitary potter – can be flexible enough to leave everything to happenstance, to give up all control. Craft requires control just as it requires responsiveness to the material at hand. Thus deliberate and emergent strategy form the end points of a continuum along which the strategies that are crafted in the real world may be found. Some strategies may approach either end, but many more fall at intermediate points.

## Effective strategies develop in all kinds of strange ways

Effective strategies can show up in the strangest places and develop through the most unexpected means. There is no one best way to make strategy.

The form for a cat collapses on the wheel, and our potter sees a bull taking shape. Clay sticks to a rolling pin, and a line of cylinders results. Wafers come into being because of a shortage of clay and limited kiln space in a studio in France. Thus errors become opportunities, and limitations stimulate creativity. The natural propensity to experiment, even boredom, likewise stimulate strategic change.

Organizations that craft their strategies have similar experiences. Recall the National Film Board with its inadvertently long film. Or consider its experiences with experimental films, which made special use of animation and sound. For 20 years, the NFB produced a bare but steady trickle of such films. In fact, every film but one in that trickle was produced by a single person, Norman McLaren, the NFB's most celebrated filmmaker. McLaren pursued a *personal strategy* of experimentation, deliberate for him perhaps (though who can know whether he had the whole stream in mind or simply planned one film at a time?) but not for the organization. Then 20 years later, others followed his lead and the trickle widened, his personal strategy becoming more broadly organizational.

Conversely, in 1952, when television came to Canada, a *consensus strategy* quickly emerged at the NFB. Senior management was not keen on producing films for the new medium. But while the arguments raged, one filmmaker quietly went off and made a single series for TV. That precedent set, one by one his colleagues leapt in, and within months the NFB – and its management – found themselves committed for several years to a new strategy with an intensity unmatched before or since. This consensus strategy arose spontaneously, as a result of many independent decisions made by the filmmakers about the films they wished to make. Can we call this strategy deliberate? For the filmmakers perhaps; for senior management certainly not. But for the organization? It all depends on your perspective, on how you choose to read the organization's mind.

While the NFB may seem like an extreme case, it highlights behavior that can be found, albeit in muted form, in all organizations. Those who doubt this might read Richard Pascale's account of how Honda stumbled into its enormous success in the American motorcycle market. Brilliant as its strategy may have looked after the fact, Honda's managers made almost every conceivable mistake until the market finally hit them over the head with the right formula. The Honda managers on site in America, driving their products themselves (and thus inadvertently picking up market reaction), did only one thing right: they learned, firsthand.[1]

### *Grass-roots strategy making*

These strategies all reflect, in whole or part, what we like to call a grass-roots approach to strategic management. Strategies grow like weeds in a garden. They take root in all kinds of places, wherever people have the capacity to learn (because they are in touch with the situation) and the resources to support that capacity. These strategies become organizational when they become collective, that is, when they proliferate to guide the behavior of the organization at large.

Of course, this view is overstated. But it is no less extreme than the conventional view of strategic management, which might be labeled the hot-house approach. Neither is right. Reality falls between the two. Some of the most effective strategies we uncovered in our research combined deliberation and control with flexibility and organizational learning.

Consider first what we call the *umbrella strategy*. Here senior management sets out broad guidelines (say, to produce only high-margin products at the cutting edge of technology or to favor products using bonding technology) and leaves the specifics (such as what these products will be) to others lower down in the organization. This strategy is not only deliberate (in its guidelines) and emergent (in its specifics), but it is also deliberately emergent in that the process is consciously managed to allow strategies to emerge en route. IBM used the umbrella strategy in the early 1960s with the impending 360 series, when its senior management approved a set of broad criteria for the design of a family of computers later developed in detail throughout the organization.[2]

Deliberately emergent, too, is what we call the *process strategy*. Here management controls the process of strategy formation – concerning itself with the design of the structure, its staffing, procedures, and so on – while leaving the actual content to others.

Both process and umbrella strategies seem to be especially prevalent in businesses that require great expertise and creativity – a 3M, a Hewlett-Packard, a National Film Board. Such organizations can be effective only if their implementors are allowed to be formulators because it is people way down in the hierarchy who are in touch with the situation at hand and have the requisite technical expertise. In a sense, these are organizations peopled with craftsmen, all of whom must be strategists.

## Strategic reorientations happen in brief, quantum leaps

The conventional view of strategic management, especially in the planning literature, claims that change must be continuous: the organization should be adapting all the time. Yet this view proves to be ironic because the very concept of strategy is rooted in stability, not change. As this same literature makes clear, organizations pursue strategies to set direction, to lay out courses of action, and to elicit cooperation from their members around common, established guide-lines. By any definition, strategy imposes stability on an organization. No stability means no strategy (no course to the future, no pattern from the past). Indeed, the very fact of having a strategy, and especially of making it explicit (as the conventional literature implores managers to do), creates resistance to strategic change!

What the conventional view fails to come to grips with, then, is how and when to promote change. A fundamental dilemma of strategy making is the need to reconcile the forces for stability and for change—to focus efforts and gain operating efficiencies on the one hand, yet adapt and maintain currency with a changing external environment on the other.

### *Quantum leaps*

Our own research and that of colleagues suggest that organizations resolve these opposing forces by attending first to one and then to the other. Clear periods of stability and change can usually be distinguished in any organization: while it is true that particular strategies may always be changing marginally, it seems equally true that major shifts in strategic orientation occur only rarely.

In our study of Steinberg Inc., a large Quebec supermarket chain headquartered in Montreal, we found only two important reorientations in the 60 years from its founding to the mid-1970s: a shift to self-service in 1933 and the introduction of shopping centers and public financing in 1953. At Volkswagenwerk, we saw only one between the late 1940s and the 1970s, the tumultuous shift from the traditional Beetle to the Audi-type design mentioned earlier. And at Air Canada, we found none over the airline's first four decades, following its initial positioning.

Our colleagues at McGill, Danny Miller and Peter Friesen, found this pattern of change so common in their studies of large numbers of companies (especially the high-performance ones) that they built a theory around it, which they labeled the quantum theory of strategic change.[3] Their basic point is that organizations adopt two distinctly different modes of behavior at different times.

Most of the time they pursue a given strategic orientation. Change may seem continuous, but it occurs in the context of that orientation (perfecting a given retailing formula, for example) and usually amounts to doing more of the same, perhaps better as well. Most organizations favor these periods of stability because they achieve success not by changing strategies but by exploiting the ones they have. They, like craftsmen, seek continuous improvement by using their distinctive competencies in established courses.

While this goes on, however, the world continues to change, sometimes slowly, occasionally in dramatic shifts. Thus gradually or suddenly, the organization's strategic orientation moves out of sync with its environment. Then what Miller and Friesen call a strategic revolution must take place. That long period of evolutionary change is suddenly punctuated by a brief bout of revolutionary turmoil in which the organization quickly alters many of its established patterns. In effect, it tries to leap to a new stability quickly to reestablish an integrated posture among a new set of strategies, structures, and culture.

But what about all those emergent strategies, growing like weeds around the organization? What the quantum theory suggests is that the really novel ones are generally held in check in some corner of the organization until a strategic revolution becomes necessary. Then as an alternative to having to develop new strategies from scratch or having to import generic strategies from competitors, the organization can turn to its own emerging patterns to find its new orientation. As the old, established strategy disintegrates, the seeds of the new one begin to spread.

This quantum theory of change seems to apply particularly well to large, established, mass-production companies. Because they are especially reliant on standardized procedures, their resistance to strategic reorientation tends to be especially fierce. So we find long periods of stability broken by short disruptive periods of revolutionary change.

Volkswagenwerk is a case in point. Long enamored of the Beetle and armed with a tightly integrated set of strategies, the company ignored fundamental changes in its markets throughout the late 1950s and 1960s. The bureaucratic momentum of its mass-production organization combined with the psychological momentum of its leader, who institutionalized the strategies in the first place. When change finally did come, it was tumultuous: the company groped its way through a hodgepodge of products before it settled on a new set of vehicles championed by a new leader. Strategic reorientations really are cultural revolutions.

### *Cycles of change*

In more creative organizations, we see a somewhat different pattern of change and stability, one that's more balanced. Companies in the business of producing novel outputs apparently need to fly off in all directions from time to time to sustain their creativity. Yet they also need to settle down after such periods to find some order in the resulting chaos.

The National Film Board's tendency to move in and out of focus through remarkably balanced periods of convergence and divergence is a case in point. Concentrated production of films to aid the war effort in the 1940s gave way to great divergence after the war as the organization sought a new raison d'être. Then the advent of television brought back a very sharp focus in the early 1950s, as noted earlier. But in the late 1950s, this dissipated almost as quickly as it began, giving rise to another creative period of exploration. Then the social changes in the early 1960s evoked a new period of convergence around experimental films and social issues.

We use the label "adhocracy" for organizations, like the National Film Board, that produce individual, or custom-made, products (or designs) in an innovative way, on a project basis.[4] Our craftsman is an adhocracy of sorts too, since each of her ceramic sculptures is unique. And her pattern of strategic change was much like that of the NFB's, with evident cycles of convergence and divergence: a focus on knick-knacks from 1967 to 1972; then a period of exploration to about 1976, which resulted in a refocus on ceramic sculptures; that continued to about 1981, to be followed by a period of searching for new directions. More recently, a focus on ceramic murals seems to be emerging.

Whether through quantum revolutions or cycles of convergence and divergence, however, organizations seem to need to separate in time the basic forces for change and stability, reconciling them by attending to each in turn. Many strategic failures can be attributed either to mixing the two or to an obsession with one of these forces at the expense of the other.

The problems are evident in the work of many craftsmen. On the one hand, there are those who seize on the perfection of a single theme and never change. Eventually the creativity disappears from their work and the world passes them by—much as it did Volkswagenwerk until the company was shocked into its strategic revolution. And then there are those who are always changing, who flit from one idea to another and never settle down. Because no theme or strategy ever emerges in their work, they cannot exploit or even develop any distinctive competence. And because their work lacks definition, identity crises are likely to develop, with neither the craftsmen nor their clientele knowing what to make of it. Miller and Friesen found this behavior in conventional business too; they label it "the impulsive firm running blind."[5] How often have we seen it in companies that go on acquisition sprees?

## To manage strategy is to craft thought and action, control and learning, stability and change

The popular view sees the strategist as a planner or as a visionary, someone sitting on a pedestal dictating brilliant strategies for everyone else to implement. While recognizing the importance of thinking ahead and especially of the need for creative vision in this pedantic world, I wish to propose an additional view of the strategist—as a pattern recognizer, a learner if you will—who manages a process in which strategies (and visions) can emerge as well as be deliberately conceived. I also wish to redefine that strategist, to extend that someone into the collective entity made up of the many actors whose interplay speaks an organization's mind. This strategist *finds* strategies no less than creates them, often in patterns that form inadvertently in its own behavior.

What, then, does it mean to craft strategy? Let us return to the words associated with craft: dedication, experience, involvement with the material, the personal touch, mastery of detail, a sense of harmony and integration. Managers who craft strategy do not spend much time in executive suites reading MIS reports or industry analyses. They are involved, responsive to their materials, learning about their organizations and industries through personal touch. They are also sensitive to experience, recognizing that while individual vision may be important, other factors must help determine strategy as well.

### *Manage stability*

Managing strategy is mostly managing stability, not change. Indeed, most of the time senior managers should not be formulating strategy at all; they should be getting on with making their organizations as effective as possible in pursuing the strategies they already have. Like distinguished craftsmen, organizations become distinguished because they master the details.

To manage strategy, then, at least in the first instance, is not so much to promote change as to know *when* to do so. Advocates of strategic planning often urge managers to plan for perpetual instability in the environment (for example, by rolling over five-year plans annually). But this obsession with change is dysfunctional. Organizations that reassess their strategies continuously are like individuals who reassess their jobs or their marriages continuously—in both cases, people will drive themselves crazy or else reduce themselves to inaction. The formal planning process repeats itself so often and so mechanically that it desensitizes the organization to real change, programs it more and more deeply into set patterns, and thereby encourages it to make only minor adaptations.

So-called strategic planning must be recognized for what it is: a means, not to create strategy, but to program a strategy already created—to work out its implications formally. It is essentially analytic in nature, based on decomposition, while strategy creation is essentially a process of synthesis. That is why trying to create strategies through formal planning most often leads to extrapolating existing ones or copying those of competitors.

This is not to say that planners have no role to play in strategy formation. In addition to programming strategies created by other means, they can feed ad hoc analyses into the strategy-making process at the front end to be sure that the hard data are taken into consideration. They can also stimulate others to think strategically. And of course people called planners can be strategists too, so long as they are creative thinkers who are in touch with what is relevant. But that has nothing to do with the technology of formal planning.

### *Detect discontinuity*

Environments do not change on any regular or orderly basis. And they seldom undergo continuous dramatic change, claims about our "age of discontinuity" and environmental "turbulence" notwithstanding. (Go tell people who lived through the Great Depression or survivors of the siege of Leningrad during World War II that ours are turbulent times.) Much of the time, change is minor and even temporary and requires no strategic response. Once in a while there is a truly significant discontinuity or, even less often, a gestalt shift in the environment, where everything important seems to change at once. But these events, while critical, are also easy to recognize.

The real challenge in crafting strategy lies in detecting the subtle discontinuities that may undermine a business in the future. And for that, there is no technique, no program, just a sharp mind in touch with the situation. Such discontinuities are unexpected and irregular, essentially unprecedented. They can be dealt with only by minds that are attuned to existing patterns yet able to perceive important breaks in them. Unfortunately, this form of strategic thinking tends to atrophy during the long periods of stability that most organizations experience (just as it did at Volkswagenwerk during the 1950s and 1960s). So the trick is to manage within a given strategic orientation most of the time yet be able to pick out the occasional discontinuity that really matters.

The Steinberg chain was built and run for more than half a century by a man named Sam Steinberg. For 20 years, the company concentrated on perfecting a self-service retailing formula introduced in 1933. Installing fluorescent lighting and figuring out how to package meat in cellophane wrapping were the "strategic" issues of the day. Then in 1952, with the arrival of the first shopping center in Montreal, Steinberg realized he had to redefine his business almost overnight. He knew he needed to control those shopping centers and that control would require public financing and other major changes. So he reoriented his business. The ability to make that kind of switch in thinking is the essence of strategic management. And it has more to do with vision and involvement than it does with analytic technique.

### *Know the business*

Sam Steinberg was the epitome of the entrepreneur, a man intimately involved with all the details of his business, who spent Saturday mornings visiting his stores. As he told us in discussing his company's competitive advantage:

"Nobody knew the grocery business like we did. Everything has to do with your knowledge. I knew merchandise, I knew cost, I knew selling, I knew customers. I knew everything, and I passed on all my knowledge; I kept teaching my people. That's the advantage we had. Our competitors couldn't touch us."

Note the kind of knowledge involved: not intellectual knowledge, not analytical reports or abstracted facts and figures (though these can certainly help), but personal knowledge, intimate understanding, equivalent to the craftsman's feel for the clay. Facts are available to anyone; this kind of knowledge is not. Wisdom is the word that captures it best. But wisdom is a word that has been lost in the bureaucracies we have built for ourselves, systems designed to distance leaders from operating details. Show me managers who think they can rely on formal planning to create their strategies, and I'll show you managers who lack intimate knowledge of their businesses or the creativity to do something with it.

Craftsmen have to train themselves to see, to pick up things other people miss. The same holds true for managers of strategy. It is those with a kind of peripheral vision who are best able to detect and take advantage of events as they unfold.

### *Manage patterns*

Whether in an executive suite in Manhattan or a pottery studio in Montreal, a key to managing strategy is the ability to detect emerging patterns and help them take shape. The job of the manager is not just to preconceive specific strategies but also to recognize their emergence elsewhere in the organization and intervene when appropriate.

Like weeds that appear unexpectedly in a garden, some emergent strategies may need to be uprooted immediately. But management cannot be too quick to cut off the unexpected, for tomorrow's vision may grow out of today's aberration. (Europeans, after all, enjoy salads made from the leaves of the dandelion, America's most notorious weed.) Thus some patterns are worth watching until their effects have more clearly manifested themselves. Then those that prove useful can be made deliberate and be incorporated into the formal strategy, even if that means shifting the strategic umbrella to cover them.

To manage in this context, then, is to create the climate within which a wide variety of strategies can grow. In more complex organizations, this may mean building flexible structures, hiring creative people, defining broad umbrella strategies, and watching for the patterns that emerge.

### *Reconcile change and continuity*

Finally, managers considering radical departures need to keep the quantum theory of change in mind. As Ecclesiastes reminds us, there is a time to sow and a time to reap. Some new patterns must be held in check until the organization is ready for a strategic revolution, or at least a period of divergence. Managers who are obsessed with either change or stability are bound eventually to harm their organizations. As pattern recognizer, the manager has to be able to sense when to exploit an established crop of strategies and when to encourage new strains to displace the old.

While strategy is a word that is usually associated with the future, its link to the past is no less central. As Kierkegaard once observed, life is lived forward but understood backward. Managers may have to live strategy in the future, but they must understand it through the past.

Like potters at the wheel, organizations must make sense of the past if they hope to manage the future. Only by coming to understand the patterns that form in their own behavior do they get to know their capabilities and their potential. Thus crafting strategy, like managing craft, requires a natural synthesis of the future, present, and past.

## TRACKING STRATEGY

In 1971, I became intrigued by an unusual definition of strategy as a pattern in a stream of decisions (later changed to actions). I initiated a research project at McGill University, and over the next 13 years a team of us tracked the strategies of 11 organizations over several decades of their history. (Students at various levels also carried out about 20 other less comprehensive studies.) The organizations we studied were: Air Canada (1937–1976), Arcop, an architectural firm (1953–1978), Asbestos Corporation (1912–1975), Canadelle, a manufacturer of women's undergarments (1939–1976), McGill University (1829–1980), the National Film Board of Canada (1939–1976), Saturday Night Magazine (1928–1971), the Sherbrooke Record, a small daily newspaper (1946–1976), Steinberg Inc., a large supermarket chain (1917–1974), the U.S. military's strategy in Vietnam (1949–1973), and Volkswagenwerk (1934–1974).

As a first step, we developed chronological lists and graphs of the most important actions taken by each organization—such as store openings and closings, new flight destinations, and new product introductions. Second, we inferred patterns in these actions and labeled them as strategies.

Third, we represented graphically all the strategies we inferred in an organization so that we could line them up to see whether there were distinct periods in their development—for example, periods of stability, flux, or global change. Fourth, we used interviews and in-depth reports to study what appeared to be the key points of change in each organization's strategic history.

Finally, armed with all this strategic history, the research team studied each set of findings to develop conclusions about the process of strategy formation. Three themes guided us: the interplay of environment, leadership, and organization; the pattern of strategic change; and the processes by which strategies form. This article presents those conclusions.

### Author's note

Readers interested in learning more about the results of the tracking strategy project have a wide range of studies to draw from. Works published to date can be found in Robert Lamb and Paul Shivastava, eds., *Advances in Strategic Management*, Vol. 4 (Greenwich, Conn.: Jai Press, 1986), pp. 3–41; *Management Science*, May 1978, p. 934; *Administrative Science Quarterly*, June 1985, p. 160; J. Grant, ed., *Strategic Management Frontiers* (Greenwich, Conn.: Jai Press, forthcoming); *Canadian Journal of Administrative Sciences*, June 1984, p. 1; *Academy of Management Journal*, September 1982, p. 465; Robert Lamb, ed., *Competitive Strategic Management* (Englewood Cliffs, N.J.: Prentice-Hall, 1984).

## Notes

1 Richard T. Pascale, "Perspective on Strategy: The Real Story Behind Honda's Success," *California Management Review*, May–June 1984, p. 47.
2 James Brian Quinn, IBM (A) case, in James Brian Quinn, Henry Mintzberg, and Robert M. James, *The Strategy Process: Concepts, Contexts, Cases* (Englewood Cliffs, N.J.: Prentice-Hall, forthcoming).
3 See Danny Miller and Peter H. Friesen, *Organizations: A Quantum View* (Englewood Cliffs, N.J.: Prentice-Hall, 1984).
4 See my article "Organization Design: Fashion or Fit?" HBR January–February 1981, p. 103; also see my book *Structure in Fives: Designing Effective Organizations* (Englewood Cliffs, N.J.: Prentice-Hall, 1983). The term *adhocracy* was coined by Warren G. Bennis and Philip E. Slater in *The temporary Society* (New York: Harper & Row, 1964).
5 Danny Miller and Peter H. Friesen, "Archetypes of Strategy Formulation," *Management Science*, May 1978, p. 921.

# 26

# TWENTY-FIVE YEARS LATER . . . THE ILLUSIVE STRATEGY

*Henry Mintzberg*

Source: A. G. Bedeian (ed.) *Management Laureates: Collection of Autobiographical Essays*, Stamford, Conn.: JAI Press, 1993, vol. 2, pp. 323–74.

## Admonitions

I was going to close this piece with advice to the young scholar that you should always take your work seriously but never yourself. I put it here instead to express my apprehensions in doing this. I think it is useful to have on record comments on how careers that were lucky enough to emerge successfully unfolded, but there is the danger that the person in question will be taken, and will take him or herself, too seriously. To have succeeded in studying something or other has never made anyone intrinsically interesting; indeed I find some of my successful colleagues terrible bores.

In line with this, I try here to avoid discussing my private life. That is my own business; the issue in question is my working life. But because the two are obviously intertwined, I would like to make a single comment here about them. When I wrote on the back cover of *Mintzberg on Management: Inside Our Strange World of Organizations* (1989) that it "is written for those of us who spend our public lives dealing with organizations and our private lives escaping from them," I was not joking. That, if anything, has characterized much of my behavior. I am intrigued by organizations; all my work has set out to understand them. But when I play, I distance myself from them as far as possible. For example, I love to cycle on back roads in Europe, but I would never dream of taking an organized tour. Sure, I need an airline to get me there, but once I get off the plane, typically with a friend or two, we just get on our bikes and go. I hate to be organized by organizations. So my fascination with them works best at a distance, in commitment at least—not space, because I love to get inside them, as an observer or temporary advisor, and sense their behavior.

To tell my career story, I shall begin with how I fell into this business—academia as a vocation—and about business itself, or at least organizations in general. Then I shall outline my career in three phases. But in order to do this, I shall present some hard data—tracks of some patterns in my behavior over time. I can explain this in terms of the title of this essay.

I spent a semester (Fall 1990) at the London Business School. A member of the strategy group there called me in Montreal in the summer to arrange a faculty seminar and I was to get back to him on the title. When I didn't, he left a message that it would be called "The Illusive Strategy." Perfect, I thought, I'll speak to that. It was an inspired suggestion (of Charles Hampden-Turner).

Strategy formation has been my most sustained subject (as will be seen in the data): it is the subject of my first article, my greatest number of articles, and my steadiest stream of articles. Much of this work has revolved around the definitions of strategy as realized (pattern in action) in addition to intended, and emergent (realized despite intentions) in addition to deliberate (intentions realized).[1] Nonetheless, my own realized strategies have, if anything, tended to be rather deliberate. At least until recently. In the talk in London, I wished to review my work at that time, which involved a rather wide-ranging collection of papers and projects. Because the patterns among them may not have been clear, I thought it would be fun to use the talk to search them out—to infer my own strategies. Hence the appropriateness of the suggested title there, and my use of it here.

In 1978, I wrote a working paper titled "Ten Years Later: Some Personal Reflections on Management and Methodology," to review the first ten years of my career (parts of which appeared in "An Emerging Strategy of Direct Research" [1979b]). So here we have "twenty-five years later," more or less.[2]

One final warning. This is my career story as told by me. It is not reality but my own reconstruction of reality through my own perceptions. I did some research for this paper—went back into old files and documents, reviewed all the c.v.s I did over the years, reread some of my earliest papers, did a systematic analysis of my publications and course teaching, and so forth. That helped me to pin some things down, but it also revealed the fallacy of my memory if not my outright biases. While such a reconstruction may be of interest in and of itself, it should be read only for what it is.

## Origins of my career

I was hiking on the moors of Somerset with a friend a few weeks before writing this when he suddenly asked, "How did you come to study organizations anyway?" "I don't know," I answered, "it just happened. . . . One thing led to another. I never really thought about it. But it's worked out quite well." I guess I should try to answer his question here, which will require a bit of personal background.

I was born to a pretty comfortable family; my father owned a successful small firm that manufactured women's dresses. It may be true, as I claimed in the preface to my first book, that as a young boy I wondered what my father, as manager, did at the office. But this was certainly no more than a passing curiosity. Overall, I think I grew up as a pretty ordinary kid, not a bad student but never one in danger of being selected "most likely to succeed."

After reasonable grades in high school, I entered engineering studies at McGill, in mechanical because I used to love to tear engines apart (although I could never quite put all of them back together again). I really wanted to do industrial engineering, but McGill had no such program. My grades were average or a bit better, but in any event, engineering grew into an excuse to do extracurricular activities. Summers were spent mostly working in factories, from die making to time studies.

When graduation came, I do not recall having very clear intentions, other than that I was determined not to work for my father. I had to know if I could make it on my own. So I halfheartedly registered for the cycle of company interviews, and after discussing the future prospects of the McGill Redmen (football team) with several personnel types who read on my c.v. that I had been sports editor of the *McGill Daily*, I walked into an interview with Canadian National Railways. Imagine, this guy had a beard! (The year was 1961; only Fidel Castro had a beard then.) Not only that, but he was a biologist, working for the railroad, and talking about these strange studies he and a mixed group of colleagues were doing under what he called "operational research." When he looked at my c.v. and asked "What did you *accomplish* as sports editor of the *McGill Daily*?," I knew this was the place for me.

So there I found myself, doing OR when it was still common sense analysis rather than a lot of greedy technique. The CN was an exciting place to be in those days, one of the most progressive railroads in the world.

It was a good way to begin. For example, at one point I found myself fishing in a hump yard. A hump yard sorts incoming trains by passing them over a hill, off which they roll one car at a time, switched into the appropriate outgoing track and braked automatically according to various parameters fed into an analog computer—the distance to the last car on the track, coefficients for the friction effects of the track and the car, and so forth—to ensure an impact speed great enough to couple and gentle enough to spare the car and its contents (about 2–4 mph. as I recall). It was wonderful, new technology. Even if the yard was littered with the debris of broken coupling gears. So a Rube Goldberg type in the CN lab made a fishing rod, with a magnet for a hook and a speedometer on the reel, and I went a-fishing—to catch a histogram of impact speeds. Amid great blasts of mating from cars labelled "chinawear—do not hump," I drew my chart of coupling speeds: a fair proportion at zero that never made it, some in the desired range, and many others on up (well into the double figures, I recall—anyone who wants to learn about organizations should just once stand next to two boxcars meeting at 12 m.p.h.). The upshot was a meeting of the executive committee in which a presentation by a regional vice president about the glories of his Montreal hump yard was followed by the flinging of my histogram on the table by our vice president of research and development. A political battle ensued, and I was learning about organizations—at the top and the bottom, as well as all that empty space in between!

I always intended to go to graduate school, certainly not one of those soft business schools with all those obnoxious (later-to-be called) "fast trackers," but for a master's degree in industrial engineering or operational research, to become a consultant to small businesses. An uncle of mine, Jack Mintzberg, with whom I was rather close, had encouraged me in this direction, in fact hired me the previous summer to develop a costing system for his tag and label company after sending me to learn about it on a course in the United States. (My c.v. still lists my very first speech—in 1963, four years before my second—to the Society of Paper Box Manufacturers of Quebec, arranged that summer by Jack. I should add that despite his directing me toward business, it was Jack, I later came to realize, who first planted the seed of an academic career in my mind. As a young man, he had worked as a research assistant for Hans Salye, the eminent physiologist, and always regretted having given in to family pressures to go into business. But if the image was set back then, it was deeply buried in my subconscious, because I recall having no pretensions whatever of a career in academia. It was not that I dismissed my academic record an insufficient; I no more aspired to be a professor than to try out for quarterback of the Green Bay Packers.)

At the suggestion of an acquaintance, I applied to the industrial engineering master's program at New York University, well ahead of time. Finding myself one day in New York, after having been accepted, I called to meet someone in the department. After getting the runaround on the telephone, I decided this would never do, and so went over to Columbia to apply to their department. Still I would not consider a business school. But, of course, MIT was not a real business school; it was then called the School of Industrial Management and it gave a Master of Science degree. There was no way I would get in with my grades, but on a lark I applied anyway. For some reason (perhaps my extracurricular activities) they accepted me, so I had a decision to make. I went to see Sebastian B. Littauer, the grand old man of industrial engineering at Columbia, and he said "Go there; we could never do for you what they will do." One of those critical moments of one's life.

And so this aspiring industrial engineer went to MIT, and within weeks was writing articles in the student newspaper condemning the excessiveness of quantitative materials in the curriculum. I even published an editorial in

November dismissing any claims that they couldn't change the program by January. (I still had a bit to learn about professional bureaucracies!) The old journalist in me had come out once again (I would likely have ended up in journalism had I not become an academic . . . maybe I did!), not only literally in my extracurricular activities but also in my attraction to the softer interpretations of reality in place of the hard core analyses that surrounded me in the classroom.

I am not sure why I applied to the doctoral program at MIT. Perhaps it was the easy thing to do (easier than getting a job), perhaps I was getting increasingly interested in some of the softer questions of management—probably a bit of both. My grades in the master's program had been good but certainly not top; my GMAT of 602 was not bad for those days (though, based on figures I have seen recently, I would probably not even be considered for the current MIT master's program).

I applied to do the degree in policy. At the time, MIT had no area of policy, no professor of policy, no doctoral concentration in policy. All that obviously suited fine someone who wanted to escape the control of organizations. That it also suited the doctoral committee is, I believe, a tribute to its members' open-mindedness. A professor of operations management named Edward (Ned) Bowman, who had just returned from a year out as assistant to the president of Honeywell Computers, and was teaching one first policy course, had just taken over the chairmanship of the committee, and on informing me of my acceptance also said he had decided to supervise me himself, to find out what this field of policy was all about.

It was an unusual course of study to say the least—in terms of American doctoral program conventions, if not European. I went into Ned's office one day to ask what I should read for my comprehensive examinations, and he replied, more or less: "I don't know. Why don't you just draw up a reading list and read it." He did add a few books to the list I drew up from my own reading, helped by a visit across the river to Roland Christensen at Harvard which had lots of policy doctoral students. I also recall vividly—though the now chaired professor of policy at Wharton does not—that after walking away from a brief meeting with Ned in the hall, he called out that "I've decided there is no future in policy." "You'll change your mind," I called back.

I had a clear mission in my studies. Theory was challenging cases in those days, inspired by the Carnegie Graduate School of Industrial Administration innovations of Bach, Simon, Cyert *et al.*, and MIT was one of the faithful adherents. But policy, and management in general, were stepchildren in these schools, often barely taught at all.[3] Why could policy not be taught conceptually as marketing and finance were then so commonly done? So I set out on a search for conceptual materials—mostly in related fields, as there was little research base in policy itself—and began to outline a theoretical approach to the field. In December 1965, just a few months into the doctoral program, I submitted a course paper titled "The Future of Business Policy," which I wrote was "in response to a request by my program supervisor, Ned Bowman, to try to define the field. The explicit objective of this paper is to argue for the recognition of Business Policy as a management discipline at MIT." I viewed the field in terms of two processes, "guiding the firm: strategy making and planning" and "leadership: purpose, relationship to society, leadership style, and power." A section on "The Research Base" categorized the "underlying research" in terms of power, game theory, the Carnegie School, military strategists, and organizational goals, and the "applied research" in terms of leadership, firm in society, business policy texts, systems analysis (PPBS), and long-range planning, all supported by numerous references. (An appendix listed forty-two books that I had read.) I concluded that while "the literature is growing rapidly," the field appears to be less developed "largely due to the fact that there has been almost no attempt to classify and identify the literature that has been printed."

Ned Bowman left MIT before I started thesis work (to take on the controllership of Yale, later the business deanship at Ohio State, before going to Wharton, with periods back at MIT in between), but he was still there for my comprehensive examinations, which must have happened in late 1965. My major was in policy (but Ned did not present me with an examination that read "Write a comprehensive examination in Policy and answer it"), with minors in "Organizational Studies" and "Information and Control Systems." My underlying discipline was Political Science, which included some weird course material on all kinds of ways to fight a nuclear war.

With the exams behind me, there was merely the question of the thesis. Strategy making was my main interest, but in truth I had no sense of what I wanted to do, and I wasted six months finding out.

Igor Ansoff's book, *Corporate Strategy* (1965), had just appeared, and I was as taken with it as everyone else. So I decided I would try to extend the application of the Ansoff model from mergers and expansions to strategic planning in general. (Another course paper I wrote in December 1965 had considered "the arguments for and against planning" and outlined a model based on the conclusion "that bureaucracies can and must plan." I also came across a thick file of thesis proposals from March to September 1966, about a "Programmed" or "An Analytical Procedure for Strategic Planning.") But, once again, I was saved from myself: I could not find an organization in which to apply the model (or, nearer to the truth, my feeble attempt to convince the new dean at MIT to let me do so in the management school failed).

Some time earlier, James Webb, who headed up NASA in the Apollo era, approached that same individual (Bill Pounds) to be studied personally, as a manager. He believed NASA would ultimately be evaluated by its technological spin-offs on this planet, and he counted among these its own management advances (including, evidently, his own managerial style). As the only doctoral student at this school of management interested in management, I was approached to do this as a thesis. I dismissed the idea quickly—studying one chief executive was no way to make your way through the bastion of science that was MIT. I did, though, get a wonderful tour of NASA installations with several faculty members.

That was in late April 1966, and immediately upon my return to MIT, a conference took place to discuss "The Impact of Computers on Management."[4] There I saw a number of impressive individuals bog down on the question for lack of a conceptual framework within which to consider managerial work. Gulick's POSDCORB (*p*lanning, *o*rganizing, *s*taffing, *d*irecting, *co*ordinating, *r*eporting, and *b*udgeting[5]) was not of help, and in their discussions, they could scarcely get beyond attempts to equate computers with programmed activities and managerial work with the unprogrammed.[5] It occurred to me, having listened to people who certainly "knew" what managers did—all were involved with management in one way or another, including a number as successful managers themselves—that they did not "know" conceptually. And without that second kind of knowing, many of the most critical issues in management simply could not even be addressed. Clearly we needed to take a closer look at what managers really do.[6]

And so, bastion of science and all that notwithstanding, I came to study managerial work for my doctoral thesis. No one had bothered to tell me that doctoral dissertations are supposed to probe narrow, researchable issues; I don't bother to tell my own doctoral students either. (One professor did once tell me that an MIT dissertation should be "elegant"; he was referring to the method, not the results, and I have always prided myself on the inelegance, or at least the simplicity, of the methodology I used to study managerial work.)

Webb was no longer available, and I decided that I would observe the activities of five chief executives. That number had no special significance, other than being several and manageable, nor did my choice of organizations, except to ensure that all were in different domains. (Years later, having done a categorization of organizations,[7] I realized there was somewhat of a bias toward professional bureaucracies and adhocracies. But I doubt this much influenced the dimensions I was studying.)

I started to write letters to possible subjects. I hit it lucky quite early. James Gaven, who headed up the Arthur D. Little consulting firm, accepted immediately by return mail. He was well known in the United States at the time as the first retired army general to have publicly criticized the Viet Nam war effort. Thus, when I received a telephone call from the secretary of John Knowles, head of the Massachusetts General Hospital, saying he wouldn't do it but that he would like to talk to me, and after he offered various reasons, I chipped in with "That's too bad because General Gaven has accepted," and without loosing a breath, Knowles added "and that's why I can't do it for at least several weeks!" (Knowles was a wonderfully extroverted subject; years later he told me someone gave him an article I did on the research with the comment, "John, this sounds exactly like you!") I do not recall having to ask more than about ten chief executives altogether; the others who accepted were Bernard O'Keefe of E.G. & G., Inc., Harry B. (for Bulova) Henshel of the Bulova Watch Company, and, of course, Charlie Brown, this one head of the Newton Massachusetts school system. They were a wonderfully cooperative group.

Jim Hekimian, an MIT professor of control with an interest in policy, took over the chairmanship of my committee, which included Charlie Myers in industrial relations, and Don Carroll in operations management. (As Jim left MIT to become dean at Northeastern, Don ended up officially signing the thesis as chairman, before he too went off deaning, at Wharton.) For the most part, they knew as much—or, I should say, as little—about the subject as I did, except for Charlie Myers who had touched on it in his book with Harbison, *Management in the Industrial World* (McGraw-Hill, 1959). But they formed a wonderfully enthusiastic support group that encouraged me to put in everything (hence the host of asides in my thesis).

When the time came to defend the thesis (an event of obvious consequence at MIT—one doctoral student showed up aside from my committee), after I presented the results, having been assured earlier by Charlie Myers that there was nothing to worry about, the committee deliberated for about twenty minutes. An anxious me was finally informed that, oh, they were just discussing the publishing possibilities.

Having been assured by someone like Charlie Myers that the thesis was publishable, I kind of dropped it in the mail to a publisher (McGraw-Hill as I recall), not quite with a note as to where to send the checks. The reply was in kind, more or less to "occupant," saying "No, thank you." Not to worry, it must have been a mistake, so I sent the thesis off to a second publisher. Perhaps a dozen publishers later, I had no contract. So Charlie Myers stepped in and proposed it to the MIT Press. It seemed headed for publication when someone on their board questioned it and out it went for another review. I met that reviewer years later, who apologized to me. Carnegie-Mellon methodology jock meets sample of five, and I was back at the beginning.

It was at that time that I surprised my wife one evening by blurting out that I knew this was an important piece of work—that I just knew it would be prominent one day—and so, in the face of all those rejection letters, I would rewrite it and proceed. I was not prone to such claims, and I was not expressing a wish or some manifestation of arrogance so much as what felt like a certainty.

And so I rewrote the thesis and resubmitted it to the whole cluster of publishers. Again they all rejected it, luckily except for Harper & Row and Random House. And so the former published *The Nature of Managerial Work* in 1973. To quote the last line of Philip Roth's *Portnoy's Complaint*:

"So (said the doctor). Now vee may perhaps to begin. Yes?" (Random House, 1967, p. 274).

## Some real hard data

My occasional diatribes notwithstanding, hard data is not a bad thing; indeed some of my own articles are full of it. It helps to pin down some of the vagueness (and in turn to create some of its own). So I thought it might be useful to present some tangible traces of my own work, before I begin to describe the phases of my career, as I see them. I took all my publications of any consequence (i.e., excluding letters, short newspaper articles, and so forth), whether good or bad, academic or not, and categorized them in three ways: first as to whether they were empirical (deriving directly from my own research, interpreting this rather narrowly as articles rooted in the research rather than drawing off it), substantially conceptual, or practitioner (intended to populize findings); second as to subject matter, comprising strategy making, managerial work, organization (including structural and power issues), management in general (including a few publications on research and on the field of policy), analysis and/or intuition, and decision making; and third, as to coauthorship. The histograms for all of this are shown in Figure 1. Books are shown shaded in; obviously each was the equivalent work of many articles.

I published my first article, called "The Science of Strategy Making," as a doctoral student in 1967, and with the exception of 1969, my second year as a professor, I have published every year ever since, from a single article in five of the twenty-five years in question to as many as six articles and two books in 1983. (Figures for 1991 include material already accepted for publication; I write this in February 1991.) Probably the most consistent substream is the empirical, almost regularly one per year, interspersed by some empty years and a few with two publications. But the conceptual stream is far fuller, with more than double the number of publications and sometimes quite frequent in a single year (e.g., 1983 with the two books and five articles). Partly this reflects my propensity to conceptualize, but it also reflects the fact that conceptual articles, especially when spun off books in which I had already worked out the issue, were easier to do than empirical ones. But I should add that I always took great care and time with almost all of my writing, books as well as articles, conceptual and practitioner-oriented as well as empirical, with five drafts or more being the norm. Practitioner publications represent a thinner stream, more sporadic, but indicating my commitment from early on to trying to reach both audiences. Indeed, in mid-1976 I took great pride in having published at the same time one article in *Administrative Science Quarterly* and another in the *Harvard Business Review*.[8]

In terms of content, it could be concluded from the data that I passed from one focus to another, initially on managerial work in the early 1970s, then over to analysis and its relationship with intuition from the mid-1970s,

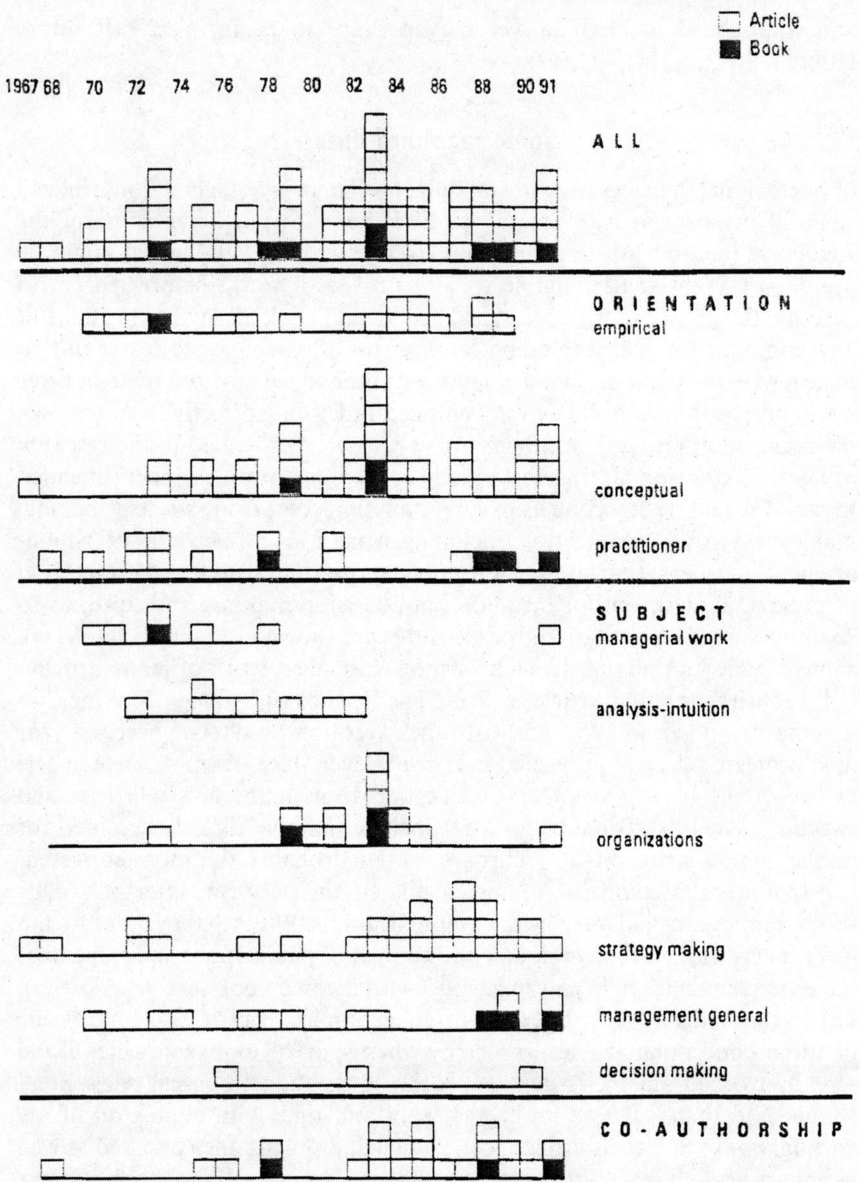


*Figure 1* Publications.

then to a heavy concentration on organizational issues (especially structure, power, and forms of organizations) from 1979 to 1984, and then to a heavier and more sustained focus on strategy making through the rest of the 1980s, with a rise at the end in the management-general category, representing especially two editions of a textbook[9] and one summary book for practitioners.[10] Three articles on decision making are shown, well spread out, the heaviest concentration of work being for the first one. That was published in 1976,[11] although the work was done in 1973 (indicating the need to take into account what can be long lead times in these figures). Management-general shows a thin trickle from early on to 1983, representing some of my practitioner articles as well as ones on research and on the field of policy. Finally, while strategy making clearly peaks as by far my heaviest concentration of articles, through most of the 1980s, that is a theme I have returned to throughout my career. Indeed, that first article as a doctoral student, in 1967, opened with a comparison of two approaches to strategy making that anticipated my much later comparison[12] of deliberate and emergent strategy:

> Man's beginnings were described in the Bible in terms of conscious planning and grand strategy. The opposing theory, developed by Darwin, suggested that no such grand design existed but that environmental forces gradually shaped man's evolution.
>
> The disagreement between the biblical and Darwinian theorists is paralleled on a more mundane level in the study of strategy-making. There are those who envision grand calculated designs for the corporate entity, and there are those who cite current practice to argue that organizational strategy evolves, shaped less by man than by his environment.[13]

I have included a histogram on coauthorship for what it may reflect. In general, I was a solo writer for most of my early years (although I did coauthor my second article with Jim Hekimian, in 1968). There was some joint work in the mid-1970s, based on a contracted monograph,[14] as well as my first article on decision making with two of my students,[15] but coauthorship became a serious and sustained activity only after Jim Waters joined the McGill faculty in 1976. Jim left McGill several years ago, and we suffered his tragic loss a short while ago. In the last few years, I have had an equally delightful collaboration with my colleague, Frances Westley, again around issues of strategy, although in recent years my variety of coauthorships has increased significantly (as can be seen, alongside everything else here, in the attached list of these publications). Finally, I should mention my collaboration with Danny Miller. Danny was my first doctoral student, and we have shared ideas closely and energetically for many years, although our formal collaboration has been restricted to that 1975 contracted monograph and one published paper called "The Case for Configuration" (1983).[16]

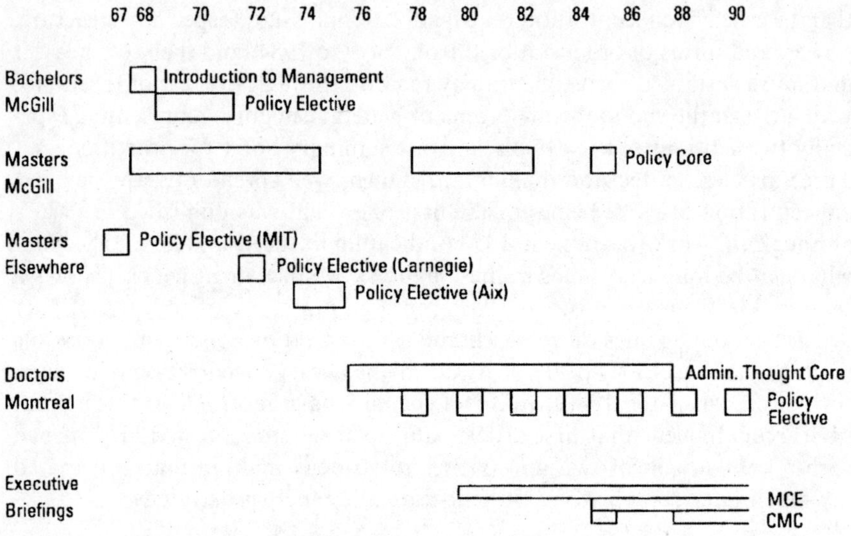

67 68 70 72 74 76 78 80 82 84 86 88 90

Bachelors McGill — Introduction to Management; Policy Elective

Masters McGill — Policy Core

Masters Elsewhere — Policy Elective (MIT); Policy Elective (Carnegie); Policy Elective (Aix)

Doctors Montreal — Admin. Thought Core; Policy Elective

Executive Briefings — MCE; CMC

*Figure 2* Teaching.

In Figure 2, I plot all my teaching activity. (My accessible records here are not complete, so there may be some inaccuracies, but this should not affect the overall patterns. The year recorded refers to the first of the whole academic year. For example, the Carnegie course shown in 1972 was actually taught in the Spring of 1973.)

As can be seen, I have not taught a great variety of courses, given the number of years. The mainstay of my teaching was mostly the MBA policy course; I was hired at McGill in 1968 to take over the full year core course that had fallen into disarray. In general, I taught one or two sections of it in almost all my years at McGill until recently, aside from periods of sabbatical or leave (to France in 1974–76 and Switzerland in the winter of 1983) and a three and a half year spell running the doctoral program in the late 1970s. I taught a similar master's elective course as a doctoral student at MIT, again as a visiting professor at Carnegie-Mellon in the Spring of 1973, and again on a sabbatical followed by a year's leave of absence in Aix-en-Provence, France in 1974–76 (technically in a "third cycle doctoral" program, but coded, as I see it, as master's level). I also taught some undergraduate courses in my early years at McGill—an introduction to management in my very first year and an elective "Seminar on Organizational Strategy" in the next three. In 1986 I negotiated myself out of McGill MBA teaching altogether to concentrate my efforts on research, writing, and doctoral training, at a reduced salary. (Figure 3 tabulates my appointments, sabbaticals and visits, etc.)

Our doctoral activity started up (as a joint program among the four Montreal universities) in 1976; I played a major role in its design and

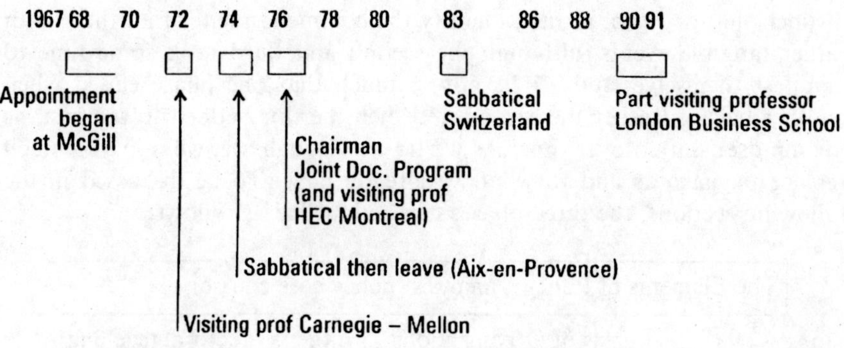


*Figure 3* Appointments.

championing, and when I returned from Aix-en-Provence in 1976, near its inception, I was asked to run it, which I did for three and a half years. For many years, I cotaught the introductory required course for all doctoral students, called "Fundamentals of Administrative Thought," and I have also offered a policy elective every second year, more or less, beginning in 1976 and occurring again right now, which remains my only teaching commitment at McGill.

Finally, the chart shows a stream of "executive briefings" beginning in 1980. This is a two-day public program that I do myself, which draws much of my work together for managers, who register from a wide variety of contexts. Originally offered by the Management Centre Europe (a Brussels-based training group associated with the American Management Association), it has become a regular activity, expanding in Europe from one program a year to two in 1985, and then to Canada on a regular basis by their sister organization in 1988.

These data suggest (to me at least) that there has always been a clear pedagogical focus in my work. In fact, one central course has always served to integrate much of my thinking and activity, including the stimulation and direction of much of my writing. In the earliest years of my career, it was the McGill MBA core policy course. After my return from France, that focus shifted to my doctoral teaching, particularly the administrative thought course. And in recent years, the two-day briefings have emerged as the focal course, directing me to particular issues and helping me to address them. As I shall specify later, the *push* of theory has gradually been replaced by the *pull* of issues in my approach to the world of organizations.

Those hard data that tell the story best I shall save for later. These are the diagrams that I have used in my publications over the years. When, as part of this exercise, I begin to consider all of them chronologically, the results were most startling: they clustered into three clearly distinct groups.

All of these findings, reinforced (or produced in the first place) by my prior beliefs, cause me to see my career as having unfolded in three fairly distinct phases. I can, in fact, identify the commencement of all three with rather tangible events, although the second and third took some time to manifest themselves fully. It is not so much that one phase ended when another began. Rather the second and then the third added to the first, as my mindset shifted over time. As we travel through life, we don't so much replace baggage as add to what we already have. To be discussed in the following sections, the three phases can be labelled as follows:

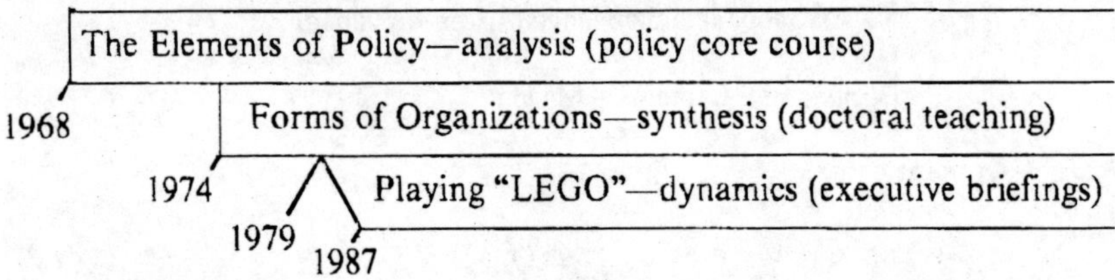


## Rectangle phase (analysis): the element of policy (from 1968)

I returned to Montreal in 1968 with not only a thesis but also an outline for a book to be called "The Theory of Management Policy." I then set out to write it, chapter-by-chapter, week-by-week, the first time I taught the McGill MBA Policy course. I am still writing it!

The MIT management school back in those days was also a bastion of theory (as was McGill's, it should be added, Canada's representative in that small club of the late 1960s), what we saw then as one of the Carnegie-inspired lights of conceptual clarity glowing in the darkness of all that Harvard case study chatter. Harvard's policy textbooks (*the* textbooks of the time) were (and remain) either devoid of conceptual material or else soft peddled bits of it lightly. Policy or general management was, as a result, almost absent from these theory-based schools. But my doctoral studies had convinced me that it need not have been: lacking was not teachable theory so much as someone to pull together all the relevant theory that did exist, much of it in related disciplines. I intended to be that someone. I simply misjudged the task, or at least my obsessive way of going about it.

The outline I had developed by 1968 was not, I suspect, much different from the earliest one I could now find, dated 1973, shown in Figure 4, which itself did not much change subsequently.[17] I opened files on each chapter, to collect notes and relevant articles. Pendaflex folders soon became boxes, and the boxes soon began to overflow and multiply. I code named each chapter TT1, TT2, and so forth (for *The Theory* of Management Policy) for purposes of filing notes, and so forth. And so I had my writing plan all set out for me—my intended strategy was well formulated, merely to be implemented.

As I wrote the chapters, I began to bind them together to hand out as a kind of text in my MBA policy course. The oldest version I have of this (and probably the first, bound at least) is dated July 1972, although I did find the

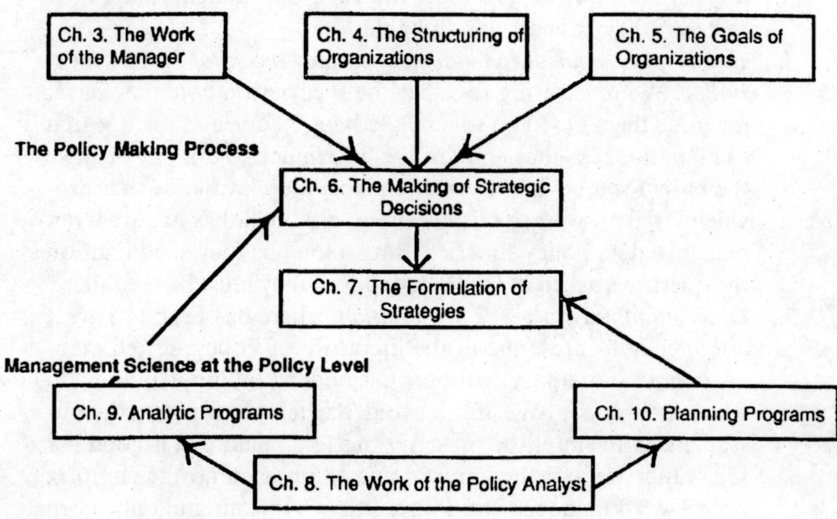


*Figure 4* Outline of "Theory of Management Policy" circa 1973.

1970–71 course outline which showed me handing out Chapters 1, 2, and 3 (the latter on goals), 4 (on structure), and 7. The 1972 text opened with a fifteen-page bibliography, followed by a working paper titled "Policy as a Field of Management Theory," which argued:

> The student of Business or Management requires a useful conceptual framework with which to view the world of Policy that he shall face during his career. He requires answers to the following questions:
>
> - What is the job of the manager?
> - How do organizations determine goals?
> - How do different organizations develop their structures and which are appropriate for each?
> - By what processes are significant decisions made?
> - What are the organizational strategies, and how are they made?
> - What is the role of management science at the Policy level?

The Management Policy Course should provide answers to these questions on the following bases:

1. *The answers to questions of Policy must be based on empirical research.* We must observe and study the management process in a systematic way. Then, what we teach our students should be researched or at least researchable.
2. *The answers should blend into an integrated theory of Management Policy.* We must bring together the theories that we now have, integrate them based on some underlying theory, and use research to fill in the gaps that remain. We have much to do, but we have the basis for a beginning. Many theories are available that provide partial answers to our questions, although they are often not recognized as Policy theories. But so long as they shed light on the questions asked in the Policy course, they must be used there.
3. *Description must precede prescription.* There has been too great a tendency to prescribe in the literature of Policy, to tell managers how to manage without first understanding why they do what they do. . . . We must avoid the temptation to arm our students with simplistic prescriptions (e.g., planning is good per se); rather we and they must come to understand the complex processes of management. Prescription is meaningful only when it is grounded in valid description.
4. *The Policy course should integrate the lessons of management science.* The Policy course is the integrative one of the MBA curriculum, linking the applied fields of marketing, finance, and production. The modern curriculum places increasing emphasis on the scientific tools of these fields (e.g., marketing research, capital budgeting, mathematical programming). The Policy course can maintain its integrative role by serving to interpret the lessons of management science for the policy maker. The Policy student should learn to assess the relevance and weaknesses of each management science technique (especially strategic planning) in the light of his or her knowledge of the actual management process. The Policy course must walk a line between behavioral science and management science, drawing on one for descriptive theory, on the other for prescriptive theory.
5. *The Policy course must link theory with practice.* Theory alone is no better than practice alone. The reality of Policy is sufficiently complex to require that the student have the opportunity to assess the relevance of theory in practice. Ideally, the students armed with theory will observe reality firsthand, via a field study or live case. Alternately, he can assess his theory in the context of a written case or business game.[18]

That working paper became Chapter 1, which was rewritten in 1974 and 1978. Chapter 2, titled "An Underlying Theory for Management Policy," sought to build some roots for the material to follow by combining the administrative theory of Herbert Simon with the general systems theory of Ludwig von Bertalanffy.[19] Although over twenty years old (and also rewritten in 1974 and 1978) and never published, I still intend eventually to turn it into some kind of article!

Chapters 3, 4, and 5 dealt with the "policy elements." There was no chapter on managerial work in that first edition, and never has been. I was just publishing my thesis as a book and knew I could easily summarize it in chapter form when necessary. I did write an early chapter on structure titled "Organizational Structure and the Coupling of Programs" (undated) which took up 67 pages in that 1973 edition, and an early chapter (dated 1970) titled "Influences and the Organizational Goal System," which took up 60 pages, the framework of which appeared in print only in one article for French speaking practitioners.[20]

Chapters 6 and 7 considered the "policy-making process," first in terms of strategic decision making (single important choices) and then strategy making (streams of choices over time). A very long version of the latter was written in the early 1970s (125 pages, undated), under the title "The Strategy Concept," although I included only parts of it in the 1973 edition. These comprised material I published as "Strategy Making in Three Modes" (1973) and three pages of propositions under the label "A General Theory of Strategy Making," each backed up by considerable text in the full version (and never published).

For Chapter 6, the 1973 edition contained one page with the words "Chapter 6 to come." It came the next year. In January 1973, I took off to Carnegie-Mellon for a semester, to soak up the energies of that famous school of administrative thought (Simon, Cyert, March, etc.), and, appropriately, I thought, to write up some data I had been collecting on the making of strategic decisions, which together with a literature review, was to become Chapter 6. Carnegie did not distract me from that task: it turned out that there was nothing left of those energies. Simon had gone off to the psychology department, Cyert was doing administration instead of writing about it, and March had long since left. For the doctoral students from Europe roaming the corridors, like me, in search of that glorious past, I became the closest thing to a resident expert on administrative theory! (I was, after all, writing a paper on decision making!) And so I did the chapter, quite large, about 80 pages, single spaced. It also remains unpublished, although its essence was captured in "The Structure of 'Unstructured' Decision Processes," (1976), with Duru Raisinghani and André Théorêt, McGill students in the MBA and doctoral programs respectively, who had helped with the earlier analysis of the data. Figure 5 reproduces a representative decision process from that article.

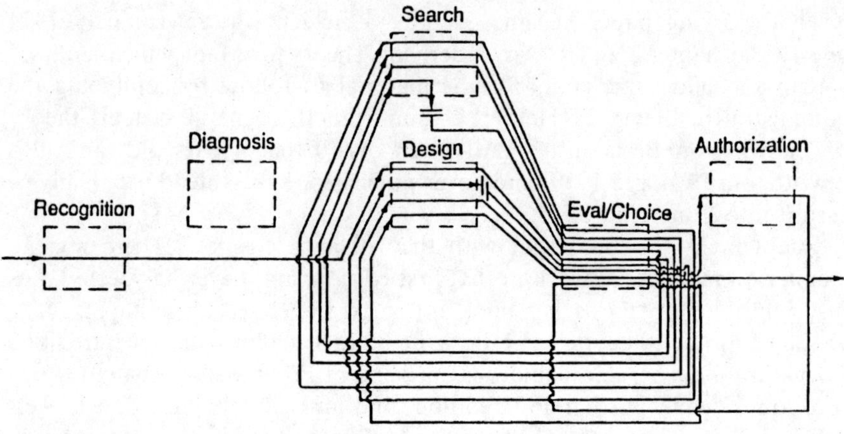


*Figure 5* Illustration of Strategic Decision Process.
*Source*: "The Structure of 'Unstructured' Decision Processes" (1976, p. 273).

The third, prescriptive section of the book, on "Management Science at the Policy Level," consisted of chapters on the work of the policy analysts and their analytic programs for decision making and planning programs for strategy making. It was represented in that 1973 edition only by a six-page piece titled "A Program for Strategic Planning" (dated January 1969), my rendition of the classic strategy model (which I now prefer to call the "design school").[21] A Chapter 8 on "The Role of the Analyst at Policy Level" did appear in 1978 (52 pages), which I shall discuss later.

And so I devoted much of what I am calling the first phase of my career (up to 1974) to writing the chapters of that book as well as to pursuing research that fitted in with those chapters—notably on strategic decision making and strategy formation. An initial proceedings publication (the only one in my reference list) outlined a major project that I was undertaking on strategy making through the analysis of patterns in behavior.[22]

Likewise, most of my publications of this period related to these chapters, two on strategy making[23] and several on managerial work, including my first book,[24] based on my thesis, and various articles spun off of it,[25] including one that delved into the information systems consequence of the findings.[26] Figure 6 shows the book's depiction of the manager's working roles. Miscellaneous publications of the period included two for Canadian practitioners[27] and one for a Canadian government publication,[28] spun off a consulting assignment, that sought to describe government activities in terms of Maslow's needshierarchy theory.[29]

I should also mention a project carried out for the U.S. National Association of Accountants and the Canadian Society of Industrial Accountants. They wondered why managers didn't use accounting information the way (accountants at least) thought they should, and were prepared to fund

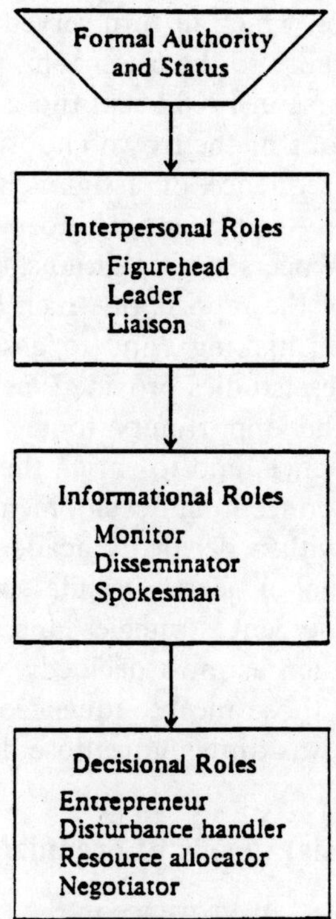


*Figure 6* The Manager's Working Roles.
*Source*: The Nature of Managerial Work (1973, p. 59).

research to find out. One project came to us, to do a kind of compendium of *Normative Models in Managerial Decision Making*, the title of the monograph published in 1975(b), coauthored with Danny Miller, who came to McGill in 1972, and Larry Gordon, a professor of accounting. But I felt they were wasting a lot of money funding original research when many of the answers were already in the published literature. So for a tiny fraction of their budget, I surveyed the literature and produced another monograph, called *Impediments to the Use of Management Information* (1975). It laid the blame on hard information itself (too limited, too aggregated, too late, unreliable), as well as on the nature of organizations (rigid objectives, politics, verbal nature of managerial work) and the nature of our own brains (cognitive limitations, biases, psychological reactions to failures).

Looking back on that phase of my career, I see myself as a rather conventional academic, except for my obsession with that textbook. I had my world neatly compartmentalized—organizations conveniently chopped up into various elements and processes—for myself probably more than for my MBA students. But they did serve as the focus of my pedagogical activity, the market force if you like, which in turn served to focus my writing and research. To bring some reality to the classroom, not to mention to myself, beginning with my first course in 1968 I sent those students out in groups to study Montreal organizations of their own choosing.[30] In fact, in the early years they were given a sequence of assignments that corresponded to the main chapters: to study one manager, to describe an organization's structure and its goals, influencers, and coalitions, to trace one of its strategic decision processes (some of the reports of which became the data base for the 1976 article on decision making), and to describe its strategy making process. Over the years, these studies provided me with a wonderful variety of examples, as well as the opportunity to test the applicability of my theoretical materials in practice, and to enrich them.

Research and especially conceptual development is what drove me in the first phase of my career, with a decidedly academic orientation, although I did do several practitioner articles. Despite some rumblings about my upcoming attention to emergent strategies and managerial intuition, in retrospect I see my work then as most decidedly deliberate and analytical. One need only look at all those nicely sequenced sets of rectangles in the figures (4, 5, and 6) that I was drawing in those days!

## Blob phase (synthesis): forms of organizations (from 1974)

Leaving for sabbatical to Aix-en-Provence in the fall of 1974 proved to be a turning point in my life, or at least coincided with one. Personally I opened up to the splendor of southern France, finding my escape from organizations in that rugged nature, and professionally an important shift began to occur in my mind.

I began serious work on a rework of the structuring chapter before I left, having read all the literature collected in my boxes and setting out to develop a detailed outline to take with me. My memory is generally awful about many details, but one event I do recall vividly in the spring of 1974 is sitting in my basement office at home when a friend dropped in, and expressing to him my intense frustration in trying to draw the huge, disparate, and awfully narrow literature on organizational structuring into some kind of comprehensive framework. Bivariate relationships concerning "administrative ratios," "amount of control," "environmental hetrogeneity," and the like just didn't help. As Danny Miller and I explained in a later article,[31] that was why the museums of organizational structuring were empty of people even if its archives were full.

Pradip Khandwalla joined the McGill Faculty of Management in 1971 after completing his doctorate at Camegie-Mellon. We soon became close colleagues and good friends. In his thesis, Pradip found that organizational effectiveness depended less on doing any particular thing (such as planning formally or decentralizing power over decision making) than on the interrelationship among several such things done (such as centralizing power *and* staying small *and* remaining informal). Early on, as I recall, I thought of this finding as configurational. There the seed was probably planted for the resolution of my frustration in the basement.

I have often tried, without success, to recall exactly how the idea of synthesizing the literature of organizational structuring around distinct configurations, or "ideal types" of organizations, came to me. All I do remember is the critical role played by the occasional insight, most notably in the work of Joan Woodward[32] on forms of technology. On at least two occasions, my struggles with anomalies in my notes were suddenly resolved as I looked through her rich description.

By the time I left for Aix in September 1974, I carried a 200-page outline of the "chapter," so specific that I wrote the first draft of what was to become a 512-page book, *The Structuring of Organizations* (1979), by December. (I keep that outline handy today, perhaps to remind myself of what I am capable of doing though never did before or since.) The full book, of course, loaded with references and quotes as befits a determined young academic, took much longer. (But later, I took much of that out for a textbook/practitioner version called *Structure in Fives* [1983].)

The first parts of the book laid out various elements of structure and the findings I had extracted from the research literature, more or less in their own terms. But this was a prelude to the last part of the book, which described five basic forms of organizations, labelled simple structure, machine bureaucracy, professional bureaucracy, diversified form, and adhocracy. Everything seemed to fall naturally into place in these five forms, so that the book achieved an integration that delighted me, down even to the link between the opening and closing stories. It remains my favorite publication, in form if not also substance. Part of the fun in doing the book was in my use of a funny little diagram which has become my logo of sorts, overlaid and distorted in various ways to integrate graphically across the text, as reproduced in Figure 7. I gave my rough sketch of it to a young American woman artist in Aix to render it clean, and she took one look and declared it obscene—"everyone will see the same thing." Well, I certainly hadn't, and over the years this pseudo-Rorschach has been described as a mushroom (in China!), my nose (by London Business School students), a telephone (at AT&T), the cross section of a rail, a woman's uterus, a kidney bean, and who knows what else. To me, it's just an organization!

The sabbatical was so enjoyable that I decided I needed another. Happily, the Aix business school (the Institute d'administration des enterprises of the Université d'Aix-Marseilles) invited me to stay another year at their expense, and McGill granted me a leave. So I set out to write the next chapter on goals and power. That went less quickly: I failed to do a detailed outline, and paid the price for it in rewrite after rewrite over the next six years or so (although it should be added that this literature was far more

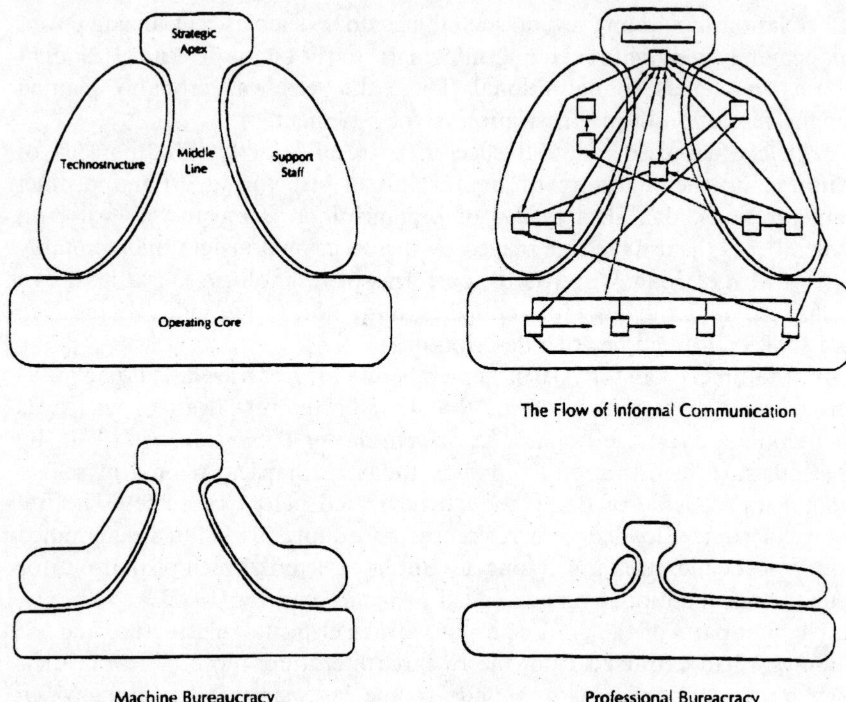


*Figure 7* Structuring Book Use of Logo.
*Source*: The Structure of Organizations: A Synthesis of the Research (1979).

diffuse and nuanced, and so far harder to integrate, than that of structure, even if I did have the notion of configuration from the outset). *Power In and Around Organizations*, exactly 700-pages long, was finally published in 1983. It laid out the elements of the power game, within and around organizations, to draw them together into configurations described in terms of power relationships. The Logo renditions of these are shown in Figure 8. (I should add that I dragged along to Aix my file on another "chapter"—two full boxes, as I recall, on strategy making—and dragged them back to Montreal two years later, unopened!)

The thought had dawned on me by the time I left Aix, perhaps as a result of having to carry around those 512 and 700 page "chapters," that my textbook was becoming something else. So, back in Montreal, I convinced Prentice-Hall, the eventual publisher of both, to label them "The Theory of Management Policy Series," so that the original conception of the textbook could at least be maintained in a series of books. One day they might even be able to issue all the "chapters" in one jacket! (With this in mind, Prentice-Hall kindly negotiated permission to reprint *The Nature of Managerial Work* in the series, which it did in 1983, and I still have contracts, dated 1977 and

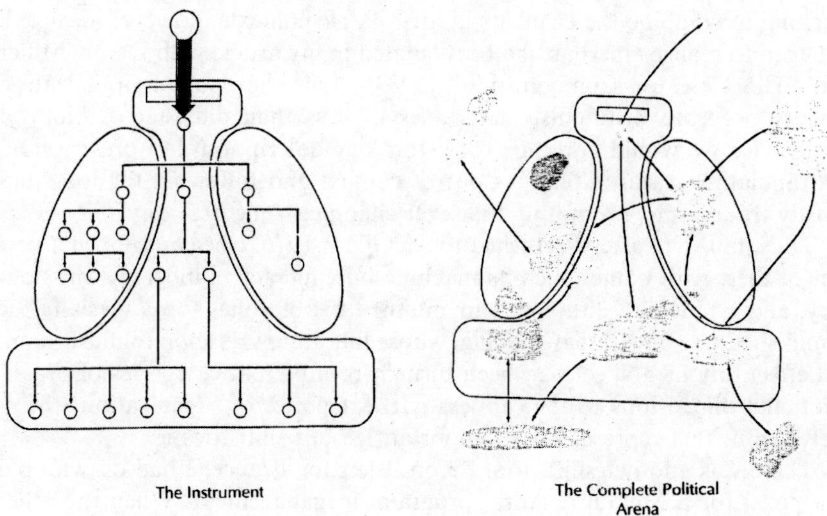


*Figure 8* Power Book Use of Logo.
*Source*: Power In and Around Organizations (1983).

1982, for one volume on decision making and another on strategy making. Maybe I should frame them!)

The significance of these two books to my work was that, whereas before them I was cutting up the world of organizations in my terms—the conceptual categories of the academic—as a result of them I began to cut that world up in its own terms—forms of whole organizations. If before I saw the world like this

managerial work

structure

power

strategy making, etc.

with the horizontal lines slicing through organizations, now I was perceiving it this way,

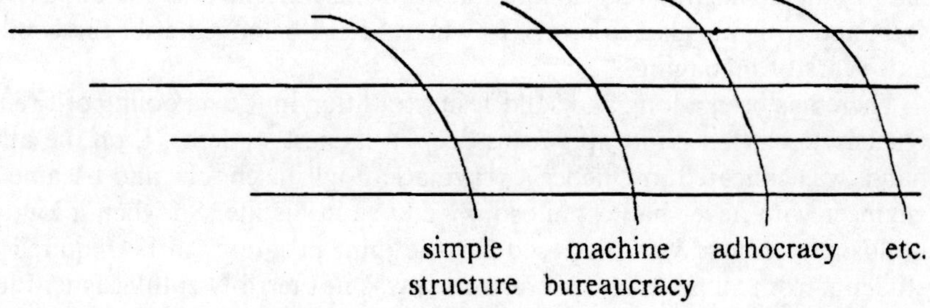

seeking to combine the elements in identifiable contexts, however idealized. I began to realize—perhaps best articulated in my article with Danny Miller on "The Case for Configuration" (1983)—that the field of organization theory needs to distinguish its species no less than did that of biology. Otherwise we would continue to distort our description and prescription, extrapolating research findings out of context and following the long and costly tradition of promoting that ever changing "one best way."

Thus, not long after I returned to McGill in 1976, I began to open a new set of files, with names such as machine bureaucracy, adhocracy, missionary, and typologies, although I maintained the old ones too, especially the unfinished one on strategy making, whose literature was soon to mushroom. In effect, my mental set had been turned from the pat categories of organizational dimensions to the (no less pat) categories of organizations themselves. But that represented an important gestalt shift for me.

There was another shift, too. Before I left for France, I had drawn up a proposal for a McGill doctoral program in management. When the other Montreal schools got word of it, given the need for approval at the level of the provincial government and the fear that our program might preempt others, they produced proposals of their own. The government committee reviewed our horse and countered with what looked like a camel—that we all get together and produce a joint doctoral program. So we sat down and did just that, and I believe (if some others don't) that the results have been excellent. Institutions are notoriously reluctant to cooperate, especially in academia. But somehow the 2 × 2 arrangement, two English, two French language schools, in each case one older and more established, the other newer and more applied, fell into a natural balance. The program was quite innovative—blending European self-study with American coursework, and involving serious cooperation in all aspects, including courses and individual student committees. Today it registers 175 students, a plurality in the policy area.

My return was greeted with a request that I run the new program, which I accepted to do. So the management of adhocracy came to life, as I entered the world of mutual adjustment—no subordinates, just peers with whom to negotiate and cajole. I learned that I could do it, also that I could think strategically, but I also learned that the "calculated chaos"[33] of practising management was not very compatible with the concentrated life of scholarship, and so I was glad to return to where I felt I belonged after three and a half years of managing.

There has been a long and solid Jesuit tradition in the schooling of French Quebec, such that philosophy runs deep in its best students. I, on the other hand, was educated in Quebec's pragmatic English schools, and became an engineer who never had a philosophy course in his life. So when a kind of philosophy course was proposed for the joint program, to be required by students from all areas and all schools, I was not terribly enthusiastic. Little did I suspect that upon my return from France, I was designated as McGill's representative to teach the course (alongside a colleague from each of the other schools). "Fundamentals of Administrative Thought" turned out to be one of the great pedagogical joys of my life; I remained with it for about ten years, using it to help socialize the incoming class into a coherent unit and to play intellectually with a wide range of ideas, as one can only do in a course that doesn't have to convey some established body of theory. A number of my ideas developed in that course, particularly concerning Herbert Simon and the role of intuition in management. I consider my (1977) review of his *New Science of Management Decision*, which grew out of work I prepared for that course, to have been an important step for me, as I shall discuss below.

I also began to teach a doctoral seminar on policy every second year, which I continue to do today. Thus, while I picked up my MBA policy course again, after completing my chairmanship of the joint doctoral program, my pedagogical focus was shifting from 23-year-old aspiring managers to thirty-plus-year-old aspiring scholars.

Configurations had entered my mind, but the elements of the original textbooks's outline hardly left my behavior. In fact, by far my most concerted effort after returning from France was my research on strategy making. It had been conceived in the early 1970s[34] around the notion of (realized) strategy as pattern in actions (originally decisions).[35] With a sizable research grant, we began to track the behaviors of organizations over time, isolating streams of activities, inferring patterns in them as strategies, combining these strategies to infer distinct periods in their histories, and finally brainstorming around the results to develop theory about the formation (not just formulation) of strategy. (So now the logic of this paper should be evident, which means, of course, that it would have to be tabulated on Figure 1 as empirical!)

I found a new colleague at McGill when I returned from France, named Jim Waters. We hit it off immediately, and after he convinced me to rename "emergent" what I had originally called "retroactive" strategy, a most productive collaboration emerged on this research, some of this also including student co-authors.[36] Of course, the configuration notion was not lost; gradually we began to see the influence of organizational form on the strategy-making process (e.g., entrepreneurial[37] adhocracy[38]; also professional bureaucracy, in a conceptual article with Cynthia Hardy, Ann Langley, and Janet Rose[39]; a first attempt by Jim and myself to draw these together;[40] and my latest book in which I added descriptions of the strategy making process to the chapters on each of the configurations[41]).

I published a variety of other articles in what I am calling this second phase of my career. A number were spun off of my two books,[42] including a few from a last section of the power book (titled "Who Should Control the Corporation?") that took me into the new realm of broader social issues.[43]

A major piece titled "Beyond Implementation: An Analysis of the Resistance to Policy Analysis" (1979), based on a Chapter 8 that I finally wrote in 1978 (52 pages), was produced for an operations research conference.

I also published two articles on research methodology. One, titled "If You're Not Serving Bill and Barbara, Then You're Not Serving Leadership" (1982), was a diatribe of sorts, done in my role as commentator for a conference on leadership research. Realizing how dismal was most of that research, I argued for the getting rid of definitions, measurements, instruments, variables, and so forth, not for shock effect but because I really believed that they didn't serve a phenomenon as fuzzy as leadership style. Bill is a close personal friend (who edited both my thesis and my latest book), and Barbara was his colleague in marketing at the National Film Board of Canada, both the kind of intelligent practitioners who, I argued, should be used as gatekeepers to decide who gets funded and published in the field of leadership research. Their comments on the papers at the conference, which I included in my own paper, merit reading in and of themselves.

The other article, "An Emerging Strategy of 'Direct Research' " (1979), outlined the approach that has characterized my own research—its descriptive and inductive nature, its use of simple ("inelegant") methodologies, the presence of a systematic focus (always addressing a clear issue if never testing a hypothesis), concern with synthesis (particularly around the notion of configuration), the need to measure, where appropriate, in real organizational terms (e.g., the pattern of store openings as opposed to "amount of control" on some perceptual 7-point scale), and always supporting systematic data by others of a richer, anecdotal nature in order to explain and not just describe what has been found (and so to theorize). Were I to add one more prescription today, it would be to cherish anomalies. Time and again, as I worked with dozens or hundreds of little notes all over the place, it was my inclination to hang onto those I could not explain, and to return to them periodically, that made all the difference. I suspect that weak theorists tend to dismiss the anomalies, while others succeed because they don't let go of them until they are explained.[44]

Finally, I published two articles in the *Harvard Business Review* during this phase of my work, each of which made a big difference in its own way. The first, "The Manager's Job: Folklore and Fact" (1975), published while I was in Aix, summarized the conclusions of my thesis for a wide practitioner audience. That it reached, with a bit of vengeance, although one additional year in Aix shielded me from its full influence.

The other, "Planning on the Left Side and Managing on the Right" (1976), had quite a different effect, on me personally. I am not particularly prone to "knocking off" an article—getting an idea, writing it up quickly, and sending it off. But on a quiet farm in the summer of 1975 in the Perigord region of France, where we were subsequently to spend many months of August, I read Robert Ornstein's, *The Psychology of Consciousness* (Freeman, 1975), about the consequences of Roger Sperry's research on the two hemispheres of the brain. I had a sense of revelation—it seemed to explain so much of what I had found in my own research, including those two kinds of knowing things, managerial work as "calculated chaos," the realization in studying strategic decision making that everything that seemed to matter (such as diagnosis and design) remained a great mystery while whatever didn't (such as the evaluation of alternatives) was crystal clear. Whether or not the physiology was correct—and that debate continues vigorously, but to my mind less a question of scientific validity than of scientists' propensities to draw inferences—to me there was clearly a critical message here.

The title came first—"Planning on the Left Side and Managing on the Right"—and then I wrote the article, rather quickly. I sent it to the *Harvard Business Review*, which accepted it, and in March 1976 I sent a copy to Herbert Simon. He replied soon after, commenting in his letter that "I believe the left-right distinction is important, but not (a) that Ornstein has described it correctly, or (b) that it has anything to do with the distinction between planning and managing or conscious-unconscious." He referred to it as "the latest of a long series of fads."[45] A day or two later, as I recall, the *Harvard Business Review* wired me to France that they needed the final draft immediately.

Herbert Simon was to me not just the most eminent management theorist of our time but one with no close equal. He had been devoting the later part of his career to intensive research on issues of human cognition, in the psychology laboratory. And here I was about to go into print in direct contradiction to his conclusions, based on the casual reading of a popular book he referred to as a "fad"! Did Simon know something I didn't, or was there some kind of block in his thinking? My heart battled with my head (or was it my right hemisphere with my left?), over whether hearts sometimes know more than heads, and after an agonizing day or two, the "right side" won.[46]

I had a comment in the original paper that both I and the *Review* editors deleted independently in the final version as too controversial: "I am tempted to raise the issue of extra-sensory perception here. There is clearly too much evidence to dismiss this as a medium of communication, at least for some people, and as Ornstein suggests, it is presumably a right hemisphere activity." Simon had picked up on this in his letter. "The temptations are so great to romanticize about human performance (and even to credit it with ESP for which there is no evidence)!" My decision turned on rereading that sentence. I am certainly no mystic, not even a numerologist (William McKelvey's worries in *Organizational Systematics: Taxonomy, Evolution, Classification* [University of California Press, 1982] about my playing with the number five notwithstanding), and I have as much trouble entertaining the notion of precognition as anyone else. But for Simon to dismiss the possibility that we pick up information in as yet unspecified ways—for example, when we "read" someone's eyes or "feel" tension in a room—struck me as a blockage. And so I decided to go with my inner "sense" instead of Herbert Simon's learned knowledge.[47]

I believe our lives are determined in large part by the occasional choice that later proves to have been a turning point. In other words, we don't get to choose critically very often, and we can, in fact, hedge and stall and do all kinds of dumb things day in and day out, but every once in a while we had better get it right. And getting it right at those times usually seems to mean listening to that inner voice, which goes by the name of "intuition," not to the babble of the social world or the logic of formal analysis.

My intuitive decision to opt for intuition subsequently opened up my work to that concept and myself to that process. It was as if I had been climbing up to a knife edge of analysis-intuition ever since I joined the operational research group at the Canadian National. The Simon letter put me right on that edge, and the decision I took began my journey down the other side.

Subsequently, my attention turned increasingly to the softer notions in management, and I broke increasingly with the long dominant rationalist view, perhaps the one real paradigm in the field, represented especially in the work of Simon himself (who, in recent years, has come to define intuition as "analyses frozen into habit"[48]). Today I am inclined to compare a "cerebral" with an "insightful" approach to management, one based on words and numbers (in academia, Harvard's words or Stanford's numbers, both equally cerebral), the other on images and "feel" (as in strategic "vision" or being "in touch"). In a recent paper on decision making (discussed in the next phase), I wrote a section that characterizes Simon's "bounded rationality" as really a "cerebral rationality" because it slights people's ability to perform great feats of synthesis (such as Simon's own writing of *Administrative Behavior* [Macmillan, 1957]).

My debate with Simon continued with some sporadic correspondence as well as a critical review in 1977 of his revised *New Science of Management Decision*. This associated excessive rationality with the excesses of the Vietnam War, especially as reflected in the "professional management" of Robert McNamara. It concluded by juxtaposing Simon's claim that "We now know a good deal about what goes on in the human head when a person is exercising judgement or having an intuition, to the point where many of these processes can be simulated on a computer"[49] with Roger Sperry's conclusion that "The right [hemisphere], by contrast [with the left] is spacial, and performs with a synthetic space-perceptual and mechanical kind of information processing not yet simulateable in computers."[50] Simon was awarded the Nobel Prize in economics in 1978; Sperry won his in physiology in 1981!

So what am I to make of this second phase of my career. This was certainly a time of loosening up and of opening up, a time of shift from the rather analytic to (what I like to think of as) more balance between the analytic and the intuitive, certainly a time in which synthesis more vigorously entered my work and thinking. I would not label my realized strategy of this period as emergent, but surely it had become less formally deliberate. One might describe it, using our own labels,[51] as umbrella in nature, guided by the notion of configuration, with, of course, that old textbook outline, now compromised by the size of its "chapters," still providing one sense of direction. I also started to become more playful in this period, both literally in my private life and figuratively in my work. One need only look back at those blob forms in Figures 7 and 8!

### Circle phase (dynamics): playing "LEGO" (from 1979/1987)

Alain Noël joined our doctoral program in September 1978, and about five months later, after having read my work on structure and power, asked me a question that was to change my thinking a second time: "Do you mean to play jigsaw puzzle or LEGO with the elements of organizations?"[52]

I had to reply that I guess it was jigsaw puzzle, at least for my readers: I was asking them to select known images of their organizations, to put the elements of structure together in one of five predetermined ways. But Alain's question so intrigued me that I soon opened a file called "LEGO," to collect examples of all those weird and wonderful organizations that refused to fit into one or other of my pat categories. It was not that I couldn't find examples of ones that did—I knew from my own experiences, and those of others, that many effective organizations conformed remarkably well. (I later began to ask the McGill MBA students to record their perception of fit with their field organizations: in just over half the cases recorded—66 out of 123—the students felt a single form fitted best.[53]) But some of the most effective organizations, and certainly many of the most interesting, did not. For example, there were seemingly bureaucratic machines that managed to innovate when they had to (McDonald's? IBM?), and what seemed like adhocracies that had rather tight control systems (Hewlett-Packard? 3M?). These became of increasing interest to me.

I show the third phase of my work as beginning on a diagonal line from 1979, when Alain first posed that question, to 1987, when I began work on a serious answer (published in *Mintzberg on Management* [1989] as "Forces and Forms in Effective Organizations"; see preferably my *Sloan Management Review* version of 1991). Here I did not so much dismiss the five forms as covert than to a set of five forces, arranged around the nodes of a pentagon, each drawing the organization in a different direction. In the middle, I added from my power book the two forces of ideology and politics (the former of "cooperation," pulling together, and the latter, "competition," pulling apart) which I described as catalytic (centripetal and centrifugal). Altogether, shown in Figure 9, this constituted what I have found to be a

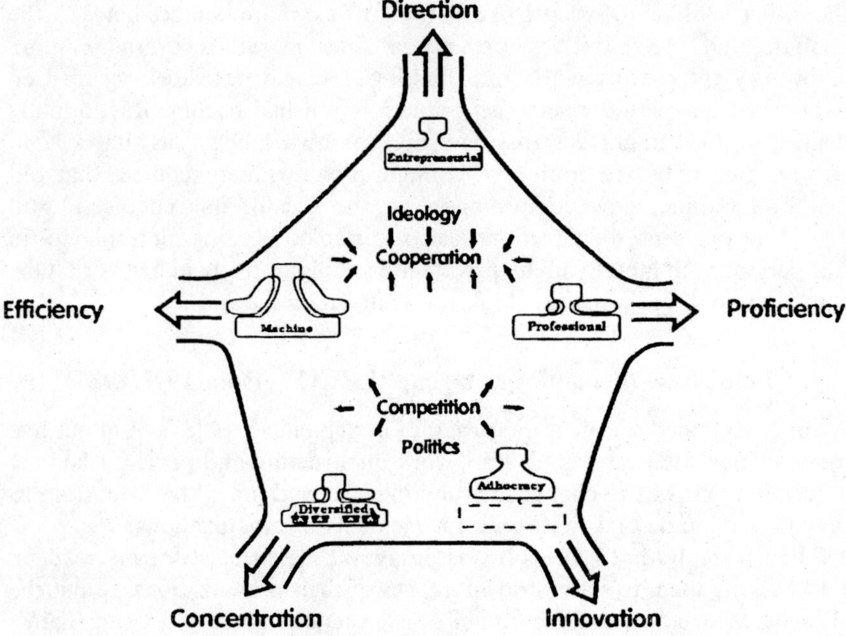


*Figure 9* Framework to Play "Organizational LEGO".
*Source*: Mintzberg on Management: Inside Our Strange World of Organizations (1989, p. 256, with modification).

most useful framework by which to diagnose the problems of organizational design.

In 1980, I was invited to do a "top management briefing" for the Management Centre Europe (MCE)—two days, me alone, with senior European executives. I guess I always subscribed to Jim Water's guide of tying a rope to a rock, the other end to your ankle, and then throwing the rock over some attractive cliff. It's called commitment. But when the time came, I was petrified, more worried than I had been for any other working engagement. I slept not a wink the night before, and making it through the first day was somewhat of a miracle. I recall in the afternoon sitting up near the ceiling of the room listening to me talking down below (a phenomenon I have heard described by others), and praying that guy wouldn't make any mistakes. Fortunately he didn't, and after a good night's sleep, and a successful second day, with all of me together on the ground, I have been doing MCE briefings ever since. By 1985, I was doing two per year, and in 1988 I began to do one regularly in Canada as well. These programs are exhausting and I limit the number, but they have come to represent the core of my thinking, focusing my writing, research, and general mental set much as did the MBA policy course when I began teaching at McGill. They force me to ask questions of relevance: how do all the concepts I teach help practicing managers to deal with serious problems.

These briefings have thus become part of a shift in my mind from the *push* of concepts to the *pull* of issues. Push promotes some idea, technique, or angle, whether transaction cost in the university or strategic planning in the corporation. It reflects the rule of the tool, that given a hammer everything begins to look like a nail. Pull begins with a problem or issue, and then draws on whatever it takes to deal with it, sometimes including concepts and techniques. Business schools, especially in America, have become prisoners of push, to their great discredit. So has much of American business practice, given its obsession with technique driven by that almighty "bottom line." I believe it is time for pull.[54]

My shift from push to pull should not be interpreted as a change to a prescriptive, applied orientation; indeed, sometimes the result has been exactly the opposite. Having to address the concerns of thoughtful managers (as Europeans in general and MCE attendees in particular tend to be) can be a helpful experience for even the most theoretical academic. To take a not incidental case in point, my description of managerial roles in *The Nature of Managerial Work* (1973) has never worked in the MCE briefings. In an effort to provide a framework by which my materials on strategy and structure (which do work) can be assessed in the attendees' own jobs, I have, therefore, had to rethink the roles.

In 1985, I served as the faculty representative on a McGill university-wide committee on budgeting problems. I proposed—seriously as an idea but with no expectation of implementation—that the university could eliminate its deficit if it paid professors for what they really did. McGill remains a very collegial and responsible institution, a place with a real sense of its own excellence despite a battering by a sometimes hostile milieu. But like any other, it has its share of faculty who have retired from research but not from drawing full salary. Since I consider research part of professors' duties—in other words, we are paid full time to work more or less full time—people who have stopped doing research should be receiving something like sixty percent of their salaries.

It soon occurred to me that I should really do just that myself, with a slightly different twist. I was becoming increasingly disillusioned with conventional management education.[55] It just did not make sense to me anymore, socially or economically, to continue the pretense of training barely experienced hotshots to be managers. The MCE experience had convinced me that management education should be reserved for people who know how organizations work, whose experience is deep as well as tacit, and whose place in the classroom is determined by their accomplishments rather than their aspirations.

So I decided to stop teaching the MBA policy course, proposing to the McGill administration that I go on reduced load and salary and concentrate my university work on writing, research, and doctoral supervision and the biannual course. In other words, I would divide my labor between scholarship in the university and application (including pedagogy) in the field. Long ago (in 1969), *Fortune* magazine published an article by S. Zalaznick titled "The MBA—the Man, the Myth, and the Method" that concluded that the real contribution of the American business schools lay not in its graduates from teaching so much as its insights from research. I always thought that to be true—now I was putting it into practice myself.

The arrangement has worked out marvellously well. All at once, I relieved myself of significant pressure (from doing what felt wrong more than from trying to do too much), clarified my efforts, and ironically, significantly increased the time I had for what I like to do best, namely scholarship. McGill has a rule of a maximum of four days of consulting per month for full-time faculty; even now, on reduced load, I do not yet reach it. Much of the time that went into MBA teaching now goes into my writing and research.

Outside the university, I do those few two-day programs, a number of one-day public conferences in Europe that I am directing more toward what I like to call "discovery conferences" (where a panel of us from theory and practice addresses some pull issue in a mostly unrehearsed way, for example, the management of strategic change), an occasional in-house workshop in the form of executive retreats, and so forth, as well as a certain amount of consulting, which tends to take on a wide variety of interesting forms. Recently, for example, I helped a couple of McKinsey consultants rethink the structure of a large South American firm and decided with people at the Brookhaven Laboratories in New York whether or not nuclear power plants are best thought of as machine bureaucracies (concluding yes and no, depending on whether one chose to play jigsaw puzzle or LEGO).[56]

These latter experiences offer me wonderful opportunities to discover issues and to root my theoretical concerns in the realities of messy practice. I do not pretend that they constitute research. (I have always considered so-called "action research" to be an attempt by some academics to have their research cake and eat the consulting fees too.) But I do find them invaluable for drawing me toward issues that seem to be significant, for exposure that frames reality in my head, and even for enhancing the scholarship in my work. Direct exposure has always been my best stimulus; lately I have been able to request tours of a fascinating variety of physical facilities, through which I also meet operating people. That has made an enormous difference—not only for the consulting work itself but also for my own development of conceptual material. At Brookhaven, for example, I asked to tour a nuclear power plant, and what I saw in just one morning made all the difference to my conclusions. Similarly, a friend in London took me out to a hospital recently, and after listening to the National Health Service regional manager talk about negotiating a new facility through the politics of the bureaucracy, followed by a tour by the head nurse who revealed her wonderful intimacy of the operations, I came home talking about "managing up" and "managing down." Where those meet—in fact, whether they meet—strikes me as a critical issue in the practice of management today. I feel privileged to have this kind of varied access to organizations at this stage in my career.

I explain all this before discussing my publications of this third phase because the order of presentation reflects the phase itself. These are the things that have increasingly begun to drive my work in the past several years. As befits more pull and closer connection to practice, my writings have also become more disparate; hence the "illusive strategy." But I should add here that when we drew conclusions about "Strategy Formation in an Adhocracy" (1985) in our own research, which we found to have oscillated between periods of convergence and divergence (typically about six years of concentration on particular product/market themes, followed by about equal periods of less focused experimentation, of "riding off in all directions"), it turned out that the organization was sometimes most effective during the periods of divergence. In other words, focused strategy is not necessarily a prerequisite to success, at least not perpetually in some kinds of organizations (which also means, I guess, that my own behavior has shifted from that of professional bureaucracy toward adhocracy!).

To make the link between my practice and my writing, I should perhaps begin with my most applied recent efforts, two books in particular. As noted earlier, I have always sought to produce a stream of work aimed at practitioners. Some of this has been easily accessible to them—articles in the *Harvard Business Review*, for example—while other material was not. And so I accepted an invitation from Bob Wallace at the Free Press to do a kind of practitioner compendium of my work. It was initially meant to be a packaging job of existing materials, but (surprise!) I ended up writing and rewriting a good part of it. The book contains some new materials (including some of the Simon exchange and the forces and forms paper discussed above, as well as other two pieces to be discussed below), and it presents the configurations renamed (as in the pentagon in Figure 9) and rewritten to encompass the dimensions of managerial work and strategy formation. The publisher calls it *Mintzberg on Management*; I prefer the subtitle *Inside Our Strange World of Organizations* (1989). The book draws together almost all of the themes in my work over the years, such that it is probably the closest thing in print to my original textbook, although not so organized, and with a particular slant (that I shall discuss below). It is aimed at the practising manager, but also, I had hoped, a far broader audience. As I noted in the introduction, in today's world of organizations, "pop organization theory" should be as important to the general public as pop psychology.

As the for second book, James Brian Quinn of the Tuck School at Dartmouth approached me a few years ago to collaborate on a textbook.

He had developed a series of excellent cases on strategic management, and proposed that I do the text. I agreed, but not in the usual way. Rather than writing it, I suggested we *design* it by pulling together the best work of other authors in the field, carefully edited for conciseness, interspersed with our own published writings. I just could not face the thought of doing a conventional "gather-around-children-while-we-tell-you-about-strategic-management" textbook. Why should intelligent students not be exposed to what intelligent writers had to say in their own words. *The Strategy Process* was published in 1988, also co-authored with Bob James, and the second edition appeared in 1991.

There is, of course, a lovely irony here. Finally given the chance to do a real policy textbook after so many years of struggling with one, indeed with most of the chapters already written and awaiting publication, I casually turned my back on it!

Turning to my work of a more scholarly nature, many of my publications up to the late 1980s were in fact manifestations of the previous phase, especially the coming to fruition of our studies of strategy formation (already listed), followed by an article called "Crafting Strategy" (1987) to draw out the broad conclusions. More recently, my pace of writing on this subject has not slowed down so much as shifted (not fully reflected in the Figure 1 histogram, due to the size and publication lag of some of this work), meaning that I continue to pursue work of the first stage too.

I took another sabbatical, this time to a tiny village in an obscure valley in the Swiss Jura mountains, during the first six months of 1984. I dragged along what amounted to many boxes of the old Chapter 7 on strategy making, and spent all that time reading and organizing it. (The analyst in me still likes to keep score, so I recorded somewhere that I read 1,495 items—I calculated it would have stood fourteen feet high.) It was all intended to write the chapter that this time I knew would be a book. Well, I was wrong again. It may be recalled that my first book, on managerial work, was 298 pages long, my second, on structuring, was 512 pages, and my third, on power, exactly 700. One need not even be the statistical jock I am to conclude that the next book in the "Theory of Management Policy Series" has to be about 900 pages long. In fact, the outline I brought home from Switzerland divided that book into two volumes, the first called *Strategy Formation: Schools of Thought*, intended to review the literature, and the second, *Strategy Formation: Towards a General Theory*, to extend the configuration notion to strategic stages across the evolution of organizations.

A number of other subsequent commitments, as well as an increasing propensity to go with ideas that come up (to be detailed below), have slowed this work down somewhat, or at least its publication, because I have in fact already produced a sizable quantity of material for the first volume. Chapter 1 on the concept of strategy has been written, and published as two articles.[57] The rest of the volume is devoted to the schools, ten in number. A lengthy chapter exists on the first, design school, much of it published in a recent article,[58] and I finished in 1985 a 358-page "chapter" on the planning school, which I am now revising for book publication. I also began work several years ago on the "positioning school" chapter, which exists as a long, untyped manuscript, one part of which has appeared as "Generic Strategies: Toward a Comprehensive Framework" (1988, also in shortened form in 1991). I might add that in doing this chapter, I was having a wonderful time playing Michael Porter: my own work may hardly be loaded with nuance and affect, but as a consummate categorizer, I was revelling in developing the rather purely logical typologies of strategy content. The chapters on the other schools—entrepreneurial, cognitive, learning, political, cultural, environmental, and configurational—remain unwritten, although I did publish a very long paper titled "Strategy Formation: Schools of Thought" (1990) that summarized them all.

Since this is my final comment on "The Theory of Management Policy," I thought it might be helpful to include an accounting of where that book now stands, which I do in Exhibit 1.[59] So near and yet so far.

*Exhibit 1* Current Status of "The Theory of Management Policy.

| *Chapter* | *Title* | *State* |
|---|---|---|
| 1 | The Field of Management Policy | Chapter (1974, 1978) and two articles |
| 2 | An Underlying Theory for Management Policy | Chapter (1974, 1978) |
| 3 | The Structuring of Organizations | Book, several articles, and chapter (1980) |
| 4 | The Nature of Managerial Work | Book and several articles |
| 5 | Power In and Around Organizations | Book and several articles (early chapter [1970] superceded) |
| 6 | The Making of Strategic Decisions | Chapter (1973) and article |
| 7 | The Formation of Strategy | Two volume outline, of which several articles and chapters, one as book manuscript (early chapter [1970] superceded) |
| 8 | The Role of the Policy Analyst | Chapter (1978) and article, also book manuscript on planning |
| 9 or 16 | Toward Effectiveness in Organizations | Article (forces and forms) |
| 9–15 | Possible chapters on seven configurations: Entrepreneurial, Machine, Diversified, Professional, Adhocracy, Ideology and the Missionary Organization, Politics and the Political Organization | Chapters in other books |

A. Concentric Cycles
- contents and levels of change

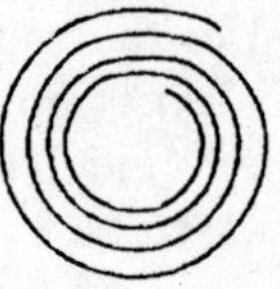

B. Circumferential Cycles
- means and processes of change

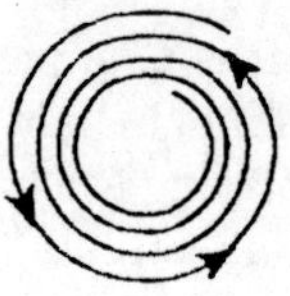

C. Spiraling Cycles
- sequences and patterns of change

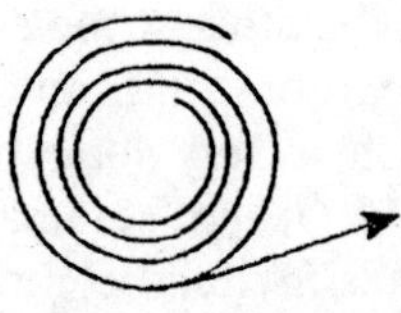

D. Spiraling Cycles
- sequences and patterns of of change

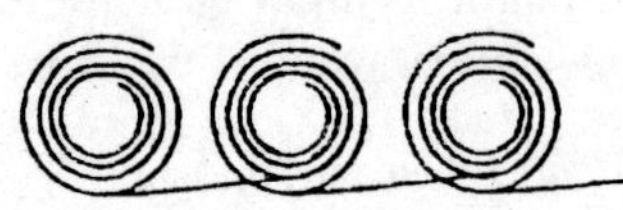

*Figure 10* Overall Cycles of Organizational Change.
*Source*: "Cycles of Organizational Change" (1993, p. 41).

Alongside the volumes on strategy formation has been my research work in that area with Frances Westley, who joined the McGill faculty in 1983. Frances is one of those rare people who came out of the push of a strong discipline and slipped ever so naturally into the pull of the management field. As a result we have developed a wonderful collaboration, of her sociological affect with my engineering effect, by which we have worked out some tricky conceptual issues with great glee. (Having made a habit of doing so just before conference presentations, we have decided that our real talent lies in "just-in-time theorizing"!) We published two articles on strategic vision,[60] and after many go-arounds are now preparing to publish another on a general model of strategic change. As shown in Figure 10, it is conceived in terms of circles and cycles, one representing the concentric levels of change, a second the means of change, a third the episodes of change, and a fourth, the evolving cycles of change.

One characteristic of this third phase of my work, as already noted, is my greater willingness to go with ideas as they come up, much as did our adhocracy, the National Film Board of Canada, in its periods of divergence. This has resulted in a number of "one-off" papers and articles, mostly co-authored, one with Joe Lampel (ex of our doctoral program) on customizing strategies (in draft), another with Maria Gonzalez (ex of our MBA program) on strategies for financial services,[61] based on a consulting assignment, a third with Angela Dumas of the London Business School on managing design.[62]

Two major activities of late have included revisiting work I did initially in the first phase of my career. I have already mentioned my return to the managerial roles because of the difficulties of using them in my MCE program. Moreover, it occurred to me, based on my own notion of emergent strategy and Karl Weick's concept of "sensemaking,"[63] that the order in which I had presented the roles (interpersonal providing information enabling decision making, as shown in Figure 6) could just as easily have been reversed; in other words, I had a list, not a theory. An invitation to speak at a celebration of the eightieth birthday of Sune Carlson, author of the classic study of managerial work titled *Executive Behavior: A Study of the Work Load and the Working Methods of Managing Directors* (1951), sent me back to this literature (specifically to my two unopened boxes of Chapter 4). There I realized that, at best, all the other descriptions were no more than lists themselves.[64] So I set out to develop something better, and last fall in London, out of a series of seminars (rocks going over cliffs, each preceded by some JITT), it all came together, quite literally so in a framework of concentric circles. [Figure 11 shows the framework as finalized in 1993.]

I think there is something to the fact that this figure (developed in considerably more detail) preceeded the outline. What matters in developing theory about managerial work, in my opinion, is not so much the fully articulated text as the comprehensive representation of the model. People need to *see* the various dimensions that appear to constitute managerial work all in one place. That way, they can begin to discuss the job of managing comprehensively and interactively. I have found this to be true as I started to use the model to develop the theory, and when I drew the diagram for Bill at dinner one evening, he immediately began using it to diagnose the problems of managing in his own firm.

For different reasons, I have for some years now wished to revisit the subject of strategic decision making. The tendency to show it as the linear unfolding of sequences of steps, in our own work[65] no less than that of others, somehow seemed to miss something important. This subject (in effect, the old Chapter 6) was not, however, on my agenda, especially given my heavy commitment to strategy formation. But with the new spirit of one-off papers, combined with a pedagogical idea I had been considering for awhile, I made room for it.

Doctoral study is really an apprenticeship. Courses are fine, as far as they go, and research assistantships can be useful, but they often subordinate the students' interests to those of the professor. So I developed the idea of a "research cell," somewhere between the two, in which a small team of selected faculty members and doctoral students could address an issue

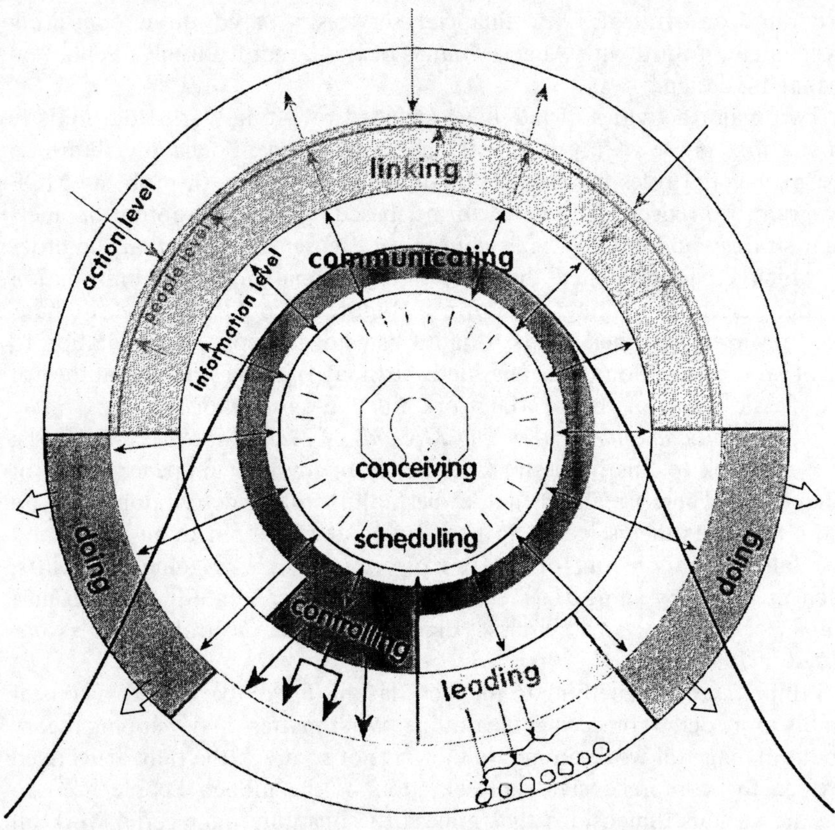


*Figure 11* Framework for Describing Managerial Work.

together. Five of us, including one other colleague and three doctoral students (from all four Montreal universities, as it happens), took on the issue of "opening up decision making," seeking to reconceive what we perceived to be this narrow line of research. A most exciting paper has resulted (submitted for publication), which opens up the concept of decision itself to the ambiguities that surround the moment of choice, opens up the decision maker to history and experience, affect, insight, and inspiration, and opens up decision making to a host of dynamic linkages such that isolated processes of decisions come to be seen as networks of issues.

Finally, there is the side of my current work I call the polemics, which address some broader social issues. Two papers were published as chapters in my last book, *Mintzberg on Management* (1989). One, called "Training Managers, Not MBAs," explains my dissatisfaction with conventional management education. And the other, "Society Has Become Unmanageable as a Result of Management," expresses my concerns about the prevailing practices of management. These chapters give the book a somewhat caustic flavor, but not, to my mind, one unwarranted in today's world of bottom-line banality. Still, I felt the need to back off after these, and so the work I continue to do on broader social issues is perhaps more provocative than polemic. Last fall, for example, invited to give a speech to a large management congress in Prague on "East Meets West," I used the occasion to do some reading and thinking on the issues facing eastern Europe. The resulting paper (just submitted for publication) emphasizes the need for grass roots strategic learning rather than formal planning in times of difficult change, and suggests that it was not capitalism that "triumphed" in the west so much as balance in our economic system, a balance that, ironically, risks being upset by these very changes.

I like what I have been doing recently. I like the style of life I have established for myself and I like the variety of work I can do, so long as it remains under the umbrella of the themes that have always rooted my work —to understand management and organizations, especially with regard to strategy (setting direction) and structure (establishing state and process). Everything seems to fit together very nicely. So I have no intentions of making any changes now; I foresee no fourth stage in the near future (but neither did I earlier foresee a second or a third). I hope to consider the issue of intuition more carefully, especially to develop the idea of an "insightful" face of management in contrast to its long dominant "cerebral" face. I wish to consider via direct exposure, certain of the trickier organizational contexts, notably the delivery of public professional services (especially health care), the management of the softer sides of government, the organization of corporations across businesses and boundaries, and the long standing problem of rendering adaptive our bureaucratic machines. I intend to redo *Structure in Fives* as "Structure in Sevens," so that I can play more elaborate LEGO; to do another research cell, on organizational effectiveness; and, of course, to keep plugging away at "Chapter 7" on strategy formation.

So where is that illusive strategy? Not so illusive, I conclude, unless one insists on the kind of deliberate plan that drove my earliest work. As my activities have grown more varied, I believe that the overall thrust has become more integrated. It all comes together around the themes that have been struggling to get out these past twenty-five years: thinking, designing, acting, and learning to achieve more effective and humane organizations. Organizations do this, biased perhaps toward that order, while I do it perhaps with a growing bias toward the opposite order. Gradually I have come closer to organizations while always maintaining my distance, being able to consider their impact more broadly while probing more narrowly into their details. Overall, I have been searching for their deceptive effectiveness, first through study of their elements, subsequently combined to describe their forms, and then exposed to reveal their dynamics, all the while attuned to their dark recesses of intuition hidden amidst the brilliance of their formal analysis. Cycling has characterized my own behavior as well as the actual theory I have been developing recently, as I have come to see organizations in increasingly dynamic terms. One need only look back at the circling and cycling diagrams I have been doing in recent years, illustrated in Figures 9, 10, and 11! Thus this third stage of my work can be depicted as follows:

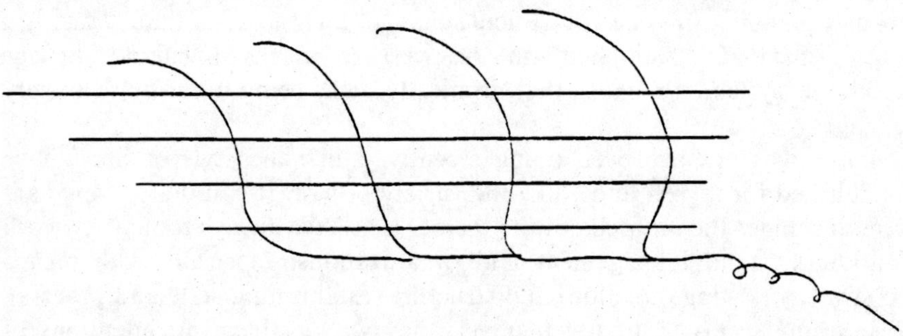

"We shall not cease from exploration," wrote T.S. Eliot in one of my favorite quotes, "and the end of all our exploring will be to arrive where we started and know the place for the first time."

This ends my story. When Art Bedeian informed me, rather casually, of the page limit, I thought to myself, who in the world would ever write that much about himself. Now look what I've done. And me who started with the admonition about not taking yourself too seriously. Could we, perhaps, just attribute this to me taking my work very seriously?

## Publications

**1967**

The science of strategy-making. *Industrial Management Review* (Spring).

**1968**

With J. Hekimian. The planning dilemma. *The Management Review* (May).

**1970**

Structured observation as a method of study managerial work. *The Journal of Management Studies* (February).

Making a science of management. *Canadian Business* (March).

**1971**

Managerial work: Analysis from observation. *Management Science* (October).

**1972**

Research on strategy-making. In *Proceedings of the Academy of Management Conference*.

A framework for strategic planning. *Canadian Forum* (January–February).

The myths of MIS. *California Management Review* (Fall).

**1973**

*The nature of managerial work*. New York: Harper & Row. (Reissued by Prentice Hall, 1983)

Policy as a field of management theory. *Journal of Business Policy* (Summer).

A new look at the senior manager's job. *Organizational Dynamics* (Winter).

Strategy-making in three modes. *California Management Review* (Winter).

Jeu des influences et buts organisationnels. *Commerce* (juin).

**1974**

A national goals hierarchy. *Optimum*.

**1975**

*Impediments to the use of management information*. Monograph of the National Association of Accountants (U.S.) and Society of Industrial Accountants (Canada).

With L. Gordon & D. Miller. *Normative models in managerial decision-making*. Monograph of the National Association of Accountants (U.S.) and Society of Industrial Accountants (Canada).

The manager's job: Folklore and fact. *Harvard Business Review* (July–August).

**1976**

With D. Raisinghani & A. Théoret. The structure of "unstructured" decision processes. *Administrative Science Quarterly* (June).

Planning on the left side and managing on the right. *Harvard Business Review* (July–August).

**1977**

Policy as a field of management theory. *Academy of Management Review* (January).

[Review of] New science of management decision. *Administrative Science Quarterly* (June).

Strategy formulation as an historical process. *International Studies of Management and Organization* (Summer).

**1978**

With W. Balke & J. Waters. Team teaching general management: Theoretically, experimentally, practically. *Exchange: The OB Teaching Journal* (June).

With J. Lorsch, J. Baughman, & J. Reece. *Understanding management*. New York: Harper & Row.

**1979**

*The structuring of organizations: A synthesis of the research*. Englewood Cliffs, NJ: Prentice-Hall.

An emerging strategy of "direct" research. *Administrative Science Quarterly* (December).

Beyond implementation: An analysis of the resistance to policy analysis [Proceedings of the 1978 IFORS Conference]. In Haley (Ed.), *Operational research '78* (pp. 106–162). Amsterdam: North-Holland.

Organizational power and goals. In Schendel and Hofer (Eds.), *Strategic management*. Boston, MA: Little, Brown.

Patterns in strategy formation. *Management Science* (May).

**1980**

Structure in 5's. *Management Science* (March).

**1981**

Configurations of organizational structure. In Meltzer and Nord (Eds.), *Making organizations humane and productive: A handbook for practitioners*. New York: Wiley.

Organization design: Fashion or fit. *Harvard Business Review* (January–February).

What is planning anyway? *Strategic Management Journal.*

**1982**

With J. Waters. Tracking strategy in an entrepreneurial firm. *Academy of Management Journal.*

A note on that dirty word efficiency. *Interfaces* (October).

If you're not serving Bill and Barbara, then you're not serving leadership. In Hunt, Sekaran, & Schriesheim (Eds.), *Leadership: Beyond establishment views*. Carbondale, IL: Southern Illinois University Press.

Commentary. In Ungson & Braunstein (Eds.), *Decision making: An interdisciplinary inquiry*. Kent Publishing.

**1983**

With D. Miller. The case for configuration. In G. Morgan (Ed.), *Beyond method.* Beverly Hills, CA: Sage.

*Structure in 5's: Designing effective organizations*. Englewood Cliffs, NJ: Prentice-Hall.

*Power in and around organizations*. Englewood Cliffs, NJ: Prentice-Hall.

With J. Waters. The mind of the strategist(s). In S. Srivasta (Ed.), *Executive mind.* San Francisco, CA: Jossey-Bass.

With C. Hardy, A. Langley, & J. Rose. Strategy formation in the university setting. *The Review of Higher Education* (Summer).

A note on the unionization of professionals from the perspective of organization theory. *Industrial Relations Law Journal.*

Why America needs, but cannot have, corporate democracy. *Organizational Dynamics* (Spring).

The case for corporate social responsibility. *Journal of Business Policy* (Fall).

**1984**

With J. Waters. Researching the formation of strategies: The history of Canadian Lady, 1939–1976. In R.B. Lamb (Ed.), *Competitive strategic management.* Englewood Cliffs, NJ: Prentice-Hall.

With W. Taylor & J. Waters. Tracking strategies in the birthplace of Canadian tycoons: The Sherbrooke Record 1946–1976. *Canadian Journal of Administrative Sciences* (June).

Power and organization life cycles. *Academy of Management Review.*

Who should control the corporation? *California Management Review* (Fall).

**1985**

With J. Waters. Of strategies, deliberate and emergent. *Strategic Management Journal.*

With A. McHugh. Strategy formation in an adhocracy. *Administrative Science Quarterly.*

The organization as political arena. *Journal of Management Studies.*

With F. Westley. Imagining strategy. *Journal of Management.*

**1986**

With P. Brunet & J. Waters. Does planning impede strategic thinking? Tracking the strategies of Air Canada from 1937 to 1976. In R. B. Lamb & P. Shivastava (Eds.), *Advances in strategic management*. Greenwich, CT: JAI Press.

Crafting strategy. *Harvard Business Review* (September–October).

Five Ps for strategy. *California Management Review* (June).

Another look at why organizations need strategies. *California Management Review.*

**1987**

With J. Jorgensen. Emergent strategy for public policy. *Canadian Public Administration* (Summer).

**1988**

With J. B. Quinn & R. M. James. *The strategy process: Concepts, contexts, and cases*. Englewood Cliffs, NJ: Prentice-Hall.

With F. Westley. Profiles of strategic vision: Levesque and Iacocca. In J. Conger & R. Kanungo (Eds.), *Charismatic leadership: The elusive factor in organizational effectiveness*. San Francisco, CA: Jossey-Bass.

Generic strategies: Toward a comprehensive framework. In R. B. Lamb & P. Shivastava (Eds.), *Advances in strategic management*. Greenwich, CT: JAI Press.

With J. Shamsie, S. Otis, & J. Waters. Strategy of design: A study of "Architects in co-partnership." In J. Grant (Ed.), *Significant developments in strategic management*. Greenwich, CT: JAI Press.

**1989**

*Mintzberg on management: Inside our strange world of organizations.* New York: Free Press.

With F. Westley. Visionary leadership and strategic management. *Strategic Management Journal.*

With A. Dumas. Managing design, designing management. *Design Management Journal* (Fall).

**1990**

With J. Waters. Does decision get in the way? *Organizational Studies.*

Strategy formation: Schools of thought. In J. Frederickson (Ed.), *Perspectives on strategic management*. Ballinger.

The design school: Reconsideration of the basic premises of strategic management. *Strategic Management Journal.*

**1991**

With J. B. Quinn. *The strategy process: Concepts, context, cases* (2nd ed.). Englewood Cliffs, NJ: Prentice-Hall.

The effective organization: Forces and forms. *Sloan Management Review.*

Managerial work: Forty years later. In the S. Carlson, *Executive behavior* (Republished edition).

With M. Gonzalez. Strategies in the financial services industry. *McKinsey Quarterly.*

Commentary. In D. Wong-Reiger & F. Reiger (Eds.), *Globalization: Separating the fad from the fact.*

## Subsequent publications

**1991**

Strategic thinking as "seeing." In J. Nasi (Ed.), *Arenas of strategic thinking*. Helsinki: Foundation for Economic Education.

Learning 1, planning 0 (Reply to Igor Ansoff). *Strategic Management Journal.*

With A. Dumas. Managing the form, function, and fit of design. *Design Management Journal* (Summer).

**1992**

Learning in (and from) Eastern Europe. *Scandanavian Journal of Management.*

**1993**

With F. Westley. Cycles of organizational change. *Strategic Management Journal.*

*The rise and fall of strategic planning*. New York: Free Press.

## Notes

1 For example, "Research on Strategy-making" (1972); "Patterns in Strategy Formation" (1979); "Of Strategies, Deliberate and Emergent" (1985); "Strategy Formation in an Adhocracy" (1985); "Emergent Strategy for Public Policy" (1987).

2 Pardon the slight ambiguity; "Ten Years Later" was meant to date from the start of my teaching career; the data I present on my publications cover exactly twenty-five distinct years, back into one year as a doctoral student.

3 See L. R. Sayles (1970, April). Whatever happened to management—Or why the dull stepchild? *Business Horizons*, 13(2), 25–34.

4 This was the title of the subsequent book of proceedings; see C. A. Myers. (Ed.) (1967). *The Impact of Computers on Management*. Cambridge, MA: M.I.T. Press.

5 See L. H. Gulick (1937). "Notes on the Theory of Organization." In L. H. Gulick & L. F. Urwick (Eds.), *Papers on the science of administration*. New York: Columbia University Press.

6 When this occurred to me I am not exactly sure. The conference was in April and I began work on the dissertation by November at the latest. I have on file a dissertation proposal called "Programmed Strategic Decision-Making" dated September. So there must have been some kind of delayed reaction. On the other hand, I did a course paper in May 1965 called "On-Line Real-Time Presidents? A Study of Computer Applications at the Presidential Level" that included interviews with two Boston chief executives and descriptions of their work. So the topic had been on my mind even before the Webb approach.
7 *The Structuring of Organizations* (1979).
8 "The Structure of 'Unstructured' Decision Processes" (1976) and "Planning on the Left Side and Managing on the Right" (1976).
9 *The Strategy Process* (1988, 1991).
10 *Mintzberg on Management* (1989).
11 "The Structure of 'Unstructured' Decision Processes (1976).
12 *Patterns in Strategy Formation* (1979).
13 "The Science of Strategy-Making" (1967), p. 71.
14 *Normative Models in Managerial Decision-Making* (1975).
15 "The Structure of 'Unstructured' Decision Processes" (1976).
16 As Danny used to be somewhat reluctant to travel and get personal exposure, we had this line about Danny Miller being the pseudonym I use for my quantitative articles.
17 See, for example, the comparable published diagrams in *The Structuring of Organizations* (1979, p. iv) and *Power In and Around Organizations* (1983, p. viii).
18 For published versions of this paper, see "Policy as a Field of Management Theory" (1973, 1977).
19 See H. A. Simon (1957). *Administrative Behavior* (2nd ed.). New York: Macmillan; and L. von Bertalanffy (1968). *General Systems Theory*. New York: Braziller.
20 "Jeu des influences et buts organisationnels" (1973).
21 See "The Design School" (1990).
22 "Research on Strategy-Making" (1972).
23 Ibid.; "Strategy-Making in Three Models" (1973).
24 *The Nature of Managerial Work* (1973).
25 "Structured Observation" (1970); "Managerial Work" (1971); "A New Look" (1973).
26 "The Myths of MIS" (1972).
27 "Making a Science of Management" (1970); "Jeu des influences et buts organisationnels" (1973).
28 "A Framework for Strategic Planning" (1972).
29 A. Maslow (1954). *Motivation and Personality*. New York: Harper and Brothers.
30 See "Team Teaching General Management" (1978).
31 "The Case for Configuration" (1983).
32 J. Woodward (1965). *Industrial Organization: Theory and Practice*. London: Oxford University Press.
33 See F. Andrews (1976, October 29). "Management: How a Boss Works in Calculated Chaos." *New York Times*, in reference to my own study of managerial work.
34 See "Research on Strategy-Making" (1972).
35 See "Does Decision Get in the Way?" (1990).
36 "Tracking Strategy in an Entrepreneural Firm" (1982); "the Mind of the Strategist(s)" (1983); "Research the Formation of Strategies" (1984); "Tracking Strategies in the Birthplace of Canadian Tycoons" (1984); "Of Strategies, Deliberate and Emergent" (1985); "Does Planning Impede Strategic Thinking?" (1986); "Does Decision Get in the Way?" (1990).

37 "Tracking Strategy" (1982).
38 "Strategy Formation in an Adhocracy" (1985).
39 "Strategy Formation in the University Setting" (1983).
40 "The Mind of the Strategist(s)" (1983).
41 *Mintzberg on Management* (1989).
42 "Organizational Power and Goals" (1979); "Structure in 5's" (1980); "Configurations of Organizational Structure" (1981); "Organization Design" (1981); "A Note on that Dirty Word Efficiency" (1982); "A Note of the Unionization of Professionals" (1983); "Power and Organization Life Cycles" (1984); "The Organization as Political Arena" (1985).
43 "Why America Needs" (1983); "The Case for Corporate Social Responsibility" (1983); "Who Should Control the Corporation?" (1984).
44 Besides, anomalies can be fun. Some people collect stamps; I collect typographical errors. I write badly, and so my secretaries over the years have obliged with wonderful ones: "statistics quo," "Karl Propper," "consultants tend to come in times of charge," and, best of all, "diversification" (what a difference an "a" makes). I use these almost subliminally in my executive programs.
45 This and subsequently referenced correspondence with Simon has been reprinted with his permission in *Mintzberg on Management* (1989), pp. 58–61.
46 I must admit to something a bit sneaky here. As Ornstein points out, there is a good deal of symbolism associated with right and left, the former correct, strong, straight (in French), masculine, and so forth, the latter "gauche" (which means left in French), "sinister" (left in Italian and Latin), mysterious, feminine, and so forth. Of course, these refer to the right and left sides of the body, which are controlled by the opposite hemispheres of the human brain. By titling the article "Planning on the Left Side and Managing on the Right," with references to hemispheres instead of arms, I was turning the effect of that symbolism to my advantage.
47 In a letter of reply to Simon, I quoted Turing ("Computing Machinery and Intelligence, *Mind*, October 1950), the great British mathematician, who wrote in his famous article (before computers) on why it should not be assumed that machines cannot think: I assume that the reader is familiar with the idea of extrasensory perception, and the meaning of the four items of it: telepathy, clairvoyance, precognition, and psychokinesis. These disturbing phenomena seem to deny all our usual scientific ideas. How we should like to discredit them! Unfortunately the statistical evidence, at least for telepathy, is overwhelming. It is very difficult to rearrange one's ideas so as to fit these new facts in . . . This argument is to my mind quite a strong one. One can say in reply that many scientific theories seem to remain workable in practice, in spite of clashing with ESP; that in fact one can get along very nicely if one forgets about it. This is rather cold comfort, and one fears that thinking is just the kind of phenomenon where ESP may be especially relevant.
48 H. A. Simon (1987, February). "Making Management Decisions: The Role of Intuition and Emotion." *The Academy of Management Executive*, pp. 58–59.
49 H. A. Simon (1977). *New Science of Management Decision*. Englewood Cliffs, NJ: Prentice-Hall, p. 81.
50 R. Sperry (1974, January). "Messages from the Laboratory." *Engineering and Science*, p. 30.
51 "Of Strategies, Deliberate and Emergent" (1985).
52 A passage written earlier for the Preface to *The Structuring of Organizations* (1979) reads:

> In retrospect, I felt I had been working on a giant jigsaw puzzle, with many missing pieces. Some of the pieces I had seemed to fit in obvious places, and once enough of them were placed, an image began to appear in my mind. Thereafter, each new piece in place clarified that image. By the time I finished, I felt I had found a logical place for all the pieces available to me.
>
> (p. xii)

53 See *Mintzberg on Management* (1989), pp. 259–260, 266.
54 This year I even redesigned my doctoral seminar in policy around pull. Whereas I used to hand out a set of readings each week on some aspect of organizations (not unexpectedly, strategy, structure, managerial work, etc.), to be discussed in class, this time the students and I identified a series of issues—organizing across borders and boundaries, managing professional institutions, effecting strategic change, and so forth—which they introduce and we all discuss each week, backed up by some related reading to stimulate understanding.
55 See *Mintzberg on Management* (1989), Chapter 5.
56 Ibid, pp. 267–268.
57 "Five Ps for Strategy" (1987); "Another Look at Why Organizations Need Strategies" (1987).
58 "The Design School" (1990).
59 The latest materials I could find in the files still reflecting a real textbook, are the bound chapters dated 1980–81 and an outline dated November 1981. The former shows Chapters 1,2,3 (now on structure), 5,6, and 8 as written, while 4 (now on managerial work) and 7 list published materials. The later outline shows efforts to incorporate the notion of configuration, with one new chapter on "Elements of Situation," another on "Configurations" themselves, and seven at the end on each configuration as well as a final one on "Transitions." I also found a document dated May 21, 1980, called "Management: Another View," that outlined a trade version of the book which was more integrated around the configurations and listed a "LEGO" chapter. Another scribbled note read "TT writing in 1976–77: concentrate on integrating the chapters." Sometime later I had crossed out the two decade 7s and replaced them with 8s, and sometime after that (in this case at least whimsically) I had crossed out the 8s and put in 9s!
60 "Profiles of Strategic Vision" (1988); "Visionary Leadership and Strategic Management" (1989).
61 "Strategies in the Financial Services Industry" (1991).
62 "Managing Design, Designing Management" (1989); I have long been fascinated with the subject of design, not just the concept in my professional work but the aesthetics in my personal reading—or preferably, looking at the pictures. In engineering school, in fact, I harbored the idea for a time of becoming a packaging consultant.
63 K. E. Weick (1979). *The Social Psychology of Organizing* (2nd ed.). Reading, MA: Addison-Wesley.
64 See "Managerial Work" (1991).
65 "The Structure of 'Unstructured' Decision Processes" (1976).

# 27

# THE FALL AND RISE OF STRATEGIC PLANNING

*Henry Mintzberg*

Source: *Harvard Business Review* 72(1) (1994): 107–14.

When strategic planning arrived on the scene in the mid-1960s, corporate leaders embraced it as "the one best way" to devise and implement strategies that would enhance the competitiveness of each business unit. True to the scientific management pioneered by Frederick Taylor, this one best way involved separating thinking from doing and creating a new function staffed by specialists: strategic planners. Planning systems were expected to produce the best strategies as well as step-by-step instructions for carrying out those strategies so that the doers, the managers of businesses, could not get them wrong. As we now know, planning has not exactly worked out that way.

While certainly not dead, strategic planning has long since fallen from its pedestal. But even now, few people fully understand the reason: *strategic planning* is not *strategic thinking*. Indeed, strategic planning often spoils strategic thinking, causing managers to confuse real vision with the manipulation of numbers. And this confusion lies at the heart of the issue: the most successful strategies are visions, not plans.

Strategic planning, as it has been practiced, has really been *strategic programming*, the articulation and elaboration of strategies, or visions, that already exist. When companies understand the difference between planning and strategic thinking, they can get back to what the strategy-making process should be: capturing what the manager learns from all sources (both the soft insights from his or her personal experiences and the experiences of others throughout the organization and the hard data from market research and the like) and then synthesizing that learning into a vision of the direction that the business should pursue.

Organizations disenchanted with strategic planning should not get rid of their planners or conclude that there is no need for programming. Rather, organizations should transform the conventional planning job. Planners should make their contribution *around* the strategy-making process rather than *inside* it. They should supply the formal analyses or hard data that strategic thinking requires, as long as they do it to broaden the consideration of issues rather than to discover the one right answer. They should act as catalysts who support strategy making by aiding and encouraging managers to think strategically. And, finally, they can be programmers of a strategy, helping to specify the series of concrete steps needed to carry out the vision.

By redefining the planner's job, companies will acknowledge the difference between planning and strategic thinking. Planning has always been about *analysis* – about breaking down a goal or set of intentions into steps, formalizing those steps so that they can be implemented almost automatically, and articulating the anticipated consequences or results of each step. "I favour a set of analytical techniques for developing strategy," Michael Porter, probably the most widely read writer on strategy, wrote in the *Economist*.[1]

The label "strategic planning" has been applied to all kinds of activities, such as going off to an informal retreat in the mountains to talk about strategy. But call that activity "planning," let conventional planners organize it, and watch how quickly the event becomes formalized (mission statements in the morning, assessment of corporate strengths and weaknesses in the afternoon, strategies carefully articulated by 5 P.M.).

Strategic thinking, in contrast, is about *synthesis*. It involves intuition and creativity. The outcome of strategic thinking is an integrated perspective of the enterprise, a not-too-precisely articulated vision of direction, such as the vision of Jim Clark, the founder of Silicon Graphics, that three-dimensional visual computing is the way to make computers easier to use.

Such strategies often cannot be developed on schedule and immaculately conceived. They must be free to appear at any time and at any place in the organization, typically through messy processes of informal learning that must necessarily be carried out by people at various levels who are deeply involved with the specific issues at hand.

Formal planning, by its very analytical nature, has been and always will be dependent on the preservation and rearrangement of established categories – the existing levels of strategy (corporate, business, functional), the established types of products (defined as "strategic business units"), overlaid on the current units of structure (divisions, departments, etc.). But real strategic change requires not merely rearranging the established categories, but inventing new ones.

Search all those strategic planning diagrams, all those interconnected boxes that supposedly give you strategies, and nowhere will you find a single one that explains the creative act of synthesizing experiences into a novel strategy. Take the example of the Polaroid camera. One day in 1943, Edwin Land's three-year-old daughter asked why she could not immediately see the picture he had just taken of her. Within an hour, this scientist conceived the camera that would transform his company. In other words, Land's vision was the synthesis of the insight evoked by his daughter's question and his vast technical knowledge.

Strategy making needs to function beyond the boxes, to encourage the informal learning that produces new perspectives and new combinations. As the saying goes, life is larger than our categories. Planning's failure to transcend the categories explains why it has discouraged serious organizational change. This failure is why formal planning has promoted strategies that are extrapolated from the past or copied from others. Strategic planning has not only never amounted to strategic thinking but has, in fact, often impeded it. Once managers understand this, they can avoid other costly misadventures caused by applying formal technique, without judgment and intuition, to problem solving.

## The pitfalls of planning

If you ask conventional planners what went wrong, they will inevitably point to a series of pitfalls for which they, of course, are not responsible. Planners would have people believe that planning fails when it does not receive the support it deserves from top management or when it encounters resistance to change in the organization. But surely no technique ever received more top management support than strategic planning did in its heyday. Strategic planning itself has discouraged the commitment of top managers and has tended to create the very climates its proponents have found so uncongenial to its practice.

The problem is that planning represents a *calculating* style of management, not a *committing* style. Managers with a committing style engage people in a journey. They lead in such a way that everyone on the journey helps shape its course. As a result, enthusiasm inevitably builds along the way. Those with a calculating style fix on a destination and calculate what the group must do to get there, with no concern for the members' preferences. But calculated strategies have no value in and of themselves; to paraphrase the words of sociologist Philip Selznick, strategies take on value only as committed people infuse them with energy.[2]

No matter how much lip service has been paid to the contrary, the very purpose of those who promote conventional strategic planning is to reduce the power of management over strategy making. George Steiner declared, "If an organization is managed by intuitive geniuses there is no need for formal strategic planning. But how many organizations are so blessed? And, if they are, how many times are intuitives correct in their judgments?"[3] Peter Lorange, who is equally prominent in the field, stated, "The CEO should typically not be . . . deeply involved" in the process, but rather be "the designer of [it] in a general sense."[4] How can we expect top managers to be committed to a process that depicts them in this way, especially when its failures to deliver on its promises have become so evident?

At lower levels in the hierarchy, the problem becomes more severe because planning has often been used to exercise blatant control over business managers. No wonder so many middle managers have welcomed the overthrow of strategic planning. All they wanted was a commitment to their own business strategies without having to fight the planners to get it!

## The fallacies of strategic planning

An expert has been defined as someone who avoids the many pitfalls on his or her way to the grand fallacy. For strategic planning, the grand fallacy is this: because analysis encompasses synthesis, strategic planning is strategy making. This fallacy itself rests on three fallacious assumptions: that prediction is possible, that strategists can be detached from the subjects of their strategies, and, above all, that the strategy-making process can be formalized.

### *The fallacy of prediction*

According to the premises of strategic planning, the world is supposed to hold still while a plan is being developed and then stay on the predicted course while that plan is being implemented. How else to explain those lockstep schedules that have strategies appearing on the first of June, to be approved by the board of directors on the fifteenth? One can just picture competitors waiting for the board's approval, especially if they are Japanese and don't believe in such planning to begin with.

In 1965, Igor Ansoff wrote in his influential book *Corporate Strategy*, "We shall refer to the period for which the firm is able to construct forecasts with an accuracy of, say, plus or minus 20 percent as the *planning horizon* of the firm."[5] What an extraordinary statement! How in the world can any company know the period for which it can forecast with a given accuracy?

The evidence, in fact, points to the contrary. While certain repetitive patterns, such as seasons, may be predictable, the forecasting of discontinuities, such as a technological innovation or a price increase, is virtually impossible. Of course, some people sometimes "see" such things coming. That is why we call them "visionaries." But they create their strategies in much more personalized and intuitive ways.

### *The fallacy of detachment*

In her book *Institutionalizing Innovation*, Mariann Jelinek developed the interesting point that strategic planning is to the executive suite what Taylor's work-study methods were to the factory floor – a way to circumvent human idiosyncrasies in order to systematize behavior. "It is through administrative systems that planning and policy are made possible, because the systems capture knowledge *about* the task." Thus "true management by exception, and true policy direction are now possible, solely because management is no longer wholly immersed in the details of the task itself."[6]

According to this viewpoint, if the system does the thinking, then strategies must be detached from operations (or "tactics"), formulation from implementation, thinkers from doers, and so strategists from the objects of their strategies.

The trick, of course, is to get the relevant information up there, so that senior managers on high can be informed about the details down below without having to immerse themselves in them. Planners' favored solution has been "hard data," quantitative aggregates of the detailed "facts" about the organization and its context, neatly packaged and regularly delivered. With such information, senior managers need never leave their executive suites or planners their staff offices. Together they can formulate – work with their heads – so that the hands can get on with implementation.

All of this is dangerously fallacious. Innovation has never been institutionalized. Systems have never been able to reproduce the synthesis created by the genius entrepreneur or even the ordinary competent strategist, and they likely never will.

Ironically, strategic planning has missed one of Taylor's most important messages: work processes must be fully understood before they can be formally programmed. But where in the planning literature is there a shred of evidence that anyone has ever bothered to find out how it is that managers really do make strategies? Instead many practitioners and theorists have wrongly assumed that strategic planning, strategic thinking, and strategy making are all synonymous, at least in best practice.

The problem with the hard data that are supposed to inform the senior manager is they can have a decidedly soft underbelly. Such data take time to harden, which often makes them late. They tend to lack richness; for example, they often exclude the qualitative. And they tend to be overly aggregated, missing important nuances. These are the reasons managers who rely on formalized information, such as market-research reports or accounting statements in business and opinion polls in government, tend to be detached in more ways than one. Study after study has shown that the most effective managers rely on some of the softest forms of information, including gossip, hearsay, and various other intangible scraps of information.

My research and that of many others demonstrates that strategy making is an immensely complex process, which involves the most sophisticated, subtle, and, at times, subconscious elements of human thinking.

A strategy can be deliberate. It can realize the specific intentions of senior management, for example, to attack and conquer a new market. But a strategy can also be emergent, meaning that a convergent pattern has formed among the different actions taken by the organization one at a time.

In other words, strategies can develop inadvertently, without the conscious intention of senior management, often through a process of learning. A salesperson convinces a different kind of customer to try a product. Other salespeople follow up with their customers, and the next thing management knows, its products have penetrated a new market. When it takes the form of fits and starts, discoveries based on serendipitous events, and the recognition of unexpected patterns, learning inevitably plays *a*, if not *the*, crucial role in the development of novel strategies.

Contrary to what traditional planning would have us believe, deliberate strategies are not necessarily good, nor are emergent strategies necessarily bad. I believe that all viable strategies have emergent and deliberate qualities, since all must combine some degree of flexible learning with some degree of cerebral control.

Vision is unavailable to those who cannot "see" with their own eyes. Real strategists get their hands dirty digging for ideas, and real strategies are built from the occasional nuggets they uncover. These are not people who abstract themselves from the daily details; they are the ones who immerse themselves in them while being able to abstract the strategic messages from them. The big picture is painted with little strokes.

### *The fallacy of formalization*

The failure of strategic planning is the failure of systems to do better than, or even nearly as well as, human beings. Formal systems, mechanical or otherwise, have offered no improved means of dealing with the information overload of human brains; indeed, they have often made matters worse. All the promises about artificial intelligence, expert systems, and the like improving if not replacing human intuition never materialized at the strategy level. Formal systems could certainly process more information, at least hard information. But they could never *internalize* it, *comprehend* it, *synthesize* it. In a literal sense, planning could not learn.

Formalization implies a rational sequence, from analysis through administrative procedure to eventual action. But strategy making as a learning process can proceed in the other direction too. We think in order to act, to be sure, but we also act in order to think. We try things, and those experiments that work converge gradually into viable patterns that become strategies. This is the very essence of strategy making as a learning process.

Formal procedures will never be able to forecast discontinuities, inform detached managers, or create novel strategies. Far from providing strategies, planning could not proceed without their prior existence. All this time, therefore, strategic planning has been misnamed. It should have been called strategic programming, distinguished from other useful things that planners can do, and promoted as a process to formalize, when necessary, the consequences of strategies that have already been developed. In short, we should drop the label "strategic planning" altogether.

## Planning, plans, and planners

Two important messages have been conveyed through all the difficulties encountered by strategic planning. But only one of them has been widely accepted in the planning community: business-unit managers must take full and effective charge of the strategy-making process. The lesson that has still not been accepted is that managers will never be able to take charge through a formalized process. What then can be the roles for planning, for plans, and for planners in organizations?

Planners and managers have different advantages. Planners lack managers' authority to make commitments, and, more important, managers' access to soft information critical to strategy making. But because of their time pressures, managers tend to favor action over reflection and the oral over the written, which can cause them to overlook important analytical information. Strategies cannot be created by analysis, but their development can be helped by it.

Planners, on the other hand, have the time and, most important, the inclination to analyze. They have critical roles to play alongside line managers, but not as conventionally conceived. They should work in the spirit of what I like to call a "soft analyst," whose intent is to pose the right questions rather than to find the right answers. That way, complex issues get opened up to thoughtful consideration instead of being closed down prematurely by snap decisions.

### *Planning as strategic programming*

Planning cannot generate strategies. But given viable strategies, it can program them; it can make them operational. For one supermarket chain that a colleague and I studied, planning was the articulation, justification, and elaboration of the strategic vision that the company's leader already had. Planning was not deciding to expand into shopping centers, but explicating to what extent and when, with how many stores, and on what schedule.

An appropriate image for the planner might be that person left behind in a meeting, together with the chief executive, after everyone else has departed. All of the strategic decisions that were made are symbolically strewn about the table. The CEO turns to the planner and says, "There they all are; clean them up. Package them neatly so that we can tell everyone about them and get things going." In more formal language, strategic programming involves three steps: codification, elaboration, and conversion of strategies.

Codification means clarifying and expressing the strategies in terms sufficiently clear to render them formally operational, so that their consequences can be worked out in detail. This requires a good deal of interpretation and careful attention to what might be lost in articulation: nuance, subtlety, qualification. A broad vision, like capturing the market for a new technology, is one thing, but a specific plan – 35% market share, focusing on the high end – is quite another.

Elaboration means breaking down the codified strategies into substrategies and ad hoc programs as well as overall action plans specifying what must be done to realize each strategy: build four new factories and hire 200 new workers, for example.

And conversion means considering the effects of the changes on the organization's operations – effects on budgets and performance controls, for example. Here a kind of great divide must be crossed from the nonroutine world of strategies and programs to the routine world of budgets and objectives. Objectives have to be restated and budgets reworked, and policies and standard operating procedures reconsidered, to take into account the consequences of the specific changes.

One point must be emphasized. Strategic programming is not "the one best way" or even necessarily a good way. Managers don't always need to program their strategies formally. Sometimes they must leave their strategies flexible, as broad visions, to adapt to a changing environment. Only when an organization is sure of the relative stability of its environment and is in need of the tight coordination of a myriad of intricate operations (as is typically the case of airlines with their needs for complicated scheduling), does such strategic programming make sense.

### *Plans as tools to communicate and control*

Why program strategy? The most obvious reason is for coordination, to ensure that everyone in the organization pulls in the same direction. Plans in the form of programs – schedules, budgets, and so on – can be prime media to communicate strategic intentions and to control the individual pursuit of them, in so far, of course, as common direction is considered to be more important than individual discretion.

Plans can also be used to gain the tangible as well as moral support of influential outsiders. Written plans inform financiers, suppliers, government agencies, and others about the intentions of the organization so that these groups can help it achieve its plans.

### *Planners as strategy finders*

As noted, some of the most important strategies in organizations emerge without the intention or sometimes even the awareness of top managers. Fully exploiting these strategies, though, often requires that they be recognized and then broadened in their impact, like taking a new use for a product accidentally discovered by a salesperson and turning it into a major new business. It is obviously the responsibility of managers to discover and anoint these strategies. But planners can assist managers in finding these fledgling strategies in their organizations' activities or in those of competing organizations.

Planners can snoop around places they might not normally visit to find patterns amid the noise of failed experiments, seemingly random activities, and messy learning. They can discover new ways of doing or perceiving things, for example, spotting newly uncovered markets and understanding their implied new products.

### *Planners as analysts*

In-depth examinations of what planners actually do suggests that the effective ones spend a good deal of time not so much doing or even encouraging planning as carrying out analyses of specific issues. Planners are obvious candidates for the job of studying the hard data and ensuring that managers consider the results in the strategy-making process.

Much of this analysis will necessarily be quick and dirty, that is, in the time frame and on the ad hoc basis required by managers. It may include industry or competitive analyses as well as internal studies, including the use of computer models to analyze trends in the organization.

But some of the best models that planners can offer managers are simply alternative conceptual interpretations of their world, such as a new way to view the organization's distribution system. As Arie de Geus, the one-time head of planning at Royal Dutch/Shell, wrote in his HBR article "Planning as Learning" (March–April 1988), "The real purpose of effective planning is not to make plans but to change the . . . mental models that . . . decision makers carry in their heads."

### *Planners as catalysts*

The planning literature has long promoted the role of catalyst for the planner, but not as I will describe it here. It is not planning that planners should be urging on their organizations so much as any form of behavior that can lead to effective performance in a given situation. Sometimes that may even mean criticizing formal planning itself.

When they act as catalysts, planners do not enter the black box of strategy making; they ensure that the box is occupied with active line managers. In other words, they encourage managers to think about the future in creative ways.

Such planners see their job as getting others to question conventional wisdom and especially helping people out of conceptual ruts (which managers with long experience in stable strategies are apt to dig themselves into).

To do their jobs, they may have to use provocation or shock tactics like raising difficult questions and challenging conventional assumptions.

## Left- and right-handed planners

Two very different kinds of people populate the planning function. One is an analytic thinker, who is closer to the conventional image of the planner. He or she is dedicated to bringing order to the organization. Above all, this person programs intended strategies and sees to it that they are communicated clearly. He or she also carries out analytic studies to ensure consideration of the necessary hard data and carefully scrutinizes strategies intended for implementation. We might label him or her the *right-handed planner*.

The second is less conventional but present nonetheless in many organizations. This planner is a creative thinker who seeks to open up the strategy-making process. As a "soft analyst," this planner is prepared to conduct more quick and dirty studies. He or she likes to find strategies in strange places and to encourage others to think strategically. This person is somewhat more inclined toward the intuitive processes identified with the brain's right hemisphere. We might call him or her the *left-handed planner*.

Many organizations need both types, and it is top management's job to ensure that it has them in appropriate proportions. Organizations need people to bring order to the messy world of management as well as challenge the conventions that managers and especially their organizations develop. Some organizations (those big, machine-like bureaucracies concerned with mass production) may favor the right-handed planners, while others (the loose, flexible "adhocracies," or project organizations) may favor the left-handed ones. But both kinds of organization need both types of planners, if only to offset their natural tendencies. And, of course, some organizations, like those highly professionalized hospitals and educational systems that have been forced to waste so much time doing ill-conceived strategic planning, may prefer to have very few of either!

## The formalization edge

We human beings seem predisposed to formalize our behavior. But we must be careful not to go over the formalization edge. No doubt we must formalize to do many of the things we wish to in modern society. That is why we have organizations. But the experiences of what has been labeled strategic planning teach us that there are limits. These limits must be understood, especially for complex and creative activities like strategy making.

Strategy making is not an isolated process. It does not happen just because a meeting is held with that label. To the contrary, strategy making is a process interwoven with all that it takes to manage an organization.

Systems do not think, and when they are used for more than the facilitation of human thinking, they can prevent thinking.

Three decades of experience with strategic planning have taught us about the need to loosen up the process of strategy making rather than trying to seal it off by arbitrary formalization. Through all the false starts and excessive rhetoric, we have learned what planning is not and what it cannot do. But we have also learned what planning is and what it can do, and perhaps of greater use, what planners themselves can do beyond planning. We have also learned how the literature of management can get carried away and, more important, about the appropriate place for analysis in organizations.

The story of strategic planning, in other words, has taught us not only about formal technique itself but also about how organizations function and how managers do and don't cope with that functioning. Most significant, it has told us something about how we think as human beings, and that we sometimes stop thinking.

## References

1 Michael Porter, "The State of Strategic Thinking," *Economist*, May 23, 1987, p. 21.

2 Philip Selznick, *Leadership in Administration: A Sociological Interpretation* (New York: Harper & Row, 1957).

3 George Steiner, *Strategic Planning: What Every Manager* Must *Know* (New York: Free Press, 1979), p. 9.

4 Peter Lorange, "Roles of the CEO in Strategic Planning and Control Processes," in a seminar on The Role of General Management in Strategy Formulation and Evaluation, cosponsored by E.S.S.E.C., E.I.A.S.M., and I.A.E. (Cergy, France: April 28–30, 1980), p. 2.

5 H. Igor Ansoff, *Corporate Strategy: An Analytic Approach to Business Policy for Growth and Expansion* (New York: McGraw-Hill, 1965), p. 44.

6 Mariann Jelinek, *Institutionalizing Innovation: A Study of Organizational Learning Systems* (New York: Praeger, 1979), p. 139.

28

# THE ART AND SCIENCE OF PLANNING AT THE BUSINESS UNIT LEVEL

*Paul Miesing and Joseph Wolfe*

Source: *Management Science* 31(6) (1985): 773–81.

This paper attempts to relate the conditions that require different planning approaches. A theoretical planning framework is presented that considers the confidence of causal linkages coupled with the extent of environmental change. Prior planning research is synthesized to speculate on the appropriate leadership and decision-making styles for single-businesses, nondiversified firms, or divisions of diversified firms. Examples of computational, consensual, contingency, and conceptual planning systems are also provided.

## Introduction

All organizations must attempt to channel individual effort to obtain unified purpose(s). Therefore, the planning framework adopted by top managers is important: they facilitate the formulation of goals and strategies, influence the behavioral processes that emerge, and direct the method of communicating, coordinating, and controlling members' behaviors so that a consistency of action occurs. In this way, desired organization objectives are established. The environment, through domain consensus, will determine if the plans are realized (Duncan 1972).

Corporate planning systems result in a master blueprint of the actions required to ensure long-term growth and prosperity. Some authors contend that this process is an art, whereas others argue it is a science. In actuality, the planning process is both. The difficulty lies in ascertaining where on the continuum the organization lies. Since what works well in a stable environment may not succeed under turbulent conditions, a rational decision model is most applicable when the decision maker can perfectly forecast environmental change. Environmental anticipation, although not always possible, is one of the Thompson's (1967) strategies for dealing with uncertain environments.

According to many (Cyert and March 1963, Duncan 1972, Emery and Trist 1965, Simon 1977, Thompson 1967), difficulties arise under the following conditions:

1 when the complexity of the decision exceeds the comprehension of the individual;
2 when required resources exceed the capacity of the organization to acquire them;
3 when the organization faces more contingencies than it is able to keep under surveillance; and
4 when competitor actions nullify proactive strategies.

Thompson distinguishes different situations by specifying two major determinants of decision strategies. They are (1) beliefs about cause-effect relations, and (2) preferences regarding possible outcomes. By dichotomizing each as being either certain or uncertain, Thompson (1967, pp. 134–135) posits the four resultant decision types as being computational, judgmental, compromise, or inspirational.

The degree of environmental certainty depends in large part on environmental complexity and stability. According to Duncan (1972), stable environments have a limited number of outcomes whereas dynamic environments present a vast range of consequences. In addition, constantly changing conditions make it "... difficult to have available the relevant information for the decision-making situation. When the environment is changing, the system must continually learn to readapt. The system cannot rely on past procedures and practices; rather, it is faced with a new situation in which its members will have to learn new methods" (Duncan 1972, p. 321).

This paper synthesizes Thompson's causality dimension and Duncan's environmental stability dimension. Considering environmental stability, decisions can be made in either a programmatic or incremental manner, with each containing different degrees of confidence regarding the consequences of action (see Table 1). Programmatic decisions occur when the environment is stable enough so that the continuity of the past can be safely maintained. Dynamic conditions require more of an incremental approach to situations in response to changing states of nature.

The likelihood of achieving a desired result also determines the planning system selected. Decisions can be made synoptically when learning and feedback information is swift and sure, such as when causal linkages are relatively certain. Cohen and Cyert refer to this environment as being disjointed since "... the causal links among the sectors of the environment are relatively short and events in one sector are likely to have only minor effects in other sectors" (1973, p. 352). On the other hand, experience or intuition is called

*Table 1* Planning Systems Based on Causal Linkages and Environmental Change.

| Environmental Change | Known ⟵ Causal Linkages: (Synoptic Orientation) | Causal Linkages ⟶ Unknown (Behavioral Orientation) |
|---|---|---|
| Stable (Programmatic Orientation) | *Planning Style*: Computational<br>*Decision Making*: Analytical<br>*Leadership*: Authoritarian<br>*Organization*: Mechanistic<br>*Strategy*: Proactive<br>*Success*: Unity of purpose; minimal interaction; efficient<br>*Example*: Mature, dominant firms | *Planning Style*: Consensual<br>*Decision Making*: Intuitive<br>*Leadership*: Arbitrator<br>*Organization*: Collegial<br>*Strategy*: Judgemental<br>*Success*: Best estimates; democratic; cohesive and cooperative<br>*Example*: Innovator facing moderate challenge |
| Dynamic (Incremental Orientation) | *Planning Style*: Contingency<br>*Decision Making*: Incremental<br>*Leadership*: Statesman<br>*Organization*: Matrix<br>*Strategy*: Interactive<br>*Success*: Environmental scanning; close internal communications; tight control<br>*Example*: Environmental adopters | *Planning Style*: Conceptualized<br>*Decision Making*: Inspiration<br>*Leadership*: Charismatic<br>*Organization*: Organic<br>*Strategy*: Creative<br>*Success*: Exploit opportunities; thrive on ambiguity and complexity; innovative "gestalt" thinking<br>*Example*: Entrepreneurial firm |

for when causality is so unknown that all ramifications cannot be anticipated, considered, or predicted. This does not indicate that decisions in this case are irrational, only that they rely on "soft" processes such as hunches, guesses, intuition, or other behavioral orientations.

## A taxonomy of planning styles

Chakravarthy and Lorange (1984) distinguish four alternative strategic systems and organization structures based on a firm's ability to predict and respond to its environment (Lorange 1984). Their model parallels four stages of growth and development experienced by multibusiness firms as they progress through centralized, decentralized, portfolio, and matrix forms. In contrast, this paper is concerned with corporate planning for only single-businesses or nondiversified firms, or divisional planning for diversified firms. The purpose of this paper is to explain the conditions which call for either computational, consensual, contingency, or conceptual planning at the business unit level based on the extent to which the decision is structured and defined. These will be shown to be congruent with the causal textures of Emery and Trist's (1965) four organizational environments.

Although the four planning systems will be described in their pure form, it should be kept in mind that many hybrids exist in reality. For instance, the model in Table 1 presents the causal linkages and environmental change dimensions as distinct extremes, whereas they are really continua. Hence, some overlap or combinations may exist. In addition, different parts of an organization may find different systems to be more appropriate, so any one type may not be used throughout an entire organization. Furthermore, there are bound to be perceptual differences throughout an organization's hierarchy so that top managers could be utilizing one type of system in formulating strategies but lower levels may rely on another type for their execution. However, this discussion is limited to the business unit level. Finally, one system may be used as only a component part in a planning scheme which relies on a completely different system to assemble its pieces.

### *Computational planning*

Classical economic theory assumes that the interests of management coincide with those of the firm (i.e., the owners); decisions are made in some long-term rational manner in order to maximize profits; and perfect knowledge exists to do so. Based on these premises, formal and systematic models have been developed which are considered to be ideal. Some, like multivariate analysis, extrapolative techniques, and simulations, are useful for prediction and description. The purpose of these models ". . . is to quantify and relate all of the significant independent variables to the attainment of the firm's goals which in the aggregate amount to maximised shareholder net worth" (Greenwood and Thomas 1981, pp. 409–410).

Models that can accurately represent reality allow managers to understand systems relationships and to avoid unnecessary judgement while checking on their planning assumptions. Furthermore, the use of an analytical framework facilitates the formulation and evaluation of alternatives and the selection of the optimal solution as long as the objective function and parameters can be quantitatively described and the calculations can be conducted in a timely and cost-effective manner (Simon 1977). Not only does objectivity minimize personal biases, but mathematical modeling processes ". . . can provide a basis for better measuring and understanding of possible outcomes of strategy options" (Greenwood and Thomas 1981, p. 412). For these reasons, most models are used to project financial conditions of the firm (Gershefski 1970, p. B-309).

The Marketing Science Institute's project on the Profit Impact of Market Strategies (PIMS) is one of the most popular applications of mathematical models at the business unit level. This ongoing study, which attempts to find the effects of strategy and market conditions on profitability, shows a strong relationship between market share and return on investment. Such findings are touted to be useful for forecasting profits, allocating resources, measuring management performance, and appraising new business proposals (Buzzell *et al.* 1975, Schoeffler *et al.* 1974). Firms or divisions attempting to balance their product portfolios have available to them the corporate asset pricing model to minimize risk (Mullins 1982) or the growth-share matrix to allocate resources to their most productive uses (Henderson 1979; Miesing 1983), although some judgment is still required for both models.

Such normative models are viable in well-structured and stable situations where consequences are fairly predictable. Little (1970, p. B-470) suggests a "decision calculus" in order to assist managers in making decisions by developing models that are simple, robust, easy to control, adaptive, comprehensive, and commutable. But these types of models are limited because they require good historical and current data and assume that they can be effectively and efficiently implemented. With minimal group interaction, a computational planning style may reduce the motivation of organization members to accept orders since they do not participate in the decision and may not feel committed to it. The biggest failure, however, is that most quantitative models are based on theoretical and normative assumptions that give ". . . inadequate incorporation of intrinsic, stylistic objectives [i.e., noneconomic factors] in the study formulation process" and an incomplete view of causality (Hall 1973, p. 37).

What is presented in classical decision theory as a computational planning style is appropriate for Emery and Trist's placid randomized environment (Emery and Trist 1965) and is similar to Miller and Friesen's (1978, p. 927) "dominant firm" in stable and munificent environments. Their examples are Xerox and IBM during the sixties since they were authoritarian with strategies that were extrapolations from the past. Mature, dominant firms can follow this approach as long as their environment is controllable or predictable. But Miller and Friesen (1978, pp. 930–931) warn of the danger of becoming either a "stagnant bureaucracy" whose strategies remain conservative as the environment changes, such as occurred in the airline industry under de-regulation; or of becoming a "headless giant" with no strong leader to provide direction.

### *Consensual planning*

Often there is disagreement or uncertainty concerning consequences of actions, even in a stable environment. According to Cyert and March (1963, p. 83):

> First, organizational decisions depend on information, estimates and expectations that ordinarily differ appreciably from reality. These organizational perceptions are influenced by some characteristics of the organization and its procedures. The procedures provide concrete estimates—if not necessarily accurate ones. Second,

> organizations consider only a limited number of decision alternatives. The set of alternatives considered depends on some features or organizational structure and on the locus of search responsibility in the organization.

As a result, the so-called "process school" of management views organizations as coalitions of interests that negotiate, bargain, and deliberate until policy decisions are made. Since the manner in which consensus is arrived at will affect the final decision selected, the social relationships of the decision makers become more important as uncertainty increases. For this reason, Guth (1976, p. 378) views policy formulation ". . . as a process involving interactions between individual participants in the organization and the social system within which they operate."

Planning without the understanding of cause-effect relations encourages and requires the use of personal values, estimates, and perceptions. Even if outcomes are known, values are important in selecting an alternative (Andrews 1971). But as Greenwood and Thomas (1981, p. 408) point out, ". . . judgemental processes or heuristics fall short in many directions. There are built-in problems of bias, as well as problems of reliance on the intuitive ability of the entrepreneur coupled with the generally subjective character of such heuristics for strategy formulation."

The inherent subjectivity of individuals can be taken into account and balanced by a collegial style where group decision making allows members to cooperatively explore issues, share and exchange ideas, and freely brainstorm as the means of obtaining consensus. Therefore, success in this situation depends on the ability to manage the internal decision-making process until a satisficing or acceptable solution is reached. Indeed, the contribution of mathematical models is minimized due to their inability to capture the social and political atmosphere typical of strategic planning in most companies.

Pfeffer, Salancik and Leblebici (1976, p. 228) argue that social influence will more completely determine the decision outcome in the absence of universal standards for evaluating those decisions. In viewing planning as a group process, top management must reconcile differences of judgement. Success in such unstructured (and sometimes emotionally-charged) situations depends on the characteristics and attitudes of the individuals involved in the decision and the group's atmosphere. It is therefore incumbent upon top management to understand the social processes that lead to good ideas so that the members are able to obtain commitment to implement the group's decisions. An atmosphere of openness, trust, and full participation in offering suggestions and giving feedback should be encouraged.

In situations having little experience as a guide, such as when a firm seeks unexploited niches not previously recognized, expected outcomes are based on intuition and good business judgment and not on aspiration. This is typical for Emery and Trist's (1965) placid, clustered environment. For instance,

Miller and Friesen (1978, pp. 928–929) found Polaroid and Control Data to be representative of their "innovator" firms that operate under moderate challenge, i.e., in a relatively stable environment. However, Polaroid's initial responses to Kodak's entry into its instant photography market were somewhat erratic and its foray into the unprofitable instant movie film market, due in large part to the domination of Edwin Land, was a disaster.

### *Contingency planning*

Companies are increasingly forced to execute strategies in situations of growing uncertainty. Examples of recent environmental turbulence include the energy and raw materials shortages; unforeseen social, political, and technical developments; simultaneous inflationary and recessionary pressures; de-regulation; and global competition. In such cases, the outcomes of specific events are somewhat predictable but the events change far too rapidly. One method of dampening adverse effects of a turbulent environment is by negotiating with those elements which are most critical to the organization. For instance, organizations can respond to external environmental pressures by revising policy decisions through a series of compromises with affected constituent groups (Murray 1978; Thompson 1967).

Industry characteristics and competitor actions also constrain the firm's flexibility. Game theory examines the unpredictability and interaction of competitor moves where decisions are made under conflict with rivals. "The number of competitors, rivals, or buyers and sellers, together with their interests, values, goals, preferences, and resources, clearly shape the choices available to the players and thereby form part of the rules of the game" (McDonald 1975). Although the precise moves of others are not known, countermoves can be developed beforehand in anticipation of possible changes in events.

Instead of relying on a single or initial corporate plan, top management in this situation must insist on a whole battery of possible plans that can deal effectively with changing environments, reviewing and revising them more frequently. According to O'Connor (1978, p. 2), ". . . the greater the range of factors that might impinge on a company's future, the greater the number of uncertainties it must cope with. And, as a defense against this increased degree of uncertainty, a firm may decide to develop alternate scenarios of the future and/or contingency plans to cover bad guesses."

An alternative to developing scenarios beforehand is to modify objectives and plans incrementally as greater knowledge is acquired. Lindblom (1959, p. 81) contrasts the rational-comprehensive approach with his method of "successive limited comparisons," and he and Braybrooke (1963, pp. 85–86) observed that policymakers use a process of "disjointed incrementalism" that compares only marginal differences from the status quo. Ansoff (1965, p. 24) described such adaptive search as a "cascade approach" where final solutions are gradually arrived at as events evolve and results unfold. Similarly, Wrapp's (1967, p. 95) "muddling with a purpose," where policies evolve from day-to-day operating decisions, differs greatly from the formal, systematic, and comprehensive models. Quinn (1978, p. 8) found that the "power-behavioral" or the "formal systems planning" paradigms alone are unsuitable for explaining how successful planning occurs. Instead, decision makers confront unstructured situations through a process of "logical incrementalism" that combines computational and consensual elements. Ackoff's (1970, p. 18) "innovative planning," or adaptavizing, could either passively respond to a changing environment or actively influence its environment.

In a dynamic environment, described by Emery and Trist (1965) as disturbed-reactive, "muddling through" could give the appearance of having vague and inconsistent goals and means while the organization flounders from one commitment to the next with its members continuously compromising each decision in turn. To avoid this, ". . . all levels of management must be in close communication with one another to permit remedial action or changes in the strategic plan and its formulation" (Greenwood and Thomas 1981, p. 413). This can be achieved with a matrix structure which differentiates and integrates activities along the environment's dominant dimensions.

Miller and Friesen (1978, pp. 926–928) found that the "adaptive firm under moderate challenge," which fits the requirements for contingency planning, develops internal controls, scans the environment, and fosters open communications, and tends to be in such traditional industries as banking, retailing, and machine tools. On the other hand, their "adaptive firm in a very challenging environment" was identified as being in such highly technical industries as semiconductors, synthetic fibers, chemicals, and defense components. Their "giant under fire" was an oligopoly such as Heinz, DuPont, and General Motors which operates in a challenging and complex environment, but "[t]he complexity of the environment and the success of previous strategies have made this type of company reluctant to abandon its well tested orientations. Thus the firm adapts to its environment *incrementally*."

### *Conceptualized planning*

The most difficult condition exists when causal linkages are unknown and environmental change is dynamic. If logical answers are not apparent, it is easy for the planning process to consist more of nonthreatening and irrelevant conversation than an opportunity for formulating, questioning, and testing meaningful strategies and policies. Going through the motions of making decisions with a sense of futility as the organization is buffeted about by the environment can lead to an extremely lackadaisical attitude, confusion, and frustration. Success under inactive leadership comes about more by accident than by design.

Ruefli and Sarrazin's (1981, p. 1160) approach to "strategic control" in this situation is a combination of political negotiation with the external environment while using an incremental approach. They call this an "ambiguous circumstance" since planning occurs where environmental control is limited and falls somewhere in between the proactive, normative models and the reactive, incremental approach. But this situation presents a whole complex of new opportunities and relationships for the entrepreneur with vision and the daring personality to venture into a potentially hazardous environment. The organization that thrives on ambiguity and complexity, is willing to take bold action in changing its own environment and can contain its risks in doing so, and is flexible enough to react quickly to surprises will gain new technologies, products, services, and markets. Such creativity defies logic, with the final decisions unanticipated and the ultimate results unknown. But all innovations begin as ideas that, with luck and proper nurture, grow to become focal points from which the future central purposes of an organization evolve.

A conceptualizer can thrive in this environment. To Andrews (1971, pp. 228–229), the general manager is the strategic architect and firm's conceptualizer:

> To find strategic choices that are not routine and to determine a strategy uniquely adapted to external opportunity and internal strengths require the policy-making executive to be an innovator. The entrepreneurial or risk-taking element in strategy formulation often requires the strength to defy the apparent implications of industry decisions. In folklore psychology, the personalities of the critical analyst and the energetic and creative innovator-entrepreneur are supposed to be antithetical. The strategist, however, must span these opposites. Fortunately, their irreconcilability has been greatly exaggerated.

Consistent with Andrews (1971), Mintzberg (1978, p. 944) introduces "gestalt" strategies as being unique, tightly integrated, and requiring "innovative thinking, rooted in synthesis rather than analysis, based on the 'intuitive' or inexplicit processes that . . . are the products of single individuals, and only appear in organizations with strong leadership, in effect, those that use the entrepreneurial mode."

For such turbulent fields (Emery and Trist 1965), Miller and Friesen (1978, p. 928) identify the entrepreneurial firm. Exemplified by conglomerates such as Gulf & Western or Textron but equally valid for single-businesses or nondiversified firms, these companies are "run by a powerful *charismatic* chief executive who is in control of strategy making [and] . . . manipulates its environment instead of reacting to it." These companies are contrasted to the "impulsive firm" which operates without planning and whose intuition may lead to bold moves but could also end in failure if the result is an increase in environmental instability and complexity, such as the current shakeout in personal computers; and to firms that attempt "swimming upstream," such as Wheeling Steel and Franklin National Bank, whose insufficient resources resulted in high risk and desperate moves and ended ". . . in harmful incongruities among the new and old elements of the strategy" (Miller and Friesen 1978, pp. 930–931).

## Summary and conclusions

The organization's success depends on more than the cumulative individual efforts put forth by its members. Performance can be improved by (1) understanding the particular situation faced by the organization, and (2) using the appropriate planning system. In some situations, the organization's members are willing and able to take orders, know what is expected of each other, and recognize that formal structure and greater direction lead to success. In such highly-defined situations, all of the alternatives can be identified, their consequences are known, and the criteria for evaluating decisions can be easily and reliably quantified. Decision making is a matter of examining these alternatives and selecting with relative certainty the optimal one. Managers can set goals and control subordinates in a tightly-operating environment by specifying tasks and expectations, and emphasizing and rewarding their ability to conform to standards.

An orientation that clearly defines roles and clarifies goals so that decisions are internally consistent can be expected to lead to high performance when causal linkages are fully understood and the environment is relatively stable. However, this style could be dysfunctional under rapidly changing conditions or when causality is unknown. In such ill-defined situations, it would be more appropriate to rely on members' input and commitment as the group makes estimates and incremental adjustments.

Properly conducted, performance in loosely-structured decision-making situations will be improved when behavioral processes are considered and correctly administered. This is because decision makers in this situation are unaware of the criteria, alternatives, or consequences determining organizational performance. In addition, the factors to be considered are complex and cannot be easily quantified, making optimal solutions difficult to obtain. Instead, participants may resort to hypotheses, intuition, "guesstimates," experience, and luck. Unstructured situations rely on input from those responsible for performance and are willing to share decisions and information in an open atmosphere. Managers involved in this type of planning system should remove interpersonal obstacles in the decision-making group so they can work to their fullest potential.

The job of top management is to determine direction, assess the external environment, and decide the extent to which decision making is to be shared.

These managers are also responsible for enhancing and encouraging organizational performance. When the structure of the problem is changing, however, the entrepreneurial organization will adapt by finding unique, safe, secure, and protected niches, or attempt to manipulate its environment through a strategy that is bold and creative with risks carefully calculated. Rigorous analysis or specific direction from a strong leader, an open decision-making atmosphere for group members, or developing scenarios and contingencies alone may not result in high performance. The ideal combination would be to have the unity of organizational purpose that oftentimes only high structure can provide, the participative decision making required for ill-defined situations, the flexibility to respond to changing conditions, and the bold, creative decisions of the strong entrepreneur during changing and uncertain times. Effective planners realize that good decision-making abilities require analytical, intuitive, and interpersonal skills, and know when to use which planning system to their maximum advantage.

## References

ACKOFF, RUSSELL L., *A Concept of Corporate Planning*, Wiley-Interscience, New York, 1970.

ANDREWS, KENNETH R., *The Concept of Corporate Strategy*, Dow Jones-Irwin, Inc., Homewood, Ill., 1971.

ANSOFF, H. IGOR, *Corporate Strategy*, McGraw-Hill, New York, 1965.

BRAYBROOKE, DAVID AND CHARLES E. LINDBLOM, "The Strategy of Disjointed Incrementalism," Chapter 5 in *A Strategy of Decision*, The Free Press, New York, 1963.

BUZZELL, ROBERT D., BRADLEY T. GALE AND RALPH G. M. SULTAN, "Market Share—A Key to Profitability," *Harvard Business Rev.*, 53, 1 (January–February 1975), 97–106.

CHAKRAVARTHY, BALAJI S. AND PETER LORANGE, "Managing Strategic Adaptation: Options in Administrative Systems Design," *Interfaces*, 14, 1 (January–February 1984), 34–46.

COHEN, KALMAN J. AND RICHARD M. CYERT, "Strategy: Formulation, Implementation, and Monitoring," *J. Business*, 46, 3 (July 1973), 349–367.

CYERT, RICHARD M. AND JAMES G. MARCH, "Organizational Choice," Chapter 5 in *A Behavioral Theory of the Firm*, Prentice-Hall, Inc., Englewood Cliffs, N. J., 1963.

DUNCAN, ROBERT B., "Characteristics of Organizational Environments and Perceived Environmental Uncertainty," *Admin. Sci. Quart.*, 17, 3 (September 1972), 313–327.

EMERY, F. E. AND E. L. TRIST, "The Causal Texture of Organizational Environments," *Human Relations*, 18, 1 (February 1965), 21–32.

GERSHEFSKI, GEORGE W., "Corporate Models—The State of the Art," *Management Sci.*, 16, 6 (February 1970), B-303–B-312.

GREENWOOD, PAUL AND HOWARD THOMAS, "A Review of Analytical Models in Strategic Planning," *Omega*, 9, 4 (1981), 397–417.

GUTH, WILLIAM D., "Toward a Social System Theory of Corporate Strategy," *J. Business*, 49, 3 (July 1976), 374–388.

HALL, WILLIAM K., "Strategic Planning Models: Are Top Managers Really Finding Them Useful?" *J. Business Policy*, 3, 2 (Winter 1973), 33–42.

HENDERSON, BRUCE D., *Henderson on Corporate Strategy*, Abt Books, Cambridge, Mass., 1979.

LINBLOM, CHARLES E., "The Science of 'Muddling Through'," *Public Admin. Rev.*, 19, 2 (Spring 1959), 79–88.

LITTLE, JOHN D. C., "Models and Managers: The Concept of a Decision Calculus," *Management Sci.*, 16, 8 (April 1970), B-466–B-485.

LORANGE, PETER, "Strategic Control: Some Issues in Making It Operationally More Useful," Chapter 10 in Robert B. Lamb (Ed.), *Competitive Strategic Management*, Prentice-Hall, Inc., Englewood Cliffs, N.J., 1984.

MCDONALD, JOHN, *The Game of Business*, Doubleday and Company, Inc., New York, 1975.

MIESING, PAUL, "Limitations of Matrix Models as a Strategic Planning Tool," *Managerial Planning*, 31, 6 (May–June 1983), 42–45.

MILLER, DANNY AND PETER N. FRIESEN, "Archetypes of Strategy Formulation," *Management Sci.*, 24, 9 (May 1978), 921–933.

MINTZBERG, HENRY, "Patterns in Strategy Formation," *Management Sci.*, 24, 9 (May 1978), 934–948.

MULLINS, DAVID W., JR., "Does the Capital Asset Pricing Model Work?" *Harvard Business Rev.*, 60, 1 (January–February 1982), 105–114.

MURRAY, EDWIN A., JR., "Strategic Choice as a Negotiated Outcome," *Management Sci.*, 24, 9 (May 1978), 960–972.

O'CONNOR, ROCHELLE, *Planning Under Uncertainty: Multiple Scenarios and Contingency Planning*, The Conference Board, Inc., New York, 1978.

PFEFFER, JEFFREY, GERALD R. SALANCIK AND HUSEYIN LEBLEBICI, "The Effect of Uncertainty on the Use of Social Influence in Organizational Decision Making," *Admin. Sci. Quart.*, 21, 2 (June 1976), 227–245.

QUINN, JAMES B., "Strategic Change: 'Logical Incrementalism'," *Sloan Management Rev.*, 20, 1 (Fall 1978), 7–21.

RUEFLI, TIMOTHY AND JACQUES SARRAZIN, "Strategic Control of Corporate Development Under Ambiguous Circumstances," *Management Sci.*, 27, 10 (October 1981), 1158–1170.

SCHOEFFLER, SIDNEY, ROBERT D. BUZZELL AND DONALD F. HEANY, "Impact of Strategic Planning on Profit Performance," *Harvard Business Rev.*, 52, 2 (March–April 1974), 137–145.

SIMON, HERBERT A., *The New Science of Management Decision*, Prentice-Hall, Inc., Englewood Cliffs, N.J., 1977.

THOMPSON, JAMES D., "The Control of Complex Organizations," Chapter 10 in *Organizations in Action*, McGraw-Hill, New York, 1967.

WRAPP, H. EDWARD, "Good Managers Don't Make Policy Decisions," *Harvard Business Rev.*, 45, 5 (September–October 1967), 91–99.

29

# MANAGING STRATEGIC ISSUES IN A TURBULENT ENVIRONMENT

*John C. Camillus and Deepak K. Datta*

Source: *Long Range Planning* 24(2) (1991): 67–74.

A major shortcoming of conventional Strategic Planning Systems (SPS) is their lack of sensitivity in coping with changing environments. On the other hand, Strategic Issues Management Systems (SIMS), which has been recently developed to respond to 'weak' signals and turbulent environments, lack some of the visionary, enduring, motivational qualities of the SPS. This article describes how the SPS and the SIMS can be integrated so as to complement their individual strengths and mitigate their respective weaknesses. A process that can promote this integration is proposed.

Organizations, over the last decade, have felt the impact of unprecedented environmental uncertainty and how they cope with this increasing dynamism and turbulence will probably be the most important determinant of their future success or failure. More than ever, businesses need to be more sensitive and responsive to such environmental changes; not doing so can prove extremely costly, even jeopardizing their very existence. Strategic planning provides only a partial answer, with traditional planning systems often being criticized for their lack of sensitivity and inability to deal with the discontinuities and crises that arise in a dynamic and turbulent environment.[1] Organizations face a continuous barrage of stimuli, and repeated instances of corporations encountering strategic crises that could have been anticipated and defused but were not, has led to strong reservations about the ability of conventional strategic planning systems (SPS) to manage strategic change.

An alternative that has emerged in the 1980s has been termed as Strategic Issues Management, [1,2] processes and systems which are designed to be flexible, sensitive and action-oriented in order to minimize the probability of encountering strategic surprises. Proponents of Strategic Issues Management systems (SIMS) argue that these systems have the potential to play a critical role in management's efforts at formulating effective strategies. Unfortunately, as noted by the Emerging Issues Group at AT & T in their report 'The Context of Legislation', issues are not always obvious or easily identifiable and analysing them can, therefore, prove to be an uphill task. However, it is important that such analyses be done because it is only through such an analysis that considerations pertinent to corporate decisions can be drawn, making today's decisions more effective and tomorrow's decisions easier.

While both SPS and SIMS have their relative advantages, operating the two separately does have potential drawbacks. A more desirable alternative involves the reconciliation and integration of the two systems, with the SPS design being modified to overcome its shortcomings by incorporating aspects of SIMS. Moreover, such an integration is important to provide the needed convergence in terms of the actions taken due to the SPS and SIMS since one cannot function independently of the other. Ideally, effecting this integration should not detract from or change the fundamental purposes of either the SPS or the SIMS but should indeed be a move towards enabling them to meet their expected roles more powerfully. A mutually supportive and, hopefully, synergistic relationship between the two systems is clearly desirable and possible.

Our objectives in this article are to facilitate and promote this needed integration by modifying the design of the SPS to accomplish what the SIMS has been developed to do. The resultant integrated system incorporates the advantages of the conventional SPS without the shortcomings to which the SIMS was intended to respond.

## Strategic planning and Strategic Issues Management Systems

A strategic planning system can be viewed as a set of organizational task definitions and procedures for ensuring that pertinent information is obtained, forecasts are made, and strategic choices are addressed and evaluated in an integrated, internally consistent and timely fashion. It deals primarily with the effort directed to the development of a purpose, the design of strategies and implementation policies by which organizational goals and objectives can be accomplished.[3] Specifically, the strategic planning activity in an organization should help executives address some basic questions about the organization, such as, 'What have been our business objectives?' or 'What has been or will be our business?' or 'What should we do to ensure that objectives are achieved?'. Potentially significant payoffs are associated with the adoption of strategic planning as evidenced by the findings of empirical research. Although the evidence is somewhat mixed, studies by Thune and House,[4] Krager and Malik[5] and Welch[6] among others have found that companies which engaged in formal strategic planning out-performed those that did not.

While the design of the SPSs adopted by organizations vary, there is a basic commonality of factors and a typical, stylized SPS framework would consist of the following activities:

- Environmental Analysis
- Defining Goals and Objectives
- Internal Analysis (Evaluating Strengths and Weaknesses)
- Formulation and Evaluation of Alternative Strategies
- Strategy Selection
- Operational Plans and Implementation
- Performance Evaluation and Feedback

A characteristic feature of the SPS is that the planning cycle is repeated at pre-specified intervals, the frequency of which would depend on factors such as the nature of the business, industry characteristics (including the extent of competition), and the degree of environmental uncertainty or turbulence faced by the firm. However, it must be understood that comprehensive planning processes in complex organizations typically cannot effectively be carried out more frequently than every 3 to 5 years. Overly frequent repetition of comprehensive planning processes can be undesirable and counter-productive, resulting in ritualistic 'form-filling' exercises rather than sensitive and creative activities.[7] On the other hand, as Hayes[8] points out, environmental volatility and changes (e.g. those brought about by the recent Iraq-Kuwait conflict) result in significant deviations from forecasts, making the elaborate strategies based on such forecasts obsolete. In such cases, rigid plans have the undesirable effect of reducing a company's flexibility, resulting in missed opportunities. The appropriate form of planning in such circumstances is 'responsiveness planning',[9] designing and using a system than can quickly detect deviations from the expected and respond to them effectively.

Like strategic planning, strategic issues management is a process of constructive adaptation to discontinuity. SIMS can be defined as a set of organizational procedures, routines and processes devoted to the perceiving, analysing, and responding to strategic issues.[10] They are designed to be flexible, sensitive and action oriented with the objective of reducing the probability of strategic surprises; particularly in terms of the negative impact of unanticipated events.

The SIM process can generally be identified by the following components:[11]

- Continuous monitoring of the environment;
- Identification of issues;
- Assessing issues, judging their likely impact and establishing priorities;
- Planning strategy and tactics for handling issues in accordance with assigned priorities; and
- Implementing tactics and planning activities.

SIMS can facilitate the realization of an organization's objectives by helping it anticipate and respond to changes in its external environment. For example, Bank of America uses strategic issues management to account for unexpected and unanticipated environmental events that might otherwise be ignored. A major objective of its issues management activity is the detection of weak signals of change in the environment, changes which might later have a significant impact on the organization.[12] Most strategic issues are triggered by threats or opportunities which originate outside the organization; they can be defined as developments which in the judgement of strategic decision makers are likely to have significant impacts on the organization's present and/or future strategies.[13]

Large organizations find it necessary to monitor and analyse a wide range of issues they consider relevant—such issues being in the areas of demographics, values/lifestyles, resources, technology, public attitudes, government policies and economic trends. Not surprisingly, firms (particularly multinationals) have started viewing issues management as being important and are more willing to commit additional resources to such activity.[14] However, most organizations are still not sure how issues can be managed or how issues management can be integrated with the planning process. While the issues management group is often an integral part of the strategic planning unit, organizations such as Atlantic Richfield Co., United Airlines, Union Carbide and Allstate Insurance have separate issues management units which work closely with their respective corporate planning units.[15] Archie Boe, CEO of Allstate (1972–1982), for example, created a Strategic Planning Committee in 1977 and an Issues Management Committee in 1978 with interlocking memberships. The Issues Management Committee was chaired by a vice-president who was also a member of the Strategic Planning Committee.[16] In addition, the approaches of organizations to the identification and analysis of issues vary considerably. In E.I. DuPont de Nemours, for example, issues management is the responsibility of the senior management while in other companies the function is delegated to staff analysts.[17] An unfortunate outcome of the popularity of SIMS is that it is often seen as a panacea by its proponents, with the result that many of its limitations are often ignored. Operated independently of the SPS, SIMS can suffer from a lack of focus and also result in substantial resources being expended without realizing the corresponding benefits.

## SPS—SIMS differences

A prerequisite to developing an integrated frame-work is an appreciation of the important differences between SPS and SIMS. The following differences have particular significance for the systems designer:

(1) Most SPSs are based on *periodic* activities, while SIMSs by their very nature, have to be *continuous* in character. An SPS usually involves a process of scanning, analysis and strategy formulation that is normally repeated at pre-set intervals. SIMS, by contrast, is *event* rather than *time-triggered* and, consequently, is a constantly ongoing process.
(2) The conventional SPS tends to respond to 'strong' signals, while SIMS is intended to pick up 'weak, not so obvious' signals.
(3) As a corollary of (1) and (2) above, the SPS focuses on issues *directly relatable* to the organization itself, while the SIMS presumably is receptive to issues having less direct or immediate effects on the corporation. Furthermore, executing the SPS itself may become somewhat narcissistic in character in that the planning process may become the superordinate goal.
(4) The output of SPS is typically characterized by a *vision* of what the organization would aspire to be; the SIMS in contrast endeavours to ascertain the *pragmatic consequences* of identified issues to focus actions which will reduce the negative impacts of and/or exploit the opportunities offered by strategic discontinuities.
(5) The orientation of the SPS towards the existing organization and the emphasis on enacting a predetermined process normally results in analysis and outputs that are significantly influenced by *existing* structure and power relationships. In contra distinction, the task forces envisaged by Ansoff[1] and King and Cleland[18] orient the SIMS to *nontraditional* modes of thought and action.
(6) Finally, given the goal orientation suggested in (4) above, the SPS would be biased towards a 'goals-means' sequence in strategy formulation. The SIMS, however, given its *ad hoc*, essentially reactive character, would inherently be limited to a 'means-goals' sequence. The paucity of related information that is characteristic of 'weak' signals would reinforce this intrinsic orientation of the SIMS.

Given the above differences, we can now examine their implications from the viewpoint of systems design.

## Implications for systems design

From the six differences that have been identified it is evident that both SPS and SIMS have features that need to be incorporated into an integrated frame-work. If we take up each of the differences, the related integrated systems design directions can be deduced.

First, the SPS is typically a time-triggered activity and its periodic character makes it an inadequate mechanism for dealing with an environment characterized by abrupt discontinuities and 'weak' signals.[1] To avoid strategic surprises and to promote aggressive, proactive strategies rather than defensive or reactive ones, it is imperative that environmental scanning of a more continuous nature be performed during the interim between the strategic planning cycles. Such scanning would generate a continuous inventory of strategic issues which need to be analysed and appropriate action responses developed. An example of a continuous issues identification programme is the highly successful TAP (Trend Analysis Program) of the American Council of Life Insurance which helped its member companies by anticipating legislative resolutions, sensitizing executives to changing public needs and enunciating issues (as formulated by a creative elite) before they reached the public agenda, thereby allowing a longer lead time for formulating strategies.

Second, the typical SPS focuses on the existing product-market-technology; a focus which is too narrow given today's business conditions. What is required is a scanning mechanism which attempts to identify discontinuities, even those not obviously and directly related to the existing product-market-technology definition. Such undirected scanning (which seeks to monitor sources of information rather than track particular developments) should increase the probability of picking up weak signals because of its nonconditioned character.

Third, in accomplishing the above two, we must not ignore the visionary character of the SPS. If the strategic visions that presumably emerge from the SPS are transitory and not enduring in character, the systematic translation of organizational aspirations into executive actions and decisions will be typified by confusion rather than coherence. Also to ask fundamental questions on a routine basis will inevitably detract from the creativity and commitment that should characterize the responses. This means that the strategic planning process cannot be a frequent activity and it is probably infeasible and certainly undesirable from a cost-effectiveness point of view to go through the entire planning process to take into account the impact of every strategic issue. The SPS modification (if any) should be only to the extent required by the importance and the impact of the issue concerned and, quite often, it need be only an incremental response.

Fourth, the SPS is organization-focused and it may be desirable to break away from the traditional modes of thought, role relationships and responsibilities. The careful design and use of task forces of a cross-functional, multi-level character may be a possible means of accomplishing this end.

Fifth, the task force approach suggested previously can contribute greatly to the effective implementation of strategic changes. Often strategic planning systems are criticized for their focus on concepts rather than actions, and issue-focused task forces with carefully delineated responsibilities can respond to this shortcoming.

## The proposed integrative planning systems model

The limitations associated with traditional SPS suggests the need for planning systems that can do more to cope with the increased environmental volatility and complexity that confronts business enterprises today. The proposed Integrative Planning Systems Framework (Figure 1) responds to this need by incorporating the design considerations mentioned above, and it provides the desired synergistic and mutually supportive relationships between the SPS and SIMS discussed earlier.

Environmental scanning, the first component of the system, is designated in the framework by (A) and (G). Any effective planning process requires a careful monitoring of the organizational environment to enable it to more effectively align its capabilities and resources with threats and opportunities. However, the scanning activity carried out at the beginning of the strategic planning process (as represented by ‘A’) is of a periodic, more directed nature. Such environmental scanning tends to focus on issues which are viewed as being important in determining the strategic direction of the organization, with the timing of the cycle being determined by the systems designer in the context of the characteristics of the organization and its perceived environment. The rest of the steps of the strategic planning process are represented by (B) through (F). However, as mentioned earlier, while periodic scanning cannot anticipate all potential discontinuities, undirected continuous scanning requires the investment of excessive resources. To make the scanning process cost-effective, we therefore propose a continuous semi-directed scanning (G) in that the key assumptions made during the comprehensive planning activity are monitored in addition to selected sources of potentially important information.

Following environmental scanning, the next step in the suggested framework is one of ‘Issues Identification’ (H). One can hardly overemphasize the importance of an early identification of the relevant issues, which provides organizations with a longer response time to develop proactive strategies. Strategic issues vary in the extent of information that is available for analysis and in the degree of consistency of that information. Sometimes both the information availability and consistency may be low resulting in significant uncertainty and ambiguity.[19] Also, special effort must be made to identify the ‘weak’ signals generated by ‘fuzzy’ environmental issues, the strategic effects of which are difficult to ascertain immediately, but which may have the potential of creating a crisis, if ignored. In addition, identifying issues early in the life cycle provides the opportunity for a thorough analysis of their potential impact on the company and the development of effective solutions before the organizational environment becomes frenetic. Efforts must be made to reduce the effect of individual biases in the identification process —consequently, it might be desirable to have executives involved in the process who do not have direct responsibility for the area being analysed.

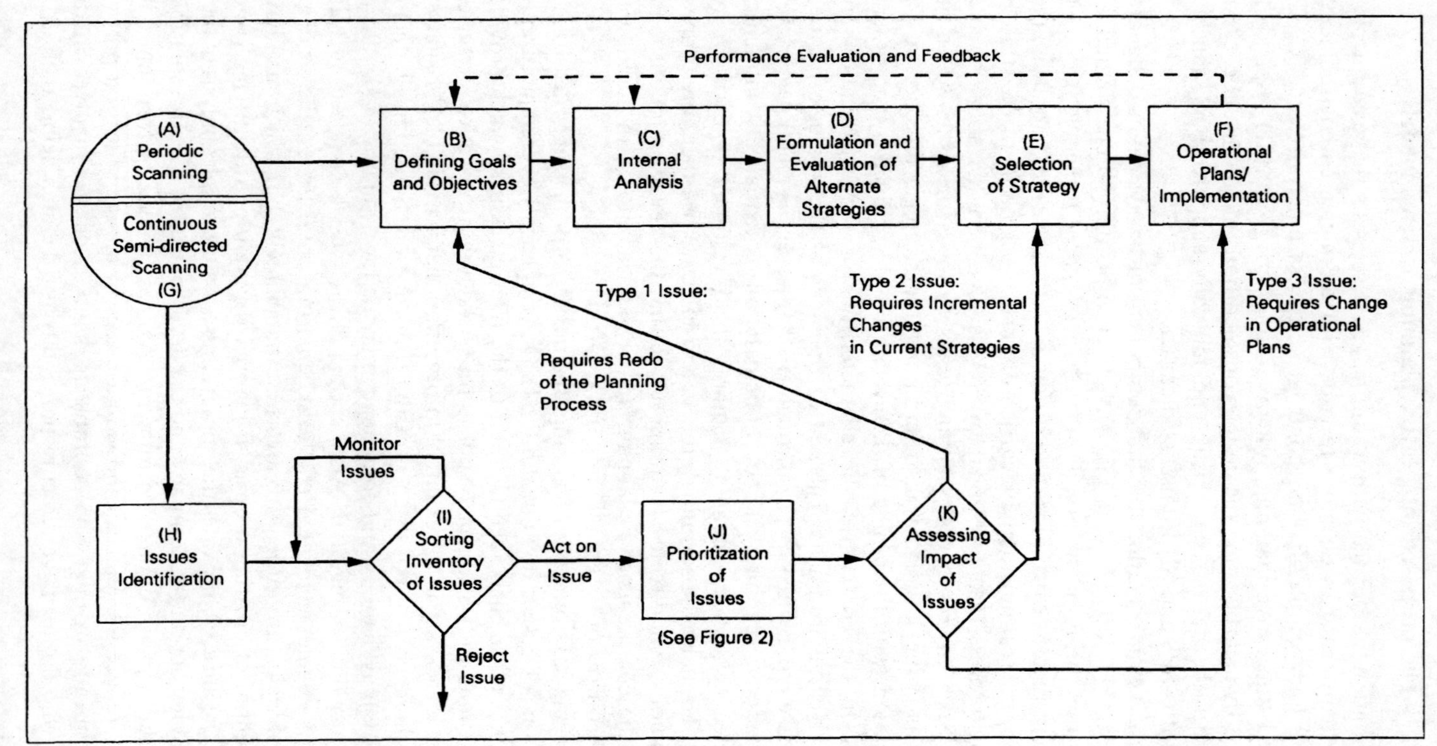


*Figure 1* Integrative planning systems framework.

Once identified, the issues need to be categorized into (1) those that have adequate clarity for immediate action, and (2) others which lack clarity and need to be closely monitored until a clearer picture emerges (permitting them to be moved over to the 'act upon' category). Alternatively, issues might be found irrelevant and be rejected at this stage. This sorting of the inventory of issues is represented by (I) in the system and is intended to be a continuous process. Once identified and categorized, issues must then be analysed and prioritized (J). The priority of an issue would obviously depend on a variety of factors, namely, the strategic relevance, the estimated cost-effectiveness (as measured by the potential impact of the issue) and the urgency (measured by the time period in which action is to be taken). This step is particularly important because, as Neubauer and Solomon[20] correctly point out, organizations are bombarded with hundreds of bits of information and an effective selection process is a must if the whole exercise is to be meaningful.

The Clarity-Priority matrix of Figure 2 can be especially useful in the sorting and prioritization processes (see step 'J' of Figure 1). The prioritized issues then serve as the input for the next critical step in the whole process, namely, assessment of the impacts of the issues on the outputs of the strategic planning process. Effects on the objectives, current strategies or operational plans are assessed to evaluate the extent to which they need to be modified to incorporate the impact of the issue. This stage requires considerable sensitivity and judgement on the part of those involved and, to

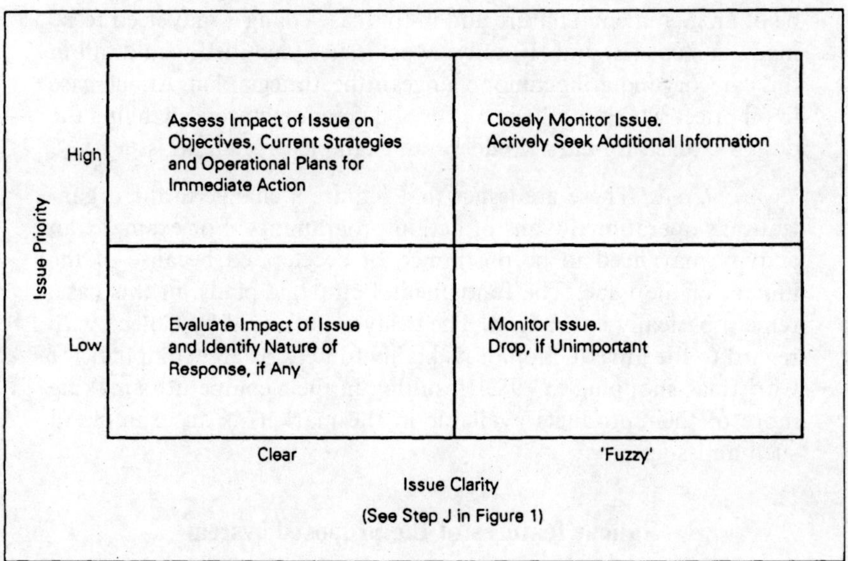


*Figure 2* The clarity-priority matrix.

avoid the effects of individual biases, is best executed by a group of executives with adequate diversity in terms of their backgrounds, hierarchial levels and functional areas.

The impacts and range of potential actions that need to be taken to address a particular issue can be visualized as falling on a continuum ranging from modest, minor changes in procedures or action plans to radical and dramatic changes.[21] However, for simplicity, we classify issues into the following three types:

*Type 1 Issues:* These are very major issues that may necessitate a redefinition of objectives and might even require an immediate redo of the comprehensive strategic planning process. Obviously such issues which require an out-of-phase strategic planning process would be very rare. The strategies chosen earlier become obsolete and the entire set of planning activities (B) through (F) needs to be redone. An unexpected major event such as the recent Gulf crisis (following Iraq's invasion of Kuwait) would be an example of such an issue for companies with significant operations in either country. Similarly, an unanticipated regulatory change in an industry would be another example.

*Type 2 Issues:* These are issues whose impact is not sufficient to require a change in the organization's objectives, but may require a re-evaluation of the current strategies leading to the selection of an alternative or slightly modified strategy. The resulting exercise would be of an incremental nature and in this case changes may need to be made in steps (E) and (F) only. Most issues identified would fall in this category requiring minor changes in the strategic plan. An increase in oil prices which results in automobile manufacturers changing the design criteria for cars would be an example of such an issue.

*Type 3 Issues:* These are issues that require a change in the organization's operational plans or action programmes. For example, an activity may need to be postponed or accelerated because of the impact of the issue. The fundamental strategic plans, in this case, remain basically unchanged. The delay experienced by Coleco with regard to the introduction of its highly touted 'Adam' computer for Christmas shopping in 1983 (resulting in their competitors making more of their products available in the market) is an example of such an issue.

## Salient features of the proposed system

The proposed system, an outcome of the integration of SPS and SIMS, has the advantage of being able to retain the positive characteristics of both. It provides strategic direction to the organization in a form similar to the SPS, but it is also responsive to strategic issues (which are continually identified and assessed) by activating necessary changes at the appropriate level.

One of the characteristic features of the proposed system is the incorporation of semi-directed, continuous environmental scanning for the identification of strategic issues. This would probably necessitate the formation of an environmental scanning unit for the purpose of identifying and doing preliminary analyses of issues. The sources for the identification of issues are many. They include, (1) appropriate literature, technical, industry as well as selected popular journals, (2) special interest groups whose activities might affect the organization, (3) professional associations, (4) organizational members with boundary-spanning roles and, (5) opinion polls. A recent addition to this list has been online databases, the use of which has been growing at a phenomenal pace.[22] These sources need to be continually tapped for a continuous stream of issues that may be relevant to the organization.

As noted earlier, a good published example of the issue identification process is the Trend Analysis Program (TAP) of the American Council of Life Insurance. Close to a hundred publications in the fields of science and technology, social sciences, business, economics, politics and government are reviewed regularly by volunteer monitors for issues that may be relevant. However, such scanning of secmingly appropriate literature, is not the only source of issues. People within the organization such as the CEO, top level executives and managers may themselves be very rich sources of relevant issues. PPG Industries, for example, encourages managers to bring up any important issue that comes to their knowledge by filling up a 'New Issues Alert' form.[23]

In Shell Oil issues identification and analysis is done jointly by senior management and staff analysts (the public affairs group) in consultation with representatives of the operating functions.[13] Staff members prepare an Issue scope paper which outlines the issue and its potential impact on Shell. Issues are reviewed by senior management who help prioritize and categorize the issues into those where immediate action needs to be taken and others which are merely to be followed. In FMC Corporation, a conglomerate with 1989 sales of S3·4bn, issues are identified, analysed and appropriate responses developed by divisional management together with Corporate Development. The issues along with responses are then sent to corporate management for ratification.[24]

Another example of a comprehensive environmental scanning, issue identification and sorting programme was at the Sun Company, a oil refiner that has diversified into other industries. This was accomplished through a 'Future Issues Committee', a free-wheeling group operating in an unstructured fashion.[25] Its members included representatives from the environmental assessment group, an officer from human resources, representatives from government affairs and the vice-chairman of Sun. The committee which met frequently considered a wide range of issues from the very fuzzy to the concrete, which were then assessed and subsequently referred to the policy-making groups in the organization. The concept is similar to that of the formation of a task force as advocated by Ansoff.[1] The scope of such a task group can be expanded to include the responsibility of following up and effecting a change in the strategic plan of the organization if required. Inclusion of a wide range of both operating and staff executives is valuable because of their different perceptions of relevant issues and their possible effects. Obviously, the degree of success enjoyed by the task force is dependent on the extent of cooperation and participation between the various people constituting the task force, a factor which has been stressed by King.[2]

Also, the proposed system ensures that issues which are 'fuzzy' but potentially important are not ignored, thereby reducing the number of crisis situations. Such issues need to be carefully monitored and any strategic or operational plans developed on the basis of an initial assessment of such issues may need to be substantially altered as a clearer, more definite picture emerges. All this points to the importance of contingency planning with alternative strategies and plans being formulated, based on different interpretations of the 'fuzzy' issue and its anticipated development.

## Conclusion

An increasingly volatile environment has resulted in executives in most organizations being continuously bombarded by a variety of strategic issues, some providing opportunities and others constituting major threats. There have been several instances where organizations have gained substantial competitive advantage because they were able to identify issues early enough, realize their strategic significance and take specific actions to seize the opportunity. The Conference Board Report[23] mentions among others, the case of two organizations (Whirlpool Corporation and PPG Industries) who, through their environmental scanning programme were able to identify and recognize the significance of key issues which enabled them to take prompt actions making them leaders in their field. On the other hand, there are many instances of companies which have suffered severe losses because of their failure to identify or respond to relevant issues. As aptly stated by the Environment Studies Group at General Electric, '. . . without proper response, societal expectation of today become the political issues of tomorrow, legislated requirements of the next day and the litigated penalties the day after that'.[23]

The environment of the 1990s promises to be full of potential surprises posing significant challenges for strategic planners. The rapidity of changes taking place in Eastern Europe, the impending changes in Western Europe as EC member countries seek to dismantle trade barriers in 1992, the explosive tensions in the Middle East and the potential for another oil shock all translate into both opportunities and threats for corporations. FMC Corporation's reactions to the recent developments in Iraq and Kuwait provides an example of an organization responding effectively to a crisis. Quick assessment of issues and the development of appropriate responses has not only resulted in FMC avoiding excessive damages but it has also helped the company gear up to take advantage of potential opportunities offered by the crisis.[26]

In addition to the obvious volatility in the global political and economic environment every industry will also need to deal with turbulence in other environmental areas. Particularly important would be the technological environment where rapid changes (e.g. breakthroughs in computer design and technology) impact not only manufacturing but also service industries like banking and financial services.[12] Managers, therefore, cannot just concern themselves with 'static optimization' embodied in the traditional SPS with the hope of developing clear cut and enduring strategies. If one were to draw an analogy, the logic behind strategic planning in the 1990s will be similar to that associated with modern conventional warfare where generals set the strategy and establish the detailed plan of action but, at the same time, continuously monitor the progress of engagement and modify strategies and tactics as and when required.

It is unlikely that strategic planning systems, as advocated in the past, will be adequate in the future; to be effective, organizations need a planning system which is sensitive in detecting and responding to critical issues that surface sporadically. What differentiates the proposed system from the traditional SPS are three important aspects that have been emphasized; continuous scanning to identify key issues; sorting and prioritization of the issues into categories based on the nature of their impact on the SPS; and the formation of task forces dedicated to carrying out the range of activities from scanning to implementation. The proposed 'sensitive systems' framework, in our view, provides executives with a powerful planning and control capability in their efforts to effectively cope with discontinuous and turbulent environments.

## References


(1) H. I. Ansoff, Strategic issues management, *Strategic Management Journal*, pp. 131–148, April–June (1980).

(2) W. R. King, Strategic issues management, in W. R. King and D. Cleland (eds.), *Strategic Planning and Management Handbook*, Van Nostrand Reinhold, New York (1987).

(3) J. C. Camillus, *Strategic Planning and Management Control*, Lexington Books (1986).

(4) S. Thune and R. House, Where long range planning pays off, *Business Horizons*, pp. 81–87, August (1970).

(5) D. W. Krager and F. A. Malik, Long range planning and organizational performance, *Long Range Planning*, pp. 60–64, December (1975).
(6) J. B. Welch, Strategic planning could improve your share price, *Long Range Planning*, pp. 144–147, April (1984).
(7) J. C. Camillus, Reconciling logical incrementalism and synoptic formalism—an integrated approach to designing planning processes, *Strategic Management Journal*, **3**, July–September (1982).
(8) R. H. Hayes, Strategic planning—forward or reverse? *Harvard Business Review*, pp. 111–119, November/December (1985).
(9) R. L. Ackoff, *A Concept of Corporate Planning*, Wiley-Interscience, New York (1970).
(10) J. E. Dutton and E. Ottensmeyer, Strategic issue management systems: forms, functions, and contexts, *Academy of Management Review*, pp. 355–365, April (1987).
(11) W. L. Renfro, Issue management: the evolving corporate role, *Futures*, **19** (5), 545–554 (1987).
(12) D. E. Raphael, Betting the bank on technology—technology strategic planning at Bank of America, *Long Range Planning*, **19** (2), 23–30, April (1986).
(13) C. B. Arrington and R. N. Sawaya, Issues management in an uncertain environment, *Long Range Planning*, pp. 17–24, December (1984).
(14) D. Nigh and P. L. Cochran, Issues management and the multinational enterprise, *Management International Review*, **27** (1), 4–12 (1987).
(15) T. G. Marx, Strategic planning for public affairs, *Long Range Planning*, **23** (1), 9–16 (1990).
(16) R. L. Heath and K. R. Cousino. Issues management: end of first decade progress report, *Public Relations Review*, **16** (1), Spring (1990).
(17) R. Zenter, Issues and strategic management, in R. B. Lamb (ed.), *Competitive Strategic Management*, pp. 634–648, Prentice Hall, Englewood Cliffs, N.J. (1984).
(18) W. R. King and D. I. Cleland, *Strategic Planning and Policy*, Van Nostrand (1978).
(19) J. E. Dutton, L. Fahey and V. K. Narayanan, Towards understanding strategic issues diagnosis, *Strategic Management Journal*, **4**, 307–323 (1984).
(20) F. Neubauer and N. Solomon, A managerial approach to environmental assessment, *Long Range Planning*, April (1977).
(21) J. E. Dutton and R. B. Duncan, The creation of momentum for change through the process of strategic issue diagnosis, *Strategic Management Journal*, **8**, 279–295 (1987).
(22) A. Rasheed and D. K. Datta, Strategic environmental scanning using online databases, *Proceedings of the 1986 Annual Meetings of the Decision Sciences Institute*, pp. 621–623 (1986).
(23) J. K. Brown, *The Business of Issues: Coping with the Company's Environments*, The Conference Board Report No. 758 (1979).
(24) S. Early, Issues and alternatives: key to FMC's strategic planning systems, *Planning Review*, **18** (3), 26–33 (1990).
(25) E. A. Weiss, How the Sun Company Addresses the Future Business Environment, Speech Given at the Public Affairs Council's Workshop on Forecasting and Managing Issues, May (1978).
(26) R. Johnson, FMC's quick reaction shows how one firm deals with Iraq crisis, *Wall Street Journal*, 16 August (1990).

# 30

# EVOLUTIONARY PERSPECTIVES ON STRATEGY

*William P. Barnett and Robert A. Burgelman*

Source: *Strategic Management Journal* 17 (1996): 5–19.

We advocate studying strategic management from an evolutionary perspective: using dynamic, path-dependent models that allow for possibly random variation and selection within and among organizations. We argue that this perspective directs our attention to some of the most interesting problems in strategic management. The papers in this special issue are summarized, along with some of their implications for the advancement of an evolutionary perspective on strategy. Collectively, the papers draw on various theoretical rationales, illustrating how an evolutionary perspective can help to integrate the diverse and otherwise separate theoretical traditions that meet within the field of strategic management.

Most strategy research offers some rationale to account for performance differences among organizations or to account for strategic differences that presumably have performance consequences. For instance, a better-performing organization may be in a market position that is protected from competition (Porter, 1980), may have unique capabilities that enable it to innovate or differentiate (Wernerfelt, 1984; Barney, 1991), may occupy a powerful position in a network of organizations (Pfeffer and Salancik, 1978; Burt, 1992), may have a structure or strategy that fits well with the challenges offered by the market (Scott, 1975; Venkatraman and Prescott, 1990), may be efficiently designed so as to minimize transaction costs (Williamson, 1991), or may have outwitted its rivals in strategic interaction (Dixit and Nalebuff, 1991; Saloner, 1991)—to mention just some of the more popular rationales. A common belief among these various schools of thought is that a theoretical rationale can be expected to correspond to empirical patterns observable at any given time. In this belief, strategy researchers typically look for cross-sectional correlations in data at a single point in time, or sometimes even in a single case at a single time. Such evidence generally is accepted as a test, or at least an illustration, of a theoretical rationale.

But through what mechanisms do these predicted results come about? We beg this question when we focus our rationale and research on what exists at a point in time, without specifying the dynamics through which these outcomes develop. As Carroll and Harrison (1994) observe, such thinking is based implicitly on what March and Olsen (1989) call the assumption of 'historical efficiency'. By making this assumption, we expect that the cause–effect relations in our rationale will play themselves out to steady-state equilibrium quickly, uniquely, and independently of the particulars of the development process. Under this assumption, 'evolution' is a rapidly optimizing force—one that brings about empirical regularities as if by a design consistent with our theoretical rationale (Nelson, 1994).[1]

Those who take an evolutionary perspective on strategy, by contrast, explicitly question how strategic outcomes develop, and in so doing treat the assumption of historical efficiency as part of the research agenda. This approach has several important consequences for our research. First, it requires that we specify a *dynamic* model. This means constructing theory that can predict patterns of change, including rates of change (the speed at which change occurs) and alternative paths of change (particular sequences of events). Dynamic models may predict convergence toward a steady state, several possible steady states, or possible ranges rather than states (Tuma and Hannan, 1984; Anderson, Arrow, and Pines, 1988). But regardless of their treatment of equilibrium conditions, evolutionary models attend to the *pace and path of strategic change*. For instance, we might model how quickly—and along which paths—organizations will grow, change their performance, or experience strategic events such as birth, restructuring, product innovation, merger, technological change, or failure. Of course, such changes are what pique the interest of strategy researchers. Thus taking an evolutionary perspective directs our attention to those occurrences that are most interesting to the field of strategic management—and yet are the least understandable through static theories and cross-sectional research designs.

Second, an evolutionary perspective allows for *variation* in the possible strategies that organizations pursue. Most theories in strategic management take the 'strategy space' of possible variants as a given and then predict which would prevail if organizations pursuing the different possible strategies were to enter into competition. But how do new strategic variants develop? How do organizations search for and learn about strategic options, especially given well-known constraints on organizational rationality (Cyert and March, 1963; March, 1981)? How adaptive is this process of search (Levinthal and March, 1981; Mezias and Lant, 1994)? These questions invite us to study the rate and path of innovation among and within existing organizations, when organizations grow (Ijiri and Simon, 1977; Penrose, 1968), when strategic initiatives are launched within firms (Burgelman, 1983a; Garud and Van de Ven, 1992), or when new jobs are created (Miner, 1990). These questions also suggest that we study the degree to which innovations are brought by existing organizations vs. through the founding of new organizations (Freeman, 1995).

In either case, an evolutionary perspective allows that many variations arise essentially at random—a possibility sometimes built into evolutionary models (Cohen, March, and Olsen, 1972; Padgett, 1982; Levinthal, 1991; Nelson, 1994). More commonly, random development represents a baseline model, serving as the null hypothesis. Theory is then challenged to explain variation or selection beyond that which arises stochastically.

Third, evolutionary inquiry asks how *selection* processes affect, and are affected by the pace and path of strategic change. Research on selection among organizations has proliferated within the research project of organizational ecology (Hannan and Freeman, 1989), with a strong emphasis on processes of organizational founding and failure. In this volume several of the studies model organizational failure rates. These studies report several findings that appear inconsistent with the assumption of historical efficiency. Selection in the auto industry favored different strategies at different points in the organizations' development (Carroll *et al.*); selection among hotel chains worked against those that were the most locally adaptive (Ingram); selection worked against software firms that relied on once-beneficial alliances (Singh and Mitchell); selection eliminated money market fund organizations that appeared to engage in the greatest amount of strategic search (Makadok and Walker); and selection among retail banks depended on the historical path of competition (Barnett and Hansen). Overall, these results add to mounting evidence that selection processes often do not function as a smoothly and rapidly optimizing force (Barron, West and Hannan, 1994; Carroll and Harrison, 1994; Barnett, 1996)—contrary to the assumption of historical efficiency.[2]

Oddly, some recoil at an emphasis on organizational failure, preferring to focus instead on instances of well-planned, sustained, excellent performance. This preference is seriously flawed on scientific grounds. One cannot adjudicate cause and effect when analyzing only today's survivors—a problem of sample-selection bias made all the worse if we focus on only the best of those survivors. Furthermore, this problem is compounded when we retrace the histories of successful organizations with our theories in mind. Such research invites retrospective rationality, as illustrated by notorious cases where strategic analysis consisted of post hoc rationalizing of events that, in fact, developed over time in unexpected and unplanned ways (Weick, 1995). Rather, in order to understand strategic success, we must study both the winners and losers—as we do in the systematic analysis of organizational failure.

Selection processes take place within organizations, as well as among them, as illustrated here by Noda and Bower, Doz, and Burgelman. A central idea of this work is 'strategic context:' the process through which new (existing) strategic variations are internally selected (deselected) and retained (abandoned) through an amendment of the firm's concept of strategy (Burgelman, 1983a, 1986). This work builds on the variation–selection–retention paradigm of cultural evolutionary theory (Campbell, 1969; Aldrich, 1979; Weick, 1979), which keeps it general enough to be applicable in various cultural contexts (Burgelman, 1988a). Other work in this vein integrates ideas from organizational ecology and strategic management (Burgelman and Singh, 1987; Burgelman, 1990). For instance, this research analyzes strategy making within firms as an intraorganizational ecological process (Burgelman, 1991, 1994; Burgelman and Mittman, 1994), where internal selection can substitute, to some extent, for external selection. A central proposition of this line of work is that external and internal selection, together, determine the fates of organizations. Those that continue to survive have an internal selection environment that reflects the relevant selection pressures in the external environment and produces externally viable new strategic variations that are internally selected and retained (Burgelman, 1988b; see also Hrebiniak and Joyce, 1985). Similarly, work on punctuated-equilibrium organizational change notes that whether organizations survive depends on how they manage through sequential cycles of reorientation and convergence (Tushman and Romanelli, 1985; Gersick, 1991; Romanelli and Tushman, 1994).

In summary, taking an evolutionary perspective on strategy means developing dynamic, pathdependent models that allow for possibly random variation and selection within and among organizations.[3] To contribute to the evolutionary perspective, it is not necessary for a study to satisfy all the components of this definition. Most careful research looks at only one or another aspect of strategic evolution, as when a study looks only at failure rates or only at variations due to innovation, but all work in this vein studies strategic dynamics. Each of the papers within this volume deals with variation and strategic search or with selection, and most have to do with both.

We organize our review beginning with the papers by Stuart and Podolny, Makadok and Walker, and Doz, which deal primarily with strategic search and organizational learning. Then we review the several papers that deal primarily with selection processes, including those by Ingram, Singh and Mitchell, Carroll *et al.*, Barnett and Hansen, Noda and Bower, and Burgelman. These papers represent a wide variety of approaches. Methodologically, they include intensive case studies, continuing a stream of process research well established in the strategy literature (e.g., Bower and Doz, 1979; Burgelman, 1983b). They also include analyses of large data sets used to obtain estimates of dynamic statistical models. Regardless of methodology, however, the papers in this issue each report an empirical analysis. This choice reflects the belief, on our part, that the greatest value of an evolutionary perspective comes in its use as a lens that can identify interesting regularities in empirical settings.

## Strategic search

How do organizations search for new strategies? This clearly is an important question, but research on strategic search is hampered by the fact that it is very difficult to measure. Stuart and Podolny make considerable progress on this problem in their study of local search in technology strategy.

### *Local search*

Stuart and Podolny study the development of technological variation among Japanese semiconductor companies. They propose to measure a firm's 'technological niche' according to the inventions on which an organization builds its own inventions. This method then allows firms to be described as either close or distant to one another in technology space, depending on whether they build on similar or different inventions. By aggregating these differences, one can characterize firms at a given time according to their relative distance from other firms in technology space. This technique permits the identification of clusters of technologically similar organizations, of organizations that are unique technologically, or of organizations that stand somewhere between different technological groupings. For instance, among the largest 10 Japanese semiconductor companies, the authors discover a cluster of technological leaders and a cluster of firms with a technological base geared toward consumer electronics. This analysis then is repeated using 'egocentric' data—a subset of the data including only firms that have at least some technological overlap with a given organization. Using this approach, the authors conduct a competitor analysis in technology space—in this case identifying the technological competitors of Mitsubishi.

Stuart and Podolny generalize this distance measure to include differences over time, both among firms and within a single firm's history. It makes a powerful tool for the evolutionary analysis of technological change, allowing one to measure the 'localness' of search by the relative distance that a firm travels in technology space over time. Using these generalized distance measures, the authors discover suprisingly stable *relative* technological positions among these companies over the period 1982–92—even though the Japanese semiconductor industry experienced extreme *absolute* change both quantitatively and qualitatively over that period. Furthermore, their analysis draws our attention to the companies that have experienced more extreme relative changes in their technological base or that have followed unique technological trajectories. Mitsubishi, for instance, shifted from the consumer electronics cluster to the technology leader cluster—a result, the authors report, of a strategic change by Mitsubishi during the study period.

One of the most attractive characteristics of Stuart and Podolny's method is that it allows one to depict technological distances both numerically and graphically. The numerical result is the familiar Euclidean distance score, measured over technology space both at a point in time and over time. Of course, the advantage of such a numerical measure is that it can be used as an independent variable in a predictive model. The distance scores can also be arrayed in two (or three) dimensions with standard techniques of multidimensional scaling, making it possible then to describe the relative technological positions of firms graphically. The plots generated by Stuart and Podolny offer compelling evidence of technological clustering, which they then corroborate by regressing the multidimensional scaling coordinates on several variables representing aspects of technology strategy. Lines bisecting these regressions clearly separate the group of technology leaders from the group based on consumer electronics technology.

Stuart and Podolny use their results to investigate whether the technological positions of these firms affect their involvement in strategic alliances. They find, interestingly, that most alliances involved firms within the group of technology leaders—developing either among leaders or between leaders and the more technologically peripheral firms based in consumer electronics. They also find that alliances especially involve firms that have changed their relative position over time.

The Stuart and Podolny study represents a considerable advance in the evolutionary study of technology strategy in particular and of strategic search generally. As the authors observe, evolutionary theories frequently emphasize—but almost never measure—relative, local change among organizations. This omission has impeded the advancement of our knowledge in this area. Using the ideas and method of Stuart and Podolny, one can now empirically model firms' time paths of search and explicitly study the relative development of technological trajectories. What's more, this approach may be able to bring empirical definition to the often-elusive 'resource base' of organizations. The authors note that, to the extent that an organization's technological position reflects its strategic capabilities, this analytical approach allows us to measure an organization's position in resource space distinct from its behavior in the market. Consequently, the authors' approach to evolutionary analysis may represent a way to study the link between strategic resources and market competitiveness without falling prey to tautological or *ex post* definitions of competence. As Stuart and Podolny suggest, future work on strategic evolution would do well to employ the ideas and methods developed in this paper.

### *Search and selection*

Makadok and Walker investigate the selection consequences of strategic search by the 233 money-market fund organizations that existed from the inception of the industry in the U.S.A. in 1975 through 1991. Strategic search is not directly observed in this study. Rather, search is inferred from an analysis of each organization's 'growth system', comprising its size, scope, performance, and cross-product subsidies—modeled so that each of these variables is allowed to affect the development of the others. Organizations with strong estimated effects among these variables have especially responsive growth systems, evidence of effective strategic policies. For instance, some organizations are more effective than others at parlaying good performance in one period into increased demand and growth in the next period. By estimating each organization's growth system for each of several time periods, Makadok and Walker are able to trace the path followed by each firm as its growth system becomes more or less responsive—presumably reflecting its search for an effective growth strategy.

The authors then speculate about the selection consequences of search and use their estimates of each firm's growth system to test two main hypotheses. First, they note that search may be adaptive, as argued in some theories of organizational learning and evolutionary economics. If search is adaptive, then the authors expect to see organizational failure rates decline as firms discover more effective growth strategies. Operationally, this would mean that firms with more responsive growth systems—those with higher estimated coefficients in their growth system—will have lower failure rates. This result should hold, moreover, after one controls separately for the *level* of each variable in the growth system. That is, it is not simply that large, broad, good-performing, well-subsidized firms are expected to survive. Rather, it is that after controlling for size, scope, performance, and subsidy, failure rates should be lower for firms with stronger estimated effects among these variables—since these are presumably the firms that have discovered more effective growth strategies. Thus Hypothesis 1 is tested by including the time-varying estimated coefficients of each organization's growth system as independent variables in a model predicting organizational failure.

Makadok and Walker are skeptical of Hypothesis 1, however, noting the plausible counter-argument that search is not adaptive. They draw on Bowman's (1963) idea that managers typically oversearch for better practices, as optimum practices are unlikely to be much better than practices near the optimum—yet attempts to reach the optimum are extremely costly and are plagued by random disturbances that prevent convergence on the optimum. Firms with the very best growth strategies are unlikely to be more viable than those with less effective growth strategies—contrary to the logic of fully adaptive search in Hypothesis 1. In fact, Makadok and Walker do not find support for Hypothesis 1—failing to reject the null hypothesis that an organization's growth system coefficients do not improve (collectively) on a failure model without these effects.

The authors also investigate a second main hypothesis, that strategic search is maladaptive, as suggested by Hannan and Freeman's (1984) structural inertia theory. This argument is based on the premise that organizations are expected to be reliable and accountable. Frequent and rapid changes in strategic policies imply reduced reliability and accountability, leading to social sanctions and ultimately to an increased likelihood of organizational failure. Makadok and Walker operationalize this idea as the cumulative change in each organization's growth system coefficients over time. Organizations with greatly changing growth policies are expected to show a great deal of cumulative change in the coefficients of their growth systems. Measures of the cumulative change in each organization's growth system, therefore, are expected to be associated with higher rates of organizational failure.

Correctly testing Hypothesis 2 requires the authors to isolate the survival implications of change *per se*—of the change process—apart from the implications of the content of organizational strategy. It is conceivable, perhaps likely, that organizations experiencing a great deal of cumulative change in their growth policies end up with extremely responsive growth systems. Nonetheless, the hazards of structural inertia come from the process of strategic change, and they threaten organizational viability apart from whatever improvements in strategic content they may have yielded. Consequently, in order to empirically model the maladaptive consequences of the change process, one must separately control for the consequences of strategy content (see Barnett and Carroll, 1995). Makadok and Walker do this in their failure models by controlling for the time-varying coefficients of each organization's growth system and then estimating the distinct effect of the cumulative amount of change in those coefficients. This procedure gives an estimate of the survival implications of change *per se*, holding constant the responsiveness of the growth policies that resulted from this change. With this model, the authors find strong support for Hypothesis 2.

### *Learning and initial conditions*

How corrigible are organizations? On the one hand, we know that initial conditions continue to have enduring consequences, and yet we also see organizations learn. Doz's study looks at this tension in the context of strategic alliances. He investigates the extent to which firms alter their collaboration in an alliance in response to feed-back, and how this process is constrained by the initial design and objectives of the alliance. Doz asks under what circumstances initial conditions foster or block interpartner learning in collaborative projects.

Doz documents change at the project level among six strategic alliances involving six companies. The emerging picture is complex. Partners start the collaboration process with a given set of initial conditions. They improve their knowledge in areas that have bearing on each of the initial conditions and re-evaluate whether the alliance should continue. The re-evaluation is based on whether the alliance appears to be efficient, adaptive, and equitable. This learning has cognitive and behavioral aspects that may or may not support one another. In some cases, cognitive learning is accompanied by behavioral learning that leads to mutual adjustment, making the initial conditions less salient. But in other cases, it is not. If cognitive and behavioral learning support each other, the alliance is likely to become stronger. Such learning seems to be facilitated when the task definition and the interface design remain somewhat open-ended at the outset so that they can change. If cognitive and behavioral learning are not mutually supportive, the alliance is likely to wind down and disband.

One especially interesting finding in Doz's study concerns the use of organizational routines. It is well known that organizations typically respond to new problems by using existing routines (March, 1981; Nelson and Winter, 1982). Doz finds a similar response in these strategic alliances: organizations tended to activate their own routines when dealing with one another, exacerbating the potential for misunderstanding, conflict, and distrust. In a related finding, Doz observed that the strategic context established by top management caused alliances to suffer if it was either extremely deterministic or extremely permissive: the former does not allow taking advantage of unanticipated strategic opportunities; the latter may lead partners to doubt their mutual commitment to the success of the alliance.

Doz's longitudinal-processual field research is a good example of how an evolutionary lens helps us to see the constraints faced by managers and to see that these constraints are often the result of previous adaptive efforts. His study identifies interesting phenomena such as the exaggerated use of organizational routines in the interface between organizational partners and the tension between determinism and permissiveness in setting the strategic context. The title of Doz's paper asks 'Initial conditions or learning processes?' But the paper's answer is initial conditions *and* learning processes. Its findings underscore the role of managers in recognizing inertial forces and, rather than denying them or simply wishing them away, taking action that alleviates or redirects them.

## Strategy and selection

Many thousands of organizations fail each year, often in the heat of competitive 'shake outs.' Despite its ubiquity, natural selection among organizations still is only rarely studied by strategy researchers. Yet scholars of many perspectives rely implicitly on selection processes to bring about their predicted outcomes. On closer examination, selection processes often generate unexpected and sometimes counterintuitive consequences.

The environment often confronts organizations with conflicting selection pressures, making it uncertain which strategies will succeed. Several of the studies in this issue illuminate this more complex view of strategy and selection.

### *Adaptation by parts vs. wholes*

A classic example of conflicting selection pressures occurs when an organization operates in more than one market. In this case, the organization faces a trade-off between highly localized adaptation and system-wide coordination. If it takes the localized-adaptation strategy, then the organization will be structured into independent units—each conforming to the demands of its own market. By contrast, if the organization takes a coordination strategy, then reliability and uniformity are preferred across an entire system.

An instance of this trade-off appears in Ingram's study of alternative naming strategies in the U.S. hotel industry. Ingram documents naming differences among all U.S. hotel chains that ever existed from 1896 to 1980, predicting and finding that this difference helped to determine which ones survived or failed. Throughout this period, U.S. hotel chains faced a choice, either to allow each of their establishments to identify with its particular locale or to adopt the name and image of the chain. Hotels pursuing the local-naming strategy were free to adapt their identities to whatever was most appropriate in their own locale—an advantage denied to hotels that adopted the name and image of a chain. By contrast, chain-named establishments had advantages due to their identification with a larger system of hotels. By adopting the common-naming strategy, a hotel changed its transactions with customers from one-time, spot market exchanges to repeated transactions. Ingram argues that this shift to repeated transactions made credible the hotel's commitment to providing valuable service, as it allowed customers to punish the hotel chain in future transactions for failing to do so. Locally named hotels, by contrast, suffered from a lack of credibility because their transactions with buyers typically were one time only, and so did not permit buyers to discipline the hotel for reneging on the contract for quality service.

Ingram predicts that this credibility gave the common-naming strategy a selection advantage over the local-naming strategy, and so he predicts lower failure rates for hotel chains adopting the common-naming strategy. Supporting this prediction, he finds those chains experienced failure rates 36 percent lower than did chains employing the local-naming strategy. This effect held despite his controls for various other independent variables, and it strengthened when aspects of organizational size were controlled in estimates from a subsample of the data.

More generally, Ingram's study nicely illustrates how one can turn the unit of selection 'problem' into an interesting research topic. An important question in theories of evolution concerns the unit that is selected or deselected. This issue is especially difficult when we study the evolution of complex organizations, as their nested, hierarchical structure makes it possible to study selection of products, divisions, establishments, or departments, as well as of entire corporations (or even networks of organizations). Ingram's approach is to allow the whole organization—the hotel chain—to be characterized by the strategies taken by its constituent establishments. In this way, he finds a compelling operationalization of the trade-off between establishment-level advantages of local adaptation and system-wide advantages of reliability.

Ingram's study compares the selection consequences of two different strategies used by a particular organizational form—in this case the multi-unit organization. An interesting, alternative comparison is to see how different organizational forms fared when using the local-naming strategy. Did locally named establishments within hotel chains have a selection advantage over single-unit hotels? Both forms of organization pursued the local-naming strategy, but the members of hotel chains conceivably benefited from their affiliation with the larger chain. Alternatively, single-unit hotels may have been individually vulnerable, but as a *population* these hotels may have been strong competitors because selection processes would be especially effective in weeding out weak variants (Barnett, 1996). Furthermore, a population of stand-alone, single-unit organizations might arguably produce greater variation to begin with than would the many members of relatively few chain organizations. Ingram's novel comparison of strategies could be extended to other comparisons where strategy and organization together affect selection processes as industries evolve.

### *The liability of collective action*

Strategic moves taken at one point in time have ongoing implications for an organization's fate. This process is illustrated by Singh and Mitchell's study of collaborative commercialization relationships in the U.S. hospital software systems industry from 1961 to 1991. In particular, they note that, once formed, alliances imply increased dependence between firms, as they come to rely on one another's capabilities. This dependence, in turn, might become hazardous if the future brings unexpected changes—the 'two-edged sword' of increased access to, and loss of control to, another organization (Selznick, 1949). Singh and Mitchell study two ways that this loss of control can make organizations more likely to fail: when a firm loses a partner because the partner fails, and when a firm's partner forms a relationship with another firm.

In the first case, losing an alliance partner to failure means losing access to the capabilities of the partner. Singh and Mitchell predict that this loss will increase a firm's failure rate—unless it can replace the failed partner with another. Here the loss of a partner is arguably an unexpected shock to the organization. At the time of their formation, no doubt such alliances are seen by all parties as beneficial. Yet by depending on these benefits, the organization makes itself vulnerable in the event that its partner fails. The empirical results support this prediction.

In the second case, where a firm's partner finds a new partner, a hazard is predicted because of a consequent change in the relationship. The firm's partner improves its negotiating position by forming a new alliance—changing the terms of trade to its benefit by reducing its dependence on any one relationship. Furthermore, Singh and Mitchell argue that if resources are constrained, then the formation of a new alliance may cause the partner to underinvest in the first alliance—harming the firm that became dependent on that alliance. In these ways, the authors expect that when a firm's partner forms new alliances, the firm's failure rate will increase. The results support this prediction, at least in specifications that allow for a time lag in the effect.

More generally, the Singh and Mitchell study suggests the usefulness of analyzing strategies with an eye for possibly adverse evolutionary consequences of policies that appear to be adaptive at the time they are implemented. By and large, our understanding of strategic alliances has remained strongly functionalist, with theorists proposing various advantages that are presumably explanations of the existence of alliances. No doubt these advantages are noted at the time of alliance formation, but it is important for us also to understand the liabilities that may result from collective action among organizations (Barnett, 1994). Singh and Mitchell offer evidence of two ways that a firm's hazard of failure might increase as a result of its past decisions to enter into alliances. Future work should continue to look into additional ways that alliance formation generates a liability of collective action.

### *Selection and initial conditions*

The strongest form of evolutionary argument holds that current organizational fates can be traced to causes at the time of founding. In their paper, Carroll, Bigelow, Seidel, and Tsai note that two popular ideas in the strategy field can be usefully thought of as this sort of 'founding conditions' argument, with contradictory implications. On the one hand, resource-based theory states that laterally diversifying firms can leverage capabilities in order to perform well in new markets (Hamel and Prahalad, 1994). This argument implies that new entrants that come from some other industry ('De Alio' entrants) will perform especially well. By contrast, theories of entrepreneurship argue that brand new 'De Novo' firms are especially adaptive to new conditions, because they are free from established routines developed for different times and places. Carroll *et al.* set out to study both of these ideas together by modeling organizational failure among all 2197 firms ever to have produced automobiles in the U.S.A. from 1885 to 1981.

To reconcile these competing stories, Carroll *et al.* go far beyond the claim that founding conditions matter, specifying detailed patterns of dynamic effects implied by both ideas. First, they expect that the resource advantages of De Alio firms will give them an initially lower failure rate, and they predict a similar advantage for De Novo firms that experience a 'preproduction' period in which the organization prepares to do business. Both of these predictions are supported by their empirical analysis.

Second, Carroll *et al.* then model the advantage of De Novo firms by specifying separate patterns of change in the failure rate for De Novo firms as compared to De Alio firms and to preproduction firms. They predict that as time passes, the advantage of existing routines and resources for De Alio and preproduction firms will become disadvantages due to inertia. De Novo firms with no preproduction experience are free from this liability, by contrast. Consequently, the initial disadvantage of the De Novo entrant is expected to reverse, so that it becomes less likely to fail. They then find evidence of this pattern—although the reversal is significant only compared to preproduction firms.

In addition, Carroll *et al.* investigate the survival implications of a De Alio entrant's industry of origin. Although the resource-based theory is not yet developed enough to make general predictions in this vein, the authors note some particular, potentially important differences among three common industries of origin: engine manufacturers, bicycle manufacturers, and carriage manufacturers. They suggest that the received wisdom among industry experts is that engine manufacturers would have an advantage as De Alio entrants into automobile production, but in fact they find the opposite—that carriage and bicycle manufacturers are the most viable De Alio entrants. The authors then explore several possible reasons for this finding.

The hypothesis tests of Carroll *et al.* are conducted with the well-developed 'density-dependent' model of organizational ecology (Hannan and Freeman, 1989; Hannan and Carroll, 1992). Carroll *et al.* use that model as a baseline, so that the basic evolutionary processes of legitimation, competition, and founding conditions are controlled. In particular, they find that failure rates of each kind of entrant fall with initial increases in the numbers of that kind of entrant—evidence of increasing legitimacy of that strategy. At high numbers, however, the effect turns competitive, so that additional increases in a given strategy predict an increase in the failure rate. Also, in addition, the number of competitors in an organization's year of founding is included as a covariate, and it predicts a higher lifetime failure rate for organizations born in a year with more competitors. This effect, known as 'density delay,' is evidence that organizations set up during scarce times suffer ongoing hazards as a result.

Carroll *et al.*'s use of a well-established model to test a strategic hypothesis is exemplary for several reasons. First, it shows that their hypothesis tests hold even after they control for processes that are known to affect organizational evolution. Second, this approach yields results that are comparable to those in other studies. Third, they study a new set of ideas within a generalizable modeling framework. This approach makes their findings more compelling than if they were to use ad hoc specifications, and it makes their novel ideas testable on other data sets. Researchers can attempt to replicate and advance their findings simply by estimating or extending their model in other organizational settings. Empirical modeling of this sort can go a long way to increase the accretion of knowledge in the strategy field.

### *The Red Queen*

Barnett and Hansen study how exposure to competition affects organizational survival, using a synthesis of organizational learning theory (March, 1988) and organizational ecology (Hannan and Freeman, 1989). They propose that an organization exposed to competition is likely to learn as a consequence (Barnett, Greve and Park, 1994). Assuming that learning is adaptive, the organization becomes a stronger competitor, triggering search and learning in its rivals. This response, in turn, strengthens competition from rivals felt by the first organization, starting the whole process over again. This reciprocal system of causality has been dubbed 'Red Queen' evolution by the biologist Van Valen (1973)—a reference to Lewis Carroll's *Through the Looking Glass*, in which Alice observes that she appears to be standing still even as she is running a race, and the Red Queen replies that in a fast world one must run just to stay still.

Barnett and Hansen argue that the Red Queen probably is very important in strategic evolution because, like an 'arms race' model, it is self-reinforcing. Even if each incremental adjustment is minor, over time this mutual incrementalism could conceivably add up to a very large difference. The authors also note, however, that it is potentially difficult to detect the consequences of this process, as each organization becomes more viable but its competitors become stronger too. As a result, net measures of performance or survival may lead us to believe wrongly that nothing has changed even when a Red Queen exists.

To overcome this problem, Barnett and Hansen model organizational failure rates as a function of two distinct, simultaneous effects. Each organization's *own* competitive experience is included in the model, because organizations with more competitive experience will be more likely to survive. At the same time, each organization's survival is allowed to depend on its *rivals*' competitive experience. Organizations with more experienced rivals are expected to be less likely to survive. Although descriptive statistics would confound these two opposing effects, Barnett and Hansen's multivariate model of organizational survival separates them into distinct terms. The key to separating these effects is in operationalizing 'competitiveness' as a property of organizations, rather than markets, allowing organizations to be stronger or weaker competitors as revealed by their effects on other organizations' viability (Barnett, 1993, 1996).

Going beyond these baseline effects, Barnett and Hansen also consider the condition under which learning may be maladaptive. Two historical constraints are considered. First, drawing on Levitt and March's (1988) idea of a 'competency trap,' Barnett and Hansen propose that competition-driven learning in the distant past is likely to have taught organizations outdated lessons. Consequently, they predict that exposure to competition in the distant past is maladaptive, making organizations both more likely to fail and weaker competitors. Whether Red Queen evolution is adaptive or maladaptive should depend on historical timing: recent experience is predicted to increase survival and competitiveness, whereas distant-past experience is predicted to have the opposite effects.

A second constraint arises when organizations compete against many different cohorts of rivals. An organization facing a single cohort of rivals shares with them a single sequence and timing of incremental adaptations. When a new cohort enters, the organization may also adapt to the challenges of this new competition, but it is constrained by adaptations made in the past to established rivals. In the same way, adaptations made in response to the new cohort of rivals constrain what can be done in response to established rivals. This pattern suggests that we should attend to the *variance* as well as the amount of competitive experience had by an organization. Organizations with their experience spread across many different cohorts of rivals—those with high variance among their competitive relationships—are more constrained in their ability to adapt to any one cohort. As these constraints increase, adaptations are less likely to exceed the costs of search and learning. Consequently, the authors predict that organizations with high variance among their competitive relationships are more likely to fail.

Barnett and Hansen empirically model these arguments together by specifying each organization's *experience distribution* in models of organizational survival. Number of competitors represents just one aspect of an organization's experience distribution: its *number of competitive relationships*. Beyond this, their arguments suggest that they also model (1) the amount of competitive experience (the *mean duration* of relationships), (2) the *historical timing* of these relationships, and (3) the *variance* in durations of these relationships. They also control for the effects of selection that might otherwise lead to spurious evidence of organizational learning. Only by modeling all of these effects together, they argue, can one detect both the adaptive and maladaptive consequences of Red Queen evolution.

The authors estimate their model using data on all 2970 retail banks ever to operate in this century in the state of Illiniois (excluding Chicago). Until recently, bank branches and holding companies were prohibited in Illinois. With only unit banks operating, each of the 650 communities within Illinois was a distinct and independent local market. These data provided ample differences in the competitive histories of organizations and their rivals—a requirement for identifying the Red Queen model. They found support for their predictions in estimates of the organizational failure rate among these banks.

Several conclusions come from the Barnett and Hansen study. First, the Red Queen model finds strong support, suggesting that a dynamic model of competitive strength may be a much better predictor of organizational success and failure than are models of static competition, which typically look at only the numbers and size distribution of competitors at a single point in time. Second, their approach is based on the idea that 'competitiveness' is a property of individual organizations, not of markets, as is usually thought to be the case. This innovation should be extremely useful for the field of strategic management, where much of our theory is based on the idea that some organizations are more competitive than others. Third, their study demonstrates that evolutionary processes have both maladaptive and adaptive consequences. Finally, Barnett and Hansen's model allows for strategic interaction among competitors, and at the same time it acknowledges that organizations are limited in their ability to strategize. The explanatory power of their model demonstrates the usefulness of basing our models on realistic assumptions when we describe the evolutionary consequences of strategic interaction.

### *Selection, initial conditions, and managerial discretion*

One of the ways in which an evolutionary perspective on strategy can be helpful is by identifying constraints on managerial action. Some of these constraints come from outside any particular organization, such as industry structures, laws, or consumer preferences. But other constraints come from within a firm, arising over its history—such as the initial conditions and organizational routines highlighted by Doz's paper. These internal constraints may limit managerial discretion in important ways.

Such internal constraints are revealed in the study by Noda and Bower. They begin their study of BellSouth and U S WEST with an interesting question: why would two organizations having similar initial market positions, similar competencies, similar structures and routines, and similar management talent embark on different courses of action when a new business opportunity arises for both? The authors then describe the different internal constraints that shaped these firms' very different strategies in cellular telephony during the period 1984 (after the breakup of AT&T) through the early 1990s.

Noda and Bower's paper shows ways in which corporate context affects the pattern of new business development with these firms. The authors use the Bower–Burgelman (B-B) process model (Bower, 1970; Burgelman, 1983c) to conceptualize the strategic decision-making processes concerning cellular telephony in BellSouth and U S WEST, and to highlight the differences between these processes in both firms. Their paper is the first to examine the usefulness of the B-B process model in a comparative study at the firm level.

Like Doz, Noda and Bower show that initial conditions associated with the corporate context are important in the strategy-making process. Top management sets the structural context, in particular the resource allocation rules. Top management also sets the initial strategic context, which reflects their 'crude strategic intent' regarding particular areas of business. Structural and strategic contexts, together, define the playing field for middle-level and operational-level managers. Managers below top management pursue business activities that give substance to the strategic context.

Although Noda and Bower confirm that top management sets the corporate context within which new business development takes shape, their findings also show that top management finds it very hard to change the pattern of resource allocation once it has been set in motion. U S WEST's CEO intended to move away from regulated businesses and focus on businesses that would allow the company to generate net income as soon as possible. He did not anticipate (as many others did not anticipate) the potential of cellular. Even though the CEO and other top managers became aware that resource allocation and key premises in the strategic context were leading U S WEST to miss out on opportunities in cellular telephony within the U.S.A., they did not change the rules and premises to avoid this unanticipated outcome. At BellSouth, in contrast, where there was initially great skepticism about the business prospects of cellular telephony at the top management level, financial rules governing resource allocation were less short-term oriented than at U S WEST, and cellular was viewed as complementary to wireline telephony rather than just as one of many potential new business opportunities. The design of corporate context thus determined patterns of escalation (BellSouth) or de-escalation (U S WEST) of commitment on the part of top management as a result of the iterations of resource allocation. The finding that structural context—in particular the resource allocation rules—was very stable highlights an important constraint on managerial discretion.

Noda and Bower also find evidence of an intraorganizational ecology in which business activities compete for resources. Initial success measured in terms of the resource allocation rules provides momentum. At U S WEST, the strategic context for new business development was less tied to telecommunications businesses than at BellSouth. Top corporate executives found that real estate and financial businesses were initially very successful and generated net income quickly. Incremental learning drove to expand nonwireless businesses (under the impulse of the managers associated with those businesses).

Finally, Noda and Bower's case data confirm that individual managers —'champions'—are important in getting a business initiative going and providing it with momentum. Their data also suggest, however, that once the business is taking shape, it becomes somewhat independent of particular individuals, as new managers replace the original champions. This result demonstrates that the unit of analysis for the B-B process model is the pattern of interlocking managerial activities, rather than the individual managers themselves.

### *Internal selection and managerial activities*

How do selection processes operate within organizations? And what patterns of managerial activities are involved in internal selection? These questions are posed in Burgelman's paper on strategic business exit (SBE). The paper studies the pattern of managerial activities involved in Intel Corporation's strategic business exit from its core business in 1984–85, dynamic random access memory (DRAM), and the redeployment of some associated distinctive competencies in the more profitable erasable programmable read-only memory (EPROM) business and, especially, the microprocessor business. The pattern of managerial activities involved in SBE was identified by using the process model of internal corporate venturing (Burgelman, 1983b) to analyze the behavioral data generated by the SBE study.

At the business level, the combined activities of operational and middle-level managers caused Intel to decline from initial dominance in DRAMs to a losing position. Some middle-level managers who embodied some of the firm's most important distinctive technical competencies deployed these competencies inflexibly, despite the fact that the industry was changing. Other middle-level managers, responding to Intel's resource allocation rules, shifted scarce manufacturing resources away from DRAMs. Operational-level managers tried to reposition Intel as a niche player in DRAMs, in an attempt to respond to internal and external conditions while taking advantage of Intel's distinctive competencies. This unsuccessful effort exacerbated Intel's loss of strategic position and reinforced the internal resource shifting and the concomitant de-escalation of commitment to DRAMs. These activities were intendedly rational, but they responded to incompatible internal and external pressures and so had the unanticipated consequence of setting Intel onto a course to exit from DRAMs.

Burgelman, like Noda and Bower, finds that at the corporate level the context set by top management had strong selective effects on the strategic actions of middle and operational managers at the business level. The resource allocation rules were a strong determinant of what the firm did, regardless of the rhetoric associated with official (or stated) corporate strategy. Like Noda and Bower in the case of U S WEST, Burgelman finds that Intel's top management did not change the resource allocation rules, even though the outcomes regarding DRAMs were not what top managers had in mind when they put the rules in place. The paper also finds that strategic business exit requires the *dissolution* of the strategic context of that business. Strategic context dissolution was found to be a complex process involving the combined but not always deliberately aligned activities of middle and top managers. By documenting the managerial activities involved in strategic context dissolution, the paper provides additional insight into the process of deinstitutionalization and a link between evolutionary and institutional perspectives.

Burgelman's paper shows some of the ways that internal selection may serve as a coordination mechanism. The paper also illustrates the intraorganizational ecology of strategy making, reporting the managerial activities that gradually decreased commitment to DRAMs and increased commitment to microprocessors. It also provides some evidence that strategic change that looks 'punctuated' at the corporate level of analysis may sometimes be the result of more gradual change taking place at lower levels in the organization.

## Conclusion

Each of the papers in this volume takes an evolutionary perspective, looking at dynamic, path-dependent processes and allowing for variation and selection within or among organizations. Each offers new insights and reveals important empirical findings. Taken collectively, they demonstrate that an evolutionary perspective may allow us to synthesize the many disparate theories now circulating in the field. The key here is that the evolutionary perspective is not inherently in contradiction with most theories of strategic management. Most rationales favored by a particular theory—efficiency, power, market position, distinctive capabilities, or whatever—usually can be understood in evolutionary perspective. In this volume, for instance, Ingram draws on economic rationale; Doz combines ideas from organizational learning theory and structural inertia theory; Singh and Mitchell analyze an asset specificity problem more often thought of as an issue for transaction cost economics; Noda and Bower as well as Burgelman combine ideas about economic incentives with an understanding of structural constraints; Stuart and Podolny use techniques and ideas from role theory in sociology; Carroll *et al.* synthesize ideas about strategic capability with structural inertia theory; Barnett and Hansen combine ideas from organizational learning theory and organizational ecology. What we advocate here is not a singular theory, but an *evolutionary perspective* that potentially can synthesize the many theoretical approaches now proliferating in the strategy field.

## Acknowledgements

This paper was written while Barnett was a fellow at the Center for Advanced Study in the Behavioral Sciences. We are grateful for financial support provided by the National Science Foundation (SES-9022192, to Barnett) and by the Stanford Graduate School of Business. Special thanks to our assistants, Regina López and Lea Richards.

## Notes

1 This 'as if' line of reasoning is rarely used explicitly (cf. Friedman, 1953), but rather is left implicit in theories that do not consider the development process.
2 In general evolutionary theory, little support remains for the idea that selection can be relied upon as an optimizing force (Gould and Lewontin, 1979; Sober, 1984; Casti and Karlqvist, 1995).
3 The problem of defining what constitutes evolutionary theory in general is not resolved (Sober, 1984). In the social sciences, most working definitions include the use of explicitly dynamic models and an allowance for randomness, variation, selection, and sometimes retention (Nelson, 1994; Aldrich, 1979).

## References

Aldrich, H. E. (1979). *Organizations and Environments*. Prentice-Hall, Englewood Cliffs, NJ.

Anderson, P. W., K. J. Arrow and D. Pines (1988). *The Economy as an Evolving Complex System*. Addison-Wesley, New York.

Barnett, W. P. (1990). 'The organizational ecology of a technological system', *Administrative Science Quarterly*, **35**, pp. 31–60.

Barnett, W. P. (1993). 'Strategic deterrence among multipoint competitors', *Industrial and Corporate Change*, **2**, pp. 249–278.

Barnett, W. P. (1994). 'The liability of collective action: Growth and change among early American telephone companies'. In J. A. C. Baum and J. V. Singh (eds.), *Evolutionary Dynamics of Organizations*. Oxford, New York, pp. 337–354.

Barnett, W. P. (1996). 'The dynamics of competitive intensity', working paper, Graduate School of Business, Stanford University.

Barnett, W. P. and G. R. Carroll (1995). 'Modeling internal organizational change', *Annual Review of Sociology*, **21**, pp. 217–236.

Barnett, W. P., H. Greve and D. Park (1994). 'An evolutionary model of organizational performance', *Strategic Management Journal*, Winter Special Issue, **15**, pp. 11–28.

Barney, J. B. (1991). 'Firm resources and sustained competitive advantage', *Journal of Management*, **17**, pp. 99–120.

Barron, D. N., E. West and M. T. Hannan (1994). 'A time to grow and a time to die: Growth and mortality of credit unions in New York City, 1914–1990', *American Journal of Sociology*, **100**, pp. 381–421.

Bower, J. L. (1970). *Managing the Resource Allocation Process*. Division of Research, Harvard Business School, Boston, MA.

Bower, J. L. and Y. Doz (1979). 'Strategy formulation: A social and political process'. In D. E. Schendel and C. W. Hofer (eds.), *Strategic Management: A New View of Business and Planning*. Little, Brown, Boston, MA, pp. 152–166.

Bowman, E. H. (1963). 'Consistency and optimality in managerial decision-making', *Management Science*, **9**, pp. 310–321.

Burgelman, R. A. (1983a). 'Corporate entrepreneurship and strategic management: Insights from a process study', *Management Science*, **19**, pp. 1349–1364.

Burgelman, R. A. (1983b). 'A model of the interaction of strategic behavior, corporate context and the concept of strategy', *Academy of Management Review*, **8**, pp. 61–70.

Burgelman, R. A. (1983c). 'A process model of internal corporate venturing in the diversified major firm', *Administrative Science Quarterly*, **28**, pp. 223–244.

Burgelman, R. A. (1986). 'Strategy making and evolutionary theory: Toward a capabilities-based perspective'. In M. Tsuchyia (ed.), *Technological Innovation and Business Strategy*. Nihon Keizai Shinbusha, Tokyo (in Japanese).

Burgelman, R. A. (1988a). 'A comparative evolutionary perspective on strategy making: Advantages and limitations of the Japanese approach'. In K. Urabe, J. Child and T. Kagono (eds.), *Innovation and Management: International Comparisons*. De Gruyter, Berlin, pp. 63–80.

Burgelman, R. A. (1988b). 'Strategy making as a social learning process: The case of internal corporate venturing', *Interfaces*, **18**, pp. 74–85.

Burgelman, R. A. (1990). 'Strategy making and organizational ecology: A conceptual integration'. In J. V. Singh (ed.), *Organizational Evolution: New Directions*. Sage, Newbury Park, CA, pp. 164–181.

Burgelman, R. A. (1991). 'Intraorganizational ecology of strategy making and organizational adaptation: Theory and field research', *Organization Science*, **2**, pp. 239–262.

Burgelman, R. A. (1994). 'Fading memories: A process theory of strategic business exit in dynamic environments', *Administrative Science Quarterly*, **39**, pp. 24–56.

Burgelman, R. A. and B. S. Mittman (1994). 'An intraorganizational ecological perspective on managerial risk behavior, performance, and survival: Individual, organizational, and environmental effects'. In J. A. C. Baum and J. V. Singh (eds.), *Evolutionary Dynamics of Organizations*. Oxford University Press, New York, pp. 53–75.

Burgelman, R. A. and J. V. Singh (1987). 'Strategy and organization: An evolutionary approach', paper presented to the Academy of Management Meetings, New Orleans.

Burt, R. S. (1992). *Structural Holes*. Harvard University Press, Cambridge, MA.

Campbell, D. T. (1969). 'Variation and selective retention in socio-cultural evolution', *General Systems*, **16**, pp. 69–85.

Carroll, G. R. and J. R. Harrison (1994). 'On the historical efficiency of competition between organizational populations', *American Journal of Sociology*, **100**, pp. 720–749.

Casti, J. L. and A. Karlqvist (eds.) (1995). *Cooperation and Conflict in General Evolutionary Processes*. Wiley, New York.

Cohen, M. D., J. G. March and J. P. Olsen (1972). 'A garbage can model of organizational choice', *Administrative Science Quarterly*, **17**, pp. 1–25.

Cyert, R. M. and J. G. March (1963). *A Behavioral Theory of the Firm*. Prentice-Hall, Englewood Cliffs, NJ.

Dixit, A. K. and B. Nalebuff (1991). *Thinking Strategically*. Norton, New York.

Freeman, J. (1995). 'Business strategy from the population level'. In C. A. Montgomery (ed.), *Resource-based and Evolutionary Theories of the Firm: Towards a Synthesis*. Kluwer, Boston, MA, pp. 219–250.

Friedman, M. (1953). *Essays in Positive Economics*. University of Chicago Press, Chicago, IL.

Garud, R. and A. H. Van de Ven (1992). 'An empirical evaluation of the internal corporate venturing process', *Strategic Management Journal*, Summer Special Issue, **13**, pp. 93–109.

Gersick, C. J. G. (1991). 'Revolutionary change theories: A multi-level exploration of the punctuated equilibrium model', *Academy of Management Review*, **16**, pp. 10–36.

Gould, S. J. and R. C. Lewontin (1979). 'The Spandrels of San Marco and the Panglossian Paradigm: A critique of the adaptationist programme'. *Proceedings of the Royal Society of London*, **205**, pp. 581–598. Reprinted in E. Sober (ed.) (1984). *Conceptual Issues in Evolutionary Biology*. MIT Press, Cambridge, MA, pp. 252–270.

Hamel, G. and C. K. Prahalad (1994). *Competing for the Future*. Harvard Business School Press, Boston, MA.

Hannan, M. T. and G. R. Carroll (1992). *Dynamics of Organizational Populations: Density, Legitimation, and Competition*. Oxford University Press, New York.

Hannan, M. T. and J. Freeman (1984). 'Structural inertia and organizational change', *American Sociological Review*, **49**, 149–164.

Hannan, M. T. and J. Freeman (1989). *Organizational Ecology*. Harvard University Press, Cambridge, MA.

Hrebiniak, L. G. and Joyce, W. F. (1985). 'Organizational adaptation: Strategic choice and environmental determinism', *Administrative Science Quarterly*, **30**, pp. 336–347.

Ijiri, Y. and H. A. Simon (1977). *Skew Distributions and the Sizes of Business Firms*. North-Holland, New York.

Levinthal, D. (1991). 'Random walks and organizational mortality', *Administrative Science Quarterly*, **36**, pp. 397–420.

Levinthal, D. and J. G. March (1981). 'A model of adaptive organizational search', *Journal of Economic Behavior and Organization*, **2**, pp. 307–333.

Levitt, B. and J. G. March (1988). 'Organizational learning', *Annual Review of Sociology*, **14**, pp. 319–340.

March, J. G. (1981). 'Footnotes to organizational change', *Administrative Science Quarterly*, **26**, pp. 563–577.

March, J. G. (1988). *Decisions and Organizations*. Basil Blackwell, Cambridge, MA.

March, J. G. and J. P. Olsen (1989). *Rediscovering Institutions: The Organizational Basis of Politics*. Free Press, New York.

Mezias, S. J. and T. K. Lant (1994). 'Mimetic learning and the evolution of organizational populations'. In J. A. C. Baum and J. V. Singh (eds.), *Evolutionary Dynamics of Organizations*. Oxford University Press, New York.

Miner, A. S. (1990). 'Structural evolution through idiosyncratic jobs', *Organization Science*, **1**, pp. 195–210.

Nelson, R. R. (1994). 'Evolutionary theorizing about economic change'. In N. Smelser and R. Swedberg (eds.), *The Handbook of Economic Sociology*. Princeton University Press, Princeton, NJ, pp. 108–136.

Nelson, R. R. and S. G. Winter (1982). *An Evolutionary Theory of Economic Change*. Harvard University Press, Cambridge, MA.

Padgett, J. (1982). 'Managing garbage can hierarchies', *Administrative Science Quarterly*, **25**, pp. 583–604.

Penrose, E. T. (1968). *The Theory of the Growth of the Firm*. Blackwell, Oxford.

Pfeffer, J. and G. R. Salancik (1978). *The External Control of Organizations*. Harper & Row, New York.

Porter, M. E. (1980). *Competitive Strategy*. Free Press, New York.

Romanelli, E. and M. E. Tushman (1994). 'Organizational transformation as punctuated equilibrium: An empirical test', *Academy of Management Journal*, **36**, pp. 701–732.

Saloner, G. (1991). 'Modeling, game theory, and strategic management', *Strategic Management Journal*, Winter Special Issue, **12**, pp. 119–136.

Scott, W. R. (1975). 'Organizational structure', *Annual Review of Sociology*, **1**, pp. 1–20.

Selznick, P. (1949). *TVA and the Grass Roots*. University of California Press, Berkeley, CA.

Sober, E. (1984). *The Nature of Selection: Evolutionary Theory in Philosophical Focus*. MIT Press, Cambridge, MA.

Tuma, N. B. and M. T. Hannan (1984). *Social Dynamics: Models and Methods*. Academic Press, New York.

Tushman, M. E. and E. Romanelli (1985). 'Organizational evolution: A metamorphosis model of convergence and reorientation'. In L. L. Cummings and B. M. Staw (eds.), *Research in Organizational Behavior*, Vol. 7. JAI Press, Greenwich, CT, pp. 171–222.

Van Valen, L. (1973). 'A new evolutionary law', *Evolutionary Theory*, **1**, pp. 1–30.

Venkatraman, N. and J. E. Prescott (1990). 'Environment-strategy coalignment: An empirical test of its performance implications', *Strategic Management Journal*, **11**(1), pp. 1–23.

Weick, K. E. (1979). *The Social Psychology of Organizing*. Addison-Wesley, Boston, MA.

Weick, K. E. (1995). *Sensemaking in Organizations*. Sage, Thousand Oaks, CA.

Wernerfelt, B. (1984). 'A resource-based view of the firm', *Strategic Management Journal*, **5**(2), pp. 171–180.

Williamson, O. E. (1991). 'Strategizing, economizing, and economic organization', *Strategic Management Journal*, Winter Special Issue, **12**, pp. 75–94.

# 31

# THE MICRO-POLITICS OF STRATEGY FORMULATION[1]

*V. K. Narayanan and Liam Fahey*

Source: *Academy of Management Review* 7(1) (1982): 25–34.

The business policy literature traditionally has emphasized the rational and normative aspects of strategy formulation in organizations. This paper develops a framework to explicate strategic decision making from a political perspective, with particular reference to the evolution of coalitions around issues. The content of a strategic decision is posited as emerging from internal dynamics. The utility of the framework is demonstrated by its comparison with the rational model of strategic decision making.

Traditional approaches to the formulation of organizational strategies, prevalent in business policy literature, have emphasized the rational and normative aspects of decision making (Bourgeois, 1980; Hofer & Schendel, 1978). Recent literature, however, suggests a growing interest in viewing strategy formulation as a political process (MacMillan, 1978; Murray, 1978; Pettigrew, 1977; Quinn, 1978). To a large extent, this interest has been stimulated by the decision process model postulated by Cyert and March (1963), primarily in the context of operating decisions (Ansoff, 1965). Although valuable efforts at enlarging the model to include strategic decisions have been undertaken (Allison, 1971; Carter, 1971), business policy literature still lacks a coherent framework within which to study strategic decision making from a political perspective.

This paper develops a framework to explicate strategic decision making triggered in organizations by strategic issues, with particular reference to the *evolution of coalitions* around issues or conflicts. The content of a strategic decision is posited as emerging from these internal dynamics. The utility of the framework is demonstrated through its comparison with the rational model of strategic decision making.

## Strategy and strategic decisions

Hofer and Schendel identify "the basic characteristics of the match an organization achieves with its environment" as the common theme underlying most definitions of strategy (content) (1978, p. 4). Mintzberg (1977), suggests that an organization's posture toward its environment is revealed as "a pattern in a stream of decisions," that is, decisions that reveal consistency over time. Following Mintzberg, this paper views strategy as the cumulative outcome of a series of strategic decisions. A *decision* here is defined as a specific commitment to action (usually a commitment of resources or enactment of precedents). *Strategic* refers to those decisions that have not been encountered before in quite the same form, for which no predetermined and explicit set of ordered responses exists in the organization, and which are important in terms of the resources committed or the precedents set (Mintzberg, Raisinghani, & Theoret, 1976; Mitroff & Emshoff, 1979).

The rational model describes strategy formulation as a set of procedures: identification of current strategy, analysis of environment, resources and gaps, identification and evaluation of strategy options, strategic choice and implementation (Andrews, 1971; King & Cleland, 1978; McNichols, 1977). Within this framework, the microeconomic assumption of a unitary voice within the firm has predominated: organizational preferences are assumed to be known and consistent, cause-effect relationships fairly well understood, and information availability sufficient to tackle most issues.

However, each of the above assumptions in particular and the rational-normative model in general can be questioned as to their representativeness of organizational realities (Murray, 1978). At the root of this questioning lies a conception of organizations as political entities, to which we now turn.

## A political conception of organizations

Fundamentally, organizations are political entities: coalitions of interests and demands emanating from within and outside organizations (Mintzberg, 1978; Thompson, 1967). Different interests and demands arise because organizations are loosely coupled systems (Weick, 1976), information bound (Simon, 1947), resource constrained (Pfeffer & Salancik, 1978), and are characterized by unclear technologies (Cohen, March, & Olsen, 1972) and differential linkages to their environments (Child, 1972; Duncan, 1972; Lawrence & Lorsch, 1967). Intraorganizational processes are dynamic: boundaries within organizations change, participation in decision domains varies, and decisions are differentially important. Under these conditions, organizations can be viewed as loose structures of interests and demands, competing for organizational attention and resources, and resulting in conflicts that are never completely resolved. As some have noted (Tushman, 1977), such a characterization typically is a political conception of organizations.

The accent of the rational-analytic conception is on strategy content. It neglects the turbulent undercurrents of organizational politics manifest in the interactions among various coalitions within the organization as they endeavor to influence strategic decisions. The political perspective brings these dynamics into sharp focus. From this perspective, the content of strategic decisions is viewed as an outcome of transactions of power and influence. Thus, political processes in organizations gain causal import in explanations of strategic decisions. The implication is that an examination of strategy content alone is insufficient to explain strategic choices. Only by investigating the organizational processes out of which strategies emerge, can one understand and explain *why* they come to be.

A dominant theme in the political conception of organizations is the role of coalitions in organizational decision making. Coalitions evolve in organizations due to limited resources, interdependence of tasks, limited availability of information, differential but limited power, and differences in and mutuality of interests (Pfeffer & Salancik, 1978; Thompson, 1967). When a single subsystem (or individual) cannot impose an organization-wide solution, coalitions are formed to enact decisions. Therefore, as Gamson (1962) has noted, coalition formation is important through its impact on the content of decisions.

Coalition behavior has been the object of inquiry by game theorists, social psychologists, and political scientists. These three disciplinary groups have adopted different philosophical approaches and have progressed relatively independently (Murnighan, 1978). Low convergence among these theories, restrictive assumptions underpinning them (as in game theory and social psychology), and differences in settings (as in political science) limit their applicability. In short, a comprehensive theory applicable to *organizational* settings has yet to be developed.

## Stages of strategic decision making

The model of strategic decision making developed in this paper is anchored in the following assumptions: (1) the ebb and flow of organizational interactions involved in such decisions may be broadly captured by a sequence of milestones or passages; (2) organizational politics manifests itself in the evolution and disintegration of coalitions; and (3) different coalitions evolve to make different decisions or similar decisions over time (Baldridge, 1971; Tushman, 1977; Warwick & Reed, 1975). These milestones and passages are presented in Figure 1. Table 1 provides in summary form the distinguishing characteristics of the various decision phases.

Broadly, the decision process encompasses two phases, gestation and resolution. The gestation phase involves a period of time when activities by

*Table 1* The Dynamics of Strategic Decision Making.

| | *Strategic Decision Stage* | | | | |
|---|---|---|---|---|---|
| *Characteristics* | *Activation* | *Mobilization* | *Coalescence* | *Encounter* | *Decision* |
| Characterization | Individual recognition of potential issues | Individual to collective level awareness | Temporal alliance of individuals with shared interests | Representation and justification of strategic alternatives | Organizational engagement around issue |
| Triggers | Recognition of symptoms, performance gaps, political ambitions, etc. | Public articulation of issues | Shared cognitive maps<br>Need to pool resources | Explicit initiation of actions | Zones of consensus |
| Process | Search for data Sense-making | Informal search for data relationships<br>Feeling out political affinities | Intracoalitional bargaining, negotiations | Power/influence ploys<br>Retrospective rationalization | Intercoalitional bargaining, negotiations, compromise |
| Content-themes | Description of symptoms, signals, discontinuities | Development of collective consciousness of symptoms<br>Questioning of assumptions, preferences, cause-effect relationships | Articulation of issue, potential programs of action | Legitimacy development<br>Goal formation Resource allocation | Strategic alternatives<br>Resource allocations Goals |
| Major actors | Individuals | Initial individuals and those whom they contact | Coalition leaders, followers | Coalition members and antagonists | "Fiduciary roles" Mediators |
| Structural determinants | Attentional processes: salience of issues, etc.<br>Formal and informal networks | Access structures<br>Social networks<br>Perceived similarity in cognitive maps | Coalition structure and processes<br>Enacted environment<br>Complexity of issue | Power/influence distribution<br>Political commitments<br>Access to information | Resource availability<br>Organization slack<br>Power/influence distribution |
| Transition mechanism | Inability to resolve issues<br>Concatenation of subjective and organization experience | Solidarity based on view of issue<br>Need to organize | Consensus of action program | Recognition of coalition's intentions and their impact | Quasiresolution of conflict |
| Outcome | Aware individual | Aware collectivity | Commitment to sponsor strategic alternatives | Explication of issue<br>Specification of claims, interests, positions | Commitment to action<br>Postponement of decision<br>Nondecision<br>Transformation into larger issue |
| Implications for strategy formulation | Organizational cognizance of strategic issues | Emergence of shape of strategic alternatives and political commitments | Specification of preferred strategic alternatives | Triggering of other strategic issues<br>Evolution of issue specific political alignments | Strategic change<br>Resource allocation<br>Political residues |

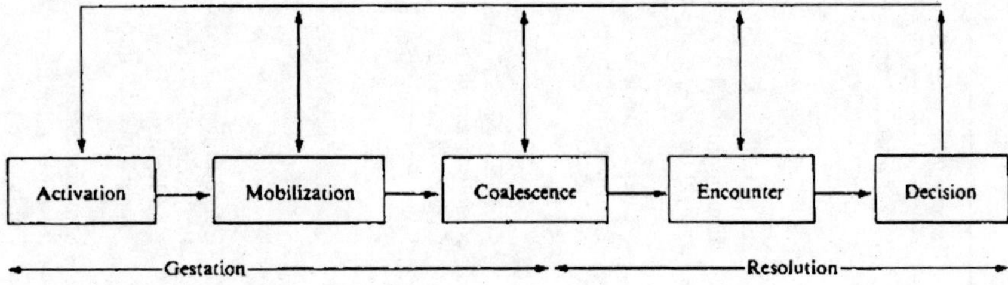


*Figure 1* The Stages of Strategic Decision Making.

selected members result in an issue (decision) being sponsored for resolution and an alternative(s) for adoption. It embraces those decisional activities that others have termed "problem formulation" (Sagasti & Mitroff, 1973), "attention directing" (Simon, 1947), "problem finding" (Pounds, 1969), or "identification" (Mintzberg *et al.*, 1976). Resolution marks a period when an organization appraises alternatives and decides whether or not to take action. Resolution has been characterized as "problem solving" (Sagasti & Mitroff, 1973), "choice" (Simon, 1947), or "selection" (Mintzberg *et al.*, 1976). The terms gestation and resolution are used here merely to indicate the emergent character of the processes, that is, the processes are not always clear to the actors involved in situ.

## *Gestation*

### *Activation*

Activation occurs when individuals become cognizant of issues or concerns salient to them. Different triggers such as performance gaps (Zaltman & Duncan, 1976), environmental opportunities (Wrapp, 1967), human needs (McClelland & Burnham, 1976), and individuals' political ambitions (Lyles & Mitroff, 1980) may activate individuals within an organization. Recent research suggests that issue recognition at the individual level is a highly intuitive and personalistic process (Lyles & Mitroff, 1980). Further, the concerns and issues that individuals focus on are influenced significantly by their attentional processes (Weick, 1969). The extent to which attentional processes focus on specific issues is a function of: (1) perceived salience of issues; (2) extent of competing claims on the individual's time and resources; (3) political factors such as anticipated retaliatory action by others (Bachrach & Baratz, 1962; Dahl, 1961); and (4) perceived ability to initiate action, fear of failure and consequent loss of credibility (Lyles & Mitroff, 1980).

The issues and concerns that arise during this stage are likely to be symptomatic and fuzzy. This is partly because informal information sources often trigger issue recognition much earlier than do signals from formal channels of communication (Aguilar, 1967; Mintzberg, 1975). As a result individuals may engage in a variety of "sense-making" (Weick, 1969) activities. The essence of this process is succinctly captured by Quinn in relating how a company president explores strategic (in this case, government related) issues:

> I start conversations with a number of knowledgeable people . . . I collect articles . . . I collect data from any reasonable source . . . from these a pattern eventually emerges. It's like fitting together a jigsaw puzzle . . . and once it's crystallized, It's not difficult to explain to others.
>
> (1978, p. 14)

The activation phase is complete when individuals have developed a sufficient level of clarity and a "language" about their concerns to be able to articulate the issues in an intelligible way to other organizational members.

### *Mobilization*

The mobilization stage entails the elevation of issue awareness from the individual to the organization level. Organizational actions are collective endeavors, and the capability to define a strategic issue and to impose or implement a solution often does not rest with a single individual or organizational subunit (Quinn, 1978). This leads individuals to mobilize around shared concerns resulting in the emergence of a collective awareness of the issue(s) (Oberschall, 1973). Activities are informal: a great deal of information is exchanged among members, and alliances begin to take shape (Wrapp, 1967). As Dennis Wrong (1980) has noted, a minimal diffuse solidarity around issues is a prerequisite for initial efforts to organize politically for issue resolution.

A network of interrelationships among individuals develops around issues during this stage. The stage is more or less protracted depending on the number of individuals activated, their political credibility, skills and commitment, and the extent of competing issues in the organization. Individuals may resort to external sources of assistance such as consultants to gain political credence and leverage (MacMillan, 1978) or to facilitate mobilization processes as in team building (Davis, 1970). In addition, structural features of the organization such as access structures (Cohen *et al.*, 1972), social networks (Roberts & O'Reilly, 1979), and perceived similarity in individuals' cognitive maps can either constrain or facilitate mobilization.

Mobilization has important implications for strategic decision making for at least two reasons. First, the broad contours of potential strategic change begin to emerge. Second, public articulation of issues tends to reshape social reality which individuals often internalize as public fact (Merton, 1957).

Thus, political commitment to decisions or potential decision outcomes builds up during this stage.

*Coalescence*

A coalition emerges as the aware collectivity grapples with the unavoidability of action to resolve strategic issues. Action requires some integration of efforts and specification of intent; these are frequently absent and unnecessary during the previous stages. As the process of decision making unfolds, a transitory alliance of individuals develops: individuals who pool their resources to obtain a desired outcome or to sponsor a set of alternatives, that is, a coalition (Gamson, 1962).

The specific content of the strategic alternative(s) ultimately sponsored by a coalition is determined by: (1) its internal structures and processes; (2) the environment that it enacts; and (3) the complexity of the issue at hand. Coalition members typically do not possess equal power/influence resources. These inequalities result in the emergence of a political structure within the coalition (MacMillan, 1978): individuals assume or are assigned political roles within it. Asymmetry of relationships among coalition members is an important structural determinant of its processes (Hickson, Hinings, Lee, Schneck, & Pennings, 1971).

The need for specificity in action requires that the emergent coalition not merely articulate its demands but aggregate into a seemingly coherent program the multiple and potentially conflicting demands of its members (Almond, 1960). As with power/influence resources, coalition members differ with respect to their aspirations, preferences, and demands (Cyert & March, 1963). Choice among alternatives in the face of divergent preferences is problematical (Arrow, 1963) and defies computational logic. This leads to bargaining and negotiations based on side payments and exercise of power as the primary mechanism by which alternatives are appraised and sponsored.

The emergent coalition possesses an identity of its own in relation to the larger organization. As Torrance (1977) notes, this identity is based on an awareness of *likeness* on the part of members and an awareness of their *differences* or estrangement from others. The environment that a coalition enacts thus is characterized by a degree of conflict. As the coalition becomes aware of its vulnerability to the actions of others (internal and external to the organization), estimates of its own political capability and the acceptability of proposed alternatives enter into the calculus of intracoalitional decision making.

In addition, intracoalitional bargaining and negotiations may be more or less protracted, depending on the nature of the extant issue(s). More complex issues require greater information processing (Galbraith, 1973), which may be reflected in more intense search for information by coalition members and the application of a greater number of criteria, that is, goals, to guide decisions (Carter, 1971). Uncertainty is absorbed by a sequence of judgments about the reliability and salience of information and by a hierarchy of threshold level goals (Carter, 1971; Cyert & March, 1963); both of these emanate from the bargaining and negotiations that are pervasive during this phase.

In summary, the gestation stage centers on the evolution of issues as organizational concerns. As Bachrach and Baratz (1962) have noted, issues have to be raised and initiated by someone before they can be resolved. The gestation phase concludes with the emergence of a coalition of interests committed to resolving an issue in a specific way.

### *Resolution*

#### *Encounter*

As the coalition begins to sponsor its preferred strategic alternative(s), decision making enters a stage in which the coalition must interact with other organizational entities (such as individuals, other coalitions, and sub-units). This stage is characterized by bilateral negotiations between groups (Carter, 1971) rather than within the same group (coalition), a characteristic of the previous stage.

The essence of a coalition's task is to prevail upon the organization to accept its preference and proposed alternatives. Some might view this as a process of seducing the organizational elites (Kelley, 1976). To achieve its purposes, the coalition engages in the deployment of *gambits*, which are defined as any strategem or means a coalition employs to achieve its goals.

#### *Gambits*

At least two types of gambits can be identified: substantive and temporal. Substantive gambits involve the form and substance of a coalition's articulation and rationalization of its position. Temporal gambits refer to the timing and sequencing of its arguments.

Substantive gambits involve efforts to alter the organization's goal structure, resource allocations, and social reality. Goal related gambits might involve selectively advocating decision criteria that favor the coalition's position (or goals) and demonstrating that proposed courses of action are in keeping with the preferences of others in the organization. Resource allocation gambits involve demonstrating the instrumentality of resource commitments to the achievement of organizational goals. Such gambits might center on the promotion of specific strategic alternatives (the means) to achieve (predetermined) goals. Legitimacy gambits involve managing the symbolic or "expressive" functions of management (i.e., organizational beliefs, attitudes, perceptions, myths, symbols, etc.) to create a climate or milieu that facilitates achievement of the coalition's goals.

Temporal gambits are intended to distract organizational attention away from or focus it on specific alternatives or aspects of alternatives, selected pieces of information, and so on. They also may be intended to order the way elements of an issue are encountered by the rest of the organization. Such gambits include "kite-flying," "red herrings," detailing an alternative's advantages before its disadvantages, or selectively supporting alternatives on opportune occasions.

Both types of gambits are intended to justify (Staw, 1979) and rationalize the coalition's preferred alternatives. Information is sought to support the coalition's position and to discredit opponents' arguments; contrary evidence often is suppressed (Argyris & Schon, 1974; Mitroff & Emshoff, 1979). The need for the appearance of rationality rather than rationality per se, defined in organizational terms, underlies information search and dissemination during this stage.

The evolution and duration of this stage is as much a function of opponents' reactions and commitments as it is of the coalition's political "finesse" or the effectiveness of its gambits. Structural features such as divergency in goals, access to information, and positions in organizational hierarchy and issue related implications such as resource commitments and changes in organization structure can potentially affect the evolution of this stage.

### *Decision*

As the encounter stage draws to a close, zones of consensus and dissent become clearer: positions crystallize, and the ramifications and political implications of alternatives begin to be understood. In terms of actors, the decision revolves around "fiduciary roles" (MacMillan, 1978). All members cannot simultaneously participate in bargaining and negotiating.

The process takes place within the existing infrastructure of power distribution in the organization. The content of the deliberation is ostensibly goal specification and the appraisal of merits and demerits of various alternatives. The actors may *appear* rational, and may be *intendedly* so within the zones of consensus. However, zones of dissent typically exist, and they lead to compromise and accommodation as mechanisms of decision. As a result, resource availability, organization slack, and power distribution may significantly influence the actual decision, as well as the duration and intensity of this stage (Manns & March, 1978).

The actual decision may assume different forms: (a) commitment to some action; (b) postponement of decision to a future date; (c) nondecision or dropping the issue altogether; or (d) transformation, or portraying the issue as a symptom of a larger issue yet to be resolved. Such outcomes generally lead to a quasiresolution of conflicts. However, residues remain that may trigger other issues and lead to different coalitions in the future. Coalition evolution and strategic decisions are interactive.

Subsequent to the decision, organizational actors may be expected to indulge in some further issue related activity. Such activities include ex post uncertainty absorption to exercise a Pollyanna-Nietzsche effect (Carter, 1971), rituals of inauguration, a show of solidarity among coalitions, or a simple release of energy after the change is enacted (Beckhard & Harris, 1977). These activities are primarily symbolic and may serve to solidify or alter the existing social reality of the organization.

The stages presented here are intended to represent milestones in the evolution of a strategic decision. The actual evolution may exhibit regression, progression, cycling, and decay among these stages. For example, if a coalition cannot agree on an alternative (during coalescence), the members may revert to further mobilization (regression). A strong-willed president can impose a solution immediately after issue recognition or activation (progression). Mintzberg *et al.* (1976) note numerous examples of decision cycling. An issue may be dropped any time (decay) due to the emergence of other more salient issues, changing needs of members, or recognition of political factors that hinder resolution.

## Implications and conclusions

A number of implications of the micro-political or coalitional model of strategy for mulation presented here may be indicated by juxtapositioning the model with the more prevalent rational model of strategy determination. The two models invoke different frames of reference in describing and studying the formulation of organizational strategies. The rational model is dependent on objective frameworks; its utility lies in rendering available a normative analytical calculus to derive what Mintzberg (1977) has termed an "intended" strategy. The model takes as given a certain degree of consensus among decision makers; it assumes that strategy formulation can be understood by treating organizations as if they are centrally coordinated purposive individuals (Allison, 1971). In many cases this is a fruitful assumption as it provides a useful analytical shorthand for understanding problems of strategy. However, it obscures the persistent state of affairs within organizations that the "maker" of strategy is not a single individual but a *set* of political actors. Within the political conception of strategy formulation, consensus among political actors is not a given; it must be nurtured and developed. With respect to individual strategic decisions, the objectivity of the rational model must be couched within a political context: *the nature of alternative(s) sponsored and the extent to which they are accepted, modified, or rejected is dependent on the power/influence distribution within and across the relevant coalition(s).*

In a similar vein, the rational model can provide objective reasons why strategic decisions are chosen and why they succeed or fail (e.g., product-market choice, utilization of "synergy"). Within this perspective, failures in strategic issue recognition, development, and implementation are viewed as analytical shortfalls. Yet a political perspective adds some critical insights as to why some strategic issues do not emerge, are suppressed (i.e., never reach the decision phase), or are vigorously supported in an organization. An analysis of strategic issues as discussed in this paper sheds light on influences that hinder recognition of decision related variables and/or, if recognized, why they may not be acted on. From a political perspective, *these failures in strategic issue recognition, development, and resolution may be ascribed to political infeasibility or the insufficient power and influence of organizational actors.*

Implicit in the political perspective is the symbolic side of management: *coalitional influences in strategic decision making may be both substantive and symbolic.* Although the instrumental value of such concepts as strategic planning, product-market portfolio, distinctive competence, and synergy in strategy formulation is widely acknowledged (as in the rational model), their symbolic value generally is underemphasized. These concepts can be viewed as substantive gambits with symbolic overtones used by a coalition to achieve its desired outcomes. This enables one to understand such evidence as presented by Sarrazin (1977–78) that "planning" in certain French organizations was really a ploy by top management to centralize power.

The political perspective points to the pervasiveness of conflict among actors in the context of strategic decisions. In a conflict filled milieu, the actors may disguise intentions and withhold, distort, or manipulate information. Further, the goals that are espoused and the information that is exchanged may be laden with symbolic overtones, making it difficult to assess their reliability. The analytical rigor of the rational model is dependent on the availability of reliable data, but the collection, evaluation, and utilization of such data are highly problematical from a political perspective.

Many authors separate strategy formulation and implementation into two distinct phases (Steiner & Miner, 1977). Ritualistic assertions about the inseparability of these phases notwithstanding, the rational model generally is taken to imply that commitment to a decision can be realized after the decision is made (Andrews, 1971). From a political perspective, *commitment to a strategic decision begins to evolve during the early phases of decision making (rather than after the decision is made).* This has wide ramifications. At a minimum, such commitment can lead to conscious or unconscious distortion of information and promotion or suppression of alternatives. At the extreme, individuals may leave the organization if the alternatives they sponsor are not adopted. Or individuals thus thwarted, as noted by Wrapp (1967), may present their preferred alternatives as a mechanism to resolve an altogether different issue at yet another time.

Coalitions and strategy formulation are interactive: the residue left by such actions as strategic decisions-commitment, redistribution of resources, and quasiresolution of conflict may precipitate further coalition formation in organizations and thus serve to trigger future strategic issues. In this sense, an implicit assumption of the rational perspective that decision content can be divorced from its (organizational) context may not be fully reflective of organizational reality.

The coalitional model of strategy formulation suggests that *logical incrementalism (Quinn, 1978) is a more appropriate description of the process of strategy making than that implied in the analytical scheme of a strictly rational conception.* Alternatives must be developed, conflicting goals and evaluation criteria must be compromised, consensus must be reconciled, and political antagonists must be appeased: there are no ready-made formulae and solutions.

A critical implication of the recognition of the political milieu of the strategy formulation arena is that the politics of decision making must be managed just like its analytical or rational side. Indeed, a consequence of the coalitional model presented above is that *formulating the content of strategy inevitably entails managing its context and processes.* For instance, the processes of the generation and utilization of strategic information must be managed; these processes are problematical. In his provocative essay, Wrapp (1967) recognizes this when he points out that good managers usually utilize many more channels of information than often is recognized, so as to avoid the potential biases and the political underpinnings of information from any one source. Similarly, strategic issue identification, development, and resolution involves the management of individuals, departments, project teams, and so on, and their interrelationships. This, in turn, necessitates managing the structure and process of strategy formulation. Such structures and processes often are different from those required for implementation. Argyris and Schon (1974), Mitroff and Emshoff (1979), and others may well be right when they argue that activities such as conflict management, team building, and organization development should form an integral part of strategy formulation.

In summary, this paper has developed a framework for understanding and studying the micropolitics of strategy formulation. Currently, the rational model, which focuses on the *content* of strategies, dominates the business policy literature. The political perspective traces the influence of organizational *context* and portrays how internal political processes determine or modify strategy content. It is suspected that effective top managers have an intuitive grasp of these political processes, and it is suggested that effective strategic management entails managing the organizational context just as much as the strategic content. Development and refinement of the political perspective therefore is necessary for an understanding of strategic management.

## Note

1 The authors wish to thank Gordon Fitch for his critique of an earlier draft of this manuscript. Portions of this paper were presented at the Midwest Academy of Management Meetings, Cincinnati, 1980.

## References


Aguilar, F. *Scanning the business environment*. New York: Macmillan, 1967.

Almond, G. A. Introduction in G. A. Almond & J. S. Coleman, (Eds.), *The politics of the developing areas*. Princeton, N. J.: Princeton University Press, 1960.

Allison, G. T. *Essence of decision: Explaining the Cuban missile crisis*. Boston: Little, Brown, 1971.

Andrews, K. R. *The concept of corporate strategy*. Homewood, Ill.: Dow Jones-Irwin, 1971.

Ansoff, H. I. *Corporate strategy*. New York: McGraw-Hill, 1965.

Argyris, C., & Schon, D. A. *Theory in practice: Increasing professional effectiveness*. San Francisco: Jossey-Bass, 1974.

Arrow, K. J. *Social choice and individual values*. 2nd ed. New York: Wiley, 1963.

Bachrach, P., & Baratz, M. S. Two faces of power. *American Political Science Review*, 1962, 56, 947–952.

Baldridge, J. V. *Power and conflict in the university*. New York: Wiley, 1971.

Beckhard, R., & Harris, R. T. *Organizational transitions: Managing complex change*. Reading, Mass.: Addison-Wesley, 1977.

Bourgeois, L. J. Strategy and environment: A conceptual integration. *Academy of Management Review*, 1980, 5, 25–39.

Carter, E. E. Thc behavioral theory of the firm and top level corporate decisions. *Administrative Science Quarterly*, 1971, 16, 413–428.

Child, J. Organization structure, environment and performance—The role of strategic choice. *Sociology*, 1972, 6, 1–22.

Cohen, M. D., March, J. G., & Olsen, J. P. A garbage can model of organizational choice. *Administrative Science Quarterly*, 1972, 17, 1–25.

Cyert, R. M., & March, J. G. *A behavioral theory of the firm*. Englewood Cliffs, N. J.: Prentice-Hall, 1963.

Dahl, R. A. *Who governs? Democracy and power in an American city*. New Haven, Conn.: Yale University Press, 1961.

Davis, S. Building more effective teams. *Innovation*, 1970, 15, 32–41.

Duncan, R. G. Characteristics of organizational environments and perceived environmental uncertainty. *Administrative Science Quarterly*, 1972, 17, 313–327.

Galbraith, J. *Designing complex organizations*. Reading, Mass.: Addison-Wesley, 1973.

Gamson, W. A. Coalition formation at presidential nominating conventions. *American Journal of Sociology*, 1962, 68, 157–171.

Hickson, D. J., Hinings, C. R., Lee, C. A., Schneck, R. E., & Pennings, J. M. A strategic contingencies theory of intraorganization power. *Administrative Science Quarterly*, 1971, 16, 216–229.

Hofer, C. W., & Schendel, D. *Strategy formulation: Analytical concepts*. New York: West, 1978.

Kelley, G. Seducing the elites: The politics of decision making and innovation in organizational networks. *Academy of Management Review*, 1976, 1, 66–74.

King, W. R., & Cleland, D. T. *Strategic planning and policy*. New York: Van Nostrand Reinhold, 1978.

Lawrence, P. R., & Lorsch, J. W. *Organization and environment*. Cambridge, Mass.: Harvard University Press, 1967.

Lyles, M. A., & Mitroff, I. I. Organizational problem formulation: An empirical study. *Administrative Science Quarterly*, 1980, 25, 102–120.

MacMillan, I. C. *Strategy formulation: Political concepts*. New York: West, 1978.

Manns, C. L., & March, J. G. Financial adversity, internal competition and curriculum change in a university. *Administrative Science Quarterly*, 1978, 3, 541–552.

McClelland, D. C., & Burham, D. H. Power is the great Motivator. *Harvard Business Review*, 1976, 54(2), 100–110.

McNichols, T. J. *Policy making and executive action*. New York: McGraw Hill, 1977.

Merton, R. K. *Social theory and social structure*. Chicago: Free Press of Glencoe, 1957.

Mintzberg, H. The manager's job: Folklore and fact. *Harvard Business Review*, 1975, 53 (4), 49–61.

Mintzberg, H. Strategy formulation as a historical process. *International Studies of Management & Organization*, 1977, 7 (2), 28–40.

Mintzberg, H. Organization power and goals: A skeletal theory. In D. E. Schendel & C. W. Hofer (Eds.), *Strategic management: A new view of business policy and planning*. Boston: Little, Brown & Co., 1978, 64–80.

Mintzberg, H., Raisinghani, D. & Theoret, A. The structure of unstructured decision processes. *Administrative Science Quarterly*, 1976, 21, 246–276.

Mitroff, I. I., & Emshoff, J. R. On strategic assumptionmaking: A dialectical approach to policy and planning. *Academy of Management Review*, 1979, 4, 1–12.

Murnighan, J. K. Models of coalition behavior: Game theoretic, social psychological, and political perspectives. *Psychological Bulletin*, 1978, 85, 1132–1153.

Murray, E. A. Strategic choice as a negotiated outcome. *Management Science*, 1978, 24, 960–972.

Oberschall, A. *Social conflict and social movements*. Englewood Cliffs, N. J.: Prentice-Hall, 1973.

Pettigrew, A. M. Strategy formulation as a political process. *International Studies of Management & Organization*, 1977, 7 (2), 78–87.

Pfeffer, J., & Salancik, G. R. *The external control of organizations: A resource dependence perspective*. New York: Harper & Row, 1978.

Pounds, W. F. Processes of problem finding. *Industrial Management Review*, 1969, 11, 1–19.

Quinn, J. B. Strategic change: Logical incrementalism. *Sloan Management Review*, 1978, 20, 7–21.

Roberts, K. H., & O'Reilly, C. A. Some correlates of communication roles in organizations. *Academy of Management Journal*, 1979, 22, 42–57.

Sagasti, F. R., & Mitroff, I. I. Operations research from the viewpoint of general systems theory. *Omega*, 1973, 6, 695–709.

Sarrazin, J. Decentralized planning in a large French company: An interpretive study. *International Studies of Management & Organizations*, 1977–78, 7 (3–4), 37–59.

Simon, H. A. *Administrative behavior*. New York: MacMillan, 1947.

Staw, B. M. Rationality and justification in organizational life. In B. Staw & L. L. Cummings (Eds.), *Research in organizational behavior* (Vol. II). Greenwich, Conn.: JAI Press, 1979.

Steiner, G. A., & Miner, J. B. *Management policy and strategy*, New York: Macmillan, 1977.

Thompson, J. *Organizations in action*. New York: McGraw-Hill, 1967.

Torrance, J. *Estrangement, alienation and exploitation: A sociological approach to historical materialism*. New York: Columbia University Press, 1977.

Tushman, M. L. A political approach to organizations: A review and rationale. *Academy of Management Review*, 1977, 2, 2006–216.

Warwick, D., & Reed, T. *A theory of public bureaucracy*. Cambridge, Mass.: Harvard University Press, 1975.

Weick, K. *The social psychology of organizing*. Reading, Mass.: Addison-Wesley, 1969.

Weick, K. Educational organizations as loosely coupled systems. *Administrative Science Quarterly*, 1976, 21, 1–19.

Wrapp, H. E. Good managers don't make policy decisions. *Harvard Business Review*, 1967, 45(5), 91–99.

Wrong, D. H. *Power: Its forms, bases and uses*. New York: Harper & Row, 1980.

Zaltman, G., & Duncan, R. *Strategies for planned change*. New York: Wiley, 1976.

32

# THE CREATION OF MOMENTUM FOR CHANGE THROUGH THE PROCESS OF STRATEGIC ISSUE DIAGNOSIS

*Jane E. Dutton and Robert B. Duncan*

Source: *Strategic Management Journal* 8(3) (1987): 279–95.

This paper presents a model of how decision-makers interpret stategic issues. The model of strategic issue diagnosis identifies three critical events: activation, assessments of urgency and assessments of feasibility. The relationship of each of these interpretive assessments to the creation of momentum for change allows one to predict if and how organizations will respond to a changed decision environment. The paper further links strategic issue diagnosis to organizational responses by highlighting the systematic effect of two contextual variables—the organization's belief structure and its resources—upon the assessments in diagnosis. In this way, the model of issue diagnosis provides a framework for understanding how and why organizations respond differently to strategic issues.

## Introduction

In the wake of increasing economic adversity it is likely that organizations will be embedded in environments marked by hostility and scarcity. Recent concern with processes and structure under conditions of decline as opposed to growth (Ford, 1980; Harrigan, 1980; Hughes, 1982; Whetten, 1980) attests to the reality of these changing environmental conditions. Coupled with the increasing complexity and change in the domains of organizations (Ansoff, 1979; Tung, 1979; Makridakis and Wheelwright, 1981), environmental adversity confronts organizations and their decision-makers with a basic survival issue: how can organizational decision-makers learn to deal effectively with these changed environments?

Organizations elicit a vast array of responses to a changed decision environment. In some cases these reponses are effective in the sense that they more correctly align the organization's internal structure or systems with the demands of the external environment. In other cases the responses are less than effective and an opportunity fades or a problem intensifies.

Theoretical attempts to link different organizational responses to changes in a decision environment have been scanty at best. Research has tended to focus on the cases where organizations have failed to respond to a changed environment. Explanations have ranged from those which focus upon decision-making pathologies (Janis and Mann, 1977; Smart and Vertinsky, 1977), restrictive organizational norms (Argyris and Schon, 1978), structural impediments (Hedberg, Nystrom and Starbuck, 1976; Hage, 1980), information system deficiencies (Hedberg and Jonsson, 1978), to system-wide pathologies (Staw, Sandelands and Dutton 1981). With few exceptions these authors fail to provide an integrative mechanism for explaining how each of these different factors contributes to organizational responsiveness.

This paper proposes that a major reason organizations respond differently to changes in the environment involves how strategic issues are triggered and interpreted by decision-makers.

The term 'strategic issues' is used to describe developments or events which have not yet achieved the status of a decision event. The term *strategic* issues is used to highlight that the concern of this paper is on the developments and events which have the potential to influence the organization's current or future strategy (Ansoff, 1979; Dutton, Fahey and Narayanan, 1983). The triggering and interpretation of strategic issues is called strategic issue diagnosis (SID). Through the process of SID, changes in the decision environment are detected and interpreted. On the basis of these interpretations, forces are put into action which initiate or impede strategic change.

The focus on strategic issues and how they are processed answers the call for new, process-oriented treatments of strategy formulation and change (Fredrickson, 1983). The paper attempts to explicitly link findings generated in organization theory with the concerns of strategic management theorists, interested in the process of strategy formulation and its links to the external environment (Hofer and Schendel, 1978; Jemison, 1981; Quinn, 1980). In this way the proposed model of the strategic issue diagnosis process attempts to wed the concerns of organization theory and strategic management by showing how the early stages of the decision-making process, and the organizational context in which they take place, are systematically related to different levels and types of strategic change.

The process of strategic issue diagnosis helps to illuminate the strategic adaptation process by more clearly specifying the assessments involved in its anticipatory phase (Meyer, 1982)—when potential strategic problems or opportunities are being detected and interpreted by decision-makers. The activities which comprise this phase of adaptation are critically important for understanding how and when decision-makers in organizations intentionally respond to a changed decision environment. Strategic issue diagnosis initiates the response process by translating and focusing key environmental events into potental issues which are assessed by decision-makers. In this way, SID is part of the more general interpretive process where data confronting decision-makers are given meaning (Daft and Weick, 1984). It is proposed that the meanings formed in SID create the momentum for change through which forces for further adaptation are set into place.

The process of strategic issue diagnosis is labeled as such to distinguish it from the processes of problem-identification (Lyles and Mitroff, 1980), problem-sensing (Keisler and Sproull, 1982) or problem-solving, and to highlight the major interpretive component of the process. The process is more generalizable than problem-identification and problem-solving as it applies equally to the processing of opportunity as well as problem-initated activities (Dutton, Fahey and Narayanan, 1983). Further, by applying the label of diagnosis to the acts of triggering and interpreting, one is not bound by the analytical rigor or logical sequencing implied by the process of problem-solving. Instead, the label of diagnosis imbues the process with an interpretive and judgemental component which more closely captures the interpretation of problem or opportunity strategic issues in organizations (Dutton, Fahey and Narayanan, 1983; Daft and Weick, 1984).

Strategic issues do not activate decisionmakers' attention in packaged form. Instead, the interpretations of key issues and how they relate to the organization are highly subjective. The strategic issue diagnosis process is one of social construction (Berger and Luckman, 1967), where alternative judgements of the meaning of an event are imposed, created and legitimated in a social context. As a result, contextual influences in the form of organizational beliefs and resources importantly affect the outcomes of SID in predictable ways.

As described here, strategic issue diagnosis takes place at the top levels of the organization, i.e. it is a critical activity that takes place within the dominant coalition (Hambrick and Mason, 1984). Although this paper focuses on strategic processes at the top of the organization, strategic decisions and allocations flow out of activities taking place at multiple levels of the organization (e.g. Bower, 1970; Burgelman, 1983).

The paper specifies the logic of strategic issue diagnosis in two distinct stages. In Part I the elements in the issue diagnosis process are outlined in simplified form to identify the key components and their interrelationships. In Part II, two aspects of the organization's context, i.e. the structure of the organization's belief system and the organization's resource supply, are discussed in terms of their impact upon strategic issue diagnosis assessments. Part I builds a model to allow one to predict how decision-makers respond to strategic issues. Part II builds a foundation for explaining why organizations respond differently to similar strategic issues. Where possible, key relationships are summarized in proposition form.

## The process of strategic issue diagnosis

This paper depicts strategic issue diagnosis as an iterative, cyclical process which involves two major events. The process is activated by the recognition of some type of strategic issue—an emerging development, trend or event which is potentially relevant to the organization's strategy. Assuming a strategic issue has been recognized, the model proposes that decision-makers endeavor to understand or interpret it. Issue assessment involves two major interpretations: (1) the urgency of taking action on the issue; and (2) the feasibility of dealing with the issue. On the basis of these assessments, momentum for change is created, and the forces for organizational responses are set into place. By understanding the assessments in strategic issue diagnosis and their relationship to organizational responses, one gains theoretical understanding of how certain types of organizational change can be tied to these early stages of strategic issue diagnosis.

Each of the major events in strategic issue diagnosis—activation and issue assessments (urgency and feasibility)—is further explored below to capture the essence of the SID process. The next two sections describe each of the events and their interrelationships. In subsequent sections the influence of the organizational context is explored in terms of its impact on SID assessments. In this way organizational context is portrayed as having a major impact on organizational responses to changes in decision environments *through* its impact on issue activation or issue assessments.

The process of strategic issue diagnosis is depicted diagrammatically in Figure 1. The activation event is seen as preceding the two issue assessments. The arrows between the triggering mechanism and the issue assessments represent the ongoing possibility of issue recycling through any one of the SID events. The figure also illustrates that urgency and feasibility assessments build momentum for change, and determine whether decision-makers will favor incremental or radical responses to the strategic issue.

### *The activation of diagnosis (Event I)*

During the process of strategic issue diagnosis, decision-makers actively engage in attempts to understand a particular strategic issue. The model begins with the activation of diagnosis, i.e. the process describing what and how issues are recognized and isolated for further consideration (Mintzberg, Raisinghani and Theoret, 1976).

Insights into how strategic issues are activated can be gleaned from a wide range of research endeavors including environmental scanning (Aguilar, 1967; Kafelas and Schoederbek, 1973), decision-making (Cyert and March, 1963; Mintzberg, Raisinghani and Theoret, 1976; Downs, 1967; Segev, 1976), problem-formulation or sensing (Keisler and Sproull, 1982; Lyles and Mitroff, 1980; Pounds, 1969), and normative models of strategic diagnosis (Nutt, 1979; Ansoff, 1979).

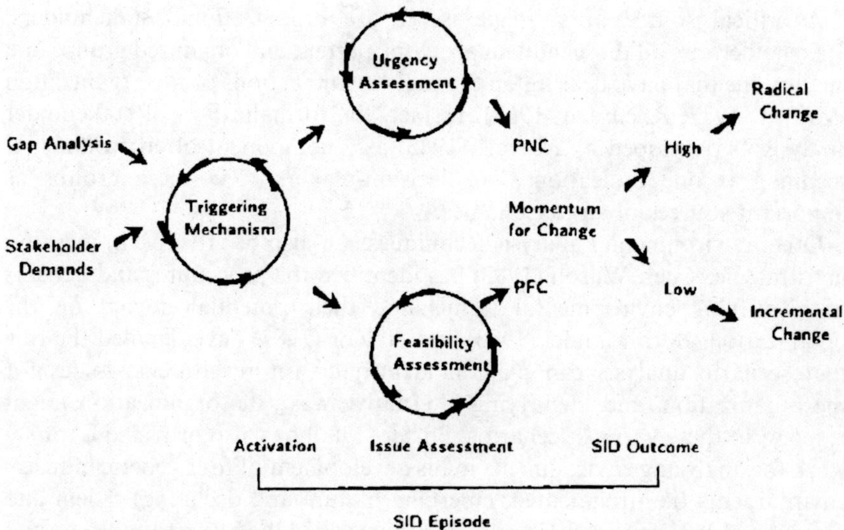


*Figure 1* Strategic events in strategic issue diagnosis.

There is a marked convergence in these works that some type of perceived inconsistency or imbalance activates the change process (Miller and Friesen, 1980). At this point it is assumed that the costs of inaction are too high to forestall further consideration. Ansoff (1975) labels these events 'strategic surprises' which are 'sudden, urgent, unfamiliar changes in the firm's perspective which threaten a major profit reversal or loss of a major opportunity'. Mintzberg, Raisinghani and Theoret (1976) label these stimuli 'action thresholds'—where stimuli accumulate to such a point that the issue must be explicitly recognized and given further decisional attention. Triggering, then, is pivotal for subsequent strategic issue diagnosis activity. It serves to focus attention upon an issue which demands further scrutiny.

Strategic issue diagnosis can be triggered through formal or informal mechanisms. Some organizations utilize strategic issue management systems that are explicitly designed to identify emerging and consequential trends in the environment (King, 1982). Other organizations rely on much more intuitive, informal systems to surface strategic issues, e.g. a rumor emerges suggesting that a major competitor is making a move which dramatically shifts the competitive structure of the industry. Whether the system which generates a strategic issue is formal or informal, the signal which launches further attentional investment is information that the status quo has changed or will change, making current modes of operating potentially ineffective, and consequently inappropriate.

A critical source of strategic issues are organizational stakeholders. Stakeholders are all those individual actors, parties, and organized groups and institutions that have bearing on the policies and actions of the organization (Mitroff, 1983; Rhenman, 1968). In fact, the formalization of stakeholder analysis as developed by Mitroff (1983) as a component of environmental scanning is one indication that decision-makers view these groups as important sources of strategic issues.

Other environmental analysis techniques can also be effective in identifying strategic issues. Wilson (1983) has identified the procedures and benefits of identifying environmental trends and their potential impact on the organization. Both Mandel (1983) and Naylor (1983) have detailed the role that scenario analysis can play in identifying future strategic issues for the organization, and identifying alternative ways the organization might respond to these various scenarios. Porter (1980) has also provided a framework for analyzing environments in his development of four generic industry environments (i.e. fragmented, emerging mature and declining). Klein and Newman (1980) have developed a technique called the Systematic Procedure for Identifying Relevant Environments (SPIRE) that is also very useful in environmental analysis. SPIRE provides a technology to identify strategically important environmental factors that either directly or indirectly have an impact on strategy formulation. All of these are examples of analytical techniques that are useful in the activation stage of diagnosis. These environmental analysis techniques will then help organizational decision-makers to better understand the pressure that organizations will face in the future. As a result, organizational decision-makers will be more able to anticipate what likely strategy or structure changes might be needed in the future (Lawrence and Dyer, 1983; Ansoff, 1984).

The perception that current actions are in-effective suggests that strategic issues are tied to an awareness of some real or anticipated performance gap) Downs, 1967, i.e. a discrepancy between desirable and actual or anticipated performance. Awareness of a real or potential gap may come about formally or informally as mentioned previously, but in either case a strategic issue emerges because of the recognition of strategic performance implications. It is this link to strategic performance that acts as the initial sorting criterion in strategic issue diagnosis. In subsequent SID assessments, issues are further sorted into those that require different types of adaptation responses.

### *Issue assessments (Event II)*

Assuming that diagnosis has been activated through the detection of some type of 'active' issue, decision-makers engage in attempts to diagnose the degree of issue urgency and feasibility. Both assessments are important in building decision-makers' interpretation of an issue and in creating the momentum for change in response to the issue. Issue urgency indicates the perceived cost of not taking action with respect to an issue, whether that action means resolving a problem or capitalizing on an opportunity (Miller, 1982). Issue urgency is a composite perception based on many judgements made about the nature of a strategic issue. Urgency captures the *perceived importance* of taking action on an issue. The greater the urgency of a strategic issue, the greater the perceived need to change the current state of affairs in the organization.

The greater perceived need to change arises because of pressures that are exerted by organizational stakeholders whose claims on the organization assure that it remains responsive to the larger environment (Mitroff, 1983). The presence of a threat that is not answered, or an opportunity that is not acted upon, induces stakeholders to apply pressures for action. In addition, at a more personal level, decision-makers' aspirations could be thwarted by not taking action on urgent issues. Thus, organizational and personal pressures motivate decision-makers to expend greater resources on issues having the highest estimated pay-off to the organization. It is this pay-off that is captured by the notion of urgency. The urgency of a particular issue serves to break down decision-makers' threshold of resistance to feedback information (Miles, 1980), increasing the probability that the issue will create momentum for change.

The urgency of a strategic issue derives from a number of salient dimensions of an issue, which draw the attention of decision-makers. The most important dimensions are those indicating how threatening the issue is to the survival of the reigning dominant coalition. Concentrating on recent behavioral research, each of these critical dimensions is described below.

The perception of an issue urgency is tied to the perception of time pressure associated with an issue. *Time pressures* can arise from deadlines embedded in an issue, e.g. where an issue surrounding future competitors' actions is linked to a specific, time-bound regulatory action. Time pressure is also tied to estimates of anticipated issue duration. Where an issue is projected to endure, the issue is likely to be judged as more urgent. For example, seasonal fluctuations in sales and costs make certain types of performance issues temporary and natural 'in the course of business'. However, if the cause or impact of the issue is expected to endure beyond some critical threshold, it is likely that the issue will be judged as urgent. This tendency is illustrated by automobile producers' responses to oil shortage. In the early 1970s the oil crisis was viewed as a temporary condition and automakers continued to produce large-scale, fuel-inefficient cars (McGinnis, 1978). However, in recent years automobile manufacturers have made a pronounced effort to produce smaller, more compact models. Responsibility for this change in strategy is due, in part, to a change in interpretations of the cause of sales declines. Performance issues came to be viewed as more enduring given the perceived permanence of OPEC's actions and its effect upon the price of petroleum products.

Assessments of urgency also depend on the *visibility* of a strategic issue to important internal and external constituencies. The perceived visibility of an issue is related to the publicity surrounding the issue and the level of issue exposure to inside and outside groups. More visible issues are more urgent for several reasons. When viewed from a competitive standpoint, failure to take action on a visible issue implies an organization's competitive edge could be whittled away as competitors and rivals respond more quickly and effectively to an emerging opportunity. Sobel's (1984) historical analysis of the auto industry indicates how both Volkswagen and Japanese manufacturers responded to the growing small car market while the U.S. 'big three' ignored this trend. In fact, increased issue exposure creates pressure to take action, whether or not the action involves eliminating a threat or capitalizing on an opportunity. Where an issue represents a threat of some type, its visibility raises the possibility of outcry or pressure for action from a wider range of the organization's internal and external stakeholders. Questions of legitimacy are raised, adding further momentum for action of some type. When U.S. auto executives began to perceive the increased demand for smaller fuel efficient cars in response to customer and government pressure, a momentum for change in the U.S. auto industry was heightened (Sobel, 1984).

A strategic issue may also be judged in terms of how responsible management believes it is for the issue's occurrence. Attributions of *responsibility* affect decision-makers' assessments of issue urgency in two competing directions. First, to the extent that decision-makers believe that the organization (as opposed to extra-organizational factors) is responsible for an issue, this responsibility attribution may increase perceived issue urgency. Ford Motor Company's admission of responsibility for the declining quality of their company's product represents a case where perceptions of responsibility increased the sense of issue urgency. The management at Ford publicly criticized their own quality standards and used this to explain the closing of one of their own plants (*Business Week*, 1980).

At the same time, attributions of internal responsibility for an issue —particularly if it involves a problem—enhance pressures to justify the appropriateness of past decisions, minimizing the severity of the strategic issue. The pressures for justification are most pronounced when single individuals or a group of individuals feel responsible for the problem (Staw, 1980). In this case, justification pressures may reduce judgements of issue urgency, thus reducing the perceived need for remedial change.

The perceptions that comprise assessments of urgency, as in judgements of responsibility described above, rely on causal analysis about an issue—its sources and its effects. Managerial beliefs are critical filters that act to screen in and screen out information relevant to an issue (Beyer, 1981). The role of organizational beliefs as filters and their link to SID will be considered systematically in a subsequent section.

Not all of these judgements are elicited in assessing the urgency of strategic issues. Instead, the salient dimensions of an issue draw the attention of decision-makers and have the most pronounced impact on this judgement (Taylor and Fiske, 1978). For example, issue responsibility may be a salient concern to some organizations because the press or media have captured the attention of constituencies internal and external to the organization. In these instances issue responsibility becomes a critical factor in urgency assessments. In other cases, factors considered in judgements of urgency are dictated by historical precedent or routines that organizations employ to sort issues into active and inactive piles (Simon, 1957). For example, organizations using annual planning reports rely upon the financial data which are conveniently available from these reports to assess pressures to act on an issue. Assessments of urgency become a routinized output of the annual planning process. Thus the depiction of urgency suggested here is an expanded model of potential factors considered in such a judgement. In reality this assessment is likely to be simplified and routinized —requiring limited investment in time or the cognitive resources of decision-makers.

The output of the urgency assessment process is a subjective interpretation of the perceived need to change the organization in some way to resolve the apparent discrepancy. When urgency is judged as low, an issue becomes inactive and is given limited, if any, further decisional attention. However, if an issue is judged as urgent, a greater need to make changes to resolve it exists, demanding further consideration. The subsequent assessments involve feasibility estimates of the likelihood of successfully resolving the strategic issue.

### *Issue feasibility (Event III)*

While the perception of urgency is one important component of diagnosis, defining and interpreting an issue also depends on judgements about the feasibility of taking action. Assessments of feasibility do not have to be made with respect to any particular alternative. In fact, at this stage in the choice process, specific alternatives and options may not have been generated by decision-makers. Rather, the model of strategic issue diagnosis proposes that decision-makers make gross judgements about the possibility of resolving an issue that systematically affect how an issue is interpreted. So, for example, if a strategic issue is identified that is familiar to one encountered in the past, e.g. a new technology is developed outside the organization that has the potential to revolutionize the organization's product mix, but decision-makers understand how to respond because they have faced a similar issue in the past, then the issue is more likely to be interpreted as an opportunity rather than a threat, and decision-makers would respond accordingly.

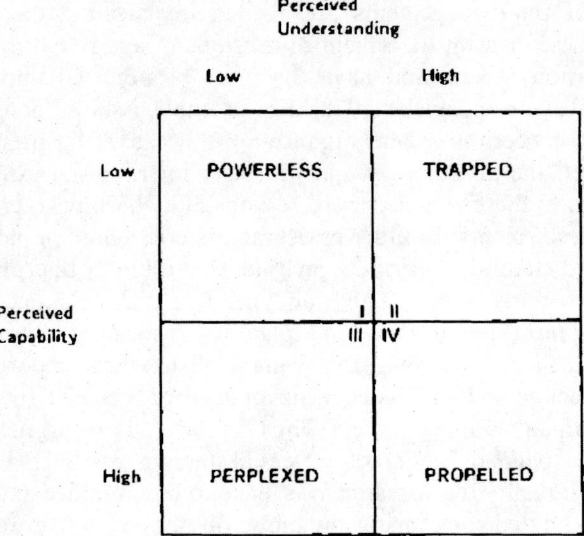


*Figure 2* Judgements in the assessment of feasibility.

Two judgements are particularly important in forming a feasibility assessment: (1) perceived issue understanding; and (2) perceived issue capability. *Issue understanding* refers to the perception that decision-makers, with some effort, could identify the means for resolving the issue. *Issue capability* describes the perception that the means for resolving the issue are available and accessible. Note that both of these judgements can be made by decision-makers without having to assume that options for resolving the issue have been generated or evaluated. Instead, the SID model proposes that asessments related to the resolution of an issue enter the diagnosis phase of a strategic issue when the issue is still being defined and interpreted.

The judgements that comprise the feasibility assessment are described in more detail below. To simplify the discussion, the four combinations of perceived understanding and capability are represented by a 2×2 matrix in Figure 2.

In Cell I decision-makers are uncertain of the means to resolve a particular issue. In addition there is a perception that the organization has neither the supply nor access to resources to resolve the issue. Decision-makers are powerless in the sense of lacking both the knowledge and means for issue resolution; consequently the issue will be interpreted as a threat. Consider the case of Chrysler Corporation and decision-makers' assessments of the feasibility of changing the situation which had caused the precipitous drop in financial performance in the late 1970s. Evidence from Chrysler's annual reports suggested that decision-makers perceived that consumer demand for their product was highly unpredictable.[1] In addition, they blamed their lack of control over government regulatory requirements for their continuing profit woes. Thus, in the case of Chrysler, although plummeting sales and market share during 1977–79 created a severe discrepancy in financial performance, decisionmakers saw the resolution of their situation as severely limited in feasibility without the assistance provided by a federal bail-out.

In Cell II, organizational decision-makers make a different set of judgements about feasibility constraints. Cell II describes the situation where strategic decision-makers believe they understand how to resolve the issue (high understanding), but do not have the resources or access to impact change (low capability). In essence decision-makers are trapped by their lack of capability for resolving the issue, although they understand what action(s) are required. This situation characterized the plight of American Motors Corporation in the late 1970s. Public statements by members of this firm suggested that consumer demand was viewed as highly predictable. However, AMC did not have the capital to quickly develop front-wheel drive, fuel-efficient cars (Sobel, 1984).

Cell III describes a different feasibility assessment. With high capability and low understanding decision-makers have the resources and access to affect change but believe they lack the understanding necessary to resolve an issue. While having the potential resources for resolving the issue, they are perplexed by their lack of means-end understanding and are likely to view the issue as ambiguous and uncertain, delaying the taking of corrective action. General Motors characterized this situation in the mid-1970s. General Motors clearly had the resources and capability to enter into the small car market, but decision-makers' uncertainty about consumer demand created reluctance in terms of making a full commitment to small cars. The statement of a high-level executive at GM to one of the authors underlines this point: 'We can get the money to develop the new line of cars, but we just don't know what the customer wants—are Americans really serious about small cars?' In 1980, GM reached the conclusion that small cars were marketable and has made the 4-year $40 billion commitment to retooling to produce their line of small cars.

In Cell IV, resolution of a strategic issue is perceived as most feasible. The resources and access to initiate change alternatives are perceived to be present, and decision-makers believe they have the knowledge necessary to understand what type of change is appropriate. In this case the issue will be perceived as an opportunity. The perceived high feasibility propels efforts to resolve an issue in the form of greater momentum for change. The situation does not imply that change is most effective when decision-makers find themselves in this cell. Rather, Cell IV captures the situation when change is most probable given its judgements about the high feasibility of change.

The importance of feasibility assessments to the process of strategic issue diagnosis is that interpretations of feasibility affect the definition of an issue and the adaptive responses of organizations. Where feasibility is perceived to be fairly low (Cell I and variants of Cells II and III), decision-makers may elicit a less venturesome response in terms of fully resolving an issue. In contrast, where perceived feasibility is high (Cell IV and variants of Cells II and III), judgements of greater understanding and capability facilitate consideration of a more radical change directed at resolving the strategic issue. In proposition form these arguments suggest the following relationship:

> *Proposition 1: The more decision-makers perceive they understand a strategic issue* and *perceive the organization has the capability for dealing with the issue, the greater the momentum for change.*

### *Translating the momentum for change into action*

The major thesis of this paper is that diagnosis influences organizational action. The process by which this occurs is revealed by linking SID assessments to the momentum for change. Assessments of urgency and feasibility have implications for the momentum for change built in response to a strategic issue. The momentum for change refers to the level of effort and commitment that top-level decision-makers are willing to devote to action designed to resolve an issue. Where this level of effort and commitment is high, decision-makers are willing and motivated to consider radical responses to an issue.

One can conceptualize the range of potential actions taken to resolve a strategic issue as falling along a continuum ranging from modest, small-scale change (e.g. change in procedures, policies, lower-level managers, etc.) to far more extensive radical and dramatic changes (Miller and Friesen, 1980). Examples of these radical changes include modifications in organizational design (e.g. the recent redesign of General Motors (*Fortune*, 1984), as well as changes in strategy (e.g. Sears' entry into the financial services industry). Any one of these radical changes, whether taking place in a small, privately owned company or a large public corporation, involves a significant reshuffling of resources and beliefs, making them significant and time-consuming events.

Within the model of strategic issue diagnosis, the relationships between assessments of feasibility, urgency, momentum for change and action are illustrated in Figure 1. As the figure implies, where the momentum for change is low, less radical changes, such as changes in scanning procedures, goal levels (standards of desirability) and control systems are more likely. However, as the momentum for change increases, more costly and more risky changes are likely to occur, such as changes in organizational design or strategy. In a sense these latter types of changes represent fundamental innovations to the organizations initiating them (Hage, 1980), compounding the difficulties associated with their comprehension and implementation.

A more precise specification of SID and the momentum for change can be gained by considering the possible combinations of urgency and feasibility.

### *The interaction of urgency and feasibility*

Thus far the discussion has implied that urgency assessments precede feasibility as the strategic issue diagnosis process unfolds. The linearity of the process has been maintained for analytical purposes only. In reality it is often the case that assessments of feasibility occur before urgency judgements. In fact various researchers have argued that judgements about the availability of solutions may serve to stimulate the detection of issues (Hewitt and Hall, 1973; March and Olsen, 1976; Starbuck, 1983). In these cases, feasibility is a forgone conclusion as a solution has already materialized. When this occurs, urgency assessments may be formed on the basis of the ease and timeliness of available solutions. Therefore, although the discussion implies that there is a specified ordering to these assessments, neither judgement necessarily takes precedence. As Figure 1 suggests, the outcomes of each assessment contribute uniquely to developing a momentum for change.

There are infinite combinations of urgency-feasibility assessments. To simplify the discussion of their interaction, four combinations of assessment outcomes are represented in a 2×2 matrix in Figure 3. The cells show the

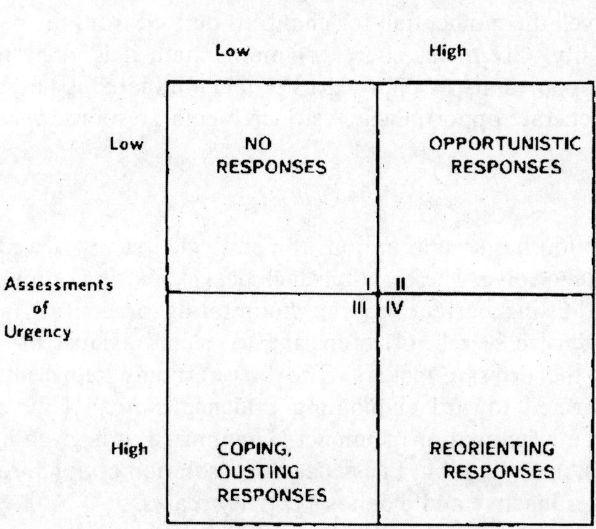


*Figure 3* Interaction of urgency and feasibility assessment and their relationship to organizational responses.

link between assessments in strategic issue diagnosis and organizational responses. At a more general level these examples help to disentangle the relationship between interpretations and actions in organizations.

### *Cell I*

Cell I represents a case when the strategic issue is inactive and decision-makers are unconcerned with its resolution. Where an issue is judged as not urgent and its resolution is perceived as infeasible, impetus to take action is absent, and the momentum for change is extremely low, if it exists at all.

### *Cell II*

A strategic issue diagnosis episode may produce an outcome where the issue is judged as feasible to resolve, but it is not viewed as urgent. In this case it is likely that change will occur, but not very rapidly. The change is more likely to be incremental than radical (Miller and Friesen, 1980; Tushman and Romanelli, 1985), although the magnitude of the change will depend upon the level of available resources and understanding of decision-makers. For example, an acquisition candidate may come to the awareness of decision-makers which looks extremely attractive. Suddenly an opportunity has materialized which was not anticipated. Although an acquisition was not part of the competitive strategy, its perceived feasibility may induce consideration of a strategic change. In fact, as decision-makers ponder this possibility, it is likely that the disturbance will be judged as more urgent. Within this cell the momentum for change is derived from the perception of issue feasibility. Given this source of momentum, it is likely that Cell II pertains to opportunity as opposed to problem-initiated issues, and correspondingly generate opportunistic, yet incremental, responses.

### *Cell III*

An organization has several options if a strategic issue is viewed as urgent, but infeasible to solve. These options include: (1) ignoring or minimizing the issue; (2) adjusting current scanning/monitoring or control mechanisms; (3) more intensive search; (4) preparing to defend against the change; or (5) ousting the decision-makers. The first response represents a coping response directed toward eliminating evidence that an issue exists. If a strategic issue is ignored or its impact is minimized, it is given little, if any, further decisional attention. In essence this resolution option means that the issue becomes inactive and diagnosis activity ceases.

Decision-makers may also choose to alter the type of information which is collected by changing the organization's scanning, monitoring or control systems. These change alternatives eliminate the strategic issue by altering its implications for strategic performance. The underlying cause of the strategic issue is not eliminated, but the symptoms indicating its existence are minimized.

The changes which result from assessments of low feasibility represent incremental adjustments in current operations which seem to minimize the impact of a strategic issue. The changes considered by decision-makers represent coping attempts, but ones which will most likely fail to bring about any radical response or change. When strategic issue diagnosis produces this sort of outcome, change responses may do more harm than good. If a strategic issue persists, yet its resolution is perceived as infeasible by organizational decision-makers, pressures for justification and retrospective rationality may ensue (Staw, 1980). Under these conditions decision-makers may engage in a more intensive search to confirm the existence of the issue. Alternatively, they may selectively attend to information which confirms the correctness of past decisions in attempts to erase evidence that change is required.

The perseverance of an urgent strategic issue coupled with the perception of infeasible resolution contributes to the crisis-like character of a decision situation. Information processing becomes distorted (Smart and Vertinsky, 1977), evidence of groupthink pathologies emerges (Janis, 1972), and decision processes and outcomes become more rigidified (Staw, Sandelands and Dutton, 1981). If this occurs, decision-makers are likely to try and defend against the change as a reactive move to minimize its impact.

The persistence of a crisis-like situation without resolution begins to dismantle the base of legitimacy upon which top decision-makers' authority rests. As legitimacy is questioned the probability that decision-makers will be replaced increases over time. Thus another possible response to a situation of high urgency and low feasibility is the ousting of top management. In fact, studies of management (e.g. Gamson and Scotch, 1964; Allen, Panian and Lotz, 1979) and organizational turnaround strategies (e.g. Schendel, Patton and Riggs, 1976) provide support for this relationship. However, further studies suggest that the forces to replace management in the wake of urgent and infeasible issues may be tempered by the distribution of ownership in the firm (Salancik and Pfeffer, 1980).

### *Cell IV*

The case where a strategic issue is viewed as urgent and change is perceived as feasible results in a final set of change responses. In this cell, issue diagnosis is hypothesized to create the greatest momentum for change. Where high perceived feasibility exists, decision-makers will consider more radical changes involving reorientations (Normann, 1977; Tushman and Romanelli, 1985) for alleviating the present strategic issue. These reorientations may involve reformulations of the organization's strategy that alter the means utilized to reach the organization's goals, or the nature of the goals themselves.

Alternatively, these orientations may involve major changes in the organization's design as attempts to realign the organization with new environmental conditions.

A recent study of university responses to changes in federal regulations provides some support for this relationship (Ottensmeyer, 1982). The research suggests that the most radical actions to impact the regulation were made by universities when the impact of the regulation was viewed as great (high urgency), and actions taken to impact the regulatory process were viewed as politically efficacious (high feasibility).

In summary, assessments of urgency and feasibility act in concert to create the momentum for change in response to a particular strategic issue. Where momentum for change is greater, decision-makers are more willing to consider radical as opposed to incremental change. This relationship is expressed in the following proposition:

*Proposition 2 The more a strategic issue is diagnosed by organizational decision-makers as urgent and feasible to resolve, the greater the momentum for change, and the more radical the change outcome.*

## Contextual influences

The model of strategic issue diagnosis described above suggests that the process takes place in a sterile and objective environment removed from the beliefs, resources and commitments of the organization. However, each diagnosis episode is closely related to the context in which it takes place, and in particular to the organization in which the episodes occur. The purpose of this section is to propose that organizational factors affect how strategic issues are diagnosed. Organizational characteristics affect diagnosis assessments in systematic ways. In this way the strategic issue process provides a theoretical rationale for why organizations respond differently to similar strategic issues.

This section highlights two organizational characteristics which act upon strategic issue events. The discussion focuses on the role of the structure of organizational beliefs and the availability of resources in strategic issue diagnosis assessments. However, the discussion only begins to capture the complexity of social, economic, and political forces at work in the creation of momentum for change. By outlining these factors the discussion reveals the subtle yet profound influence of beliefs and resources on adaptation *through* their effect on strategic issue diagnosis.

### *Organizational beliefs*

Organizational beliefs represent shared understandings about the relationships between objects, properties and ideas (Sproull, 1981). Particularly relevant for strategic issue diagnosis are the beliefs used by decision-makers to interpret situations and to make judgements about feasible courses of action. Recent research suggests that three categories: (1) beliefs about risk preference; (2) beliefs about self-sufficiency, and (3) vision of distinctive competence (Donaldson and Lorsch, 1983) are important. These shared understandings act as filters through which management perceives the realities facing the firm (Donaldson and Lorsch, 1983:79), and thus they critically influence interpretations made in SID episodes.

Miles and Snow (1978) have perhaps come the closest to articulating how organizations vary in terms of beliefs. They argue that there are three major sets of beliefs about the nature of management which correspond to three dominant schools of management thought: the traditional model, human relations model, and human resources model. They argue, further, that different strategic types—analyzers, prospectors, reactors and defenders—have different sets of dominant beliefs. Although their results are preliminary, initial studies indicate that defender and reactor organizations tend to share traditional and human relations beliefs, while analyzers and prospectors tend to hold beliefs more consistent with the human resources school (Miles *et al.*, 1978). One interpretation of this find is that organizations vary in terms of the range and diversity of beliefs about the nature of management, and that these beliefs are compatible with some strategic stances and incompatible with others.

Two characteristics of the structure of belief—their complexity and the level of consensus—are particularly important in determining the activation of SID, the urgency and feasibility assessements and the resulting momentum for change. Belief complexity captures the breadth and variety of factors which are present and legitimate in a particular belief system (Brunsson, 1982).

Organizations also vary in the level of consensus over the content of these beliefs. Organizations which possess a homogeneous group of actors, have enjoyed a history of frequent and continuous success, or face a clear and identifiable threat there is likely to be a high degree of consensus over the content of beliefs. Each of these factors acts to solidify beliefs, increasing the level of agreement over their content.

Conceptually, levels of belief consensus and belief variety are independent dimensions of an organization's belief structure. In reality, however, the two dimensions are closely linked. Where organizational beliefs are simple and unvaried, consensus is easier to achieve and is sustainable over time. However, where beliefs are highly varied and complex a high level of agreement over the broader domain is more difficult to achieve. For clarification purposes these two dimensions of the belief structure organization can be combined into a single characteristic labeled belief differentiation. Where beliefs are highly varied and lack consensus, beliefs are highly differentiated. Where the beliefs are highly similar and consensual, then the belief structure is integrated.

The purpose in clarifying the meaning of this organizational characteristic is to enable a more precise specification of how belief structure impacts activation and feasibility assessments during issue diagnosis. It is proposed that a more differentiated belief structure in an organization increases the frequency of issue triggering and increases the probability that change will be perceived as feasible, in turn increasing the momentum for change.

If an organization has a highly differentiated belief structure, a more diverse set of performance expectations and results are considered legitimate during assessments of performance. Where this diversity exists more strategic issues are likely to be detected, further increasing diagnosis activity.

Returning to the research of Miles and Snow (1978), this argument suggests that analyzer organizations, holding the most varied and least consensual beliefs about management, would experience the most frequent triggering of strategic issues. Where this strategic type contains managers who believe in attending to detail and in delegating to others, they will be receptive to a wider range of issues than if either belief was advocated alone. Using this argument, the differentiation of beliefs determines the range of indicators to which decision-makers are sensitive, affecting the frequency of triggering of SID.

Yates' (1983) analysis of the American automobile industry provides an excellent example of the effect of belief differentiation on issue diagnosis. Yates points out that automobile executives lived in cultural isolation in Detroit from the non-automobile society. They lived, played and worked and thought together generating an *esprit de corps*, but isolated themselves from broader insights in contemporary society (Yates, 1983: 80). Translated into the SID model, there was less opportunity in the auto industry for issue triggers as decision-makers were exposed to singular, highly consensual views of the world.

Although the impact of organizational beliefs on urgency assessment is unclear, one can visualize a clear link to interpretations of feasibility. Where beliefs are highly differentiated the feasibility of change is increased as multiple bases for understanding how to resolve an issue are available during diagnosis. The existence of diverse views that contribute to the identification of feasible alternatives, however, is likely to delay the change process. If one assumes that agreement must be reached before change can begin, then the diversity of beliefs makes general agreement more difficult to achieve, delaying the change process.

The variety of ideas or beliefs applied to an issue increases the probability that the issue will be perceived as feasible to resolve, in turn raising the momentum for change. In fact this relationship may be one reason why organizations with more organic structures are associated with more frequent and rapid change (Lawrence and Lorsch, 1967). A more organic design is marked by greater differentiation of beliefs which translates into more frequent recognition of new strategic issues and greater perceived feasibility of change. The relationship between the belief structure of an organization and SID is summarized in the following propositions:

*Proposition 3: The more differentiated an organization's belief structure (lower concensus and more complex), the more frequently strategic issue diagnosis will be triggered.*

*Proposition 4: The more differentiated an organization's belief structure, the greater the perceived feasibility of change, and the greater the momentum for change.*

### Organizational resources

The supply of organizational resources also influences the outcomes of issue diagnosis. For example, an organization which has experienced a prolonged and rapid success builds a resource cushion which insulates decision-makers from the spur to action of performance-related strategic issues. In essence the organization experiences the 'fat cat syndrome' when resources are bountiful. Although slack resources may protect organizations from cyclical or minor vacillations in performance, this same slack can be dysfunctional in certain cases. Abundant resources can act to absorb performance shocks such that decision-makers become impervious to key changes occurring internally or externally to the organization (Cyert and March, 1963).

The supply of resources built by continued organizational success promotes 'illusions of invulnerability' in the minds of decision-makers. Although the researcher who coined this phrase was referring to a group process under stress (Janis, 1972), these illusions can result from a pattern of continuous and rapid success at the organizational level (Starbuck and Hedberg, 1977). This illusion, in turn, encourages decision-makers to underestimate the magnitude and immediacy of a strategic issue, while at the same time magnifying perceptions of understanding and capability. Success-related illusions have been known to create diastrous results when organizations diversify outside the areas in which the success was made: 'The most difficult situation is one in which the previous success is so complete that the world is viewed through glasses polished in the previous incarnation' (*Business Week*, 1981: 61).

While a resource base which is too abundant has one set of consequences for strategic diagnosis, a limited resource base has another. A restricted resource supply may reduce perceptions of feasible issue resolution. Viewed in this light, an organization may become locked into current patterns of responses not because they have become routine and habitual, but because the issues are perceived as non-resolvable due to a resource shortage. The organization requires some minimal level of resources to successfully consider or implement change (Hedberg, 1981).

A restricted resource base acts to inflate assessments to urgency. Without a resource cushion to isolate decision-makers from minor performance deviations, the importance of each disturbance is magnified, increasing the perceived need for change. At the same time hopes of resolving the discrepancy are dampened as the organization's resource capability is limited. In addition, a restricted resource supply restrains the level of knowledge and expertise which can be devoted to comprehending any given strategic issue. Consequently, the perceived feasibility of change is further constrained through a restriction in the level of perceived issue understanding.

As the previous discussion implies, the resource base of the organization has a mixed impact on the outcomes of strategic issue diagnosis. On the one hand, greater resources promote change momentum by increasing the perceived feasibility of change. On the other hand, a larger resource base discourages change by depressing issue urgency. These conflicting effects of resource base on the perceived momentum for change are captured in the following propositions.

*Proposition 5: The greater the supply of organizational resources, the less the perception of urgency, the less the perceived need to change and the less the momentum for change.*

*Proposition 6: The greater the supply of organizational resources, the greater the perceived feasibility of resolving an issue, and the greater the momentum for change.*

## Conclusions

The strategic issue diagnosis process is a critical and relatively poorly understood element of strategic decision-making (Dutton, Fahey and Narayanan, 1983; Mintzberg, Raisinghani and Theoret, 1976). This paper attempts to fill this gap by proposing a model of the critical events in the SID process. The model suggests that the process is triggered through the recognition of performance consequences of an emerging development or trend that captures the attention of decision-makers. Attention is captured by the actions of stakeholders, outputs of scanning or issues management systems, and a variety of other attention-focusing actions.

Once SID is triggered the model proposes that urgency and feasibility assessments are made that help to apply meaning and definition to an issue. These assessments rely on a number of subjective judgements about the issue (e.g. its visibility, immediacy, etc.), and the organization's relationship to the issue (e.g. responsibility for the issue's occurrence, understanding of how to resolve it, etc.).

By specifying the wide range of judgements that enter these two assessments, the complexity of the SID process becomes clear. In addition, one easily appreciates the possibility of disagreement and conflict over the meaning of a strategic issue, and how the seeds for a political decision process are planted very early—when issues are first diagnosed (Allison, 1971; Narayanan and Fahey, 1982).

This paper also presents an effort to link a key phase of strategic decision-making, i.e. strategic issue diagnosis to organizational outcomes; i.e. adaptation. In particular, the paper proposes a model of the key events which take place during the strategic issue diagnosis—when vague, illdefined events are interpreted by top-level decision-makers. The model of strategic issue diagnosis suggests that by understanding the assessments in SID and their interaction, one can predict the magnitude and type of change which an issue initiates. In this way the paper constructs a link between interpretive activities of top-level decision-makers and organizational change.

The model goes one step further, however, in trying to link decision activity and the nature of organizational adaptation. It suggests the differences in an organization's belief structure and level of resources have systematic influence on organizational adaptation. In this way strategic issue diagnosis is the pivotal activity through which beliefs and resources affect organizational change. These relationships, in turn, build the foundation for predicting why organizations respond differently to strategic issues.

From this link one can begin to disentangle how organizational differences relate to the process of strategy formulation and change. For example, the model helps our understanding of why organizations with prolonged periods of performance success have less radical responses to a changed decision environment than organizations which have not experienced this success pattern. The resource slack and undifferentiated beliefs which result from successful performance depress the probability of issue-triggering and perceptions of issue urgency and feasability, building barriers to organizational change. The American automobile industry's failure to identify the need to develop small, fuel-efficient cars in the late 1960s and 1970s is a clear example of this situation (Yates, 1983; Sobel, 1984).

The links between interpretive activities in strategic issues diagnosis and organizational change raise challenging new research opportunities. The propositions can be tested in the context of tracing how organizations within a changing market environment identify strategic issues and how these diagnoses translate into strategic choices that represent varying degrees of radical change. For example, the American automobile industry provides an opportunity to examine how organizations in the same market environment adapted differently, based on their diagnosis of strategic issues. Validation or falsification of the propositions would help to illuminate the boundaries operating on strategic choice in organizatios. Where support for the propositions is upheld, it lends credibility to the view that strategic choices have consequence for organizational action (Child, 1972).

The model presented here extends recent work on the role of cognition in strategic management (Barnes, 1984; Chittipeddi and Gioia, 1983; Ginter and White, 1982; Schwenk, 1984). It presents a model which explicitly captures how the organizational context (i.e. beliefs and resources) influences strategic change. In this extension it illustrates how organization theory helps to uncover the role of the structural and strategic context (Burgelman, 1983) in influencing the processes underpinning strategic change.

## Acknowledgements

The authors greatly appreciate the comments of Susan J. Ashford, Larry L. Cummings, Charles McGee, Joseph Moag, Robert H. Miles, Denise Rousseau, Lance E. Sandelands, and three anonymous reviewers on earlier drafts of this paper. This paper was supported by a grant from the Tenneco Fund Program at the Graduate School of Business Administration, New York University. The authors also appreciate the support of the J. L. Kellogg Strategy Chair and the AACSB Doctoral Fellowship in preparation of this paper.

## Note

1 A comparision was made of interpretations for financial performance for the 1977–79 period for General Motors. Chrysler Corporation, Ford Motor Company and American Motors Company, based upon an analysis of statements made in the annual reports. Further information in this pilot study can be obtained from the authors.

## References

Aguilar, F. *Scanning the Business Environment*, Macmillan, New York, 1967.

Allen, M. P., S. K. Panian and R. E. Lotz. 'Managerial succession and organizational performance: a recalcitrant problem revisited', *Administrative Science Quarterly*, **24**, 1979, pp. 167–180.

Allison, G. *Essence of Decision: Explaining the Cuban Missile Crisis*, Little, Brown, Boston, MA, 1971.

Ansoff, I. 'Managing strategic surprise by response to weak signals', *California Management Review*, Winter 1975, pp. 21–33.

Ansoff, I. *Strategic Management*, John Wiley & Sons, New York, 1979.

Ansoff, I. *Implanting Strategic Management*, Prentice-Hall, Englewood Cliffs, NJ, 1984.

Argyris, C. and D. A. Schon. *Organizational Learning: A Theory of Action Perspective*, Addison-Wesley, Reading, MA, 1978.

Barnes, J. H. 'Cognitive biases and their impact on Strategic planning', *Strategic Management Journal*, **5**, 1984, pp. 129–138.

Berger, P. and T. Luckman. *The Social Construction of Reality*, Doubleday, New York, 1967.

Beyer, J. M. 'Ideologies, values and decision making in organizations'. In Nystrom, P. and W. Starbuck (eds), *Handbook of Organization Design*, vol. 1, Oxford University Press, London, 1981, pp. 166–202.

Bower, J. *Managing the Resource Allocation Process*, Harvard University Press, Boston, MA, 1970.

Brunsson, N. 'The irrationality of action and action rationality decisions: ideologies and organizational actions', *Journal of Management Studies*, **19** (1), 1982, pp. 29–44.

Burgelman, R. 'A process model of internal corporate venturing in the diversified firm', *Administrative Science Quarterly*, **28**, 1983, pp. 223–244.

*Business Week*, 'Driving to rebuild Ford for the future', August 4, 1980, pp. 70–71.

*Business Week*, 'Schlumberger: the star of the oil fields tackles semi-conductors', February 16, 1981, pp. 60–70.

Child, J. 'Organizational structure, environment and performance: the role of strategic choice', *Sociology*, **6**, 1972, pp. 1–22.

Chittipeddi, K. and D. Gioia. 'A cognitive psychological perspective on the strategic management process'. Paper presented at Academy of Management Annual Meeting, Dallas, Texas, August 1983.

Cyert, R. M. and J. G. March. *A Behavioral Theory of the Firm*, Prentice-Hall, Englewood Cliffs, NJ, 1963.

Daft, R. and K. Weick. 'Toward a model of organizations as interpretation systems', *Academy of Management Review*, **9**, 1984, pp. 284–295.

Donaldson, G. and J. Lorsch. *Decision Making at the Top: The Shaping of Strategic Direction*, Basic Books, New York, 1983.

Downs, A. *Inside Bureaucracy*, Little, Brown, Boston, MA, 1967.

Dutton, J. E., L. Fahey and V. K. Narayanan. 'Toward understanding strategic issue diagnosis', *Strategic Management Journal*, **4**, 1983, pp. 307–324.

Ford, J. D. 'The occurrence of structural hysteresis in declining organizations', *Academy of Management Review*, **5**, 1980, pp. 589–598.

*Fortune*, 'GM's unlikely revolutionist', March 19, 1984, pp. 107–112.

Fredrickson, James W. 'Strategic process research: questions and recommendations', *Academy of Management Review*, **8**, 1983, pp. 465–475.

Gamson, W. and N. Scotch. 'Scapegoating in baseball', *American Journal of Sociology*, **70**, 1964, pp. 69–76.

Ginter, P. M. and D. D. White. 'A social learning approach to strategic management; a theoretical foundation', *Academy of Management Review*, **7**, 1982, pp. 253–261.

Habermas, T. *Legitimations Crisis* (T. McCarthy, trans.) Beacon Press, Boston, MA, 1975.

Hage, J. *Theories of Organizations: Form, Process and Transformation*, John Wiley & Sons, New York, 1980.

Hambrick, D. and P. Mason. 'Upper echelons: the organization as a reflection of its top managers', *Academy of Management Review*, **9**, 1984, pp. 193–206.

Harrigan, K. R. *Strategies for Declining Business*, D. C. Heath, Lexington, MA, 1980.

Hedberg, B. 'How organizations learn and unlearn'. In Nystrom, P. and W. Starbuck (eds), *Handbook and Organization Design*, vol. 1, Oxford University Press, New York, 1981, pp. 3–28.

Hedberg, B. and S. Jonsson. 'Designing semi-confusing information systems for organizations in changing environments', *Accounting, Organizations and Society*, **3**, 1978, pp. 47–64.

Hedberg, B., P. Nystrom and W. H. Starbuck. 'Camping on seesaws: prescriptions for a self-designing organization', *Administrative Science Quarterly*, **21**, 1976, pp. 41–65.

Hewitt, J. P. and P. M. Hall, 'Social problems, problematic situations, and quasi-theories', *American Sociology Review*, **38**, 1973, pp. 367–374.

Hofer, C. W. and D. Schendel. *Strategy Formulation: Analytical Concepts*, West, St Paul, MN, 1978.

Hughes, K. *Corporate Responses to Declining Rates of Growth*, D. C. Heath, Lexington, MA, 1982.

Janis, I. L. *Victims of Groupthink*, Houghton-Mifflin, Boston, New York, 1972.

Janis, I. L. and L. Mann. *Decision Making*, Free Press, New York, 1977.

Jemison, David B. 'The contributions of administrative behavior to strategic management', *Academy of Management Review*, **6**, 1981, pp. 601–608.

Kafelas, A. and P. P. Schoederbek. 'Application and implementations: scanning the business environment—some empirical results', *Decision Sciences*, **4**, 1973, pp. 63–74.

Keisler, S. and L. Sproull. 'Managerial response to changing environments: perspectives on problem sensing from social cognition', *Administrative Science Quarterly*, **27**, 1982, pp. 548–570.

King, W. 'Strategic issue analysis and planning'. Working paper, Graduate School of Business, University of Pittsburgh, 1980.

King, W. 'Using strategic issue analysis in long range planning', *Long Range Planning*, **15**, 1982, 45–49.

Klein, H. and W. Newman. 'How to use SPIRE: a systematic procedure for identifying relevant environments for strategic planning', *Journal of Business Strategy*, **1**, 1980, pp. 32–45.

Lawrence, P. R. and D. Dyer. *Renewing American Industry*, Harvard University Press, Boston, MA, 1983.

Lawrence, P. R. and J. W. Lorsch. *Organization and Environment*, Harvard University Press, Boston, 1967.

Lyles, M. and I. Mitroff. 'Organizational problem formulation: an empirical study', *Administrative Science Quarterly*, **25**, 1980, pp. 102–119.

MacCrimmon, K. R. and R. N. Taylor. 'Decision making and problem solving', in M. P. Dunnette (ed.), *Handbook of Industrial and Organizational Psychology*, Rand McNally, Chicago, IL, 1976, pp. 1397–1453.

McGinnis, L. 'Organizational adaptation to environment in the U.S. automotive industry: GM vs. AMC'. In Miles, R. H. (ed.), *Organizational Adaptation to Environment; A Preliminary Set of Case Histories*. Working Paper No. 7, Research Program on Government Business Relations, Yale School of Organization and Management, New Haven, CT, Spring 1978.

Makridakis, S. and S. Wheelwright. 'Forecasting an organization's future'. In Nystrom, P. and W. Starbuck (eds), *Handbook of Organizational Design*, vol. 1, Oxford University Press, New York, 1981, pp. 122–139.

Mandel, T. 'Future scenarios and their uses in corporate stategy'. In Albert, K. (ed.), *The Strategic Management Handbook*, McGraw-Hill, New York, 1983, pp. 10.1–10.21.

March, J. G. and J. P. Olsen. *Ambiguity and Choice in Organizations*, Universitetsforlaget, Bergen, Norway, 1976.

Meyer, A. 'Adapting to environmental jolts', *Administrative Science Quarterly*, **27**, 1982, pp. 515–538.

Miles, R. E. and C. C. Snow. *Organizational Strategy, Structure and Process*, McGraw-Hill, New York, 1978.

Miles, R. E., C. C. Snow, A. D. Meyer and H. H. Coleman, Jr. 'Organizational strategy, structure and process', *Academy of Management Review*, **3**, 1978, pp. 546–562.

Miles, R. H. *Macro Organizational Behavior*, Goodyear Publishing Company, Santa Monica, CA, 1980.

Miller, D. 'Evolution and revolution: a quantum view of structural change in organizations', *Journal of Management Studies*, **19**(12), 1982, pp. 131–151.

Miller, D. and P. Friesen. 'Archetypes of organizational transition', *Administrative Science Quarterly*, **25**(2), 1980, pp. 246–275.

Mintzberg, H., D. Raisinghani and A. Theoret. 'The structure of unstructured decision processess', *Administrative Science Quarterly*, **21**, 1976, pp. 246–275.

Mitroff, I. *Stakeholders of the Organizational Mind*, Jossey Bass, San Francisco, CA, 1983.

Narayanan, V. K. and L. Fahey. 'The micro-politics of strategy formulation', *Academy of Management Review*, **7**(1), 1982, pp. 25–34.

Naylor, M. 'Planning for uncertainty—the scenario-strategy matrix'. In Albert, K. (ed.), *The Strategic Management Handbook*, McGraw-Hill, New York, 1983, pp. 22.1–22.11.

Normann, R. *Management for Growth*, John Wiley & Sons, Chichester, 1977.

Nutt, P. C. 'Calling out and calling off the dogs: managerial diagnosis in public service organizations', *Academy of Management Review*, **4**, 1979, pp. 203–214.

Otley, D. T. and A. J. Berry. 'Control, organizations and accounting', *Accounting, Organizations and Society*, **5**(2), 1980, pp. 231–244.

Ottensmeyer, E. 'Strategic organizational adaptation and the regulatory environment: a study of universities during a time of regulatory change'. Unpublished Ph.D. dissertation, Indiana University, 1982.

Pfeffer, J. and G. Salancik. *The External Control of Organizations*, Prentice-Hall, New York, 1978.

Porter, M. *Competitive Strategy*, Free Press, New York, 1980.

Pounds, W. F. 'The process of problem finding', *Industrial Management Review*, **11**, 1969, pp. 1–19.

Quinn, J. B. *Strategies for Change: Logical Incrementalism*, Richard D. Irwin, Homewood, IL, 1980.

Rhenman, E. *Industrial Democracy and Industrial Management*, Tavistock, London, 1968.

Rubin, I. 'Universities in stress: decision making under conditions of reduced resources', *Social Science Quarterly*, **58**, 1977, pp. 242–254.

Rumelt, R. *Strategy, Structure and Economic Performance*, Harvard University Press, Boston, MA, 1974.

Salancik, G. R. and J. Pfeffer. 'Effects of ownership and performance on executive tenure in U.S. corporations', *Academy of Management Journal*, **23**, 1980, pp. 653–664.

Schendel, D., G. R. Patton and J. Riggs. 'Corporate turnaround strategies: a study of profit decline and recovery', *Journal of General Management*, **3**(3), 1976, pp. 3–11.

Schwenk, C. R. 'Cognitive simplification processess in strategic decision making', *Strategic Management Journal*, **5**, 1984, pp. 111–128.

Segev, E. 'Triggering the strategic decision-making process', *Management Decision*, **14**, 1976, pp. 229–238.

Simon, H. A. *Administrative Behavior*, 2nd edn, Macmillan, New York, 1957.

Smart, C. and I. Vertinsky, 'Designs for crisis decision units', *Administrative Science Quarterly*, **22**, 1977, p. 640–657.

Snow, C. and D. Hambrick. 'Measuring organizational stategies: some theoretical and methodological problems', *Academy of Management Review*, **5**, 1980, pp. 527–538.

Sobel, R. *Car Wars*, Dutton, New York, 1984.

Sproull, L. 'Beliefs in organizations'. In Nystrom, P. and W. Starbuck (ed.), *Handbook of Organizational Design*, Oxford University Press, Oxford, 1981, pp. 203–225.

Starbuck, W. 'Organizations as action generators', *American Sociological Review*, **48**, 1983, pp. 91–102.

Starbuck, W. H. and B. Hedberg. 'Saving an organization from a stagnating environment'. In Thorelli, H. (ed.), *Strategy + Structure = Performance*, Indiana Press, Bloomington, IN, 1977, pp. 249–258.

Staw, B. M., L. Sandelands and J. Dutton. 'Threat rigidity cycles in organizational behavior', *Administrative Science Quarterly*, **26**, 1981, pp. 501–524.

Taylor, S. E. and S. T. Fiske. 'Salience, attention and top of the head phenomena'. In Berkowitz, L. (ed.), *Advances in Experimental Social Psychology*, Academic Press, New York, 1978.

Thompson, J. D. *Organizations in Action*, McGraw-Hill, New York, 1967.

Tung, R. 'Dimensions of organizational environments: an exploratory study of their impact on organization structures', *Academy of Management Journal*, **22**, 1979, pp. 672–693.

Tushman, M. and E. Romanelli. 'Organizational evolution: Interactions between external and emergent processess and strategic choice'. In Staw, B. and L. L. Cummings (eds), *Research in Organizational Behavior*. vol. 8, JAI Press, Greenwich, CT, 1985.

Weick, K. 'Cognitive processes in organizations'. In Staw, B. (ed.), *Research in Organizational Behavior*, vol. 1, JAI Press, Greenwich, CT, 1979, pp. 41–74.

Whetten, D. A. 'Organizational decline: a neglected top in organizational science', *Academy of Management Review*, **5**, 1980, pp. 477–588.

Wilson, I. 'The benefits of environmental analysis'. In Albert, K. (ed.), *The Strategic Management Handbook*, McGraw-Hill, New York, 1983, pp. 9.1–9.19.

Yates, B. *The Decline and Fall of the American Automobile Industry*, Empire Books, New York, 1983.

# 33

# STRATEGIC MANAGEMENT ARCHETYPES

*J. G. Wissema, H. W. van der Pol and H. M. Messer*

Source: *Strategic Management Journal* 1(1) (1980): 37–47.

## Summary

In the recruitment of managers it is increasingly necessary to attune the choice of candidate to the strategy of the company or its subsidiary.

In this paper—coauthored by specialists in the fields of management recruitment and corporate strategy—the authors develop classifications of strategies and of management archetypes. Linking of these classifications leads to an approach that can assist both managersemployees and managers-employers when filling management vacancies. In addition, the approach can be used to assist management development programmes and to relate management planning to strategic planning.

Perhaps the most important problem for leaders of all kinds of organizations is concerned with the manning of positions of leadership, most of all their own succession. This task seems just as important as the establishment of the objectives and strategies of the organization. These main tasks of top management as we see them can be formulated as the attraction, allocation and motivation of men and means on behalf of the organization and its component parts, in dynamic balance with the establishment of the objectives and strategies.

Much has been written about the criteria according to which managers are selected. The term *management development* refers to the process of interrelating management functions to a logical and practical whole, together with the recruitment and selection of managers to man these functions. In connection with management development a number of fundamental questions arise, including the following two key questions:

(1) What determines whether or not someone will function well in a particular function in a particular organization?
(2) What determines why one person provides leadership, the other follows?

From the literature it emerges that there is no such a thing as a general formula for leadership. The choice of a leader is strongly dependent on the situation and the community for which he is to provide leadership. A participatory style of management, for instance, is not always the most effective style. However, the amount of participation present or desired has an effect upon the choice of the most suitable candidate. Katz and Kahn (1966) noted as early as 1966 that the tasks of managers must be derived from the goals of the organization.

## Characteristics of managers

Delineation of manager-stereotypes can be useful in the selection process because it forces one towards a choice, both of the 'profile' of the candidate and of the person once the profile is sketched. In principle stereotypes can be written from many points of view, starting, for example, from the style of leadership or from affinity with the task which must be fulfilled. Almost all manager typologies build upon the concepts already used by Lewin, Lippitt and White (1939), i.e. authoritarian, democratic, laissez-faire. The starting point in this case is, therefore, the style of cooperation and leadership. Mintzberg (1976) used a classification which is based upon the assumed principle-differentiating functions of the two halves of the brain, which induces him to suppose that some are more suited, or feel more attracted to planning, or staff-work in general, while in others the preference is for management in line-work. The fact that these preferences are so deeply-rooted in everyone's psychological and physiological makeup would then explain the discrepancy between staff managers and line managers. Insofar as the term typology can be employed in this instance, this has thus relation both to the aptitude and to the work-content of the person concerned.

Another approach is based on an analysis of the manager's job. Form the insights that management is, in a very broad sense, a problem-solving activity that can be described as a complex information process. Ansoff and Brandenburg (1969) derive a description of a manager consisting of a connected chain of ten basic processes. Within this chain they identify four different subcycles. Four archetypal roles are then described that correspond to the requirements of the different natures of the jobs as described by the subcycles. This analysis, logical and intuitively appealing, is used by the authors to analyse the role of general management in the future.

Leaders change, through their personal and professional development. To what extent can someome of one type change to another, as the situation demands? Theobald (1977) describes the results of an investigation (questionnaire method) by Schubart among 2444 German managers and the 9 types which resulted. More important than this are his comments that a typing has something final about it and that an individual can only move over with difficulty from one type to another. Theobald also draws attention to behavioural limits, particularly in the sense that particular success curves are peculiar to particular types.

We can summarize the above into two conclusions, which are, at the same time, starting points for the approach we have developed. These are:

(1) leaders can change but are, in all probability, not so flexible that they can function optimally in every kind of organization;
(2) the effectiveness of a leader depends, among other things, on the nature of the situation in which he is to operate.

In the practice of management development the reciprocal character, not only of the organization, but also of the *strategy* in relation to the manager-type should always be perceived. This has led us to develop a typology of managers which is based upon possible business strategies. This typology adds to those which start from various styles of leadership and can be used together with the latter in delineation of the person sought.

## The allocation of sets of capabilities

Not only management development but also the allocation of other 'capabilities' such as information systems, research, marketing and so on must be linked to the strategy of the part of the organization concerned. The theory of corporate strategy has concerned itself mainly with the establishment of objectives, with 'gap-analysis' (analysis of the development of costs and yields with fixed policy) and to the provision of instruments for portfolio management. Studies of the 'capabilities' needed for execution of the strategy have only recently emerged.

Ansoff *et al.* (1976) have described a system to allow the 'capabilities' of an undertaking to be adjusted to the level of turbulence of the environment in which it proceeds. This description marks a breakthrough because it is the first to note that different parts of companies or organizations mostly have different strategies and that the 'package of capabilities' of the various parts must be adjusted to these.

## Typology of strategic situations

This implies that a number of possible strategies for change must be formulated to allow the packages of capabilities to be described. We have taken as the starting point for the description of strategies the *strategic starting situation* which we characterize like other post BCG portfolio models on the basis of what we call the *external potential* and the *internal potential*. By these we mean the situation *of* the market and the situation of the company in the market.

The situation *of* the market can be characterized with the aid of the well-known lifecycle theory. This theory comes down, briefly, to the fact that in the development of a product or service a number of phases can be distinguished. For our purposes the division into phases:

I introduction
II growth
III saturation
(IV) decline

seems appropriate for use, in which connection we note that the presence of the fourth phase is not a *conditio sine qua non*. On the contrary, the vast majority of products, admittedly with continuing adaptation, can maintain themselves in the market for a long time.

The situation *in* the market, i.e. the competitive situation, is determined by a large number of factors, among which the size of the market share is dominant (Buzzel *et al.* (1975)). Other factors are power over distribution, reputation of the brand, exclusivity of know-how, quality of the service organization and so on. Following a method of analysis which we shall not describe here we can measure the internal potential and define it as H (High), M (Moderate), or L (Low).

Setting out the external and internal potentials in relation to each other provides us with a strategic grid (Figure 1), in which 12 or 9 situations are distinguishable according to whether a decline/end phase comes into question. The reader will recognize these situations straight away. MII stands for a product-market combination (PMC) which operates in a growing market and which takes up, according to the strength of competition, a middle position, for example as a good 'follow-the-leader'. HIII denotes the attractive position of a strong market position in a saturated market, occupied by some manufacturers of branded goods. HI is the situation of an innovatory PMC, HII that of a 'first-to-the-market' market-leader.

Although the above typing is described in terms of a product-market combination of a manufacturing or trading undertaking, it is immediately clear that it is directly applicable to the services sector and to official bodies. The battle against terrorism can, for example, be typified as a growth market, the municipal cleansing service as a saturated market (i.e. no further explosive growth). In the case of a monopolist situation like the position of a government agency the concept 'strength of competition' is to be interpreted as the qualitiative position of the agency with respect to other (national or local) authorities.

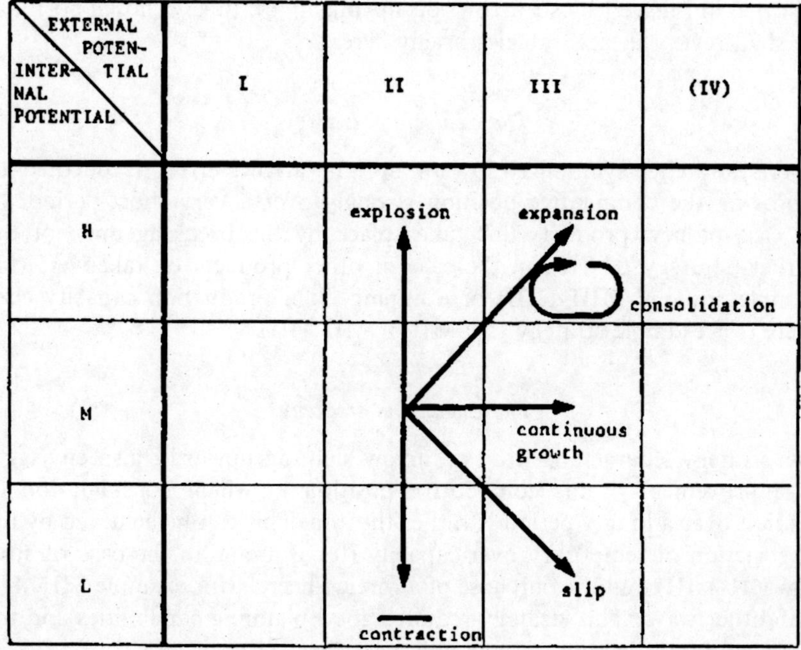


*Figure 1* The main PMC-strategies.

It is to be noted that the company or organization has influence upon the internal potential, but that the external potential nearly always presents itself to the individual concerned as a circumstance upon which he can exert little or no influence. For insiders of strategic planning we would note, in addition, that if the concept 'external potential' is restricted to 'growth of the market' and the concept 'internal potential' to 'market share', while both concepts are subsequently characterized as large or small, the grid reduces to the four position grid of BCG.

## Typology of strategies

With the above system the strategic situations of the PMC's of an organization can be charted and a strategy of change for each PMC chosen on this basis. We define a *PMC strategy* in this connection as the route from the current strategic position to the desired strategic position. The occupation of the desired strategic position is the *PMC objective.* Just as the strategic positions can be referred to as HII, MIII, etc., the strategies can be denoted by MII–MIII, MI–HII, etc., very much like chess notation.

It is now evident that there are only six kinds of PMC strategies and that therefore six sets of capabilities must also be described. These strategies are indicated in Figure 1 by six arrows occupying an arbitrarily chosen position. We shall review these strategies briefly here.

### *The explosion strategy*

In this strategy, symbolized by an upright arrow, effort is devoted to improving the competitive position strongly over a very short period. In the case of new products this takes place by the breaking open of the market (strategy LI–HI), in the case of other products by takeovers (for example strategy MIII–HIII) or dumping from production capacity elsewhere (for example strategy LII–MII or MII–HII).

### *The expansion strategy*

This strategy, characterized by an arrow slanting upwards, also envisages an improvement in the competitive position in which consolidation of position over a longer period is rather the aim. This can be achieved by the construction of temporary over-capacity (for example in the case of strategy MII–HIII), but the purchase of a foreign license (for example LII–MII) or in other ways. This strategy requires good planning capabilities and the ability to dare to accept considerable risks.

### *The continuous growth strategy*

This strategy (horizontal arrow) envisages maintenance of the competitive position. This implies that there must be added investment in good time in a growing market (for example strategy MI–MII or MII–MIII) but in such a way that substantial overcapacity is avoided. This requires still more accurate judgement and timing than in the case of the expansion strategy. The continuous growth strategy is less spectacular than the strategies mentioned above, but no less demanding.

### *The slip strategy*

This strategy, also well-named 'nil-growth in a growing market' and indicated by an arrow slanting downwards, is only possible starting from positions HI, HII, MI and MII. Here the market is growing, but the PMC deliberately gives up maintenance of the competitive position, which must primarily be read as abandonment of maintenance of market share. The reason for this, at first sight perhaps strange, behaviour is that the product is not strong, that it could perhaps be strengthened with, for example, a strategy MII–HIII, but that the means required could be better employed elsewhere in the company. Even MII–MIII is regarded as too costly. Application of the slip strategy implies: no expansion of capacity, no promotional activities, at the most some price campaigns, no further investment. Every penny is saved: a blown-off rooftile is, so to speak, not replaced. One continues as long as the proceeds exceed the costs, in the knowledge that one will stop once this is no longer the case. It is therefore essential in the case of this strategy that a worsening of the competitive position is accepted and, as a consequence, that activity will, in due course, also be brought to an end. The capabilities required lie, above all, in acceptance of the situation, which is not really one for the entrepreneur: the PMC must, after all, continuously let chances go by. The art is to stretch out activities for as long as possible with as little money as possible.

### *The consolidation strategy*

This strategy is only applicable in a saturated market or in a diminishing but not wholly extinct market. Its symbol is the curved arrow; another name, 'nil-growth in a stabilized market'. In this connection nil-growth must, however, not be interpreted too literally. A certain amount of growth, parallel with growth in population or prosperity, is allowed. Substantial growth through continuing opening up of new markets is, however, excluded.

In the saturated phase (and certainly in the declining phase) there is often a shakingout process by which companies with a strong competitive position manage, by way of the effects of scale, to squeeze out smaller enterprises.

The consolidation strategy requires above all, therefore, dexterity, adaptability over the short term and artistry in arriving continuously in the market with cost-savings and initiatives, with few resources. The risk, particularly with strategy HIII–HIII, is that changes are discerned too late.

### *The contraction strategy*

In the case of negative growth, shown by a vertical arrow pointing downwards, activity is considerably reduced or ended (closure or sale); termination is indicated by a small horizontal line beneath the arrow. The social element always predominates in this case, and much creativity, caution, readiness to deliberate and steadfastness are necessary.

## Typology of managers

On the basis of the six strategic 'directions' described above the most adequate sets of capabilities required for the realization of the PMC objective can be described.

In this paper we will limit ourselves to the description of types of managers corresponding to the strategies. The division into six types (as well as other typologies developed in the course of time) is naturally debatable, having regard to the overlap which exists between the various types.

*Table 1*

| *Strategic direction* | *Type of manager* |
|---|---|
| Explosive growth | Pioneer |
| Expansion | Conqueror |
| Continuous growth | Level-headed |
| Consolidation | Administrator |
| Slip strategy | Economiser |
| Contraction | Insistent diplomat |

Nevertheless the division is, in our experience, meaningful, since the various types are very recognizable, not only to managers themselves but also to others. The model developed can provide valuable support in making discussion of the types of manager desired possible and by making visible pitfalls in which managers can end up whenever they wish to, or have to, change to another strategic direction.

We have described each type of manager on the basis of a group of five viewpoints, i.e. conformity, sociability, activity, pressure to achieve and style of thinking. The first four of these viewpoints are personality factors; the fifth (style of thinking) has much to do with intelligence, apart from personality.

We shall not here go into the correlations that exist between the various personality factors. We have made these selections specifically on the basis of a brief investigation and on the grounds of high degree of recognizability. Description of types of manager on the basis of personality factors has the advantage that it brings in a certain measure of systematization, and that the types are not plucked relatively at random from experience.

The six different strategic directions and the six types of manager corresponding with them are brought together in Table 1. Within the framework of this paper it would be going too far to describe all these types in detail on the basis of the five chosen characteristics and we are, therefore, restricting ourselves to a schematic rendering. (Tables 2–7.)

*Table 2* Pioneer.

| *Behavioural characteristics* | *Characteristics of a 'pioneer'* |
|---|---|
| Conformity | Very flexible, very creative, divergent |
| Sociability | Very extrovert, much flair and glamour but driven by circumstances and solitary, mistrustful |
| Activity | Hyperactive, restless, anticipatory, uncontrolled |
| Pressure to achieve | Stormy, daredevil, seeking challenges, motivated by anything unique |
| Style of thinking | Intuitive-irrational, thinking disconnectedly, original, divergent |

*Table 3* Conqueror.

| *Behavioural characteristics* | *Characteristics of a 'conqueror'* |
|---|---|
| Conformity | Appropriately non-conformist, creatively structured towards anything new |
| Sociability | Selectively extrovert, forms small groups of chosen individuals |
| Activity | Energetic, reacts to 'weak signals', nervous with great self-control |
| Pressure to achieve | Increasing sphere of influence, calculated risks |
| Style of thinking | Capable of seeing beyond limits, generalist, rational |

*Table 4* Level-headed ruler.

| *Behavioural characteristics* | *Characteristics of a 'level-headed ruler'* |
|---|---|
| Conformity | Strongly structured, 'according to the time-table', security |
| Sociability | Amicable, team-worker, maintains grip, well-regarded |
| Activity | Directed to objective, stable, according to agreement |
| Pressure to achieve | Level-headed growth, satisfaction through control of the situation |
| Style of thinking | Solid, systematic, penetrating, specialist |

*Table 5* Administrator.

| *Behavioural characteristics* | *Characteristics of an 'administrator'* |
|---|---|
| Conformity | Reproducible, routine, docile |
| Sociability | Introvert, training |
| Activity | Stable-static, via procedures, waits and sees, 'yes, but' |
| Pressure to achieve | Maintaining of *status quo*, defending of territory |
| Style of thinking | Solid and conformist vision, connection with earlier situations |

*Table 6* Economiser.

| *Behavioural characteristics* | *Characteristics of an 'economiser'* |
|---|---|
| Conformity | Bureaucratic, dogmatic, rigid |
| Sociability | Procedural-dirigistic |
| Activity | *Laissez-faire*, doing what has to be done, little initiative |
| Pressure to achieve | Reactive behaviour, stimuli from outside |
| Style of thinking | Legalistic, everything according to precedent |

*Table 7* Insistent diplomat.

| *Behavioural characteristics* | *Characteristics of an 'insistent diplomat'* |
|---|---|
| Conformity | Maximal flexibility within a fixed objective, accepted restrictions |
| Sociability | Considerate/human, takes others into account, decisive/ inspiring confidence, allays emotion |
| Activity | Steady, retentive but flexible |
| Pressure to achieve | More strategic/directed towards the long term than tactical/ directed towards the short term, directed towards objectives but also carefully measured input |
| Style of thinking | Broad, relativistic, manysided |

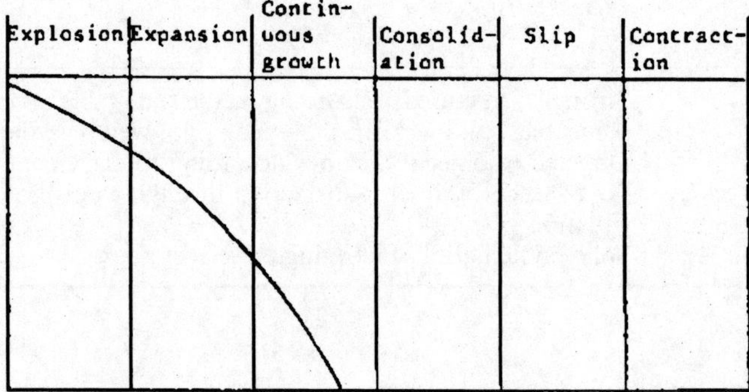


*Figure 2* Effectiveness of a 'pioneer'.

## Effectiveness of manager types in the case of a particular strategy

From the models of the six strategic directions and the six types of manager it is possible to indicate approximately effectiveness and chance of success according to type.

Limiting ourselves to two types of manager it is possible to 'read-off' quickly from Figures 2 and 3 in which strategic direction a particular type of manager is more or less successful.

It is thus possible to make clear in a simple way that the pioneer manager type can scarcely function in a consolidation phase and that the insistent diplomat can function in several situations but has at the same time clear limitations.

We shall not here go into the various reasons why a particular type of manager functions badly in particular strategies and will confine ourselves to observing that behavioural patterns are required from him in such situations

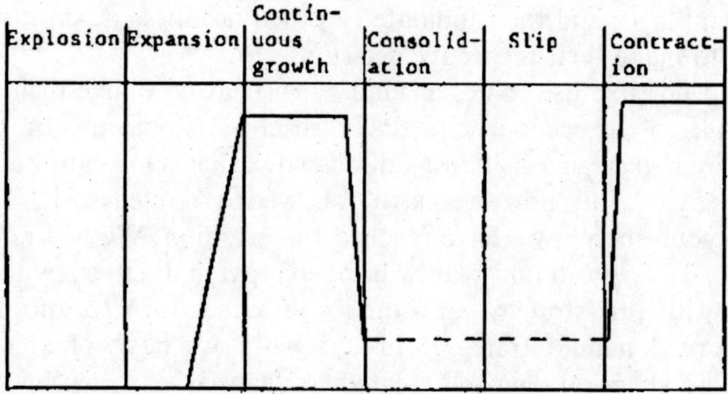


*Figure 3* Effectiveness of an 'insistent diplomat'.

which are not in accordance with the behavioural tendencies inseparably linked to his person. The pioneer driven to despair on learning that no more money is available for new developments and who for this reason proceeds further with discoveries, but in his free time, or proceeds further independently, may serve as an example. No more can an insistent diplomat function well in an explosive strategy, because he is lacking in the creativity and energy required.

Despite all the simplifications it is possible by means of the abovementioned diagrams to give a verdict regarding the desired behaviour of managers in the case of particular strategic directions and it will also be clear why a particular type of manager may well fail whenever the strategic direction has become other than 'his'.

## Applications of the method

The approach described above can be used in companies and non-profit organizations as an addition to their management promotion and selection procedures, provided that the strategies of the components of the organization are defined in the way we described. When a profile of the new manager is being drawn, one can use the descriptions of stereotypes of Lewin *et al.* (1939). Ansoff and Brandenburg (1969) and the above types. These stereotypes have all been defined from different angles and can be used simultaneously. A warning should be made against the 'labelling' of a management function and, even worse, of a manager. One could never explicitly demand, say, a manager of a pioneer type, nor label anyone as a pioneer; real people exhibit something of all the types. However, the strategy of the PMC can be part of the profile of the management function and the preference of a manager for certain types of strategy as well as his previous experience in terms of types of strategy can be part of his personal profile.

Both the employer and the candidate can then use these descriptions when they have to make their respective decisions.

A second possible use comes around when PMC's change their strategy. Such changes often occur when a PMC reaches its objective, in the sense of the desired strategic position as discussed earlier. One can then ask the manager, say: 'Until now we have followed a strategy MII–HIII and thanks to your energy, we have reached this position. We will now follow HIII–HIII. Do you think you will be happy and effective in leading the PMC with this strategy, or would you rather turn to another PMC with a more dynamic strategy?' In our work we have often seen wise pioneers who abandon their self-created company when it reaches the stage of maturity. On the other hand, we know a typical MII–MII company that could diversify with a new LI–MII strategy where the management is rightly aware that they will have to recruit a new manager for this job, because they themselves are not geared for it. It is certainly no disgrace but rather a sign of good management when a management team realizes that a discrepancy is going to arise between their desired and available capabilities.

It would be desirable were many managers to take the decision to select another position, and allow their places to be taken by another manager, more adequate at that juncture. This awareness can prevent much conflict and terminal events such as bankruptcy, heart attacks and such like. A sensible management sees its own limitations, knows how to live with them and accepts their consequences.

This brings us to a third possible application of our approach, namely its addition to management planning and management development. In this way, it can serve as the *trait d'union* between the corporate strategy procedures and the management development procedures, a link that is painfully lacking in most companies. From the projected activities of the company, one can generate the future management need, taking into account divestment or new activities. From an overview of the present management characteristics, one can identify the 'management gap'. This may lead to a reconsideration of the strategies chosen, which can be overambitious in view of present management capabilities and recruitment limitations.

On the other hand, the 'gap' may serve as the basis for management training, recruitment and job rotation. In this way, management planning and corporate strategy are in equilibrium. It goes without saying that such an integrated planning system is extremely complex because so many parameters are needed to describe the present and future management capabilities and the strategic archetypes are only one of them. However, with the increasing demands on managers, we expect that good management is becoming increasingly scarce and that management planning systems will be needed more urgently than before.

## References

Ansoff, H. I., and R. G. Brandenburg. 'The general manager of the future', *California Management Review*, **11**, Spring 1969, pp. 61–72.

Ansoff, H. I., R. P. Declerck, and R. L. Hayes. 'From strategic planning to strategic management', in book with the same title, Wiley, Chichester, 1976.

Buzzel, R. D. *et al.* 'Market share, a key to profitability', *Harvard Business Review*, January–February 1975, pp. 97–106.

Katz, D. and R. L. Kahn. *The social psychology of organisation*, Wiley, New York, 1966.

Lewin, K., R. Lippitt, and R. K. White. 'Patterns of aggressive behaviour in experimentally created social climates', *Journal of Social Psychology*, **10**, 1939, pp. 271–299.

Mintzberg, H. 'Planning on the left side and managing on the right', *Harvard Business Review*, July–August 1976, pp. 49–58.

Theobald, A. *Die Macher, eine Typologie des Chefs*, Mosaik Verlag, München, 1977, p. 22.

34

# STRATEGY AS OPTIONS ON THE FUTURE

*Peter J. Williamson*

Source: *Sloan Management Review*, Spring (1999): 117–26.

> "It is a great piece of skill to know how to guide your luck even while waiting for it."
>
> — *Baltasar Gracián (1601–1658)*

In 1984, *The Economist* asked sixteen people — four finance ministers, four chairman of multinational companies, four Oxford University economics students, and four London dustmen (or garbage collectors) — to generate ten-year forecasts. they were the kinds of forecasts that underpin many long-term, strategic plans: the average growth rate in Organization for Economic Cooperation and Development countries over ten years, the average inflation rate in OECD countries, the exchange rate between pound sterling and the U.S. dollar, the price of oil, and the year when Singapore's GDP per capita would overtake Australia's (double Singapore's at the time). In 1994, *The Economist* checked the sixteen people's forecasts against what had actually happened.

On average, the forecasts were more than 60 percent too high or too low. The average forecasted price of oil, for example, was $40 compared with an actual price of just $17. All the respondents said Singapore's GDP per capita would never overtake Australia's, but that had actually happened in 1993. The most accurate forecasters were the London dustmen and the chairmen of multinational companies (a tie for first place): the finance ministers came in last. But the performance of every group was quite abysmal. The unpalatable fact is that no one can predict the long-term economic and market environment with any real accuracy.

Yet many strategic plans are meticulously constructed on these foundations of sand, perched on top of forecasts that, in all probability, will prove to be hopelessly off the mark. Consider how many companies approach strategic planning: The numbers in the long-term plan are dominated by a sales forecast that is produced by product and customer type or region (often a projection of around five years); the companies then allocate the investment to business units consistent with achieving the long-term sales forecast. Then they compute the implied costs and profits, and the process iterates until they produce an acceptable "long-term plan." The plans often include erudite SWOT analysis (strengths, weaknesses, opportunities, and threats) or other market and trend analyses, but the decisions are made on the basis of forecast sales, investments, and costs.[1] The forecasts are often heavily influenced by straight-line projections with forecasts of sales growth of existing products in existing markets. This implies that the company will maintain significant percentages of its costs as fixed, so that when these are spread over the greater sales volume, profits will grow.

The large forecast error in projecting variables like those in *The Economist* experiment and, hence, sales levels over the long run creates problems for the kind of strategic planning I described above. Companies will tend to overinvest in building assets and capabilities that are highly specific to a particular strategy, relative to what would be optimal if the planning approach explicitly acknowledged that its forecasts would most likely be off the mark. A framework that encourages planners to optimize the configuration of investments on the assumption that they know the sales volume for particular products and markets will underinvest in flexibility.

By making investment decisions on "single line" forecasts, a company risks becoming a prisoner of its existing investments in capabilities and market understanding. Rapidly repositioning a company when investments in the capabilities and market knowledge necessary have not been made in advance will leave it like "an aircraft carrier turning on a dime." The company will suffer "diseconomies of time compression" (extra costs of trying to accelerate the rate of change).[2] Contrast this with a company that has invested in experiments to understand potential new markets and in seeding new capabilities (such as a small-scale project to supply a particular product direct to customers). These investments, and the learning they produce, effectively create a portfolio of strategic options on the future, a series of alternative "launching pads" that the company can use to rapidly change its strategic direction in response to market developments. A competitor that has aligned its investments with a single, and different, trajectory will struggle to catch up in the race to reposition.

For example, in 1990, USX (formerly United States Steel) had the choice of investing in new equipment to gain experience in a new steel-casting technology — compact strip production (CSP) — or in equipment using its traditional hot-rolling technology. USX chose to invest further in the hot rolling. A competitor, Nucor Steel, piloted the CSP technology and, in the process, created an option not available to USX. Commenting on USX's ability to catch up once CSP had proven successful, Nucor's CEO remarked:

"It will take them two years to build a plant and another year to get it running properly. We've got at least three-and-a-half to four years on them."[3]

My message is that, while companies may focus on executing a single strategy at any point in time, they must also build and maintain a portfolio of strategic options on the future. Building that portfolio of options requires investments in developing new capabilities and learning about new, potential markets. By putting in place a set of strategic options on the future, a company will be able to reposition itself faster than competitors that have focused all their investments on "doing more of the same." But this requires changes to traditional strategy processes and a new way of thinking about how planning and opportunism interact in determining strategy.

Next I discuss a strategy that embodies a coherent portfolio of options, sketch a process managers can use to develop this kind of strategy, and explain how planning and management opportunism can reinforce each other. Establishing a portfolio of future options involves four main steps:

- Uncovering the hidden constraints on the company's future.
- Establishing processes for building new strategic options.
- Optimizing the portfolio of strategic options.
- Combining planning and opportunism.

## Step 1. Uncover the hidden constraints

Successful companies often get ahead of competitors by focusing on a particular segment of customers or geographic market and learning more about their behavior and needs than anyone else. The companies design a profit-generating engine, based on a particular price, margin, and cost structure, that is underpinned by investments in the capability to source, produce, distribute, and support a product or service that these customers value. Over time, this profit engine is continually fine-tuned, often reaping economies of scale, scope, and learning. For example, Frank Winfield Woolworth, who founded Woolworth Corporation in 1879, pioneered the idea of selling merchandise at no more than five cents. He refined this "five and dime" profit engine to become a finely-tuned general merchandising machine. Initial concepts of "no frills" service, cheap products, and items that were nonperishable formed the core. The Woolworth Corporation subsequently developed competencies in managing a wide product range while keeping stock turnover high, competencies in site selection and development, and logistics to reap economies of scale from a chain of stores.

When its founder died in 1919, Woolworth boasted a chain of 1,081 stores with sales of $119 million (an incredible figure for its day). The power of the formula was reflected in the company's New York headquarters building at 233 Broadway; at 792 feet, it was the world's tallest building until the

Chrysler building was completed in 1930. After World War II, the company continued to improve on the winning formula, adding new competencies in the management of advertising, consumer credit, and self-service, and in site selection and management in the new retailing environment of U.S. suburbs.

Woolworth's strategy had the advantages of focus: it was able to deepen its existing competencies and incrementally expand both its competency base and its knowledge of different market environments. However, competitors were developing retail formats that required both competencies and market knowledge that were outside the "box" in which Woolworth was operating. Competitors like Wal-Mart (general-merchandise, discount superstores) attacked on one flank, while specialty "category killers" like Toys-R-Us attacked on the other.

Despite a decline in its overall sales figures in real terms, Woolworth failed to invest in creating new capabilities or understanding the behavior of shoppers using the new retail format so it could expand into either superstores or specialty retailing. When, in the late 1980s, Woolworth eventually tried to respond with its own discount and specialty stores, it ran into a hidden constraint: while the strategy made sense, Woolworth didn't really have the option to change its strategy quickly, because it had not invested in creating new capabilities and knowledge outside its existing formula. Thus, by 1995, Woolworth was forced to sell its new specialty stores "Kids Mart" and "Little Folks," established in the early 1990s, because of poor profitability. The company had become a prisoner of its past.

In 1993, Woolworth closed 400 stores in the United States and sold its 122 Canadian Woolco stores to Wal-Mart. In 1997, Woolworth shut down its last general-merchandise store in the United States. It had refined and polished its economic engine and deepened its narrow range of competencies into almost perfect extinction. The company had invested in new strategic options too late to build the competencies and knowledge necessary to pursue a new strategy.

In the quest to achieve challenging new missions, Woolworth managers kept bumping up against two constraints: they didn't really understand the customers they needed to attract to achieve a new, broader strategy; and they didn't have the capabilities to compete with rivals that were already established. When they decided to respond to lost sales caused by market changes, well-established Woolworth managers kept hitting the dual constraints. They had not invested in real options soon enough to replace their dying profit engine and were caught in a box *(see Figure 1)*.

Woolworth did, however, invest in one new strategic option that partially saved it, when, in 1974, it backed an experiment in specialty retailing — "Foot Locker." Using new capabilities in the retailing of athletic footwear and its market knowledge, Woolworth exercised this option to build a chain of athletic-shoe stores when growth in the market took off in the 1980s.

It subsequently introduced new formats, including Lady Foot Locker in 1982 and Kids Foot Locker in 1987. Over time, Woolworth opened more than 7,100 specialty stores, and in June 1998, it changed its corporate name to Venator Group. In some ways, this is an example of successfully repositioning a company whose core business had become obsolete. But, in fact, Woolworth paid a high price for failing to recognize the hidden constraints on its strategy choices and underinvestment in new strategic options. Venator is a much smaller company; it now occupies only half the floors in that famous New York skyscraper, which it sold in April 1998.

To avoid becoming a prisoner of hidden constraints, a company must build new capabilities and simultaneously expand its knowledge of new market segments and customer behavior. If the outcome of uncertain market developments falls within the range of that portfolio of options, the company will then be able to exercise one or more relevant options. Thus the company will be able to outperform the competitors that have not made these investments. Alternatively, it will be able to close the competitive gap with rivals that already possess the necessary capabilities and market knowledge.

Companies should distinguish between capability constraints and market knowledge constraints (see the "existing" box in *Figure 1*). Some companies' options are not seriously constrained by their market knowledge. Through various processes I describe later, they have created a large internal pool of knowledge about new customers and competitive behavior. This may include knowledge about new potential users of the company's products or services, new geographic segments, existing users with changed needs and buying behavior, or competitors changing the rules of the game. The dilemma these companies face is that market knowledge itself can still leave them with few ways to exploit that knowledge (other than, perhaps, selling it to someone else). The "trader" is a company with potentially valuable market information, but no capability to use it to create value except by

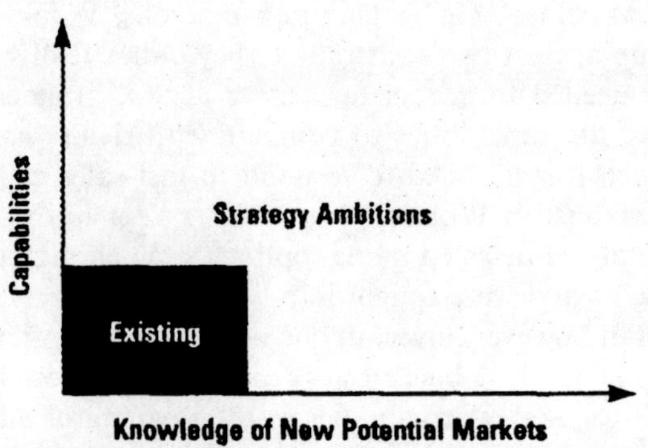


*Figure 1* Hidden Constraints: Narrow Capabilities and Market Knowledge.

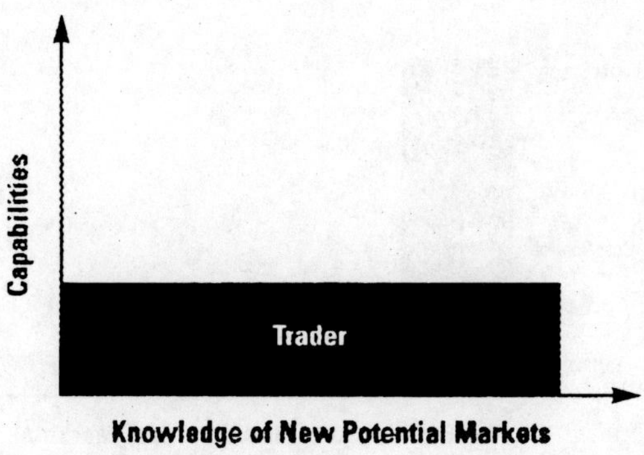


*Figure 2* The Trader (Aware but Incapable).

trading the information or using it to arbitrage a commodity (*see Figure 2*). Obviously, some profitable companies are based on trading information, but for most, this option does not allow them to leverage their existing competence base and therefore support an adequate return on their asset and skill bases.

To avoid having capabilities that are too narrow to exploit the knowledge of different markets and customer behaviors, such a company needs to systematically expand its pool of value-creating capabilities (adding, for example, the capability to manufacture products or deliver services that utilize that market knowledge). For example, the British trading house, Inchcape, had a geographic reach extending from southeast Asia to the Americas, the Caribbean, India, Europe, and Africa, with interests in more than 500 companies in forty-four countries. It became a professional distributor, marketer, and seller of the products and technologies of its "principals" (the owners of the branded products and services it traded) and a provider of specialist services. As a trader, it successfully expanded its options into new markets (the horizontal dimension in Figure 2). But as the principals for whom Inchcape acted as agent became more familiar with the local markets, they wanted more control over their market positioning and built the scale to cover the fixed costs of local operations. They began to invade Inchcape's business. As a traditional trader, it had few places to turn. With finelyhoned trading skills, but lacking the breadth of capabilities to add value in other ways, its strategic options were tightly circumscribed. Some of Inchcape's competitors, like Swire Pacific, for example, had invested more in creating options by developing new capabilities in areas such as property development and airline management. By the time that pure trading as a mechanism for extracting profit from local knowledge came under serious threat, Swire used these expanded capabilities to extract an increasing proportion of total profit from its local knowledge in new ways.[4]

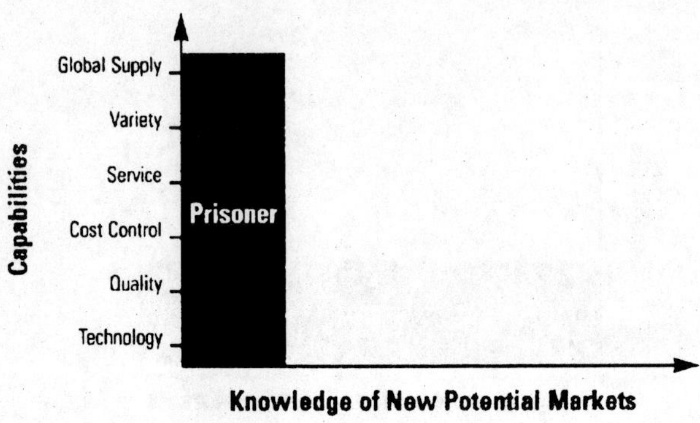


*Figure 3* The Prisoner (Capable but Unaware).

Some companies have the opposite problem: they have created formidable capabilities but are prisoners of their lack of market knowledge (*see Figure 3*). AT&T, immediately after deregulation, had capabilities in technology, communications infrastructure, and experience in sales and customer service. As a result of domestic regulation and government monopolies overseas, however, the potential of AT&T's capabilities was imprisoned by a lack of market experience outside the long-distance, voice, and data sector in the United States. These constraints meant that AT&T could not fully utilize its existing capabilities so that it had underutilized capacity for value creation (in the sense that the marginal costs of using these capabilities would have been less than the marginal revenues earned had AT&T had the option to broaden its offering and the range of markets it served). Gradually, AT&T has opened new strategic options by building its knowledge base of the markets for new domestic service and users in national markets overseas. It is thus able to increase the effective capacity utilization of its existing capabilities.

To develop new strategic options, therefore, two sets of processes are required: (1) processes that fundamentally expand the company's capabilities, and (2) processes that expand the company's knowledge of new markets and market behavior. However, opening new options does not necessarily imply unrelated, or even related diversification in the traditional sense.[5] Strategic options on the future are not full-fledged new businesses. Instead they are the "doors to the future" that are created when a company undertakes pilot projects, reconnaissance, and experiments that expand its knowledge of alternative market segments and value propositions and that seed new organizational capabilities.

In the case of Woolworth, the relevant options turned out to be experiments with new retailing formats, which can be seen as a type of related diversification. But, alternatively, new options can often involve finding new ways to either deliver enhanced value to or reduce the costs of serving an existing customer segment, as in Monsanto's use of biotechnology to replace traditional chemicals in its weed-control business or Schwab's introduction of "E-Schwab." In almost every case, however, creating new options involves some combination of fundamentally extending the company's existing capabilities and, at the same time, its knowledge of customer and market behavior. E-Schwab, for example, requires new capabilities in the design and management of an Internet interface between the customer and Schwab's internal systems. Many E-Schwab customers use the existing telephone trading system, but they are likely to behave differently in electronic trading. Schwab needed to understand, for example, which customers would pay a price premium and how it could change its ability to build customer loyalty.[6]

I am not arguing that companies should develop an infinite number of capabilities or exploit them across every possible market. Such approaches would eventually drown in diseconomies of complexity as the variety of activities increased.[7] There is an optimal portfolio of options that a company can create in order to strike the right balance between the cost of creating and maintaining an option and the payoffs in the ability to reposition itself more rapidly and at lower costs.

What do these processes look like? How broad a range of options should a company create? Woolworth, for example, continually expanded its capabilities and knowledge of customer behavior within its existing retailing format; its error was to limit the range of new options, given the rate and nature of changes occurring in its industry.

## Step 2. Establish processes

As we have seen, creating new strategic options combines expansion of the company's knowledge about new, potential markets or customer behaviors with simultaneous development of new capabilities. The processes need to minimize the costs of building and maintaining the portfolio of strategic options — a particularly important factor given that many options are likely to remain unexercised.

Cost-effective methods of expanding knowledge about new potential markets and customer behavior include leveraging customers' and suppliers' knowledge and learning from "maverick" competitors and related industries. Market research is perhaps the most obvious way to leverage customers' knowledge. Traditional market research is limited by the current perceptions and orthodoxies of existing consumers. Companies should focus on customers' complaints to understand their perceptions of the existing offering. In some industries, companies can become partners with customers that have articulated an unserved need.

The geographic periphery of the company's existing markets or concentrations of highly sophisticated customers can also supply knowledge about potential new customer segments or emerging customer behavior. The company must ensure the right environment for the broad potential of these adaptations. It may enter a new market simply to learn what is potentially relevant for its global operations, rather than earn profits from that market directly. The costs of such a market are an investment in expanding the portfolio of strategic options.

Partnerships with leading-edge suppliers, exchange of technical information, or purchase of minority equity stakes in suppliers with potentially innovative technologies are processes that can provide the raw material to generate new options. Likewise, the company can scan related industries for potentially applicable technologies, service systems, or patterns of changing customer behavior as a way to form new options.

Companies should continually ask which companies are breaking the rules in the industry. A company with a single strategy, from which sales and efficiency must be optimized, dismisses these competitors as irrelevant or as following a different strategy. However, the behavior of maverick competitors can be a source of ideas for creating a portfolio of strategic options.

Analogous processes build the new capabilities that allow a company to expand its strategic options. Leonard-Barton analyzed the processes, including building a company's capabilities base through problem solving, experimentation, importing knowledge, and implementing and integrating new capabilities.[8] The combination of capability-building initiatives involved in a total quality management system includes physical and technical systems, managerial systems, and values and norms, all aligned to the process of building a new capability, in this case "quality."

Acer used these processes to grow from a small electronics company in Taiwan to become the third largest supplier of personal computers in the world (*see Figure 4*). Just like its competitors, Acer lacked a reliable crystal ball to forecast the future, but had a broad sense of which markets it should learn about to expand its strategic options. Acer recognized that because Americans are sophisticated PC buyers, understanding these customers would give it a head start against competitors in other global markets. That understanding would open many options for Acer both to respond more rapidly and to lead change as other markets followed the U.S. lead. According to Acer's Chairman Stan Shih, this is why Acer has maintained its presence in the United States despite sometimes extended periods of local financial losses.[9]

Acer also knew it would be suicidal to attack the established PC giants across a broad front, so it concentrated on understanding the Asian consumers. Most of the major PC suppliers had traditionally sold only to the high-end, high-price segment of Asian markets. Acer developed capabilities, products, and consumer understanding so it could access the much lower-price mainstream markets in Asia. After rounds of redesigns to cut costs, interspersed with test marketing, Acer learned how to sell

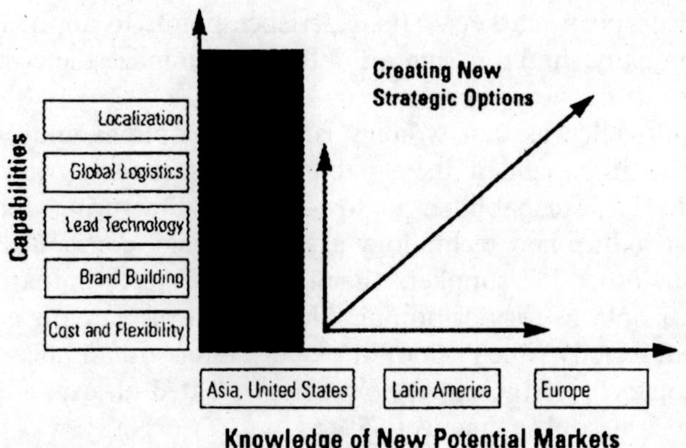


*Figure 4* Creating Strategic Options at Acer.

computers to the mass-market segment in emerging Asian economies ahead of competitors. This opened new options to enter other low-price, emerging markets like Mexico, South Africa, and Russia.

Acer didn't follow a strategy of straight-line forecasting based on its existing products and procedures. When it entered a new market, it didn't always know exactly what product it would sell to whom. Its initial investment in entering a market amounted to buying an option. Rather than simply selling its products to the kinds of customers it served at home, Acer invested in partnerships with local distributors and suppliers designed to maximize its opportunities to learn about the market and further develop its capabilities. In the United States, partnerships with discount retailers taught Acer how to use a previously underserved channel. Its alliance with California-based Frog Design built its capability to develop nontraditional computer designs and ergonomics. It subsequently exercised this option when it launched the unconventional, sleek, grey "Aspire" — a multimedia home PC.

In Mexico, competitors like IBM and HP believed that only large corporations could afford branded personal computers, while private consumers bought low-quality clones. Acer invested with its local partner in working with small- and medium-sized companies to discover a gap in the market of smaller businesses. It then used its capabilities to create a suitable product. Having established a new option, it moved aggressively to exercise it, building its market share in Mexico to 32 percent by 1996.

Acer did not exercise all the options it created. In 1996, Acer built an assembly plant in Lappeenranta, Finland, from which it could efficiently supply computers to Russian distributors. Developments in Russia during 1996 and 1997, including the rapid emergence of strong, domestic competitors, meant that the Russian market became less attractive than when Acer had made the investment. However, given Finland's membership in the European Union, Acer could easily transfer resulting excess capacity into other European markets.[10] Its experience points to another important factor: a company should design an option to minimize the costs incurred, should it decide not to exercise it.

Acer's approach was that strategy is creating options and exercising in new markets. It expanded its capabilities in successive waves, by first exploiting its basic capabilities in low-cost manufacturing and flexibility to rapidly introduce new technology as a supplier of components and subassemblies to other PC suppliers. Each wave of Acer's initiatives opened new, broader options for positioning. No amount of planning could enable it to pinpoint exactly which option it would exercise in an uncertain future. Unlike Woolworth or Inchcape, however, it created an expanded strategic space in which it could maneuver.

## Step 3. Optimize the portfolio

How does a manager know if he or she has created the right portfolio of strategic options for the future? First, by setting aside traditional spreadsheets. Instead, managers need to consider two factors:

1. What alternative capabilities might profitably meet probable customers' needs? (For example, digital or analog technology, localization or individual customization, high levels of variety, reduced lead times, bundled products and services, and so on.)
2. Which potential future markets (geographic, customer, or nonuser segments) or new customer behavior (such as effects of e-commerce) does the company need to know about?

If they stay at the level of future capabilities and potential new markets, far above the detail of unit sales and prices, companies can probably forecast with reasonable accuracy. In 1984, the same year as *The Economist* forecasting competition, John Naisbitt analyzed 6,000 U.S. newspapers to isolate ten "megatrends." They were developments such as "customers would demand a combination of high-tech combined with high-touch," "globalization would mean a combination of more shared production with more cultural assertiveness in individual markets," or customers would demand an "option explosion," not just chocolate or vanilla, but a huge variety of alternative product or services.[11] Most of these broad "predictions" came to pass, largely because they were not predictions at all, but trends already underway that simply gathered pace over time. They are exactly the views that companies need to assess the capabilities necessary to generate a sound portfolio of strategic options. What kind of capabilities does a company need to increase options and provide future customers with more variety? What does this mean for operations, for inventory systems, for salesforce training? The answers will obviously differ by industry and by company.

Various techniques exist to develop needed alternative capabilities and to understand market environments or customer behavior. One approach is scenario planning.[12] Hamel and Prahalad suggest isolating potential "discontinuities" by looking for the likely collision of different trends that will create a step-change in the environment.[13] An example of such discontinuity is the combination of a twenty-four-hour demand for news broadcasts, emergence of a new cable media distribution channel, and development of low-cost satellite communications.

Once a company lists alternative new capabilities and market environments and behavior, it can create a table of its main alternatives (*see Table 1*). Not all combinations of future potential discontinuities and possible capabilities required to underpin competitive advantage will be technically feasible (Internet-mobile telephony convergence and analog technology, for example). Once planners identify the feasible options, they must decide whether to make the necessary investment to include a particular option in the portfolio. In looking at Table 1, for example, each competitor has to decide whether to include option 3 and option 8 in its portfolio by investing in the continued development of analog technology. These decisions should result from three considerations:

- The costs of creating and maintaining the option.
- The estimated probability that the company will exercise the options.
- The probability that creating the option will itself spawn future options, even if it remains unexercised (e.g., a company may value option 3 or option 8, not for its direct profit-making potential, but because of its capacity to open future options that rely on analog technology).

*Table 1* Portfolio of Options for the Mobile Telephone Business.

| | *Capability Requirement* | | |
|---|---|---|---|
| *Market Discontinuity* | *Analog Engineering* | *Digital GSM Engineering* | *Other Digital Engineering* |
| Mobile telephones competing to replace fixed-line services inside large corporations | | Option 1 | Option 2 |
| Emergence of lifestyle uses and the mobile telephone as a "fashion accessory" | Option 3 | Option 4 | Option 5 |
| Internet, voice, and data applications converge | | Option 6 | Option 7 |
| Entertainment media and mobile telephony converge | Option 8 | | Option 9 |

When strategy is viewed as the creation of options on the future, minimizing the costs of creating and maintaining them becomes a critical managerial concern. The costs can be reduced by careful design of efficient experiments, test marketing, and prototyping; by sharing the costs in partnership with interested; customers or suppliers; and by leveraging new information sources.

In attempting to optimize the company's portfolio of options, management must clearly distinguish between the cost of investing in the option and the cost of exercising that option (the latter being the cost of scaling up the option into a profit-generating business). In the case of Woolworth, for example, the cost of its initial experiment to establish its first Foot Locker store was the cost of creating an option to move into specialty retailing. If Woolworth had not exercised this option, the cost would have amounted to writing off the cost of the experiment. The cost of exercising the option included all the investments required to establish and operate a competitive chain of stores that achieved the minimum efficient scale. The cost of Acer's option on the Russian market amounted to the investment in its Finnish plant less the expected present value of cash it could obtain from selling the product elsewhere in Europe if it decided not to exercise the option to enter Russia. The costs of exercising its Russian option, meanwhile, would have included the costs of investing in brand building and distribution capacity in Russia, and so on. This distinction is critical because the decision whether to include a particular option in a portfolio should be made by comparing the estimated value of that option with the *cost of creating the option*, not with the costs of exercising it.[14]

By viewing the first role of good strategy as the creation of a portfolio of options for the future, that strategy's success does not rest on the ability to predict continuing trends. Depending on the future environment, not all options will be exercised. However, those discarded are not wasted, but serve the useful purpose of insurance against an uncertain future.

## Step 4. Combine planning and opportunism

Planning and opportunism both have an essential role in the strategy process. A company can plan the successive capabilities needed and new potential markets in order to create sufficient strategic space — the room to maneuver in the future. It can plan the proactive creation of strategic options.

A company cannot plan the precise options to select: exactly which products and services will it sell to which customers in which markets at what prices? That is the purview of opportunism. For example, as part of building its "localization" capability, Acer began assembling its product in a suburb of Mexico City in 1993. By careful planning, it expanded its strategic options in respect of the market. During the peso crisis in December 1994, Acer exploited one of these strategic options. Having shifted a significant part of its cost structure to Mexico, it broke with the industry custom of quoting U.S. dollar prices and listed its products in pesos. When the computer market shrank by 40 percent, it launched a new model, continued to buy TV time, and targeted new customers, winning prestigious contracts to supply the national, state-owned power company and the main public university. Its market share rocketed, allowing it to retain a 32 percent market share when the market improved by 1996. Through timely opportunism, Acer decisively exercised its option to its advantage. It didn't predict the peso crisis, but when unexpected events unfolded, it had the strategic option to turn adversity to its advantage.

Another example of the interplay between strategic options and unexpected opportunities is the introduction of Acer's "fast food" model of PC supply. When Acer began to build its original localization capability, it didn't need to know exactly how to use it. It knew that localization would become an important capability and that, having analyzed the possibilities, the investment in this option was justified. Having this strategic option allowed Acer to outpace its competitors when the market moved toward "customized" PCs. Opportunism guided Acer's tactics for using its localization capability and market knowledge to gain a specific competitive advantage.

A critical element is to keep tactical opportunism within the bounds of the company's overall direction and to rule out the options that would cause it to wander from its long-term mission. The selection and management of a portfolio of options, with some options expiring and new ones added, based on the decision rules I discussed earlier, is a good way to set bounds. To make "bounded opportunism" work in practice, every manager should ask the following question about each tactical opportunity: "Is it a weed or a flower?" An unexpected opportunity that diverts the company from pursuing its long-term mission is a "weed." Meanwhile, opportunities that allow it to take advantage of its options to accelerate progress toward long-term goals are "flowers." In this way, top management can set bounds that are sensitively applied without crushing the organization's entrepreneurial spirit.

## Conclusion

Traditional strategic planning draws from forecasts of parameters like market growth, prices, exchange rates, and input costs. As *The Economist* experiment aptly demonstrates, we are unable to predict those variables five or ten years in advance with any accuracy. Spreadsheets try to predict exactly what products and services to sell to which customers in what volumes at what prices. In the process, these traditional frameworks lead to betting everything on straight-line strategies and risk boxing the company into a corner when reality inevitably turns out differently from predictions.

The trends we can predict with reasonable confidence — more localization, increased variety, and faster response times — can't be acted on by classic strategic planning systems driven by forecasts of sales, prices, and costs. Strategic planning systems deploy exactly the input we have no way to accurately predict, while discarding the new capabilities and knowledge of new market segments that will give companies the option to respond to broad, long-term trends.

To break from this trap, companies need to understand that successful strategy must combine both planning and opportunism. Planning builds new capabilities and augments knowledge of new, potential markets and customer behavior. Because investing in these options costs money, however, the number of strategic options must be optimized and managed. Actively managing a portfolio of strategic options allows a company room to maneuver and reposition. Short-term opportunism must determine which precise option a company chooses to exercise.

## References

The author would like to thank José F. P. dos Santos, Constantinos Markides, and the anonymous referees for their helpful comments on an earlier draft. Remaining errors are, of course, the responsibility of the author.

1 These techniques are well described in: R. M. Grant, Contemporary Strategy Analysis, second edition (Oxford: Blackwell Business, 1995).

2 See I. Dierickx and and K. Cool, "Asset Stock Accumulation and Sustainability of Competitive Advantage," *Management Science*, volume 35, December 1989, pp. 1504–1514.

3 R. Wrubel, "The Ghost of Andy Carnegie?." *Financial World*, volume 1, September 1992, p. 50.

4 P. Lasserre and C. Butler. "The Inchcape Group (A): The End of an Era" (Fontainebleau, France INSEAD, case 04/93-317, 1993); and C. Kennedy, "Can Two Hongs Get It Right?," *Director*, February 1996, pp. 34–40.

5 See, for example:
M. Lubatkin and S. Chetterjee, "Extending Modern Portfolio Theory to the Domain of Corporate Strategy: Does it Apply?." *Academy of Management Journal*, volume 37, September 1994, pp. 109–36.

6 A. DeMeyer, "E* Trade, Charles Schwab, and Yahoo!: The Transformation of On-line Brokerage" (Fontainebleau, France: INSEAD, case 05/98-4757. 1998).

7 P. J. H. Schoemaker, "Strategy, Complexity, and Economic Rent," *Management Science*, volume 36, October 1990, pp. 31–43.

8 D. Leonard-Barton, *Wellsprings of Knowledge* (Boston: Harvard Business School Press, 1995).

9 P. J. Williamson and D. Clyde-Smith, "The Acer Group: Building an Asian Multinational (Fontainebleau, France: INSEAD, case 01/98-4712, 1998).

10 "Laptops from Lapland," *The Economist*, 6 September 1997, pp. 89–90.

11 J. Naisbitt, *Megatrends* (New York: Simon & Schuster, 1984).

12 See, for example:
C. A. R. McNulty, "Scenario Development for Corporate Planning," *Futures*, April 1977; or A. de Geus, "Planning as Learning," *Harvard Business Review*, volume 66, March–April 1988, pp. 70–74.

13 G. Hamel and C. K. Prahalad, *Competing for the Future* (Boston: Harvard Business School Press, 1994), p. 145.

14 The subject of valuing real options is a large topic in its own right. There is insufficient space to cover it here. For relevant techniques and methods, see, for example:
M. Amram and N. Kulatilaka, *Real Options: Managing Strategic Investment in an Uncertain World* (Boston: Harvard Business School Press, 1999).

# Part 3

# STRATEGY REFLECTING THE ORGANISATION

# 35

# THREE MODELS OF STRATEGY[1]

*Ellen Earle Chaffee*

Source: *Academy of Management Review* 10(1) (1985): 89–98.

Three models of strategy that are implicit in the literature are described—linear, adaptive, and interpretive. Their similarity to Boulding's (1956) hierarchical levels of system complexity is noted. The strategy construct is multifaceted, and it has evolved to a level of complexity almost matching that of organizations themselves.

Researchers and practitioners have used the term strategy freely—researchers have even measured it—for over two decades. Those who refer to strategy generally believe that they are all working with the same mental model. No controversy surrounds the question of its existence; no debate has arisen regarding the nature of its anchoring concept.

Yet virtually everyone writing on strategy agrees that no consensus on its definition exists (Bourgeois, 1980; Gluck, Kaufman, & Walleck, 1982; Glueck, 1980; Hatten, 1979; Hofer & Schendel, 1978; Lenz, 1980b; Rumelt, 1979; Spender, 1979; Steiner, 1979). Hambrick (1983) suggested that this lack of consistency is due to two factors. First, he pointed out, strategy is multidimensional. Second, strategy must be situational and, accordingly, it will vary by industry.

The literature affirms Hambrick's assessment that strategy is not only multidimensional and situational but that such characteristics are likely to make any consensus on definition difficult. Strategy also suffers from another, more fundamental problem; that is, the term strategy has been referring to three distinguishable mental models, rather than the single model that most discussions assume. Beyond reflecting various authors' semantic preferences, the multiple definitions reflect three distinct, and in some ways conflicting, views on strategy. This paper seeks to analyze the ways strategy has been defined and operationalized in previous treatises and studies.

It highlights those aspects of strategy on which authors in the field appear to agree and suggests three strategy models that are implicit in the literature.

## Strategy: areas of agreement

A basic premise of thinking about strategy concerns the inseparability of organization and environment (Biggadike, 1981; Lenz, 1980a). The organization uses strategy to deal with changing environments. Because change brings novel combinations of circumstances to the organization, the substance of strategy remains unstructured, unprogrammed, nonroutine, and nonrepetitive (Mason & Mitroff, 1981; Mazzolini, 1981; Miles & Cameron, 1982; Narayanan & Fahey, 1982; Van Cauwenbergh & Cool, 1982). Not only are strategic decisions related to the environment and nonroutine, but they also are considered to be important enough to affect the overall welfare of the organization (Hambrick, 1980).

Theorists who segment the strategy construct implicitly agree that the study of strategy includes both the actions taken, or the content of strategy, and the processes by which actions are decided and implemented. They agree that intended, emergent, and realized strategies may differ from one another. Moreover, they agree that firms may have both corporate strategy ("What businesses shall we be in?") and business strategy ("How shall we compete in each business?"). Finally, they concur that the making of strategy involves conceptual as well as analytical exercises. Some authors stress the analytical dimension more than others, but most affirm that the heart of strategy making is the conceptual work done by leaders of the organization.

Beyond these general factors, agreement breaks down. Yet the differences in point of view are rarely analyzed. Only the existence of multiple definitions of strategy is noted and, as in Mintzberg (1973), definitions are sometimes grouped by type. Analysis reveals that the strategy definitions in the literature cluster into three distinct groups.

## Three models of strategy

The name assigned to each model of strategy represents its primary focus. Although these descriptions represent a collective version of similar views, each model also includes many variations of its central theme. Moreover, as will be shown later, the three models are not independent. However, for present purposes, the three models will be treated according to their independent descriptions in the literature.

### *Model I: Linear strategy*

The first model to be widely adopted is linear and focuses on planning. The term linear was chosen because it connotes the methodical, directed, sequential action involved in planning. This model is inherent in Chandler's definition of strategy.

> Strategy is the determination of the basic long-term goals of an enterprise, and the adoption of courses of action and the allocation of resources necessary for carrying out these goals.
>
> (1962. p. 13)

According to the linear view, strategy consists of integrated decisions, actions, or plans that will set and achieve viable organizational goals. Both goals and the means of achieving them are results of strategic decision. To reach these goals, organizations vary their links with the environment by changing their products or markets or by performing other entrepreneurial actions. Terms associated with the linear model include strategic planning, strategy formulation, and strategy implementation.

The linear model portrays top managers as having considerable capacity to change the organization. The environment is, implicitly, a necessary nuisance "out there" that is composed mainly of competitors. Top managers go through a prototypical rational decision making process. They identify their goals, generate alternative methods of achieving them, weigh the likelihood that alternative methods will succeed, and then decide which ones to implement. In the course of this process, managers capitalize on those future trends and events that are favorable and avoid or counteract those that are not. Because this model was developed primarily for profit-seeking businesses, two of its important measures of results are profit and productivity.

Several assumptions that underlie the linear model are not made explicit in most discussions, but they nonetheless follow from the authors' tendency to emphasize planning and forecasting. For example:

> Conceptually, the process [of strategic planning] is simple: managers at every level of a hierarchy must ultimately agree on a detailed, integrated plan of action for the coming year; they [start] with the delineation of corporate objectives and [conclude] with the preparation of a one-or two-year profit plan.
>
> (Lorange & Vancil, 1976, p. 75)

If a sequential planning process is to succeed, the organization needs to be tightly coupled, so that all decisions made at the top can be implemented throughout the organization. This tight coupling assumption enables intentions to become actions. A second assumption arises from the time-consuming and forward-looking nature of planning. In other words, though decisions made today are based on beliefs about future conditions, they may not be implemented until months, even years, from now. In order to believe that making such decisions is not a waste of time, one must assume either

*Table 1* Summary of Linear Strategy.

| *Variable* | *Linear Strategy* |
|---|---|
| Sample definition | "... determination of the basic longterm *goals* of an enterprise, and the adoption of courses of *action* and the allocation of resources necessary for carrying out these *goals*" (Chandler, 1962, p. 13, italics added). |
| Nature of strategy | Decisions, actions, plans Integrated |
| Focus for strategy | Means, ends |
| Aim of strategy | Goal achievement |
| Strategic behaviors | Change markets, products |
| Associated terms | Strategic planning, strategy formulation and implementation |
| Associated measures | Formal planning, new products, configuration of products or businesses, market segmentation and focus, market segmentation and focus, market share, merger/ acquisition, product diversity |
| Associated authors[a] | Chandler, 1962<br>Cannon, 1968<br>Learned, Christensen, Andrews, & Guth, 1969<br>Gilmore, 1970<br>Andrews, 1971<br>Child, 1972<br>Drucker, 1974<br>Paine & Naumes, 1974<br>Glueck, 1976<br>Lorange & Vancil, 1976<br>Steiner & Miner, 1977 |

[a]Classified by their *definitions* of strategy. Classification is not intended to imply that authors omit discussion of topics relevant to other models.

that the environment is relatively predictable or else that the organization is well-insulated from the environment. Also, most authors explicitly assume that organizations have goals and that accomplishing goals is the most important outcome of strategy.

Major characteristics of the linear model and the names of several authors whose definitions of strategy are consistent with this model are listed in Table 1. Note that though the authors' definitions of strategy constitute grounds for classifying them in the model, nearly all authors extend their discussions of strategy into areas that are relevant to more than one model.

As the dates in these citations suggest, interest in the linear model waned in the mid-1970s. Ansoff and Hayes (1976) suggested that the emphasis moved away from the linear model as the strategic problem came to be seen as much more complex. Not only does it involve several dimensions of the managerial problem and the process, but also technical, economic, informational, psychological, and political variables as well. The model that arose next is labeled here the adaptive model of strategy.

### *Model II: Adaptive strategy*

Hofer's definition typifies the adaptive model of strategy, characterizing it as

> concerned with the development of a viable match between the opportunities and risks present in the external environment and the organization's capabilities and resources for exploiting these opportunities.
>
> (1973, p. 3)

The organization is expected continually to assess external and internal conditions. Assessment then leads to adjustments in the organization or in its relevant environment that will create "satisfactory alignments of environmental opportunities and risks, on the one hand, and organizational capabilities and resources, on the other" (Miles & Cameron, 1982, p. 14).

The adaptive model differs from the linear model in several ways. First, monitoring the environment and making changes are simultaneous and continuous functions in the adaptive model. The time lag for planning that is implicit in the linear model is not present. For example, Miles and Snow (1978) portray strategic adaptation as recurring and overlapping cycles with three phases: the entrepreneurial phase (choice of domain), the engineering phase (choice of technology), and the administrative phase (rationalizing structure and process, and identifying areas for future innovation).

Second, the adaptive model does not deal as emphatically as the linear model with decisions about goals. Instead, it tends to focus the manager's attention on means, and the "goal" is represented by coalignment of the organization with its environment. Third, the adaptive model's definition of strategic behaviors goes beyond that of the linear model to incorporate not only major changes in products and markets, but also subtle changes in style, marketing, quality, and other nuances (Hofer, 1976a; Shirley, 1982).

A fourth difference follows from the relative unimportance of advance planning in the adaptive model. Thus, as might be expected, strategy is less centralized in top management, more multifaceted, and generally less integrated than in the linear model. However, top managers in the adaptive model still assume overall responsibility for guiding strategy development.

Finally, in the adaptive model the environment is considered to be a complex organizational life support system, consisting of trends, events, competitors, and stakeholders. The boundary between the organization and its environment is highly permeable, and the environment is a major focus of attention in determining organizational action. Whether taken proactively or reactively. action is responsive to the nature and magnitude of perceived or anticipated environmental pressures.

In sum, the adaptive model relies heavily on an evolutionary biological model of organizations. The analogy is made explicit in the following passage:

> As a descriptive tool, strategy is the analog of the biologist's method of "explaining" the structure and the behavior of organisms by pointing out the functionality of each attribute in a total system (or strategy) designed to cope with or inhabit a particular niche. The normative use of strategy has no counterpart in biology (as yet!), but might be thought of as the problem of designing a living creature . . . to exist within some environment . . .
>
> (Rumelt, 1979, pp. 197–198)

As interest in strategy as adaptation increased so, too, did attention to the processes by which strategy arises and is carried out. Beginning with Mintzberg's (1973) modes of strategy making, a number of discussions have been presented to deal with the social, political, and interactive components of strategy (Fahey, 1981; Ginter & White, 1982; Greenwood & Thomas, 1981; Guth, 1976; Hofer, 1976b; E. Murray, 1978; J. Murray, 1978–79; Narayanan & Fahey, 1982; Tabatoni & Jarniou, 1976). Each of the authors dealt with organizational processes in the adaptive strategy model.

Adaptive strategy rests on several assumptions. The organization and its environment are assumed to be more open to each other than is implied in the linear model. The environment is more dynamic and less susceptible to prediction in the adaptive model. It consists of competitors, trends, and—of increasing importance—stake-holders. Rather than assuming that the organization must *deal with* the environment, the adaptive model assumes that the organization must *change with* the environment.

The adaptive model attempts to take more variables and more propensity for change into account than does the linear model. Table 2 lists terms that reflect this complexity, along with those authors whose strategy definitions fit the adaptive model. It also outlines the characteristics of the model. A number of authors using the adaptive model suggest that it can successfully handle greater complexity and more variables than the linear model. However, opinion is mounting that the situation is complex in other ways. To meet this need, a third model of strategy is emerging.

### *Model III: Interpretive strategy*

Development of interpretive strategy parallels recent interest in corporate culture and symbolic management outside the strategy literature (Dandridge, Mitroff, & Joyce, 1980; Deal & Kennedy, 1982; Feldman & March, 1981;

*Table 2* Summary of Adaptive Strategy.

| *Variable* | *Adaptive Strategy* |
|---|---|
| Sample definition | ". . . concerned with the development of a viable match between the opportunities and risks present in the external environment and the organization's capabilities and resources for exploiting those opportunities" (Hofer, 1973, p. 3). |
| Nature of strategy | Achieving a "match"<br>Multifaceted |
| Focus for strategy | Means |
| Aim of strategy | Coalignment with the environment |
| Strategic behaviors | Change style, marketing, quality |
| Associated terms | Strategic management, strategic choice, strategic predisposition, strategic design, strategic fit, strategic thrust, niche |
| Associated measures | Price, distribution policy, marketing expenditure and intensity, product differentiation, authority changes, proactiveness, risk taking, multiplexity, integration, futurity, adaptiveness, uniqueness |
| Associated authors[a] | Hofer, 1973<br>Guth, 1976<br>Hofer & Schendel, 1978<br>Litschert & Bonham, 1978<br>Miles, Snow, Meyer, & Coleman, 1978<br>Miller & Friesen, 1978<br>Mintzberg, 1978<br>Dill, 1979<br>Steiner, 1979<br>Rumelt, 1979<br>Hambrick, 1980<br>Bourgeois, 1980<br>Snow & Hambrick, 1980<br>Quinn, 1980<br>Jemison, 1981<br>Kotler & Murphy, 1981<br>Green & Jones, 1981<br>Hayman, 1981<br>Jauch & Osborn, 1981<br>Gluck *et al.*, 1982<br>Chackravarthy, 1982<br>Hatten, 1982<br>Shirley, 1982<br>Camillus, 1982<br>Miles & Cameron, 1982<br>Galbraith & Schendel, 1983 |

[a]Classified by their *definitions* of strategy. Classification is not intended to imply that authors omit discussion of topics relevant to other models.

Meyer & Rowan, 1977; Peters, 1978 Peters & Waterman, 1982; Pfeffer, 1981; Smircich & Morgan, 1982; Weick & Daft, 1983). The parameters of the emerging interpretive model of strategy are still unclear. However, a recurring theme suggests that the model is based on a social contract, rather than an organismic or biological view of the organization (Keeley, 1980) that fits well with the adaptive model. The social contract view portrays the organization as a collection of cooperative agreements entered into by individuals with free will. The organization's existence relies on its ability to attract enough individuals to cooperate in mutually beneficial exchange.

The interpretive model of strategy further assumes that reality is socially constructed (Berger & Luckmann, 1966). That is, reality is not something objective or external to the perceiver that can be apprehended correctly or incorrectly. Rather, reality is defined through a process of social interchange in which perceptions are affirmed, modified, or replaced according to their apparent congruence with the perceptions of others.

Strategy in the interpretive model might be defined as orienting metaphors or frames of reference that allow the organization and its environment to be understood by organizational stakeholders. On this basis, stakeholders are motivated to believe and to act in ways that are expected to produce favorable results for the organization. "Metaphors" is plural in this definition because the maintenance of social ties in the organization precludes enforcing agreement on a single interpretation (Weick & Daft, 1983).

Pettigrew (1977) provided an early example of the interpretive model by defining strategy as the emerging product of the partial resolution of environmental and intraorganizational dilemmas. Although his emphasis on the political and processual nature of strategy might be considered compatible with the adaptive model, he offered several innovative contributions. Among them are: (1) his interest in the management of meaning and symbol construction as central components of strategy and (2) his emphasis on legitimacy, rather than profit, productivity, or other typical goals of strategy.

Van Cauwenbergh and Cool (1982) defined strategy broadly as calculated behavior in nonprogrammed situations. They went on to posit middle management's central position in the strategy formulation process, as well as to point out that managing the organizational culture is a powerful tool in the hands of top management. The authors concluded by suggesting that their views differed from the traditional strategy literature in three ways: (1) organizational reality is incoherent in nature, not coherent; (2) strategy is an organization-wide activity, not just a top management concern; and (3) motivation, not information, is the critical factor in achieving adequate strategic behavior. Congruent with these authors' interest in organizational culture, Dirsmith and Covaleski dealt with what they called strategic norms, or

*Table 3* Summary of Interpretive Strategy.

| *Variable* | *Interpretive Strategy* |
|---|---|
| Sample definition | Orienting metaphors constructed for the purpose of conceptualizing and guiding individual attitudes of organizational participants |
| Nature of strategy | Metaphor<br>Interpretive |
| Focus for strategy | Participants and potential participants in the organization |
| Aim of strategy | Legitimacy |
| Strategic behaviors | Develop symbols, improve interactions and relationships |
| Associated terms | Strategic norms |
| Associated measures | Measures must be derived from context, may require qualitative assessment |
| Associated authors[a] | Pettigrew. 1977<br>Van Cauwenbergh & Cool, 1982<br>Dirsmith & Covaleski, 1983<br>Chaffee, 1984 |

[a]Classified by their *definitions* of strategy. Classification is not intended to imply that authors omit discussion of topics relevant to other models.

> institutional level action postures . . . that serve to guide acceptable behavior. [S]trategic norms involve the establishment of maps of reality or images held of organizations and environments.
>
> (1983, p. 137)

The new themes in these writings suggest a strategy model that depends heavily on symbols and norms. Hatten (1979) saw this change as moving from the goal orientation of the linear model to a focus on desired relationships, such as those involving sources of inputs or customers. He envisaged a new theory of strategy that was oriented toward managerial perceptions, conflict and consensus, as well as the importance of language. The relatively few entries in Table 3 indicate that the model is too new to have become well-developed.

Rather than emphasizing *changing with* the environment, as is true of the adaptive model, interpretive strategy mimics linear strategy in its emphasis on *dealing with* the environment. There is, however, an important difference. The linear strategist deals with the environment by means of organizational actions that are intended to affect relations instrumentally, but the interpretive strategist deals with the environment through symbolic actions and communication.

Interpretive strategy, like adaptive strategy, assumes that the organization and its environment constitute an open system. But in interpretive strategy the organization's leaders shape the attitudes of participants and potential participants toward the organization and its outputs; they do not make physical changes in the outputs. This attitude change seeks to increase credibility for the organization or its output. In this regard, interpretive strategy overlaps with the adaptive model. For example, when an adaptive strategist focuses on marketing to enhance product credibility, the strategist's behavior could be classified as interpretive. Because strategy is multifaceted, however, examining marketing in combination with other strategic moves permits surer classification into either the adaptive or interpretive model.

A final noteworthy distinction between the adaptive and interpretive models relates to the ways in which each conceptualizes complexity. Adaptive strategy arose from and attempts to deal with structural complexity, notably conflicting and changing demands for organizational output. Interpretive strategy emphasizes attitudinal and cognitive complexity among diverse stakeholders in the organization.

Each of the three models may be summarized briefly. In linear strategy, leaders of the organization plan how they will deal with competitors to achieve their organization's goals. In adaptive strategy, the organization and its parts change, proactively or reactively, in order to be aligned with consumer preferences. In interpretive strategy, organizational representatives convey meanings that are intended to motivate stakeholders in ways that favor the organization. Each model provides a way of describing a certain aspect of organizational functioning to which the term *strategy* has been applied. By analogy, one would have three descriptions of a single phenomenon if a geologist, a climatologist, and a poet were to model the Grand Canyon.

One value of diverse models, whether they relate to strategy or the Grand Canyon, is that they provide options. In future development of strategy, one might delineate the circumstances under which one model of strategy is more appropriate than the others. However, before such delineation is warranted, the models and their interrelationships require further theoretical attention.

As noted earlier, the three strategy models may not be independent of one another, although so far they have been treated separately in both the literature cited and this discussion. The basis for suggesting that the models are interrelated is that they show some similarity to a well-known hierarchy of systems in which each level incorporates the less complex levels that precede it [Boulding, 1956]. If the strategy models were analogous to the systems hierarchy, the relationships among the models would also be hierarchical. The systems hierarchy has certain similarities to the three strategy models. Certain characteristics at each set of system levels match those of one of the strategy models. Furthermore, similarities between each level of systems and one of the strategy models suggest that an organization that functions at a given level in the systems hierarchy will benefit from using the corresponding model of strategy.

Therefore, relating the strategy models to the systems hierarchy makes three contributions toward elaborating on the strategy construct. First, it suggests a means of ordering and interrelating the disparate, more narrowly focused definitions of strategy in the existing literature. Second, discrepancies between system levels and strategy models suggest areas in which the models could profitably be developed. Third, the analogy provides a bridge for moving from a survey of theoretical literature to its implications for practice.

## The hierarchy of strategy models

Boulding (1956) developed a nine-level hierarchical framework that was keyed to all classes of systems, including human systems. At the most basic level were three classes that Pondy and Mitroff (1979) grouped together under the metaphor of a machine. In the highest of the three machine classes, a control mechanism regulates system behavior according to an externally prescribed target or criterion. Information flows between the regulator and the system operator. Linear strategy shows similar properties in that the executive is expected to control the organization according to predetermined goals and to change the goals when circumstances warrant.

The three intermediate classes constitute the biological set, the highest of which is the internal image system. At this level, because the system has differentiated receptors, it is imbued with detailed awareness of its environment. Awareness is organized into an image, but the system is not self-conscious. Other characteristics of the biological set include its having the same internal differentiation as the environment, as well as its having a generating mechanism that produces behavior. Adaptive strategy corresponds to the biological level, in that the model calls for the organization to scan, anticipate, and respond to various elements in its environment.

Boulding's most complex set of system levels is the cultural set. It consists of the symbol processing level, in which the system is a self-conscious user of language, and the multicephalous level, a collection of individuals acting in concert and using elaborate systems of shared meaning. Boulding's third level in the cultural set is transcendental, not fully specified. The cultural set is analogous to interpretive strategy. Weick and Daft (1983) place interpretation at level 6, the highest biological level, but they identify interpretation as a cultural phenomenon. Wherever it is placed, interpretive strategy, like the cultural level of systems, emphasizes the importance of symbol manipulation, shared meaning, and cooperative actions of individuals. Although the emphases are the same, interpretive strategy is not as fully developed as its correspondence to the cultural level might imply.

Each level in Boulding's hierarchy subsumes those that preceded it. If the same were true of the strategy models, then adaptive strategy would incorporate linear strategy, and interpretive strategy would incorporate both adaptive and linear strategies. Although the evolution of the strategy construct proceeded sequentially through the hierarchy, beginning at the machine level and recently reaching the cultural level, the shift from each level to the next abandoned, rather than incorporated, the preceding level(s). Boulding's cultural level is more complex than his biological level precisely because it builds on the base of the machine and biological levels. Interpretive strategy ignores linear and adaptive strategy. Dealing with stakeholder attitudes is not inherently more complex than dealing with consumer preferences, nor is conveying productive interpretations necessarily more complex than achieving coalignment with the environment. No interpretive strategist has evaluated the extent to which linear and adaptive strategy are subsumed in the "higher" model. Moreover, the adaptive strategists have largely ignored the linear model.

Some hints at relating the three models have appeared in the literature. For example, Weick and Daft (1983) suggested that one criterion of effective interpretation is detailed knowledge of the particulars of the environment (adaptive model) so that the phenomenon to be interpreted may be seen in context. Another paper implied that the models constitute a series of stages through which the organization itself moves over time as it becomes more sophisticated and adept at strategic management (Gluck *et al.*, 1982). The authors stated that organizations start with financial and forecast-based planning (linear model), then shift to strategic analysis (adaptive model), and finally achieve strategic management (interpretive model). Cummings (1983) outlined two major themes in the literature: management by information (linear/adaptive) and management by ideology (interpretive). Cummings argued that both themes must be integrated to achieve an instrumental organization that serves the purposes of its participants. But he did not explain in operational terms how integration occurs. In the only empirical study that relates directly to the strategy models, Chaffee (1984) found that organizations recovering from decline used adaptive strategy, but it was their use of interpretive strategy that differentiated them from organizations unable to recover. However, like Cummings and like Gluck and his colleagues, Chaffee did not deal with how or why the two models were integrated in organizational functioning.

It is important to integrate each lower level model with models that represent more complex systems because organizations exhibit properties of all levels of system complexity. Adaptive and interpretive strategies that ignore less complex strategy models ignore the foundations on which they must be built if they are to reflect organizational reality. Furthermore, a comprehensive interpretive strategy probably requires some planning as would fit with a linear strategy and some organizational change as would fit with an adaptive strategy; and a viable adaptive strategy may well require some linear planning. But rather than building toward a sophisticated construct that equals the complexities for which it is intended, strategists have selected three key themes and treated them separately. Each may have value as far as it goes, but none integrates all levels of complexity and options for action that are inherent in an organization.

Finding three models of strategy holds implications for organizations, for managers, and for future development of the strategy construct. Even at this point, without deepening the adaptive and interpretive models to include lower levels of complexity, the analysis specifies three diverse ways of viewing the organizational problem and three classes of potential solutions. The models may be used conceptually to examine an organizational situation and consider alternatives for coping with it. For example, a manager might consider whether predictions about the declining demand for a product are: (a) based on firm evidence that will provide sufficient lead time for a planning task force to convene and generate alternatives to deal with the decline, (b) fundamental shifts in consumer preferences that could be addressed by modifying the product or replacing it with another, or (c) symptomatic of a loss of confidence among the buying public that could be remedied by better marketing to build legitimacy.

Futhermore, strategic decision making may profit from an analysis of a given situation's level of complexity. If an organization or a problem exhibits characteristics that are predominantly mechanistic, a linear strategy is called for. Adaptive strategies can be applied when issues of supply and demand are especially salient. Complex interpretive strategies may be reserved for situations in which modifying the attitudes of organizational stakeholders is the primary key to success.

The full value of strategy cannot be realized in practical terms, however, until theorists expand the construct to reflect the real complexities of organizations. Each successive level of strategy should incorporate those that are less complex. Then researchers can examine the ways this construct behaves in real organizations. Ultimately, the construct may emerge as a unitary merger of the three models, such as an interpretive model that incorporates adaptive and linear strategy. Or it may emerge as a hierarchy of three models: a mechanistic linear model; a biological adaptive model incorporating linear strategy; and a cultural interpretive model, incorporating both linear and adaptive strategy. Theoreticians also may find value in still greater model differentiation. Perhaps this can be done by specifying a hierarchy that contains a model of strategy for each of Boulding's nine levels of system complexity.

Whatever the end products maybe—and whether or not they finally relate to Boulding's hierarchy—it is time for strategy theoreticians and researchers to begin putting the pieces together. During the past 20 years, the strategy literature has greatly evolved. Today, in fact, it has almost arrived at the point at which it is capable of reflecting the actual level of complexity at which organizations operate. The way is now open to capitalize, both theoretically and empirically, on the richness of that complexity.

## Note

1 The research reported here was supported by a contract (#400-83-0009) from the National Institute of Education. An abbreviated version was presented at the annual meeting of the Academy of Management, Boston, 1984, and appears in the *Proceedings* of the meeting. The author is grateful to Jane Dutton for several excellent suggestions.

## References

Andrews, K. R. *The concept of corporate strategy*. Homewood, IL: Irwin, 1971.

Ansoff, H. I., & Hayes, R. L. Introduction. In H. I. Ansoff, R. P. Declerck, & R. L. Hayes (Eds.), *From strategic planning to strategic management*. New York: Wiley, 1976, 1–12.

Berger, P., & Luckmann, T. *The social construction of reality*. New York: Doubleday, 1966.

Biggadike, E. R. The contributions of marketing to strategic management. *Academy of Management Review*, 1981, 6, 621–632.

Boulding, K. E. General systems theory—The skeleton of science. *Management Science*, 1956, 2, 197–208.

Bourgeois, L. J., III. Strategy and environment: A conceptual integration. *Academy of Management Review*, 1980, 5, 25–39.

Camillus, J. G. Reconciling logical incrementalism and synoptic formalism—An integrated approach to designing strategy planning processes. *Strategic Management Journal*, 1982, 3, 227–283.

Cannon, J. T. *Business strategy and policy*. New York: Harcourt Brace Jovanovich, 1968.

Chaffee, E. E. Successful strategic management in small private colleges. *Journal of Higher Education*, 1984, 55, 212–241.

Chakravarthy, B. S. Adaptation: A promising metaphor for strategic management. *Academy of Management Review*, 1982, 7, 35–44.

Chandler, A. D., Jr. *Strategy and structure*. Cambridge, MA: MIT Press, 1962.

Child, J. Organizational structure, environment, and performance: The role of strategic choice. *Sociology*, 1972, 6, 1–22.

Cummings, L. L. The logics of management. *Academy of Management Review*, 1983, 8, 532–538.

Dandridge, T. C., Mitroff. I., & Joyce, W. F. Organizational symbolism: A topic to expand organizational analysis. *Academy of Management Review*, 1980, 5, 77–82.

Deal, T. E., & Kennedy, A. A. *Corporate cultures: The rites and rituals of corporate life*. Reading. MA: Addison-Wesley, 1982.

Dill, W. R. Commentary. In D. E. Schendel & C. W. Hofer (Eds.), *Strategic management: A new view of business policy and planning*. Boston: Little, Brown, 1979, 47–51.

Dirsmith, M. W., & Covaleski, M. A. Strategy, external communication and environment context. *Strategic Management Journal*, 1983, 4, 137–151.

Drucker, P. F. *Management: Tasks, responsibilities, practices*. New York: Harper & Row, 1974.

Fahey, L. On strategic management decision processes. *Strategic Management Journal*, 1981, 2, 43–60.

Feldman, M., & March, J. G. Information in organizations as signal and symbol. *Administrative Science Quarterly*, 1981, 26, 171–186.

Galbraith, C., & Schendel, D. An empirical analysis of strategy types. *Strategic Management Journal*. 1983, 4, 153–173.

Gilmore, F. F. Formulating strategy in smaller companies. *Harvard Business Review*, 1970, 49(5), 71–81.

Ginter, P. M., & White, D. D. A social learning approach to strategic management: Toward a theoretical foundation. *Academy of Management Review*, 1982, 7, 253–261.

Gluck, F., Kaufman, S., & Walleck, A. S. The four phases of strategic management. *Journal of Business Strategy*, 1982, 2(3), 9–21.

Glueck, W. F. *Business policy: Strategy formation and management action*. New York: McGraw-Hill, 1976.

Glueck, W. F. *Strategic management and business policy*. New York: McGraw-Hill, 1980.

Green, J., & Jones, T. Strategic development as a means of organizational change: Four case histories. *Long Range Planning*, 1981, 14(3), 58–67.

Greenwood, P., & Thomas, H. A review of analytical models in strategic planning. *Omega*, 1981, 9(4), 397–417.

Guth, W. D. Toward a social system theory of corporate strategy. *Journal of Business*, 1976, 49, 374–388.

Hambrick, D. C. Operationalizing the concept of business-level strategy in research. *Academy of Management Review*, 1980, 5, 567–575.

Hambrick, D. C. Some tests of the effectiveness and functional attributes of Miles and Snow's strategic types. *Academy of Management Journal*, 1983, 26, 5–25.

Hatten, K. J. Quantitative research methods in strategic management. In D. E. Schendel & C. W. Hofer (Eds.), *Strategic management: A new view of business policy and planning*. Boston: Little, Brown, 1979, 448–467.

Hatten, M. L. Strategic management in not-far-profit organizations. *Strategic Management Journal*, 1982, 3, 89–104.

Hayman, J. *Relationship of strategic planning and future methodologies*. Paper presented at the 1981 Annual Convention of the AERA, Los Angeles, 1981.

Hofer, C. W. Some preliminary research on patterns of strategic behavior. *Academy of Management Proceedings*, 1973, 46–59.

Hofer, C. W. *Conceptual scheme for formulating a total business strategy*. Boston: HBS Case Services, 1976a.

Hofer, C. W. Research on strategic planning: A survey of past studies and suggestions for future efforts. *Journal of Economics and Business*. 1976b, 28, 261–286.

Hofer, C. W., & Schendel, D. *Strategy formulation: Analytical concepts*. St. Paul, MN: West, 1978.

Jauch, L. R., & Osborn, R. N. Toward an integrated theory of strategy. *Academy of Management Review*, 1981, 6, 491–498.

Jemison, D. B. The contributions of administrative behavior to strategic management. *Academy of Management Review*, 1981, 6, 633–642.

Keeley, M. Organizational analogy: A comparison of organismic and social contract models. *Administrative Science Quarterly*, 1980, 25, 337–362.

Kotler, P., & Murphy, P. E. Strategic planning for higher education. *Journal of Higher Education*, 1981, 52, 470–489.

Learned, E. P., Christensen, C. R., Andrews, K. R., & Guth, W. R. *Business policy*. Homewood, IL: Irwin, 1969.

Lenz, R. T. Strategic capability: A concept and framework for analysis. *Academy of Management Review*, 1980a, 5, 225–234.

Lenz, R. T. Environment, strategy, organization structure and performance: Patterns in one industry. *Strategic Management Journal*, 1980b, 1, 209–226.

Litschert, R. J., & Bonham, T. W. Conceptual models of strategy formulation. *Academy of Management Review*, 1978, 3, 211–219.

Lorange, P., & Vancil, R. F. How to design a strategic planning system. *Harvard Business Review*, 1976, 54(5), 75–81.

Mason, R. O., & Mitroff, I. I. *Challenging strategic planning assumptions*. New York: 1981.

Mazzolini, R. How strategic decisions are made. *Long Range Planning*, 1981, 14(3), 85–96.

Meyer, J. W., & Rowan, B. Institutionalized organizations: Formal structure as myth and ceremony. *American Journal of Sociology*, 1977, 83, 340–363.

Miles, R. E., & Snow, C. C. *Organizational strategy, structure, and process*. New York: McGraw-Hill, 1978.

Miles, R. E., Snow, C. C., Meyer, A. D., & Coleman, H. J., Jr. Organizational strategy, structure, and process. *Academy of Management Review*, 1978, 3, 546–563.

Miles, R. H., & Cameron, K. S. *Coffin nails and corporate strategies*. Englewood Cliffs, NJ: Prentice-Hall, 1982.

Miller, D., & Friesen, P. Archetypes of strategy formulation. *Management Science*, 1978, 24, 253–280.

Mintzberg, H. Strategy-making in three modes. *California Management Review*, 1973, 16(2), 44–53.

Mintzberg, H. Patterns in strategy formation. *Management Science*, 1978, 24, 934–948.

Murray, E. A. Strategic change as a negotiated outcome. *Management Science*, 1978, 24, 960–972.

Murray, J. A. Toward a contingency model of strategic decision. *International Studies of Management and Organization*, 1978–79, 8, 7–34.

Narayanan, V. K., & Fahey, L. The micro-politics of strategy formulation. *Academy of Management Review*, 1982, 7, 25–34.

Paine, F. T., & Naumes, W. *Strategy and policy formation: An integrative approach*. Philadelphia: Saunders, 1974.

Peters, T. J. Symbols, patterns, and settings: An optimistic case for getting things done. *Organizational Dynamics*, 1978, 7(2), 3–23.

Peters, T. J., & Waterman, R. H., Jr. *In search of excellence: Lessons from America's best-run companies*. New York: Harper & Row, 1982.

Pettigrew, A. M. Strategy formulation as a political process. *International Studies of Management and Organization*, 1977, 7, 78–87.

Pfeffer, J. Management as symbolic action: The creation and maintenance of organizational paradigms. In L. L. Cummings & B. M. Staw (Eds.), *Research in organizational behavior*. Greenwood, CT: JAI Press, 1981, 1–52.

Pondy, L. R., & Mitroff, I. I. Beyond open system models of organization. In B. M. Staw (Ed.), *Research in organizational behavior*. Greenwood, CT: JAI Press, 1979, 3–39.

Quinn, J. B. *Strategies for change: Logical incrementalism*. Homewood, IL: Irwin, 1980.

Rumelt, R. P. Evaluation of strategy: Theory and models. In D. E. Schendel & C. W. Hofer (Eds.), *Strategic management: A new view of business policy and planning*. Boston: Little, Brown. 1979, 196–212.

Shirley, R. C. Limiting the scope of strategy: A decision based approach. *Academy of Management Review*, 1982, 7, 262–268.

Smircich, L., & Morgan, G. Leadership: The management of meaning. *Journal of Applied Behavioral Science*, 1982, 18(3), 257–273.

Snow, C. C., & Hambrick, D. C. Measuring organizational strategies: Some theoretical and methodological problems. *Academy of Management Review*, 1980, 5, 527–538.

Spender, J. C. Commentary. In D. E. Schendel & C. W. Hofer (Eds.), *Strategic management: A new view of business policy and planning*. Boston: Little, Brown, 1979, 383–404.

Steiner, G. A. *Strategic planning*, New York: Free Press, 1979.

Steiner, G. A., & Miner, J. B. *Management policy and strategy*. New York: Macmillan, 1977.

Tabatoni, P., & Jarniou, P. The dynamics of norms in strategic management. In H. I. Ansoff, R. P. Decleick, & R. L. Hayes (Eds.), *From strategic planning to strategic management*. London: Wiley, 1976, 29–36.

Van Cauwenbergh, A., & Cool, K. Strategic management in a new framework. *Strategic Management Journal*, 1982, 3, 245–265.

Weick, K. E., & Daft, R. L. The effectiveness of interpretation systems. In K. S. Cameron & D. A. Whetten (Eds.), *Organizational effectiveness: A comparison of multiple models*. New York: Academic Press, 1983, 71–93.

36

# THE THEORY OF BUSINESS STRATEGY

*Carl Shapiro*

Source: *RAND Journal of Economics* 20(1) (1989): 125–37.

## 1. Introduction

The field of industrial organization has been transformed during the past twenty years. In the 1950s and 1960s, I.O. was predominantly an empirical field with little theory to guide either industry analysis or cross-section regression studies. During the 1980s, by contrast, there has been an intense flurry of activity in I.O. devoted to the development of new theory. This new wave of research consists almost exclusively of game-theoretic studies of behavior and performance in imperfectly competitive markets.

In his companion piece Franklin Fisher argues that the game-theoretic approach to industrial organization has been unsuccessful. My aim here is to provide one participant's view of what industrial organization economists have learned from the recent theoretical research and where the field of industrial organization should go during the 1990s.

## 2. The theory of business strategy

Industrial organization economists are both blessed and cursed: our field encompasses a wide range of business behavior that is a rich arena in which to apply economic principles, but the very richness of business strategy defies simple and general theories. In analyzing behavior in concentrated markets, one must face questions like these: What is the timing of investment and pricing decisions? Which costs are recoverable and which are sunk? What information does each firm have about its rivals' actions or market conditions, and when does the firm acquire this information?

Game theory has emerged as the predominant methodology for analyzing business strategy. Much of the work in the new I.O. involves specifying a game among competing firms and solving that game in extensive form using the noncooperative solution concept of Nash equilibrium or one of its refinements. Using extensive-form games to model strategic interactions has the virtue of forcing the analyst to think carefully and to be quite precise about the specific nature of competition. At this time, game theory provides the only coherent way of logically analyzing strategic behavior.

A metatheme that emerges from this research is that the predictions of the model concerning the character of the equilibrium in the game tend to be quite sensitive to the exact specification of the firms' strategies and the timing of actions. This is not a new notion; it has been appreciated for at least 100 years that the Cournot (1838) equilibrium (Nash equilibrium in quantities) and the Bertrand (1883) equilibrium (Nash equilibrium in prices) generate very different predictions, given the same cost and demand conditions. Sequential moves, *à la* von Stackelberg (1934), yield yet another outcome.

Critics such as Fisher see this sensitivity of equilibrium behavior to the specification of the extensive form of the game as evidence that the game-theoretic approach has failed, especially since the "correct" specification may be hard to discern from available industry information. This complaint is reminiscent of the old lament that "there is no theory of oligopoly" (since several competing theories have yet to be rejected).

The fact of the matter is that competitive strategy in practice encompasses a wide variety of strategic and tactical decisionmaking, from the pricing of products to investment in production and distribution facilities to contracting practices with customers and input suppliers to research and development expenditures. There is no reason to expect or strive for a single unified oligopoly theory that would deliver unique predictions to armchair theorists, independent of the particulars of how competition is played out in a given industry.

The diversity of predictions in different game-theoretic models reflects our broadening understanding of business strategy. With our new game-theoretic tools, we can carefully analyze a much wider range of competitive strategy than was previously possible, and we know better what to look for in doing case studies and industry analysis. The theory tells us the conditions under which different outcomes occur and what factors are most critical in shaping behavior and performance in concentrated industries. The new theories also help us understand what we observe happening in concentrated industries, although rather detailed information is necessary to know which piece of theory best applies in any particular setting.

I like to think of our emerging theory of oligopolistic behavior as analogous to the theory of evolution. crudely put, the basic hypothesis in the theory of evolution is that living species adapt to their environment to survive and prosper. It is a general theory that is meant to apply throughout the biological world. Applying the theory of evolution to individual species, however, reveals a stunning diversity of tactics employed in different settings by different species. Some animals produce a few young and nurture them carefully, while others produce a multitude of offspring, only a small percentage of which survive to reproduce. Some plants use animals to spread their seeds, others use wind or water. And so on.

The theory of strategic competition is in a similar, if less developed, state. We have some general working hypotheses about firms' behavior: they seek to maximize profits and they behave noncooperatively. We also assume that there is some pool of common knowledge about the environment that is shared by all participants. As with the theory of evolution, however, we see a striking diversity of available and adopted strategies when we look across different industries with different underlying structures. In one industry the firms tacitly collude by using meeting-the-competition clauses and display periods of successful collusion interspersed with fiercely competitive phases. In another industry R&D is the crucial dimension of competition, and we see a series of major innovations followed by licensing and imitation. In a third industry incumbents keep potential entrants out of the market by establishing large installed bases of users. And so on.

Even the term "oligopoly theory" is in need of replacement. It conjures up such stale topics as the traditional static models of oligopoly (Cournot vs. Bertrand) and the misguided and internally inconsistent theory of conjectural variations. The explosion of game-theoretic work in I.O. is better described as the "theory of business strategy."[1]

By the theory of business strategy I mean the growing collection of models of business rivalry—along many dimensions—in concentrated markets. The emphasis in this literature is on the *dynamics of strategic actions* and in particular on the role of *commitment* in strategic settings. Under conditions of imperfect information, the focus is on information transmission and reception. The diversity of models of business strategy does not indicate any failure of the new I.O.; rather it is an indication that we are using appropriate technology. We are finally developing theories that address the richness of business behavior, from R&D to information sharing to product design, and more.

With its emphasis on strategic commitment, the theory of business strategy takes the field of I.O. in the opposite direction from that of the well-known theory of contestable markets (Baumol, Panzar, and Willig, 1982). Contestability theory applies when there are no sunk costs. This translates into a complete absence of strategic behavior, since any action that is costlessly reversible has no commitment or strategic value. Since sunk costs are ubiquitous, I regard strategic theories of rivalry as appropriate and natural, in contrast to contestability theory, which appears to be an empty box.

As we explore strategic behavior and broaden the scope of business practices included in our models, we are finding a common theme running through the theory of business strategy: The timing of strategic decisions and the ability of large firms to make commitments are the key to understanding business strategy. The new I.O. develops the themes articulated by Thomas Schelling in his classic book *The Strategy of Conflict*, rather than refining static models of oligopolistic interactions.

But enough by way of general remarks. The proof of the pudding is in the eating.

## 3. Examples of the theory of business strategy

When I teach industrial organization, I organize the theory of business strategy around the various dimensions of strategic behavior that are amenable to study using the tools of the new I.O. See my survey paper (Shapiro, 1989) for a more complete treatment of these many types of conduct.[2]

One of the themes of the theory of business strategy is that we should distinguish *strategic* decisions, which involve long-lasting commitments, from *tactical* decisions, which are short-term responses to the current environment. In the language of game theory, the strategic decisions determine the evolution of state variables that provide a setting in which current tactics are played out. The examples below are organized by the dimension of strategic behavior being examined.

### *Investment in physical capital*

It is natural to begin with investment in physical capital as our first example of a strategic variable. Investments in physical capital can serve a strategic role because they alter the investing firm's optimal behavior in the future. We now understand that any investment that lowers a firm's marginal costs can constitute credible commitment to compete more vigorously in the future. A firm can gain an advantage by investing if its own more vigorous behavior in the future will lead its rivals to respond by competing less vigorously or by staying out of the market altogether. See Spence (1979), Dixit (1980), and Eaton and Lipsey (1981).[3]

For investment to play a strategic role, it must be observable to rival firms. The investment also must not be recoverable. Costlessly reversible actions never constitute commitments and have no strategic role. This principle tells us that the fraction of any investment that is sunk will be important in evaluating its strategic role. The principle also suggests that firms may try to convert recoverable costs into sunk costs for some strategic purposes.[4]

The mechanics and analytics of strategic investment in physical capital depend upon the timing of investment decisions, the possibility of entry and exit, and the nature of the tactical (pricing or output) competition that will prevail in the future. We now understand these relationships much better than ten years ago.

### *Investment in intangible assets*

Physical capital is hardly the only way in which firms make investments. Many investments generate know-how or intellectual property. Learning-by-doing and the funding of R&D are prominent examples of investment in intangible assets. Since these types of investments can require very long planning horizons, they are natural objects of study in the theory of business strategy.

The dynamics of competition in technologically advancing, hi-tech industries are shaped by firms' efforts to take a technological lead. Performance in such industries is unquestionably a crucial aspect of overall industrial performance. And we now have a set of tools and models to evaluate such performance.

I see the theory of technological competition as a particularly successful line of research within the broad area I am calling the theory of business strategy. We have learned a great deal about the many aspects of the process of innovation: the dynamics of patent races, the persistence of monopoly, the adoption of new technologies, imitation and its effects on the pace of innovation, the licensing of intangible property, spillovers in R&D, and research joint ventures.[5]

In fact, many of the questions studied in the recent theoretical literature on R&D were not even posed properly before the use of game theory in I.O. For example, Katz (1986) shows that, in deciding whether to engage in cooperative research (and how to structure a cooperative research agreement), a firm must consider how the sharing of research results will affect subsequent product-market competition and how the nature of product-market competition and the presence of spillovers in the research process will affect all firms' incentives to contribute to the cooperative research effort. Our analytics must reflect this forward-looking decision process.

Our understanding of the licensing of intangible property also has been advanced by using game-theoretic tools. Shapiro (1985) discusses the role of cross-licensing of patents as a device for facilitating collusion: if competitors can sign binding cross-licensing contracts that involve per unit royalties, they often can use such contracts to enforce the fully collusive outcome. Katz and Shapiro (1987) show how the prospect of obtaining a license on favorable terms may dramatically alter rivalry to secure a patent. Grossman and Shapiro (1987) develop a model of dynamic R&D competition in which the effects of research joint ventures, intermediate patents, and patent licensing can be studied. Before this work, we had little theory to guide us in thinking about the effects of patent licensing or research joint ventures on the pace of technological advance and on the extent of diffusion of innovations.

The game-theoretic approach to studying the many aspects of R&D rivalry is logically compelling and has been fruitful. This research has the potential to provide valuable insights for the design of patent policy as well as for understanding the nature of technological competition. For example, Scotchmer and Green (1988) explore the effects of different patent policies, including first-to-file vs. first-to-invent rules for establishing priority. I anticipate further progress in this area, especially in analyzing markets where there is a sequence of innovations.

### *Strategic control of information*

Industrial organization economists are now beginning to use relatively new methods of game theory—in particular, Bayesian equilibrium and Bayesian perfect equilibrium—to examine strategic behavior in the context of asymmetric information. This coming together of the economics of information with the economics of strategic behavior has made it possible to examine theoretically many longstanding issues in I.O. and to explain a variety of observed behavior that previously defied explanation. I call this "strategic control of information" because firms act strategically to affect their rivals' beliefs about market conditions.

For example, we now have a start on a theory explaining how a firm may build a reputation as a tough competitor through predatory tactics. Such predatory tactics can occur in equilibrium so long as the prey is uncertain about the profitability of predation to the predator. See Kreps and Wilson (1982) and Kreps, Milgrom, Roberts, and Wilson (1982) for the basic theory, Saloner (1987) for an analysis of predation and mergers, and Roberts (1987) for a more thorough description of this line of research. This research provides one example of how the theory of business strategy has improved our understanding of conduct in concentrated markets. Previously, some antitrust analysts had argued that predation could never be profitable. That position has now been shown to be flawed.[6]

Strategic control of information can also be used for purposes of entry deterrence, since preentry actions may affect (potential) entrants' beliefs about the profitability of entering the market. Milgrom and Roberts (1982) and Harrington (1986) show how pricing behavior is affected by the threat of entry. Alternatively, firms may simply make announcements that will delay or deter entry, if the information revealed is unfavorable to entrants and can be verified as accurate.

The behavior of established oligopolists also can be altered by asymmetric information. Riordan (1985) shows how traditional Cournot competition is intensified in the presence of uncertainty about demand that is serially correlated. And information exchange among oligopolists can now be rigorously examined; for example, Shapiro (1986) examines how traditional Cournot competition is affected by private cost information, including the possibility of direct information exchange among rivals through a trade association.

### *Horizontal mergers*

The antitrust treatment of horizontal mergers is a perennially important policy topic in I.O. The theory of business strategy can be harnessed to provide new insights about the strategic effects of horizontal mergers. In this policy context we can hope for theories that inform, not replace, the in-depth industry analysis undertaken by antitrust authorities in response to a merger request.

Mergers are properly viewed as a consolidation of industry-specific assets and can be modelled as a change in the structure of ownership of assets. The effect of such a structural change on tactical competition and market performance can be studied by using a twostage game in which firms first combine assets and then engage in pricing and output competition.

Salant, Switzer, and Reynolds (1983), Perry and Porter (1985), and Farrell and Shapiro (1989b) have used this approach to obtain new predictions and insights about the effects of horizontal mergers. Farrell and Shapiro (1989b) provide a general treatment of horizontal mergers that builds on Cournot oligopoly theory. They show that the responses to a merger by large non-participant firms are crucial to evaluating the welfare effects of profitable mergers. Farrell and Shapiro also derive a very general but simple, necessary and sufficient condition for a merger to raise price and show that mergers generating no synergies cause price to rise. Finally, they provide a rather general condition under which profitable mergers raise welfare.

### *Network competition and product standardization*

In many important industries—especially telecommunications and computers —consumers value products more highly if many others are using compatible equipment. In such industries, there is a natural set of state variables, namely the installed bases of the competing brands. These installed bases are commonly the object of intensive strategic competition. The theory of business strategy allows us to develop theories of competition in such network industries. The role of sponsors that control proprietary technologies, the incentives to develop compatible products, and the possibility that the market will get stuck with an inferior technology are all amenable to analysis using game-theoretic tools. Farrell and Saloner (1986) and Katz and Shapiro (1986b, 1989) are several prominent examples.

### *Contracting*

Whenever contracts constitute genuine commitments, they can serve a strategic function. A growing literature seeks to explain the form of various contracts written by participants in a larger strategic conflict. Virtually any contract written by a firm that is engaged in strategic conflict can be modified to yield an advantage in that struggle, if the contract is observable to rivals and is credible.

We are beginning to understand how contracts can be designed for such strategic purposes. Aghion and Bolton (1987) show how an incumbent firm can sign long-term contracts with its customers to deter entry, even though the customers recognize that entry would be to their advantage. Holt and Scheffman (1987) and Salop (1986) discuss the possible role of meet-the-competition clauses and most-favored-customer clauses in facilitating collusion. Vickers (1985) and Fershtman and Judd (1987) show how the owner of an oligopolist can increase profits by compensating managers on the basis of sales as well as profits.[7] Brander and Lewis (1986) show how the mix of debt and equity affects the behavior of an oligopolist, and thus is not neutral, in a strategic setting.

### *Other dimensions of business strategy*

One of the most exciting aspects of the theory of business strategy is its flexibility in analyzing a wide range of business strategies. In addition to those highlighted above, the game-theoretic approach to business strategy has generated new insights into many topics, a selective sampling of which follows.

Ghemawat and Nalebuff (1985, 1989) have explored the dynamics of exit in declining industries. They identify a strategic *dis*advantage associated with size in declining industries. Their theories predict that larger firms will be the first to downsize or exit in unfavorable conditions, even in the presence of modest scale economies. Ghemawat and Nalebuff provide some limited evidence to support their theory.[8] Fudenberg and Tirole (1986) have modelled the exit decision as a war of attrition if there is asymmetric information about costs. Dixit and Shapiro (1986) show how entry and exit processes are linked.

In many industries, buyers must incur substantial switching costs in choosing a new supplier. Such *lock-in* naturally creates some *ex post* market power for the supplier. The implications of this *ex post* market power for *ex ante* competition have been explored by Klemperer (1987a, 1987b) and Farrell and Shapiro (1988, 1989a). In two-period models Klemperer studies the intense *ex ante* competition followed by *ex post* market power that characterizes markets with switching costs. He explores the effect of switching costs on firms' profits and on buyers. In a many-period model Farrell and Shapiro (1988) show how switching costs can serve to encourage rather than discourage entry. In their 1989 paper they analyze long-term contracts with asymmetric information about switching costs.

Product selection is naturally modelled as a strategic choice; it is followed by and affects pricing competition. Shaked and Sutton (1982) show how firms may position their products so as to diminish subsequent pricing competition. Judd (1985) provides a fine example of why game-theoretic reasoning is essential to a logical analysis of product selection. In particular, he points out the importance of considering product *withdrawal* when studying product selection. A firm cannot deter entry through product proliferation, for example, unless it is credible that these products would be continued in the event of entry. This is an example of a simple point that, once made, is self-evident, but required game-theoretic reasoning to be appreciated.

An especially influential application of the theory of business strategy has been to international trade. Brander and Spencer (1983) show how strategic trade policies can benefit domestic oligopolists in their competition with foreign rivals. Eaton and Grossman (1986) show how the nature of product-market competition affects optimal trade policy in oligopolistic industries. Bulow, Geanakoplos, and Klemperer (1985) show how presence in one market can be a strategic advantage or disadvantage in another market, either through cross-market demand or cost effects.

The same game-theoretic tools that have made these advances possible have been used successfully in several other major areas of industrial organization and its neighboring fields: consumer protection, advertising, consumer search, and product quality; the regulation of natural monopolies; managerial compensation schemes; vertical practices; insurance markets; law and economics, etc.[9]

In summary, the new I.O. has permitted us to examine a far wider range of business behavior than we could have even a short time ago. Although more time is needed to sort out the empirically significant effects from the theoretical curiosities, there seems little doubt that we have a powerful lens through which to view business strategy.

## 4. Game theory, industrial organization, and Professor Fisher

When I was a graduate student at M.I.T., the required econometrics course had a reputation of truly tesing—and surely frightening—all aspiring economists at M.I.T. Along with the associated econometrics project, it was rightly viewed as a centerpiece of the graduate program. At the helm in this econometrics class was the more-than-slightly intimidating Professor Franklin Fisher.

If you know fear, you can imagine the mood of the class as we shifted in our seats while Professor Fisher prepared to return our graded midterm exams to us. This mood was hardly lightened as Professor Fisher proceeded to explain the intricacies hidden in the exam questions, which the bulk of us had failed to fathom. Apparently, our collective performance was the weakest he had seen in his many years teaching econometrics at M.I.T.

The effort exerted by the class in the wake of this midterm disaster was truly impressive. And by the time the final arrived, we really had learned a lot about econometrics. Only later did we learn that every class was treated to the same performance after the midterm.

In his companion piece, "Games Economists Play: A Noncooperative View," Professor Fisher attacks "oligopoly theory," charging that little or no progress has been made despite the surge of theoretical activity in I.O.

If Professor Fisher's article was written in the same vein as his criticism of our econometrics class, with the aim of pushing industrial organization theorists to develop more general theories that are amenable to parameter estimation, capable of direct empirical falsification, and useful for practitioners, then I can only hope that his motivational techniques are as successful as they were in his econometrics class. If his statements about the lack of value of the new industrial organization are to be taken at face value, however, then it seems to me that he is fairly far from the mark.

Most of Fisher's attacks are directed at "static, one-shot oligopoly theory." This is a straw man. If his main point is that the static theory of pricing and output competition has advanced rather little since Cournot wrote 150 years ago and Bertrand wrote 100 years ago, I would agree that the pace of progress viewed over the entire 150 years since 1838 has been modest. I also have some sympathy with his criticism of supergame theory, with its great multiplicity of equilibria. Even here, however, and even if one accepts Fisher's view that the central question of oligopoly theory is whether oligopolists will succeed in achieving the joint profit-maximizing solution,[10] there have been some notable recent advances, e.g., the work of Abreu (1986, 1988).[11]

But in my view Fisher's emphasis on the shortfalls of static oligopoly theory is quite out-of-date and entirely out-of-touch with the theoretical advances of the past ten to fifteen years. The whole point of the theory of business strategy is that static models are inadequate, that commitments and timing matter a great deal, that imperfect information has a profound impact on firms' behavior, and that we can study an enormous range of business behavior, not just pricing and output competition, by using a single set of game-theoretic tools (though not in single model).

Contrary to Fisher's assertions, we do have a powerful methodology for analyzing business behavior, from both a positive and a normative perspective. Strategic competition can be viewed as a dynamic game in which long-lived strategic decisions serve as commitments, thereby determining the movement of underlying state variables or assets that have a direct impact on the firms' short-run or tactical decisions. Furthermore, game theory gives us a methodology for understanding the relationship between strategic decisions and tactical competition.

Most fundamentally, I think Professor Fisher is misguided in seeking a single "generalizing" theory of oligopoly. First, a very general theory may be of quite limited usefulness if it fails to match real-world conditions. General equilibrium theory suffers this fate. Second, a search for a single generalizing theory of oligopoly denies the very richness of business behavior that makes I.O. so interesting. We do have some general themes emerging from the theory of business strategy—the importance of timing and the role of commitment—but to seek a single theory of strategic behavior is both unwise and fruitless.

To illustrate the shortcomings of Fisher's line of argument, let me discuss two examples that Fisher himself uses to attack the new I.O.: product preannouncements and the use of oligopoly theory to inform horizontal merger analysis.

As Fisher reports in his article, he testified in the I.B.M. case that good-faith product announcements could never be premature, i.e., anticompetitive by virtue of coming sooner than they should. Farrell and Saloner (1986) have shown that this general claim is false in industries where network externalities are significant. Early announcements can cripple the ability of new entrants to develop enough of an installed base to allow them to compete with the incumbent.

Fisher is quite right to point out that Farrell and Saloner have only shown what *can* happen, not necessarily what did happen. As is often the case in the theory of business strategy, their model warns us not to make premature general statements and directs us to those industry features that are most relevant. Farrell and Saloner merely pointed out a theoretical possibility, along with a set of industry conditions to look for to see whether preannouncement has in fact occurred. Fisher is the one who made the general statement about the procompetitive nature of product preannouncements, and he erred because he did not account for network externalities. If users in the computer industry cared little about compatibility with each other, then I would agree that Farrell and Saloner's analysis would have little possible applicability to the I.B.M. case. But there seems little doubt that network externalities are an essential aspect of the computer industry.

Fisher also scoffs at the use of game-theoretic methods in evaluating horizontal mergers, although he offers no constructive alternative. I believe that my joint work with Joe Farrell (1989b) has produced valuable insights by taking the game-theoretic approach.[12] We examine a two-stage game in which firms first merge (combine assets) and then engage in Cournot competition. We allow for differences across firms in their efficiencies and for synergies associated with the merger.

Fisher argues that using Cournot equilibrium to study mergers is silly since Cournot competition is static. This criticism misses the point in several ways. First, there is considerable empirical support for the existence of a smooth positive relationship between market concentration and price-cost margins, as predicted by the Cournot model. Although firms do not engage in static quantity setting, the Cournot model thus has some practical claim on our attention as we try to relate industrial concentration to output and pricing behavior. Whatever complex repeated game the firms actually play, if the outcome is close to Cournot, it makes good sense to use Cournot oligopoly to summarize the basic properties of tactical competition following a strategic decision such as a merger.

Second, the insights that are unearthed by using Cournot oligopoly theory to examine the welfare consequences of mergers have application even if the firms' tactical competition is considerably different from the Cournot equilibrium. Farrell and I show, for example, by using no more than basic welfare accounting methods, that the welfare effects of a merger depend critically on the output responses by nonparticipant firms that have large markups before the merger. So long as the larger firms are those with the most market power and thus the largest markups (as in the Cournot equilibrium), our qualitative findings will be valid. For example, our finding that for any given price change a merger is more desirable, the more it *increases* concentration (as measured by the Herfindahl index with Cournot oligopoly), while derived in a Cournot model, is much more general.

But more important is the basic idea of viewing a merger as a strategic act with implications for subsequent tactical competition. This approach tells us to examine how the merger will commit the participants to altered behavior, and helps us identify just how a merger will alter subsequent competition in prices or output. Such modelling of a merger is of course natural within the theory of business strategy. But by looking at how a merger alters the participants' behavior, and thus overall industry behavior, one can determine how the merger will affect both the mix of output and total output in the industry. And these are the factors that determine the welfare effects of the merger.

Will Farrell's and my theory, or others', make unnecessary careful industry analysis by those who must pass antitrust judgment on horizontal mergers? Certainly not; careful empirical examination will remain essential. But such case-by-case analysis will gain useful direction and guidance from the theory. Our theory gives simple conditions in terms of market shares and the responses by nonparticipants in the merger under which a profitable merger will raise welfare. And we identify conditions on the participants' costs under which a merger is likely to raise or lower price. In this way the theory of business strategy can serve as a useful guide to the practitioner to indicate what variables are important in evaluating a horizontal merger.

## 5. Where do we go from here?

So far I have argued that the introduction of game-theoretic tools into the study of oligopolistic competition has made it possible to analyze carefully a whole range of questions that were not previously amenable to economic analysis. This leaves open the question of just how to use this theory or extend it.

Despite my favorable view of the usefulness of the theory of business strategy, I suspect that we are running into diminishing returns in the use of game theory to develop simple models of business strategy. Many of the most important aspects of strategic behavior have now been subjected to such game-theoretic analysis. The basic analytics of different dimensions of strategic behavior (different types of investment, the relationship between strategic and tactical variables, etc.) have been explored. Although I expect that in the years ahead there will be continuing advances along the lines of the past decade, I would be surprised if we learned as much in the next decade by using this same approach as we have learned in the past decade. I believe that other participants share the same sense of diminishing returns.

What does this view imply for I.O. in the 1990s? I expect and hope that we will see a marriage of the theory of business strategy and the tools of industry analysis. In other words, I believe that the most useful contributions of the 1990s will come from consolidating what we have learned in the 1970s and 1980s with the more detailed empirical approach of the 1940s and 1950s. For the theory of business strategy ultimately to demonstrate its utility and stand the test of time, it must prove helpful in analyzing particular industries or identifying behavioral regularities that apply across industries.

The integration of game-theoretic analysis and industry studies is only beginning, but I for one find the early returns encouraging. Let me give a few selective examples and confine myself to some of the dimensions of business strategy that I have discussed above. Besen and Johnson (1986) systematically apply the theory of network externalities and product standardization to study compatibility standards in the broadcasting industry. Holt and Scheffman (1985) use the theory of meet-or-release contracts and most-favored-customer clauses to examine tacit collusion in the market for lead-based gasoline additives. Gilbert and Lieberman (1987) examine the role of strategic investment in chemical processing industries. Bresnahan and Reiss (1987) explore the role of strategic factors in deterring entry into small, isolated retail and professional markets in the United States. Further examples abound; I refer the reader to Bresnahan (1989) and Schmalensee (1988) for recent surveys of empirical work in industrial economics.

These papers are the vanguard in the coming together of the theory of business strategy and industry analysis. I see this alliance as the ultimate test of the success of the theory of business strategy. I also regard this union as the most promising direction for ongoing work in industrial organization.

The theory of business strategy has taught us that we must look closely at an industry and understand the type of competition that prevails in it if we are to make any reliable predictions of industry behavior and performance and how they are affected by an exogenous or structural change. We now know enough about strategic behavior to return to industry studies with a powerful theoretical framework and structure to guide us through the rich world of strategic rivalry.

## Notes

I thank Avinash Dixit, Joe Farrell, Gene Grossman, Alvin Klevorick, Barry Nalebuff, John Vickers, and the Editorial Board for valuable comments on an earlier draft.

1 Of course, the more applied field of corporate strategy has a long and rich history. Economists have much to learn from scholars who have studied corporate behavior and corporate strategy in detail. I hope the learning will be mutual, as economists undertake more case studies to test their theories and as corporate strategy experts integrate game-theoretic insights into their work.

2 Schmalensee (1988) provides a broader survey of the current state of industrial economics.

3 Modelling investment as a commitment has also informed the older debate on prices vs. quantities as modes of behavior in oligopoly theory; see Kreps and Scheinkman (1983) and Davidson and Deneckere (1986).

4 In games against horizontal competitors this is often an appropriate strategy. But in vertical relationships it may be important to minimize the degree of commitment or lock-in to retain bargaining power.

5 As a few representative contributions among many, see Dasgupta and Stiglitz (1980), Lee and Wilde (1980), Reinganum (1981), Fudenberg and Tirole (1983 and 1985), Katz and Shapiro (1985, 1986a, and 1987), Shapiro (1985), Katz (1986), Harris and Vickers (1985 and 1987), and Grossman and Shapiro (1987); see Reinganum (1989) for a survey of the area.

6 Of course, none of this proves that predation has occurred in any specific application. But the new theory exposes the limitation of previous arguments, alerts us to the possibility of predation, and gives us some guidance in our attempts to detect predation and distinguish it from legitimate competition.

7 Katz (1988) points out that the lack of observability, and hence the lack of credibility, of such contracts may undermine their strategic role.

8 But Whinston (1988) shows how different behavior is possible if downsizing cannot be done continuously.

9 Indeed, game-theoretic contributions are now considered important throughout economics; for example, they are used to examine the time-consistency of government policy in macroeconomics and the nature of employment contracts in labor economics.

10 As I hope is clear by now, I do not believe that the question of whether joint profit maximization is achieved is the central question in the theory business strategy. It is one question, and often an interesting one, but the emphasis of the theory is on how firms behave in the many situations where joint profit maximization is not achieved.

11 Oligopolistic supergames with imperfect monitoring also expose some key tensions in dynamic oligopoly. See especially Green and Porter (1984) and Abreu, Pearce, and Stacchetti (1986) for game-theoretic extensions of Stigler's classic (1964) article. I do not focus on these games, however, since they are confined to pricing or output competition without any strategic variables (long-lasting commitments). It is also worth noting the interesting theoretical developments regarding renegotiation in oligopolistic supergames; see Farrell and Maskin (1987), Bernheim and Ray (1987), and Pearce (1987). These papers address some of Fisher's concerns about the multiplicity of equilibria in supergames.

12 Fisher's article predates my work with Farrell on horizontal mergers.

## References

ABREU, D. "Extremal Equilibria of Oligopolistic Supergames." *Journal of Economic Theory*, Vol. 39 (1986), pp. 191–225.

——. "On the Theory of Infinitely Repeated Games with Discounting." *Econometrica*, Vol. 56 (1988), pp. 383–396.

——, PEARCE, D., AND STACCHETTI, E. "Optimal Cartel Equilibria with Imperfect Monitoring." *Journal of Economic Theory*, Vol. 39 (1986), pp. 251–269.

AGHION, P. AND BOLTON, P. "Contracts and Entry Deterrence." *American Economic Review*, Vol. 77 (1987), pp. 388–401.

BAUMOL, W., PANZAR, J., AND WILLIG, R. *Contestable Markets and the Theory of Industry Structure*. New York: Harcourt Brace Jovanovich, 1982.

BERNHEIM, B. D. AND RAY, D. "Collective Dynamic Consistency in Repeated Games." Stanford University, 1987.

BERTRAND, J. "Book Review of *Théorie Mathématique de la Richesse Sociale* and of *Recherches sur les Principes Mathématiques de la Théorie des Richesses." Journal des Savants*, Vol. 67 (1883), pp. 499–508.

BESEN, S. AND JOHNSON, L. *Compatibility Standards, Competition, and Innovation in the Broadcasting Industry*. Santa Monica, Ca: RAND Report R-3453 NSF. The RAND Corporation, 1986.

BRANDER, J. A. AND LEWIS, T. R. "Oligopoly and Financial Structure: The Limited Liability Effect." *American Economic Review*, Vol. 76 (1986), pp. 956–970.

—— AND SPENCER, B. J. "Export Subsidies and International Market Share Rivalry." *Journal of International Economics*, Vol. 18 (1983), pp. 83–100.

BRESNAHAN, T. "Studies of Individual Industries" in R. Schmalensee and R. Willig, eds., *Handbook of Industrial Organization*, New York: North-Holland, 1989.

—— AND REISS, P. "Do Entry Conditions Vary across Markets?" *Brookings Papers on Economic Activity*, No. 3 (1987), pp. 833–881.

BULOW, J., GEANAKOPLOS, J., AND KLEMPERER, P. "Multimarket Oligopoly: Strategic Substitutes and Complements." *Journal of Political Economy*, Vol. 93 (1985), pp. 488–511.

COURNOT, A. A. *Researches into the Mathematical Principles of the Theory of Wealth*, English ed. of *Recherches sur les Principes Mathématiques de la Théorie des Richesses*, New York: Kelley, 1838.

DASGUPTA, P. AND STIGLITZ, J. "Uncertainty, Industrial Structure, and the Speed of R&D." *Bell Journal of Economics*, Vol. 11 (1980), pp. 1–28.

DAVIDSON, C. AND DENECKERE, R. "Long-Run Competition in Capacity, Short-Run Competition in Price, and the Cournot Model." *RAND Journal of Economics*, Vol. 17 (1986), pp. 404–415.

DIXIT, A. K. "The Role of Investment in Entry Deterrence." *Economic Journal*, Vol. 90 (1980), pp. 95–106.

—— AND SHAPIRO, C. "Entry Dynamics with Mixed Strategies" in L. G. Thomas, ed., *Strategic Planning*, Lexington: Lexington Books, 1986.

EATON, B. C. AND LIPSEY, R. G. "Capital, Commitment, and Entry Equilibrium." *Bell Journal of Economics*, Vol. 12 (1981), pp. 593–604.

EATON, J. AND GROSSMAN, G. "Optimal Trade and Industrial Policy under Oligopoly." *Quarterly Journal of Economics*, Vol. 101 (1986), pp. 383–406.

Farrell, J. and Maskin, E. "Notes on Renegotiation in Repeated Games." Unpublished Manuscript, Harvard University, 1987.

—— and Saloner, G. "Installed Base and Compatibility: Innovation, Product Preannouncements, and Predation." *American Economic Review*, Vol. 76 (1986), pp. 940–955.

—— and Shapiro, C. "Dynamic Competition with Switching Costs." *RAND Journal of Economics*, Vol. 19 (1988a), pp. 123–137.

—— and ——. "Optimal Contracts with Lock-In." *American Economic Review*, Vol. 79 (1989a), pp. 51–68.

—— and ——. "Horizontal Mergers: An Equilibrium Analysis." *American Economic Review*, Vol. 79 (1989b), forthcoming.

Fershtman, C. and Judd, K. "Equilibrium Incentives in Oligopoly." *American Economic Review*. Vol. 77 (1987), pp. 927–940.

Fisher, F. "Games Economists Play: A Noncooperative View." *RAND Journal of Economics*, Vol. 19 (1989), pp. 113–124.

Fudenberg, D. and Tirole, J. "Learning-by-Doing and Market Performance." *Bell Journal of Economics*, Vol. 14 (1983), pp. 522–530.

—— and ——. "Preemption and Rent Equalization in the Adoption of New Technology." *Review of Economic Studies*, Vol. 52 (1985), pp. 383–402.

—— and ——. "A Theory of Exit in Duopoly." *Econometrica*, Vol. 54 (1986), pp. 943–960.

Ghemawat, P. and Nalebuff, B. "Exit." *RAND Journal of Economics*, Vol. 16 (1985), pp. 184–193.

—— and ——. "The Devolution of Declining Industries." *Quarterly Journal of Economics*, Vol. 104 (1989), forthcoming.

Gilbert, R. and Lieberman, M. "Investment and Coordination in Oligopolistic Industries." *RAND Journal of Economics*, Vol. 18 (1987), pp. 17–33.

Green, E. and Porter, R. "Noncooperative Collusion under Imperfect Price Information." *Econometrica*, Vol. 52 (1984), pp. 87–100.

Grossman, G. and Shapiro, C. "Dynamic R&D Competition," *Economic Journal*, Vol. 97 (1987), pp. 372–387.

Harrington, J. "Limit Pricing When the Potential Entrant Is Uncertain of Its Cost Function." *Econometrica*, Vol. 54 (1986), pp. 429–437.

Harris, C. and Vickers, J. "Perfect Equilibrium in a Model of a Race." *Review of Economic Studies*, Vol. 52 (1985), pp. 193–209.

—— and ——. "Racing with Uncertainty." *Review of Economic Studies*, Vol. 54 (1987), pp. 1–21.

Holt, C. and Scheffman, D. "The Effects of Advance Notice and Best-Price Policies: Theory, with Applications to *Ethyl*." Thomas Jefferson Center Working Paper, University of Virginia, 1985.

—— and ——. "Facilitating Practices: The Effects of Advance Notice and Best-Price Policies." *RAND Journal of Economics*, Vol. 18 (1987), pp. 187–197.

Judd, K. "Credible Spatial Preemption." *RAND Journal of Economics*, Vol. 16 (1985), pp. 153–166.

Katz, M. L. "An Analysis of Cooperative Research and Development." *RAND Journal of Economics*, Vol. 17 (1986), pp. 527–543.

——. "Game-Playing Agents: Contracts as Commitments." Unpublished Manuscript, University of California at Berkeley, 1988.

—— AND SHAPIRO, C. "On the Licensing of Innovations." *RAND Journal of Economics*, Vol. 16 (1985), pp. 504–520.

—— AND ——. "How to License Intangible Property." *Quarterly Journal of Economics*, Vol. 101 (1986a), pp. 567–590.

—— AND ——. "Technology Adoption in the Presence of Network Externalities." *Journal of Political Economy*, Vol. 94 (1986b), pp. 822–841.

—— AND ——. "R&D Rivalry with Licensing or Lmitation." *American Economic Review*, Vol, 77 (1987), pp. 402–420.

—— AND ——. "Product Introduction with Network Externalities." Princeton University, 1989.

KLEMPERER, P. "Markets with Consumer Switching Costs." *Quarterly Journal of Economics*, Vol. 102 (1987a), pp. 375–394.

——. "The Competitiveness of Markets with Switching Costs." *RAND Journal of Economics*, Vol. 18 (1987b), pp. 138–150.

KREPS, D. AND SCHEINKMAN, J. "Quantity Precommitment and Bertrand Competition Yield Cournot Outcomes." *Bell Journal of Economics*, Vol. 14 (1983), pp. 326–337.

—— AND WILSON, R. "Reputation and Imperfect Information." *Journal of Economic Theory*, Vol. 27 (1982), pp. 253–279.

——, MILGROM, P., ROBERTS, D. J., AND WILSON, R. "Rational Cooperation in the Finitely-Repeated Prisoner's Dilemma." *Journal of Economic Theory*, Vol. 27 (1982), pp. 245–252.

LEE, T. AND WILDE, L. "Market Structure and Innovation: A Reformulation." *Quarterly Journal of Economics*, Vol. 94 (1980), pp. 429–436.

MILGROM, P. AND ROBERTS, D. J. "Limit Pricing and Entry under Incomplete Information: An Equilibrium Analysis." *Econometrica*, Vol. 50 (1982), pp. 443–459.

PEARCE, D. "Renegotiation-Proof Equilibria: Collective Rationality and Intertemporal Cooperation." Yale University, 1987.

PERRY, M. AND PORTER, R. "Oligopoly and the Incentive for Horizontal Merger." *American Economic Review*, Vol. 75 (1985), pp. 219–227.

REINGANUM, J. "On the Diffusion of New Technology: A Game-Theoretic Approach." *Review of Economic Studies*, Vol. 48 (1981), pp. 395–405.

——. "The Timing of Innovation: Research, Development and Diffusion" in R. Schmalensee and R. Willig, eds., *Handbook of Industrial Organization*, New York: North-Holland, 1989.

RIORDAN, M. "Imperfect Information and Dynamic Conjectural Variations." *RAND Journal of Economics*, Vol. 16 (1985), pp. 41–50.

ROBERTS, D. J. "Battles for Market Share: Incomplete Information, Aggressive Strategic Pricing, and Competitive Dynamics" in T. Bewley, ed., *Advances in Economic Theory, Invited Papers from the 5th World Congress*, New York: Cambridge University Press, 1987.

SALANT, S., SWITZER, S., AND REYNOLDS, R. "Losses Due to Merger: The Effects of an Exogenous Change in Industry Structure on Cournot-Nash Equilibrium." *Quarterly Journal of Economics*, Vol. 98 (1983), pp. 185–199.

SALONER, G. "Predation, Mergers, and Incomplete Information." *RAND Journal of Economics*, Vol. 18 (1987), pp. 165–186.

SALOP, S. "Practices That Credibly Facilitate Oligopoly Coordination" in J. Stiglitz and F. Mathewson, eds., *New Developments in the Analysis of Market Structure*, Cambridge: MIT Press, 1986.

SCHELLING, T. *The Strategy of Conflict*. New York: Oxford University Press, 1960.

SCHMALENSEE, R. "Industrial Economics: An Overview." *Economic Journal*, Vol. 98 (1988), pp. 643–681.

SCOTCHMER, S. AND GREEN, J. "Novelty and Disclosure in Patent Law." Working Paper No. 88–7, Program in Law and Economics, Boalt Hall, University of California at Berkeley, 1988.

SHAKED, A. AND SUTTON, J. "Relaxing Price Competition through Product Differentiation." *Review of Economic Studies*, Vol. 49 (1982), pp. 3–14.

SHAPIRO, C. "Patent Licensing and R&D Rivalry." *American Economic Review*, Vol. 53 (1985), pp. 433–446.

——. "Exchange of Cost Information in Oligopoly." *Review of Economic Studies*, Vol. 53 (1986), pp. 433–446.

——. "Theories of Oligopoly Behavior" in R. Schmalensee and R. Willig, eds., *Handbook of Industrial Organization*, New York: North-Holland, 1989.

SPENCE, A.M. "Investment Strategy and Growth in a New Market." *Bell Journal of Economics*, Vol. 10 (1979), pp. 1–19.

STIGLER, G. "A Theory of Oligopoly." *Journal of Political Economy*, Vol. 72 (1964), pp. 44–61.

VICKERS, J. "Delegation and the Theory of the Firm." *Economic Journal*, Vol. 95 (1985), pp. 138–147.

VON STACKELBERG, H. *Marktform und Gleichgewicht*. Vienna: Springer, 1934.

WHINSTON, M. "Exit with Multiplant Firms." *RAND Journal of Economics*, Vol. 19 (1988), pp. 568–588.

# Part 4

# STRATEGY AND INFORMATION

# 37

# MANAGEMENT MISINFORMATION SYSTEMS

*Russell L. Ackoff*

Source: *Management Science* 14(4) (1967): B147–B156.

Five assumptions commonly made by designers of management information systems are identified. It is argued that these are not justified in many (if not most) cases and hence lead to major deficiencies in the resulting systems. These assumptions are: (1) the critical deficiency under which most managers operate is the lack of relevant information, (2) the manager needs the information be wants, (3) if a manager has the information he needs his decision making will improve, (4) better communication between managers improves organizational performance, and (5) a manager does not have to understand how his information system works, only how to use it. To overcome these assumptions and the deficiencies which result from them, a management information system should be imbedded in a management control system. A procedure for designing such a system is proposed and an example is given of the type of control system which it produces.

The growing preoccupation of operations researchers and management scientists with Management Information Systems (MIS's) is apparent. In fact, for some the design of such systems has almost become synonymous with operations research or management science. Enthusiasm for such systems is understandable: it involves the researcher in a romantic relationship with the most glamorous instrument of our time, the computer. Such enthusiasm is understandable but, nevertheless, some of the excesses to which it has led are not excusable.

Contrary to the impression produced by the growing literature, few computerized management information systems have been put into operation. Of those I've seen that have been implemented, most have not matched expectations and some have been outright failures. I believe that these near- and far-misses could have been avoided if certain false (and usually implicit) assumptions on which many such systems have been erected had not been made.

There seem to be five common and erroneous assumptions underlying the design of most MIS's, each of which I will consider. After doing so I will outline an MIS design procedure which avoids these assumptions.

## Give them more

Most MIS's are designed on the assumption that the critical deficiency under which most managers operate is the *lack of relevant information.* I do not deny that most managers lack a good deal of information that they should have, but I do deny that this is the most important informational deficiency from which they suffer. It seems to me that they suffer more from an *over abundance of irrelevant information.*

This is not a play on words. The consequences of changing the emphasis of an MIS from supplying relevant information to eliminating irrelevant information is considerable. If one is preoccupied with supplying relevant information, attention is almost exclusively given to the generation, storage, and retrieval of information: hence emphasis is placed on constructing data banks, coding, indexing, updating files, access languages, and so on. The ideal which has emerged from this orientation is an infinite pool of data into which a manager can reach to pull out any information he wants. If, on the other hand, one sees the manager's information problem primarily, but not exclusively, as one that arises out of an overabundance of irrelevant information, most of which was not asked for, then the two most important functions of an information system become *filtration* (or evaluation) and *condensation.* The literature on MIS's seldom refers to these functions let alone considers how to carry them out.

My experience indicates that most managers receive much more data (if not information) than they can possibly absorb even if they spend all of their time trying to do so. Hence they already suffer from an information overload. They must spend a great deal of time separating the relevant from the irrelevant and searching for the kernels in the relevant documents. For example, I have found that I receive an average of forty-three hours of unsolicited reading material each week. The solicited material is usually half again this amount.

I have seen a daily stock status report that consists of approximately six hundred pages of computer print-out. The report is circulated daily across managers' desks. I've also seen requests for major capital expenditures that come in book size, several of which are distributed to managers each week. It is not uncommon for many managers to receive an average of one journal a day or more. One could go on and on.

Unless the information overload to which managers are subjected is reduced, any additional information made available by an MIS cannot be expected to be used effectively.

Even relevant documents have too much redundancy. Most documents can be considerably condensed without loss of content. My point here is best made, perhaps, by describing briefly an experiment that a few of my colleagues and I conducted on the OR literature several years ago. By using a panel of well-known experts we identified four OR articles that all members of the panel considered to be "above average," and four articles that were considered to be "below average." The authors of the eight articles were asked to prepare "objective" examinations (duration thirty minutes) plus answers for graduate students who were to be assigned the articles for reading. (The authors were not informed about the experiment.) Then several experienced writers were asked to reduce each article to 2/3 and 1/3 of its original length only by eliminating words. They also prepared a brief abstract of each article. Those who did the condensing did not see the examinations to be given to the students.

A group of graduate students who had not previously read the articles were then selected. Each one was given four articles randomly selected, each of which was in one of its four versions: 100%, 67%, 33%, or abstract. Each version of each article was read by two students. All were given the same examinations. The average scores on the examinations were then compared.

For the above-average articles there was no significant difference between average test scores for the 100%, 67%, and 33% versions, but there was a significant decrease in average test scores for those who had read only the abstract. For the below-average articles there was no difference in average test scores among those who had read the 100%, 67%, and 33% versions, but there was a significant *increase* in average test scores of those who had read only the abstract.

The sample used was obviously too small for general conclusions but the results strongly indicate the extent to which even good writing can be condensed without loss of information. I refrain from drawing the obvious conclusion about bad writing.

It seems clear that condensation as well as filtration, performed mechanically or otherwise, should be an essential part of an MIS, and that such a system should be capable of handling much, if not all, of the unsolicited as well as solicited information that a manager receives.

## The manager needs the information that he wants

Most MIS designers "determine" what information is needed by asking managers what information they would like to have. This is based on the assumption that managers know what information they need and want it.

For a manager to know what information he needs he must be aware of each type of decision he should make (as well as does) and he must have an adequate model of each. These conditions are seldom satisfied. Most managers have some conception of at least some of the types of decisions they must make. Their conceptions, however, are likely to be deficient in a very critical way, a way that follows from an important principle of scientific economy: the less we understand a phenomenon, the more variables we require to explain it. Hence, the manager who does not understand the phenomenon he controls plays it "safe" and, with respect to information, wants "everything." The MIS designer, who has even less understanding of the relevant phenomenon than the manager, tries to provide even more than everything. He thereby increases what is already an overload of irrelevant information.

For example, market researchers in a major oil company once asked their marketing managers what variables they thought were relevant in estimating the sales volume of future service stations. Almost seventy variables were identified. The market researchers then added about half again this many variables and performed a large multiple linear regression analysis of sales of existing stations against these variables and found about thirty-five to be statistically significant. A forecasting equation was based on this analysis. An OR team subsequently constructed a model based on only one of these variables, traffic flow, which predicted sales better than the thirty-five variable regression equation. The team went on to *explain* sales at service stations in terms of the customers' perception of the amount of time lost by stopping for service. The relevance of all but a few of the variables used by the market researchers could be explained by their effect on such perception.

The moral is simple: one cannot specify what information is required for decision making until an explanatory model of the decision process and the system involved has been constructed and tested. Information systems are subsystems of control systems. They cannot be designed adequately without taking control in account. Furthermore, whatever else regression analyses can yield, they cannot yield understanding and explanation of phenomena. They describe and, at best, predict.

## Give a manager the information he needs and his decision making will improve

It is frequently assumed that if a manager is provided with the information he needs, he will then have no problem in using it effectively. The history of OR stands to the contrary. For example, give most managers an initial tableau of a typical "real" mathematical programming, sequencing, or network problem and see how close they come to an optimal solution. If their experience and judgment have any value they may not do badly, but they will seldom do very well. In most management problems there are too many possibilities to expect experience, judgement, or intuition to provide good guesses, even with perfect information.

Furthermore, when several probabilities are involved in a problem the unguided mind of even a manager has difficulty in aggregating them in a valid way. We all know many simple problems in probability in which untutored intuition usually does very badly (e.g., What are the correct odds that 2 of 25 people selected at random will have their birthdays on the same day of the year?). For example, very few of the results obtained by queuing theory, when arrivals and service are probabilistic, are obvious to managers; nor are the results of risk analysis where the managers' own subjective estimates of probabilities are used.

The moral: it is necessary to determine how well managers can use needed information. When, because of the complexity of the decision process, they can't use it well, they should be provided with either decision rules or performance feed-back so that they can identify and learn from their mistakes. More on this point later.

## More communication means better performance

One characteristic of most MIS's which I have seen is that they provide managers with better current information about what other managers and their departments and divisions are doing. Underlying this provision is the belief that better interdepartmental communication enables managers to coordinate their decisions more effectively and hence improves the organization's overall performance. Not only is this not necessarily so, but it seldom is so. One would hardly expect two competing companies to become more cooperative because the information each acquires about the other is improved. This analogy is not as far fetched as one might first suppose. For example, consider the following very much simplified version of a situation I once ran into. The simplification of the case does not affect any of its essential characteristics.

A department store has two "line" operations: buying and selling. Each function is performed by a separate department. The Purchasing Department primarily controls one variable: how much of each item is bought. The Merchandising Department controls the price at which it is sold. Typically, the measure of performance applied to the Purchasing Department was the turnover rate of inventory. The measure applied to the Merchandising Department was gross sales; this department sought to maximize the number of items sold times their price.

Now by examining a single item let us consider what happens in this system. The merchandising manager, using his knowledge of competition and consumption, set a price which he judged would maximize gross sales. In doing so he utilized price-demand curves for each type of item. For each price the curves show the expected sales and values on an upper and lower

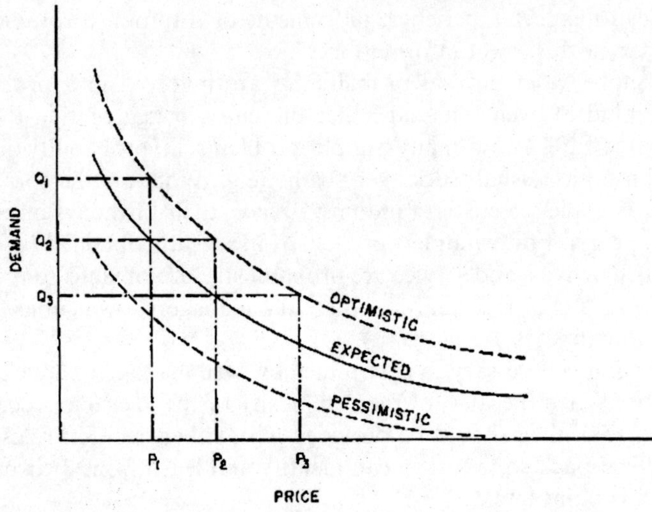


*Figure 1* Price-demand curve.

confidence band as well. (See Figure 1.) When instructing the Purchasing Department how many items to make available, the merchandising manager quite naturally used the value on the upper confidence curve. This minimized the chances of his running short which, if it occurred, would hurt his performance. It also maximized the chances of being over-stocked but this was not his concern, only the purchasing manager's. Say, therefore, that the merchandising manager initially selected price $P_1$ and requested that amount $Q_1$ be made available by the Purchasing Department.

In this company the purchasing manager also had access to the price-demand curves. He knew the merchandising manager always ordered optimistically. Therefore, using the same curve he read over from $Q_1$ to the upper limit and down to the expected value from which he obtained $Q_2$, the quantity he actually intended to make available. He did not intend to pay for the merchandising manager's optimism. If merchandising ran out of stock, it was not his worry. Now the merchandising manager was informed about what the purchasing manager had done so he adjusted his price to $P_2$. The purchasing manager in turn was told that the merchandising manager had made this readjustment so he planned to make only $Q_3$ available. If this process—made possible only by perfect communication between departments—had been allowed to continue, nothing would have been bought and nothing would have been sold. This outcome was avoided by prohibiting communication between the two departments and forcing each to guess what the other was doing.

I have obviously caricatured the situation in order to make the point clear: when organizational units have inappropriate measures of performance which put them in conflict with each other, as is often the case, communication between them may hurt organizational performance, not help it. Organizational structure and performance measurement must be taken into account before opening the flood gates and permitting the free flow of information between parts of the organization. (A more rigorous discussion of organizational structure and the relationship of communication to it can be found in [1].)

## A manager does not have to understand how an information system works, only how to use it

Most MIS designers seek to make their systems as innocuous and unobtrusive as possible to managers lest they become frightened. The designers try to provide managers with very easy access to the system and assure them that they need to know nothing more about it. The designers usually succeed in keeping managers ignorant in this regard. This leaves managers unable to evaluate the MIS as a whole. It often makes them afraid to even try to do so lest they display their ignorance publicly. In failing to evaluate their MIS, managers delegate much of the control of the organization to the system's designers and operators who may have many virtues, but managerial competence is seldom among them.

Let me cite a case in point. A Chairman of a Board of a medium-size company asked for help on the following problem. One of his larger (decentralized) divisions had installed a computerized production-inventory control and manufacturing-manager information system about a year earlier. It had acquired about $2,000,000 worth of equipment to do so. The Board Chairman had just received a request from the Division for permission to replace the original equipment with newly announced equipment which would cost several times the original amount. An extensive "justification" for so doing was provided with the request. The Chairman wanted to know whether the request was really justified. He admitted to complete incompetence in this connection.

A meeting was arranged at the Division at which I was subjected to an extended and detailed briefing. The system was large but relatively simple. At the heart of it was a reorder point for each item and a maximum allowable stock level. Reorder quantities took lead-time as well as the allowable maximum into account. The computer kept track of stock, ordered items when required and generated numerous reports on both the state of the system it controlled and its own "actions."

When the briefing was over I was asked if I had any questions. I did. First I asked if, when the system had been installed, there had been many parts whose stock level exceeded the maximum amount possible under the new system. I was told there were many. I asked for a list of about thirty and for some graph paper. Both were provided. With the help of the system designer and volumes of old daily reports I began to plot the stock level of the first listed item over time. When this item reached the maximum "allowable" stock level it had been reordered. The system designer was surprised and said that by sheer "luck" I had found one of the few errors made by the system. Continued plotting showed that because of repeated premature reordering the item had never gone much below the maximum stock level. Clearly the program was confusing the maximum allowable stock level and the reorder point. This turned out to be the case in more than half of the items on the list.

Next I asked if they had many paired parts, ones that were only used with each other; for example, matched nuts and bolts. They had many. A list was produced and we began checking the previous day's withdrawals. For more than half of the pairs the differences in the numbers recorded as withdrawn were very large. No explanation was provided.

Before the day was out it was possible to show by some quick and dirty calculations that the new computerized system was costing the company almost $150,000 per month more than the hand system which it had replaced, most of this in excess inventories.

The recommendation was that the system be redesigned as quickly as possible and that the new equipment not be authorized for the time being.

The questions asked of the system had been obvious and simple ones. Managers should have been able to ask them but—and this is the point—they felt themselves incompetent to do so. They would not have allowed a handoperated system to get so far out of their control.

No MIS should ever be installed unless the managers for whom it is intended are trained to evaluate and hence control it rather than be controlled by it.

## A suggested procedure for designing an MIS

The erroneous assumptions I have tried to reveal in the preceding discussion can, I believe, be avoided by an appropriate design procedure. One is briefly outlined here.

### *1. Analysis of the decision system*

Each (or at least each important) type of managerial decision required by the organization under study should be identified and the relationships between them should be determined and flow-charted. Note that this is *not* necessarily the same thing as determining what decisions *are* made. For example, in one company I found that make-or-buy decisions concerning parts were made only at the time when a part was introduced into stock and was never subsequently reviewed. For some items this decision had gone unreviewed for as many as twenty years. Obviously, such decisions should be made more often; in some cases, every time an order is placed in order to take account of current shop loading, underused shifts, delivery times from suppliers, and so on.

Decision-flow analyses are usually self-justifying. They often reveal important decisions that are being made by default (e.g., the make-buy decision referred to above), and they disclose interdependent decisions that are being made independently. Decision-flow charts frequently suggest changes in managerial responsibility, organizational structure, and measure of performance which can correct the types of deficiencies cited.

Decision analyses can be conducted with varying degrees of detail, that is, they may be anywhere from coarse to fine grained. How much detail one should become involved with depends on the amount of time and resources that are available for the analysis. Although practical considerations frequently restrict initial analyses to a particular organizational function, it is preferable to perform a coarse analysis of all of an organization's managerial functions rather than a fine analysis of one or a subset of functions. It is easier to introduce finer information into an integrated information system than it is to combine fine subsystems into one integrated system.

### 2. *An analysis of information requirements*

Managerial decisions can be classified into three types:

(a) Decisions for which adequate models are available or can be constructed and from which optimal (or near optimal) solutions can be derived. In such cases the decision process itself should be incorporated into the information system thereby converting it (at least partially) to a control system. A decision model identifies what information is required and hence what information is relevant.

(b) Decisions for which adequate models can be constructed but from which optimal solutions cannot be extracted. Here some kind of heuristic or search procedure should be provided even if it consists of no more than computerized trial and error. A simulation of the model will, as a minimum, permit comparison of proposed alternative solutions. Here too the model specifies what information is required.

(c) Decisions for which adequate models cannot be constructed. Research is required here to determine what information is relevant. If decision making cannot be delayed for the completion of such research or the decision's effect is not large enough to justify the cost of research, then judgment must be used to "guess" what information is relevant. It may be possible to make explicit the implicit model used by the decision maker and treat it as a model of type (b).

In each of these three types of situation it is necessary to provide feedback by comparing actual decision outcomes with those predicted by the model or decision maker. Each decision that is made, along with its predicted outcome, should be an essential input to a management control system. I shall return to this point below.

### *3. Aggregation of decisions*

Decisions with the same or largely overlapping informational requirements should be grouped together as a single manager's task. This will reduce the information a manager requires to do his job and is likely to increase his understanding of it. This may require a reorganization of the system. Even if such a reorganization cannot be implemented completely what can be done is likely to improve performance significantly and reduce the information loaded on managers.

### *4. Design of information processing*

Now the procedure for collecting, storing, retrieving, and treating information can be designed. Since there is a voluminous literature on this subject I shall leave it at this except for one point. Such a system must not only be able to answer questions addressed to it; it should also be able to answer questions that have not been asked by reporting any deviations from expectations. An extensive exception-reporting system is required.

### *5. Design of control of the control system*

It must be assumed that the system that is being designed will be deficient in many and significant ways. Therefore it is necessary to identify the ways in which it may be deficient, to design procedures for detecting its deficiencies, and for correcting the system so as to remove or reduce them. Hence the system should be designed to be flexible and adaptive. this is little more than a platitude, but it has a not-so-obvious implication. No completely computerized system can be as flexible and adaptive as can a man-machine system. This is illustrated by a concluding example of a system that is being developed and is partially in operation. (See Figure 2.)

The company involved has its market divided into approximately two hundred marketing areas. A model for each has been constructed as is "in" the computer. On the basis of competivive intelligence supplied to the service marketing manager by marketing researchers and information specialists he and his staff make policy decisions for each area each month. Their tentative decisions are fed into the computer which yields a forecast of expected performance. Changes are made until the expectations match what is desired. In this way they arrive at "final" decisions. At the end of the month the computer compares the actual performance of each area with what was predicted. If a deviation exceeds what could be expected by chance, the company's OR Group then seeks the reason for the deviation,

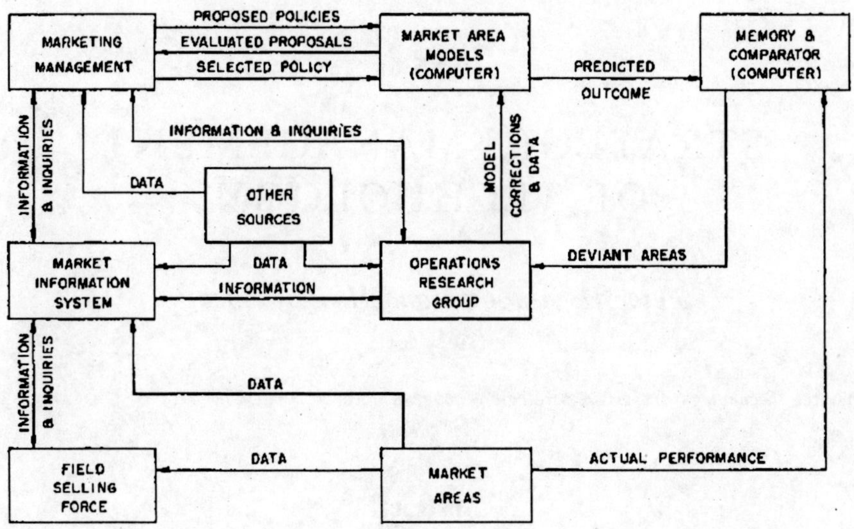


*Figure 2* Simplified diagram of a market-area control system.

performing as much research as is required to find it. If the cause is found to be permanent the computerized model is adjusted appropriately. The result is an adaptive man-machine system whose precision and generality is continuously increasing with use.

Finally it should be noted that in carrying out the design steps enumerated above, three groups should collaborate: information systems specialists, operations researchers, *and managers*. The participation of managers in the design of a system that is to serve them, assures their ability to evaluate its performance by comparing its output with what was predicted. Managers who are not willing to invest some of their time in this process are not likely to use a management control system well, and their system, in turn, is likely to abuse them.

## Reference

1 SENGUPTA, S. S., AND ACKOFF, R. L., "Systems Theory from an Operations Research Point of View," *IEEE Transactions on Systems Science and Cybernetics*, Vol. 1 (Nov. 1965), pp. 9–13.

38

# STRATEGIC MANAGEMENT OF TECHNOLOGY

*Peter H. Antoniou and H. Igor Ansoff*

Source: *Technology Analysis & Strategic Management* 16(2) (2004): 275–91.


## Abstract

This article deals with technology as it relates to strategy design. It addresses the different views of reality between general managers and the organization's technologists. This becomes increasingly important in high levels of turbulence. It examines the role of the general management and technological myopia as major influencer in the decision-making process. The thrust of this article is on the assessment of gaps between management and technologists and methods to close them. The article completes with the role of management in managing and driving technological innovation while integrating technology strategy in the organization's strategy.


Technology was been the driving force in the 20th century and it promises to hold the same if not greater importance during the 21st. The creation, development and application of technology are major forces, which make organizations successful. The most successful and admired organizations are those that are in the forefront of technological innovations.

While general management is responsible for the firm's strategic direction, it frequently fails to manage the organization's technological innovation process in both low and high technology industries.[1]

On one hand the focus of technology in low technology organizations is primarily in utilizing and expanding technology innovation.[2] On the other, technology in high technology organizations is one of the critical determining factors of firms' future success.[3]

It is expected that high technology turbulence is going to increase and to become one of the critical determining factors for organizations' future success. The emphasis in this article will be on the high technology turbulence levels.

Examples of general managements that have been unsuccessful in managing firms' technological innovations were Apple and IBM in the mid to late 1980s. In both cases their general managers did not see the emerging technological as well as the business discontinuities and changes associated with them. Therefore management became the enemy of their own successes. In both cases their general managers were asked to resign.

## Technology challenges to general management

The management of organizations' technological innovation is part of organizations' strategic development, since new technologies, product prototypes and the subsequent stream of new products are developed and explored there.

Selection of the wrong technologies and products as well as downstream mismanagement of firms' profit making processes can lead to a decline of organizations' profitability.[4] Other organizations do not wish to risk too much innovation, because it is costly, and can be made obsolete by rival innovation. So firms have split the difference through the sale of technology licenses and participation in technology-sharing compacts that pay huge dividends to the economy as a whole—and thereby made innovation a routine feature of economic life.[5]

### *Technology impacts on firms' strategy*

There are two groups of variables that influence organizations' choice of technology strategy: external and internal. The external variables are: technological progress, technology life cycle, product life cycle and competitive dynamics. The internal ones are: leadership role and power centre. These variables are illustrated in Figure 1.

The interpretation and assessment of the external and internal variables help general management choose the firm's technology strategy by:

- forecasting the future technological turbulence,
- diagnosing the organization's present technological aggressiveness,
- determining the organization's future technology gap, and
- designing actions and priorities for future technology development.

There are external and internal variables that influence the organization's development and direction.[6] The external variables are technological progress, type of technology cycle, product life cycle and competitive dynamics. The internal ones are leadership role and power centre. These are described below:

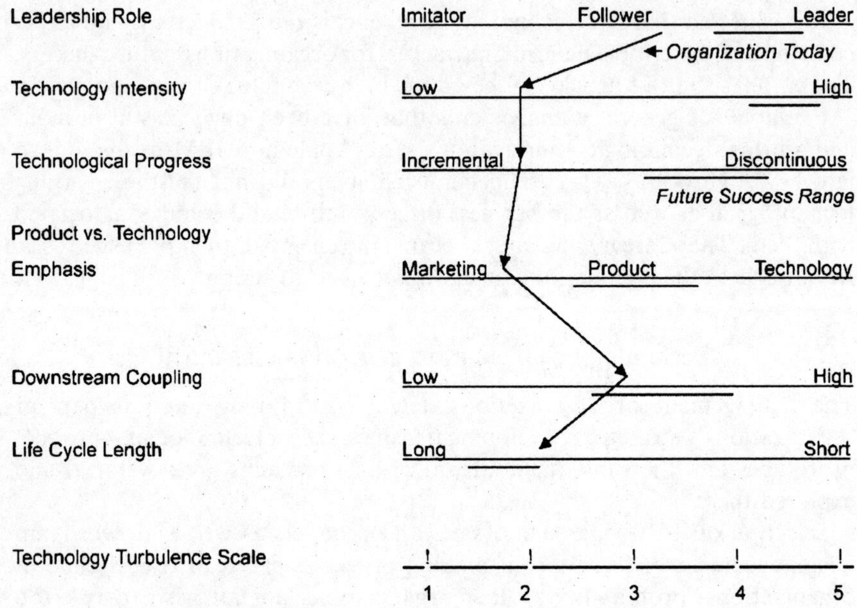


*Figure 1* Technology strategy components.

### *Technological progress*

It assesses the competitive dynamics of technology, technological product differentiation, use of technology as a competitive tool and the technological intensity of the market. Technological progress can be:

- incremental where it is expected that extensions of existing technologies will prevail, i.e. the hygiene or industrial detergent industries, or
- discontinuous where inventions of new proliferating technologies are expected to emerge, i.e. digital technology in photography.

### *Technology cycle*

It determines the length of the cycle, the frequency of introduction of new technologies to the market, and the number of competing technologies. The discussion on the different types of technology life cycles in turbulent environments is included in the second section of this chapter.

### *Product life cycle*

It varies according to the frequency of new product introduced to the market, the length of the life cycles and technologies incorporated in successive products.

### *Competitive dynamics*

They include product differentiation based on technology, use of technology as a competitive tool as well as technological responses due to consumer pressures and governmental regulations. These dynamics influence the competitive and technological intensity of the organization's technological environment.

The remaining two variables, leadership role and power centre are the internal ones and relate to an organization's desired position in the future.

### *Leadership role*

It helps assess organizations' future competitive position in the market. The firm's role can be imitator, follower or leader. To make the decision on which role to play, general management needs to assess the:

- competence level of the organization's technologists,
- existence or not of technological obsolescence, the firm's technologists,
- organization's research leadership abilities,
- organization's leadership position in the market,
- organization's abilities to provide product/service support,
- processes that exist now *vs.* the ones that need to be in place to provide future product/service support.

### *Power centre*

It identifies the departments within the firm where the stimulus for new technology development originates. The different departments include production, marketing, R&D or general management.

The process for determining the external and internal factors affecting the firm's technology strategy are included in the book titled *Implanting Strategic Management*, authored by Ansoff and McDonnell.[7]

## Technological myopia

To assure future success, an organization's strategic direction should be determined by anticipating the future needs of the environment.[8] In today's turbulent environment, misinterpretation of the future environment will have impacts on the firm's future. To succeed in these environments, general managers need to have the mindset and skills to interpret the direction the environment is taking.

Addressing the problem of technological myopia is progressively becoming critical to the success of firms.[9] Before general managers address problems relating to the firm's technologies, they need to realize that they themselves

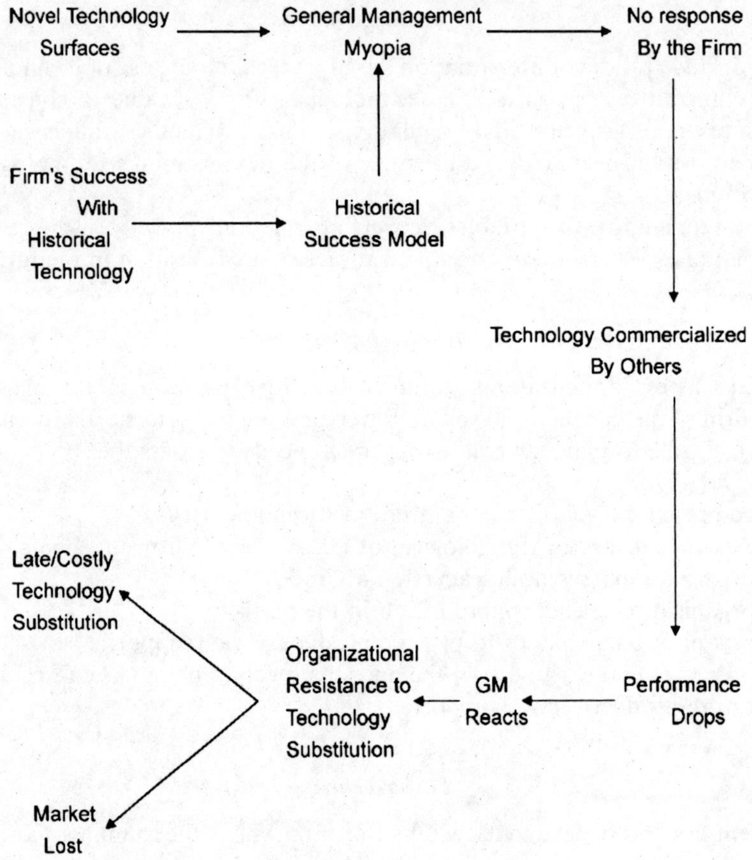


*Figure 2* Technological myopia during technology substitution.

might be myopic. General managers' myopia needs to be treated first before addressing the existence or not of technological myopia.

Myopic general managers refuse to foresee new technological directions.[10] Therefore, myopic general managers do not support technological developments in the direction that would be the most successful for their firm's future.

Figure 2 illustrates the events associated with technological myopia and its impact during technology substitution.

An example elaborating on Figure 2 can be seen in the actions taken by Mr Erstnam Akers, Louis Gerstner's predecessor at IBM, who took the company's reins in 1985. When Mr Akers joined IBM, he found a firm that had '. . . developed the feeling that it could do no wrong. An absolute myopia developed about what was really happening out there with the customers'.[11] Mr Akers did not interpret the demand, features and technological applications of personal computers correctly. He neither saw the shift of technology from hardware to software, nor the future potential of the personal computers. Personal computers were perceived as self-standing instruments and were viewed as hardware pieces with limited capabilities. As a result, Mr Akers did not see the value of expanding into the personal computer hardware industry where each unit is sold at a ridiculously low price in comparison to that of mainframes.

Lack of a correct interpretation of the trends in the computer industry and IBM's past successes on mainframe computers caused Mr Akers to think that '. . . mainframe computers were here to stay forever'.

Based on this view, IBM's general management made its decision to focus on mainframe computers based on the expertise and technical knowledge of individuals whose background and experience were in mainframe technology and were equally myopic.

IBM's lack of response encouraged competitors to introduce clones of the (PS/2) personal computers, thus, eroding IBM's market share.

In 1988, when Mr Akers reacted belatedly and inconclusively, IBM's financial performance had been declining for two consecutive years. IBM reacted with a late and costly technology substitution.

In order to assess the direction of an organization's technology environments and reduce technological myopia, the collection of necessary information should come from a wide range of unbiased sources, from within as well as from outside the firm.

General managers need to seek advice especially from outside the firm in order to:

- examine the existence of technological myopia of the firm's technologists, and
- understand and get an unbiased view of the future technology developments in the firm's industry.

The analysis of the information from within as well as from outside the organization forces general managers to question their organization's technological competence in the industry.

In turbulent environments general managers are the ones assessing and interpreting the information on organizations' technology developments.

Assessment and interpretation of information on future technologies encompasses dealing with employees and outside experts whose knowledge and expertise is in a field where general managers might not have the desired background or knowledge. Therefore, general managers need to develop some knowledge in the technology field and most importantly to develop their skill in using experts and asking experts 'expert questions'. The development of these skills is discussed later in this article.

## The role of general management in technology innovation

In managing an organization's technology innovation in turbulent environments, general managers should:

- guide organization's forecasting units,
- direct organization's technology innovation process,
- assure the level of competence of the firm's technologists,
- direct marketing and production for timely introduction of products/ services to the market, and
- choose the organization's technology strategy.

In turbulent environments the use of cutting edge technology is a critical success factor. Therefore, general managers need to assure that the firm has up-to-date technology that will support firms' business strategy.[12]

There are two types of technology cycles in turbulent environments: fertile and turbulent. Each technology life cycle requires a different response from the firm.

Figure 3 illustrates the demand life cycle and the types of technology life cycle in turbulent environments.

As shown in Figure 3, fertile life cycles exist when the basic technology is long lived within the demand life cycle and products proliferate offering incrementally better performance. In fertile technologies, product development becomes a critical factor in economic success. The newest and best performing product captures the market. This usually takes place by

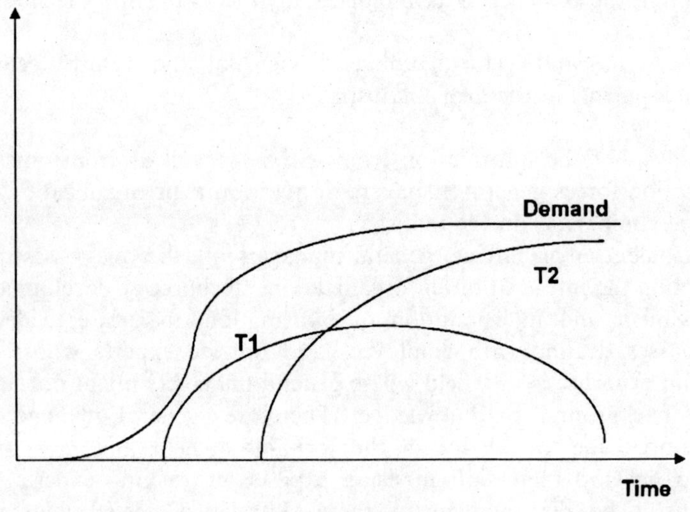


*Figure 3* Technology life cycle.

developing additional applications, uses or extensions of existing technologies, for example, the watch industry or the glass sheet industry.

In turbulent technology cycles, there is technology substitution of one or more technology life cycles within the demand life cycle.

Success in turbulent technology cycles requires the invention of new technologies that replace the existing ones, for example, in the office automation or the audio industry.

The effects of technology substitution in turbulent technology cycles are further reaching than that of the fertile life cycles. Technology substitution threatens obsolescence of the firm's entire investment in the preceding technology.

The role of general managers is to guide their firm's forecasting units in collecting and interpreting information on the organization's future environment. This information will indicate whether the firm will be operating in fertile, turbulent or both fertile and turbulent environments.

### *The role of general managers in directing firms' technology innovation process*

Based on the information general managers receive on the organization's future technology environments from outside as well as from within the organization, general managers decide on their firm's R&D direction.

Transition to a new technology is difficult within the organization, not only financially, but also culturally and politically.[13] The new technology challenges the historical success model held by both technologists and general managers. It also threatens the position of power and influence within the firm.[14]

The problem of transition to a new technology is further aggravated when the technology life cycle is both fertile and turbulent. When a new technology surfaces, the firm is already deeply involved in the competitive struggle of product proliferation. Its R&D is committed to this struggle and can become an obstacle to the firm's transition to the new substituting technology.[15]

This is exactly what happened at Eastman Kodak when digital technology emerged as the next generation of technology in image processing.

General managers need to decide whether the organization will be operating in:

- fertile technology cycle, thus requiring investment in extension of technologies to satisfy future needs, or
- turbulent technology cycle, thus requiring investment in invention of technologies to satisfy future needs, or
- both, fertile and turbulent, thus requiring separation of firms' efforts between extension and invention of future technologies.

General managers do not always interpret future direction of technology correctly. An example is Remington typewriters. Remington's technological advantage was the 'feather touch' feature of its typewriter. This is what gave Remington a differentiating advantage in the marketplace. Under management's direction, Remington's R&D division focused on how to extend the existing technology by trying to make the 'feather touch' more 'feather touch'. IBM surpassed Remington by introducing a replacement technology, the electric typewriter and the new 'ball' design, which made IBM well known in the 1970s.

The same case scenario occurred later with IBM. IBM was still introducing new and upgraded models of the electric 'ball' technology typewriters, while IBM's competitors gained market advantage by introducing a completely different type of technology, the word processors and later the desk top computers. These products/technologies replaced typewriters completely.

The challenge to management is to be realistic in assessing the consequences of the new technology. It is easy to rationalize that a new technology will revolutionalize the products and produce a large-scale revival of demand. This is not likely to occur, unless the advances are so revolutionary as to make obsolete the products that already saturate the marketplace.

## The role of general managers in assuring the level of competence of their firm's technologists

Technologists play a significant role in introducing new technologies and consequently products/services to the market. Their role is to focus on the development of new technologies and products. They hold in their hands the creative process of new technology development.

Technology is translated into new inventions, new applications and new products and services. New technologies are obtained through long-term investment directly impacting firms' short-term profitability.

It is necessary for general managers and their firm's technologists to communicate pertinent information to each other in order for general managers to determine the firm's future direction. Particularly in turbulent environments, general managers become involved in the management of technology and articulate the products and services general management wants. Furthermore, general managers need to assure themselves that the necessary technological expertise exists within the firm to develop the needed products/services.

### *Technological obsolescence of organizations' technologists*

In high turbulent environments the problem of obsolescence of a firm's technologists could develop. When a new technology evolves it is likely that the expertise of the existing technologists could become obsolete. It is necessary for general managers to assess whether their firm's technologists have the needed expertise for the new technology.

Obsolete technologists can become an obstacle to the firm's technological innovation. They are usually the ones who introduced a technology with a successful stream of products/services, which is becoming obsolete. They do not see the next technological wave.

When there is technological obsolescence, general management separates the firm's technologists, based on the expertise of the technologists, into three groups. The first group consists of the technologists who are experts on the existing technology. Their focus is on extension and support of existing technologies.

The second group is of technologists whose expertise is in the existing technology but are trainable in the new technology the firm wants to develop in the future. This group would focus on training in and the development of the new technology and would later be screened based on the individual's progress and development.

Technologists, whose expertise lies in the next generation of technologies the firm wishes to develop in the future, form the third group. Their instructions are to develop the new generation of technology and they are given the appropriate resources. These technologists are separated as a group because they should not be 'contaminated' or 'stifled' by the technologists and mindsets committed to the previous technology.

A company that followed this approach successfully is Eastman Kodak. General management separated the technologists of image processing into two groups. The first was comprised of technologists of the silver halide technology, which Eastman Kodak pioneered and with which it dominates the US and global markets. The focus of this group is on the proliferation of the halide technology. The second group is focusing on the digital technology, its creation, evolution and the generation of products that Eastman Kodak will be adopting in the near future.

Other companies that followed this approach successfully are Walt Disney with the animation group and Lockheed with the Stealth project.

## Gaps between general managers and technologists

In relating with each other, general managers and technologists have different views of reality and are typically confronted with several gaps in understanding each other. These gaps are the semantic gap, the objectives/value gap and the information gap. These gaps are illustrated in Figure 4.

The semantic gap arises from differences in language and perception of success factors between general managers and the firm's technologists.

While general managers focus on operationalizing technological advancements, technologists perceive technological advancements and breakthroughs as the critical success factors in their profession. Technologists typically

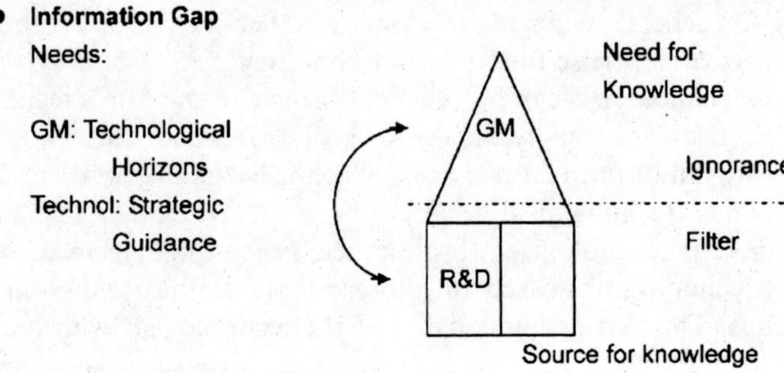


- **Semantic Gap**
  - Mentality Differences
  - Language Differences
  - Implicit Knowledge "Fingerspitzengefuhl"

*Figure 4* Gaps between general management and technologists.

perceive technological variables as the decisive parameters in advocating new investment.

The key is how general managers and technologists communicate their needs so that each one utilizes their implicit knowledge.[16]

The objectives/value gap arises from the difference in what is perceived to be important.

General managers concentrate on the commercial impact of technology and are interested in providing support for technological advancements based on expected commercial impact.

The emphasis of technologists is more on the thrill of discovery that is translated in the optimization of knowledge, research, social progress and the professional prestige associated with it. The firm's profitability can be more of a hindrance rather than a stimulus for technologists. Profitability usually stifles the development process, questioning the researchers' reasoning of further exploration in every step. While technologists see a technological innovation as enough of a reason to bring it to the market, general managers need to realize its profit potential.

The information gap arises from the knowledge and information that general managers and technologists need from each other. On one hand, general managers need to have knowledge of the technological prospects in order to decide on future technology development. Technologists, on the other hand, need to have strategic guidance to direct the technology efforts for research and exploration.

Knowledge on new technologies is often vague and difficult to quantify since prospects, risks, costs and consequences are usually in the hands of the technologists. In addition, this knowledge will have to be communicated in a language that general management understands.

Technologists are usually ignorant of the language general management uses, the way information is interpreted and the way the decision-making process takes place. Technologists are not usually aware of what is needed to bring new products to the market and the downstream costs associated with new product/service introduction. In addition to the downstream costs, technologists do not realize the time and costs related to developing the new capabilities needed to support the introduction of the new technology.

General managers may also be ignorant of technological developments that make transmission of information even more complicated. General managers may not understand the new proposed technology and may also not understand the language associated with it.

Another issue that complicates the communication process even further is that needed knowledge and information is usually buffered by layers of management who do not understand technological consequences either.

To summarize, while technologists are the source of technological knowledge, general managers and technologists do not speak the same language and do not have common objectives, thus making the communication process difficult and the interpretation of information even harder.

Deciding on a new product/service is difficult for general managers. General managers do not fully understand the technology and do not have the knowledge to interpret the technological information. General managers are faced with taking risks on new technology developments without having a clear idea of the real costs involved.

### *Eliminating the gaps between general managers and their organizations' technologists*

There are three things that general managers can do to eliminate gaps between them and their firm's technologists:

(1) Develop direct communication channels between general managers and their organizations' technologists. This allows general managers to provide direct strategic direction and assessment of new product development. The more direct the communication channel the less the likelihood for misinterpretation.
(2) Establish a dual rewards system for the organization's technologists. First, rewarding the technologists for the financial contribution of their technologies to the firm's success. Second, allowing the technologists to pursue their personal research objectives.
(3) Establish an education system where general managers learn the dynamics of technology and the technologists learn the dynamics of profit making.

## The role of general managers in directing marketing and production for timely introduction of new products/services to the market

Timing of new product introduction is a major concern, since, if the organization is too early in introducing a new technology to the market, the consumers might not be ready to accept it. At the same time, if the organization is late, competition may have a first entry advantage.[17]

When a new technology/product is invented, there are consequences for the organization's product line and profitability. The moment a new technology and its products are introduced to the market they displace the previous generation of products and services. Organizations phase out displaced products/services with the associated loss in future sales of an already depreciated technology expense.

When new technologies and products are invented, general management faces a conflict between near and long-term profitability.[18] On one hand, to maintain and increase near term profitability, it is more beneficial for a firm not to introduce a new technology and product line; but the longer the organization waits the higher the probability that its competitors will enter the market first. On the other hand, a firm has to introduce new technologies, products and services to gain long-term profitability. The decision rests in the hands of general managers to decide on the optimum timing for the introduction of new products and services to the market for maximum profitability.[19]

In addition to future losses from not taking further advantage of an already depreciated technology, there are additional costs associated with introducing a new technology to the market. These costs are comprised of expenditures on in house support and marketing efforts for new products/services. These costs are in addition to the ones incurred to develop the new technology. Therefore the introduction of a new product to the market is not taken lightly by general management.

There are two approaches to the innovation process and the introduction of products/services to the market: the uncontrolled and the controlled innovation processes. These processes are illustrated in Figure 5.

The top part of Figure 5 illustrates the uncontrolled innovation process where general managers have little influence in new product development with near and long-term effects in organizations' profitability.

There are certainly a number of examples of incidents where companies were either too early or too late in the introduction of a new technology/product to the market, with direct effects on the firm's profitability. Incidents of this type have occurred in the audio industry and the digital technology when new technology and products were introduced to the market too soon.

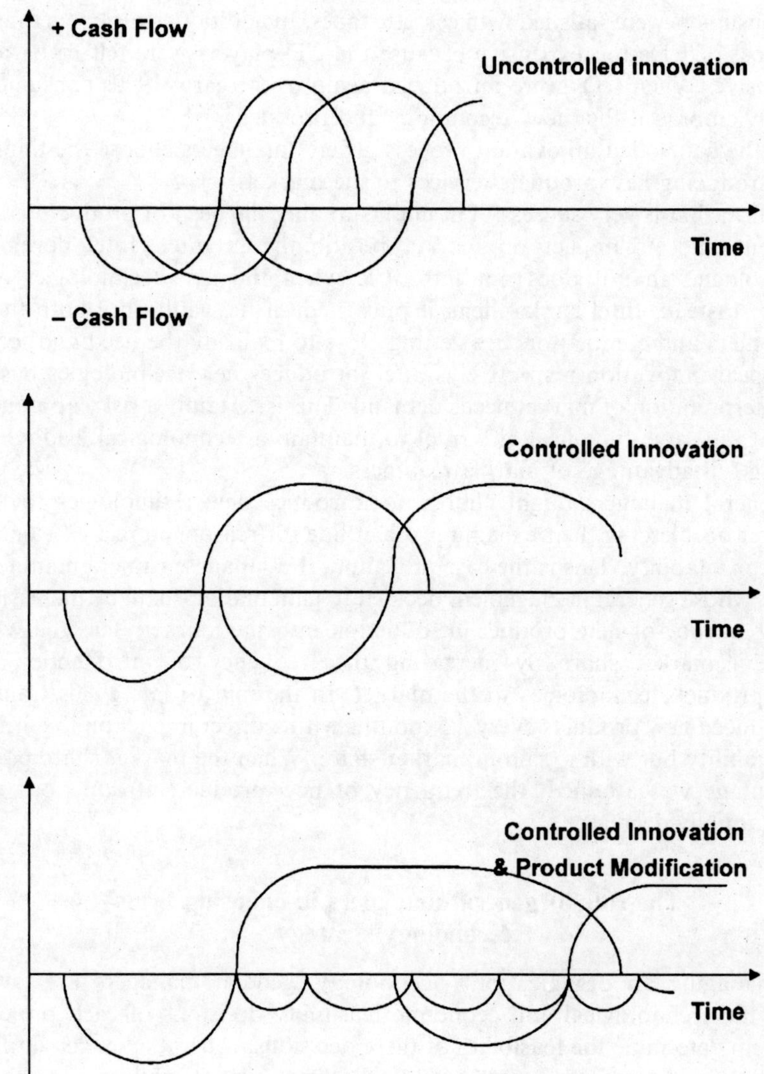


*Figure 5* Controlling product development.

Digital technology was invented in 1972 and CDs were first introduced to the market in the late 1970s. Consumers did not react favourably to the new technology. At that time consumers were happy with LPs and 8-track tapes. CDs were again introduced to the market in the early 1980s and again the consumers did not respond.

Consumers were satisfied with cassette tapes. In addition, consumers found the cost of CDs too expensive because the CD players were felt to be too expensive. When CDs were introduced again in the early 1990s consumers largely embraced the 'new' technology and product.

In the controlled innovation process general managers choose the timing of introducing new products/services to the market.

A firm that is very successful in understanding the need of product development and its impact on market positioning is Intel. Intel develops technologies that it does not introduce when the new technologies are ready. Instead, Intel banks them; it puts them in the vault until both their customers and competitors are getting close to realizing the need and technological innovation respectively. Intel introduces new technologies based on interpretation of market needs/demand. This is certainly a risky approach but at the same time it allows Intel to maintain a technological lead while taking full advantage of market readiness.

General managers might choose to introduce new technologies to the market obsolescing their existing product line for reasons unrelated to near term profitability. This is the case of Canon, the Japanese camera manufacturer, whose general management decided to gain market share by increasing the frequency of new product introduction into the market. The goal was to gain market share by increasing the frequency of introduction of new products/technologies to the market. In the mid to late 1980s Canon introduced new products every 2.5 months with a direct impact on the firm's profitability but with a gain in market share. When the market share point advantage was attained, the frequency of new product introduction was substantially decreased.

## The role of general managers in choosing firms' technology strategy

In managing an organization's technology, general managers are faced with the technological and economic feasibility decisions of each project. To help determine the feasibility of these decisions, general managers utilize information from within and outside the firm. The feasibility assessment constantly influences general managers' decisions to buy or develop new technologies.

There are three major areas that general managers focus on while addressing issues in managing firms' technology:

(1) Identification of future technologies and their impact on their organization's environment;
(2) Assessment of the firm's internal technology capability; and
(3) Integration of technology in the organization's strategy.

One of the tools that general managers can use to determine an organization's future technologies is a technology surveillance system. This tool is installed in the organization to track technology developments and their impact on the firm and the organization's environment. This is accomplished by identifying and assessing trends, opportunities, discontinuities and threats of the organization's future environment.

This technological information system collects and analyses information pertinent to general managers' decision-making needs. This system helps determine the intensity of technology innovation and its relative importance to the organization and the organization's future technology environment.

Another area that a general manager needs to assess is the organization's internal technology capability. General managers could identify the strength of the firm's technological capability by assessing the existence of a gap between the future technology turbulence and the organization's technological capability. Based on the existence and size of gaps general management would develop action priorities.

Particularly in high technology turbulent environments, general managers need to install a flexible organization based on innovative cultures.[20] General managers would be involved in the management of the organization's technology innovation and have expertise in technology management.

One way, which fosters technology innovation, is establishing a project management system within the firm. The project system encourages different avenues of creativity that are then channelled into profitable development projects. The profitability estimates for each project should include the entire streams of costs associated from research to market.

Another area, mentioned earlier, is educating general managers and R&D managers in an effort to foster better understanding and communication between them.[21] On one hand, general managers would be educated on the dynamics and economics of the R&D process as well as in the behaviour of creative technologists. On the other, R&D managers would be educated on the strategic management decision-making process and feasibility assessment decisions.

General managers need to develop their skills in utilizing the information provided by experts when dealing with technologists in the firm and those in the technology field.

### *General managers' expertise in using experts*

The skill of general managers in using experts is valuable both in an outside the firm. This skill entails asking experts the kinds of questions which will provide answers that general managers understand and can use in their decision-making process. Honing this skill helps general managers to communicate in fields where, in the majority of times, they do not have the needed expertise.

The following are some ways to develop general managers' skills in using experts:

(1) Cultivate the experts: keeping track of the outcomes predicted by the experts *vs.* the actual outcome. This helps general managers learn the experts' bias towards higher or lower expectations.
(2) Develop cross-ideological communication skill: managers and experts have norms and aspirations that they bring to work. An understanding of these norms and their influence on experts' behaviour is helpful in evaluating the experts' proposals.
(3) Use the advice of several experts: engage in discussions with different experts in the field so as to confront opinions and identify trends and technological developments.
(4) Acquire sufficient knowledge in the field: managers who rely on experts should acquire sufficient knowledge about the respective fields of the experts in order to be able to judge the experts' method of analysis and its applicability to the problem to be solved.

## Integration of technology in the firm's strategy

There are two parts supporting the organizations' future business strategy: the technology strategy and the societal strategy. Integration of these strategies is illustrated in Figure 6.

A major component of this integration is the installation of a surveillance system. This system collects information pertinent to the firm's strategic, technological and societal needs. Based on this information, general managers decide on the types of technologies to explore in the development of future projects.

Technology decisions go hand in hand with an organization's societal strategy. Firms must be aware of changes in the socio-political environment and recognize how the 'rules of the game' will impact the firm's future behaviour. Societal changes influence both the speed and impact of new technology introduction on the society. The societal changes in turn influence organizations' development of technology.

An organization's future technology is a decisive factor on its future survival. Future trends, opportunities and threats are translated into decisions on:

- technology substitution: whether to foster extension or invention of new technologies, and
- technology acquisition: whether to buy or develop the next generation of technology.

General managers are constantly faced with the techno-economical decision for every project and its affects on the organization's profitability.

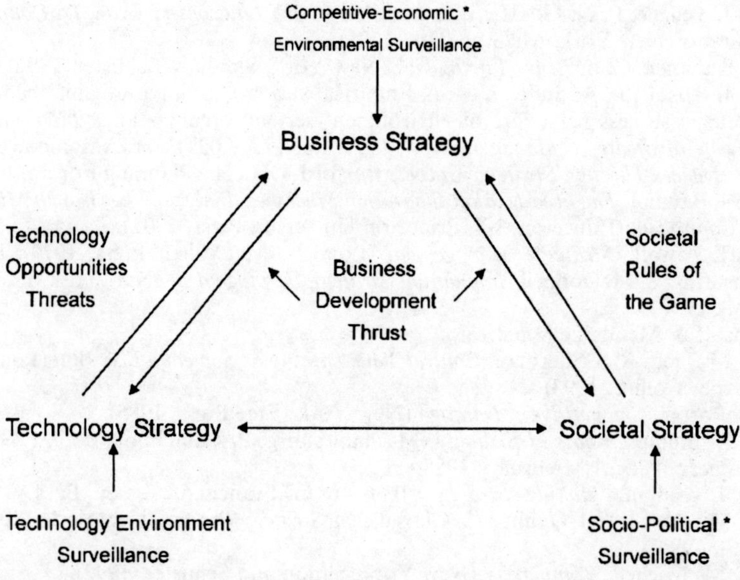


*Figure 6* Integration of business, technology and societal strategies.

General managers are responsible to the firm's investors to provide an acceptable return on their investment. Usually, investors are interested in the near term profitability of the firm as measured by quarterly performance. Investment in technology is often translated into a short-term decrease in profits. Investors are resistant to a decrease in profits, but without investment in technology future profitability is threatened.

General managers are faced with the challenge in trying to find the optimal investment decision balancing between near term profitability and medium to long-term investments in technology.

However in turbulent environments, general managers who are directly involved in business strategy development are more successful than those who let the firm's strategists propose future plans. The signs are that the successful organizations in the 21st century will depend on technology. Technology strategy becomes an important component in the job of the general manager.

## Notes and references

1 H. I. Ansoff, The concept of strategic management, *The Journal of Business Policy*, 2(4), 1972, p. 3; T. Khalil, *Management of Technology* (New York, McGraw Hill, 2000).

2 G. J. Tellis & P. N. Golder, *Will & Vision—How Latecomers Grow To Dominate Markets* (New York, McGraw Hill, 2001).
3 L. Kahaner, *Competitive Intelligence* (New York, Simon & Schuster, 1996).
4 H. I. Ansoff, P. A. Sullivan *et al.*, Empirical support for a paradigmic theory of strategic success behaviors of environment serving organizations, *International Review of Strategic Management*, 4, 1993, pp. 173–202; P. H. Antoniou, *Competitiveness Through Strategic Success* (Oxford, OH, The Planning Forum, 1994).
5 W. J. Baumol, *The Free-Market Innovation Machine: Analyzing the Growth Miracle of Capitalism* (Princeton, NJ, Princeton University Press, 2002).
6 H. I. Ansoff, *Strategic Management* (London, MacMillan Press, 1979); H. I. Ansoff & E. McDonnell, *Implanting Strategic Management* (New York, Prentice Hall, 1990).
7 Ansoff & McDonnell, *ibid.*
8 N. M. Tichy & S. Sherman, *Control Your Destiny or Someone Else Will* (London, Harper Collins, 1993).
9 M. Porter, *Competitive Advantage* (New York, Free Press, 1985).
10 T. R. Phillips, *Roots of Strategy* (Mechanicsburg, PA, Stackpole Books, 1985).
11 *Business Week*, 15 February 1988.
12 T. J. Galpin, *Making Strategy Work* (San Francisco, Jossey Bass, 1997); H. Mintzberg, J. B. Quinn & S. Ghosal, *The Strategy Process* (New York, Prentice Hall, 1999).
13 W. M. Michell, *Complexity* (New York, Simon and Schuster, 1992).
14 G. W. Dauphinais, G. Means & C. Price, *Wisdom of CEO* (New York, Wiley, 2000); F. E. Emery & E. L. Trist, The causal texture of organizational environments, *Human Relations*, 18, 1963, pp. 20–26.
15 M. A. Mische, *Strategic Renewal* (New York, Prentice Hall, 2001).
16 M. Tusman & E. Romanelli, Organizational evolution: a metamorphosis model of convergence and reorientation, in: B. Staw & L. Cummings L (Eds), *Research in Organizational Behavior*, Vol. 7 (Greenwich, CT, JAI Press, 1985), pp. 171–222.
17 R. Cross, S. P. Bogarti & A. Parker, Making invisible work visible: using social network analysis to support strategic collaboration, *California Management Review*, 44(2), 2002, pp. 25–41.
18 H. I. Ansoff, *The New Corporate Strategy* (New York, Wiley, 1988).
19 M. Tripsas, Understanding the timing of technology transitions, *Working Paper* #02-028, Harvard Business School, 2001.
20 P. C. Nutt, Surprising but true: half of the decisions in organizations fail, *Academy of Management Executive*, 13, 1999, pp. 75–70.
21 Kakabadse, From individual to team to cadre: tracking leadership for the third millennium, *Strategic Change* 9(1), 2000, pp. 5–16. D. A. Nadler, *Champions of Change* (San Francisco, Jossey Bass, 1998).

# Part 5

# CASE STUDIES

# 39

# CORPORATE ECONOMIC PERFORMANCE

## Diversification strategy versus market structure

*H. Kurt Christensen and Cynthia A. Montgomery*

Source: *Strategic Management Journal* 2(4) (1981): 327–43.

**Summary**

This paper incorporates both diversification strategy and market structure variables in a study of corporate economic performance. A subsample of 128 firms from Rumelt's 1974 study was updated and utilized to investigate the possibility that market structure variables might moderate or confound the diversification/performance relationship he reported. Study results indicate that performance differences could be demonstrated for some of Rumelt's categories, but, across the range of categories, a hypothesis of performance differences was rejected. As expected, categories associated with distinctly high or distinctly low economic performance were also associated with significant differences in a series of market structure variables.

Researchers from several disciplines have sought to identify factors which influence corporate economic performance. Strategic management researchers have sought to relate corporate economic performance to the major direction-setting decisions made by the firm. For a new and growing firm, these decisions frequently relate to the degree and manner in which its product line and served market should be extended. For an older firm which wishes to continue to grow, the key decisions generally relate to the degree and manner in which it should diversify into different businesses (Chandler, 1962; Scott, 1971).

Starting from a very different perspective, researchers in industrial organization economics have been guided by a conceptual framework which examines possible relationships among (1) the structure of the industry (or industries) in which the firm operates, (2) the conduct of the firms within that industry, and (3) the level of economic performance both of the individual firms and of their associated industries. This effort has yielded an extensive literature, much of which supports the proposition that firm profits are strongly influenced by the structure of the market or markets in which the firm operates (Scherer, 1970).

These two streams of research have developed in large measure independently of each other. It is the purpose of the present research to incorporate both diversification strategy and market structure variables in a study of corporate economic performance.

## Overview of study and hypotheses

The publication of Richard P. Rumelt's book, *Strategy, Structure, and Economic Performance* in 1974 represented a watershed in the study of diversification strategy. In that work, Rumelt made two major contributions. First, building on the earlier work of Wrigley (1970), he developed a nine-category measure of diversification strategy. Second, he demonstrated a statistical linkage between diversification strategy and economic performance.

In assigning companies to a diversification strategy category, Rumelt utilized three ratios, the latter two of which he developed specifically for his study.

1. *Specialization ratio:* 'The proportion of a firm's revenues that can be attributed to its largest single business.' (Rumelt, 1974:14)
2. *Related ratio:* 'The proportion of a firm's revenues attributable to its largest group of related businesses.' (Rumelt, 1974:16)
3. *Vertical ratio:* 'The proportion of the firm's revenues that arise from all by-products, intermediate products, and end products of a vertically integrated sequence of processing activities.' (Rumelt, 1974:23)

By developing measures of relatedness and verticality, Rumelt overcame some of the limitations both of Wrigley's four-category scheme and of product-count measures employed in industrial organization economics studies of diversification, (Rumelt's categories are defined in Appendix A.)

Utilizing the improved classification scheme and multiple measures of economic performance, Rumelt found that seven of his nine diversification categories clustered into high, medium and low performance groups. A summary of Rumelt's findings appears in Tables 1 and 2.

It is noteworthy that both categories classified as high performers diversified by building on a single strength or resource associated with the

*Table 1* Financial characteristics of the strategic categories.

| | *Sales growth* | *Earnings growth* | *Earnings per share growth* | *Relative standard deviation of EPS* | *Price/ earnings ratio* | *Return on capital* | *Return on equity* | *Equity/ capital ratio* | *Internal financing ratio* | *Risk premium ratio* |
|---|---|---|---|---|---|---|---|---|---|---|
| Est. category means: | | | | | | | | | | |
| Single | $7.17^{--}$ | $4.81^{--}$ | $3.92^{--}$ | $16.13^{-}$ | $14.60^{---}$ | 10.81 | 13.20 | 0.781 | 0.580 | $0.378^{--}$ |
| Dominant-vertical | $7.42^{--}$ | $7.34^{-}$ | $5.14^{-}$ | 22.79 | $15.68^{--}$ | $8.24^{---}$ | $10.18^{---}$ | $0.724^{---}$ | $0.662^{-}$ | $0.329^{---}$ |
| Dominant-constrained | 9.48 | 9.08 | 7.60 | 23.15 | 15.92 | $12.71^{+++}$ | $14.91^{++}$ | $0.807^{+}$ | $0.609^{--}$ | $0.658^{++}$ |
| Dominant-linked-unrelated | 6.93 | 8.10 | 6.11 | 16.63 | 15.41 | 8.69 | 10.28 | 0.758 | 0.601 | $0.221^{-}$ |
| Related-constrained | 9.62 | $10.39^{++}$ | $8.56^{+++}$ | $15.91^{--}$ | $19.19^{+++}$ | $11.97^{+++}$ | $14.11^{+++}$ | $0.800^{++}$ | 0.729 | $0.775^{+++}$ |
| Related-linked | 8.06 | 7.15 | 5.57 | 17.58 | $19.27^{+++}$ | 10.43 | 12.28 | 0.798 | 0.681 | 0.451 |
| Unrelated-passive | $6.10^{-}$ | 7.78 | 5.96 | 20.90 | $13.77^{--}$ | 9.40 | $10.38^{-}$ | $0.830^{+}$ | 0.616 | $0.357^{-}$ |
| Acquisitive-conglomerate | $20.64^{+++}$ | $18.64^{+++}$ | $9.46^{+}$ | $39.28^{+++}$ | 17.43 | 9.56 | 13.13 | $0.591^{---}$ | $1.970^{+++}$ | 0.516 |
| Est. overall mean | 9.01 | 8.72 | 6.57 | 20.11 | 17.02 | 10.52 | 12.64 | 0.769 | 0.732 | 0.516 |
| Est. residual $\sigma$ | 6.06 | 8.73 | 8.02 | 18.63 | 5.45 | 5.05 | 5.33 | 0.142 | 0.400 | 0.456 |
| Partial $R^2$ (per cent) | 20.00 | 11.40 | 5.50 | 8.80 | 10.30 | 9.40 | 9.60 | 13.00 | 36.40 | 7.40 |
| Sig. $F_1$-ratio test | 0.001 | 0.001 | — | 0.005 | 0.001 | 0.005 | 0.001 | 0.001 | 0.001 | 0.015 |
| Sig. $F_2$-ratio test | 0.05 | 0.1 | — | — | 0.001 | 0.001 | 0.005 | 0.025 | — | — |

The *F*-ratio was used to test the hypothesis that category effects were zero (all category means are equal). The $F_2$-ratio was used to test the hypothesis that category effects are zero if the acquisitive-conglomerate category is excluded. The table shows the significance levels at which these hypotheses can be rejected.

*Source*: Richard Rumelt. *Strategy, Structure, and Economics Performance*, Harvard University Press, Cambridge, Massachusetts, 1974, p. 92. Reprinted by permission. Estimated mean values of the Equity/Capital Ratio, Internal Financing Ratio, Price/Earnings Ratio, and Risk Premium Ratio are expressed as ratios. All others are expressed as percentages. The plus or minus signs following an estimated category mean indicate that it differed significantly ('+' for a positive deviation, '–' for a negative deviation) from the overall mean (*t*-ratio test). One sign indicates a deviation significant at the 0.1 level, two signs indicate the 0.5 level, and three signs the 0.01 level.

Each of the performance variables is defined in Rumelt, 1974, pp. 168–70.

*Table 2* Strategy performance in Rumelt's study.

| *Strategy performance* | | |
|---|---|---|
| *High* | *Medium* | *Low* |
| Dominant-constrained<br>Related-constrained | Related-linked<br>Single<br>Acquisitive-conglomerate | Dominant-vertical<br>Unrelated-passive |

(Two of Rumelt's categories, dominant-linked and dominant-unrelated, were not clearly associated with any cluster.)
*Source*: Richard Rumelt, *Strategy, Structure, and Economic Performance*, Harvard University Press, Cambridge, Massachusetts, 1974, p. 94. Reprinted by permission.

*Table 3* A selected listing of research studies investigating the relationship between firm or industry performance and market structure variables

| | *Market share* | *Market concentration* | *Market growth* | *Firm size* |
|---|---|---|---|---|
| Gutmann (1964) 53 firms | | | + | |
| Hall and Weiss (1967) 341 firms | | + | | + |
| Collins and Preston (1968) 20 2-digit, 213 4-digit industries | | + | | |
| Miller (1969) 106 minor IRS industries | | + | | |
| Shepherd (1972) 231 firms | + | + | | – |
| Gale (1972) 106 firms | + | + | ± | + |
| Bass (1973) 97 food firms | + | ± | ± | + |
| Meehan and Duchesneau (1973) 186 firms in 32 4-digit industries | | + | | |
| Rhoades (1973) 241 4-digit industries | | + | + | |
| Dalton and Penn (1976) 97 food firms | + | + | – | ± |
| Patton (1976) Firms in U.S. brewing industry, 1952–1971 | ± | | | |
| Bass, Cattin, and Wittink (1978) 63 firms | + | ± | + | ± |

+ indicates a positive correlation with performance
– indicates a negative correlation with performance
± indicates mixed results; correlations in both directions

original business (constrained diversification). The low performers, on the other hand, reflected both sides of the diversification spectrum. The unrelated passive firms are among the most highly diversified in the study, while the dominant vertical firms were far less diversified.

Rumelt's work has commonly been interpreted to mean that various diversification profiles lead to varied performance levels. However, the correlational nature of Rumelt's results cannot support such conclusions, a caution Rumelt himself noted (1974:156). Beyond the difficulty of establishing causality scientifically, the linkage has not been examined rigorously for potential moderating or confounding effects. That is, rival explanations for the observed linkage have not been ruled out. In particular, research from industrial organization economics raises the possibility that market structure variables account for some or all of the differences Rumelt observed between diversification strategy and corporate economic performance.

The present study draws five rival explanations from industrial organization economics for the observed relationship between diversification strategy and firm performance. Most of these explanations are related to the firm's environment, and specifically to the characteristics of the markets in which they participate. These potentially moderating or confounding variables are market share, market concentration, market growth, market profitability and absolute firm size. Table 3 presents a summary of representative findings on the relationship between these variables and firm or industry profitability.

This study hypothesized that systematic differences in market structure variables would be found across Rumelt's strategy categories. In particular, it was expected that Rumelt's high performers would possess more favourable market characteristics (e.g. higher market shares), and his low performers would possess less favourable market characteristics (e.g. lower market shares) than other firms in the sample.

Specifically, it was expected that

*A. Constrained diversifiers have larger weighted market share indices,*[1] *and unrelated diversifiers have smaller weighted market share indices than other firms in the sample.*

This expectation is consistent with the types of diversification these firms have pursued (natrow versus broad) and with the research which indicates that firms with large market shares are better performers than firms with small market shares (Shepherd, 1972; Bass, 1973; Buzzell *et al.*, 1975; Bass *et al.*, 1978).

*B. Constrained diversifiers are located in more highly concentrated markets, and unrelated diversifiers in less concentrated markets than other firms in the sample.*

It is reasonable to expect that some markets are more conducive to specialization than others, and that, in turn, those markets will be more concentrated than markets where specialization is not as advantageous. Alternatively, high market shares (which by definition are more likely to occur in highly concentrated markets) could encourage firms to maintain constrained product lines and to reap the advantages therein.

A positive relationship between market concentration and profitability has been shown in many studies, including Collins and Preston (1968); Miller (1969); Gale (1972), and Dalton and Penn (1976).

C. *Constrained diversifiers' markets are growing faster than those of other firms in the sample, and unrelated diversifiers' markets are growing slower than those of other firms in the sample.*

The expectation is in line with Bass' 'defensive diversification' conclusion where growth was found to be a significant correlate of success for firms with little diversification and not a significant correlate for highly diversified firms (Bass *et al.*, 1977:193).

Among others, the following work has shown a positive relationship between growth of served markets and firm or industry profitability: Gutmann (1964), Rhoades (1973), and Bass *et al.* (1978).

D. *Constrained diversifiers are located in more profitable markets, and unrelated diversifiers in less profitable markets than other firms in the sample.*

The expectation that profitable firms will be located in profitable markets seems to be intuitive, yet few rigorous studies have demonstrated this point. The Strategic Planning Institute's work with the PIMS database is probably the best known work leading to this conclusion (Schoeffler, 1977). Additionally, in an extension to *Strategy, Structure, and Economic Performance*, Rumelt reported that market profitability varied among strategy categories, and that the profitability associated with constrained firms' markets was higher than that associated with the markets of other types of diversifiers (Rumelt, 1977).

E. *On average, unrelated diversifiers are larger, and constrained-diversifiers are smaller than other firms in the sample.*

This finding would be consistent with economists' suggestion that non-maximization of profits can result when large firm size leads to inefficiency, poor communication, slow reaction time, etc.

Empirical research on the relationship between firm size and profitability has produced conflicting results (for example, see Hall and Weiss, 1967; Shepherd, 1972; Dalton and Penn, 1976; Bass *et al.*, 1978). Hence, past evidence in support of this hypothesis is not strong. However, because the relationship is problematic, its potential influence should be evaluated.

Unless one or more of these hypotheses can be rejected, one must admit the possibility that the relationships Rumelt observed between diversification strategy and performance were in some part due to differences in one or more of these structural variables.

## Time frame and sample composition

The present work focuses on the time frame from 1972–1977. The focus was guided by the availability of market share data and necessitated the updating of Rumelt's classifications up to 1977. The updating process itself became an integral part of the research, providing an opportunity to evaluate both the inter-rater reliability of Rumelt's 1974 classifications and the reproducibility of his results in a different time frame.

Financial constraints related to the procurement of market share data[2] prohibited the study of firms in all ten of Rumelt's strategy categories.[3] Selection among the ten was based on the significance each category played in Rumelt's overall conclusions (see Table 2).

Both of the high performing categories (dominant-constrained and related-constrained), and two of the medium performers (related-linked and single business) were included. The selection of these categories, along with the dominant-linked, allowed for a comparison between constrained and linked diversifiers. A choice between the low performers led to a selection of the unrelated portfolio category which included most of the firms which had previously been designated as unrelated-passives. It was judged that unrelated portfolio firms would represent best the high end of the diversification continuum (additionally, the selection decision was influenced by the imprecision involved in determining the diversification status of vertically integrated firms.)

For classification decisions, this study made use of line-of-business data reported in Securities and Exchange Commission Form 10-Ks and in company annual reports. Regulations requiring companies to report some data at the line-of-business level were put into effect between the time of Rumelt's initial study and this study. Thus, more refined data were available for this study.

Beginning with 139 *Fortune* 500 firms in these categories, five were eliminated due to post-1974 merger and acquisition activity, two were eliminated due to unreliability of financial data; and four were eliminated due to strategy changes during the 1975–77 period.

Classifications for 125 of the remaining 128 firms matched Rumelt's, and classification changes were needed for the other three. The overall high degree of inter-rater agreement between this study's classifications and Rumelt's suggests that his category classification system is reliable. Commonly voiced fears that the system was unreliable owing to its degree of dependence on qualitative judgements were not borne out. Indeed, the availability of line-of-business data reduces the extent to which making Rumelt-type strategy classifications is a judgemental process.

Furthermore, the line-of-business data reduced the amount of time needed to make the classification decisions. In this capacity, they are a most useful facilitator of strategic management research. The fact that their high level of aggregation makes them unsuitable for some research questions (e.g. competitive strategy in a narrowly-defined market) does not necessarily reduce their usefulness for making categorical strategy classifications.

## Results

### *Performance by strategy category*

The next step in the analysis was to determine whether, for the new time period and sample, significant differences in performance could be demonstrated across the strategy categories (see Table 4.)

*F*-tests were used both in Rumelt's research and in the present study to determine whether there were statistically significant differences among the performance means across the strategy categories. Rumelt (Table 1) had found statistically significant differences, thereby supporting his conclusion that diversification strategy and performance were associated. In contrast, none of the overall *F*-ratios in Table 4 approaches significance at the 0.1 level.[4] Therefore, there are no statistical grounds for asserting that significant performance differences exist over the range of categories in this sample.

This study, like Rumelt's, utilized *t*-tests to compare individual category means to the mean of the remainder of the sample. The results of the *t*-tests in Table 4 suggest some agreement with Rumelt's results. Measuring performance as return on invested capital, unrelated-diversifiers clearly were less successful, and related-constrained diversifiers were more successful than other firms in the sample. The dominant-constrained firms' higher than average returns on assets and equity suggest that they, too, were better than average performers. Additionally, the ROCRR risk measure, which divides average ROIC by its standard deviation, indicates that unrelated firms as well as dominant-linked and single business firms were riskier than other firms in the sample, while related-constrained firms were less risky than others.

Although the *t*-tests indicate that Rumelt's results were in some sense replicated here, the lack of significant *F*-ratios in Table 4 cannot be dismissed lightly. The disparity in overall significance (*F*-ratios) between this study's results and Rumelt's was puzzling and unexpected. Various possible explanations for the difference were evaluated, including an assessment of chronological/economic differences between the samples. As important as these issues are, the examination indicated that it was not likely that they would cause a differential impact across firms. Instead, the most likely

*Table 4* Performance by strategy category.

| | *GSALES‡* | *GEPS* | *ROIC* | *ROA* | *ROE* | *ROCRR* | *ROIC77* | *ROA77* | *ROE77* |
|---|---|---|---|---|---|---|---|---|---|
| Est. category means | | | | | | | | | |
| Single (19)* | 0.1703 | 0.0990 | 0.1106 | 0.0555 | 0.1041 | 6.755$^{--}$ | 0.1180 | 0.0589 | 0.1140$^{-}$ |
| Dominant-constrained (13) | 0.1467 | 0.1202 | 0.1353 | 0.0768$^{++}$ | 0.1399$^{++}$ | 10.546 | 0.1300 | 0.0779$^{++}$ | 0.1407 |
| Dominant-linked (3) | 0.1204$^{--}$ | 0.2735 | 0.1157 | 0.0831$^{+}$ | 0.1489 | 4.195$^{---}$ | 0.1515$^{++}$ | 0.0908$^{++}$ | 0.1572$^{+}$ |
| Related-constrained (39) | 0.1416 | 0.1473 | 0.1297$^{+}$ | 0.0614 | 0.1296 | 10.967$^{+}$ | 0.1247 | 0.0672 | 0.1296 |
| Related-linked (39) | 0.1319 | 0.1484 | 0.1174 | 0.0606 | 0.1090$^{-}$ | 9.598 | 0.1134 | 0.0600 | 0.1413 |
| Unrelated-portfolio (15) | 0.1227 | 0.1489 | 0.1075$^{--}$ | 0.0725 | 0.1443$^{+}$ | 7.500$^{-}$ | 0.1298 | 0.0742 | 0.1354 |
| Overall Mean | 0.1407 | 0.1410 | 0.1208 | 0.0637 | 0.1185 | 9.317 | 0.1220 | 0.0662 | 0.1333 |
| Sig. *F-ratio* | 0.6676 | 0.7758 | 0.4860 | 0.4866 | 0.7033 | 0.2789 | 0.9573 | 0.6716 | 0.4844 |

The plus or minus signs following a category mean indicate that it differed significantly ('+' for a positive deviation, '–' for a negative deviation) from the overall mean for the other five categories. The *F*–ratio was used to test the hypothesis that category effects were absent.

* Sample size.

+ = significant at the 0.1 level; ++ = significant at the 0.05 level; +++ = significant at the 0.01 level.

‡ See Appendix B for definitions of column headings.

*Table 5* Performance by strategy category with vertically integrated firms included.

| | *GSALES*‡ | *GEPS* | *ROIC* | *ROA* | *ROE* | *ROCRR* | *ROIC77* | *ROA77* | *ROE77* |
|---|---|---|---|---|---|---|---|---|---|
| Est. category means | | | | | | | | | |
| Single (19)* | 0.1703 | 0.0990 | 0.1106 | 0.0555 | 0.1041 | $6.755^{--}$ | 0.1180 | 0.0589 | 0.1140 |
| Dominant-constrained (13) | 0.1467 | 0.1202 | 0.1353 | $0.0768^{+++}$ | $0.1399^{+++}$ | 10.546 | $0.1300^{++}$ | $0.0779^{+++}$ | $0.1407^{+}$ |
| Dominant-linked (3) | $0.1204^{---}$ | $0.2735^{+}$ | 0.1157 | $0.0831^{+}$ | $0.1489^{+}$ | $4.195^{--}$ | $0.1515^{++}$ | $0.0908^{++}$ | $0.1572^{++}$ |
| Related-constrained (39) | 0.1416 | 0.1473 | $0.1297^{+++}$ | 0.0614 | 0.1296 | $10.967^{++}$ | 0.1247 | 0.0672 | 0.1296 |
| Related-linked (39) | 0.1319 | 0.1484 | 0.1174 | 0.0606 | 0.1090 | 9.598 | 0.1134 | 0.0600 | $0.1413^{++}$ |
| Unrelated-portfolio (15) | 0.1227 | 0.1489 | 0.1075 | 0.0725 | 0.1443 | $7.500^{-}$ | 0.1298 | 0.0742 | 0.1354 |
| Vertical (31) | $0.1730^{+}$ | $0.0757^{--}$ | $0.0874^{---}$ | $0.0451^{---}$ | $0.0846^{--}$ | $6.311^{---}$ | $0.0957^{---}$ | 0.0470 | $0.0969^{---}$ |
| Overall Mean | 0.1470 | 0.1282 | 0.1143 | 0.0600 | 0.1119 | 8.731 | 0.1169 | 0.0625 | 0.1261 |
| Sig. *F*-ratio | 0.4490 | 0.4800 | 0.0165 | 0.0903 | 0.4664 | 0.0767 | 0.6616 | 0.2124 | 0.0295 |

* Sample size.

+ = significant at the 0.1 level; ++ = significant at the 0.05 level; +++ = significant at the 0.01 level.

‡ See Appendix B for definitions of column headings.

explanation appeared to be related to sample composition and the properties of the *F*-test.

When performance data for 31 vertically integrated firms were added to the analysis, *F*-ratios for key performance variables became significant (ROIC, ROA, ROCRR) (see Table 5.) Recalling that

$$F = \frac{\text{Mean square between}}{\text{Mean square within}}$$

and noting that the vertically integrated firms were distinctly low performers in both samples, suggests that the unusually poor performance of the vertically integrated firms forced several of the *F*-ratios to significance. This finding demonstrates that the *F*-ratio is sensitive to category extremes and indicates that one must be cautious to conclude that significant differences exist across all or most categories when the analysis includes an extreme group.

It is interesting to note, however, that the overall patterns from the *t*-tests in Tables 4 and 5 are similar, and basically in support of Rumelt's findings. Constrained firms do appear to be the strongest performers in the sample, and the unrelated firms tend to be the weakest. Considered *in toto* this information indicates that distinct categories of performers can be identified, but, for any given variable, clear distinctions across the range of firms are unlikely.

## Market structure variables

The next step in the analysis was to test for possible moderating or confounding effects of the market structure variables. The *F*-test was again utilized to determine whether statistically significant differences in market structure variables existed across the sample. Table 6 presents strategy category means for several market structure variables. Note that PROF1, the weighted return on assets measure associated with the firms' markets, differed significantly across strategy categories. Additionally, differences in the weighted market share variable approached significance (*F*-ratio = 0.1067).

Two individual categories displayed interesting and significant differences. Unrelated portfolio firms were found to have lower market shares, to be positioned in less profitable and less concentrated markets[5] and to be significantly smaller than other firms in the sample. Related-constrained firms, on the other hand, were found to be in more profitable, faster growing, and more highly concentrated markets than other firms. Each of these findings was in the direction hypothesized except for firm size.

*Table 6* Strategy category means for firm-specific and market variables

| | *SHARE*‡ | *PROF1* | *PROF2* | *CON1* | *CON2* | *CON3* | *CON4* | *GROW* | *FSIZE* |
|---|---|---|---|---|---|---|---|---|---|
| Est. category means | | | | | | | | | |
| Single (19)* | 0.0771 | 0.0596 | 0.1206 | 0.4489 | 0.5760 | 0.7218 | 0.8338 | 0.1149 | 0.1138 |
| Dominant-constrained (13) | 0.0963 | 0.0658 | 0.1283 | 0.4367 | 0.5634 | 0.7224 | 0.8397 | 0.1206 | 0.1123 |
| Dominant-linked (3) | 0.1190 | 0.0545 | 0.1141 | 0.4053 | 0.5292 | 0.6982 | 0.8260 | 0.1242 | 0.1152 |
| Related-constrained (39) | 0.0724 | $0.0693^{+++}$ | $0.1343^{++}$ | 0.4248 | 0.5691 | $0.7409^{+}$ | $0.8604^{+}$ | $0.1276^{+}$ | 0.1114 |
| Related-linked (39) | 0.0729 | 0.0613 | 0.1244 | 0.4270 | 0.4270 | 0.5535 | 0.8423 | 0.1185 | $0.1110^{--}$ |
| Unrelated-portfolio (15) | $0.0242^{---}$ | $0.0529^{---}$ | $0.1144^{--}$ | 0.4048 | 0.5258 | $0.6804^{-}$ | $0.8064^{--}$ | 0.1195 | $0.1141^{+}$ |
| Overall mean | 0.0711 | 0.0629 | 0.1259 | 0.4275 | 0.5591 | 0.7199 | 0.8419 | 0.1212 | 0.1121 |
| Sign *F*-ratio | 0.1067 | 0.0714 | 0.2723 | 0.9617 | 0.9186 | 0.7058 | 0.5785 | 0.7718 | 0.2023 |

* Sample size.
+ = significant at the 0.1 level; ++ = significant at the 0.05 level; +++ = significant at the 0.01 level.
‡ See Appendix B for definitions of column headings.

Reviewing the hypotheses: significant market profitability differences (hypothesis D) were found across the categories in the sample, while significant concentration (hypothesis B) differences at the 20-firm and 50-firm levels were found for two strategy categories.[6] Significant market share (hypothesis A) and growth (hypothesis C) differences were found for one category. A firm size (hypothesis E) difference was found for one category in the opposite from expected direction. These results indicate that differences in diversification strategy go beyond skeletal patterns of product linkages and include the characteristics of the markets in which firms participate.

## Conclusions and implications

The evidence presented here supports the view that performance differences exist among some, though not all, of Rumelt's categories. In turn, those differences appear to be linked to characteristics of the markets in which the firms operate.

Rather than being viewed as a system for differentiating among a range of firms, Rumelt's category scheme can perhaps best be viewed as a means for distinguishing a few distinct groups from other firms in general. The results of the *t*- and *F*-tests are consistent with this interpretation. In particular, two distinct profiles emerge from this work: one for the related-constrained, and the other for the unrelated portfolio diversifiers. These firms are distinguished not only by their product linkages and performance levels, but also by the characteristics of the markets in which they participate.

*Ex post facto* research studies such as this one cannot support causal statements; however, economic theory in conjunction with this research suggests that market structure variables influence firm performance and diversification strategy. The rationale behind the direction of the market structure-performance linkage has been well-argued in the economics literature. The direction of the influence between market structure and strategy is based on the concept of defensive diversification (for example, see Bass *et al.*, 1977). This concept suggests that firms located in markets which constrain their growth or profitability are the most likely candidates for diversification. Firms or businesses in 'low opportunity' markets are likely to find a similar lack of opportunity in markets which they could enter through constrained diversification. Therefore, they are more likely to pursue unrelated diversification.

These relationships are depicted in Figures 1 and 2. Figure 1 shows that related-constrained firms tend to be high return, low accounting risk performers in part because they operate in growing, highly concentrated, highly profitable markets. They can achieve this level of performance while participating only in markets which enable them to capitalize on their core strength (the dominant-constrained firms appear to have a profile much like that of the related-constrained firms, although the linkages are not statistically significant).

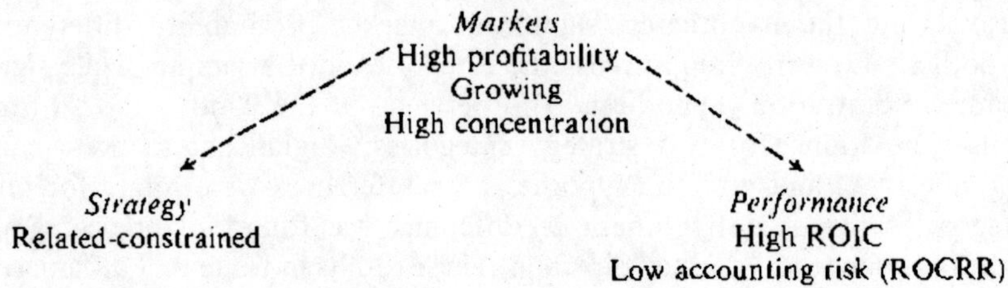


*Figure 1* Proposed relationships among market structure, firm performance, and related-constrained diversification strategies.

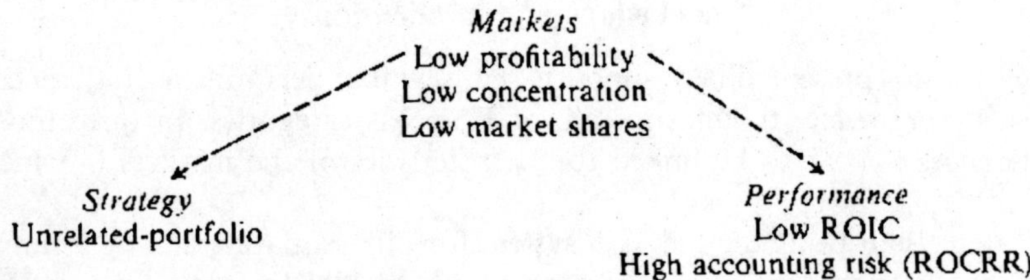


*Figure 2* Proposed relationships among market structure, firm performance, and unrelated-portfolio diversification strategies

Figure 2 shows that unrelated-portfolio firms tend to be low return, high accounting risk performers in part because they operate in highly fragmented, low profitability markets.

This study's findings have important implications for practising managers. First, following a strategy of constrained diversification is not sufficient to assure high earnings. The constrained diversifiers appear to be more profitable in part because they operated in very profitable, highly concentrated markets, and were able to acquire large shares in those markets. These firms' above-average market shares also suggest that they possess a sufficient level of the skills and resources critical to success in these high opportunity markets—a condition which may have developed due to diversification close to the original business. Successful performance is the outcome of market opportunity combined with the capacity to take advantage of that opportunity. In diversification planning, it is unwise to fail to analyse either.

Second, the rather uninspiring performance of unrelated-portfolio firms suggests the dangers of inattention to market structure in entry decisions or of knowingly entering highly fragmented, low profit markets. To the degree such markets are entered because businesses can be purchased for attractive prices, a longer-run point of view is needed. If these businesses are acquired because of unrealistic expectations of improving performance with new ownership, a hard look at market structure variables can lead to more realistic assessments of turnaround potential.

However, the performance problems of the unrelated-portfolio firms may be deeper than this: they may lack critical skills or resources needed to participate successfully in faster growing, more concentrated markets. Additionally, the objectives and control systems of unrelated-portfolio diversifiers may discourage the application of resources to activities expected to yield high, but delayed, returns.

Of necessity, this study has left unanswered many questions about diversification and corporate economic performance. In addition to the questions which emerge directly from the findings of this study, there is a need to examine the management systems, organizational structures and managerial styles conducive to a high level of economic performance in diversified firms (Bettis, Hall and Prahalad, 1978). As the separate research traditions that study corporate economic performance become integrated, both research and managerial practice will be enriched.

## Appendix A

### *Definitions of Rumelt's categories*[7]

*Single business:* Any firm which derives 95 per cent or more of its revenues from one business.

*Dominant business:* Any firm which derives 70–94 per cent of its revenues from its largest single business.

Dominant firms were divided into four sub-classifications:

*Dominant vertical:* Any dominant firm with a high vertical ratio.

*Dominant constrained:* Any dominant firm which diversified by building on a single strength or resource associated with the original business.

*Dominant linked:* Any dominant firm which diversified on the basis of one of several strengths or resources. The particular strength or resource varied across the different businesses in the firm.

*Dominant unrelated:* Any dominant firm whose diversification activities are not related to the dominant business.

*Related business:* Any firm deriving less than 70 per cent of its sales from a single business and possessing a high relatedness ratio.

Related firms were divided into two sub-classifications:

*Related constrained:* Any related firm which diversified by building on a single strength or resource associated with the original business.

*Related linked:* Any related firm which diversified on the basis of one of several strengths or resources. The particular strength or resource varied across the different businesses in the firm.

*Unrelated business:* Any firm deriving less than 70 per cent of its sales from a single business and possessing lower relatedness ratios.

Unrelated firms were divided into two sub-classifications:

*Multi-business:* Any unrelated firm containing a few large unrelated businesses.

*Unrelated-portfolio:* Any unrelated firm containing many unrelated businesses.

## Appendix B

Definitions of performance measures used in the study

| Name | Defined as | Prior use |
|---|---|---|
| GSALES | | |
| Sales growth 1973–1977 | Average per cent change over period $\frac{100}{N}\frac{X_N - X_L}{X_L}$ | Ansoff *et al.*, 1971 |
| GEPS | | |
| Growth in earnings per common share 1973–1977 | Average per cent change over period $\frac{100}{N}\frac{X_N - X_L}{X_L}$ | Ansoff *et al.*, 1971 |
| ROIC, ROIC77 | | |
| Return on invested capital, average 1975–1977, 1977 | $\frac{\text{Net income A. T. + interest}}{\text{Shareholders' equity + L–T debt}}$ | Rumelt, 1974*<br>Bass, 1973* |
| ROA, ROA77 | | |
| Return on assets average 1975–1977, 1977 | $\frac{\text{Net income after taxes}}{\text{Total assets}}$ | Rumelt, 1974*<br>Widely employed return measure |
| ROE, ROE77 | | |
| Return on equity average 1975–1977, 1977 | $\frac{\text{Net income after taxes}}{\text{Bk. value of shareholders' equity}}$ | Rumelt, 1974*<br>Widely employed return measure |
| ROCRR | | |
| Risk adjusted return, 1973–1977 | $\frac{\text{Average return on invested capital}}{\text{s.d. of return on invested capital}}$ | Rumelt, 1977 |

* These authors also employed these measures in subsequent research.

Definitions of market variables used in the study

| *Market variables* | | |
|---|---|---|
| $m_{ij4}$ = the percentage of firm $i$'s total sales that are in 4-digit market $j$ | | |
| $m_{ij3}$ = the percentage of firm $i$'s total sales that are in 3-digit market $j$ | | |
| SHARE<br>Weighted market share | $MS_i = \frac{\Sigma_j m_{ij4} M_{ij}}{\Sigma m_{ij+}}$ | $M_{ij}$ = Firm $i$'s share 4-digit market $j$ |
| PROF1<br>Weighted industry ROA | $P1 = \frac{\Sigma_j m_{ij3} \mathrm{ROA}_j}{\Sigma m_{ij^3}}$ | $\mathrm{ROA}_j$ = ROA associated with 3-digit market $j$ |
| PROF2<br>Weighted industry ROE | $P2 = \frac{\Sigma_j m_{ij3} \mathrm{ROE}_j}{\Sigma m_{ij^3}}$ | $\mathrm{ROE}_j$ = ROE associated with 3-digit market $j$ |
| CON1<br>Four-firm concentration | $\mathrm{CON}_{1-4} = \Sigma_j m_{ij4} \mathrm{con}_{j,1-4}$ | |
| CON2<br>Eight-firm concentration | | |
| CON3<br>Twenty-firm concentration | | |
| CON4<br>Fifty-firm concentration | | |
| GROW<br>Growth of firm's markets, 1972–1976 | $GR = \Sigma_j m_{ij4} GR_j$ | $\mathrm{GR}_j$ = annuity measure of shipment growth (in dollars) in 4-digit market |
| FSIZE<br>Firm size average 1975–1977 | $\frac{1}{\text{Log assets}}$ | |

## Notes

1 Variable definitions are given in Appendix B.

2 This study utilized the market share data of Economic Information Systems available through the Lockheed Dialogue System. These data are subdivided by 4-digit S.I.C. category.

3 In 1977 Rumelt slightly revised his original classification system of nine strategy categories. A working paper, 'Diversity and profitability' details this change.

4 A significance level of 0.1 was selected to balance the likelihood of Type I and Type II errors. The precision of estimates extracted from large scale economic surveys suggests that more exactness cannot be demanded from the data at hand.

Additionally, when attempting to reproduce previously stated results, care should be taken to avoid unnecessary Type II (β) errors.

5 It is interesting to note that it is not the 4-firm or 8-firm concentration levels that differ by strategy category. Rather, it is the 20-firm and 50-firm levels. This suggests that the overall number of firms in a market and the associated size of barriers to entry differ between some strategy categories.

6 Overall statements on performance and market structure differences are based on the sample of 128 firms (i.e. not on the sample including the vertically integrated firms). Sales breakdown data were not available for the vertically integrated firms, and in the interest of consistency it seems appropriate to compare market structure differences from 128 firms to performance differences from the same rather than an expanded sample. That the performance means of the unrelated portfolio firms were not significantly different in the expanded sample should be noted, but evaluated with respect to the extremes presented by the vertically integrated firms and the properties of the statistical tests employed. Compared to other non-extreme categories (Table 4), the unrelated portfolio firms were lower than average performers. That perspective is carried through in additional discussions.

7 Sources: Rumelt, 1974: 9–32. The discussion of unrelated business categories is contained in Rumelt, 1977.

## References


Ansoff, H. Igor, Richard G. Brandenburg, Fred E. Porter, and Raymond Radosevich. *Twenty Years of Acquisition Behaviour in America*, Associated Press, London, 1971.

Bass, Frank M. 'Market structure and profitability—analysis of the appropriateness of pooling cross-sectional industry data'. Paper No. 242, Institute for Research in the Behavioral, Economic, and Management Sciences, Krannert Graduate School of Management, Purdue University, October, 1973.

Bass, Frank M., Phillippe Cattin, and Dick R. Wittink. 'Market structure and industry influence on profitability', in H. Thorelli (ed.) *Strategy + Structure = Performance*, Indiana University Press, Bloomington, Indiana, 1977.

Bass, Frank M., Phillippe Cattin, and Dick R. Wittink. 'Firm effects and industry effects in the analysis of market structure and profitability'. *Journal of Marketing Research*, XV, February 1978, pp. 3–10.

Bettis, Richard, William Hall, and C. K. Prahalad. 'Diversity and performance in the multibusiness firm'. *AIDS 1978 Proceedings*, Atlanta: American Institute for Decision Sciences, 1978, pp. 210–212.

Buzzell, Robert D., Bradley T. Gale, and Ralph G. M. Sultan. 'Market share—a key to profitability', *Harvard Business Review*, 53, January–February 1975, pp. 97–106.

Chandler, Alfred D. *Strategy and Structure: Chapters in the History of the Industrial Enterprise*, M.I.T. Press, Cambridge, Mass., 1962.

Collins, Norman R., and Lee E. Preston. *Concentration and Price-Cost Margins in Manufacturing Industries*, University of California Press, Berkeley, 1968.

Dalton, James A., and David W. Penn. 'The concentration-profitability relationship: is there a critical concentration ratio?', *The Journal of Industrial Economics*, XXV, December 1976, pp. 133–142.

Gale, Bradley T. 'Market share and rate of return'. *The Review of Economics and Statistics*, LIV, No. 4, November 1972, pp. 412–423.

Gutmann, Peter M. 'Strategies for growth', *California Management Review*, Summer, 1964, pp. 31–66.

Hall, Marshall, and Leonard Weiss. 'Firm Size and Profitability', *The Review of Economics and Statistics*, XLIX, No. 3, August 1967, pp. 319–331.

Meehan, James W., Jr., and Thomas D. Duchesneau. 'The critical level of concentration: an empirical analysis', *The Journal of Industrial Economics*, XXII, No. 1, September 1973, pp. 21–36.

Miller, Richard A. 'Market structure and industrial performance: relation of profit rates to concentration, advertising intensity, and diversity', *The Journal of Industrial Economics*, XVIII, No. 2, April 1969, pp. 104–118.

Montgomery, Cynthia A. 'Diversification, market structure, and firm performance: an extension of Rumelt's model'. *Ph.D. Dissertation*, Purdue University, West Lafayette, Indiana, 1979.

Patton, Richard G. 'A simultaneous equation model of corporate strategy: the case of the U.S. brewing industry'. *Ph.D. Dissertation*, Purdue University, West Lafayette, Indiana, 1976.

Rhoades, Stephen A. 'The effect of diversification on industry profit performance in 241 manufacturing industries: 1963', *Review of Economics and Statistics*, May 1973, pp. 146–155.

Rumelt, Richard P. *Strategy, Structure, and Economic Performance*, Division of Research, Graduate School of Business Administration, Harvard University, Boston, 1974.

Rumelt, Richard P. 'Diversity and profitability'. Paper MGL-51, Managerial Studies Center, Graduate School of Management, University of California, Los Angeles, 1977.

Rumelt, Richard P. 'Data bank on diversification strategy and corporate structure'. Paper MGL-55, Managerial Studies Center, Graduate School of Management, University of California, Los Angeles, 1978.

Scherer, F. M. *Industrial Market Structure and Economic Performance*, Rand McNally, Chicago, 1970.

Schoeffier, Sidney. 'Nine basic findings on business strategy'. PIMS-LETTER No. 1. The Strategic Planning Institute, 1977.

Scott, Bruce R. 'Stages of corporate development'. Harvard Business School, Boston, Mass.: Intercollegiate Case Clearing House, ICCH #9-371-294, 1971.

Shepherd, William G. 'The elements of market structure', *The Review of Economics and Statisties*, LIV, No. 1, February 1972, pp. 25–37.

Wrigley, Leonard. 'Divisional autonomy and diversification', *Unpublished Doctoral Dissertation*, Harvard Business School, 1970.

40

# ON STRATEGIC MANAGEMENT DECISION PROCESSES

*Liam Fahey*

Source: *Strategic Management Journal* 2(1) (1981): 43–60.


## Summary

This paper attempts to bridge the divide between rational/analytical and behavioural/political conceptions of strategic decision making. The linkages and interactions between these approaches to the making of strategic decisions are explored in the context of a specific decision arena—strategic energy management.


## Introduction

Most analysts of the concepts of 'strategy' would generally agree with Hofer and Schendel's (1978: 4) delineation of strategy as 'the basic characteristics of the match an organization achieves with its environment.' Implicit in any definition or consideration of organizational strategy (or strategy formulation, strategic planning, etc.) is some concept of decision making. As noted by Mintzberg, Raisinghani, and Theoret (1976), and Quinn (1978), among others, few researchers of managerial behaviour or administrative processes have paid much empirical attention to explicating the *organizational* processes involved in strategic decision making. The research reported here, which is part of a larger study (Fahey, 1978), represents one endeavour to do so. The study examines the analytical and political processes which influence strategic decision making in the context of energy management in a sample of six large (i.e. annual sales in excess of $250 million) multi-divisional firms.

The literature on strategic decision making (i.e. the processes involved in choosing a firm's strategy) has historically been dominated by a highly *normative* or rational stance. A comprehensive, step-by-step set of procedures are usually postulated as those which *should* be included in any framework designed to formulate a total firm strategy (Ansoff, 1965; Ackoff,

1970; Katz, 1970; Vancil and Lorange, 1975). These steps typically include identification of the firm's mission, the establishment of goals and objectives and the specification of product/market strategies (i.e. the resource allocation decisions) after the firm has scanned its environment(s) to determine those opportunities which best match its capabilities.

A less populous but nonetheless significant body of literature focuses on the roles of behavioural and political factors in organizational strategy making in such contexts as government (Lindblom, 1959; Allison, 1971), educational establishments (March and Olsen, 1976) and industrial firms (Chandler, 1962; Bower, 1970; and Carter, 1971). The behavioural/political perspective focuses upon the dynamics of the interactions among individuals and organizational sub-units as they endeavour to influence strategic decisions.

The conceptual work of Astley *et al.* (1979), Grant and King (1979), Bower and Doz (1979), Mintzberg (1979), Anderson and Paine (1975), Guth (1976), and the empirical endeavours of Quinn (1977, 1978), and Mintzberg, Raisinghani, and Theoret (1976), are indicative of a recent movement toward an integration of analytical/intellectual and behavioural/political processes in strategy making. The unifying theme of this movement is that the 'technical' (Astley *et al.*, 1979) or analytical rubric of strategy formulation is not sufficient to describe and explain the process of strategic decision making and its outcome, i.e. implemented strategy. The processes involved in the acquisition and utilization of organizational power, influence and control must be incorporated into our explanatory paradigms of strategic decision making (MacMillan, 1978).

## Research scope and objectives

Although the Mintzberg *et al.* study is the most comprehensive and illuminating set of insights into the nature of strategic decision processes which has yet emerged, one must concur with their conclusion that 'we have, however, barely scratched the surface of organizational decision making' (1976: 274). Their work included only one decision in each organization; it may be that major differences exist within organizations across individual decisions. Similarly there may be significant differences in the way different organizations make the same decision. A noticeable absence in the decision making literature is the interaction(s) between the elements or phases in decision making and organizational structure. Perhaps most critical from the perspective of our understanding of how strategy is formulated is the lack of empirical attention to the interrelationships among individual decisions and their integration into what ultimately becomes manifest as the organization's implemented strategy.

The objectives of this research were to explore interrelationships between the two perspectives on strategy making noted above and specifically to examine the above mentioned gaps in our knowledge about strategy making in the context of strategic energy management in large multi-divisional firms. Strategic energy management was defined for the purpose of this study as 'those decision processes, procedures, behaviours and investments which are designed to improve the effectiveness and efficiency of the firm's energy resources'. Strategy here refers to the firm's choice of investment options to pursue improved energy utilization efficiency or enhanced energy supply availability.

The central focus of this research was to trace strategic energy decisions through the organizational structure, paying particular attention to corporate headquarters–division interaction. Although other studies have investigated corporate-division decision making linkages (Berg, 1965; Lorsch and Allen, 1973), the emphasis in most studies of strategic management in multi-divisional firms has been on strategy content rather than the decision processes leading to strategic choice (Berg and Pitts, 1979). It will be noted that the emphasis in this study is on strategic energy management as a set of interrelated decisions and not on any one individual decision. This approach was adopted to allow exploration of the complexities and interactions in a single management decision arena (i.e. the management of energy resources) as opposed to detailing the specifics of the decision process in the context of a single decision.

Strategic energy management was chosen as the arena within which to investigate strategic decision processes for a number of reasons. The turbulence in the energy environment during the 1970s when considered as a major environmental or resource supply uncertainty could be hypothesized to provoke strategic responses on the part of large multi-divisional firms. As well as the firm-environment effectiveness dimensions of strategy, energy management has major implications for internal operating efficiency. Also, many energy management decisions would certainly fall within most authors' definition of strategic decisions in terms of importance if measured by 'actions taken, resources committed or precedents set' (Mintzberg *et al.*, 1976: 246) or as parameters along which firm–environment interaction is manifest (Katz, 1970; Steiner and Miner, 1977). For these reasons, an analysis of strategic energy decisions may generate findings which are relevant to strategic decisions in other decision arenas.

## Research method

### *Study sample*

Eleven large multi-divisional firms were identified as potential research sites. The primary criteria for inclusion in the sample were that the firm be large (only one firm had sales less than $500 million) and have a number of distinct divisions. These firms represented a variety of industries. A broad spectrum of energy intensity levels was also manifest in the sample firms:

defining energy intensity as total energy costs as a percentage of total operating costs, the initial sample firms ranged in energy intensity from five per cent to twenty-five per cent.

In order to pursue the goals of this research, it was essential that energy management be an established component of corporate management activity at corporate headquarters level. In three firms, it was clearly evident that in keeping with their overall management approach, energy management was a decentralized activity: divisions had autonomous decision making power with regard to the acquisition and utilization of energy resources. Corporate headquarters personnel had little input into energy related decisions. Thus, energy decision making in these three firms will not be reported in this paper.

Of the remaining eight firms, it was possible to collect requisite data in at least one division of each of six firms. The findings that are reported in this paper are therefore based on the data collected in six large multidivisional firms.

### *Data collection*

Interviews with two to five key energy management personnel at corporate headquarters and one to four at the division level were the primary mode of data collection. A structured research instrument was developed to ensure that a core set of issues and questions were covered in each firm. In some cases, follow-up in-person interviews and in many cases follow-up telephone interviews were conducted.

Several procedures were used to verify the accounts of executives: (1) where possible, executives were asked to document their accounts of the decision making process in general or specific decisions in particular. For instance, in some firms, it was possible to review the corporate or division energy management plan and programmes, objectives, etc.; (2) the details of one executive's account were checked against those of others; (3) where uncertainties or inconsistencies arose, follow-up in-person or telephone interviews were conducted; (4) personal and corporate anonymity was guaranteed to all interviewees.

## Study findings

Although there were obvious dissimilarities in the approaches to strategic energy management adopted by these six firms, a sufficient number of themes and commonalities appear with reasonable consistency to facilitate development of a model of strategic energy management decision making in these firms. This general model or depiction of strategic decision making is presented and briefly described in three segments: (1) the linkages between firms' organization structure and strategic energy management; (2) strategic

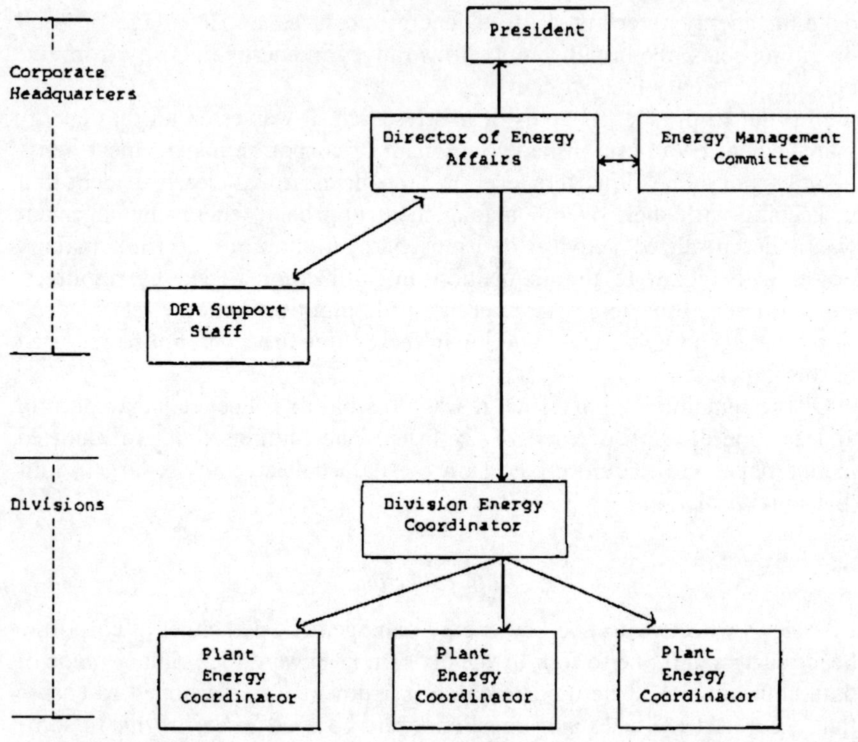


*Figure 1* Energy management organization structure in large multi-divisional firms.

energy management decision making as an intellectual–analytical endeavour; and (3) the behavioural–political processes involved in strategic energy management decision making. Each of these segments summarizes part of the study's findings and provides the basis from which the propositions in the final section of the paper are developed.

### *Strategic energy management and organization structure*

Figure 1 is a generalized summary of the principal actors in corporate energy management with specific energy management responsibilities. Although the position titles, the relationships between positions and the specific roles and responsibilities vary from one firm to another, major elements of the positions shown in Figure 1 and their interrelationship can be found in each firm.

The energy management decision making system [EMDMS] which revolves around the organization structure depicted in Figure 1, is shown in Figure 2. Figure 2 summarizes the major energy management decision points, their sequence and interaction as well as their linkage to the principal energy

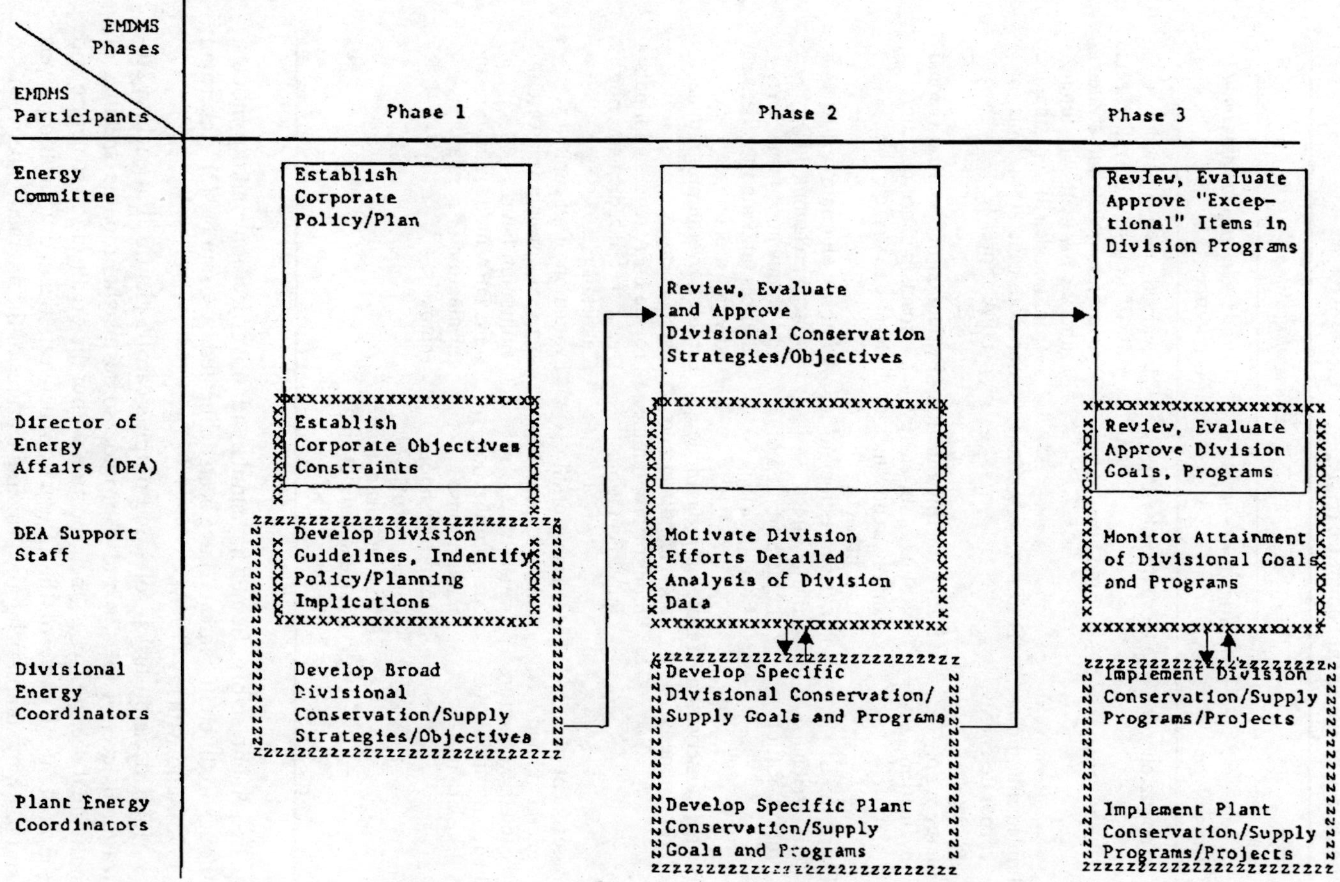


*Figure 2* Energy management decision making system in large, multi-divisional firms.

*Table 1* Major features of interaction between director of energy affairs (DEA) and energy management committee (EMC).

| | *Locus of decision* | |
|---|---|---|
| *Decision type* | *Director of energy affairs (DEA)* | *Corporate energy management committee* |
| Corporate energy policy | Developed by DEA. | Reviewed and evaluated by EMC to insure that it reflects corporate policy and strategies and is consistent with inputs from (e.g. legal) departments. |
| Implementation of corporate energy policy | Direct responsibility. | Serves to generate support for DEA efforts. |
| Energy supply evaluation | Data gathering function evaluation of energy supply trends, major firm impacts. | Evaluation of specific divisional impacts, finance restraints, legal barriers, etc. |
| Energy mix, conversion, fuel allocation | Make suggestions to EMC; direct implementation of EMC decisions. | Authorize alternate fuel back-up systems; recommend development of firms' energy sources; allocate fuels between divisions, plants, etc. |
| Energy conservation programmes | Develop programme specifics; direct and monitor programme implementation. | Establish overall programme guidelines. Provide DEA requested inputs e.g., specialized engineering assistance. |
| Assessment of energy related capital expenditures | Assessment of all capital expenditures which have energy utilization implications. | Evaluation of all capital expenditures above a certain minimum figure. |
| Federal/state/local legislation | Monitor regulatory developments. Assess and disseminate current and potential implications. | Assist DEA in identification and evaluation of regulatory impacts. |

management actors. Somewhat similar adaptive decision making models, though in different contexts, have been delineated by Grant (1972), Ackerman (1973), and Murray (1976).

Major decision tasks, roles and outputs can be identified at each organizational level. Tables 1 and 2 provide some insight into the specifics of individual decision types, their location within the organization structure and the content of some of the interaction between these organization levels and roles, by summarizing the principal features of the interaction between the Director of Energy Affairs (DEA) and the Energy Management Committee

*Table 2* Major features of interaction between director of energy affairs office (DEAO) and division energy coordinators (DECs).

| *Decision type* | *Locus of decision*<br>*Office of director of energy affairs (DEAO)* | *Division energy coordinator* |
|---|---|---|
| Implementation of corporate policy | Identify general implications of corporate energy policy for each division.<br>Evaluate divisional constraints, peculiarities, limitations, etc.<br>Establish corporate objectives. | Detail divisional implications of corporate energy policy.<br>Provide divisional viewpoint on corporate energy policy: constraints, peculiarities, etc. |
| Corporate objectives/ divisional goals | Work with DECs on developing divisional goals. | Work with DEAO on developing divisional goals. |
| Energy conservation programme | Evaluate division programmes.<br>Monitor division progress on each programme element.<br>Establish agreed bench-marks to evaluate division progress.<br>Develop reporting system to facilitate monitoring and evaluation. | Develop detailed division programme in conjunction with plant energy coordinators.<br>Provide progress reports to DEAO on each programme element. |
| Energy supply | Monitor corporate and divisional energy mix.<br>Identify potential energy shortages and their implications.<br>Establish programme criteria for installation of alternative fuel back-up systems. | Develop division energy demand projections.<br>Assess alternative energy back-up system requirements.<br>Create contingency plans for alternative systems (e.g. foreign oil embargo, industrial dispute in coal industry, etc.). |
| Energy related capital expenditures | Solicit and evaluate major capital expenditures in divisions conservation and supply programmes. | Detail conservation and supply programme capital expenditures.<br>Itemize energy implications of non-energy specific capital expenditures. |

(EMC) and the DEA and the Division Energy Coordinators (DECs)—the most significant energy management decision making relationships.

The decision making processes and roles shown in Figure 2 and Tables 1 and 2 are themselves characterized by behavioural and political activities or phenomena. Table 3 identifies a number of behavioural and political characteristics of strategic energy management decision making at selected decision points. The behaviours noted in Table 3 centre around interactions between different organization levels.

*Table 3* Political and behavioural processes in corporate energy management.

| | *Division energy coordinators (DECs)* | *Office of director of energy affairs* | *Energy management committee (EMC)* |
|---|---|---|---|
| Development of corporate policy/plan | Become familiar with HOEM personnel and procedures, extent of<br>HO expectations, and requirements. | Negotiate EM blueprint and specific 'policy' compromise with EMC.<br>Sell notion of EM to divisions. | Sell idea of EM to corporate functional groups.<br>Facilitate role of DEA's office within HO and its interactions with divisions. |
| Initial development of division plans | DECs plead special case to corporate headquarters.<br>Invoke assistance of division management.<br>Attempt to create alignments with DEA's office and EMC. | Negotiate with DECs as to appropriate division EM objectives and guidelines. | Bargaining within EMC as to appropriate resources allocation criteria.<br>Coalitions emerge (within EMC and with DEA's office & DEC's) based on desired direction for corporate EM policy/plans. |
| Review of initial division plans | | Identify and evaluate commitment of divisions to EM.<br>Assess receptivity of divisions to HO 'push' for EM. | Reflect their own individual and functional group interests.<br>Time allocation difficulties.<br>Partial ignorance regarding individual division EM decisions. |
| Development of specific division plans/ programmes | 'Packaging' of data for presentation to HO.<br>Efforts to instil 'slack' in programmes.<br>Utilization of alignments with DEA's office and EMC. | Determine appropriate means to motivate division efforts.<br>Attempt to identify division management biases and perceptions. | Pressure DEA's office to support EMC pet projects. |
| Review of division plans/programmes | | Determination of exceptions.<br>Interpretation and presentation of division data to EMC. | Function group interests and alignments in determining programme/project tradeoffs. |

Key: EM: Energy Management
HOEM: Head Office Energy Management
HO: Head Office (Corporate level)

### *Analytical processes*

From the perspective of strategic decision making as an intellectual or analytical process, the energy management decision making system (EMDMS) described in Figure 2 can be conceptualized in three distinct phases, each comprising a number of specific stages or routines. Phase 1 establishes the thrust and impetus for the overall framework of corporate energy management. Its principal tasks are the development or revision of the corporate energy policy/planning document which entails broad corporate energy management policy guidelines, strategies, objectives and constraints, and more specifically, the development of a broad energy management plan for each division. These two tasks are largely performed at the corporate headquarters level by the DEA, his supporting staff and the EMC.

The corporate energy management policy and plan are by design, non-specific; they merely set forth general objectives, an estimate of the resources that will be available for capital expenditures, an identification and assessment of the areas where capital investment may be required, a consideration of past successes or failures in the attainment of energy conservation and supply of goals, etc. The approach adopted by management to establishing the broad outlines of a corporate policy manifests many of the characteristics prescribed for top level policy making by Wrapp (1967) and Quinn (1978), among others: management through the collective voice of the DEA and the EMC makes public within the organization its commitment to the concept of energy management without at this stage specifying the tasks to be accomplished or the precise goals to be achieved.

The significance of the corporate energy policy/plan is that it provides a sense of direction for the work of the DEA's support staff and the DECs in their initial efforts to establish division energy management plans—the second stage of Phase 1 activities, its major output, and by far the most time consuming element. The divisions' broad energy management plans provide an opportunity for corporate headquarters (specifically, the DEA's support staff) to review the strengths and weaknesses of each division's energy management approach, as well as the identification of divisions' energy related constraints, characteristics and requirements.

The specific purpose of Phase 2 of the EMDMS is to develop detailed division energy conservation and supply programmes. As shown in Figure 2, it is a three-stage process. First, the DEA and EMC review, evaluate and approve or reject the general division plans. The purpose of this review process is to ensure that division energy management activities are consistent with the corporate energy policy/plan.

The second major stage of Phase 2 activities involves the DEA and his support staff working in close conjunction with the DEC and other division management in the development of specific division conservation and supply programmes. A programme ultimately consists of a set of specific investment proposals defined in terms of costs, savings, timing, problems created or solved by the investment, etc.

The final stage in Phase 2 is the formulation of these energy management programmes by each division. This is primarily the responsibility of DECs in conjunction with plant energy coordinators (PECs) and division management. The decision processes involved in the development of general programmes and specific projects within divisions are themselves quite complex and too involved to be elaborated here.

Implementation of the energy management programmes which evolve from Phases 1 and 2 is the primary focus of Phase 3. First, the DEA's office reviews, evaluates, and recommends division energy conservation and supply programmes which are the output of Phase 2. Major items of capital expenditure and/or programmes or individual projects which the DEA's office claims are 'exceptional' are referred to the EMC for review and evaluation.

Regular planning procedures designed to facilitate continued interaction with division personnel (especially DECs) provide a rich data base on a number of facets of division energy management activities and processes—a knowledge base which becomes critical to corporate headquarters' understanding, evaluation, control, and stimulation of division energy management efforts. This knowledge base evolves over time as the DEA's office monitors the success or failure of divisions in implementing their energy management programmes.

### *Behavioural and political processes*

The EMDMS described above is embedded in and reflects the political and behavioural nature of organizational decision making discussed by many authors (e.g. Pettigrew, 1973; Carter, 1971; Allison, 1971; Cyert and March, 1963; and Bower, 1970). Power relationships and organization alignments become evident in the formulation of plans; and bargaining and negotiation processes characterize many decisions. In short, it is evident from the data that strategic decision making is not simply a matter of explicating alternatives, and choosing between them on the basis of readily available criteria which have been agreed upon in advance as appropriate by all decision participants.

It will be noted from Table 3 that different behavioural or political processes and activities may impact different stages of the phases of the overall decision process. For instance, the initial efforts to formulate division energy management plans are often characterized by intense bargaining and negotiation between the DECs (often with the active support of division management) and the DEA's office.

DEAs and their office staff also indicated that cultivating an alliance with individual members of the EMC was a necessity if a smooth-working relationship was to emerge between the DEA's office and the EMC. This aspect of the DEA office's role reflects, of course, the lack of consensus and diversity of perspective which was evident within the EMCs. Establishing the broad outlines of a corporate energy policy or investigating the implications of specific energy decisions inevitably brought to the surface existing and potential areas of conflict within the EMC between different groups or functions (i.e. R&D engineering, facilities planning, etc.). Many 'decisions' which emanated from EMC deliberations were commonly described as 'compromises'.

Within Phase 2, a major task for the DEA's office is the assessment of divisions' commitment to energy management and the stimulation of divisions to improve their energy efficiency. Both these endeavours were described by some DEA office personnel as requiring more organizational acumen than analytical prowess. A number of factors were suggested by DEAs and their support staff as being at least as indicative of divisional commitment to energy management as their formal written plans: (1) knowledge of the power structure within divisions; (2) the nature of overt and covert division and functional area decision making criteria; (3) decision makers' personal goals; and (4) division personnel biases and perceptions with respect to energy management in general and specific projects in particular. An understanding of these phenomena facilitates choice of the appropriate means by corporate headquarters to attempt to spur division efforts to formulate comprehensive energy supply and conservation programmes.

Monitoring the implementation of programmes during Phase 3 provides insights into the phenomena discussed above for corporate headquarters personnel. However, the acquisition of this type of organizational knowledge or the institutionalization of this form of organizational learning requires that corporate headquarters staff be attuned to the identification and examination of these phenomena—which is itself a behavioural or political process.

## Study implications and discussion

To help guide future research on the complex nature of strategy making, some implications of the study's findings are presented here in the form of propositions. These propositions are tentative, but they are suggestive of patterns which are evident in the data previously presented.

*Proposition 1: The initiation of a structured approach to strategic management is critically dependent in its early stages upon a high degree of organized advocacy, i.e. it is predominantly a political process.*

We are assuming here that the notion of systematically managing the firm's energy resources has been sanctioned by top management. However, the process of formulating strategy does not happen, it must be managed

(Saunders, 1972; Ansoff, Declerck, and Hayes, 1976). This would seem to be especially true in the early stages of the evolution of a structured planning or decision making process where the organization has little experience in formally explicating strategy, objectives, assumptions, etc., and has little knowledge about the *process* of doing planning. The formal, structured approach to energy management has reached the highest state of development in those firms where top corporate management was explicit in its commitment to improving energy resource utilization, and a leadership role was assumed by an individual (a DEA) who was willing to tackle the difficulties involved in weaving the notion of energy management into the organizational fabric. In effect, the DEA becomes the 'advocate' for energy management within the organization, a task which all the DEAs suggested was their major role upon assuming their positions.

*Proposition 2a: The formulation of strategy and the establishment of specific goals/objectives is an interrelated, iterative and interactive process.*

*Proposition 2b: The formulation of objectives and goals is considerably more 'problematical' than 'rational'.*

In all the firms studied, the specifics of energy management objectives and goals at both the headquarters and division levels are modified at many stages in the overall planning process. The EMC, DECs and the DEA's offices continually establish and modify overall energy management objectives and specific programme or project goals as they proceed through the strategy formulation and implementation process. Energy efficiency goals and energy supply goals are modified as problems or crises emerge and as opportunities for efficiency improvement or supply enhancement arise: goals are a function of the problems and opportunities facing the firm (Andrews, 1971). From descriptions of the overall planning process and analysis of specific decisions there is little support for the contention that goal establishment and the evaluation of alternative strategies (i.e. investment options) are separate and sequential elements in strategy formulation.

It will, of course, be noted that Proposition 2a flies in the face of most of the normative literature on strategy formulation: the choice of goals/objectives and strategy formulation are often represented as separate and sequential elements in strategy making (Ansoff, 1965; Steiner and Miner, 1977; King and Cleland, 1978).

It has also been noted that stated objectives and goals can hardly be taken at face value (Perrow, 1961); they are themselves the outcome of a decision process. Objectives and goals are the result of compromise (Cyert and March, 1963). The bargaining and negotiating inherent in compromise are also apparent from the data described in this study: the filtering of information (e.g. DEA office staff preparing analyses of division proposals for the EMC), bargaining for resource allocations (both between headquarters and divisions and within individual divisions), conflicts in perspectives and interests (the diverse interests represented within EMCs), the use of informal as opposed to formal channels (e.g. the alignments created by division DECs) all help to illustrate that objectives and goals are not fixed and static but rather reflect the organizational dynamics of strategy development. Goals as constraints (Simon, 1964), as targets and as criteria of evaluation reflect the ebb and flow of the strategy formulation process; they are as much the outcome of the behavioural and political processes at work in strategy making as they are the consequence of its intellectual or analytical facets.

*Proposition 3: For many individual decisions the evaluation and selection phase (i.e. 'the choice among alternatives') may be of less significance than the search for and development of the alternatives.*

Economic theory and decision theory assume that the decision alternatives are known and a decision criterion is available. Empirical research of capital budgeting decisions (Carter, 1971; Bower, 1970), detailed mapping of specific investment decisions (Cyert, Simon, and Trow, 1956; Pettigrew, 1973) and the analysis of general strategic decision processes (Mintzberg, Raisinghani, and Theoret, 1976) suggest that not only are these assumptions a misrepresentation of reality but that they focus on the least significant (and certainly the least interesting) aspects of the decision process.

The data in this study support these contentions. A number of instances can be cited where investment options ('projects') were considered at the division level, rejected for some reason, and consequently not forwarded to headquarters. These projects would therefore not come within the purview of the principal review, evaluation and choice (i.e. approve or reject) stage of the planning process. Even those 'programmes' (i.e. a set of projects) or individual projects which survived to the evaluation/choice stage were often packaged by division personnel so that they would 'look good' to headquarters staff, and even DEA office staff were not shy in some cases to present alternatives to the EMC in a favourable light.

These observations would seem to be especially critical in those decision contexts where obvious solutions were not readily available (e.g. proven conservation or supply technologies) to solve perceived problems or realize apparent opportunities. In these instances, the decision problem is characterized by a high degree of uncertainty; no one is even sure how to go about analysing the problem. Under these circumstances the choice or decision criteria which apply to the rejection of alternatives at the early phases of a decision process are often not explicated but can be just as significant in determining the ultimate choice or outcome as those criteria which are applied to the alternatives which survive these early decision phases. Many interviewees could identify a variety of reasons why entire projects or specific alternatives within a given project did not receive thorough exploration and development. A notable characteristic of many of these cited reasons is their relatively 'soft' nature (e.g. perceptions of higher management level reactions, incompatibility with other functional area interests, incongruity with technological capabilities, degree of technological appropriateness, uncertainty with regard to resource availability, etc.) compared to the professed ultimate choice criteria (e.g., ROI, projected savings, degree of elimination of supply risk, etc.).

> *Proposition 4: The initial phases of the decision process (i.e. search and early screening activities), are complex, multiorganizational level phenomena and are frequently characterized by a high degree of political activity.*

It is commonly suggested that strategic issues, problems or 'challenges' (Hofer, 1975) are ill structured, complex and not readily amenable to the analytical techniques found in management science or operations research. This is reflected in the paucity of studies (with the notable exception of Mintzberg *et al.*, 1976) which have attempted to systematically determine how organizations become aware of strategic challenges, what analytical processes are brought to bear on these issues and what factors affect the diagnostic skills and procedures which organizations employ endeavouring to understand a strategic problem or opportunity.

In the case of the strategic decisions investigated in this study, the identification and early analysis of strategic options could take place at many organizational levels: the EMC, DEA, DEA office staff, DECs, division management and engineering functions were all identified as frequent sources or sponsors of potential energy strategy options. What is more critical from a decision making perspective is an appraisal of the processes and influences which inhibit or facilitate the transformation of tentative ideas into fully developed alternatives. Defining the financial costs and benefits of projects was rarely described as straightforward and was often cited as a source of disagreement and conflict. Factors not readily demarcated in financial terms such as the impact on production of closing down a furnace for a short period or the adequacy of various energy supply levels, were often the source of intense disagreement between organization levels. Many options were cited as embroiled in conflict due to inadequacy of data, uncertainty of potential gains, potential for significant non-energy implications and 'fit' with previous or projected resource commitments. In those cases where benefits do not clearly outweight the associated costs and problems, diagnosing and screening options can be subject to delays through 'requests for clarification', requests for further data analysis, postponement of 'action' to future meetings and establishment of task forces. Unless a project or option has a very forceful advocate, organizational decision making procedures provide many avenues for delaying its development into a fully documented proposal.

Some decisions studied where the 'benefits' were suggested as clearly outweighing the 'costs' were also characterized by a number of 'interrupts' in the early decision phases. Each decision must be considered as a component of ongoing organization activity which may involve linkages to (for example) the firm's production system, research and development activities, facilities planning programmes, non-energy related investments and, of course, capital allocation decisions in general. The analysis of these implications draws more organization levels and functions into the decision process and thus tends to lead to a more protracted decision process. Almost all the interviewees questioned indicated that the greater the number of organization levels and functions involved, the less the consensus as to a specific alternative's consequences and the greater the disagreement as to the criteria which should be applied in their assessment since each organization level or function views a project or a specific alternative from the vantage point of its own interests. Thus, a decision process in its early stages may go through a number of cycles or feedback loops before a project proposal (i.e. a set of alternatives with regard to a specific decision) is ready for final evaluation.

*Proposition 5: The decision process is dependent upon the complexity of the decision.*

A major goal of this study was to determine whether significant differences exist in the decision process with regard to individual decisions (even within the same firm). It will be seen from Figure 2 that the extent of the review, evaluation, and choice procedure is dependent upon the decision involved. For example, if it is regarded as an 'exceptional item' (e.g., capital expenditures above a threshold level, the decision would establish a new precedent, etc.) the decision is the prerogative of the EMC.

A high degree of variability in the extent of interaction between organization levels is also evident across decisions (see also Tables 1 and 2). The DEA's office plays a large role in the development of some projects while in others it is almost entirely a function of division personnel. Within divisions, DECs reported major differences in the extent of interaction with plant management, the engineering function and division general management.

Even with respect to decision types (e.g. conservation *vs.* supply decisions) major differences at a general level can be noted. Energy supply decisions such as building new storage capacity or conversion to alternate fuels and conservation decisions can differ with respect to: (1) frequency of occurrence (supply decisions occurring much less frequently; (2) degree of criticalness (supply decisions being more critical); (3) the initial impetus for each decision (supply decisions often having a problem stimulus—

supply interruptions—conservation decisions being usually opportunity oriented, e.g. knowledge of existing inefficiencies and/or exploitation of new technologies or processes); (4) the extent to which information gathering and evaluation is required (conservation decisions generally requiring greater diversity of information—thus, a wider number of information sources); (5) the number of alternative courses of action identified (supply decisions usually entail fewer options); and (6) the length of time involved in decision making (after a supply interruption some decisions were made very quickly, whereas some conservation decisions may be prolonged for many months, if not years).

From these differences across (and within) decision types it will not be surprising to discover that some decision processes are considerably more repetitive and circular than others: the individual phases in the decision process or the stages in the decision (planning) system are repeated a number of times before a decision is made. This would seem to be especially the case where the alternatives are characterized by a high degree of uncertainty and/or the decision considered is new to the organization. This evidence suggests that the search, alternative development, evaluation and choice phases differ across decision types and even across decisions within the same decision type or classification.

> *Proposition 6: The structure and process of decision making systems may be a better predictor of strategic choices and behaviour (i.e. decision outcomes) than organizational structure*, per se, *or firms product/market configuration.*

The literature on strategy and structure (for example, Chandler, 1962; Salter, 1970; Scott, 1971; Channon, 1973; Rumelt, 1974) suggests that organization structure should and generally does follow changes in strategic posture. However, the findings to date with regard to the linkages between strategy, structure and economic performance have been less than conclusive (Grinyer and Norburn, 1974; Steiner and Miner, 1977; Galbraith and Nathanson, 1978). Moreover, relatively little attention has been paid to organization structure as an inhibitor or facilitator of strategic chance. Any major choice in strategy flows from some given organization structure (i.e. strategy is influenced by—or follows—structure, to some extent) but this linkage has received very sparse conceptual and empirical treatment.

The dominant concept of structure in the context of strategy/structure relationships has been heavily influenced by organization chart notions. Structure has been primarily conceived as some mixture of functional, divisional, and multi-divisional forms or as some set of product/market configurations. A supplementary route to examine the structure/strategy relationship may be to focus on the structure of strategic decision making processes. The structure of a decision making process is defined here as the organizational systems and procedures which have been established to facilitate decision making in some particular context (e.g. energy management).

The argument here is that the structure and process of decision making in determining 'strategic choice' (Child, 1972) or 'strategic posture' (Katz, 1970) is only partially influenced by organization structure, *per se*, or the firm's product/market configuration. Although a divisionalized structure was common to all firms in the original sample, the energy management decision making structure varied considerably from highly centralized to highly decentralized. The more systematized decision processes entail structured procedures and roles and are reflected in more formal, comprehensive and consistent strategy, i.e. energy management plans. Thus, the performance of firms in terms of improved energy efficiency may be more a function of the structure and process of energy management decision making employed by firms than their formal organizational structure. If this is the case, then, the structure of strategic decision making may help to explain why firms with similar organization structures (in the organization chart sense) or with similar product/market characteristics often adopt quite different strategies or why a particular firm will choose a new strategic posture. It also implies that strategy–structure theorists and researchers need to redefine extant notions of structure to include decision making process elements and to consider alternate concepts of structure as determinants of strategy.

*Proposition 7: A structured or formal planning approach to strategy formulation and implementation does not necessarily imply 'rationality' in the 'maximizing' mode.*

Various authors (e.g. Mintzberg, 1973; Guth, 1976; Steiner and Miner, 1977) have described and summarized a variety of decision making processes or modes in the context of strategy formulation such as the entrepreneurial mode, adaptive decision making, disjointed incrementalism, bureaucratic politics, intuitive-anticipatory planning, and formal-structured planning. These approaches to strategic decision making are generally discussed in their pure form with occasional efforts to delineate their interaction through 'mixing the modes' (Mintzberg, 1973).

Within these descriptions of strategy making, the formal-structured planning process is closest to the thrust and philosophy of economic and decision theory; objectives are established, strategies or alternative courses of action to systematically pursue these objectives are developed and a preferred strategy is chosen. The economist's notion of 'rationality', i.e. the choice of the most efficient means to achieve predetermined ends/goals, is clearly evident in the normative underpinnings of the formal-structured approach to planning (Guth, 1976).

However, it is also evident from the data in this study that the economists' concept of rationality must be tempered by recognition of behavioural and political processes. The choice of goals as discussed in Proposition 2b is itself problematical. Second, the choice of 'means' (i.e. energy management programmes or specific projects) is affected by behavioural and political processes; different organization levels and functional areas evaluating programmes and projects in accordance with their own interests does not necessarily result in the most 'rational' (i.e. most cost efficient) choices. For instance, DECs reported a number of projects were rejected or reformulated due to criticisms by plant and other division management interests; criticisms that were often not based on energy-related considerations. Potential alternatives within a given programme or project often did not reach the final evaluation stage (see, Proposition 3). Also, for those programmes or projects which survived to the final evaluation/choice stage within the formal decision making system (e.g. decisions on projects facing the EMC) such factors as the commitment of specific individuals and groups to individual projects and the particular political alignments supporting projects often influenced the eventual outcome. Thus, rationality as a concept when considered within an organizational context is more aptly described by the engineering of choice (March, 1978) than by the assumptions underlying economic or decision theory.

## Conclusion

A strategic energy management decision making system has evolved in these large multi-divisional firms. To further our understanding of such systems, they can be delineated in terms of their structure (i.e. organization level roles, responsibilities, tasks, etc.) and processes (i.e. interaction across organizational levels, political activities, information transmission, etc.). Also, specific decisions can be traced through and related to the overall decision making system.

Strategic decision making emerges as a complex, multi-organizational level phenomenon, with many individual decisions simultancously in process. The analytical and political/behavioural dimensions of strategic decision making can be investigated separately and collectively. However, the investigation of both dimensions is required to understand, explain and predict strategic decision content and outcomes. The findings of this study particularly emphasize that behavioural and political processes can critically impact any stage of a decision making system or any phase of a specific decision process. As a consequence, 'rationality' or the appearance of rationality, can assume many guises, some of which will not be evident if we confine our explorations to the intellectual and analytical components of strategy making.

The findings of this paper stated in the form of propositions need to be tested in a variety of organizational forms and in different decision contexts. Indeed, much further research is required to move us toward a more formal and comprehensive synthesis of the intellectual/analytical and behavioural/political processes that are necessarily involved in organizational strategy making.

## References

Ackerman, Robert W. 'How companies respond to social demands', *Harvard Business Review*, July–August 1973, pp. 88–98.

Ackoff, Russell L. *A Concept of Corporate Strategy*, Wiley, New York, 1970.

Allison, Graham *T. Essence of Decision: Explaining the Cuban Missile Crisis*, Little, Brown, Boston, 1971.

Anderson, Carl R., and Frank T. Paine. 'Managerial perceptions and strategic behavior', *Academy of Management Journal*, December 1975, pp. 811–823.

Andrews, Kenneth R. *The Concept of Corporate Strategy*, Dow Jones-Irwin, Homewood, Illinois, 1971.

Ansoff, H. Igor. *Corporate Strategy*, McGraw-Hill, New York, 1965.

Ansoff, H. Igor, R. P. Declerck, and R. L. Hayes. *From Strategic Planning to Strategic Management*, Wiley, Chichester, 1976.

Astley, W. Graham, Runo Axelsson, Richard J. Butler, David J. Hickson, and David C. Wilson. 'The dialectics of strategic decision making', University of Bradford Management Centre, England, March 1979, unpublished manuscript.

Berg, Norman. 'Strategic planning in conglomerate companies', *Harvard Business Review*, May–June 1965, pp. 79–92.

Berg, Norman, and Robert A. Pitts. 'Strategic management: the multi-business corporation', in Dan E. Schendel and Charles W. Hofer (eds), *Strategic Management*, Little, Brown and Company, Boston, 1979.

Bower, J. L. *Managing the Resource Allocation Process: A Study of Corporate Planning and Investment*, Division of Research, Harvard Business School, Boston, 1970.

Bower, Joseph L., and Yves Doz. 'Strategy formulation: a social and political process', in Dan E. Schendel and Charles W. Hofer, *Strategic Management: A New View of Business Policy and Planning*, Little, Brown, Boston, 1979.

Carter, E. E. 'The behavioral theory of the firm and top level corporate decisions', *Administrative Science Quarterly*, December 1971, pp. 413–428.

Chandler, Alfred D. *Strategy and Structure*, MIT Press, Cambridge, Mass., 1962.

Channon, Derek F. *The Strategy and Structure of British Enterprises*, Graduate School of Business Administration, Harvard University, Boston, 1973.

Child, John. 'Organizational structure, environment and performance—the role of strategic choice', *Sociology*, January 1972, pp. 1–22.

Cyert, R. M., and J. G. March. *A Behavioral Theory of the Firm*, Prentice-Hall, Englewood Cliffs, N.J., 1963.

Cyert, R. M., H. A. Simon, and D. B. Trow. 'Observation of business decision', *Journal of Business*, 29, 1956, pp. 237–248.

Fahey, Liam. 'An exploratory study of the process of energy management in industrial firms', *unpublished doctoral dissertation*, University of Pittsburgh, 1978.

Galbraith, Jay R., and Daniel A. Nathanson. *Strategy Implementation: The Role of Structure and Process*, West Publishing Company, St. Paul, 1978.

Grant, John H. 'Management implications of systems oriented strategies within selected industrial firms: a developmental model', *unpublished doctoral dissertation*, Harvard University, 1972.

Grant, John H., and William R. King. 'Strategy formulation: analytical and normative models', in Dan E. Schendel and Charles W. Hofer, *Strategic Management: A New View of Business Policy and Planning*, Little, Brown, Boston, 1979.

Grinyer, Peter H., and David Norburn. 'Strategic planning in 21 U.K. companies', *Long Range Planning*, August 1974, pp. 80–89.

Guth, William D. 'Toward a social system theory of corporate strategy', *Journal of Business*, 49, July 1976, pp. 374–388.

Hofer, Charles W. 'Toward a contingency theory of business strategy', *Academy of Management Journal*, December 1975, pp. 784–810.

Hofer, Charles W., and Dan Schendel. *Strategy Formulation: Analytical concepts*, West Publishing Company, St. Paul, 1978.

Katz, Robert L. *Management of the Total Enterprise*. Prentice-Hall, Englewood Cliffs, N.J., 1970.

King, William R., and David I. Cleland. *Strategic Planning and Policy*, Nostrand Reinhold Publishing Company, New York, 1978.

Lindblom, Charles E. 'The science of muddling through', *Public Administration Review*, Spring 1959, pp. 79–88.

Lorange, Peter, and Richard F. Vancil. 'How to design a strategic planning system', *Harvard Business Review*, September–October 1976, pp. 75–81.

Lorsch, J. W., and S. A. Allen. 'Managing diversity and interdependence: an organizational study of multidivisional firms', Division of Research, Harvard Business School, Boston, 1973.

MacMillan, Ian C. *Strategy Formulation: Political Concepts*, West Publishing Company, St. Paul, 1978.

March, James G. 'Bounded rationality, ambiguity, and the engineering of choice', *The Bell Journal of Economics*, March 1978, pp. 587–608.

March, J. G., and J. P. Olsen, (eds). *Ambiguity and Choice in Organization*, Universitetsforlaget, Norway, 1976.

Mintzberg, Henry. 'Organization power and goals: a skeletal theory', in Dan E. Schendel and Charles W. Hofer, *Strategic Management: A New View of Business Policy and Planning*. Little, Brown, Boston, 1979.

Mintzberg, Henry. 'Strategy making in three modes', *California Management Review*, Winter 1973, pp. 44–53.

Mintzberg, Henry, Duru Raisinghani, and Andre Theoret. 'The structure of "unstructured" decision processes', *Administrative Science Quarterly*, June 1976, pp. 246–276.

Murray, Edward A. 'The social response process in commercial banks'. *Academy of Management Review*, July 1976, pp. 5–15.

Perrow, Charles. 'The analysis of goals in complex organizations', *American Sociological Review*, December 1961, pp. 854–866.

Pettigrew, Andrew. *The Politics of Organizational Decision Making*, Tavistock, London, 1973.

Quinn, James Brian. 'Strategic goals: process and politics', *Sloan Management Review*, Fall 1977, pp. 21–38.

Quinn, James Brian. 'Strategic change: logical incrementalism', *Sloan Management Review*, Fall 1978, pp. 7–21.

Rumelt, R. *Strategy, Structure and Economic Performance*, Harvard University Press, Cambridge, Mass., 1974.

Salter, Malcolm. 'Stages of corporate development', *Journal of Business Policy*, 2, 1970.

Saunders, Charles E. 'What should we know about strategy formulation', *Proceedings, Academy of Management*, 1972.

Scott, Bruce R. 'Stages of corporate development', *9–371–294, BP 998*, Intercollegiate Case Clearing House, Harvard Business School, 1971.

Simon, H. A. 'On the concept of organizational goal', *Administrative Science Quarterly*, June 1964, pp. 1–22.

Steiner, George A., and John B. Miner. *Management Policy and Strategy*, Macmillan, New York, 1977.

Vancil, Richard F., and Peter Lorange. 'Strategic planning in diversified companies,' *Harvard Business Review*, January–February 1975, pp. 81–91.

Wrapp, H. E. 'Good managers don't make policy decisions', *Harvard Business Review*, September–October 1967, pp. 91–99.

# 41

# RISK AND THE RELATIONSHIP AMONG STRATEGY, ORGANIZATIONAL PROCESSES, AND PERFORMANCE

*David B. Jemison*

Source: *Management Science* 33(9) (1987): 1087–101.

Performance is an important variable in strategic management research. But, although managers must deal with performance on two dimensions, its level (return) and the variation in that level (risk), performance has traditionally been studied only in terms of return. This paper reports the results of a study of business strategy content and processes where performance was operationalized as both return and risk.

In a field study of 20 firms in the banking industry in one state, different strategies were found to be associated with differences in risk but not in return. The effects of processes on performance were varied; some processes were associated with risk only, some with return only, and others with both risk and return.

These results suggest that the relationships among strategy, processes and performance are more complex than most researchers have acknowledged. Further theoretical and managerial insights may be gained into these relationships if risk is included as a dimension of performance in strategic management research.

## Introduction

The covariation of strategy, organizational processes, and performance is an important and unresolved issue in strategic management and comes from a prevailing assumption that a firm's performance is optimized by a strategy that aligns its capabilities with environmental requirements (e.g., Andrews 1971; Mintzberg 1978). Extant research in this area has viewed performance in terms of its level (return). However, empirical studies show that firms may experience a negative correlation between level of performance (return) and variation in that performance level (risk) (Bowman 1980; Bettis and

Hall 1982). This, of course, contradicts classical economic theory, which suggests that higher performance levels will accrue to firms that undertake more risk. These findings suggest that risk and return may be tapping two different dimensions of performance and that prior studies of strategy, organizational processes, and performance may mask important relationships among the variables if performance is considered only in terms of return.

This study jointly examines strategy content, organizational processes, performance level (return) and performance variation (risk) at the business strategy level. The results indicate that strategy content, organizational processes, and performance do covary systematically. They also suggest that the type of variation depends on whether performance is characterized as return or risk.

Scholars from a variety of disciplines have explored the richness and multiplicity of the relationships among strategy, processes, and performance. Industrial organization economists have provided valuable insights into the range of profitability available in certain industries (e.g., Caves *et al.* 1974; Scherer 1970; Ravenscraft 1983). Research on multi-industry data bases such as PIMS has identified the types of strategies that are associated with profitability in certain settings (e.g., Schoeffler *et al.* 1974; MacMillan *et al.* 1982). Finally, researchers from organization behavior have explored the association of organizational processes and performance (e.g., Venkatraman and Camillus 1984; Van de Ven and Drazin 1985).

Although these studies have provided important insights, they have not simultaneously examined the interaction of these variables and have pursued the question from different theoretical perspectives and units of analysis. This has not led to an integrated understanding of the relationships among these variables or to gestalts, which Miller (1981) argues are not only possible but also potentially more enlightening than bivariate studies.

## Risk and return

The traditional conception of performance in strategic management research has been an accounting figure representing the firm's profit levels or a representative ratio such as return on investment. This perspective on return as performance level will be augmented here by adding risk, variation in performance level.

Risk is an elusive concept with many interpretations. Ball and Brown (1969) point out that risk is an *ex ante* concept that we can only measure *ex post*. Most literature relating risk and return considers risk *ex post* as the variation in a firm's returns (Ball and Brown 1969; Libby and Fishburn 1977). But managers deal with risk as a continuing phenomenon and as such their decisions are affected by both *ex post* experiences (the results of which can be measured in an accounting sense) and *ex ante* presumptions about their future experiences.

Because we cannot use *ex post* variation in return to explain *ex ante* risk taking, this study will use variation in return *ex post* as an indicator of the risk that exists. In this light, managers will have recognized the existence of this risk and will have developed strategies and organizational processes accordingly.

Beyond measurement, the perspective from which risk is viewed is also important. That is, should risk be seen from the managers' perspective, the owners' perspective, or both? A review by Libby and Fishburn (1977) indicates that variability of returns is a common operationalization of risk from an internal managerial accounting perspective. Risk from the owner's perspective is considered differently, most commonly in light of the securities markets and the risk associated with ownership of a particular security.[1] Beaver, *et al.* (1970) have shown that accounting measures of risk are good surrogates for securities market measures of risk. Thus, accounting measures of risk will be used in this study.

## Method

### *Sample*

A sample of 20 banks was taken from a population of 43 Indiana banks between $125 and $550 million in 1979 assets. The banks studied were not large, money center banks but community-oriented firms that provided a range of loans for businesses as well as individuals. The upper bound of this size range allowed a focus on business strategy by concentrating on banks whose primary activities were local banking and had not expanded into a variety of other financial services.[2] The lower bound provided a minimum size above which industry experts and banking managers said there would be division of labor for key organizational decisions. In addition, the internal validity was increased by studying firms in the same industry subject to similar environmental circumstances.

### *Data*

Three types of data were used in the study: archival data about the firm's performance (return and risk) and the content of their business strategies; questionnaire data from the firms' senior managers regarding organizational processes; and interviews with the firms' CEOs. Archival data for the period 1975–1979 for the 43 banks were used to develop risk and return measures and 1979 data were used to identify business strategies (Sheshunoff 1980). In-depth questionnaire and interview data from senior managers in 20 of these banks were used to test the hypotheses regarding organizational processes. Further details about the sample and data sources are available from the author.

*Measurement*

Performance level (return) for each bank was operationalized as the average return on assets for the five-year period (1975–1979). Performance variation (risk) for each bank is the standard deviation of its return on assets over the same five-year period (Bettis and Mahajan 1985; Beaver *et al.* 1970; Libby and Fishburn 1977).

Strategy content was operationalized by grouping the sample firms on the basis of a cluster analysis of three key dimensions related to business strategy over which the managers had control: product mix, pricing, and internal operating efficiency. Clustering was done with the BMD-P2M clustering algorithm that uses a Euclidean distance measure to link cluster centroids in a stepwise fashion (Dixon 1981).

The variables used in developing the strategy clusters were first identified by the author as representative of basic components of a business strategy for firms in this industry (Ansoff 1965; Schendel and Hofer 1979) and were then cross validated by a series of interviews with industry experts: four CEOs at banks in the sample that did not participate in the questionnaire phase of the project, the head of the industry trade association, and three professors of finance whose research focused on financial institutions. Therefore, the strategy content variables used in the cluster analysis reflect a conceptual link to the components of a business strategy that are grounded in the practice of the industry (Morrison 1967). Table 1 describes the operationalization of these variables and Table 2 presents the strategies derived from the clustering procedure.

The organizational process variables used in this study reflect managerial processes that prior research has related to differences in strategy, return, and risk. They are decision centralization (Lawrence and Lorsch 1967; Thompson 1967), planning activities (Ansoff *et al.* 1970; Kudla 1980), types and extent of environmental interaction (Hambrick 1981; Pfeffer and Salancik 1978), departmental interdependence (Thompson 1967; Williamson 1975), and influence on strategic decisions (Hickson *et al.* 1971; Jemison 1981). The operationalization of these variables, the scales used, and the reliabilities in this study are summarized in Table 3.

*Table 1* Variables Used in Developing Strategy Clusters.

| *Strategic Dimension* | *Variable Operationalization* |
|---|---|
| Product Mix | Loans to retail customers as a percent of total loans |
| Pricing Policies | Difference between interest received on loans and investments and interest paid on deposits and borrowed funds as percent of average assets |
| Efficiency | Total assets divided by number of employees (Assets/Employees) |

*Table 2* Strategy Types Results of Cluster Analysis Comparison of Cluster Means with Sample Means.

| *Strategic Variable* | *Sample* (n = *43*) | *Strategy 1* *Focused Retailer* (n = *18*) | *Strategy 2* *High-priced Inefficient* (n = *12*) | *Strategy 3* *Focused Commercial* (n = *13*) |
|---|---|---|---|---|
| Product Mix[a] | 54.9 | 63.0**** | 53.0 | 44.3**** |
| Pricing Policies[b] | 4.7 | 4.64 | 5.09**** | 4.46** |
| Efficiency[c] | 979 | 1009 | 857*** | 1070** |

Reflects significant difference from sample mean, *t*-test.
$^{****}p < 0.001$.
$^{***}p < 0.01$.
$^{**}p < 0.05$.
[a] Higher score means more consumer loans as percent of total loans.
[b] Higher score means higher relative prices.
[c] Higher score means more efficient.

A mailed questionnaire to gather data on the process variables was sent to 164 executives at 20 of the banks in late 1979. (Note this gives the questionnaire data a temporal correspondence with the archival data on performance and strategy content.) These executives were recommended by their CEOs as having an input into their firm's strategic decisions. Each executive completed the questionnaire privately and mailed it directly to the researcher to insure anonymity. A total of 141 questionnaires were returned, of which 135 were usable, an 83% response rate. The number of usable questionnaires ranged from 5 to 11 per firm with no less than a 69% response rate in any one bank. There were no material differences between respondents and nonrespondents on managerial level, function, or firm size. A complete description of the process variables, the instruments used, the data gathering procedures, and the analytical methodology is available from the author.

## Hypotheses

The primary issue addressed in this study is whether the conceptualization of performance as both return and risk affects the existing relationships among business strategy, organizational processes, and performance. Traditional economic theory suggests that if risk and return are related, then the strategies and processes associated with that performance would also be related. But, because risk and return have been found to be negatively correlated (Bowman 1980; Bettis and Hall 1982) and because risk as a dimension of performance has not been considered before in either business-level strategy or organizational process studies, they are considered separately among the hypotheses tested here to test for possibly differential

*Table 3* Organizational Process Variables Summary of Operationalization.

| *Organizational Process Variable* | *Measures* | *Reliability* Chronbach's α* | *Scale Source* |
|---|---|---|---|
| Decision Centralization | The place in the hierarchy where a variety of decisions are made. (Lower scores indicate more centralization.) | 0.71 | Lenz (1978) |
| Planning Activities | The extent to which strategic planning is —formalized —operationalized. (Higher scores indicate more formalization or operationalization). | 0.91 | Lenz (1978) |
| Environmental Interaction | | | |
| —Amount of Interaction | Percent of time dealing with outsiders | | |
| —Type of Interaction | Boundary spanning activities: | | Jemison (1981) |
| | Customer contact | 0.82 | |
| | Input acquisition | 0.88 | |
| | Information control | 0.90 | |
| | Representing the firm to outsiders | 0.73 | |
| | Information acquisition | 0.65 | |
| | (Higher scores indicate more interaction) | | |
| Departmental Interdependence | Your dependence on others | 0.87 | Rousseau (1978) |
| | Others' dependence on you | 0.93 | |
| | (Higher scores indicate more dependence) | | |
| Distribution of Influence on Strategic Decisions | Influence of a department on a series of strategic decisions (Higher scores indicate more influence). | 0.95 | Hinings *et al.* (1974) |

* Reliability figures are based upon multiple raters for each measure.

effects. As such, three general questions form the basis for the more specific hypotheses tested here:

1. Are there differences in return and risk across business strategy types?
2. Are there differences in organizational processes between firms with high and low return and high and low risk?
3. Are the organizational processes that differ by high and low return the same as those that differ by high and low risk?

### *Question 1: Are there differences in risk and return across strategy types?*

While there is evidence that certain business-level strategies improve return (e.g., Hambrick 1983; Hatten *et al.* 1979; MacMillan *et al.* 1982; Schoeffler *et al.* 1974) there is no empirical evidence relating business strategies and risk. In contrast, at the corporate level, there is evidence that certain diversification strategies can improve return (Rumelt 1974). Recent studies at the corporate level also indicate that risk and return may be negatively correlated (Bowman 1980; Rumelt 1977) and that certain diversification strategies may improve the risk/return relationship for a firm (Bettis and Hall 1982; Bettis and Mahajan 1985).

While prior research in strategic management has not extensively considered performance in terms of both return and risk, fields such as accounting and finance have. Their evidence indicates that managers do consider the riskiness of their decisions (Libby and Fishburn 1977; MacCrimmon and Wehrung 1986). Thus, it appears that risk is an important variable that needs to be included in strategic management research, especially at the business strategy level.

Major themes in strategic management have emphasized the need to develop a business strategy that responds to the particular needs of the environment (Bourgeois 1980; Hambrick 1983). In this industry, the strategy content variables identified by industry experts were product mix, pricing, and internal operating efficiency. Thus, following prior research, we would expect both higher returns and more consistent performance (lower risk) from banks whose strategies targeted a particular market segment allowing the management group to develop an in-depth understanding of the customers' needs and providing the opportunity to build continuing relationships that are important, especially in small town banking. Other firms would find it difficult to penetrate these barriers, except by more innovative services or lower prices.

> H1a. *Strategies that are more focused on a particular market segment will have lower risk than those that are less focused.*
> H1b. *Strategies that are more focused on a particular market segment will have higher returns than those that are less focused.*

Beyond the importance of matching business strategy and environment, prior research suggests that internal consistency in that business strategy is important (Porter 1980; Woo and Cooper 1981). In this industry, internal consistency would involve expense control, allowing managers in a bank with an established market position to prevent existing competitors or new entrants from undercutting their firm on the basis of price. This is very important in this industry since in essence banks sell a fungible commodity, money. Thus, we would expect banks who are able to control expenses better than others to experience higher as well as more consistent returns.

H1c. *Low risk firms will be more efficient than high risk firms.*
H1d. *High return firms will be more efficient than low return firms.*

### *Question 2: Are there differences in organizational processes between firms with high and low return and high and low risk?*

A substantial amount of research has explored the various relationships among organizational processes, structure, and performance. Central among these researchers are contingency theorists who have examined the relationship of performance and a variety of organization structure and process variables including technology (Woodward 1965; Perrow 1972), organization structure (Hall 1977), and the environment (Lawrence and Lorsch 1967; Burns and Stalker 1961).

This search for the right combination of conditions associated with superior performance is important but to date the findings have been inconclusive (Dalton *et al.* 1980; Venkatraman and Camillus 1984; Drazin and Van de Ven 1985). Miller (1981) contends that these inconclusive findings are due to the narrow-mindedness of contingency theory and argues that more open, gestalt-oriented approaches are needed. A related explanation, proposed here, is that performance has been conceptualized too narrowly as only return. Accordingly, Hypotheses 2 through 6 test for differences in five organizational processes that both prior research and industry practice suggest would be associated with variation in return and risk: decision centralization, planning activities, environmental interaction, departmental interdependence, and distribution of influence on strategic decisions.

Although prior research has related *decision centralization* to return in stable environments (Lawrence and Lorsch 1967; Lenz 1978) and as a result of technology (Thompson 1967), risk has not been considered. Decision centralization in this industry is expected to be related to high return and low risk for several reasons. Due to the stability of the banking industry in Indiana at the time of the study and the mediating nature of a bank's technology (Thompson 1967), banks must centrally control their policies regarding the sources and costs of funds as well as their ultimate use and pricing. A greater degree of decision centralization would insure consistency in funds acquisition and allocation which would lead to both lower overall costs in a stable environment and more equitable treatment of customers. Thus, because of the need to control the cost of inputs and to insure the consistency of outputs, better performing banks are hypothesized to have more decision centralization.

H2a. *Low risk firms will have more decision centralization than high risk firms.*
H2b. *High return firms will have more decision centralization than low return firms.*

The effectiveness of *planning activities* as a way to improve performance is subject to much debate in strategic management. While some studies find that strategic planning yields better results (e.g., Ansoff *et al.* 1970; Karger and Malik 1975), others suggest that there is no systematic relationship between strategic planning and economic performance (Grinyer and Norburn 1975; Kudla 1980). Frederickson (1984), studying firms in a stable environment, found a positive relationship between a comprehensive strategic decision making processes and performance (measured as return). This study's purpose was not to test the impact of strategic planning on economic performance but instead to explore whether there were differences in strategic planning activities of firms associated with high and low risk and return especially since the relationship between planning and risk has not been explored.

Two aspects of strategic planning activities are examined for their relationship to risk and return: the formality of a firm's planning activities and the extent to which aspects of the plan are operationalized and objectives are converted into measurable outcomes. In this industry, we would expect both the formalization of the planning process and the operationalization of the plan to be associated with lower risk because of the advantages it would provide managers in understanding and developing a consistent approach in their business and the way in which it interacts with the environment.

H3a. *Low risk firms will have more formalized strategic planning processes than high risk firms.*
H3b. *Low risk firms will have more completely operationalized objectives than high risk firms.*
H3c. *High return firms will have more formalized strategic planning processes than low return firms.*
H3d. *High return firms will have more completely operationalized objectives than low return firms.*

The environment is also acknowledged to have an important impact on firm performance (Bourgeois 1980; Caves 1980). This occurs as managers interact with their firm's environment in attempts to affect it and are simultaneously affected by it (Weick 1979). Because all the banks in this sample operated within a relatively similar environment, we can test the relative importance of environmental interaction on firm performance in a somewhat "controlled" situation. Two aspects of *environmental interaction*, amount and type, are hypothesized to affect risk and return. Because of the environmental similarity of the sample banks' environment, it is hypothesized that firms with greater absolute levels of environmental interaction will experience higher returns and lower risks. Better performance would result because the interactions would increase the information available to managers, allowing a better understanding of competitive and market trends as well as provide an image of bank interest and involvement to customers and competitors.

> H4a. *Greater absolute levels of environmental interaction will be present in low risk firms than in high risk firms.*
> H4b. *Greater absolute levels of environmental interaction will be present in high return firms than in low return firms.*

While the absolute amount of interaction is hypothesized to be important, the actual segments of the environment with which the managers choose to interact are also expected to be important. If managers cope effectively with key segments of the environment, their firms should experience better performance (Pfeffer and Salancik 1978; Thompson 1967). Although this is conceptually appealing, selecting a particular type of environmental interaction for hypothesis testing must be guided by both theory and a knowledge of the industry. In this industry, two types of environmental interaction are hypothesized to be associated with better performance. Customer contact is seen to be important to maintain customer relationships and understand evolving customer needs. Information acquisition about environmental trends is seen to be important to control costs of funds and maintain competitive pricing policies.

> H4c. *More environmental interaction directed to customer contact and information acquisition will be present in low risk than in high risk firms.*
> H4d. *More environmental interaction directed to customer contact and information acquisition will be present in high return than in low return firms.*

*Departmental interdependence* within a firm reflects the interaction of various organizational subunits in the performance of their duties. Some firms' operations may require substantial interaction; others may have subunits that are quite autonomous. Although there are many ways to organize, a firm with a mediating technology, such as a bank (Thompson 1967), needs coordination among departments to acquire funds and make loans in a consistent and profitable fashion. These interdependencies may affect performance because of inefficiencies that accrue to inappropriate methods of organization (Galbraith and Nathanson 1977; Williamson 1975). Because of the needs in this industry to coordinate the activities of different departments, to acquire funds, and to make loans consistently to customers, banks with high return and low risk are hypothesized to be more interdependent.

H5a. *Low risk firms will have more departmental interdependence than high risk firms.*
H5b. *High return firms will have more departmental interdependence than low return firms.*

The *distribution of influence on strategic decisions* reflects the distribution of power among groups within the firm. Prior research in intraorganizational power has established that influence accrues to those within the firm whose activities enable them to deal with the strategic contingencies facing the firm, especially those present in the environment (Hinings *et al.* 1974; Jemison 1981; Pfeffer and Salancik 1978). But to date, no research has shown an association between relative influence on strategic decisions and firm performance.

This study explores the extent to which a firm's risk and return varies as managers who interact with the environment also have influence over strategic decisions. Because of the importance of the environment in strategic decision making, it is hypothesized that firms giving more influence on strategic decisions to managers who interact with the environment will have higher returns and lower risk.

H6a. *Low risk firms will give more influence over strategic decisions to groups that interact with the environment than high risk firms.*
H6b. *High return firms will give more influence over strategic decisions to groups that interact with the environment than low return firms.*

### *Question 3: Are the organizational processes that differ by high and low return the same as those that differ by high and low risk?*

Hypotheses 2 through 6 beg an important question: "If there are differences in processes associated with risk and return, will the differences be consistent?" Contingency theory suggests that a firm must match its organizational processes and structure to its environment if it is to perform well (Van de Ven and Drazin 1985). But, because performance has dual components of return and risk, the particular organizational processes associated with better performance in terms of return may not be the same as those processes associated with better performance in terms of risk. For example, one might expect that managers whose firms are operating in more volatile environments would decentralize more decisions and engage in more environmental interaction with the expectation of reducing risk. Influence patterns would also be expected to be associated with differences in the levels of return and risk. Additionally, because of managerial risk preferences (MacCrimmon and Wehrung 1986), internal power distribution patterns may be quite different in firms that have low risk with compared to those with high return.

H7. *The organizational processes that differ by high and low return will be different from those that differ by high and low risk.*

## Results and discussion

The hypotheses were tested using one-way analysis of variance and regression analysis. The results, in general, support the hypotheses and suggest that our conception of the strategy-process-performance relationship should be expanded to include performance in terms of both return and risk.

### *Hypothesis 1: Strategy content, risk, and return*

As indicated in Table 4, Hypothesis 1b, that banks focused on particular market segments would have higher returns than less highly focused banks, was not supported. In addition, Hypothesis 1d, that banks with high returns would be more efficient than those with low returns was also not supported. However, hypotheses 1a and 1c, that banks with more focused strategies and with greater efficiency, respectively, would have less risk, was supported. The Strategy 2 bank (High Priced, Inefficient) had a risk level that was significantly about twice that of Strategy 1 (Focused Retailer) and Strategy 3 (Focused Commercial). This finding argues that although different

*Table 4* Performance Difference Across Strategies.
(Risk and Return)
(Means Reported)

| *Performance* | *Sample* (n = *43*) | *Strategy 1* *Focused* *Retailer* (n = *18*) | *Strategy 2* *High Priced* *Inefficient* (n = *12*) | *Strategy 3* *Focused* *Commercial* (n = *13*) |
|---|---|---|---|---|
| RETURN[a] | 0.85 | 0.84 | 0.79 | 0.96 |
| RISK[b] | 1.13 | 0.10 | 0.18*** | 0.09 |

Reflects significant difference from sample mean, *t*-test.
***$p < 0.01$.
[a] Average Return on Assets 1975–1979.
[b] Standard Deviation of Return on Assets 1975–1979.

*Table 5* Organizational Process Variables One-Way ANOVA by Return and Risk. (Mean Reported)

| | *RETURN* | | | *RISK* | | |
|---|---|---|---|---|---|---|
| | *High* n = *10* | *Low* n = *10* | F-*Statistic* | *High* n = *11* | *Low* n = *9* | F-*Statistic* |
| *Decision Centralization* | 2.58 | 2.80 | 4.85** | 2.63 | 2.79 | 0.14 |
| *Planning Approach* | | | | | | |
| —Formalization | 1.77 | 1.85 | 0.11 | 1.59 | 2.14 | 7.75*** |
| —Operationalization | 3.11 | 3.49 | 2.13 | 3.22 | 3.41 | 0.49 |
| *Environmental Interaction* | | | | | | |
| —Amount of Interaction (% time dealing with outsiders) | 36.5 | 37.8 | 0.12 | 35.8 | 39.1 | 0.78 |
| —Customer Contact | 10.8 | 10.9 | 0.00 | 10.9 | 10.7 | 0.10 |
| —Input Acquisition | 13.6 | 14.3 | 0.95 | 13.7 | 14.3 | 0.60 |
| —Information Control | 11.3 | 10.9 | 0.56 | 11.2 | 11.0 | 0.25 |
| —Representative | 9.4 | 9.9 | 0.96 | 9.4 | 10.0 | 1.24 |
| —Information Acquisition | 10.1 | 9.8 | 0.70 | 9.8 | 10.2 | 1.6 |
| *Departmental Interdependence* | | | | | | |
| —You on Others | 3.11 | 3.24 | 0.51 | 3.16 | 3.20 | 0.06 |
| —Others on You | 3.03 | 3.04 | 0.002 | 2.9 | 3.3 | 3.90** |
| *Distribution of Influence on Strategic Decisions* (see Table 6) | | | | | | |

***$p < 0.01$.
**$p < 0.05$.

strategies may have similar returns, the risk associated with them is quite different and should be considered separately. As such, the results suggest that the risk component of performance should be an important consideration in research on business strategy content and performance.

### *Hypothesis 2: Decision centralization, risk, and return*

Hypothesis 2b, that decision centralization would be greater in high return banks, was supported, while Hypothesis 2a, that decision centralization would be greater in low risk banks, was not supported (Table 5). Because banks sell money, an essentially fungible commodity, they must control the policies regarding the sources and cost of that money as well as its uses and pricing at a high level in the firm. This centralization in high return banks also follows from Lawrence and Lorsch (1967), given the stable nature of the banking environment at the time of the study. When coupled with the significant findings in Hypothesis 2b, the lack of significance in Hypothesis 2a suggests that return and risk as aspects of performance are indeed different and should be treated as such by researchers and managers when considering process-performance relationships.

### *Hypothesis 3: Planning, risk, and return*

Hypothesis 3a, that lower risk would be associated with more formalized planning systems, was strongly supported (Table 5). In this sample, systematically thinking about the future was associated with a reduction in the variance in return. Hypothesis 3b, that lower risk firms would have more completely operationalized objectives than higher risk firms, was not supported. Similarly, Hypotheses 3c and 3d that high return firms would have respectively more formalized planning and more completely operationalized objectives than low return firms was not supported. The finding that planning activities were not seen to be to be associated with higher returns supports the doubts about the effectiveness of improving returns through strategic planning in service firms, at least in this industry (Rue 1973). In addition, the findings show that as indications of performance, risk and return are associated with different types of organizational processes.

### *Hypothesis 4: Environmental interaction, risk, and return*

In this sample, neither frequency of interaction nor focus on a particular environmental segment was associated with significant performance differences as measured by either return or risk. As Table 5 indicates, Hypotheses 4a and 4b were not supported; there were no significant differences in the amount of environmental interaction associated with risk or return. Similarly, Hypotheses 4c and 4d were not supported; there were no significant differences by type of environmental interaction between high and low risk and return. Accordingly, in this industry, merely interacting with the environment or a key component of it does not seem to be associated with an increase in return or a reduction in risk. This finding is very interesting because it suggests that, in the same industry, neither the amount nor the type of environmental interaction is associated with return or risk. If strategic management researchers are to continue to emphasize the environment as an important variable, a better understanding is needed about why aspects of the environment and managers' interactions with it are strategic.

### *Hypothesis 5: Departmental interdependence, risk, and return*

Two types of departmental interdependence were tested for association with return and risk, the dependence of the respondent's department on other departments (you on others) and the dependence of other departments on the respondent's department (others on you).[3] Hypothesis 5b, that related departmental interdependence to return, was not supported (Table 5). Hypothesis 5a was supported; managers in low risk firms reported significantly more dependence on them by others than did managers in high risk firms.

These findings raise interesting questions about the role of perceived self-importance and organizational performance (in this case lower risk). One explanation consistent with the industry will be explored here. We would expect better interdepartmental coordination to be associated with reduced risk in this industry. As hypothesized, managers in lower risk firms reported significantly more dependence on them by others than reported by their counterparts in higher risk firms. But there were no differences between high and low performing firms (both risk and return) on departments' perceptions of their dependence on others. This implies that managers in low risk firms may have had a better self-image and a perception that they were important to the firm. This self-perception may have been associated with greater incentives for coordination among departments which in turn would lead to a reduction in risk in this industry.

### *Hypothesis 6: Influence on strategic decisions, return and risk*

Hypotheses 6a and 6b, that in low risk and high return firms respectively, more influence over strategic decisions would be given to groups that interact with the environment than in high risk and low return firms were strongly supported (Table 6). The influence on strategic decisions associated with the various boundary spanning roles is substantially higher in low risk firms than in high risk firms (adjusted $R^2 = 0.25$ for low risk vs 0.09 for high risk). Similarly, the adjusted $R^2$ for influence on strategic decisions associated

*Table 6* Environmental Interaction and Influence on Strategic Decisions Multiple Regression by Risk & Return.
(Standardized Betas Reported)

| | *Return* | | *Risk* | |
|---|---|---|---|---|
| *Boundary Spanning Role* | *High* n = *67* | *Low* n = *68* | *High* n = *79* | *Low* n = *56* |
| —Information Control | 0.35**** | | 0.23** | 0.22* |
| —Customer Contact | 0.16* | 0.26** | | 0.39**** |
| —Information Acquisition | | | | |
| —Input Control | 0.25*** | 0.13* | | 0.33**** |
| —Representative | 0.35*** | | 0.22** | 0.15* |
| $R^2$ | 0.32 | 0.08 | 0.12 | 0.30 |
| Adjusted $R^2$ | 0.28 | 0.04 | 0.09 | 0.25 |

****$p < 0.001$.
***$p < 0.01$.
**$p < 0.05$.
*$p < 0.10$.
Dependent variable = Influence on Strategic Decisions
Independent variable = Type of environmental interaction as operationalized by Boundary Spanning Roles

with the various boundary spanning roles is 0.28 for high return firms and 0.04 for low return firms.

These findings offer new insights into the issue of environmental interaction, power distribution, and financial performance. The common, significant finding from these data is that both higher returns and lower risks accrue to those firms whose managers have the internal power to cope with the external environment. These results also offer insights into the questions regarding environmental interaction and performance raised by the results of Hypothesis 4. Recall that no significant differences in the patterns of environmental interaction were associated with return or risk (Table 5). When coupled with the results of Hypothesis 6, these results suggest that it is not enough to merely interact with the environment. Better performance accrues to firms whose managers both interact with the environment and also have influence over strategic decisions. Performance is improved because these managers couple their knowledge of the environment with their intraorganizational influence, allowing the firm's strategy to reflect the demands and opportunities present in the environment.

### *Hypothesis 7: Process differences associated with return and risk*

The results support Hypothesis 7, indicating that the organizational processes associated with high and low return are different from those associated with high and low risk (Tables 5 and 6). Significant differences between high and low return firms were found in decision centralization, types of boundary spanning roles with influence on strategic decisions, and the extent to which boundary spanning was associated with influence on strategic decisions. In contrast, significant differences in high and low risk firms were found in the extent of planning formalization, departmental interdependence, the types of boundary spanning roles with strategic decision influence, and the extent to which those roles were associated with influence on strategic decisions. These differences reinforce the argument that risk and return are two different dimensions of organizational performance and suggest that researchers should distinguish between them when studying processes and performance.

## Conclusions and implications

The findings of this study allow some tentative conclusions about the interrelationship of business-level strategy, organizational processes, and performance in strategic management research. Although it is important to recognize the limitations of a study in a single industry, the results of this study raise several important questions about our conception of performance, the importance of environmental interaction, the relative contribution of strategy and processes to performance, and the organizational processes associated with strategy types.

This study suggests that the relationship of strategy, processes, and performance is more complex than most researchers have acknowledged. This study found that organizational processes and strategy were related to both return and risk. In addition, the processes that varied with return were different from those that varied with risk. This suggests that our conception of performance should be expanded to include both return and risk. If the risk dimension of performance were included in strategic management research, a degree of richness could be added to our understanding of these basic process-performance relationships in a variety of settings given the importance of risk in managerial decisions.

For example, in situations where there is little variation in strategy content and return, process differences may be better understood by considering risk. Moreover, the relationship of strategy content and processes with return and risk raises questions about the nature of managerial goals and risk preferences. Specifically, most research has focused on strategies that are intended to achieve certain levels of return. The relationship of risk to managerial decisions about strategy and organizational processes has not been explored by researchers as either an alternative model for or as an impediment to those decisions.

These findings also suggest that the concept of "fit" between a firm's environment, strategy, organizational processes, and performance should be expanded to include both risk and return. Since the organizational processes associated with return and risk are different, requirements for fit would be expected to be different as well.

Another common theme that emerges from this research is the importance of translating environmental interaction into organizational decisions. These results showed that firms with either high return or low risk consistently gave more organizational power to people interacting with the environment than did firms with poorer performance of either type (lower return or higher risk). This suggests that if firms (at least in this industry) give power to those who can cope most effectively with the environment they will experience better performance. It is also important to note that there were no performance differences among the sample firms in the types of environmental interaction (types of boundary spanning roles) in which managers engaged (Table 5). However, the fact that the influence of some of these roles was much greater among better performers (Table 6) suggests an important association between performance and power distribution within firms that has yet to be explored by organizational researchers.

The setting of this research offers possibilities to strategic management researchers interested in simultaneously exploring process and content issues. One problem in such research is deciding the extent to which one should control for either strategy content or strategic process variables. These results suggest that by standardizing on the industry dimension, researchers can control for content while still allowing for variance on both content and process. Promising research sites may include industries in which managers have limited flexibility in strategic options because of high entry or exit barriers, associated resource requirements, regulation, or managerial perspective. This would control for strategy content to an extent but simultaneously allow the researcher to study content and process-related actions within that particular arena. Thus, for a particular industry, the researcher could develop hypotheses that relate organizational processes to aspects of strategy content that would be expected to be associated with a competitive advantage in that industry.

Finally, this research offers insights into the relative importance of strategy content and organizational processes on performance. This study was conducted at a time when managers in the sample firms had relatively little flexibility to drastically or quickly change strategy content because of regulatory barriers, investments in people, or market image. The results here indicated that performance differences (especially with respect to return) were more closely linked with processes than with strategic variables. Support is provided for Miller and Friesen's (1977) argument that organizational processes may be more important in certain stages of a firm's life than strategy content. Even though a firm's strategic flexibility may be reduced due to regulation, exit barriers, etc., performance differences are still possible because of the strategic management of organizational processes. Empirical support is thus provided for the common argument in strategic management that it is not enough to have a good strategy; execution and management practice are equally important.[4]

## Notes

1 The Capital Asset Pricing Model (CAPM) provides a way for a security owner to conceptualize and operationalize the risk attendant on holding a particular security (Sharpe 1964; Lintner 1965). Jensen (1972) provides a comprehensive review of the CAPM.

2 Two of the banks in the sample had formed a holding company for such purposes. Care was taken to use only content data related to their commercial banking activities and questionnaires for process data were not set to people whose activities were outside commercial banking.

3 Department as used here refers to either the department or to the area of the firm for which the executive completing the questionnaire had responsibility.

4 Support for this research was provided by the Strategic Management Program, Graduate School of Business, Stanford University, and the Indiana University Foundation. This paper has benefitted from the helpful comments of Rich Bettis, Jay Bourgeois, Robert Burgelman, Jim Fredrickson, Don Hambrick, Tom Lenz, Janet Near, Steve Wheelwright and two anonymous referees.

## References

Andrews, K. R., *The Concept of Corporate Strategy*, Dow Jones-Irwin, Homewood, IL, 1971.

ASOFF, H. I., *Corporate Strategy*, McGraw-Hill, New York, 1965.

——, J. AVNER, R. G. BRANDENBURG, F. E. PORTNER AND R. RADOSEVICH, "Does Planning Pay? The Effects of Planning on Success of Acquisitions of American Firms," *Long Range Planning*, 3, 2(1970), 2–7.

BALL, R. AND P. BROWN, "Portfolio Theory and Accounting," *J. Accounting Res.*, (Autumn 1969), 300–323.

BEAVER, W. H., P. KETTLER AND M. SCHOLES, "The Association Between Market Determined and Accounting Determined Risk Measures," *Accounting Rev.*, 45(1970), 654–682.

BETTIS, R. A. AND V. MAHAJAN, "Risk/Return Performance of Diversified Firms," *Management Sci.*, 31 (1985), 785–799.

—— AND W. K. HALL, "Diversification Strategy, Accounting Determined Risk, and Accounting Determined Return," *Acad. Management J.*, 25(1982), 254–264.

BOURGEOIS, L. J., "Strategy and Environment: A Conceptual Integration," *Acad. Management Rev.*, (Spring 1980), 17–31.

BOWMAN, E. H., "A Risk Return Paradox for Strategic Management," *Sloan Management Rev.*, (Spring 1980), 17–31.

BURNS, T. AND G. STALKER, *The Management of Innovation*, Tavistock, London, 1961.

CAVES, R. E., "Industrial Organization, Corporate Strategy, and Structure: A Survey," *J. Economic Lit.*, 16 (1980), 64–92.

——, *American Industry: Structure, Conduct, Performance*. 4th ed., Prentice-Hall, Englewood Cliffs, NJ, 1977.

——, B. T. GALE AND M. E. PORTER, "Interfirm Profitability Differences," *Quart. J. Economics*, 88 (1974), 181–192.

DALTON, D. R., W. P. TUDOR, M. J. SPENDOLINI, G. J. FIELDING AND L. W. PORTER, "Organization Structure and Performance; A Critical Review," *Acad. Management Rev.*, 5(1980), 49–64.

DIXON, W. J. (ED.), *BMDP Statistical Software*, University of California Press, Berkeley, 1981.

DRAZIN, R. AND A. H. VAN DE VEN, "Alternative Forms of Fit in Contingency Theory," *Admin. Sci. Quart.*, 30(1985), 514–539.

FREDERICKSON, J. W., "The Comprehensiveness of Strategic Decision Processes: Extension, Observations, Future Directions," *Acad. Management J.*, 27, 3(1984), 445–466.

GALBRAITH, J. AND D. NATHANSON, *Strategy Implementation: The Role of Structure and Progress*, West Publishing Company, St. Paul, 1978.

GREEN, P. E., *Analyzing Multivariate Data*, Dryden Press, Hinsdale, IL, 1978.

GRINYER, P. H. AND D. NORBURN, "Planning for Existing Markets: Perceptions of Chief Executives and Financial Performance," *J. Roy. Statist. Soc., Ser. A*, 139(1975), 70–97.

HALL, R. H., *Organizations: Structure & Process*. 2nd Ed., Prentice-Hall, Englewood Cliffs, NJ, 1977.

HAMBRICK, D. C., "High Profit Strategies in Mature Capital Goods Industries: A Contingency Approach," *Acad. Management J.*, 26(1983), 697–707.

——, "Environment, Strategy, and Power Within Top Management Teams," *Admin. Sci. Quart.*, 26 (1981), 253–276.

HICKSON, D. J., C. R. HININGS, C. A. LEE, R. E. SCHNECK AND J. M. PENNINGS, "A Strategic Contingencies Theory of Intraorganizational Power," *Admin. Sci. Quart.*, 16(1971), 216–219.

HININGS, C. R., D. J. HICKSON, J. M. PENNINGS AND R. E. SCHNECK, "Structural Conditions of Intraorganizational Power," *Admin. Sci. Quart.*, 17(1974), 22–44.

JEMISON, D. B., "Organizational vs. Environmental Sources of Influence in Strategic Decision Making," *Strategic Management J.*, 2(1981), 77–89.

JENSEN, M. C., "Capital Markets: Theory and Evidence," *Bell J. Economics and Management*, 3 (Autumn 1972).

KARGER, D. W. AND Z. A. MALJK, "Long Range Planning and Organizational Performance," *Long Range Planning*, 8, 6(1975), 6–64.

KUDLA, R. J., "The Effects of Strategic Planning on Common Stock Returns," *Acad. Management J.*, 23(1981), 5–20.

LAWRENCE, P. R. AND J. W. LORSCH, "*Organization and Environment*," Division of Research, Harvard Business School, Boston, 1967.

LENZ, R. T., "Strategic Interdependence and Organizational Performance: Patterns in One Industry," unpublished doctoral dissertation, Indiana University, 1978.

——, "Environment, Strategy, Organization Structure, and Performance: Patterns in One Industry," *Strategic Management J.*, 1(1980), 209–266.

LIBBY, R. AND P. C. FISHBURN, "Behavioral Models of Risk Taking in Business Decisions: A Survey and Evaluation," *J. Accounting Res.*, 15(1977), 272–292.

LINTNER, J., "The Valuation of Risk Assets and the Selection of Risky Investments in Stock Portfolio and Capital Budgets," *Rev. Economics and Statist.*, 47(1965), 13–37.

MACCRIMMON, K. R. AND D. A. WEHRUNG, *Taking Risks: The Management of Uncertainty*, Free Press, New York, 1986.

MACMILLAN, I. C., D. C. HAMBRICK AND D. L. DAY, "The Product Portfolio and Profitability—A PIMS- Based Analysis of Industrial-Product Businesses," *Acad. Management J.*, 25(1982), 733–755.

MILLER, D., "Toward a new Contingency Approach: The Search for Organizational Gestalts," *J. Management Studies*, 18(1981), 1–26.

—— AND P. H. FRIESEN, "Strategy-Making in Context: Ten Empirical Archetypes," *J. Management Studies*, 14(1977), 253–280.

MINTZBERG, H., "Patterns of Strategy Formulation," *Management Sci.*, 24(1978), 934–948.

MORRISON, D. C., "Measurement Problems in Cluster Analysis," *Management Sci.*, 13(1967), 175–180.

PERROW, C., *Complex Organizations: A Critical Essay*, Scott-Foresman & Co., Glencoe, IL, 1981.

PFEFFER, J. AND G. R. SALANCIK, *The External Control of Organizations: A Resource Dependence Perspective*, Harper & Row, New York, 1978.

PORTER, M. E., *Competitive Strategy*, Free Press, New York, 1980.

RAVENSCRAFT, D. J., "Structure Performance Relationships at the Line of Business and Industry Level," *Rev. Economic and Statist.*, 65(1983), 22–31.

ROUSSEAU, D. M., "Technological Differences in Job Characteristics, Employee Satisfaction and Motivation: A Synthesis of Job Design Research and Socio-technical Systems Theory," *Organizational Behavior and Human Performance*, 19 (1978), 18–42.

RUE, L. W., "Theoretical and Operational Implications of Long Range Planning on Selected Measures of Financial Performance in US Industry," Unpublished doctoral dissertation, Georgia State University, 1973.

RUMELT, R. P., "Diversity and Profitability," Paper MGL-SI, Managerial Studies Center, Graduate School of Management, University of California, Los Angeles, 1977.

——, *Strategy, Structure and Economic Performance*, Harvard University Press, Boston, 1974.

SCHENDEL, D. E. AND C. W. HOFER, *Strategic Management*, Little, Brown, Boston, 1979.

—— AND R. G. PATTON, "Simultaneous Equation Model of Corporate Strategy," *Management Sci.*, 24 (1978), 1611–1621.

SCHERER, F. M., *Industrial Market Structure and Economic Performance*, Rand McNally College Publishing Co., Chicago, 1970.

SCHOEFFLER, S., R. D. BUZZELL AND D. F. HEANY, "The Impact of Strategic Planning on Profit Performance," *Harvard Business Rev.*, 52 (1974), 137–145.

SHARPE, W. F., "Capital Asset Prices: A Theory of Market Equilibrium Under Conditions of Risk," *J. Finance*, 19 (1964), 425–442.

SHESHUNOFF AND CO., *Banks of Indiana: 1980*, Sheshunoff and Company, Austin, TX.

THOMPSON, J. D., *Organizations in Action*, McGraw-Hill, New York, 1967.

VAN DE VEN, A. H. AND R. DRAZIN, "The Concept of Fit in Contingency Theory," in B. M. Staw and L. L. Cummings (Eds.), *Research in Organizational Behavior*, 7, JAI Press, Greenwich, CT, 1985, 333–365.

VENKATRAMAN, N. AND J. C. CAMILLUS, "Exploring the Concept of Fit in Strategic Management," *Acad. Management Rev.*, 9 (1984), 513–525.

WEICK, K., *The Social Psychology of Organizing*, Addison-Wesley, Reading, MA, 1979.

WILLIAMSON, O., *Markets and Hierarchies*, The Free Press, New York, 1965.

WOO, C. Y. Y. AND A. C. COOPER, "Strategies of Effective Low Share Businesses," *Strategic Management J.*, 2, 2(1981), 301–318.

WOODWARD, JOAN, *Industrial Organization: Theory and Practice*, Oxford University Press, London, 1965.

42

# STRATEGY, STRATEGY MAKING, AND PERFORMANCE – AN EMPIRICAL INVESTIGATION

*Eli Segev*

Source: *Management Science* 33(2) (1987): 258–69.

The purpose of this paper is to study the effect of the relationships between strategic type and strategy-making mode on organizational performance. Two important typologies were used in this study, one stressing strategic type, the other, strategy-making mode. Hypotheses were stated on strategy "fit" of specific strategy type with strategy-making modes, where strategic fit contributes to organizational performance. As part of a larger study of strategy formulation, the two top executives in each of 126 kibbutz-owned industrial enterprises evaluated their organization's strategic type as Defender, Prospector, Analyzer, or Reactor, and its strategy-making mode as Entrepreneurial, Adaptive and Planning. The executives typed their organizations using textual descriptions of strategies. The findings clearly indicate links between the two typologies, i.e. associations between strategic types and strategy-making modes, and that certain combinations are more conducive to enhancing organizational performance than others. When nonoptimal stragies are adopted they result in lower levels of performance. The paper also relates the primary discussion on the relationship between the strategy type and strategy-making mode typologies to the content-process dilemma on which it sheds some light.

## Introduction

This paper focuses on strategy and strategy making and the relationships between two important typologies, each stressing one of these concepts. Miles and Snow (1978) proposed a typology of strategic types based for the most part on the organization's orientation toward product-market development. They suggested four strategic types: Defenders, Analyzers, Prospectors and Reactors. The first three enjoy similar degrees of success, while the last is a strategic failure. Snow and Hambrick (1980; p. 528) observe that in this typology: "the focus has been primarily on strategy and its correlates, not the process used to formulate and implement strategies". Later studies (such as Hambrick 1981, 1983; Snow and Hrebiniak 1980) clearly operationalized this typology and used it to categorize strategy content.

While Miles and Snow and others were studying strategy as part of a broader holistic approach to the organization-environment adaptation cycle, other researchers were addressing the same question from a different point of view, and developing a parallel typology to describe the strategy-making process.

Mintzberg (1973) suggested three modes of strategy-making: the Entrepreneurial, the Adaptive and the Planning. He focused mainly on the motives for decisions, who makes them, how alternatives are evaluated, the decisions' horizons, linkages, organizational goals, flexibility of modes, age of organization, and types of environments beneficial to each mode. Mintzberg thus laid emphasis on the process by which strategies emerge, rather than on their content. He also explicitly refrained from suggesting a mutually exclusive typology (see Miller 1983 for another point of view). Later, in 1979, Mintzberg developed a five-faceted typology for organizational structure which naturally related to his strategy-making modes. The modes, however, are more useful than the structural typology in strategy formulation studies. This approach was later elaborated upon in a series of studies carried out by Miller (1979, 1981, 1983), Miller and Friesen (1978, 1980a, b), Miller *et al.* (1982). Though these studies focus mainly on strategy formulation, they also discuss organizational adaptation and relate to product-market strategies.

Burgelman (1983) suggested a parallel between Minbtzberg's and Miles and Snow's typologies; this is of particular interest, in view of his later study of the interplay of process and content in internal corporate ventures, and his conclusions, which indicate the need for research on process and content in business-level strategy (Burgelman 1984).

Several authors have developed conceptual schemes relating to the content-process dilemma (Bourgeois 1980; Camillus 1981; Jemison 1981; Venkatraman and Camillus 1984). One source has even described the dichotomy as a "disciplinary and methodological artifact". From the literature, then, content and process emerge as two distinct, but related concepts, and there appears to be no direct causal relationship between strategy (content) and strategy making (process) but rather a relationship arising from and attributable to the holistic nature of an open social system (Van de Ven 1979).

In contingency theory an assertion of fit implies a relationship between two variables, which in turn predicts a third variable (Schoonhoven 1981). The assertion studied in this paper is: there is a relationship between strategy making as typified by Mintzberg and strategy as typified by Miles and Snow, and this relationship affects organizational performance.[1]

A recent survey of empirical studies (Segev 1984) relating to business-level strategies, suggested certain relationships among strategy, strategy making, and organizational performance. The mutual relations between the two typologies indicate that Miles and Snow's four strategy types occur in all the possible combinations with Mintzberg's three strategy-making modes, and that some combinations are more conducive to high performance than others.

## Hypotheses

In the Entrepreneurial mode as defined by Mintzberg (1973), strategy making is characterized by active search for new opportunities. Power is centralized in the hands of the chief executive, dramatic forward leaps are made in the face of uncertainty, and growth is the dominant goal of the organization. Of the four strategic types suggested by Miles and Snow (1978), the Prospector is most compatible with the Entrepreneurial mode of strategy making (Burgelman 1983). Organizations of the Prospector type value being "first in" in new product and market areas, even when some of their efforts do not prove to be highly profitable. Theirs is a broad product-market domain which is periodically redefined, and the organization responds rapidly to early signs of opportunity (Miles and Snow 1978, pp. 40–67).

The Reactor is the strategic type least compatible with the Entrepeneurial mode. Reactor organizations take less risks than their competitors; they respond only when forced to by environmental pressures; they are not even aggressive in maintaining their established products and markets (Miles and Snow 1978, pp. 81–93).

The Defender is depicted as a "grey" mid-range strategic type whose compatibility with the Entrepreneurial mode is rather low. These organizations look for and locate relatively stable niches in product or service areas, and then strive to maintain them. They may take initiatives in offering higher quality, superior service, or lower prices, but this is to protect their domain rather than to move aggressively. They try to do the best job possible in a limited area, but tend to ignore changes in the industry (Miles and Snow 1978, pp. 31–48).

Hambrick (1983) suggested that Miles and Snow's (1978) fourth strategic type, the Analyzer, is a hybrid Defender-Prospector. Organizations of this type are quick in following new developments in the industry, but new opportunities are carefully selected and pursued while maintaining a stable limited line of products or services. These organizations grow and innovate, but they are frequently "second-in" and seldom "first-in" (Miles and Snow 1978, pp. 68–80). The compatibility of the Analyzer with the Entrepreneurial mode is hypothesized therefore to be high, but lower than that of the Prospector. Thus:

> Proposition 1. *Ranking of the four strategic types according to their compatibility with the Entrepreneurial mode of strategy making is: Prospector, Analyzer, Defender, Reactor.*

According to our hypothesis, high compatibility between strategy and strategy-making mode implies better performance. Hence:

> Proposition 2. *Prospectors conforming more to the Entrepreneurial mode perform better than other Prospectors.*

The Adaptive mode of strategy making, as defined by Minzberg (1973), reflects a division of power among members of a complex coalition and clear goals do not exist. Solutions to existing problems are reactive rather than a proactive search for new opportunities, and disjointed decisions are made in incremental, serial steps. While the Entrepreneurial and Planning modes (discussed below) imply better performance, the Adaptive mode inherently implies a lower level of performance, even in conjunction with the most compatible strategy type.

Of the four strategic types, the Reactor is the most compatible with the Adaptive mode (Burgelman 1983). It is precisely those factors which contribute to low compatibility with the Entrepreneurial mode that make for a positive relationship with the Adaptive mode: inconsistent product-market orientation, lack of aggressiveness, low level of risk taking, response rather than initiative, and submission to environmental pressures.

The Prospector is the least compatible with the Adaptive mode of strategy making: the characteristic initiative, which often leads to a new round of competitive activity, the periodic redefinition of the broad product-market domain, the constant drive to be "first-in" in products and markets, and the high level of risk taking, even when some prospects of profitability are low, all reduce compatibility with the Adaptive mode.

The literature on Defenders and Analyzers (Snow and Hrebiniak 1980) indicates that they are fairly compatible with the Adaptive mode. These two strategy types maintain a limited line of products or services, and are assiduous in protecting their niches. The Defenders tend to ignore industrial changes that have no direct influence on the current areas of their operation, and to adopt their competitors' strategy, with certain marginal modifications in areas such as quality, price, and service. The Analyzers also monitor the actions of their major competitors, but their "me-too" innovations reduce their compatibility with the Adaptive mode. Thus:

> Proposition 3. *The ranking of the four strategic types according to their compatibility with the Adaptive mode of strategy making is: Reactor, Analyzer and Defender, Prospector.*

Reactors, then, are hypothesized to have a "tight fit" with the Adaptive mode of strategy making. Compatibility with this mode is hypothesized to reduce performance, and so:

Proposition 4. *Reactors which conform more to the Adaptive mode perform worse than other Reactors.*

Analysts play a major role in the Planning, the third strategy-making mode suggested by Mintzberg (1973). Assessment of the costs and benefits of competing proposals is systematically analyzed, and decisions and strategies are integrated.

The Defender has been shown to exhibit characteristics compatible with the Planning mode (Burgelman 1983), the most important being concentration on internal efficiency; possession of information on major competitors; ability to maintain and protect a secure niche for relatively long periods; and the making of decisions on how to be different from their competitors.

Analyzers, hybrids of Defenders and Prospectors, are also compatible with the Planning mode. Certain intrinsic characteristics of the Analyzer are indicative of this compatibility: careful monitoring of major competitors; the focus on products or services which are more cost efficient than those of the competitors; the gradual change in existing product-markets; and the careful selection of new avenues of development.

Two of the four strategic types are expected to exhibit low compatibility with the Planning mode, but for very different reasons. The 'trigger happy' Prospectors are notably quick to react, they periodically redefine their domain, and are more than usually innovative, willing to take risks, and engage in competitive action. All these characteristics point to low compatibility with the Planning mode. At the same time, the Reactor's conservatism, lack of consistent product-market domain and initiative, reaction to external actions, and very low risk taking, also point to lack of compatibility with the Planning mode. Thus:

Proposition 5. *The ranking of the four strategic types according to their compatibility with the Planning mode of strategy making is: Defender, Analyzer, Prospector and Reactor.*

The proposition related to performance is:

Proposition 6. *Defenders which conform more to the Planning mode perform better than other Defenders.*

## Findings[2]

### *Strategy and strategy making*

In order to investigate the level of conformity between the strategy making modes and strategic type (Propositions 1, 3, and 5), analysis of variance and mean comparisons were performed on the three strategy-making mode

*Table 1* Analysis of Variance of Strategy Making Modes by Strategic Type* and Least Significant Difference Post-Hoc Test of Difference Among Groups (General Manager Evaluations).

| | *Strategy Making Modes* | | |
|---|---|---|---|
| *Strategic Type* | *Entrepreneurial* | *Adaptive* | *Planning* |
| Total Population | 4.39<br>(109) | 3.49<br>(108) | 2.92<br>(109) |
| Defenders | 4.15<br>(27) | 3.52<br>(27) | 2.93<br>(27) |
| Prospectors | 4.97<br>(31) | 2.87<br>(30) | 3.19<br>(31) |
| Analyzers | 4.49<br>(39) | 3.49<br>(39) | 2.80<br>(40) |
| Reactors | 3.17<br>(12) | 5.00<br>(12) | 2.55<br>(11) |
| F Value | 4.205 | 5.785 | 0.505 |
| Significance of F | 0.007 | 0.001 | — |

COMPARISONS AMONG GROUPS**

*ENTREPRENEURIAL MODE*

| | 1 | 2 | 3 | 4 |
|---|---|---|---|---|
| 1. Defenders | — | | | |
| 2. Prospectors | 0.05 | — | | |
| 3. Analyzers | N.S. | N.S. | — | |
| 4. Reactors | 0.1 | 0.01 | 0.05 | — |

*ADAPTIVE MODE*

| | 1 | 2 | 3 | 4 |
|---|---|---|---|---|
| 1. Defenders | — | | | |
| 2. Prospectors | N.S. | — | | |
| 3. Analyzers | N.S. | 0.1 | — | |
| 4. Reactors | 0.01 | 0.01 | 0.01 | — |

* Mean
(# of cases)
** Level of significance, N.S. = Not Significant

measures by strategic type. Table 1 presents the analyses of variances and the Least Significant Difference test among the means of the groups. The General Manager (GM) evaluations for both strategic type and strategy-making modes were used. A comparable analysis of the Kibbutz Secretary (KS) evaluations is presented in Table 2.

The first and the third propositions are supported by the data; the fifth remains unsupported. The mean of the degree to which the organizations

*Table 2* Analysis of Variance of Strategy Making Modes by Strategic Type* and Least Significant Difference Post-Hoc Test of Difference Among Groups (Kibbutz Secretary Evaluations).

| | *Strategy Making Modes* | | |
|---|---|---|---|
| *Strategic Type* | *Entrepreneurial* | *Adaptive* | *Planning* |
| Total Population | 4.09<br>(76) | 4.05<br>(78) | 2.82<br>(77) |
| Defenders | 3.71<br>(21) | 4.36<br>(22) | 2.52<br>(21) |
| Prospectors | 4.79<br>(14) | 3.29<br>(14) | 3.20<br>(15) |
| Analyzers | 4.23<br>(30) | 3.71<br>(31) | 2.93<br>(30) |
| Reactors | 3.55<br>(11) | 5.36<br>(11) | 2.55<br>(11) |
| F Value | 1.732 | 4.298 | 0.648 |
| Significance of F | 0.168 | 0.008 | — |

COMPARISONS AMONG GROUPS**

*ENTREPRENEURIAL MODE*

| | 1 | 2 | 3 | 4 |
|---|---|---|---|---|
| 1. Defenders | — | | | |
| 2. Prospectors | 0.1 | — | | |
| 3. Analyzers | N.S. | N.S. | — | |
| 4. Reactors | N.S. | 0.1 | N.S. | — |

*ADAPTIVE MODE*

| | 1 | 2 | 3 | 4 |
|---|---|---|---|---|
| 1. Defenders | — | | | |
| 2. Prospectors | 0.1 | — | | |
| 3. Analyzers | N.S. | N.S. | — | |
| 4. Reactors | 0.1 | 0.1 | 0.1 | — |

* Mean
(# of Cases)
** Level of Significance, N.S. = Not Significant

categorized as Reactors conformed to the Entrepreneurial mode of strategy making (3.17) is significantly smaller than those of the three other strategic types, and the Prospectors' mean (4.97) is significantly higher than that of the Defenders (4.15). Thus, the *first proposition*, which claimed a rank order of Prospector, Analyzer, Defender, Reactor for strategic types on the Entrepreneurial mode of strategy making, is largely supported by the data. Note also that the Analyzers' mean (4.49) is not significantly different from that of the Prospectors or of the Defenders. (Analysis of the Kibbutz Secretaries' evalutions—which are only marginally different for the strategic types-significance of $F$ is 0.168—also revealed that the Reactors' mean is lower than that of the Prospectors and the latter is higher than that of the Defenders.)

The mean of the degree to which the organizations categorized as Reactors conformed to the Adaptive mode of strategy making (5.00) is significantly higher than those of the three other strategic types, and the Prospectors' mean (2.87) is significantly lower than that of the Analyzers (3.49). Thus, *Proposition* 3, which claimed a rank order of Reactors, Analyzers and Defenders, Prospectors on the Adaptive mode of strategy making, is largely supported by the data. Note that the Defenders' mean (3.52) is not significantly different from that of the Analyzers. (Analysis of KS evaluations shows that the Defenders' mean is significantly higher than that of the Prospectors, and that the highest mean is for Reactors.)

Since the analysis of variance for the Planning mode proved nonsignificant by strategic type, no post-hoc comparisons were made and *Proposition* 5 remains unsupported by the data.

### *Strategy typelstrategy-making mode fit and performance*

To test Propositions 2, 4 and 6 regarding performance as a function of the degree of fit between the strategic type and the strategy-making mode, within each strategic type, Pearson $r$ correlations were calculated between the strategy-making modes and the measures of performance (see Tables 3 and 4).

All three propositions gained some support from the data. Lines 5 and 6 of Table 3 provide slight support for *Proposition* 2. Only one measure of the performance of the Prospectors (KS, 0.60 $p = 0.007$) is significantly positively correlated with the Entrepreneurial mode of strategy making. (The analysis of the relationships between the performance measures of the Prospectors and the Kibbutz Secretaries' evaluations, Table 4, lines 5 and 6, showed nonsignificance.)

Lines 9 and 10 of both Tables 3 and 4 indicate strong support for *Proposition* 4. Reactors which conform more to the Adaptive mode perform worse (–0.78 $p = 0.001$ and –0.57 $p = 0.121$, according to General Manager evaluations, and: –0.75 $p = 0.004$ and –0.68 $p = 0.016$ according to the Kibbutz Secretaries' evaluations). Note that the correlation coefficients are stronger than for the total population (lines 1 and 2).

Lines 3 and 4 of Table 3 support *Proposition* 6. Significant positive correlations were found between the performance of Defenders employing the Planning mode (0.33 $p = 0.057$; 0.56 $p = 0.006$). Note that these relationships are stronger than for the total population (lines 1 and 2). The analysis of the Kibbutz Secretaries' evaluations (Tables 4, lines 3 and 4) gave disappointing results.

*Table 3* Pearson R Correlations Between Performance Measures and Strategy Making Modes by Strategic Type (General Manager Evaluations).

| Line No. | Strategic Type | Performance Measures | Strategy Making Modes: Entrepreneurial | Adaptive | Planning |
|---|---|---|---|---|---|
| 1 | Total | GM | 0.18<br>(102)<br>0.032 | −0.35<br>(102)<br>0.000 | 0.23<br>(102)<br>0.009 |
| 2 | Population | KS | 0.31<br>(67)<br>0.006 | −0.40<br>(66)<br>0.000 | 0.18<br>(66)<br>0.076 |
| 3 | | GM | 0.33<br>(24)<br>0.057 | −0.43<br>(24)<br>0.017 | 0.33<br>(24)<br>0.057 |
| 4 | Defenders | KS | 0.50<br>(19)<br>0.014 | −0.60<br>(19)<br>0.003 | 0.56<br>(19)<br>0.006 |
| 5 | | GM | 0.03<br>(26)<br>0.441 | 0.07<br>(25)<br>0.372 | 0.29<br>(26)<br>0.076 |
| 6 | Prospectors | KS | 0.60<br>(16)<br>0.007 | −0.31<br>(16)<br>0.125 | 0.29<br>(16)<br>0.137 |
| 7 | | GM | −0.02<br>(35)<br>0.447 | −0.07<br>(36)<br>0.352 | −0.10<br>(36)<br>0.286 |
| 8 | Analyzers | KS | 0.25<br>(22)<br>0.132 | −0.25<br>(21)<br>0.138 | −0.24<br>(22)<br>0.140 |
| 9 | | GM | −0.37<br>(12)<br>0.118 | −0.78<br>(12)<br>0.004 | 0.40<br>(11)<br>0.111 |
| 10 | Reactors | KS | −0.84<br>(6)<br>0.018 | −0.57<br>(6)<br>0.121 | 0.93<br>(5)<br>0.012 |

Table Entries: Pearson R Coefficient of Correlation
(Number of Observations)
Significance Level

GM = General Manager
KS = Kibbutz Secretary

*Table 4* Pearson R Correlations Between Performance Measures and Strategy Making Modes by Strategic Type (Kibbutz Secretary Evaluations).

| *Line No.* | *Strategic Type* | *Performance Measures* | *Strategy Making Modes* *Entrepreneurial* | *Adaptive* | *Planning* |
|---|---|---|---|---|---|
| 1 | Total | GM | 0.20<br>(71)<br>0.047 | −0.42<br>(73)<br>0.000 | 0.20<br>(69)<br>0.042 |
| 2 | Population | KS | 0.10<br>(69)<br>0.204 | −0.38<br>(71)<br>0.001 | 0.17<br>(69)<br>0.077 |
| 3 | | GM | 0.12<br>(17)<br>0.334 | −0.36<br>(18)<br>0.071 | 0.23<br>(17)<br>0.185 |
| 4 | Defenders | KS | −0.28<br>(18)<br>0.171 | 0.10<br>(19)<br>0.348 | −0.12<br>(18)<br>0.318 |
| 5 | | GM | −0.00<br>(13)<br>0.494 | −0.50<br>(13)<br>0.043 | −0.01<br>(14)<br>0.486 |
| 6 | Prospectors | KS | −0.10<br>(12)<br>0.490 | −0.07<br>(12)<br>0.410 | 0.20<br>(12)<br>0.271 |
| 7 | | GM | 0.29<br>(25)<br>0.077 | −0.31<br>(26)<br>0.062 | 0.07<br>(25)<br>0.367 |
| 8 | Analyzers | KS | 0.07<br>(20)<br>0.363 | −0.33<br>(27)<br>0.048 | 0.20<br>(26)<br>0.162 |
| 9 | | GM | −0.24<br>(11)<br>0.235 | −0.75<br>(11)<br>0.004 | 0.64<br>(11)<br>0.017 |
| 10 | Reactors | KS | 0.03<br>(10)<br>0.464 | −0.68<br>(10)<br>0.076 | 0.36<br>(10)<br>0.153 |

Table Entries: Pearson R Coefficient of Correlation
(Number of Observations)
Significance Level
GM = General Manager
KS = Kibbutz Secretary

## Discussion

The findings clearly indicate links between the two typologies: Mintzberg's strategy-making modes and Miles and Snow's strategy types. The Entrepreneurial mode of strategy making is mostly employed by Prospectors and Analyzers, less by Defenders, and least by Reactors. The Adaptive mode is used mainly by Reactors, less by Analyzers and Defenders and least by Prospectors. No conclusions about the planning mode may be made on the basis of the findings of this study. A study of a population which applies the Planning mode more intensively than the population studied in this research is required before conclusions may be drawn.

Generally, the hypothesized relationships between the two typologies are clearly strengthened by the findings of the study, and the theoretically suggested parallel of Burgelman (1983) was empirically supported.

The propositions related to the effects of strategic fit on the performance of the organization are only partially supported. Prospectors conforming more to the Entrepreneurial mode of strategy making exhibited better performance on only one (out of four) performance indicators. Stronger support was found for the Planning mode-performance relationships of Defenders, and conformity with the Adaptive mode clearly reduces the performance of Reactors. Thus, though the findings do not strongly support the claim that strategic fit affects performance, the indications are clearly in this direction.

Given that performance is affected by industry, the relationships found between performance and strategy-making mode, by strategic type, are very interesting. A finer typology based on strategy/strategy making combinations is indicated. In Miles and Snow's terms, some organizations do not properly implement strategy: nonoptimal strategies may exist at any point in time, and result in lower levels of performance. Thus, the main findings of the study are the relationships between the strategic type typology and the typology of strategy-making modes, and the effect of the strategy/strategy making fit on organizational performance.

It is important to note that no causality between the two typologies was assumed and, of course, none was found. It may be hypothesized that a given mode of strategy making is more conducive to a specific strategy type, or that each strategy type will differently facilitate strategy making modes. A mutual alignment process probably affects both, but only a longitudinal study can address this question.

## Conclusions

The findings of our study of the two presumed parallel typologies, strategy type and strategy-making mode, and the effect of their fit on the performance of a rather unique type of economic organization, provide indications as to the nature of strategic management. Broad product-markets, "first-in" innovation strategy in markets and products, and quick response to opportunities fit better the Entrepreneurial mode of strategy making. To enhance their performance, organizations which pursue a niche-seeking strategy should carry out systematic analysis and integrate their decisions and strategies. The worst that organizations with complex and cumbersome managerial coalitions and no clearly-defined goals can do is operate without a consistent product-market orientation, and submit to environmental pressures. This will further reduce their already low level of performance.

Various constraints on both strategy type and strategy-making mode may hinder organizations in their striving for "pure" fit. In this study, degrees of compatibility between strategy and strategy making other than "tight fit" were observed. Thus, organizations do not have to conform to "ideal" types. This is consistent with Mintzberg's (1973) suggestion of "mixed" modes, and Miles and Snow's observation that, on the average, for any given industry, the level of performance of Defenders, Prospectors and Analyzers is similar. A higher level of performance, however, requires a higher degree of fit.

The relationships found in this study between the two typologies and the indicated effect of strategy/strategy making fit on organizational performance shed some light on the content-process dilemma. Admittedly, neither typology lends itself to simple categorization as process or content orientated. Both deal with strategy in an holistic approach to the organization-environment adaptation cycle. Each, however, has a different focus. Miles and Snow focus on strategy content, as do we in our operationalization of their typology, while Mintzberg's typology focuses on process and not on the strategies themselves. Thus, certain conclusions, and suggestions for future studies, may be made on the basis of this study.

This study supports the notion that the process-content dichotomy is an artifact of convenience and that the two are integral components of any organization-environment adaptation process, that is, of strategic management. Because this adaptation is holistic, fit exists between the essence of strategies and the processes whereby they are formulated. Better compatibility between strategy content and process enhanced organizational performance.

These initial conclusions may be much refined by future studies. First, content and process in business-level strategy should be directly operationalized and studied. Though typologies are very convenient tools for studies, they may mask by their halo effect the distinctions between content and process. One approach to alleviate this effect is to decompose each strategic type, or strategy making mode, into its basic facets, identify and amalgamate identical facets, recluster the facets into process and content groups (an initial experiment yielded three groups: mostly process, mostly content, conjoint facets) and then operationalize and measure each facet independently. Using the above approach it may be possible to focus on the studied typologies, or use other typologies (e.g. Porter 1980; Miller and Friesen 1978).

Since the administrative behavior paradigm addresses process, while the business policy paradigm addresses content, as do the industrial organization and marketing paradigms (Jemison, 1981), the simultaneous study of content and process will contribute to the integration of knowledge in these areas. Two of the most important topics on which such studies may shed new light are the role of strategy makers and their values in both strategy making and strategy, and the process whereby the organizational environment affects strategy.

It is important that studies on the process-content dilemma will focus on the various strategic levels (business, corporate), as well as on specific strategic issues, such as foreign direct investment, turnarounds, or technological innovation strategies. The limitations of the cross-sectional questionnaire type surveys may be greatly overcome by the application of complementary methodologies, such as laboratory experiments based on large business-games (a study currently conducted), or secondary analysis of in-depth written case studies.

Findings of studies employing different approaches for strategy measurement, such as investigator inference, external assessment and objective indicators, as well as other methods for operationalizing business-level strategy, such as textual descriptions of strategy, measurement of parts of strategies, and multivariate measurement of strategy would, we believe, endorse the conclusions of this study.

This study focused on a population of relatively small organizations which operate in a single national environment, ownership being of a single kind. The universality of the findings may therefore be questioned, even though these particular characteristics are eminently suitable for carrying out a study on strategy/strategy making relationships in a business-level environment. Though there is no *a priori* reason to assume uniqueness of this particular population, repetition of the study in more generalized populations (such as PIMS) is called for.[3]

## Notes

1 Research on organizational strategy has produced four concepts on which theory in the area rests: *strategy* (Andrews *et al.* 1965; Andrews 1971; Chandler 1962; Glueck 1976; Boston Consulting Group 1968; Hofer and Schendel 1978; Mintzberg 1978; Rumelt 1974), *strategy making* (Aharoni 1966; Allison 1971; Ansoff 1965; Bower 1970; Cyert and March 1963; MacMillan 1978; Mintzberg 1973), *organizational structure* (Chandler 1962; Channon 1973; Child 1972; Galbraith and Nathanson 1978; Lawrence and Lorsch 1967; Perrow 1970; Woodward 1965), and *environment* (Anderson and Paine 1975; Duncan 1972; Emery and Trist 1965; Lawrence and Lorsch 1967; Schendel and Hofer 1979).

These four meta-concepts are depicted as components of a broader process—an organization-environment adaptation cycle. Chandler (1962), Channon (1973), Child (1972), and Galbraith and Nathanson (1978) studied the compatibility of strategy and organizational structure. Burns and Stalker (1962), and Lawrence and Lorsch (1967) identified viable environment-structure combinations. Mintzberg (1973) discussed compatibility of strategy-making modes and environment, while Miles and Snow (1978) and Hambrick (1983) discussed compatibility of strategic types with environment. The findings of these studies indicate that the four meta-concepts may form gestalts. Miller (1981) suggested a limited number of such gestalts, each a specific combination of strategic components (see also Miller and Friesen 1978). Thus, fit between strategy and strategy making is conceptualized and defined here as the way the two must be joined in a particular configuration to achieve completeness which results in higher performance.

Van de Ven (1979) suggested four different conceptual meanings of fit; the one adopted here is based on the hierarchical theory of the holistic nature of an open social system. Since the strategy/strategy making relationship is always observed in the context of a specific organizational structure and organizational environment, one may be led to assume that this context is the reason for fit between strategy and strategy-making, and thus defer to another of Van de Ven's (1979) meanings of fit: a spurious result of the context. Since in this case the other factors, namely organizational structure and environment, are conceptually defined, and the theory specifically indicates associations rather than that either strategy making or strategy are the results of other factors, fit in our context is not a spurious result. (The two other meanings of fit suggested by Van de Ven are clearly irrelevant here, since they imply interaction effect or direct causation.)

2 A detailed methodological appendix, containing a discussion of the population, the executives, the sample, the variables and measures-including the operationalization of the performance measure, and the survey instrument, is available upon request from the TIMS editorial offices in Providence, Rhode Island. The study focused on kibbutz-owned industrial enterprises in Israel. A kibbutz (plural: kibbutzim) is a collective settlement, based on agriculture and industry. The industrial enterprises are businesses operating in a single industry. When a kibbutz decides to diversify into a new and unrelated field, a new plant is established under separate management. Thus, this specific population is especially suitable for studying business, or product-market, strategies.

The General Manager of a kibbutz industrial enterprise is usually elected by the members of the kibbutz. The Kibbutz Secretary acts for all practical purposes as the chief executive officer of the kibbutz and as the Chairperson of the Board of Directors of the industrial enterprise.

Questionnaires, to which both the General Manager and the Kibbutz Secretary were requested to reply, were sent to a target population composed of 290 industrial enterprises. Data collection was performed between March and May 1983. Two mailings yielded 126 usable General Managers' questionnaires (43.5%) and 99 Kibbutz Secretary questionnaires (34%). For 85 industrial enterprises (29.3%), completed questionnaires were received from both. The two evaluations are compared and discussed, the analysis focusing on the evaluation of the general managers, since they are the chief executive officers of their respective organizations.

Following Snow and Hrebiniak (1980), self-typing of textual descriptions of strategy was used in this study. Mintzberg's (1973) three strategy-making modes were also operationalized for self-typing of textual descriptions, and pre-tested. Level of performance was operationalized by several measures. The two executives' evaluations of performance, for which the data are more complete, were used as surrogates for all performance measures.

3 Partial financial support was provided by JIM—the Jerusalem Institute of Management.

## References

Aharoni, Yair, "The Foreign Investment Decision Process," Division of Research, Graduate School of Business Administration, Harvard University, Boston, 1966.

ALLISON, GRAHAM T., *Essence of Decision: Explaining the Cuban Missile Crisis*, Little, Brown, Boston, 1971.

ANDERSON, CARL R. AND FRANK T. PAINE, "Managerial Perceptions and Strategic Behavior," *Acad. Management J.*, 18, 4 (1975), 811–823.

ANDREWS, K. R., *The Concept of Corporate Strategy*, Dow Jones-Irwin, Homewood, Ill., 1971.

——, E. LEARNED, C. R. CHRISTENSEN AND W. GUTH, *Business policy: Text and Cases*, Irwin, Homewood, Ill., 1965.

ANSOFF, H. IGOR, *Corporate Strategy*, McGraw-Hill, New York, 1965.

Boston Consulting Group Staff, *Perspectives on Experience*, Boston Consulting Group, Boston, 1968.

BOWER, JOSEPH, "Managing the Resource Allocation Process," Division of Research, Graduate School of Business Administration, Harvard University, Boston, 1970.

BOURGEOIS, L. J. III, "Strategy and Environment: A Conceptual Integration," *Acad. Management Rev.*, 5, 1 (1980), 25–39.

BURGELMAN, ROBERT A., "Corporate Entrepreneurship and Strategic Management: Insights from a Process Study," *Management Sci.*, 29, 12 (December 1983), 1349–1364.

——, "On the Interplay of Process and Content in Internal Corporate Ventures: Action and Cognition in Strategy-Making," *Acad. Management Proc.* 1984, 2–6.

BURNS, T. AND G. STAKLER, *The Management of Innovation*, Tavistock, London, 1961.

CAMILLUS, J. C., "Corporate Strategy and Executive Action: Transition Stages and Linkage Dimensions," *Acad. Management Rev.*, 6, 2 (1981), 253–259.

CHANDLER, ALFRED D., *Strategy and Structure*, MIT Press, Cambridge, 1962.

CHANNON, D., "Strategy and Structure in British Enterprise," Division of Research, Graduate School of Business Administration, Harvard University, Boston, 1973.

CHILD, J., "Organizational Structure, Environment, and Performance: The Role of Strategic Choice," *Sociology*, 6 (1972), 1–22.

CYERT, R. M. AND J. G. MARCH, *A Behavioral Theory of the Firm*, Prentice-Hall, Englewood Cliffs, N.J., 1963.

DUNCAN, ROBERT G., "Characteristics of Organizational Environments and Perceived Environmental Uncertainty," *Admin. Sci. Quart.*, 17, 2 (1972), 313–327.

EMERY, F. E. AND E. L. TRIST, "The Causal Texture of Organizational Environments," *Human Relations*, 18 (1965), 21–32.

GALBRAITH, J. R. AND D. A. NATHANSON, *Strategy Implementation: The Role of Structure and Process*, West, St. Paul, Minn., 1978.

GLUECK, WILLIAM F., *Business Policy: Strategy Formation and Management Action*, McGraw-Hill, New York, 1976.

HAMBRICK, D. C., "Operationalizing the Concept of Business-Level Strategy in Research," *Acad. Management Rev.*, 5, 4 (1980), 567–575.

——, "Environment, Strategy and Power within Top Management Teams," *Admin. Sci. Quart.*, 26 (1981), 253–275.

——, "Some Tests of the Effectiveness and Functional Attributes of Miles and Snow's Strategic Types," *Acad. Management J.*, 26, 1 (1983), 5–26.

——, J. C. MACMILLAN AND R. R. BARABOSA, "Business Unit Strategy and the Changes in the Product R&D Research," *Management Sci.*, 29, 7 (July 1983), 757–769.

HOFER, C. W. AND D. SCHENDEL, *Strategy Formulation: Analytical Concepts*, West Publishing, St. Paul, 1978.

JEMISON, D. B., "The Importance of an Integrative Approach to Strategic Management Research," *Acad. Management Rev.*, 6, 4 (1981), 601–608.

LAWRENCE, PAUL AND JAY LORSCH, "Organization and Environment," Division of Research, Harvard Business School, Boston, 1967.

MACMILLAN, I. C., *Strategy Formulation: Political Concepts*, West Publishing, St. Paul, Minn., 1978.

MILES, R. E. AND C. C. SNOW, *Organizational Strategy, Structure, and Process*, McGraw-Hill, New York, 1978.

MILLER, D., "Strategy, Structure and Environment: Context Influences upon Some Bivariate Association," *J. Management Studies*, 16 (1979), 294–316.

——, "Toward a New Contingency Approach: The Search for Organizational Gestalts," *J. Management Studies*, 18, 1 (1981), 1–26.

——, "The Correlates of Entrepreneurship in Three Types of Firms," *Management Sci.*, 29, 4 (1983), 770–791.

—— AND P. FRIESEN, "Archetypes of Strategy Formation," *Management Sci.*, 24, 9 (1978), 921–933.

—— AND ——, "Archetypes of Organizational Transition," *Admin. Sci. Quart.*, 25 (1980a), 268–299.

—— AND ——, "Momentum and Revolution in Organizational Adaptation," *Acad. Management J.*, 23, 4 (1980b), 591–614.

——, M. F. R. KETS DE VRIES AND J. H. TOULOUSE, "Top Executive Locus of Control and Its Relationship to Strategy Making, Structure, and Environment," *Acad. Management J.*, 25, 2 (1982), 237–253.

MINTZBERG, H., "Strategy Making in Three Modes," *California Management Rev.*, 16, 2 (1973), 44–53.

——, "Patterns in Strategy Formation," *Management Sci.*, 24, 9 (1978), 934–948.

——, *The Structuring of Organizations*, Prentice-Hall, Englewood Cliffs, N.J., 1979.

PERROW, C., *Organizational Analysis: A Sociological View*, Brooks/Cote Monterey, Cal., 1970.

RUMELT, R. P., *Strategy, Structure and Economic Performance*, Harvard University Press, Boston, 1974.

SCHENDEL, D. AND C., W. HOFER, (Eds.), *Strategic Management*, Little, Brown and Co., Boston, 1979.

SCHOONHOVEN, C. B., "Problems With Contingency Theory: Testing Assumptions Hidden Within the Language of Contingency Theory," *Admin. Sci. Quart.*, 26 (1981), 349–377.

SEGEV, E., "Business Level Strategies and Strategy Making," Working Paper No. 827/84, Faculty of Management, Tel Aviv University, August 1984.

SNOW, CHARLES C. AND DONALD C. HAMBRICK, "Measuring Organizational Strategies: Some Theoretical and Methodological Problems," *Acad. Management Rev.*, 5, 4 (October 1980), 527–538.

—— AND L. G. HREBINIAK, "Strategy, Distinctive Competence, and Organizational Performance," *Admin. Sci. Quart.*, 25 (1980), 317–335.

VAN DE VEN, A. H., "Review of Aldrich's (1979) Book—*Organization and Environments*," *Admin. Sci. Quart.*, 24 (1979), 320–326.

VENKATRAMAN, N. AND J. C. CAMILLUS, "Exploring the Concept of 'Fit' in Strategic Management," *Acad. Management Rev.*, 9 (1984), 513–525.

WOODWARD, J., *Industrial Organization*, Oxford University Press, London, 1965.

# 43

# STRATEGIC INTENT

*Gary Hamel and C. K. Prahalad*

Source: *Harvard Business Review* 67(3) (1989): 63–76.

Today managers in many industries are working hard to match the competitive advantages of their new global rivals. They are moving manufacturing offshore in search of lower labor costs, rationalizing product lines to capture global scale economies, instituting quality circles and just-in-time production, and adopting Japanese human resource practices. When competitiveness still seems out of reach, they form strategic alliances – often with the very companies that upset the competitive balance in the first place.

Important as these initiatives are, few of them go beyond mere imitation. Too many companies are expending enormous energy simply to reproduce the cost and quality advantages their global competitors already enjoy. Imitation may be the sincerest form of flattery, but it will not lead to competitive revitalization. Strategies based on imitation are transparent to competitors who have already mastered them. More-over, successful competitors rarely stand still. So it is not surprising that many executives feel trapped in a seemingly endless game of catch-up, regularly surprised by the new accomplishments of their rivals.

For these executives and their companies, regaining competitiveness will mean rethinking many of the basic concepts of strategy.[1] As "strategy" has blossomed, the competitiveness of Western companies has withered. This may be coincidence, but we think not. We believe that the application of concepts such as "strategic fit" (between resources and opportunities), "generic strategies" (low cost versus differentiation versus focus), and the "strategy hierarchy" (goals, strategies, and tactics) has often abetted the process of competitive decline. The new global competitors approach strategy from a perspective that is fundamentally different from that which underpins Western management thought. Against such competitors, marginal adjustments to current orthodoxies are no more likely to produce competitive revitalization than are marginal improvements in operating efficiency. (The sidebar "Remaking Strategy" describes our research and summarizes the two contrasting approaches to strategy we see in large multinational companies.)

Few Western companies have an enviable track record anticipating the moves of new global competitors. Why? The explanation begins with the way most companies have approached competitor analysis. Typically, competitor analysis focuses on the existing resources (human, technical, and financial) of present competitors. The only companies seen as a threat are those with the resources to erode margins and market share in the next planning period. Resourcefulness, the pace at which new competitive advantages are being built, rarely enters in.

In this respect, traditional competitor analysis is like a snapshot of a moving car. By itself, the photograph yields little information about the car's speed or direction – whether the driver is out for a quiet Sunday drive or warming up for the Grand Prix. Yet many managers have learned through painful experience that a business's initial resource endowment (whether bountiful or meager) is an unreliable predictor of future global success.

Think back: In 1970, few Japanese companies possessed the resource base, manufacturing volume, or technical prowess of U.S. and European industry leaders. Komatsu was less than 35% as large as Caterpillar (measured by sales), was scarcely represented outside Japan, and relied on just one product line – small bulldozers – for most of its revenue. Honda was smaller than American Motors and had not yet begun to export cars to the United States. Canon's first halting steps in the reprographics business looked pitifully small compared with the $4 billion Xerox powerhouse.

If Western managers had extended their competitor analysis to include these companies, it would merely have underlined how dramatic the resource discrepancies between them were. Yet by 1985, Komatsu was a $2.8 billion company with a product scope encompassing a broad range of earth-moving equipment, industrial robots, and semi-conductors. Honda manufactured almost as many cars worldwide in 1987 as Chrysler. Canon had matched Xerox's global unit market share.

The lesson is clear: Assessing the current tactical advantages of known competitors will not help you understand the resolution, stamina, or inventiveness of potential competitors. Suntzu, a Chinese military strategist, made the point 3,000 years ago; "All men can see the tactics whereby I conquer," he wrote, "but what none can see is the strategy out of which great victory is evolved."

Companies that have risen to global leadership over the past 20 years invariably began with ambitions that were out of all proportion to their resources and capabilities. But they created an obsession with winning at all levels of the organization and then sustained that obsession over the 10- to 20- year quest for global leadership. We term this obsession "strategic intent."

On the one hand, strategic intent envisions a desired leadership position and establishes the criterion the organization will use to chart its progress.

Komatsu set out to "encircle Caterpillar." Canon sought to "beat Xerox." Honda strove to become a second Ford – an automotive pioneer. All are expressions of strategic intent.

At the same time, strategic intent is more than simply unfettered ambition. (Many companies possess an ambitious strategic intent yet fall short of their goals.) The concept also encompasses an active management process that includes focusing the organization's attention on the essence of winning, motivating people by communicating the value of the target, leaving room for individual and team contributions, sustaining enthusiasm by providing new operational definitions as circumstances change, and using intent consistently to guide resource allocations.

**Strategic intent captures the essence of winning**. The Apollo program – landing a man on the moon ahead of the Soviets – was as competitively focused as Komatsu's drive against Caterpillar. The space program became the scorecard for America's technology race with the USSR. In the turbulent information technology industry, it was hard to pick a single competitor as a target, so NEC's strategic intent, set in the early 1970s, was to acquire the technologies that would put it in the best position to exploit the convergence of computing and telecommunications. Other industry observers foresaw this convergence, but only NEC made convergence the guiding theme for subsequent strategic decisions by adopting "computing and communications" as its intent. For Coca-Cola, strategic intent has been to put a Coke within "arm's reach" of every consumer in the world.

**Strategic intent is stable over time**. In battles for global leadership, one of the most critical tasks is to lengthen the organization's attention span. Strategic intent provides consistency to short-term action, while leaving room for reinterpretation as new opportunities emerge. At Komatsu, encircling Caterpillar encompassed a succession of medium-term programs aimed at exploiting specific weaknesses in Caterpillar or building particular competitive advantages. When Caterpillar threatened Komatsu in Japan, for example, Komatsu responded by first improving quality, then driving down costs, then cultivating export markets, and then underwriting new product development.

**Strategic intent sets a target that deserves personal effort and commitment**. Ask the CEOs of many American corporations how they measure their contributions to their companies' success, and you're likely to get an answer expressed in terms of shareholder wealth. In a company that possesses a strategic intent, top management is more likely to talk in terms of global market leadership. Market share leadership typically yields shareholder wealth, to be sure. But the two goals do not have the same motivational impact. It is hard to imagine middle managers, let alone blue-collar employees, waking up each day with the sole thought of creating more shareholder wealth. But mightn't they feel different given the challenge to "beat Benz" – the rallying cry at one Japanese auto producer? Strategic intent gives

**Remaking strategy**

Over the last ten years, our research on global competition, international alliances, and multinational management has brought us into close contact with senior managers in the United States, Europe, and Japan. As we tried to unravel the reasons for success and surrender in global markets, we became more and more suspicious that executives in Western and Far Eastern companies often operated with very different conceptions of competitive strategy. Understanding these differences, we thought, might help explain the conduct and outcome of competitive battles as well as supplement traditional explanations for Japan's ascendance and the West's decline.

We began by mapping the implicit strategy models of managers who had participated in our research. Then we built detailed histories of selected competitive battles. We searched for evidence of divergent views of strategy, competitive advantage, and the role of top management.

Two contrasting models of strategy emerged. One, which most Western managers will recognize, centers on the problem of maintaining strategic fit. The other centers on the problem of leveraging resources. The two are not mutually exclusive, but they represent a significant difference in emphasis – an emphasis that deeply affects how competitive battles get played out over time.

Both models recognize the problem of competing in a hostile environment with limited resources. But while the emphasis in the first is on trimming ambitions to match available resources, the emphasis in the second is on leveraging resources to reach seemingly unattainable goals.

Both models recognize that relative competitive advantage determines relative profitability. The first emphasizes the search for advantages that are inherently sustainable, the second emphasizes the need to accelerate organizational learning to outpace competitors in building new advantages.

Both models recognize the difficulty of competing against larger competitors. But while the first leads to a search for niches (or simply dissuades the company from challenging an entrenched competitor), the second produces a quest for new rules that can devalue the incumbent's advantages.

Both models recognize that balance in the scope of an organization's activities reduces risk. The first seeks to reduce financial risk by building a balanced portfolio of cash-generating and cash-consuming businesses. The second seeks to reduce competitive risk by ensuring a well-balanced and sufficiently broad portfolio of advantages.

Both models recognize the need to disaggregate the organization in a way that allows top management to differentiate among the investment needs of various planning units. In the first model, resources are allocated to product-market units in which relatedness is defined by common products, channels, and customers. Each business is assumed to own all the critical skills it needs to execute its strategy successfully. In the second, investments are made in core competences (microprocessor controls or electronic imaging, for example) as well as in product-market units. By tracking these investments across businesses, top management works to assure that the plans of individual strategic units don't undermine future developments by default.

Both models recognize the need for consistency in action across organizational levels. In the first, consistency between corporate and business levels is largely a matter of conforming to financial objectives. Consistency between business and functional levels comes by tightly restricting the means the business uses to achieve its strategy – establishing standard operating procedures, defining the served market, adhering to accepted industry practices. In the second model, business-corporate consistency comes from allegiance to a particular strategic intent. Business-functional consistency comes from allegiance to intermediate-term goals or challenges with lower-level employees encouraged to invent how those goals will be achieved.

employees the only goal that is worthy of commitment: to unseat the best or remain the best, worldwide.

Many companies are more familiar with strategic planning than they are with strategic intent. The planning process typically acts as a "feasibility sieve." Strategies are accepted or rejected on the basis of whether managers can be precise about the "how" as well as the "what" of their plans. Are the milestones clear? Do we have the necessary skills and resources? How will competitors react? Has the market been thoroughly researched? In one form or another, the admonition "Be realistic!" is given to line managers at almost every turn.

But can you *plan* for global leadership? Did Komatsu, Canon, and Honda have detailed, 20-year strategies for attacking Western markets? Are Japanese and Korean managers better planners than their Western counterparts? No. As valuable as strategic planning is, global leadership is an objective that lies outside the range of planning. We know of few companies with highly developed planning systems that have managed to set a strategic intent. As tests of strategic fit become more stringent, goals that cannot be planned for fall by the wayside. Yet companies that are afraid to commit to goals that lie outside the range of planning are unlikely to become global leaders.

Although strategic planning is billed as a way of becoming more future oriented, most managers, when pressed, will admit that their strategic plans reveal more about today's problems than tomorrow's opportunities. With a fresh set of problems confronting managers at the beginning of every planning cycle, focus often shifts dramatically from year to year. And with the pace of change accelerating in most industries, the predictive horizon is becoming shorter and shorter. So plans do little more than project the present forward incrementally. The goal of strategic intent is to fold the future back into the present. The important question is not "How will next year be different from this year?" but "What must we do differently next year to get closer to our strategic intent?" Only with a carefully articulated and adhered to strategic intent will a succession of year-on-year plans sum up to global leadership.

Just as you cannot plan a ten- to 20- year quest for global leadership, the chance of falling into a leadership position by accident is also remote. We don't believe that global leadership comes from an undirected process of intrapreneurship. Nor is it the product of a Skunk Works or other technique for internal venturing. Behind such programs lies a nihilistic assumption: that the organization is so hidebound, so orthodox ridden, the only way to innovate is to put a few bright people in a dark room, pour in some money, and hope that something wonderful will happen. In this Silicon Valley approach to innovation, the only role for top managers is to retrofit their corporate strategy to the entrepreneurial successes that emerge from below. Here the value added of top management is low indeed.

Sadly, this view of innovation may be consistent with reality in many large companies.[2] On the one hand, top management lacks any particular point of view about desirable ends beyond satisfying shareholders and keeping raiders at bay. On the other, the planning format, reward criteria, definition of served market, and belief in accepted industry practice all work together to tightly constrain the range of available means. As a result, innovation is necessarily an isolated activity. Growth depends more on the inventive capacity of individuals and small teams than on the ability of top management to aggregate the efforts of multiple teams toward an ambitious strategic intent.

In companies that have overcome resource constraints to build leadership positions, we see a different relationship between means and ends. While strategic intent is clear about ends, it is flexible as to means – it leaves room for improvisation. Achieving strategic intent requires enormous creativity with respect to means: Witness Fujitsu's use of strategic alliances in Europe to attack IBM. But this creativity comes in the service of a clearly prescribed end. Creativity is unbridled but not uncorralled, because top management establishes the criterion against which employees can pretest the logic of their initiatives. Middle managers must do more than deliver on promised financial targets; they must also deliver on the broad direction implicit in their organization's strategic intent.

Strategic intent implies a sizable stretch for an organization. Current capabilities and resources will not suffice. This forces the organization to be more inventive, to make the most of limited resources. Whereas the traditional view of strategy focuses on the degree of fit between existing resources and current opportunities, strategic intent creates an extreme misfit between resources and ambitions. Top management then challenges the organization to close the gap by systematically building new advantages. For Canon, this meant first understanding Xerox's patents, then licensing technology to create a product that would yield early market experience, then gearing up internal R&D efforts, then licensing its own technology to other manufacturers to fund further R&D, then entering market segments in Japan and Europe where Xerox was weak, and so on.

In this respect, strategic intent is like a marathon run in 400-meter sprints. No one knows what the terrain will look like at mile 26, so the role of top management is to focus the organization's attention on the ground to be covered in the next 400 meters. In several companies, management did this by presenting the organization with a series of corporate challenges, each specifying the next hill in the race to achieve strategic intent. One year the challenge might be quality, the next it might be total customer care, the next, entry into new markets, and the next, a rejuvenated product line. As this example indicates, corporate challenges are a way to stage the acquisition of new competitive advantages, a way to identify the focal point for employees' efforts in the near to medium term. As with strategic intent, top management is specific about the ends (reducing product development times by 75%, for example) but less prescriptive about the means.

Like strategic intent, challenges stretch the organization. To preempt Xerox in the personal copier business, Canon set its engineers a target price of $1,000 for a home copier. At the time, Canon's least expensive copier sold for several thousand dollars. Trying to reduce the cost of existing models would not have given Canon the radical price-performance improvement it needed to delay or deter Xerox's entry into personal copiers. Instead, Canon engineers were challenged to reinvent the copier – a challenge they met by substituting a disposable cartridge for the complex image-transfer mechanism used in other copiers.

Corporate challenges come from analyzing competitors as well as from the foreseeable pattern of industry evolution. Together these reveal potential competitive openings and identify the new skills the organization will need to take the initiative away from better-positioned players. (The exhibit "Building Competitive Advantage at Komatsu" illustrates the way challenges helped Komatsu achieve its intent.)

For a challenge to be effective, individuals and teams throughout the organization must understand it and see its implications for their own jobs. Companies that set corporate challenges to create new competitive advantages (as Ford and IBM did with quality improvement) quickly discover that engaging the entire organization requires top management to do the following:

- *Create a sense of urgency*, or quasi crisis, by amplifying weak signals in the environment that point up the need to improve, instead of allowing inaction to precipitate a real crisis. Komatsu, for example, budgeted on the basis of worst-case exchange rates that overvalued the yen.
- *Develop a competitor focus at every level through widespread use of competitive intelligence.* Every employee should be able to benchmark his or her efforts against best-in-class competitors so that the challenge becomes personal. For instance, Ford showed production-line workers videotapes of operations at Mazda's most efficient plant.
- *Provide employees with the skills they need to work effectively* – training in statistical tools, problem solving, value engineering, and team building, for example.
- *Give the organization time to digest one challenge before launching another.* When competing initiatives overload the organization, middle managers often try to protect their people from the whipsaw of shifting priorities. But this "wait and see if they're serious this time" attitude ultimately destroys the credibility of corporate challenges.
- *Establish clear milestones and review mechanisms* to track progress, and ensure that internal recognition and rewards reinforce desired behaviors. The goal is to make the challenge inescapable for everyone in the company.

It is important to distinguish between the process of managing corporate challenges and the advantages that the process creates. Whatever the actual challenge may be – quality, cost, value engineering, or something else – there is the same need to engage employees intellectually and emotionally in the development of new skills. In each case, the challenge will take root only if senior executives and lower-level employees feel a reciprocal responsibility for competitiveness.

We believe workers in many companies have been asked to take a disproportionate share of the blame for competitive failure. In one U.S. company, for example, management had sought a 40% wage-package concession from hourly employees to bring labor costs into line with Far Eastern competitors. The result was a long strike and, ultimately, a 10% wage concession from employees on the line. However, direct labor costs in manufacturing accounted for less than 15% of total value added. The company thus succeeded in demoralizing its entire blue-collar workforce for the sake of a 1.5% reduction in total costs. Ironically, further analysis showed that their competitors' most significant costs savings came not from lower hourly wages but from better work methods invented by employees. You can imagine how eager the U.S. workers were to make similar contributions after the strike and concessions. Contrast this situation with what happened at Nissan when the yen strengthened: Top management took a big pay cut and then asked middle managers and line employees to sacrifice relatively less.

Reciprocal responsibility means shared gain and shared pain. In too many companies, the pain of revitalization falls almost exclusively on the employees least responsible for the enterprise's decline. Too often, workers are asked to commit to corporate goals without any matching commitment from top management – be it employment security, gain sharing, or an ability to influence the direction of the business. This onesided approach to regaining competitiveness keeps many companies from harnessing the intellectual horsepower of their employees.

Creating a sense of reciprocal responsibility is crucial because competitiveness ultimately depends on the pace at which a company embeds new advantages deep within its organization, not on its stock of advantages at any given time. Thus, the concept of competitive advantage must be expanded beyond the scorecard many managers now use: Are my costs lower? Will my product command a price premium?

Few competitive advantages are long lasting. Uncovering a new competitive advantage is a bit like getting a hot tip on a stock: The first person to act on the insight makes more money than the last. When the experience curve was young, a company that built capacity ahead of competitors, dropped prices to fill plants, and reduced costs as volume rose went to the bank. The first mover traded on the fact that competitors undervalued market share – they didn't price to capture additional share because they didn't understand how market share leadership could be translated into lower costs and better margins. But there is no more undervalued market share when each of 20 semiconductor companies builds enough capacity to serve 10% of the world market.

Keeping score of existing advantages is not the same as building new advantages. The essence of strategy lies in creating tomorrow's competitive advantages faster than competitors mimic the ones you possess today. In the 1960s, Japanese producers relied on labor and capital cost advantages. As Western manufacturers began to move production offshore, Japanese companies accelerated their investment in process technology and created scale and quality advantages. Then, as their U.S. and European competitors rationalized manufacturing, they added another string to their bow by accelerating the rate of product development. Then they built global brands. Then they de-skilled competitors through alliances and out-sourcing deals. The moral? An organization's capacity to improve existing skills and learn new ones is the most defensible competitive advantage of all.

To achieve a strategic intent, a company must usually take on larger, better-financed competitors. That means carefully managing competitive engagements so that scarce resources are conserved. Managers cannot do that simply by playing the same game better – making marginal improvements

Building Competitive Advantage at Komatsu

| *Corporate Challenge* | *Protect Komatsu's Home Market Against Caterpillar* | *Reduce Costs While Maintaining Quality* | *Make Komatsu an International Enterprise and Build Export Markets* | *Respond to External Shocks That Threaten Markets* | *Create New Products and Markets* |
|---|---|---|---|---|---|
| **Programs** | **early 1960s** Licensing deals with Cummins Engine, International Harvester, and Bucyrus-Erie to acquire technology and establish benchmarks<br>**1961** Project A (for Ace) to advance the product quality of Komatsu's small and midsize bulldozers above Caterpillar's<br>**1962** Quality circles companywide to provide training for all employees | **1965** Cost Down (CD) program<br>**1966** Total CD program | **early 1960s** Develop Eastern bloc countries<br>**1967** Komatsu Europe marketing subsidiary established<br>**1970** Komatsu America established<br>**1972** Project B to improve the durability and reliability and to reduce costs of large bulldozers<br>**1972** Project C to improve payloaders<br>**1972** Project D to improve hydraulic excavators<br>**1974** Establish presales and service departments to assist newly industrializing countries in construction projects | **1975** V-10 program to reduce costs by 10% while maintaining quality; reduce parts by 20%; rationalize manufacturing system<br>**1977** ¥180 program to budget companywide for 180 yen to the dollar when exchange rate was 240<br>**1979** Project E to establish teams to redouble cost and quality efforts in response to oil crisis | **late 1970s** Accelerate product development to expand line<br>**1979** Future and Frontiers program to identify new businesses based on society's needs and company's know-how<br>**1981** EPOCHS program to reconcile greater product variety with improved production efficiencies |

to competitors' technology and business practices. Instead, they must fundamentally change the game in ways that disadvantage incumbents: devising novel approaches to market entry, advantage building, and competitive warfare. For smart competitors, the goal is not competitive imitation but competitive innovation, the art of containing competitive risks within manageable proportions.

Four approaches to competitive innovation are evident in the global expansion of Japanese companies. These are: building layers of advantage, searching for loose bricks, changing the terms of engagement, and competing through collaboration.

The wider a company's portfolio of advantages, the less risk it faces in competitive battles. New global competitors have built such portfolios by steadily expanding their arsenals of competitive weapons. They have moved inexorably from less defensible advantages such as low wage costs to more defensible advantages such as global brands. The Japanese color television industry illustrates this layering process.

By 1967, Japan had become the largest producer of black-and-white television sets. By 1970, it was closing the gap in color televisions. Japanese manufacturers used their competitive advantage – at that time, primarily, low labor costs – to build a base in the private-label business, then moved quickly to establish world-scale plants. This investment gave them additional layers of advantage – quality and reliability – as well as further cost reductions from process improvements. At the same time, they recognized that these cost-based advantages were vulnerable to changes in labor costs, process and product technology, exchange rates, and trade policy. So throughout the 1970s, they also invested heavily in building channels and brands, thus creating another layer of advantage: a global franchise. In the late 1970s, they enlarged the scope of their products and businesses to amortize these grand investments, and by 1980 all the major players – Matsushita, Sharp, Toshiba, Hitachi, Sanyo – had established related sets of businesses that could support global marketing investments. More recently, they have been investing in regional manufacturing and design centers to tailor their products more closely to national markets.

These manufacturers thought of the various sources of competitive advantage as mutually desirable layers, not mutually exclusive choices. What some call competitive suicide – pursuing both cost and differentiation – is exactly what many competitors strive for.[3] Using flexible manufacturing technologies and better marketing intelligence, they are moving away from standardized "world products" to products like Mazda's minivan, developed in California expressly for the U.S. market.

Another approach to competitive innovation, searching for loose bricks, exploits the benefits of surprise, which is just as useful in business battles as it is in war. Particularly in the early stages of a war for global markets, successful new competitors work to stay below the response threshold of their larger, more powerful rivals. Staking out underdefended territory is one way to do this.

To find loose bricks, managers must have few orthodoxies about how to break into a market or challenge a competitor. For example, in one large U.S. multinational, we asked several country managers to describe what a Japanese competitor was doing in the local market. The first executive said, "They're coming at us in the low end. Japanese companies always come in at the bottom." The second speaker found the comment interesting but disagreed: "They don't offer any low-end products in my market, but they have some exciting stuff at the top end. We really should reverse engineer that thing." Another colleague told still another story. "They haven't taken any business away from me," he said, "but they've just made me a great offer to supply components." In each country, the Japanese competitor had found a different loose brick.

The search for loose bricks begins with a careful analysis of the competitor's conventional wisdom: How does the company define its "served market"? What activities are most profitable? Which geographic markets are too troublesome to enter? The objective is not to find a corner of the industry (or niche) where larger competitors seldom tread but to build a base of attack just outside the market territory that industry leaders currently occupy. The goal is an uncontested profit sanctuary, which could be a particular product segment (the "low end" in motorcycles), a slice of the value chain (components in the computer industry), or a particular geographic market (Eastern Europe).

When Honda took on leaders in the motorcycle industry, for example, it began with products that were just outside the conventional definition of the leaders' product-market domains. As a result, it could build a base of operations in underdefended territory and then use that base to launch an expanded attack. What many competitors failed to see was Honda's strategic intent and its growing competence in engines and power trains. Yet even as Honda was selling 50cc motorcycles in the United States, it was already racing larger bikes in Europe – assembling the design skills and technology it would need for a systematic expansion across the entire spectrum of motor-related businesses.

Honda's progress in creating a core competence in engines should have warned competitors that it might enter a series of seemingly unrelated industries – automobiles, lawn mowers, marine engines, generators. But with each company fixated on its own market, the threat of Honda's horizontal diversification went unnoticed. Today, companies like Matsushita and Toshiba are similarly poised to move in unexpected ways across industry boundaries. In protecting loose bricks, companies must extend their peripheral vision by tracking and anticipating the migration of global competitors across product segments, businesses, national markets, value-added stages, and distribution channels.

Changing the terms of engagement – refusing to accept the front-runner's definition of industry and segment boundaries – represents still another form of competitive innovation. Canon's entry into the copier business illustrates this approach.

During the 1970s, both Kodak and IBM tried to match Xerox's business system in terms of segmentation, products, distribution, service, and pricing. As a result, Xerox had no trouble decoding the new entrants' intentions and developing countermoves. IBM eventually withdrew from the copier business, while Kodak remains a distant second in the large copier market that Xerox still dominates.

Canon, on the other hand, changed the terms of competitive engagement. While Xerox built a wide range of copiers, Canon standardized machines and components to reduce costs. It chose to distribute through office product dealers rather than try to match Xerox's huge direct sales force. It also avoided the need to create a national service network by designing reliability and serviceability into its product and then delegating service responsibility to the dealers. Canon copiers were sold rather than leased, freeing Canon from the burden of financing the lease base. Finally, instead of selling to the heads of corporate duplicating departments, Canon appealed to secretaries and department managers who wanted distributed copying. At each stage, Canon neatly sidestepped a potential barrier to entry.

Canon's experience suggests that there is an important distinction between barriers to entry and barriers to imitation. Competitors that tried to match Xerox's business system had to pay the same entry costs – the barriers to imitation were high. But Canon dramatically reduced the barriers to entry by changing the rules of the game.

Changing the rules also short-circuited Xerox's ability to retaliate quickly against its new rival. Confronted with the need to rethink its business strategy and organization, Xerox was paralyzed for a time. Its managers realized that the faster they downsized the product line, developed new channels, and improved reliability, the faster they would erode the company's traditional profit base. What might have been seen as critical success factors – Xerox's national sales force and service network, its large installed base of leased machines, and its reliance on service revenues – instead became barriers to retaliation. In this sense, competitive innovation is like judo: The goal is to use a larger competitor's weight against it. And that happens not by matching the leader's capabilities but by developing contrasting capabilities of one's own.

Competitive innovation works on the premise that a successful competitor is likely to be wedded to a recipe for success. That's why the most effective weapon new competitors possess is probably a clean sheet of paper. And why an incumbent's greatest vulnerability is its belief in accepted practice.

Through licensing, outsourcing agreements, and joint ventures, it is sometimes possible to win without fighting. For example, Fujitsu's alliances in Europe with Siemens and STC (Britain's largest computer maker) and in the United States with Amdahl yield manufacturing volume and access to Western markets. In the early 1980s, Matsushita established a joint venture with Thorn (in the United Kingdom), Telefunken (in Germany), and Thomson (in France), which allowed it to quickly multiply the forces arrayed against Philips in the battle for leadership in the European VCR business. In fighting larger global rivals by proxy, Japanese companies have adopted a maxim as old as human conflict itself: My enemy's enemy is my friend.

Hijacking the development efforts of potential rivals is another goal of competitive collaboration. In the consumer electronics war, Japanese competitors attacked traditional businesses like TVs and hi-fis while volunteering to manufacture next generation products like VCRs, camcorders, and CD players for Western rivals. They hoped their rivals would ratchet down development spending, and, in most cases, that is precisely what happened. But companies that abandoned their own development efforts seldom reemerged as serious competitors in subsequent new product battles.

Collaboration can also be used to calibrate competitors' strengths and weaknesses. Toyota's joint venture with GM, and Mazda's with Ford, give these automakers an invaluable vantage point for assessing the progress their U.S. rivals have made in cost reduction, quality, and technology. They can also learn how GM and Ford compete – when they will fight and when they won't. Of course, the reverse is also true: Ford and GM have an equal opportunity to learn from their partner-competitors.

The route to competitive revitalization we have been mapping implies a new view of strategy. Strategic intent assures consistency in resource allocation over the long term. Clearly articulated corporate challenges focus the efforts of individuals in the medium term. Finally, competitive innovation helps reduce competitive risk in the short term. This consistency in the long term, focus in the medium term, and inventiveness and involvement in the short term provide the key to leveraging limited resources in pursuit of ambitious goals. But just as there is a process of winning, so there is a process of surrender. Revitalization requires understanding that process, too.

Given their technological leadership and access to large regional markets, how did U.S. and European countries lose their apparent birthright to dominate global industries? There is no simple answer. Few companies recognize the value of documenting failure. Fewer still search their own managerial orthodoxies for the seeds of competitive surrender. But we believe there is a pathology of surrender that gives some important clues. (See the sidebar "The Process of Surrender.")

It is not very comforting to think that the essence of Western strategic thought can be reduced to eight rules for excellence, seven S's, five competitive forces, four product life-cycle stages, three generic strategies, and innumerable two-by-two matrices.[4] Yet for the past 20 years, "advances" in strategy have taken the form of ever more typologies, heuristics, and laundry lists, often with dubious empirical bases. Moreover, even reasonable concepts like the product life cycle, experience curve, product portfolios, and generic strategies often have toxic side effects: They reduce the number of strategic options management is willing to consider. They create a preference for selling businesses rather than defending them. They yield predictable strategies that rivals easily decode.

Strategy recipes limit opportunities for competitive innovation. A company may have 40 businesses and only four strategies – invest, hold, harvest, or divest. Too often, strategy is seen as a positioning exercise in which options are tested by how they fit the existing industry structure. But current industry structure reflects the strengths of the industry leader, and playing by the leader's rules is usually competitive suicide.

Armed with concepts like segmentation, the value chain, competitor benchmarking, strategic groups, and mobility barriers, many managers have become better and better at drawing industry maps. But while they have been busy mapmaking, their competitors have been moving entire continents. The strategist's goal is not to find a niche within the existing industry space but to create new space that is uniquely suited to the company's own strengths – space that is off the map.

This is particularly true now that industry boundaries are becoming more and more unstable. In industries such as financial services and communications, rapidly changing technology, deregulation, and globalization have undermined the value of traditional industry analysis. Mapmaking skills are worth little in the epicenter of an earthquake. But an industry in upheaval presents opportunities for ambitious companies to redraw the map in their favor, so long as they can think outside traditional industry boundaries.

Concepts like "mature" and "declining" are largely definitional. What most executives mean when they label a business "mature" is that sales growth has stagnated in their current geographic markets for existing products sold through existing channels. In such cases, it's not the industry that is mature, but the executives' conception of the industry. Asked if the piano business was mature, a senior executive at Yamaha replied, "Only if we can't take any market share from anybody anywhere in the world and still make money. And anyway, we're not in the 'piano' business, we're in the 'keyboard' business." Year after year, Sony has revitalized its radio and tape recorder businesses, despite the fact that other manufacturers long ago abandoned these businesses as mature.

A narrow concept of maturity can foreclose a company from a broad stream of future opportunities. In the 1970s, several U.S. companies thought that consumer electronics had become a mature industry. What could possibly top the color TV? they asked themselves. RCA and GE, distracted by opportunities in more "attractive" industries like mainframe computers,

**The process of surrender**

On the battles for global leadership that have taken place during the past two decades, we have seen a pattern of competitive attack and retrenchment that was remarkably similar across industries. We call this the process of surrender.

The process started with unseen intent. Not possessing long-term, competitor-focused goals themselves, Western companies did not ascribe such intentions to their rivals. They also calculated the threat posed by potential competitors in terms of their existing resources rather than their resourcefulness. This led to systematic underestimation of smaller rivals who were fast gaining technology through licensing arrangements, acquiring market understanding from downstream OEM partners, and improving product quality and manufacturing productivity through companywide employee involvement programs. Oblivious of the strategic intent and intangible advantages of their rivals, American and European businesses were caught off guard.

Adding to the competitive surprise was the fact that the new entrants typically attacked the periphery of a market (Honda in small motorcycles, Yamaha in grand pianos, Toshiba in small black-and-white televisions) before going head-to-head with incumbents. Incumbents often misread these attacks, seeing them as part of a niche

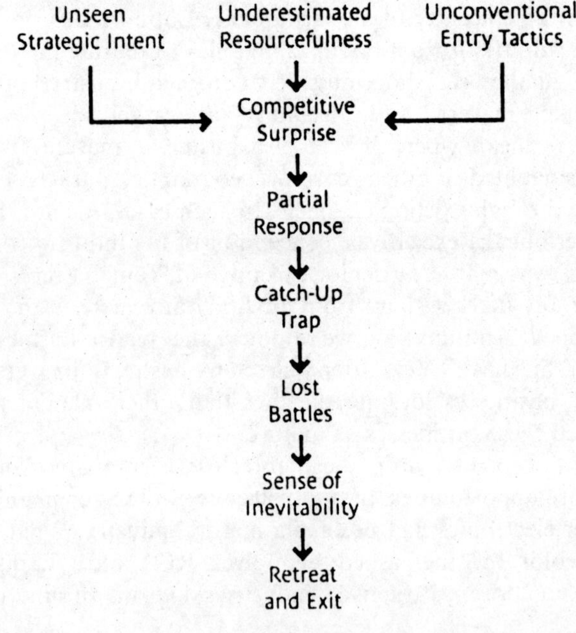

strategy and not as a search for "loose bricks." Unconventional market entry strategies (minority holdings in less-developed countries, use of nontraditional channels, extensive corporate advertising) were ignored or dismissed as quirky. For example, managers we spoke with said Japanese companies' position in the European computer industry was nonexistent. In terms of brand share that's nearly true, but the Japanese control as much as one-third of the manufacturing value added in the hardware sales of European-based computer businesses. Similarly, German auto producers claimed to feel unconcerned over the proclivity of Japanese producers to move upmarket. But with its low-end models under tremendous pressure from Japanese producers, Porsche has now announced that it will no longer make "entry level" cars.

Western managers often misinterpreted their rivals' tactics. They believed that Japanese and Korean companies were competing solely on the basis of cost and quality. This typically produced a partial response to those competitors' initiatives: moving manufacturing offshore, outsourcing, or instituting a quality program. Seldom was the full extent of the competitive threat appreciated – the multiple layers of advantage, the expansion across related product segments, the development of global brand positions. Imitating the currently visible tactics of rivals put Western businesses into a perpetual catchup trap. One by one, companies lost battles and came to see surrender as inevitable. Surrender was not inevitable, of course, but the attack was staged in a way that disguised ultimate intentions and side-stepped direct confrontation.

left Japanese producers with a virtual monopoly in VCRs, camcorders, and CD players. Ironically, the TV business, once thought mature, is on the verge of a dramatic renaissance. A $20 billion-a-year business will be created when high-definition television is launched in the United States. But the pioneers of television may capture only a small part of this bonanza.

Most of the tools of strategic analysis are focused domestically. Few force managers to consider global opportunities and threats. For example, portfolio planning portrays top management's investment options as an array of businesses rather than as an array of geographic markets. The result is predictable: As businesses come under attack from foreign competitors, the company attempts to abandon them and enter other areas in which the forces of global competition are not yet so strong. In the short term, this may be an appropriate response to waning competitiveness, but there are fewer and fewer businesses in which a domestic-oriented company can find refuge. We seldom hear such companies asking, Can we move into emerging markets overseas ahead of our global rivals and prolong the profitability of this business? Can we counterattack in our global competitors' home market and slow the pace of their expansion? A senior executive in one successful global company made a telling comment: "We're glad to find a competitor managing by the portfolio concept – we can almost predict how much share we'll have to take away to put the business on the CEO's 'sell list.'"

Companies can also be overcommitted to organizational recipes, such as strategic business units (SBUs) and the decentralization an SBU structure implies. Decentralization is seductive because it places the responsibility for success or failure squarely on the shoulders of line managers. Each business is assumed to have all the resources it needs to execute its strategies successfully, and in this no-excuses environment, it is hard for top management to fail. But desirable as clear lines of responsibility and accountability are, competitive revitalization requires positive value added from top management.

Few companies with a strong SBU orientation have built successful global distribution and brand positions. Investments in a global brand franchise typically transcend the resources and risk propensity of a single business. While some Western companies have had global brand positions for 30 or 40 years or more (Heinz, Siemens, IBM, Ford, and Kodak, for example), it is hard to identify any American or European company that has created a new global brand franchise in the past ten to 15 years. Yet Japanese companies have created a score or more – NEC, Fujitsu, Panasonic (Matsushita), Toshiba, Sony, Seiko, Epson, Canon, Minolta, and Honda among them.

General Electric's situation is typical. In many of its businesses, this American giant has been almost unknown in Europe and Asia. GE made no coordinated effort to build a global corporate franchise. Any GE business with international ambitions had to bear the burden of establishing its credibility and credentials in the new market alone. Not surprisingly, some once-strong GE businesses opted out of the difficult task of building a global brand position. By contrast, smaller Korean companies like Samsung, Daewoo, and Lucky-Goldstar are busy building global-brand umbrellas that will ease market entry for a whole range of businesses. The underlying principle is simple: Economies of scope may be as important as economies of scale in entering global markets. But capturing economies of scope demands interbusiness coordination that only top management can provide.

We believe that inflexible SBU-type organizations have also contributed to the de-skilling of some companies. For a single SBU, incapable of sustaining an investment in a core competence such as semiconductors, optical media, or combustion engines, the only way to remain competitive is to purchase key components from potential (often Japanese or Korean) competitors. For an SBU defined in product market terms, competitiveness means offering an end product that is competitive in price and performance. But that gives an SBU manager little incentive to distinguish between external sourcing that achieves "product embodied" competitiveness and internal development that yields deeply embedded organizational competencies that can be exploited across multiple businesses. Where upstream component-manufacturing activities are seen as cost centers with cost-plus transfer pricing, additional investment in the core activity may seem a less profitable use of capital than investment in downstream activities. To make matters worse, internal accounting data may not reflect the competitive value of retaining control over a core competence.

Together, a shared global corporate brand franchise and a shared core competence act as mortar in many Japanese companies. Lacking this mortar, a company's businesses are truly loose bricks – easily knocked out by global competitors that steadily invest in core competences. Such competitors can coopt domestically oriented companies into long-term sourcing dependence and capture the economies of scope of global brand investment through inter-business coordination.

Last in decentralization's list of dangers is the standard of managerial performance typically used in SBU organizations. In many companies, business unit managers are rewarded solely on the basis of their performance against return on investment targets. Unfortunately, that often leads to denominator management because executives soon discover that reductions in investment and head count–the denominator–"improve" the financial ratios by which they are measured more easily than growth in the numerator: revenues. It also fosters a hair-trigger sensitivity to industry downturns that can be very costly. Managers who are quick to reduce investment and dismiss workers find it takes much longer to regain lost skills and catch up on investment when the industry turns upward again. As a result, they lose market share in every business cycle. Particularly in industries where there is fierce competition for the best people and where competitors invest relentlessly, denominator management creates a retrenchment ratchet.

The concept of the general manager as a movable peg reinforces the problem of denominator management. Business schools are guilty here because they have perpetuated the notion that a manager with net present value calculations in one hand and portfolio planning in the other can manage any business anywhere.

In many diversified companies, top management evaluates line managers on numbers alone because no other basis for dialogue exists. Managers move so many times as part of their "career development" that they often do not understand the nuances of the businesses they are managing. At GE, for example, one fast-track manager heading an important new venture had moved across five businesses in five years. His series of quick successes finally came to an end when he confronted a Japanese competitor whose managers had been plodding along in the same business for more than a decade.

Regardless of ability and effort, fast-track managers are unlikely to develop the deep business knowledge they need to discuss technology options, competitors' strategies, and global opportunities substantively. Invariably, therefore, discussions gravitate to "the numbers," while the value added of managers is limited to the financial and planning savvy they carry from job to job. Knowledge of the company's internal planning and accounting systems substitutes for substantive knowledge of the business, making competitive innovation unlikely.

When managers know that their assignments have a two- to three-year time frame, they feel great pressure to create a good track record fast. This pressure often takes one of two forms. Either the manager does not commit to goals whose time line extends beyond his or her expected tenure. Or ambitious goals are adopted and squeezed into an unrealistically short time frame. Aiming to be number one in a business is the essence of strategic intent; but imposing a three- to four-year horizon on the effort simply invites disaster. Acquisitions are made with little attention to the problems of integration. The organization becomes overloaded with initiatives. Collaborative ventures are formed without adequate attention to competitive consequences.

Almost every strategic management theory and nearly every corporate planning system is premised on a strategy hierarchy in which corporate goals guide business unit strategies and business unit strategies guide functional tactics.[5] In this hierarchy, senior management makes strategy and lower levels execute it. The dichotomy between formulation and implementation is familiar and widely accepted. But the strategy hierarchy undermines competitiveness by fostering an elitist view of management that tends to disenfranchise most of the organization. Employees fail to identify with corporate goals or involve themselves deeply in the work of becoming more competitive.

The strategy hierarchy isn't the only explanation for an elitist view of management, of course. The myths that grow up around successful top managers–"Lee Iacocca saved Chrysler," "Carlo De Benedetti rescued Olivetti," "John Sculley turned Apple around" – perpetuate it. So does the turbulent business environment. Middle managers buffeted by circumstances that seem to be beyond their control desperately want to believe that top management has all the answers. And top management, in turn, hesitates to admit it does not for fear of demoralizing lower-level employees.

The result of all this is often a code of silence in which the full extent of a company's competitiveness problem is not widely shared. We interviewed business unit managers in one company, for example, who were extremely anxious because top management wasn't talking openly about the competitive challenges the company faced. They assumed the lack of communication indicated a lack of awareness on their senior managers' part. But when asked whether they were open with their own employees, these same managers replied that while they could face up to the problems, the people below them could not. Indeed, the only time the workforce heard about the company's competitiveness problems was during wage negotiations when problems were used to extract concessions.

Unfortunately, a threat that everyone perceives but no one talks about creates more anxiety than a threat that has been clearly identified and made the focal point for the problem-solving efforts of the entire company. That is one reason honesty and humility on the part of top management may be the first pre-requisite of revitalization. Another reason is the need to make "participation" more than a buzzword.

Programs such as quality circles and total customer service often fall short of expectations because management does not recognize that successful implementation requires more than administrative structures. Difficulties in embedding new capabilities are typically put down to "communication" problems, with the unstated assumption that if only downward communication were more effective – "if only middle management would get the message straight" – the new program would quickly take root. The need for upward communication is often ignored, or assumed to mean nothing more than feedback. In contrast, Japanese companies win not because they have smarter managers but because they have developed ways to harness the "wisdom of the anthill." They realize that top managers are a bit like the astronauts who circle the Earth in the space shuttle. It may be the astronauts who get all the glory, but everyone knows that the real intelligence behind the mission is located firmly on the ground.

Where strategy formulation is an elitist activity, it is also difficult to produce truly creative strategies. For one thing, there are not enough heads and points of view in divisional or corporate planning departments to challenge conventional wisdom. For another, creative strategies seldom emerge from the annual planning ritual. The starting point for next year's strategy is almost always this year's strategy. Improvements are incremental. The company sticks to the segments and territories it knows, even though the real opportunities may be elsewhere. The impetus for Canon's pioneering entry into the personal copier business came from an overseas sales subsidiary – not from planners in Japan.

The goal of the strategy hierarchy remains valid – to ensure consistency up and down the organization. But this consistency is better derived from a clearly articulated strategic intent than from inflexibly applied top-down plans. In the 1990s, the challenge will be to enfranchise employees to invent the means to accomplish ambitious ends.

We seldom found cautious administrators among the top managements of companies that came from behind to challenge incumbents for global leadership. But in studying organizations that had surrendered, we invariably found senior managers who, for whatever reason, lacked the courage to commit their companies to heroic goals – goals that lay beyond the reach of planning and existing resources. The conservative goals they set failed to generate pressure and enthusiasm for competitive innovation or give the organization much useful guidance. Financial targets and vague mission statements just cannot provide the consistent direction that is a pre-requisite for winning a global competitive war.

This kind of conservatism is usually blamed on the financial markets. But we believe that in most cases, investors' so-called short-term orientation simply reflects a lack of confidence in the ability of senior managers to conceive and deliver stretch goals. The chairman of one company complained bitterly that even after improving return on capital employed to over 40% (by ruthlessly divesting lackluster businesses and downsizing others), the stock market held the company to an 8:1 price/earnings ratio. Of course, the market's message was clear: "We don't trust you. You've shown no ability to achieve profitable growth. Just cut out the slack, manage the denominators, and perhaps you'll be taken over by a company that can use your resources more creatively." Very little in the track record of most large Western companies warrants the confidence of the stock market. Investors aren't hopelessly short-term, they're justifiably skeptical.

We believe that top management's caution reflects a lack of confidence in its own ability to involve the entire organization in revitalization, as opposed to simply raising financial targets. Developing faith in the organization's ability to deliver on tough goals, motivating it to do so, focusing its attention long enough to internalize new capabilities – this is the real challenge for top management. Only by rising to this challenge will senior managers gain the courage they need to commit themselves and their companies to global leadership.

## Notes

1 Among the first to apply the concept of strategy to management were H. Igor Ansoff in *Corporate Strategy: An Analytic Approach to Business Policy for Growth and Expansion* (McGraw-Hill, 1965) and Kenneth R. Andrews in *The Concept of Corporate Strategy* (Dow Jones-Irwin, 1971).
2 Robert A. Burgelman, "A Process Model of Internal Corporate Venturing in the Diversified Major Firm," *Administrative Science Quarterly*, June 1983.
3 For example, see Michael E. Porter, *Competitive Strategy* (Free Press, 1980).
4 Strategic frameworks for resource allocation in diversified companies are summarized in Charles W. Hofer and Dan E. Schendel, *Strategy Formulation: Analytical Concepts* (West Publishing, 1978).
5 For example, see Peter Lorange and Richard F. Vancil, *Strategic Planning Systems* (Prentice-Hall, 1977).

44

# DESIGN, LEARNING AND PLANNING

## A further observation on the design school debate

*Michael Goold*

Source: *Strategic Management Journal* 13(2) (1992): 169–70.

I have enjoyed the debate between Henry Mintzberg and Igor Ansoff about the merits of the design school of strategic management (Mintzberg, 1990, 1991; Ansoff, 1991). These articles articulate two different approaches to strategic management well, and, in Mintzberg 1991, move towards a synthesis or at least a reconciliation between them.

Alas, however, the polemics and the prejudices get in the way of moving forward towards a real synthesis. Mintzberg, 1991, gives a good account of why *both* incremental learning *and* deliberate planning are needed, of why both processes should 'intertwine'. But this reconciliation is sandwiched between colorful passages that condemn planning and extol learning. These were summed up in Mintzberg's eventual score sheet: Learning 1, Planning 0. This hardly represents a balance between or an intertwining of the two approaches.

Mintzberg may claim that his prejudices are necessary to counter the prejudice of others in favor of the planning school. And it is true that his work has brought out aspects of strategic management that may previously have been neglected. But there is equal danger in going too far in the other direction.

We can focus these issues around the motorcycle industry report by BCG (1975) that Mintzberg refers to, and of which I was a coauthor. Mintzberg is severe on the BCG report ('never bothered to ask' about how Honda developed their strategy, 'mistake' was in 'what it left out'), and from the perspective of the historian he is probably correct. The report does not dwell on how the Honda strategy was evolved and on the learning that took place. However, the report was commissioned for an industry in crisis, with the brief of identifying commercially viable alternatives. The perspective required was managerial ('what should we do now?'), not historical ('how did this situation arise?'). And for most executives concerned with strategic management the primary interest will always be 'what should we do now?'.

Given such an interest, what would a Mintzbergian learning approach recommend? This is not clear from Mintzberg's article, but presumably it would be 'try something, see if it works and learn from your experience'. Indeed there is some suggestion that one should specifically try 'probable nonstarters'. For the manager, such advice would be unhelpful, even irritating. 'Of course, we should learn from experience,' he will say 'but we have neither the time nor the money to experiment with endless, fruitless nonstarters' Where the manager needs help is with what he should try to make work. This, surely, is exactly where strategic management thinking should endeavor to be useful.

In this context, the BCG analysis of Honda's success is much more valid (Boston Consulting Group, 1975). Its purpose was to discern what lay behind and accounted for Honda's success, in a way that would help others to think through what strategies would be likely to work. In this sense, one might even locate it as much in the learning (i.e. learning from the success of others) as in the planning school. Paradoxically, the approach is close to one adopted by Mintzberg elsewhere (Mintzberg, 1978), in that it tries to discern patterns in Honda's strategic decisions and actions, and to use these patterns in identifying what works well and badly. How Honda arrived at their patterns is not the focus of attention, nor should it be, given the purpose of the work.

None of this is to deny that, in following through whatever strategy is chosen, a willingness to learn for experience and refine the chosen strategy is vital. Here Mintzberg's crusade is valuable and important, particularly for managers who might otherwise suffer from tunnel vision. But we can do better than starting with random experiments and we can use both planning and learning from others in selecting the strategies to try. I see no contest between planning and learning, rather a collaboration. But, if a score sheet must be drawn up, something like Planning 1, Learning 1 is surely a fairer reflection of the contribution of both sides.

## References

Ansoff, H. I. 'Critique of Henry Mintzberg's 'The Design School: Reconsidering the basic premises of strategic management', *Strategic Management Journal*, **12**(6), 1991, pp. 449–461.

Boston Consulting Group. *Strategy Alternatives for the British Motorcycle Industry*, Her Majesty's Stationery Office, London, 1975.

Mintzberg, H. 'Patterns in strategy formation', *Management Science*, May 1978, pp. 934–948.

Mintzberg, H. 'The Design School: Reconsidering the basic premises of strategic management', *Strategic Management Journal*, **11**(6), 1990, pp. 171–195.

Mintzberg, H. 'Strategy formation: Schools of thought'. In J. Frederickson (ed.), *Perspectives on Strategic Management*, pp. 105–235, Harper Business, New York, 1990.

Mintzberg, H. 'Learning 1, planning 0: Reply to Igor Ansoff'. *Strategic Management Journal*, **12**(6), 1991, pp. 463–466.

45

# COMPETING ON CAPABILITIES

## The new rules of corporate strategy

*George Stalk, Philip Evans and Lawrence E. Shulman*

Source: *Harvard Business Review* 70(2) (1992): 57–69.

In the 1980s, companies discovered time as a new source of competitive advantage. In the 1990s, they will learn that time is just one piece of a more far-reaching transformation in the logic of competition.

Companies that compete effectively on time – speeding new products to market, manufacturing just in time, or responding promptly to customer complaints – tend to be good at other things as well: for instance, the consistency of their product quality, the acuity of their insight into evolving customer needs, the ability to exploit emerging markets, enter new businesses, or generate new ideas and incorporate them in innovations. But all these qualities are mere reflections of a more fundamental characteristic: a new conception of corporate strategy that we call "capabilities-based competition."

For a glimpse of the new world of capabilities-based competition, consider the astonishing reversal of fortunes represented by Kmart and Wal-Mart:

In 1979, Kmart was king of the discount retailing industry, an industry it had virtually created. With 1,891 stores and average revenues per store of $7.25 million, Kmart enjoyed enormous size advantages. This allowed economies of scale in purchasing, distribution, and marketing that, according to just about any management textbook, are crucial to competitive success in a mature and low-growth industry. By contrast, Wal-Mart was a small niche retailer in the South with only 229 stores and average revenues about half of those of Kmart stores – hardly a serious competitor.

And yet, only ten years later, Wal-Mart had transformed itself and the discount retailing industry. Growing nearly 25% a year, the company achieved the highest sales per square foot, inventory turns, and operating profit of any discount retailer. Its 1989 pretax return on sales was 8%, nearly double that of Kmart.

Today Wal-Mart is the largest and highest profit retailer in the world – a performance that has translated into a 32% return on equity and a market valuation more than ten times book value. What's more, Wal-Mart's growth has been concentrated in half the United States, leaving ample room for further expansion. If Wal-Mart continues to gain market share at just one-half its historical rate, by 1995 the company will have eliminated all competitors from discount retailing with the exception of Kmart and Target.

## The secret of Wal-Mart's success

What accounts for Wal-Mart's remarkable success? Most explanations focus on a few familiar and highly visible factors: the genius of founder Sam Walton, who inspires his employees and has molded a culture of service excellence; the "greeters" who welcome customers at the door; the motivational power of allowing employees to own part of the business; the strategy of "everyday low prices" that offers the customer a better deal and saves on merchandising and advertising costs. Economists also point to Wal-Mart's big stores, which offer economies of scale and a wider choice of merchandise.

But such explanations only redefine the question. *Why* is Wal-Mart able to justify building bigger stores? Why does Wal-Mart alone have a cost structure low enough to accommodate everyday low prices and greeters? And what has enabled the company to continue to grow far beyond the direct reach of Sam Walton's magnetic personality? The real secret of Wal-Mart's success lies deeper, in a set of strategic business decisions that transformed the company into a capabilities-based competitor.

The starting point was a relentless focus on satisfying customer needs. Wal-Mart's goals were simple to define but hard to execute: to provide customers access to quality goods, to make these goods available when and where customers want them, to develop a cost structure that enables competitive pricing, and to build and maintain a reputation for absolute trustworthiness. The key to achieving these goals was to make the way the company replenished inventory the centerpiece of its competitive strategy.

This strategic vision reached its fullest expression in a largely invisible logistics technique known as "cross-docking." In this system, goods are continuously delivered to Wal-Mart's warehouses, where they are selected, repacked, and then dispatched to stores, often without ever sitting in inventory. Instead of spending valuable time in the warehouse, goods just cross from one loading dock to another in 48 hours or less.

Cross-docking enables Wal-Mart to achieve the economies that come with purchasing full truckloads of goods while avoiding the usual inventory and handling costs. Wal-Mart runs a full 85% of its goods through its warehouse system – as opposed to only 50% for Kmart. This reduces Wal-Mart's costs of sales by 2% to 3% compared with the industry average. That cost difference makes possible the everyday low prices.

But that's not all. Low prices in turn mean that Wal-Mart can save even more by eliminating the expense of frequent promotions. Stable prices also make sales more predictable, thus reducing stockouts and excess inventory. Finally, everyday low prices bring in the customers, which translates into higher sales per retail square foot. These advantages in basic economics make the greeters and the profit sharing easy to afford.

With such obvious benefits, why don't all retailers use cross-docking? The reason: it is extremely difficult to manage. To make cross-docking work, Wal-Mart has had to make strategic investments in a variety of interlocking support systems far beyond what could be justified by conventional ROI criteria.

For example, cross-docking requires continuous contact among Wal-Mart's distribution centers, suppliers, and every point of sale in every store to ensure that orders can flow in and be consolidated and executed within a matter of hours. So Wal-Mart operates a private satellite-communication system that daily sends point-of-sale data directly to Wal-Mart's 4,000 vendors.

Another key component of Wal-Mart's logistics infrastructure is the company's fast and responsive transportation system. The company's 19 distribution centers are serviced by nearly 2,000 company-owned trucks. This dedicated truck fleet permits Wal-Mart to ship goods from warehouse to store in less than 48 hours and to replenish its store shelves twice a week on average. By contrast, the industry norm is once every two weeks.

To gain the full benefits of cross-docking, Wal-Mart has also had to make fundamental changes in its approach to managerial control. Traditionally in

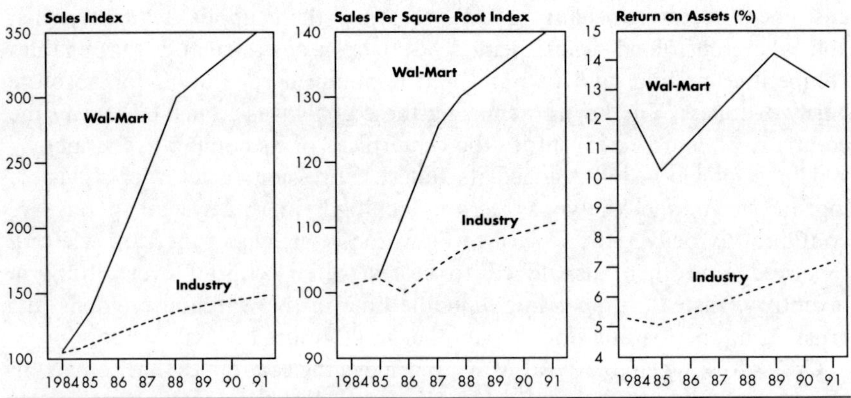


Capabilities Help Wal-Mart Outperform Its Industry.
*Source*: The Boston Consulting Group.

the retail industry, decisions about merchandising, pricing, and promotions have been highly centralized and made at the corporate level. Cross-docking, however, turns this command-and-control logic on its head. Instead of the retailer pushing products into the system, customers "pull" products when and where they need them. This approach places a premium on frequent, informal cooperation among stores, distribution centers, and suppliers – with far less centralized control.

The job of senior management at Wal-Mart, then, is not to tell individual store managers what to do but to create an environment where they can learn from the market – and from each other. The company's information systems, for example, provide store managers with detailed information about customer behavior, while a fleet of airplanes regularly ferries store managers to Bentonville, Arkansas headquarters for meetings on market trends and merchandising.

As the company has grown and its stores have multiplied, even Wal-Mart's own private air force hasn't been enough to maintain the necessary contacts among store managers. So Wal-Mart has installed a video link connecting all its stores to corporate headquarters and to each other. Store managers frequently hold videoconferences to exchange information on what's happening in the field, like which products are selling and which ones aren't, which promotions work and which don't.

The final piece of this capabilities mosaic is Wal-Mart's human resources system. The company realizes that its frontline employees play a significant role in satisfying customer needs. So it set out to enhance its organizational capability with programs like stock ownership and profit sharing geared toward making its personnel more responsive to customers. Even the way Wal-Mart stores are organized contributes to this goal. Where Kmart has 5 separate merchandise departments in each store, Wal-Mart has 36. This means that training can be more focused and more effective, and employees can be more attuned to customers.

Kmart did not see its business this way. While Wal-Mart was fine-tuning its business processes and organizational practices, Kmart was following the classic textbook approach that had accounted for its original success. Kmart managed its business by focusing on a few product-centered strategic business units, each a profit center under strong centralized line management. Each SBU made strategy – selecting merchandise, setting prices, and deciding which products to promote. Senior management spent most of its time and resources making line decisions rather than investing in a support infrastructure.

Similarly, Kmart evaluated its competitive advantage at each stage along a value chain and subcontracted activities that managers concluded others could do better. While Wal-Mart was building its ground transportation fleet, Kmart was moving *out* of trucking because a subcontracted fleet was cheaper. While Wal-Mart was building close relationships with its suppliers,

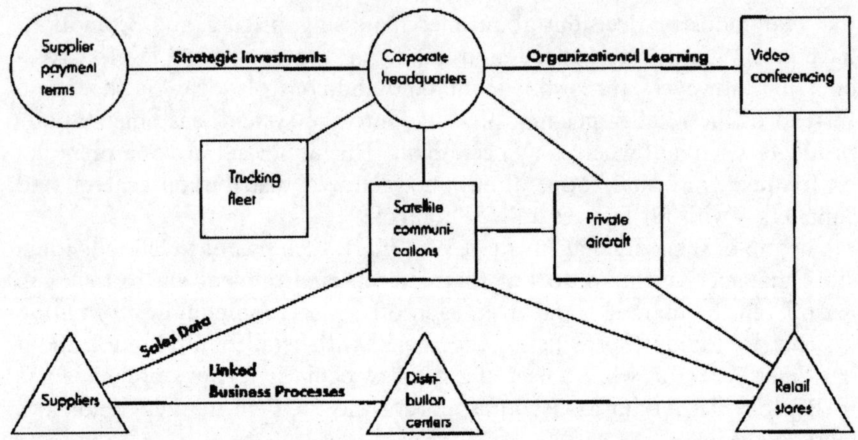


Mapping Capabilities: Inventory Replenishment at Wal-Mart.
At Wal-Mart, building capabilities begins with strategic investments: good payment terms to suppliers, a dedicated trucking fleet, satellite communications, company-owned aircraft, and videoconferencing. These investments enable suppliers to respond quickly to sales data beamed directly from stores, distribution centers to deliver new orders in less than 48 hours, and store managers to share best practice. The result: linked business processes that give Wal-Mart its competitive edge.

Kmart was constantly switching suppliers in search of price improvements. While Wal-Mart was controlling all the departments in its stores, Kmart was leasing out many of its departments to other companies on the theory that it could make more per square foot in rent than through its own efforts.

This is not to say that Kmart managers do not care about their business processes. After all, they have quality programs too. Nor is it that Wal-Mart managers ignore the structural dimension of strategy: they focus on the same consumer segments as Kmart and still have to make traditional strategic decisions like where to open new stores. The difference is that Wal-Mart emphasizes behavior – the organizational practices and business processes in which capabilities are rooted – as the primary object of strategy and therefore focuses its managerial attention on the infrastructure that supports capabilities. This subtle distinction has made all the difference between exceptional and average performance.

## Four principles of capabilities-based competition

The story of Kmart and Wal-Mart illustrates the new paradigm of competition in the 1990s. In industry after industry, established competitors are being outmaneuvered and overtaken by more dynamic rivals.

- In the years after World War II, Honda was a modest manufacturer of a 50 cc. engine designed to be attached to a bicycle. Today it is challenging General Motors and Ford for dominance of the global automobile industry.

- Xerox invented xerography and the office copier market. But between 1976 and 1982, Canon introduced more than 90 new models, cutting Xerox's share of the mid-range copier market in half.[1] Today Canon is a key competitor not only in mid-range copiers but also in high-end color copiers.
- The greatest challenge to department store giants like Macy's comes neither from other large department stores nor from small boutiques but from The Limited, a $5.25 billion design, procurement, delivery, and retailing machine that exploits dozens of consumer segments with the agility of many small boutiques.
- Citicorp may still be the largest U.S. bank in terms of assets, but Banc One has consistently enjoyed the highest return on assets in the U.S. banking industry and now enjoys a market capitalization greater than Citicorp's.

These examples represent more than just the triumph of individual companies. They signal a fundamental shift in the logic of competition, a shift that is revolutionizing corporate strategy.

When the economy was relatively static, strategy could afford to be static. In a world characterized by durable products, stable customer needs, well-defined national and regional markets, and clearly identified competitors, competition was a "war of position" in which companies occupied competitive space like squares on a chessboard, building and defending market share in clearly defined product or market segments. The key to competitive advantage was *where* a company chose to compete. *How* it chose to compete was also important but secondary, a matter of execution.

Few managers need reminding of the changes that have made this traditional approach obsolete. As markets fragment and proliferate, "owning" any particular market segment becomes simultaneously more difficult and less valuable. As product life cycles accelerate, dominating existing product segments becomes less important than being able to create new products and exploit them quickly. Meanwhile, as globalization breaks down barriers between national and regional markets, competitors are multiplying and reducing the value of national market share.

In this more dynamic business environment, strategy has to become correspondingly more dynamic. Competition is now a "war of movement" in which success depends on anticipation of market trends and quick response to changing customer needs. Successful competitors move quickly in and out of products, markets, and sometimes even entire businessess –a process more akin to an interactive video game than to chess. In such an environment, the essence of strategy is *not* the structure of a company's products and markets but the dynamics of its behavior. And the goal is to identify and develop the hard-to-imitate organizational capabilities that distinguish a company from its competitors in the eyes of customers.

Companies like Wal-Mart, Honda, Canon, The Limited, or Banc One have learned this lesson. Their experience and that of other successful companies suggest four basic principles of capabilities-based competition:

1. The building blocks of corporate strategy are not products and markets but business processes.
2. Competitive success depends on transforming a company's key processes into strategic capabilities that consistently provide superior value to the customer.
3. Companies create these capabilities by making strategic investments in a support infrastructure that links together and transcends traditional SBUs and functions.
4. Because capabilities necessarily cross functions, the champion of a capabilities-based strategy is the CEO.

A capability is a set of business processes strategically understood. Every company has business processes that deliver value to the customer. But few think of them as the primary object of strategy. Capabilities-based competitors identify their key business processes, manage them centrally, and invest in them heavily, looking for a long-term payback.

Take the example of cross-docking at Wal-Mart. Cross-docking is not the cheapest or the easiest way to run a warehouse. But seen in the broader context of Wal-Mart's inventory-replenishment capability, it is an essential part of the overall process of keeping retail shelves filled while also minimizing inventory and purchasing in truckload quantities.

What transforms a set of indvidual business processes like cross-docking into a strategic capability? The key is to connect them to real customer needs. A capability is strategic only when it begins and ends with the customer.

Of course, just about every company these days claims to be "close to the customer." But there is a qualitative difference in the customer focus of capabilities-driven competitors. These companies conceive of the organization as a giant feedback loop that begins with identifying the needs of the customer and ends with satisfying them.

As managers have grasped the importance of time-based competition, for example, they have increasingly focused on the speed of new product development. But as a unit of analysis, new product *development* is too narrow. It is only part of what is necessary to satisfy a customer and, therefore, to build an organizational capability. Better to think in terms of new product *realization*, a capability that includes the way a product is not only developed but also marketed and serviced. The longer and more complex the string of business processes, the harder it is to transform them into a capability – but the greater the value of that capability once built because competitors have more difficulty imitating it.

Weaving business processes together into organizational capabilities in this way also mandates a new logic of vertical integration. At a time when cost pressures are pushing many companies to out-source more and more activities, capabilities-based competitors are integrating vertically to ensure that they, not a supplier or distributor, control the performance of key business processes. Remember Wal-Mart's decision to own its transportation fleet in contrast to Kmart's decision to subcontract.

Even when a company doesn't actually own every link of the capability chain, the capabilities-based competitor works to tie these parts into its own business systems. Consider Wal-Mart's relationships with its suppliers. In order for Wal-Mart's inventory-replenishment capability to work, vendors have to change their own business processes to be more responsive to the Wal-Mart system. In exchange, they get far better payment terms from Wal-Mart than they do from other discount retailers. At Wal-Mart, the average "days payable," the time between the receipt of an invoice from a supplier and its payment, is 29 days. At Kmart, it is 45.

Another attribute of capabilities is that they are collective and cross-functional – a small part of many people's jobs, not a large part of a few. This helps explain why most companies underexploit capabilities-based competition. Because a capability is "everywhere and nowhere," no one executive controls it entirely. Moreover, leveraging capabilities requires a panoply of strategic investments across SBUs and functions far beyond what traditional cost-benefit metrics can justify. Traditional internal accounting and control systems often miss the strategic nature of such investments. For these reasons, building strategic capabilities cannot be treated as an operating matter and left to operating managers, to corporate staff, or still less to SBU heads. It is the primary agenda of the CEO.

Only the CEO can focus the entire company's attention on creating capabilities that serve customers. Only the CEO can identify and authorize the infrastructure investments on which strategic capabilities depend. Only the CEO can insulate individual managers from any short-term penalties to the P&Ls of their operating units that such investments might bring about.

Indeed, a CEO's success in building and managing capabilities will be the chief test of management skill in the 1990s. The prize will be companies that combine scale and flexibility to outperform the competition along five dimensions:

- *Speed.* The ability to respond quickly to customer or market demands and to incorporate new ideas and technologies quickly into products.
- *Consistency.* The ability to produce a product that unfailingly satisfies customers' expectations.

- *Acuity*. The ability to see the competitive environment clearly and thus to anticipate and respond to customers' evolving needs and wants.
- *Agility*. The ability to adapt simultaneously to many different business environments.
- *Innovativeness*. The ability to generate new ideas and to combine existing elements to create new sources of value.

## Becoming a capabilities-based competitor

Few companies are fortunate enough to begin as capabilities-based competitors. For most, the challenge is to become one.

The starting point is for senior managers to undergo the fundamental shift in perception that allows them to see their business in terms of strategic capabilities. Then they can begin to identify and link together essential business processes to serve customer needs. Finally, they can reshape the organization – including managerial roles and responsiblities – to encourage the new kind of behavior necessary to make capabilities-based competition work.

The experience of a medical-equipment company we'll call Medequip illustrates this change process. An established competitor, Medequip recently found itself struggling to regain market share it had lost to a new competitor. The rival had introduced a lower priced, lower performance version of the company's most popular product. Medequip had developed a similar product in response, but senior managers were hesitant to launch it.

Their reasoning made perfect sense according to the traditional competitive logic. As managers saw it, the company faced a classic no-win situation. The new product was lower priced but also lower profit. If the company promoted it aggressively to regain market share, overall profitability would suffer.

But when Medequip managers began to investigate their competitive situation more carefully, they stopped defining the problem in terms of static products and markets. Increasingly, they saw it in terms of the organization's business processes.

Traditionally, the company's functions had operated autonomously. Manufacturing was separate from sales, which was separate from field service. What's more, the company managed field service the way most companies do – as a classic profit center whose resources were deployed to reduce costs and maximize profitability. For instance, Medequip assigned full-time service personnel only to those customers who bought enough equipment to justify the additional cost.

However, a closer look at the company's experience with these steady customers led to a fresh insight: at accounts where Medequip had placed one or more full-time service representatives on-site, the company renewed its highly profitable service contracts at three times the rate of its other accounts. When these accounts needed new equipment, they chose Medequip twice as often as other accounts did and tended to buy the broadest mix of Medequip products as well.

The reason was simple. Medequip's on-site service representatives had become expert in the operations of their customers. They knew what equipment mix best suited the customer and what additional equipment the customer needed. So they had teamed up informally with Medequip's sales-people to become part of the selling process. Because the service reps were on-site full-time, they were also able to respond quickly to equipment problems. And of course, whenever a competitor's equipment broke down, the Medequip reps were on hand to point out the product's shortcomings.

This new knowledge about the dynamics of service delivery inspired top managers to rethink how their company should compete. Specifically, they redefined field service from a stand-alone function to one part of an integrated sales and service capability. They crystallized this new approach in three key business decisions.

First, Medequip decided to use its service personnel *not* to keep costs low but to maximize the lifecycle profitability of a set of targeted accounts. This decision took the form of a dramatic commitment to place at least one service rep on-site with selected customers – no matter how little business each account currently represented.

The decision to guarantee on-site service was expensive, so choosing which customers to target was crucial; there had to be potential for considerable additional business. The company divided its accounts into three categories: those it dominated, those where a single competitor dominated, and those where several competitors were present. Medequip protected the accounts it dominated by maintaining the already high level of service and by offering attractive terms for renewing service contracts. The company ignored those customers dominated by a single competitor – unless the competitor was having serious problems. All the remaining resources were focused on those accounts where no single competitor had the upper hand.

Next Medequip combined its sales, service, and order-entry organizations into cross-functional teams that concentrated almost exclusively on the needs of the targeted accounts. The company trained service reps in sales techniques so they could take full responsibility for generating new sales leads. This freed up the sales staff to focus on the more strategic role of understanding the long-term needs of the customer's business. Finally, to emphasize Medequip's new commitment to total service, the company even taught its service reps how to fix competitors' equipment.

Once this new organizational structure was in place, Medequip finally introduced its new lowprice product. The result: the company has not only stopped its decline in market share but also *increased* share by almost 50%. The addition of the lower priced product has reduced profit margins, but the overall mix still includes many higher priced products. And absolute profits are much higher than before.

This story suggests four steps by which any company can transform itself into a capabilities-based competitor:

*Shift the strategic framework to achieve aggressive goals.* At Medequip, managers transformed what looked like a no-win situation – either lose share or lose profits – into an opportunity for a major competitive victory. They did so by abandoning the company's traditional function, cost, and profit-center orientation and by identifying and managing the capabilities that link customer need to customer satisfaction. The chief expression of this new capabilities-based strategy was the decision to provide on-site service reps to targeted accounts and to create cross-functional sales and service teams.

*Organize around the chosen capability and make sure employees have the necessary skills and resources to achieve it.* Having set this ambitious competitive goal, Medequip managers next set about reshaping the company in terms of it. Rather than retaining the existing functional structure and trying to encourage coordination through some kind of matrix, they created a brand new organization – Customer Sales and Service – and divided it into "cells" with overall responsibility for specific customers. The company also provided the necessary training so that employees could understand how their new roles would help achieve new business goals. Finally, Medequip created systems to support employees in their new roles. For example, one information system uses CD-ROMs to give field-service personnel quick access to information about Medequip's product line as well as those of competitors.

*Make progress visible and bring measurements and reward into alignment.* Medequip also made sure that the company's measurement and reward systems reflected the new competitive strategy. Like most companies, the company had never known the profitability of individual customers. Traditionally, field-service employees were measured on overall service profitability. With the shift to the new approach, however, the company had to develop a whole new set of measures – for example, Medequip's "share-by-customer-by-product," the amount of money the company invested in servicing a particular customer, and the customer's current and estimated lifetime profitability. Team members' compensation was calculated according to these new measures.

*Do not delegate the leadership of the transformation.* Becoming a capabilities-based competitor requires an enormous amount of change. For that reason, it is a process extremely difficult to delegate. Because capabilities are cross-functional, the change process can't be left to middle managers. It requires the hands-on guidance of the CEO and the active involvement of top line managers. At Medequip, the heads of sales, service, and order entry led the subteams that made the actual recommendations, but it was the CEO who oversaw the change process, evaluated their proposals, and made the final decision. His leading role ensured senior management's commitment to the recommended changes.

This top-down change process has the paradoxical result of driving business decision making down to those directly participating in key processes – for example, Medequip's sales and service staff. This leads to a high measure of operational flexibility and an almost reflex-like responsiveness to external change.

## A new logic of growth: the capabilities predator

Once managers reshape the company in terms of its underlying capabilities, they can use these capabilities to define a growth path for the corporation. At the center of capabilities-based competition is a new logic of growth.

In the 1960s, most managers assumed that when growth in a company's basic business slowed, the company should turn to diversification. This was the age of the multibusiness conglomerate. In the 1970s and 1980s, however, it became clear that growth through diversification was difficult. And so, the pendulum of management thinking swung once again. Companies were urged to "stick to their knitting" – that is, to focus on their core business, identify where the profit was, and get rid of everything else. The idea of the corporation became increasingly narrow.

Competing on capabilities provides a way for companies to gain the benefits of both focus and diversification. Put another way, a company that focuses on its strategic capabilities can compete in a remarkable diversity of regions, products, and businesses and do it far more coherently than the typical conglomerate can. Such a company is a "capabilities predator" – able to come out of nowhere and move rapidly from nonparticipant to major player and even to industry leader.

Capabilities-based companies grow by transferring their essential business processes – first to new geographic areas and then to new businesses. Wal-Mart CEO David Glass alludes to this method of growth when he characterizes Wal-Mart as "always pushing from the inside out; we never jump and backfill."

Strategic advantages built on capabilities are easier to transfer geographically than more traditional competitive advantages. Honda, for example, has become a manufacturer in Europe and the United States with relatively few problems. The quality of its cars made in the United States is so good that the company is exporting some of them back to Japan.

In many respects, Wal-Mart's move from small towns in the South to large, urban, northern cities spans as great a cultural gap as Honda's move beyond Japan. And yet, Wal-Mart has done it with barely a hiccup. While the stores are much bigger and the product lines different, the capabilities are exactly the same. Wal-Mart simply replicates its system as soon as the required people are trained. The company estimates that it can train enough new employees to grow about 25% a year.

But the big payoff for capabilities-led growth comes not through geographical expansion but through rapid entry into whole new businesses. Capabilities-based companies do this in at least two ways. The first is by "cloning" their key business processes. Again, Honda is a typical example.

Most people attribute Honda's success to the innovative design of its products or the way the company manufactures them. These factors are certainly important. But the company's growth has been spearheaded by less visible capabilities.

For example, a big part of Honda's original success in motorcycles was due to the company's distinctive capability in "dealer management," which departed from the traditional relationship between motorcycle manufacturers and dealers. Typically, local dealers were motorcycle enthusiasts who were more concerned with finding a way to support their hobby than with building a strong business. They were not particularly interested in marketing, parts-in-ventory management, or other business systems.

Honda, by contrast, managed its dealers to ensure that they would become successful businesspeople. The company provided operating procedures and policies for merchandising, selling, floor planning, and service management. It trained all its dealers and their entire staffs in these new management systems and supported them with a computerized dealer-management information system. The part-time dealers of competitors were no match for the better prepared and better financed Honda dealers.

Honda's move into new businesses, including lawn mowers, outboard motors, and automobiles, has depended on re-creating this same dealer-management capability in each new sector. Even in segments like luxury cars, where local dealers are generally more service-oriented than those in the motorcycle business, Honda's skill at managing its dealers is transforming service standards. Honda dealers consistently receive the highest ratings for customer satisfaction among auto companies selling in the United States. One reason is that Honda gives its dealers far more autonomy to decide on the spot whether a needed repair is covered by warranty. (See the sidebar, "How Capabilities Differ from Core Competencies: The Case of Honda.")

But the ultimate form of growth in the capabilities-based company may not be cloning business processes so much as creating processes so flexible and robust that the same set can serve many different businesses. This is the case with Wal-Mart. The company uses the same inventory-replenishment system that makes its discount stores so successful to propel itself into new and traditionally distinct retail sectors.

Take the example of warehouse clubs, no-frills stores that sell products in bulk at a deep discount. In 1983, Wal-Mart created Sam's Club to compete with industry founder Price Club and Kmart's own PACE Membership Warehouse. Within four years, Sam's Club sales had passed those of both Price and PACE, making it the largest wholesale club in the country. Sam's 1990 sales were $5.3 billion, compared with $4.9 billion for Price and $1.6

billion for PACE. What's more, Wal-Mart has repeated this rapid penetration strategy in other retail sectors, including pharmacies, European-style hypermarkets, and large, no-frills grocery stores known as superstores.

While Wal-Mart has been growing by quickly entering these new businesses, Kmart has tried to grow by acquisition, with mixed success. In the past decade, Kmart has bought and sold a number of companies in unrelated businesses such as restaurants and insurance–an indication the company has had difficulty adding value.

This is not to suggest that growth by acquisition is necessarily doomed to failure. Indeed, the company that is focused on its capabilities is often better able to target sensible acquisitions and then integrate them successfully. For example, Wal-Mart has recently begun to supplement its growth "from the inside out" by acquiring companies–for example, other small warehouse clubs and a retail and grocery distributor–whose operations can be folded into the Wal-Mart system.

It is interesting to speculate where Wal-Mart will strike next. The company's inventory-replenishment capability could prove to be a strong competitive advantage in a wide variety of retail businesses. In the past decade, Wal-Mart came out of nowhere to challenge Kmart. In the next decade, companies such as Toys "R" Us (Wal-Mart already controls as much as 10% of the $13 billion toy market) and Circuit City (consumer electronics) may find themselves in the sights of this capabilities predator.

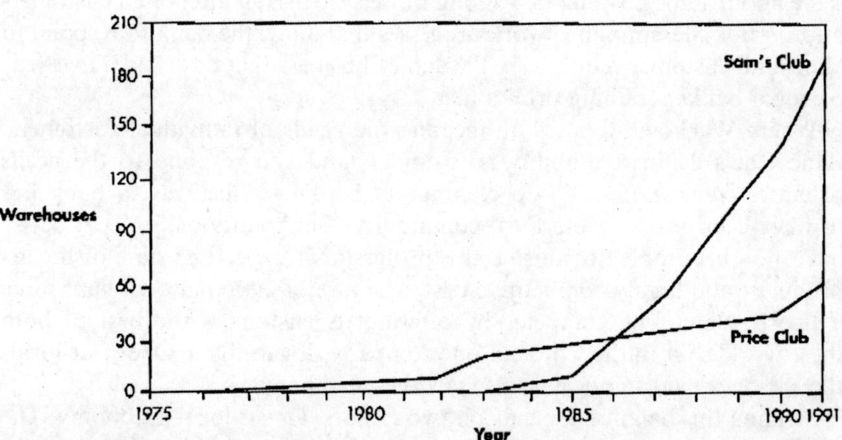


Portrait of a Capabilities Predator.

By applying capabilities developed in its core business, Wal-Mart was able to penetrate the wholesale club market quickly. Its unit, Sam's Club, overtook industry leader Price Club in a mere four years.

## The future of capabilities-based competition

For the moment, capabilities-based companies have the advantage of competing against rivals still locked into the old way of seeing the competitive environment. But such a situation won't last forever. As more and more companies make the transition to capabilities-based competition, the simple fact of competing on capabilities will become less important than the specific capabilities a company has chosen to build. Given the necessary long-term investments, the strategic choices managers make will end up determining a company's fate.

If Wal-Mart and Kmart are a good example of the present state of capabilities-based competition, the story of two fast-growing regional banks suggests its future. Wachovia Corporation, with dual headquarters in Winston-Salem, North Carolina and Atlanta, Georgia, has superior returns and growing market share throughout its core markets in both states. Banc One, based in Columbus, Ohio, has consistently enjoyed the highest return on assets in the U.S. banking industry. Both banks compete on capabilities, but they do it in very different ways.

Wachovia competes on its ability to understand and serve the needs of individual customers, a skill that manifests itself in probably the highest "cross-sell ratio"–the average number of products per customer – of any bank in the country. The linchpin of this capability is the company's roughly 600 "personal bankers," frontline employees who provide Wachovia's mass-market customers with a degree of personalized service approaching what has traditionally been available only to private banking clients. The company's specialized support systems allow each personal banker to serve about 1,200 customers. Among those systems: an integrated customer-information file, simplified work processes that allow the bank to respond to almost all customer requests by the end of business that day, and a five-year personal banker training program.

Where Wachovia focuses on meeting the needs of individual customers, Banc One's distinctive ability is to understand and respond to the needs of entire *communities*. To do community banking effectively, a bank has to have deep roots in the local community. But traditionally, local banks have not been able to muster the professional expertise, state-of-the-art products, and highly competitive cost structure of large national banks like Citicorp. Banc One competes by offering its customers the best of both these worlds. Or in the words of one company slogan, Banc One "out-locals the national banks and out-nationals the local banks."

Striking this balance depends on two factors. One is local autonomy. The central organizational role in the Banc One business system is played not by frontline employees but by the presidents of the 51 affiliate banks in the Banc One network. Affiliate presidents have exceptional power within their own region. They select products, establish prices and marketing strategy, make credit decisions, and set internal management policies. They can even overrule the activities of Banc One's centralized direct-marketing businesses. But while Banc One's affiliate system is highly decentralized, its success also depends on an elaborate, and highly centralized, process of continuous organizational learning. Affiliate presidents have the authority to mold bank products and services to local conditions, but they are also expected to learn from best practice throughout the Banc One system and to adapt it to their own operations.

Banc One collects an extraordinary amount of detailed and current information on each affiliate bank's internal and external performance. For example, the bank regularly publishes "league tables" on numerous measures of operating performance, with the worst performers listed first. This encourages collaboration to improve the weakest affiliates rather than competition to be the best. The bank also continously engages in work-flow re-engineering and process simplification. The 100 most successful projects, known as the "Best of the Best," are documented and circulated among affiliates.

Wachovia and Banc One both compete on capabilities. Both banks focus on key business processes and place critical decision-making authority with the people directly responsible for them. Both manage these processes through a support system that spans the traditional functional structure, and senior managers concentrate on managing this system rather than controlling decisions. Both are decentralized but focused, single-minded but flexible.

But there the similarities end. Wachovia responds to individual customers en masse with personalization akin to that of a private banker. Banc One responds to local markets en masse with the flexibility and canniness of the traditional community bank. As a result, they focus on different business processes: Wachovia on the transfer of customer-specific information across numerous points of customer contact; Banc One on the transfer of best practices across affiliate banks. They also empower different levels in the organization: the personal banker at Wachovia, the affiliate president at Banc One.

Most important, they grow differently. Because so much of Wachovia's capability is embedded in the training of the personal bankers, the bank has made few acquisitions and can integrate them only very slowly. Banc One's capabilities, by contrast, are especially easy to transfer to new acquisitions. All the company needs to do is install its corporate MIS and intensively train the acquired bank's senior officers, a process that can be done in a few months, as opposed to the much longer period it takes Wachovia to train a new cadre of frontline bankers. Banc One has therefore made acquisitions almost a separate line of business.

If Banc One and Wachovia were to compete against each other, it is not clear who would win. Each would have strengths that the other could not match. Wachovia's capability to serve individual customers by cross-selling a wide range of banking products will in the long term probably allow the company to extract more profit per customer than Banc One. On the other hand, Wachovia cannot adapt its products, pricing, and promotion to local market conditions the way Banc One can. And Wachovia's growth rate is limited by the amount of time it takes to train new personal bankers.

Moreover, these differences are deep-seated. They define each of the two companies in ways that are not easy to change. Capabilities are often mutually exclusive. Choosing the right ones is the essence of strategy.

## Note

1 See T. Michael Nevens, Gregory L. Summe, and Bro Uttal, "Commercializing Technology: What the Best Companies Do," HBR May–June 1990, p.154.

# 46

# QUALITY MANAGEMENT THROUGH VISIONARY LEADERSHIP

*Sonny Nwankwo and Bill Richardson*

Source: *Managing Service Quality* 6(4) (1996): 44–7.

## Abstract

States the importance of leadership in fostering a quality culture in organizations is widely acknowledged. However, research on leadership can be conducted at multiple levels of analysis. This has resulted in the complexity, diversity and ambiguity of information that typifies the leadership task. Identifies the visionary transformer leaders as the requisite leadership type for achieving success through quality-led strategic change. In the context of illustrations drawn from organizational experience of the past decade, and using Ansoff's growth vector as an underpinner, discusses how visionary translormer leaders use quality management strategy to secure the future of their organizations.

In highly competitive and homogeneous markets competitive moves are quickly copied. In such conditions, the very planned and autocratic approaches of the corporate planner and the classical administrator are unsuited to take the dominant influence positions in the strategic configuration.

Britain's declining industrial performance is well monitored and the situation endures wherein many UK companies are desperately in need of a recovery strategy. At the heart of the problem is the inability to come to terms with new environmental conditions of dynamism and hostility and a failure to continue to "delight" customers. Wider political, legal and societal issues increasingly affect today's organizations. For example, traditional "steady state" enterprises such as gas and telecommunications can now be threatened by decartelization and other information freeing, "perfect market" oriented legislation. In such circumstances the problem of "managerial obsolescence" intensifies in scale and scope. For many organizations, entrenched in traditional approaches to organization, there is a need for early and substantial reorganization towards improved environmental responsiveness, incorporating greater consumer satisfaction and more efficient operations – the hallmarks of quality management. This requires a thorough review of some of the taken-for-granted assumptions about organizational leaders in engineering successful turnarounds. Such a review might open up alternative forms of analysis within the orthodox formulation of leadership dynamics and could, perhaps, lead to a reconceptualization of leadership paradigms – widening and clarifying means for improving organizational responsiveness to the discontinuities of our time.

This paper explains why the "visionary transformer leader" has become a leader for our times and focuses on some of the important aspects of vision management. Using Ansoff's [1] growth vector as underpinner, the paper goes on to examine the espoused rationales of the visionary leader for adopting and implementing quality-driven strategic development. Illustrations from famous-name, visionary-led contexts of the past decade are interwoven into the text.

## Quality as a strategic weapon

Today, virtually all organizations are affected by the quality movement. Both empirical and anecdotal evidence suggest that organizations which successfully implanted the quality culture enjoy relative competitive advantage and superior growth in earnings[2]. It is no surprise, therefore, that strategists are concertedly exploring the quality domain with a view to, among other things, containing the complexities of modern business operating conditions and providing a counterbalance to the increasing vulnerability of market positions. According to much of the management literature on the topic, setting the strategic agenda, implementing and sustaining the quality culture falls, first, within the domain of organizational leaders[3]. Competence in quality management, therefore, underpins the visionary leader's approach to organizing a vision living organization system.

## Visionary leadership

These days, there is a discernible move away in strategic thinking from a preoccupation with attractive products and markets towards those competences[3] and capabilities[4,5] which underpin them. This perhaps explains the increasing attention to strategic leadership in contemporary management literature[6,7]. Essentially, the organization is a reflection of its leaders[8]. However, Finkelstein and Hambrick[9] argue that leaders vary in their:

> experiences, capabilities, values and personalities; these differences in turn cause executives to differ in their awarcness and interpretation of strategic stimuli, their aspiration levels, their beliefs about causation, even their beliefs about what it is they are trying to accomplish and how urgent it is.

Interpersonal and inspirational aspects of leadership embed the visionary transformer leader.

Ten characteristics of the successful visionary are: imaginative, experienced, intuitive and analytical; seeks excellence; oriented towards action; empowerer; calculating risk taker; independent; passion for achievement and workaholism; reward oriented; optimistic; powerful.

She/he is a leader who has special skills in creating new marketplace positions and in transforming traditionally "stuck" organizations and reorienting them towards the implementation of a winning vision of how and where the organization will compete. This is the leader who gains the commitment of his/her organization's people to the achievement, in a more pragmatic rather than linearsequential planned way, of the vision. She/he so clearly creates change through very personal leadership. The visionary, more clearly than any of the other leaders, creates an organization which reflects his/her own personality, style and preferences. She/he is the leader who "wins hearts and minds" and charismatically takes the organization into a new successful era. The process of visionary leadership involves the design of a desired future and the motivation of others in the organization to share it and commit themselves to taking personal responsibility for its achievement.

The term "vision management" is comparatively new to the modern management literatute[10]. The concept of vision management, however, has always underpinned leadership activity[11]. Mindful of the tendency for managers to see their world in terms of fashionable theory (for example, they might perceive "quality" as a current problem because theory is extolling it as such) we can nevertheless point to research studies which support the need for vision management to take a leading place in modern strategic systems[12,13].

## Visionary leadership, quality and product-market development strategy

Quality as a differentiator is a key ingredient in the successful visionary's organizational transformation recipe. Looking back over the past decade or so, it is clear that many UK-based visionary leaders have used the concept of quality to improve their marketplace performances. Visionaries have been seen to grow their organizations' competitive strengths through using quality as an underpinner of the following product-market developments.

### *Regaining lost ground*

For many organizations the strategic challenge has not been one of taking the organization into quality but, regaining its former marketplace position through getting it back to quality and closer to its customers and differentiating itself in the eyes of customers from its competitors. Often this enables the organization to obtain price premiums compared to its competitors. For example, Jaguar's return to quality and concomitantly, profitability in the 1980 was largely due to John Egan's quality-driven management approach. At British Airways (BA), leadership came from two people at the top: Lord King and Sir Colin Marshall. With their assistance, the BA culture eventually became more customer focused, somewhat more sensitive to cost, productivity and profits, and more encouraging of initiative from employees. BA now prides itself as the "world's favourite airline". At SAS, the new culture emerged after Jan Carlzon became chief executive officer in 1981. That culture placed a high premium on serving targeted groups of customers, was more supportive of leadership up and down the hierarchy, was somewhat more concerned with making a profit and paid a great deal of attention to employees.

### *Consolidating existing market position*

Practical applications of the quality concept also lie at the heart of mass market leaders' continued success. In industries where goods are often homogeneous and customers shop around, firms watch what is happening in the marketplace, follow the moves of competitors and, if possible, try to be the first with original marketing approaches. Quality of service and customer responsiveness is essential to competing effectively on an ongoing basis. British Telecom, under the leadership of Ian Vallance, instituted "Operation Sovereign" and quality-based cultural change programmes in its efforts to maintain its position in an increasingly competitive marketplace.

### *Moving into new products and/or new markets*

Greendale Electronics Limited, struggling in the low technology production industry in the early 1980s, moved into high profitability through entering the higher value-added, high technology, electronic components manufacturing segment. Success came from a new organizational attention to quality which extends to the point of refusing to make products to "inferior customer specification". Greendale's newly incumbent managing director Colin Wemyss argued that, "In the end, there is only one answer and that is quality. That is where we defeat them" – an assertion which is difficult to refute when backed by net asset growth from £23,000 to £538,000 and share price up from 5p to £1.65 over a five-year period.

A similar theme runs through the success story of BSC Cumbria Engineering where, after initial trauma and failure, improved quality assurance schemes have enabled a transition away from its steel fabrications base (and poor prospects) into commercial success in nuclear equipment manufacture. Another famous-name, UK example of a visionary-led, quality oriented organizational reorientation through new market development is that of ICI in the mid-1980s. Under Sir John Harvey-Jones, the company undertook a cultural rite of passage from product orientation to market orientation.

### *Creating new markets*

In talking with visionaries about their market positions comparative to other marketplace players, it is often difficult to obtain from them a clear evaluation of how they stand competitively speaking. Sometimes this is not so much because they have failed to monitor their marketplaces but more to do with their having created a new marketplace – one which has been created because of the new way in which the visionary's organization operates. In the early days of this operation the visionary probably does not have direct "interfirm" rivals. Customers have been seen to "flock" to the newly created marketplaces of George Davies' Next (when his affordable exclusivity concept changed the face of high-street fashion retailing in the 1980s and attracted customers prepared to pay the 10 per cent-above-Marks & Spencer's prices his organization charged) or to the "speciality" retail operation of Kroustie European Bread Ltd. The ability to "redefine the mundane" is a tremendous success generator and a strong indication that a successful visionary is at work at the helm of the organization. Anita Roddick's leadership of Body Shop provides another example of a visionary who, over the past decade or so, has created a new market within the general cosmetics industry.

### *Attracting higher prices*

Visionary-led organizations tend to create their better-than-average performances through improving "top lines" (prices) more than they do through reducing "bottom lines" (costs of operations). Their abilities to provide particularly attractive products and services command premium prices. Of course, charging higher prices in conditions where customers are prepared to pay, is perhaps the easiest way of all to improved productivity and successful financial performance. The customer-responsive, quality-based operations of visionary-led organizations can lock in customers, at least in the early stages of the "new" operation, and create huge price-premium-based profit outcomes. Bill Gates' ability to do this through his Microsoft organization made him the second-richest man in the USA in the mid-1990s.

In the UK, and in a smaller organizational setting, Martin Port is developing a successful business retailing speciality bread. People working with Martin describe how he attends personally to the detail of any new operations – at the outset of a new venture he is a "tremendous worrier". They also comment on his great concern to ensure that, after systems have been set up, each aspect of the operation produces a high quality outcome. Once the new venture is up and running he hands over to his managers but keeps a watchful eye over things and goes back in again if the venture is not operating to his satisfaction.

### *Pleasing powerful customers*

In an increasingly quality conscious organizational world some big corporations have insisted that their smaller suppliers obtain a recognized quality certificate such as that provided under the standard BS 5750. This has provided an opportunity for some early compliers to "steal a march" on more tardy competitors by entrenching themselves with powerful customers and at the same time getting inside what becomes a barrier to potential future entrants into quality accredited markets.

### *Gaining cost-improvement-based productivity*

Although visionary organizations seem most often to emphasize quality in its external, differentiating role, it makes much sense for the quality concept to be applied in its lower (if not "least") cost producing capacity. First, it should be obvious that a differentiated position will only produce good financial performance if costs of production are maintained at lower than the level of sales turnover. Some potentially successful visionary leaders have failed to create successful organization because they have emphasized a marketingled approach to the exclusion of the marketing-controlled approach. Second, in reorientation situations where a new leader is called on to improve the flagging performance of an established organization, a first area for productive attack is often the "operating slack" which has built up in the system over previous years. In this context, the quality literature of the past decade has provided some impressive examples of efficiency savings being generated by quality improvement programmes. Importantly, preventive quality control, because of its propensity to reduce costs associated with quality appraisal and quality failure, is seen as the key to release the massive savings available.

### *Quality and people-empowerment strategy*

According to the literature, the visionary leader is adept at empowering his personnel. An empowered individual is one who is committed to the organizational cause and who has been given discretion to make decisions at "critical moments" and to act in self-chosen ways for the betterment of the organization. Kanter[14] provides an impressive array of illustrations.

## Conclusion

This era of quality movement throws up new challenges for organizational leaders. These challenges (and problems) are still being investigated and the requisite skills being honed. This paper shows how visionary leaders are facing up to the task of leading their organizations through the discontinuities of our time. Visionary leaders focus on quality, and exemplify the critical leadership competence in quality management, as a basis for successful strategic development.

## References

1 Ansoff, I., *Corporate Strategy*, Penguin, London, 1987.
2 Powell, T., "Total quality management as competitive advantage: a review and empirical study", *Strategic Management Journal*, Vol. 16, 1995, pp. 15–37.
3 Nwankwo, S. and Richardson, B., "Reviewing service quality in the public sector", in Curwen *et al.* (Eds), *Public Sector in Transition*, Pavic, Sheffield, 1994.
4 Prahalad, C. and Hamel, G., "The core competence of the corporation", *Harvard Business Review*, May/June 1990, pp. 79–91.
5 Stalk, G., Evans, P. and Shulman, L., "Competing on capabilities: the new rules for corporate strategy", *Harvard Business Review*, March/April 1992.
6 Nichols, J., "The strategic leadership star, a guiding light in delivering value to the customer". *Management Decision*, Vol. 32 No. 8, 1994, pp. 21–6.
7 Taylor, B., "The new strategic leadership – driving change, getting results", *Long Range Planning*, Vol. 28 No. 5, 1995, pp. 71–81.
8 Hambrick, D. and Mason, P., "Upper echelons: the organization as a reflection of its top managers", *Academy of Management Review*, Vol. 9, 1984, pp. 193–206.
9 Finkelstein, S. and Hambrick, D., *Strategic Leadership*, West Publishing, St Paul, MN, 1996.
10 Larwood, L., Falbe, C., Kriger, M. and Miesing, P., "Structure and meaning of organizational vision". *Academy of Management Journal*, Vol. 38 No. 3, 1995, pp. 740–69.
11 Quigley, J., "Vision how leaders develop it, share it, and sustain it?", *Business Horizons*, September/October 1994, pp. 37–41.
12 Schoemaker, P., "How to link strategic vision to core capability", *Sloan Management Review*, Fall 1992, pp. 67–81.
13 Collins, J. and Porras, J., "Building a visionary company", *Califomia Management Review*, Vol. 37 No. 2, 1995, pp. 80–100.
14 Kanter, R. M., *When Giants Leam to Dance: Mastering the Challenges of Strategy, Management and Careers in the 1990s*, Unwin Hyman, London, 1990.

# Part 6

# STRATEGIC THINKING: THE PAST

# 47

# STRATEGY CHANGES

## Possible worlds and actual minds

*Edward H. Bowman*

Source: J. W. Frederickson (ed.) *Perspectives on Strategic Management*, New York: Harper Business, 1990, pp. 9–37.

> Once or twice she had peeped into the book her sister was reading, but it had no pictures or conversation in it, and "what is the use of a book," thought Alice, "without pictures or conversation?"
>
> —Lewis Carroll, *Alice in Wonderland* (p. 19)

> The thought crept in: it was probably more useful to go back than to go on. It was just faintly possible he might learn more from what he had left out of his forty years of reporting than to go on and add more observation.
>
> —Theodore White, *In Search of History* (p. 3)

This chapter examines strategy as it has changed over the past three decades, primarily in several university courses but also in the "real world." Part of the argument put forward will be that the courses we teach are influenced by strategy thought in the industrial enterprise, and that this thought, in turn, is influenced by the secular state of the economy. We shall look at two courses in order to discuss this history and to explore the current state of strategy research. Comments about this research, how it is changing, and what changes we might prefer, will end the chapter. I believe a discussion of the two courses, one professional and the other research, offers a chance to argue for what isn't available, based on what is.

## Experience in two courses

### *The professional course*

The academic field of policy/strategy went through a major shift, virtually a birth, in the 1960s and has subsequently gone through two minor shifts in the 1970s and 1980s. Before the sixties, many business schools required a business policy course as a capstone to graduate education in their MBA programs. The course was offered toward the end of the program and had the task of "tying together" all the functional courses previously taken in the program. The course was to be not only integrative but "professional"; that is, it was to correspond to the issues as faced by top management in the world of practice.

One unintended consequence of such a course design was that it became difficult to prepare young faculty for this task in their own graduate education. There was not a visible or cohesive field of research, published and available for study, and consequently, the road to promotion and tenure for young faculty was not an easy one. Though all of the above observations may still be relevant, it is clear that they have also started to become dated.

The strategy area started to change in the 1960s. It became more focused as a field of its own, not just an amalgam of other fields. As the field started to develop rapidly, new books and then other literature became available, more research started to appear, and elective, follow-on courses were added. Numerous doctoral programs in strategy were eventually a consequence of these changes. These programs, in turn, created markets in business schools for strategy faculty members. So far, the progression sounds quite good, but the story is not without problems. We will return to the earlier decade to understand those problems.

Three books became available in the 1960s, at the time I was introducing a new MBA course in business policy and strategy. I built the course around these books. Alfred Chandler's (1962) *Strategy and Structure*, written at MIT, is the exemplar of business history books. It explored the history of four large American corporations in the early part of this century as they grew in response to a changing economic environment, diversified, and changed their organizations. Chandler introduced a number of ideas about corporate strategy based, according to him, not on a priori theory but on his understanding of the stories as they unfolded. Though a historian, Chandler is also an empiricist in the following sense. Howard Gardner (1985:8), in his recent book *The Mind's New Science*, discusses the history of philosophy: "In philosophy, I trace the perennial dispute between those of a rationalist persuasion (who view the mind as actively organizing experiences on the basis of pre-existing schemes), and those of an empiricist bent (who treat mental processes as a reflection of information obtained from the environment)." Hence, Chandler is a true empiricist. This distinction between rationalists and empiricists is an important one that will reappear again in this chapter.

The second book appearing in the 1960s was from the more rationalist school–it was certainly not empirical. Igor Ansoff at Carnegie-Mellon wrote the first book to be titled *Corporate Strategy* (1965). It took a programmatic approach to the topic and laid out an explicit sequence of issues to be considered. I think it is fair to call this work an engineering treatment–it certainly was written from an engineer's perspective. It took an analytic approach to the decisions embedded in corporate strategy: What would be the product/market? What would be the competitive advantage? What would be the synergy (the first use of this label)? What would be the "growth vector"? And what would be the make-or-buy choices? This book, as well as the Chandler book, placed substantial emphasis on diversification; we shall return to this point.

The third book of importance was more of a textbook than the first two. It was *Business Policy: Text and Cases* by Learned, Christensen, Andrews, and Guth (1965). In the style of the Harvard Business School, half of the book was cases. But the other half of the book, written largely by Ken Andrews, had chapters devoted to the issues of strategy formulation (Book I) and strategy implementation (Book II). As with Ansoff, *Business Policy* presented a rationalist view of the construction of corporate strategy, but the constructs presented were, according to the authors, "a simple practitioner's theory, a kind of Everyman's conceptual scheme" (p. viii). The business cases, of course, supply one form of empiricism. Again, many of the cases dealt with the issues of diversification, expansion, and growth.

### *History parallels*

I believe one can make the argument that the emphasis on growth, expansion, and diversification in the 1960s is, at least in part, a reflection of the American economy at that time. Opportunities seemed to be everywhere, and a firm could look at its own strengths and decide where the next move might be made. In contrast, little consideration had to be given to threats from foreign competition. To paraphrase an expression, the United States was the most favored nation. Therefore, American firms could, essentially, consider their own wishes and strengths and plan for future growth in a relatively unconstrained fashion.

Three partners at McKinsey wrote a paper some years later that captured the spirit of this argument. In "Strategic Management for Competitive Advantage," Gluck, Kaufman, and Walleck (1980) made the case that over time strategy thinking had gone through at least four stages—budgets, long-range planning, strategic planning, and strategic management. The stage in the 1960s was long-range planning. (By extension, budgeting would have been the stage in the 1940s and 1950s—and only the young would think that budgets were never new and didn't go through the classical diffusion process.)

Long-range planning considered the balanced development of all the functions of the business so that growth would not be constrained by the "logistics" of any element—people, equipment, technology, products, finances. But it was essentially, though not entirely, a look *within* the firm. *The New Yorker* (1987) made the same distinction concerning writers and poets. There, the distinction was between "mirror-writers" (for example, Emily Dickinson) and "window-writers" (Walt Whitman). In strategy, the emphasis in the 1960s was on the mirror.

The next stage in the McKinsey group's formulation is strategic planning, where the recommendation is to look outside the firm, that is, through the window, not in the mirror. The focus in this transition period (the 1970s) is on the specific industry. Industrial organization, theory from economics deals almost entirely with this orientation, and Michael Porter's book *Competitive Strategy* (published in 1980, but preceded by his articles in the 1970s) is the exemplar for this period. My strategy course for MBA students made this transition comfortably.

The emphasis of this period was on the firm within its industry and on the important actors with whom it must cope—suppliers, competitors, potential entrants, substitute products, and customers. As is traditional in economics, all of these actors were considered adversaries who tended to drive profits toward zero (at least with respect to "excess profits," or "rents"). Therefore, as the American economy offered expansion in the 1960s, so it offered stagnation (or "stagflation") in the 1970s, which change corresponded to the strategy field's emphasis on industry focus, industrial organization, and transition.

In the 1980s, we move into global competitiveness (balance-of-payments trauma) and a somewhat wider set of strategic considerations. In this period, the literature focus widens considerably (Porter 1985; Hayes and Wheelwright 1984; Rappaport 1986; Itami/Roehl 1987; Teece 1987), as do the strategic issues. We now see the McKinsey "strategic management" stage, which deals with a strategic treatment of all the elements of the firm—people, skills, technology, information, finance—to see if they are consistent with strategy and can be made more *competitive*. The industrial world sees "restructuring" on every hand, which is in part a response to the "market for corporate control." This shift acknowledges the pervasive nature of global competition.

Although some actors were identified as adversaries by industrial organization theory and economics, strategy now has more explicit input from sociology, and a resulting reconsideration of those actors in a potentially nonadversarial relationship. This is clearly the case in the sequence of suppliers, competitors, and customers; each and every one may be our partner. Early sourcing, technology sharing, quality cooperation, and just-in-time inventories are now the new look in suppliers. Customers may now be thought of as our best source of new product ideas, and they use our computers and information systems for logistics (and by extension, all of the previous ideas about suppliers hold because we are their suppliers). Even competitors may now be viewed as engaged in a cooperative (nonzero-sum game) relationship. For example, chemical industry firms share expertise on toxic spills and lobby Washington together; these firms even return to the old-fashioned idea of cooperative-mutual insurance underwriting for environmental risk because, for a while, the commercial insurance industry abandoned them (Bowman and Kunreuther 1988).

So the American economy, in the brief span of three decades since the birth of strategy as an academic endeavor (and since the beginning of my MBA course as well), has taken us from opportunities to transition to difficulty, from diversification to focus to global competitiveness, and from long-range planning to strategic planning to strategic management.

During the span of these three decades, the complex issue of the firm's performance measures has also shifted. While the issue of goals and performance may continue to be viewed from the standpoint not only of the firm itself but also of the firm in society (social welfare) and the top management in the firm (agency), the major performance concern for the firm may have shifted from growth to return on investment, to market over book value ratio (or Tobin's Q). The society, the firm, and the top-level manager continue to have interacting goals that are made more complex by the trade-off between short-term and long-term considerations. These complexities may reflect, in part, the shifts over the three decades mentioned earlier.

The industrial world, consulting practice, and even the professional literature seem to have followed the same path through the 1960s, 1970s, and 1980s. However, systematic and empirical strategy research has followed a less clear path. The "professional" course for MBAs that I have taught at three schools (Yale, MIT, and Wharton) during these three decades was relatively easy to map to the above pattern, using a combination of conceptual material and business cases, because the history of strategy practice has been followed reasonably closely in the professional literature of strategy. Research developments have not followed this history as closely.

### *The research course*

A research course that I began fifteen years ago has been a somewhat more taxing exercise. In 1973 I decided to offer a research seminar in corporate strategy, essentially for doctoral students. I searched for two dozen articles for the seminar—two each for twelve or thirteen weeks—that were (1) published, (2) empirical, (3) research, and (4) about strategy—and this was fifteen years ago. I still teach the course, and for each reading, the students and I discuss "questions or topics, received theory and literature, methods of research, data sources, tests and treatments, alternative approaches, findings and conclusions, presentation style, problems and flaws, meaning to managers, and other comments."

It probably is no surprise that it took me quite a while to find the twenty-four papers that I was looking for from the journals that existed then. I wanted a course that was organized around what I thought was fairly interesting and good strategy research. In my judgment, there were no journals in strategy at that time. With a few odds and ends from elsewhere, the articles were pulled primarily from six, more general journals: *Administrative Science Quarterly, Management Science*, and *Bell Journal of Economics and Management Science* (since known as the *Bell Journal of Economics*, and now known as the *Rand Journal of Economics*); and three school Journals —*Harvard Business Review, Sloan Management Review*, and *California Management Review*.

It has been possible since that time to greatly modify my collection of research articles, especially with the introduction of the *Strategic Management Journal* at the beginning of the 1980s. (Yet it may surprise today's professors that I still occasionally use some papers from that first set of selections, like Pfeffer's [1972] "Size and Composition of Corporate Boards of Directors," Fouraker and Stopford's [1968] "Organizational Structure and Multinational Strategy," and Altman's [1973] "Predicting Railroad Bankruptcies in America.") With two dozen research articles, it is possible to cover *many* kinds of problems, theoretical fields, methodologies, data sources, and presentation styles. Over the years it has become easier to find articles that touch on most major facets of our field of strategy.

Along with the research articles covered in this doctoral seminar, I always try to have book reports in the spirit of the articles. That is, I want each student to report on a research book—not a text, not a speculative book, but a *research* work for which some author/researcher has gone out and looked at a particular problem, gathered descriptive material, applied some theory, and explained to the reader what it meant, in book form. Finding such books was even more difficult than finding the articles because I wanted about a dozen. Something that we really lack (to go to a conclusion before developing the argument) is good research books in strategy written by people who have done a big enough job that they can write books about their work. I will eventually mention five or six that I like, but there should be twenty or thirty available to us.

One positive difference from a decade ago that I see in strategy today, one which is manifest in my research seminar, is that we've brought in theories from a number of other domains. We are now doing fairly interesting strategy research based on half a dozen related theoretical fields—finance theory, industrial organization theory, population ecology theory, transaction costs theory, resource dependency theory, and behavioral decision theory. Ten years ago one would have had to stretch to find a single good study—which we would agree was a strategy study—that drew on the theories of these fields.

In my research seminar I have at least one paper from each of these six fields. In finance, I use a paper by Amihud and Lev (1981), who look at agency theory and diversification. They argue that firms diversify, if the manager controls the firm, to protect against employment risks of the top managers. This paper has the added advantage that its authors demonstrate their argument with two completely different types of data and analysis. In industrial organization, I use a chapter on the corn wet milling oligopoly from a book by Porter and Spence (1982); it is a very involved study using scenario analysis and simulation with corporate data. It has the attribute of "rational expectations" (about competitor behavior) as an important element of the analysis. (Note that all of these studies have data; I don't use papers that lack some kind of strong evidence. They may not all have the same kind of evidence, but they are all empirical works.) I also use a paper related to population ecology: Langton's (1984) work on Wedgwood Pottery and how it developed over an interesting fifty-year period two centuries ago. It is a combination of bureaucracy theory and social Darwinism, showing the interaction of internal and external developments. (It should be noted that Perrow [1985] wrote a scathing criticism of the article in the next journal issue from a power and welfare standpoint, and that Langton had a chance to respond.)

Intellectual exchanges or arguments like the one between Langton and Perrow are quite useful, but they are not as common in our field as they should be. Perhaps this is a sign of the immaturity of strategy literature. Laudan (1977: 46–47) makes an important point in this regard:

> If we look at the reception of Darwin's evolutionary biology, Freud's psychoanalytic theories, Skinner's behaviorism, or modern quantum mechanics, the same pattern repeats itself. Alongside of the rehearsal of empirical anomalies and solved empirical problems, both critics and proponents of a theory often invoke criteria of theoretical appraisal which have nothing whatever to do with a theory's capacity to solve the empirical problems of the relevant scientific domain. . . . Rather than seeking to learn something about the complex nature of scientific rationality from such cases, philosophers (with regret) and sociologists (with delight) have generally taken them as tokens of the irrationality of science as actually practiced.

For transaction costs theory, I use a paper by Walker and Webber (1984) that examines organization boundaries and vertical integration, drawing on Williamson's (1975) work. It looks in a new way at external sourcing by the automobile industry. For resource dependency, I use a paper by Hirsch (1975) that compares the ability of the pharmaceutical and phonograph record industries to cope with important facets of their respective environments. It shows how important "gatekeepers" can be. For behavioral decision theory, I use my own paper (Bowman 1982) on risk seeking by troubled firms, which draws on Tversky and Kahneman's (1981) prospect theory. It moves beyond a standard financial view of corporate risk.

I offer the above articles as illustrations of the way that I think our field is changing by drawing on the best new theories from a wide variety of disciplines. We do this in part because we don't have our own central paradigm. But *even if we did*, these theories ought to be brought in; I feel that they enrich the strategy field.

## Observations from research

### *No central paradigm*

The above discussion illustrates an often discussed characteristic of the strategy field—it has no central paradigm. The lack of a central paradigm in strategy will probably continue and is undoubtedly due to a number of factors. One reason is that the underlying social science fields on which strategy currently draws are economics and sociology—or to stretch just a bit, the rational and the natural (Scott 1981; Pfeffer 1982). These two perspectives are very different, yet they are both useful. The contrast between them on one issue—the purpose of the firm—highlights their differences. Though "maximization" (from economics) is sometimes utilized as a concept in strategy, purpose and performance are still at issue. Therefore, academics are still asking, "What is one to maximize?" and, "Who is the actor?" The sociologists' questions would be "Why and how should the firm survive?" and "For what function?"

Another reason for the continued absence of a central paradigm is that the interests represented in strategy are as disparate as those between physics and civil engineering, as between theory and practice. There is a big difference between positive science and professional design. (One meaning of *design*, as noted later, is Simon's [1969] process of changing *existing* situations into *preferred* ones. To oversimplify, it is the distinction between "what is" and "how to.") While they may be related to each other, their practitioners consider almost entirely different questions. One of the problems in graduate education for strategy is that one can make a reasonable case for including major elements from both positive science and professional design. Another problem is that most faculty specialize in only one of these areas and neither understand nor appreciate the other. It is a little bit like Adam Smith's pin makers, who specialize in either the heads or the points of the pins.

Because the problems of design are so broad—and one can consider strategy as an exercise in design—it is unlikely that either school will ever be dominant. This is particularly true when we consider the four levels of strategy now extant in the literature. I refer to institutional strategy, corporate strategy, business strategy, and functional strategy. To be brief, institutional strategy deals with fitting the firm comfortably into the legal, political, and social environments in which it operates; corporate strategy deals with the allocations, interactions, reinforcements, and economies of scale and scope among various business units of a firm, as well as choosing those units; business strategy deals with how a unit will position itself within a particular product market, considering the many dimensions available to it; and functional strategy deals with how a function (for example, marketing, R&D, or human resources) might seek to respond to the demands and opportunities it encounters. How could one central paradigm really cope with all these issues? What might result from attempts to provide a central paradigm is "reductionism," where much of the situation is assumed away by those constructing their preferred model. Reductionism in constructing a central paradigm is an ever present tendency and carries the risk of riding roughshod over the issues.

I generally believe that it is not bad that strategy does not have a central paradigm; we should continually bring in research work that is based on related areas (as I have illustrated). However, my research seminar continues to be based primarily on the mainstream of strategy work. Therefore, I should mention at least two articles out of the many that are somewhat closer to our central focus. I use the Woo and Cooper (1981) paper, "Strategies of Effective Low Share Businesses." They use Profitability Impact of Market Strategy (PIMS) data in a comparative analysis across types of industries of high share/low share and high profit/low profit businesses; they also cleverly analyze business strategy within these pseudo-industries. I also use Bourgeois' (1980) "Performance and Consensus," which investigates the relationships between top management teams' goals and strategy consensus on the one hand, and the performance of their firms on the other. Its empirical challenge to conventional planning wisdom is refreshing.

We are fortunate in strategy to have many research articles such as these to draw from. They present theoretical foundations, report analyses, provide evidence, draw conclusions, and ruminate on the import of their findings. Though these articles are unevenly distributed across the various levels of strategy (that is, institutional, corporate, business, and functional)—an issue to be discussed later—at least some are available as illustrations of each of the levels, and I am able to sample from each level for the research seminar.

### *Strategy research books*

As mentioned earlier, my research seminar also incorporates a discussion of research books. The books that I offer as examples are Chandler (1962), Bower (1970), Allison (1971), Cohen and March (1974), Rumelt (1974), Miles and Snow (1978), and Miles and Cameron (1982). Each of these books actually takes a *detailed* look at an important problem. They all have data; they all draw some conclusions; and they are all written in the depth that allows you to really get a sense of what the authors are talking about. You can read some studies that leave you asking, "Did this author really tell me anything?" The people who wrote the above books found something important in their research. I will read them again, and I can tell you about these books after I have read them.

There are no doubt other books that I could use as illustration, but these few will serve the purposes of my argument. Chandler (1962), mentioned earlier as part of my professional course for MBAs, still qualifies in my mind as a research book. Similarly, Bower's (1970) *Managing the Resource Allocation Process* gives us some sense of how large resource commitments are made within the diversified firm, how these are influenced by various levels of managers within the firm (with different roles), and how these commitments are derived from the developing strategy of the firm. Allison's (1971) *Essence of Decision*, though admittedly not about strategy, is a splendid empirical investigation of decision making in a crisis atmosphere (the Cuban Missile Crisis) and illustrates three very different modes of thought regarding organizational behavior.

As business educators we are dealing with two kinds of practitioners, the manager and the academic, both of whom can learn from examples. The manager typically learns from case studies, with which he or she can identify. The first, third, and fifth chapters of Allison's book present the models (and theories) that he wishes to explain. The second, fourth, and sixth chapters tell the story of the Cuban Missile Crisis, each chapter relying to *some* extent on the theory chapter preceding it. Over and over in my professional course in strategy, in which I also use this book, I have asked manager-students which set of chapters they appreciate most. The answer is always the story chapters. The story chapters are "peopled" and narrative. To quote Alice, they have both "pictures and conversations."

The academic practitioner also learns by example, even when it is theory that is being learned. I have found that one of the best kinds of comparative analysis (an extension here of Glaser and Strauss's [1967] arguments) is a Ph.D. student discussion comparing one published research piece with another. What did the different authors assume? What theories did they draw on? What were the differences in the constructs that they developed? How did they obtain their data? What statistical methodologies did they use (if any, if appropriate, and if powerful)? What conclusions did they reach? This "discovery of grounded theory" is itself a theory of practice.

The difference between the manager and the academic is, of course, the nature of their practice. Borrowing from Herbert Simon's (1969) ideas, one can argue that a, perhaps *the*, key element in research for the academic practitioner is the idea of design. How will this study be put together? For academics, a systematic investigation and group discussion of exemplars is perhaps the best kind of education. After such formal training, the academic must continue to learn from examples for the next forty or fifty years. The process can be discovered by the individual, but it should be enhanced with the appropriate treatment during the more formal education years.

To return to my identification of research books, the Cohen and March (1974) book *Leadership and Ambiguity*, which was reissued in 1986 with added appendixes, develops their "garbage can" theory of organizational decision making in the context of American college presidencies. The Rumelt (1974) book, *Strategy, Structure, and Economic Performance*, is an early study of the relationship between strategy, structure, and performance. Here the reader is offered a taxonomy of relative diversification, as well as the empirically grounded, apparent superiority of relatedness in diversification (something Ansoff [1965] had developed conceptually).

The Miles and Snow (1978) book, *Organization Strategy, Structure, and Process*, is a good example of a research book that has been extended with enough theory and commentary that some may use it as a textbook. Nevertheless, they investigated in some depth a series of industries, and companies within the industries, in order to develop (not unlike the "discovery of grounded theory" proposed by Glaser and Strauss) the theory of generic types of strategy, to understand their underlying rationale, and to describe the derivative behavior that one can anticipate with each generic type.

The Miles and Cameron (1982) book, *Coffin Nails and Corporate Strategy*, is also a splendid research book; it explored tobacco industry firms as they responded to the threat posed by the surgeon general's report on smoking. It is here that one sees generic strategies in use, as well as the stages in strategic response—domain defense (institutional strategy), domain offense (business strategy), and domain creation (corporate strategy). In addition, and beyond the usual industrial organization theory of competition, one observes cooperation with competitors and the important role of the government—something present in many of our industries.

## Changes preferred

Based on my view of the past three decades, there are a number of changes that I believe are needed in strategy research. They are offered as *additions* to our agenda; it is not subtractions from our present orientation but additions to future explorations that I prefer.

### *More research books*

The first of my preferences is for more research books. One of the interesting and somewhat puzzling aspects of research books is that, although the field of strategy has many fewer than I would like, it has more than most of our sister fields in the business school. If one explores the fields of marketing and finance, for instance, one finds that they are prolific with research activity but seem to have few research books.

Research books in strategy offer many advantages over what we normally see in journal articles. For example, a topic can be investigated both more deeply and more richly. The theory, developed or received, can be full enough so that the constructs of interest can be well argued and justified by the author. Too often in a journal article the author must move too quickly from received theory, through surrogate variable and constructs, to measurement. Similarly, all too often the measurement is driven by the variables available, as in PIMS, and the constructs for which the measured variables are taken are not well thought out.

Books can also offer protection against reductionism, whereas a paper, apparently for reasons of space, must emphasize only a central argument. One especially common result of this problem appears in the concluding paragraphs of many papers, which offer normative statements for the manager. A classic ploy here is to take (a) a static analysis of (b) the correlation between/among variables, and then turn it into (c) a dynamic recommendation for (d) a causal chain between/among variables. While poorly written research books may also do this, fewer space limitations give book authors an opportunity to discuss at some length such suggestions for practice.

A further advantage of a research book, if the author has sought both theoretical patterns and empirical evidence, is that it offers the chance not only to inform the empirical story with the theoretical overlay but to use the empirical work to critique the theory. Though an article may do this as well, it is less likely to do so. In addition to comparing theory to evidence, a book may offer the opportunity to compare and contrast several theories in the context of a particular empirical problem (Kuhn 1970; Laudan 1977).

A fourth advantage of the research book is that the author can include in it much more institutional material than would fit in an article. For instance, a company, its product lines, its organization structure, its people, and its history can all be described in a book. "Other things being equal" is an argument that does not have to be made. Other things are really never equal, and the book offers an opportunity to show how and why.

Finally, research books seem to offer a better opportunity to break new ground than do articles. While admittedly I argue we have no central paradigm, if there is to be a paradigm shift a la Kuhn (1970), it is more likely to come in a book. A research book offers a forum for the iconoclast, whose ideas and position may not be well received by reviewers versed in the current state of the field.

It is important to emphasize that I do not bemoan the lack of research books for their own sake. It is my perception that such books are the best vehicle for conveying the richness of many strategy phenomena. Therefore, their continued absence prevents us from understanding important phenomena and answering important questions. Taken to its extreme, this trend will deprive the strategy area of much of the integrating effort that is needed to make sense of the increasingly specialized work that has come to dominate it.

### *Narrative versus paradigmatic*

Jerome Bruner (1986), the dean of cognitive psychologists, has written a new book entitled *Actual Minds, Possible Worlds*. He talks about two modes of thought—the "narrative" and the "paradigmatic." The narrative mode tells the story; it shows meaning; you get a sense of what is going on. The paradigmatic mode is scientific; it has evidence of a different kind. It uses a method of science, but often it doesn't show the same kind of thing as the narrative mode. I believe that the field of strategy is drifting too far toward the paradigmatic mode. I will let Professor Bruner (1986: 11–14) make his own points:

> There are two modes of cognitive function . . . irreducible to one another. . . . Arguments convince one of their truth, stories of their lifelikeness. The one verifies by eventual appeal to procedure for establishing formal and empirical proof. The other establishes not truth but verisimilitude. . . . Perhaps Richard Rorty (1979) is right in characterizing the mainstream of Anglo-American philosophy (which, on the whole he rejects) as preoccupied with the epistemological question of how to know truth—which he contrasts with the broader question of how we come to endow experience with meaning, which is the question that preoccupies the poet and the storyteller. . . . The logico-scientific mode (I shall call it paradigmatic hereafter) deals in general causes . . . [and] is driven by principled hypothesis. . . . Narrative mode . . . Strives to put its timeless miracles into the particulars of experience, and to locate the experience in time and space. . . . [Scientists'] salvation is to wash the stories away when causes can be substituted for them. . . . Narrative deals with the vicissitudes of human intentions.

I am not a strong advocate of case studies and case presentations per se, but I would like to see some good studies on strategy that are "peopled" —that is, studies that have people with names, who are doing things, studies that help you think about why they are doing those things. I don't see much good strategy research of this kind. Research that deals with Bruner's "vicissitudes of human intentions" and presents Perrow's (1986) "feel" of the organization will have to be built around the behavior of individual people—real actors. Allison's book and Chandler's book are examples of this style of research. While academics may differ from practitioners, I believe that everyone's ability to remember and make sense out of an argument is often enhanced by this human perspective.

Research in strategy, as in most fields, may be characterized as deductive or inductive, although the labels don't always fit specific works very well. Nevertheless, Thomas Kuhn's (1970) idea can be used here: deductive work is largely normal science as it draws on an accepted theory or paradigm to explore some derivative issues. Inductive work is more akin to empiricism, as mentioned earlier. Glaser and Strauss (1967) developed an appreciation for this inductive type of work in their oft-cited book, *The Discovery of Grounded Theory*. Some of the current work in strategy falls in this category and deserves to be continued. However, the suggestions of Glaser and Strauss should be followed more closely. For example, the idea of comparative analysis drawing on multiple field studies is attractive, especially where theory is weak. The systematic development of formal theory from substantive theory—to the general from the specific—is also useful. None of this means that received theory, which would normally precede deductive work, should be ignored. However, it does mean that received theory should not strongly drive a strategy study.

This issue is further illustrated by Charles Perrow (1986: 164–176) in his book *Complex Organizations*, in which he develops a case for the "institutional school." He notes that "after the arid and dense forest of two-variable propositions . . . and the axiomatic edifice . . . it is a pleasure to read about a real organization confronting real problems in real time and space. . . . Above all, the descriptive and historical nature of this school gives us a 'feel' for how organizations operate." While Perrow is speaking of the institutional school in organization studies and sociology, Galbraith (1987: 129) commends the institutional school in economics: "In the United States . . . economics divides today as between classicists (the overwhelming number) and institutionalists, between those committed to the inevitable and constant equilibrium and those who, with much less claim to scientific precision, accept a world of evolution and continuing change."

For the study of strategy, I believe we need many more active institutionalists. Rich empirical work would increase our understanding of the many issues involved and may also be transformed or used directly for professional education purposes. There is always the risk that the professor would rather interact intellectually with other professors and doctoral students than with executives. While the first interaction is obviously worthwhile, to miss the second is folly. Most of us exist in professional business schools that, as with all professional schools, exist to help the professions—the worldly managers and managers-to-be.

### *Less logical positivism*

Another change in strategy research would be directly related to the above and would be a move away from the overly strong emphasis on logical positivism. Several years ago, there was a review by Roger Evered of the

Schendel and Hofer (1979) book. In his review, Evered (1980: 536–542) despaired over the drift he saw toward logical positivism:

> Positivism would be even more disastrous for policy/strategy than for other areas of social sciences. . . . The ideal research paradigm is presumed already known and important inquiry options are closed out too early. . . . Very little regard [is given] to the inherent epistemological assumptions of what is proposed in relation to the focal phenomena of the field.

Using a positivist perspective, an investigator can get data, make statements, and get results that are significant, but have quite modest R squares. Often he or she is working with a large received data base accumulated by others for quite different purposes. With cluster analysis, factor analysis, and regression analysis, an investigator can feed in the data and get a small relationship. One wonders, "What really did they find out?" Maybe not much. Given the progress that statistics for the social sciences has made in the last three decades, one must offer criticism with some care. However, I am sometimes left with the impression that a kind of Gresham's law is at work. Is the bad money of statistical methodology driving out the good money of strategic substance? I am not saying we shouldn't do this kind of work; I simply hope that we don't continue down this road to the point where 90 percent of the empirical work in strategy can be described this way.

One of the potential problems of positivism mentioned earlier is the rapid journey made by an author/researcher from theory to construct, to surrogate variable, to measurement, to subsequent analysis. Often, but of course not always, we as authors do not give enough attention to the particular constructs that we are using. Do they really make sense? Have they been explored in all their relationships? Do they truly serve the purpose for which we use them? A different kind of criticism of positivism and its derivative work is that the issue may not really be very important; or at the extreme, it is trivial. While importance may be in the eye of the beholder, at least two groups might supply the straw vote. We should ask ourselves: Are other researchers interested in it? Are practitioners interested in it?

Donald Schon (1983: 39–46), in *The Reflective Practitioner*, develops a strong argument that questions the positivist school, especially when it comes to useful knowledge for practice:

> Increasingly we have become aware of the importance to actual practice of phenomena—complexity, uncertainty, instability, uniqueness, and value-conflict—which do not fit the model of Technical Rationality. Now, in the light of the Positivist origins of Technical Rationality, we can more readily see why these phenomena

> are so troublesome. . . . From the perspective of Technical Rationality, professional practice is a process of problem *solving*. Problems of choice of decision are solved through the selection from available means, of the one best suited to established ends. But with the emphasis on problem solving, we ignore problem *setting*, the process by which we define the decision to be made, the ends to be achieved, the means which may be chosen. In real world practice, problems do not present themselves to the practitioners as given. . . . Herbert Simon, whose *The Sciences of the Artificial* has aroused a great deal of interest in professional circles . . . most clearly links the predicament of professional knowledge to the historical origins of the Positivist epistemology practice. Simon believes that all professional practice is centrally concerned with what he calls "design," that is, with the process of "changing existing situations into preferred ones" (Simon 1969: 55). But design in this sense is precisely what the professional schools do not teach. The older schools have a knowledge of design that is "intellectually soft, intuitive, informal and cookbooky," and the newer ones, more absorbed into the general culture of the modern university, have become schools of natural science.

While Schon, and to some extent Simon, are talking about professional education, I am arguing that these aspects of design (that is, changing existing situations to preferred ones) should be a component of a strategy research portfolio. We should study issues of design in an empirical context in order to describe them better. The practitioner and the researcher are doubly linked: the researcher supplies insights, relationships, and theory for the practitioner. But the practitioner supplies puzzles, ideas, judgments, and priorities for the researcher.

### *Higher order theory*

An additional issue for strategy research is the need for a higher order of theoretical research. For example, where is the analogue for cognitive science at the level of the firm? Is it artificial intelligence? Is it a modern-day version of cybernetics (Steinbruner 1974)? Gardner (1985: 16) summarized how progress was made in another field by noting that "Wiener (1984) . . . concluded that there were important analogies between feedback aspects of engineering devices and the homeostatic process by which the human nervous system sustains purposive activity. These ideas of planning, purpose, and feedback, developed with mathematical precision, were directly antithetical to the behaviorist credo."

While there has been a healthy reaction to naive normative ideas in strategy by such prolific authors as Simon (1969), Cohen and March (1986), Mintzberg

(1978), Pfeffer (1972), and Weick (1987), we may now have reached the point where we will have to move back and forth on an upward path of sophistication between the rational and the natural, between the normative and the positive (admittedly not quite the same polarity). New and more abstract theoretical work may be called for. What is unusually difficult in this regard will be an empirical grounding to help demonstrate the reality of this theoretical work.

Though a call for such work may seem antithetical to the reality of institutionalism, it does not run counter to the larger scheme that encourages pluralism. As I argued in an earlier piece on epistemology:

> At this stage in the development of managerial education and investigation, the mixed strategy of using all approaches is probably better than the reliance on only one or two, especially where students and managers may differ markedly in the ability to learn from the different approaches. A mixed strategy not only allows the possibility for reinforcement and/or a productive dialectic, but given the explicitly different perspectives, offers the chance for a future response to issues of corporate strategy which is *robust*.
>
> (Bowman 1974: 49)

I believe research in strategy should become broader in its viewpoints, topics, methodologies, and theories—rather than narrower, as may be preferred by some. While science is a noble calling, it is not the only intellectual or academic approach to truth. Nor do I wish the world to believe that issues of strategy are only in some way derived from social science. At one time I felt that economics was the slighted aspect of strategy literature:

> The kinds of topics developed by economists which are of some interest are entrepreneurship, innovation and diffusion, portfoiio selection and capital asset pricing, international trade, industrial organization and concentration, oligopoly and game theory, monopolistic competition, discretionary behavior, input-output analysis, capital budgeting and investment and the growth of the firm. . . . It can be noted with some interest that most of the literature and books addressed to corporate strategy directly . . . pay very little if any attention to the economics literature. If a single major criticism were to be leveled at the corporate strategy literature, this is perhaps the one.
>
> (Bowman 1974: 40)

It is surprising, at least to me, how this situation has changed in fifteen years. The above epistemology paper was written in the same season that my research seminar was started. Certainly one would not make that comment today about the lack of connection between economic theories and strategy. What I believe may be missing today are more papers in areas like business history. While there are at least two polar views of history, each can contribute to our understanding of this field. Those of the Annales school, as exemplified by Fernard Braudel (1986), argue that it is the major underlying forces (geography, politics, economics, technology) that determine history. Contrarily, those adherents of what some call the Schumpeterian school of business history argue that it is particular actors (for example, entrepreneurs) who shape historical outcomes. An example of *both* schools of thought, perhaps classified as sociology by some, is Langton's (1984) study of the development of the Wedgwood Potteries in the last half of the eighteenth century. Here one reads not only about the specific actions and decisions of Josiah Wedgwood but also about the growing British transportation system, which opened up national markets. Alfred Chandler's *Strategy and Structure* is another, more extended example, from a period 150 years later.

It should be emphasized that we need not choose between the old and the new history; battle lines do not need to be drawn, as they recently were in the *New York Times Book Review*. In "The Ugly Historians," Neil McKendrick (1988: 14) notes that "when the new historian cannot conceal his contempt for a history that persists in studying important people, significant events, and successful historical movements, it is hardly surprising that the old historian will take delight in making mock of statements such as one writer's observation that 'Mickey Mouse may be in fact more important to an understanding of the 1930's than Franklin Roosevelt!' " Both the old and the new history make useful contributions to our understanding of strategy; good history is good research.

### *More longitudinal and individual work*

Professor Ed Zajac and I have done a study (Zajac and Bowman 1985) on the publications of the last five years in the *Strategic Management Management Journal*. We specified characteristics *a, b, c, d*, and *e* of empirical research and classified each paper according to those characteristics. We were able to draw some conclusions and provide some observations. But two characteristics were dropped because we didn't get enough variance— "individual versus organization," and "longitudinal versus cross-sectional." Less than 10 percent of the articles focused on the individual level of decision making vis-à-vis strategy, so we couldn't use it because the remaining 90 percent had to do with the organization as a unit. Similarly, less than 10 percent of the studies were really longitudinal, and 90 percent were essentially cross-sectional; so we couldn't use that characteristic either. I think that both of these findings are disheartening. That is, I would encourage strategy researchers to do more work on individual people making strategic decisions, in truly longitudinal studies.

When we do not do longitudinal studies, we are likely to miss phenomena such as retrospective rationality, learning, escalation, and most elements of a game theoretic nature. If we miss the individual decision maker, we are likely to miss issues of cognition, bounded rationality, heuristics, and image and representation. There is general agreement on the complexity and uncertainty associated with strategic decision making. However, research programs in strategy that explicitly deal with issues of bounded rationality are strangely lacking in the academy.

### *More levels of strategy*

Of the four levels of strategy currently found in our literature—from top to bottom: institutional, corporate, business, and functional—we see a lot of work on the corporate strategy and business strategy levels. I think to some extent we slight the institutional level; we should be interested in the issues of how a corporation fits itself comfortably into the social environment and the body politic. For instance, problems of hazardous waste in the chemical industry are enormously important to that industry (Bowman and Kunreuther 1988). This is an institutional problem of the kind that strategy research typically ignores.

Many problems or issues in institutional strategy point toward the sociological notions contained in resource dependency. Strategy research, for instance, rarely gives explicit consideration to the government, its laws, and its agencies as a crucial part of the firm's environment. Likewise, we are only now starting to look at the functional correspondence to strategy of the firm. Marketing, R&D, manufacturing, and finance, even if they have their own research, should be a part of our research endeavor. And at all levels of strategy, though we are doing some, we are not doing enough internationally focused research.

### *Foreground versus background*

"Figure versus ground," or "foreground versus background" (contrasts drawn from both art and psychology), are terms that people like Jim March use. A connected issue for strategy, which has not been well enough developed in either the general/theoretical literature or in specific research studies, is "today versus tomorrow." I am not referring to the common cry (Hayes and Abernathy 1980) that finance theory, investment analysts, and mobile managers short-change the future. I am referring to the fact that most students of strategy focus on today's strategy problems and on ways of coping with them. Surely I agree that one must survive today in order to fight tomorrow. But to focus on today's problems may miss the nuances of tomorrow's world. Some of the work on strategy should be concerned with how managers address this trade-off. For example, how do you develop talent that can make strategic decisions in the future when you can't spend money today on future strategies because you hardly know what the problems are?

My colleague Aron Katsenelinboigen (1984) writes that a major difference in chess styles between nineteenth- and twentieth-century masters is that one searched for material advantage while the other searches for positional advantage. The former weights the independent value of each piece in an exchange. The latter considers the relational arrangement of the pieces for a particular game and "his chances to parry his opponent's future moves" (p. 10). This metaphor correlates directly to the concern for foreground versus background, or for either today's strategies or tomorrow's.

Even in the planning literature a similar distinction exists—between "Cooks-Tour" planning and "Lewis-and-Clark" planning. James Schlesinger (1966: 7, 8), cabinet officer under several U.S. presidents, writes that "Cooks-Tour planning . . . rests, implicitly or explicitly, on the supposition that the future is sufficiently certain that we can chart a straight course years in advance. In it, direction, speed, size of commitment, and achievement milestones (not decision points) are indicated at least with rough precision." By contrast, what he terms "Lewis-and-Clark planning . . . acknowledges that many alternative courses of action and forks in the road will appear, but their precise character and timing cannot be anticipated. . . . The planning function . . . is to prepare to cope with [the] uncertain terrain of the future." He adds that the cost of acquiescence to the organization pressures for precise planning "is neglect of uncertainties, lost flexibility, neglected and suppressed options, and less-than-optimal adjustment to changing opportunities and threats existing in the external environment."

The ideas of Katsenelinboigen and Schlesinger highlight the difference between the particular focus on efficiency and the general/contingency focus on survival. Strategy research looks too much at the first and not enough at the second.

A recent piece of research I undertook, published as "The Concerns of the CEO" (Bowman 1986), further illustrates my point. By far the most salient concern of the twenty-six CEOs interviewed was "management development." They were strongly concerned with whether and/or how their associates would be prepared to deal with the problems of the firm. Upon reflection, I believe this concern can be interpreted as addressing tomorrow's strategy problems. One can sensibly allocate resources today to deal with today's strategy problems. But as previously asked, how can you deal with tomorrow's problems when you don't even know what they will be? I believe that one of the only ways to deal with tomorrow's problems is to work on the robustness of the organization and on the protection of its core skills. This, I feel, is largely in the hands of the many top and middle managers who have to cope with these problems.

Nelson and Winter (1982) discuss the skills of the organization and how these core skills, largely tacit, become the competitive advantage of the firm.

They comprise in large part the "invisible assets" that Itami/Roehl (1987) argue must be mobilized. Strategy researchers pay little attention to these skills. Perhaps the main concern of corporate strategy (as distinct from business strategy) should be with the development of these organizational skills, this tacit knowledge that provides for and protects against the future. Nobel laureate Robert Solow (1988: 10) suggests that "the major source of economic growth in modern industrial economies is the advance of knowledge." I argue that this is analogous to the future prosperity of the individual firm. Strategy research must reflect this knowledge-building for the future.

## Overall agenda

If we wish to encourage pluralism in both theory and research methods, as well as in the style of presentation and in discourse, it may take some changes in the academy. Those of us who have lived there for a long time know this is problematic. Tenure is, I suppose, both the problem and the solution. How can we expect untenured faculty to pursue the long-term course outlined above? For example, while senior faculty in strategy can argue the benefits, the quality, and the contribution of publications (articles, essays, chapters, monographs, and books) that go beyond a logical positivist perspective, it is not clear how well received these arguments will be in many business schools. One solution for the younger professor going through this process would be the support of a group—an invisible college—of faculty at good schools who understand and appreciate such work. However, for this "college" to be built, more faculty must recognize the limits of positivism and become advocates for an enlarged perspective.

What will probably be even more difficult will be strategy research taking on the coloration of history, philosophy, and design. These are all accepted parts of the modern university, but they have not yet been accepted in the "modern" business school. The idea that tenure can be both the problem and the solution encompasses the possibility that more senior faculty, once they have tenure, can devote their efforts to these broader forms of research. Unless the young faculty member is unusually creative and lucky and the institution is broadminded, the research efforts I speak for here may have to come from those further along in their careers. Interestingly enough, I can think of examples of both young iconoclasts and older reformists; we need to value both.

My argument for research in strategy has been for broadening rather than narrowing. It has been geared toward including more fields of related theory, and even new theories, rather than toward a primary search for a central paradigm; toward the uncertainties of the future rather than the complexities of the present; toward the skills of the background that go beyond the choices of the foreground; toward the narrative to complement the paradigmatic; toward institutional and functional strategies, to add to the corporate and business strategies; and toward the individual and longitudinal studies rather than the solely organizational and cross-sectional. I argue for inclusion of the historian, the institutionalist, and the empiricist, rather than for their exclusion.

Many of the above choices can be reflected in research regardless of its forum. However, I believe that research books offer the best hope of satisfying these wishes. Therefore, as a group of academics we should encourage colleagues, at various stages of their careers, who have not considered a research project culminating in a book, to undertake one.

## Note

The author wishes to thank Professors Kathleen Conner, Deborah Dougherty, and Paul Tiffany for their helpful draft comments, and the Reginald H. Jones Center for its support.

## References

Allison, G. T. 1971. *Essence of Decision: Explaining the Cuban Missile Crisis.* Boston: Little, Brown and Company.

Altman, E. 1973. "Predicting Railroad Bankruptcies in America." *Bell Journal of Economics and Management Science* 4, no. 1 (Spring): 184–211.

Amihud, Y., and B. Lev. 1981. "Risk Reduction as a Managerial Motive for Conglomerate Mergers." *Bell Journal of Economics* 12, no. 2 (Fall): 605–617.

Ansoff, H. I. 1965. *Corporate Strategy: An Analytic Approach to Business Policy for Growth and Expansion.* New York: McGraw-Hill Book Company.

Bourgeois, L. J., III. 1980. "Performance and Consensus." *Strategic Management Journal* 1, no. 2 (July–August): 227–248.

Bower, J. L. 1970. *Managing the Resource Allocation Process.* Boston: Harvard Business School, Division of Research.

Bowman, E. H. 1974. "Epistemology, Corporate Strategy, and Academe." *Sloan Management Review* 15, no. 2 (Winter): 35–50.

——. 1982. "Risk Seeking by Troubled Firms." *Sloan Management Review* 23, no. 4 (Summer): 33–42.

——. 1986. "Concerns of the CEO." *Human Resource Management* 25, no. 2 (Summer): 267–286.

——, and H. Kunreuther. 1988. "Post-Bhopal Behavior at a Chemical Company." *Journal of Management Studies* 25, no. 4 (July): 387–401.

Braudel, F. 1986. *The Wheels of Commerce.* Civilization and Capitalism, 15th–18th Century, Vol. 2. New York: Harper & Row.

Bruner, J. 1986. *Actual Minds, Possible Worlds.* Cambridge, Mass.: Harvard University Press.

Carroll, L. 1865. Reprint. *Alice's Adventures in Wonderland.* London: Octopus Books, 1978.

Chandler, A. D., Jr. 1962. *Strategy and Structure: Chapters in the History of American Enterprise.* Cambridge, Mass.: MIT Press.

Cohen, M. D., and J. G. March. 1986. *Leadership and Ambiguity: The American College President*. 2d ed. Boston: Harvard Business School Press.

Evered, R. 1980. Review of *Strategic Management: A New View of Business Policy and Planning*, edited by D. E. Schendel and C. W. Hofer. *Administrative Science Quarterly* 25, no. 3 (September): 536–542.

Fouraker, L. E., and J. M. Stopford. 1968. "Organizational Structure and Multinational Strategy." *Administrative Science Quarterly* 13, no. 1 (June): 47–64.

Galbraith, J. K. 1987. *Economics in Perspective: A Critical History*. Boston: Houghton Mifflin Company.

Gardner, H. 1985. *The Mind's New Science: A History of the Cognitive Revolution*. New York: Basic Books.

Glaser, B. G., and A. L. Strauss. 1967. *The Discovery of Grounded Theory: Strategies for Qualitative Research*. New York: Aldine de Gruyter.

Gluck, F. W., S. P. Kaufman, and A. S. Walleck. 1980. "Strategic Management for Competitive Advantage." *Harvard Business Review* 58, no. 4 (July–August): 154–161.

Hayes, R. H., and W. J. Abernathy. 1980. "Managing Our Way to Economic Decline." *Harvard Business Review* (July–August): 67–77.

Hayes, R. H., and S. C. Wheelwright. 1984. *Restoring Our Competitive Edge: Competing Through Manufacturing*. New York: John Wiley & Sons.

Hirsch, P. M. 1975. "Organizational Effectiveness and the Institutional Environment." *Administrative Science Quarterly* 20, no. 3 (September): 327–344.

Itami, H. with T. W. Roehl. 1987. *Mobilizing Invisible Assets*. Cambridge, Mass.: Harvard University Press.

Katsenelinboigen, A. 1984. *Some New Trends in Systems Theory*. Intersystems Publications.

Kuhn, T. S. 1970. *The Structure of Scientific Revolutions*. 2d ed. Chicago: University of Chicago Press.

Langton, J. 1984. "The Ecological Theory of Bureaucracy: The Case of Josiah Wedgwood Pottery Industry." *Administrative Science Quarterly* 29, no. 3 (September): 330–354.

Laudan, L. 1977. *Progress and Its Problems: Toward a Theory of Scientific Growth*. Berkeley: University of California Press.

Learned, E. A.; C. R. Christensen; K. R. Andrews; and W. D. Guth. 1965. *Business Policy: Text and Cases*. Homewood, Ill.: Richard D. Irwin.

McKendrick, N. 1988. "The Ugly Historians" (A review of T. S. Hamerow, *Reflections on History and Historians* [Madison: University of Wisconsin Press, 1987] and Gertrude Himmelfarb, *The New History and the Old* [Cambridge, Mass.: Harvard University Press, The Belknap Press, 1987]). *New York Times* (7 ebruary): 14.

Miles, R. E., and C. C. Snow. 1978. *Organization Strategy, Structure, and Process*. New York: McGraw-Hill Book Company.

Miles, R. H., and K. S. Cameron. 1982. *Coffin Nails and Corporate Strategy*. Englewood Cliffs, N. J.: Prentice-Hall.

Mintzberg, H. 1978. "Patterns in Strategy Formation." *Management Science* 16, no. 2, pp. 44–53.

Nelson, R. R., and S. G. Winter. 1982. *An Evolutionary Theory of Economic Change*. Cambridge, Mass.: Harvard University Press.

*The New Yorker*. 1987. "Briefly Noted," October 5.

Perrow, C. 1985. "Comment on Langton's Ecological Theory of Bureaucracy." *Administrative Science Quarterly* 30: 278–288.

——. 1986. *Complex Organizations: A Critical Essay*. 3d ed. New York: Random House.

Pfeffer, J. 1972. "Size and Composition of Corporate Boards of Directors: The Organization and Its Environment." *Administrative Science Quarterly* 17, no. 2(June): 218–228.

——. 1982. *Organizations and Organization Theory*. Marshfield, Mass.: Pitman.

Porter, M. 1980. *Competitive Strategy*. New York: Free Press.

——. 1985. *Competitive Advantage*. New York: Free Press.

——, and A. M. Spence. 1982. "The Capacity Expansion Process in a Growing Oligopoly: The Case of Corn Wet Milling." In *The Economics of Information and Uncertainty*, edited by J. McCall, ch. 8, pp. 259–309. Chicago: University of Chicago Press.

Rappaport, A. 1986. *Creating Shareholder Value: The New Standard for Business Performance*. New York: Free Press.

Rorty, R. 1979. *Philosophy and the Mirror of Nature*. Princeton, N. J.: Princeton University Press.

Rumelt, R. P. 1974. *Strategy, Structure, and Economic Performance*. Boston: Harvard Business School, Division of Research.

Schendel, D. E., and C. W. Hofer, eds. 1979. *Strategic Management: A New View of Business Policy and Planning*. Boston: Little, Brown and Company.

Schlesinger, J. 1966. "Organization Structures and Planning." Rand Paper, P-3316 (25 February).

Schon, D. A. 1983. *The Reflective Practitioner: How Professionals Think in Action*. New York: Basic Books.

Scott, W. R. 1981. *Organizations: Rational, Natural, and Open Systems*. Englewood Cliffs, N. J.: Prentice-Hall.

Simon, H. A. 1969. *The Sciences of the Artificial*. Cambridge, Mass.: MIT Press. Solow, R. 1988. "Short-Run Gain or Long-Run Health." *Technology Review* 91, no. 2 (February/March): 10 (MIT insert).

Steinbruner, J. D. 1974. *The Cybernetic Theory of Decision: New Dimensions of Political Analysis*. Princeton, N. J.: Princeton University Press.

Teece, D. J., ed. 1987. *The Competitive Challenge: Strategies for Industrial Innovation and Renewal*. Cambridge, Mass.: Ballinger Publishing Company.

Tversky, A., and D. Kahneman. 1981. "The Framing of Decisions and the Psychology of Choice." *Science* 211, no. 4481 (30 January): 453–458.

Walker, G., and D. Webber. 1984. "A Transaction Cost Approach to Make-or-Buy Decisions." *Administrative Science Quarterly* 29, no. 3 (September): 373–391.

Weick, K. E. 1987. "Substitutes for Strategy." In *The Competitive Challenge: Strategies for Industrial Innovation and Renewal*, edited by D. J. Teece, ch. 10, pp. 221–234. Cambridge, Mass.: Ballinger Publishing Company.

White, T. H. 1978. *In Search of History: A Personal Adventure*. New York: Warner Books.

Wiener, N. 1948. *Cybernetics, or, Control and Communication in the Animal and the Machine*. New York: MIT Press.

Williamson, O. 1975. *Markets and Hierarchies: Analysis and Antitrust Implications.* New York: Free Press.

Woo, C. Y. Y., and A. C. Cooper. 1981. "Strategies of Effective Low Share business." *Strategic Management Journal* 2, no. 3 (July–September): 301–318.

Zajac, E. J., and E. H. Bowman. 1985. "Perspectives and Choices in Strategy Research." Reginald H. Jones Center Working Paper 85–15.

48

# THE ADOLESCENCE OF STRATEGIC MANAGEMENT, 1980–1985

## Critical perceptions and reality

*Donald C. Hambrick*

Source: J. W. Fredrickson (ed.) *Perspectives on Strategic Management*, New York: Harper Business, 1990, pp. 237–53.

In 1980, the field of strategy was at a crossroads. The Schendel and Hofer (1979) volume, summarizing the views of many of the leading figures of the field, had just the year before called for rechristening "business policy" as "strategic management." And 1980 was also the year two new journals—*Strategic Management Journal (SMJ)* and *Journal of Business Strategy (JBS)*—dealing exclusively with the topic of strategy were created, which greatly multiplied the printed pages available for the field's work.

The distance traveled since 1980 has been substantial. For instance, possibly twice as much strategy research has been done in the past five years as in the preceding twenty. But we still seem to be at a crossroads: not fully sure of where we've been, much less where we're headed; not sure we always like what we see in our research, much less that we can expect others to like it. Many of the weaknesses do not lie in individual pieces of research. Each is typically competent and contributes in its own way. Rather, our problem lies in our general inability or hesitance to reflect broadly upon our field—its context, its purpose, its comparative advantages, its rocky adolescence. This lack of introspection is what makes volumes such as this one so important.

When Jim Fredrickson asked me to participate in the symposium that spawned this book, my immediate reaction was to pull out a notepad and start thinking of all of my general impressions and pet peeves about what had been going on in the field of strategy for the last several years. But then my dyed-in-the-wool empiricist tendencies took over.

Why not study it? So that is what I did, along with Chandru Rajam, a doctoral student at Penn State, where I was on sabbatical. We conducted a large-scale, systematic study of strategy research published between 1980 and 1985. We chose 1980 as the starting year because, as noted above, it is a relatively clean point of demarcation in our field: the start of two new journals; publication of Mike Porter's (1980) immensely important book; and a year following the publication of the Schendel and Hofer (1979) book rechristening the field. We closed with 1985 because we were doing the project in early 1986.

It is useful now to discuss how the study was conducted. Then we will turn to our analyses and findings, many of which I leave to the reader to interpret.

## Description of the study

So much was written in the field between 1980 and 1985 that there was no way that we could study everything. Nor did we choose to study a random sample, since such a sample would not be very meaningful. We decided instead to identify and study the fifty works, among those published between 1980 and 1985, that were most cited by other works published during the same period. To do this, we conducted an exhaustive analysis of all of the reference lists of all strategy-oriented and top management-oriented articles in *Academy of Management Journal (AMJ), Academy of Management Review (AMR), Administrative Science Quarterly (ASQ)*, and *Harvard Business Review (HBR)*, and of all articles in *JBS* and *SMJ*. In total, the reference lists of 479 articles were studied to determine the post-1980 works they cited most often. We used a weighting system (described in appendix 6–1) to adjust for publication date since, of course, more recent works have inherently less opportunity to be cited. The list of fifty most noted works is reported in appendix 6–2.

Two legitimate concerns can be raised about the time frame of the study. First, it can be argued that six years is a very thin slice of the field's existence to study. This is true; however, earlier eras of the field have been analyzed elsewhere (Hofer 1976; Saunders and Thompson 1980; Jauch 1983). As noted above, the six years we focus on appear to be a somewhat well-defined "adolescent" period for the field; obviously, we encourage studies of this type to examine strategy research for the second half of the 1980s.

The second timing concern is whether the list of the fifty most-noted works would hold together if a longer citation period were allowed. Fortunately, the two years that have lapsed between the initial analysis and this writing allow us to address this concern systematically. Namely, we examined all the strategy-oriented articles appearing during 1986 and 1987 (a total of 146) in the six journals listed above in order to observe the degree to which they, too, cited the fifty "most-noted" works from 1980–1985. The results were striking. The Pearson correlation between the original recency-adjusted scores (as reported in appendix 6–2) and the number of citations in 1986–1987 articles was .76 ($p < .001$). Appendix 6–3 reports the number of 1986–1987 citations for the first ten works in the list, the second ten, and so on, clearly confirming that the composition of the list, and even its general order, is stable over time.

A final caveat should be expressed about this list: *It is not a "bit parade."* By identifying the "fifty most-noted works," one has done just that: identified the fifty most-noted works. Works are just as often cited for their limitations and weaknesses as they are for their contributions. Moreover, the tendency for a work to be cited is a function of its topic, particularly whether the topic is of central concern to the field or highly specialized. Therefore, this list should not be taken as any sort of popularity index.

## The issues addressed

There are many things that these fifty works might tell us about the recent development of the field of strategy. However, we must limit our discussion to some manageable scope. Therefore, this analysis will focus on a handful of concerns–six to be exact–that people both within and outside the field seem to be voicing more and more.

I do not have definitive proof that these are the most burning issues among us; but as I visit colleagues around the country, these are the concerns that come out, time and again, about the field of strategy in the eighties:

- "We have broken too sharply from our past; we've discarded our legacy."
- "We are using increasingly sterile data that lack organizational richness and texture."
- "We are doing too much number-crunching, often without any theoretical aim."
- "Our models and methods are too static."
- "Our research is based on restrictive and naive assumptions about managerial roles."
- "Our research is overly concerned with performance and prescription."

In the sections that follow, I will use data from our study to shed light on the validity of each of these concerns. As noted earlier, I will concentrate on reporting the findings and will leave much of the interpretation to the reader.

### *Broken from our past?*

A concern I often hear voiced is that the field of strategy has discarded its legacy. In its quest for legitimacy and maturity, and with an influx of newly trained researchers, the field is accused of scrapping its origins, ignoring a substantial theoretical, methodological, and practical tradition. To the extent that this continual reinvention and redefinition is occurring, it no doubt aggravates any identity crisis the field may have.

An approach to studying this issue is to examine continuity in researchers and exemplars in the field. Chuck Hofer's 1976 paper, in which he examined essentially everything that had been written in the field at the time, serves as one basis for comparison. In fact, it is hard to identify anything then in the field of strategy that was excluded from that article's reference list. The reference list cites works by 105 different authors; that is, 105 different people after accounting for multiple and joint authorships. In turn, our set of fifty works from the early eighties had fifty-eight different authors. What is the overlap between the two lists? Seven people. This signals a radical demarcation between who did research in the sixties and seventies, and who did it in the early eighties.

If one uses the Schendel and Hofer (1979) book as another basis for comparison, the conclusion is the same. The book had forty-two contributors, carefully selected as the field's leading thinkers. The overlap with our list is five people. This small, hence extraordinary, group consists of Arnold Cooper, John Grant, Ian MacMillan, Henry Mintzberg, and Ian Mitroff. Although needing verification, I would guess that few other fields, in any two nearly adjacent five-year periods, would have such radical changes in their principal figures.

Another way of looking at continuity is in terms of the field's exemplars, or the kinds of works that the field draws upon. Evered (1980) tallied the most commonly cited works by contributors to the Schendel and Hofer volume. In order of frequency, they were Chandler (1962), Ansoff (1965), Boston Consulting Group (1968), Rumelt (1974), Andrews (1971), Allison (1971), and Hofer's (1975) contingency article. By comparison, if one looks at the reference lists of our fifty early 1980s works, the most common entries were Porter (1980), Miles and Snow (1978), Child (1972), Thompson (1967), Andrews (1971), and Chandler (1962). So, there is some overlap. Interestingly, by their vintage, Lawrence and Lorsch, Child, and Thompson could have been more prominent in the Schendel and Hofer volume. Their recent emergence adds evidence of a shift in the paradigms and the literature bases the field of strategy has tended to draw upon.

### *Sterile data?*

The next concern often heard is that strategy researchers are using increasingly sterile data that lacks richness and texture and is detached from the phenomena being studied. Others writing in this volume—Ned Bowman, Dick Daft, and Vicki Buenger—have echoed this criticism. Judging the "richness" of data is, of course, a matter of taste. However, knowing the means of data collection is helpful to anyone making that judgment.

*Table 1* Data Sources for Twenty-three Empirical Projects.*

| | |
|---|---|
| Archival | 15 |
| Survey | 9 |
| Interview/observation | 10 |
| Laboratory | 0 |

*Adds to more than twenty-three owing to multiple data sources.

Among our fifty early 1980s works, twenty-three were empirical. Table 1 reports their data sources. (Some used more than one kind of data.) Fifteen were archival (six of which were based on the PIMS data set), nine used survey data, ten used interview and observation data, and none used laboratory data. Thus, there appears to be a reasonable spread. If we assume that laboratory studies are most remote from organizational reality, the criticism of sterility seems ill founded. Conversely, if we assume that only interview and observation data can qualify as textured, then over 40 percent (ten of the twenty-three) of the empirical studies qualify. Eclecticism seems to exist. Strategy researchers appear not to have abandoned talking to managers or getting inside organizations.

In a related vein, Ned Bowman raises concern in this book about the lack of recent empirical books in the field. Such projects, which Ned appropriately contends often carry the most texture and richness, were indeed in short supply among our fifty works. In fact, there were only three: Harrigan's (1980) book on decline, Quinn's (1980) book on logical incrementalism, and the Peters and Waterman (1982) book. (I consider Peters and Waterman not only to be an unequivocally empirical project but also, in major ways, to be literature-based and theory-based. For instance, it is often forgotten that the first nearly 100 pages present a very substantial literature review.) All the other books, of which there were eight, were texts or quasi-texts. So, it seems Ned Bowman is right: there has not been much in the way of research-oriented empirical books recently.

### *Too much aimless number-crunching?*

The next concern often heard is that strategy researchers are doing too much atheoretical number-crunching. The critics say that, in their attempt to escape being labeled "soft," strategists will factor, cluster, regress, and LOGIT everything in sight.

Have we really fallen into a "numbers mentality"? Dare I now say, "Let's look at the numbers?" Adapting a system set forth by Dick Daft (1980) in a review of *ASQ* works, we can classify the twenty-three early 1980s empirical projects according to how they present their data, or by what Dick would call "the richness of the language." The results are as follows (these will add

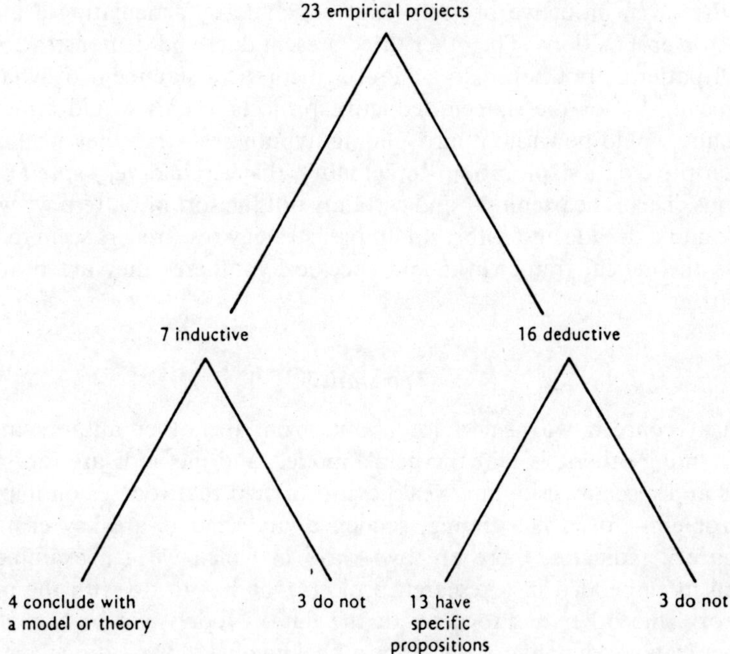


*Figure 1* Theoretical Focus of Twenty-three Empirical Projects.

up to more than twenty-three because data can be presented in multiple ways): four were qualitative, three were quantitative with no significance tests, seven were bivariate with significant tests, and eleven were multivariate. There is a clear tendency toward multivariate number-crunching, the kind of reporting that Dick Daft would call "low-variety language." I know my own research has made me a party to this trend, but I have to share Dick and Ned's concern about it.

We now turn to the other part of the criticism—that a great deal of strategy research is without any theoretical focus. To start an examination of this issue, we need to first identify whether the twenty-three empirical projects in our study were primarily inductive or deductive in their intent. As figure 1 indicates, seven were inductive and sixteen were deductive. Proponents of inductive research might be troubled by this lopsidedness. However, I am not at all sure the proportions are amiss. For instance, any halfway promising theory ought to be tested at least three to five times with different types of samples, different control variables, and so on. Thus, we might expect the general proportion of emphasis on theory generation as opposed to theory testing to be about one to four. The fact that the ratio is one to two supports my own concern that we have far too many untested or undertested ideas in our field.

Of the seven inductive projects, four conclude by articulating a model, theory, or propositions. The other three present data and demonstrate some general patterns, but never do achieve a theoretical statement of what the data mean. As for the sixteen deductive projects, critics would anticipate that many would be without any guiding hypotheses—that they would just be descriptive data exploration. In actuality, thirteen had very specific propositions. This is heartening—and certainly not the sort of pattern we would have found a decade ago. More and more, strategy researchers seem to have concise theoretical frameworks and specific hypotheses they are trying to work from.

### *Too static?*

The next concern we hear a lot about, from the other authors in this book, among others, is that the field's models and methods are too static. This is an especially crippling weakness for a field that focuses on managerial problems, for which timing, sequence, and change are key elements. As figure 2 indicates, there are two ways in which we can examine the dynamism embedded in a research project. One has to do with the model or theory, the other has to do with the data. Models can be thought of as either static or dynamic. A dynamic model involves flows—growth, stages, sequence, decay, timing, and so on. In turn, data can be categorized as either cross-sectional (gathered for a specific point of time) or longitudinal (gathered for multiple time periods).

As figure 2 portrays, the majority of the twenty-three empirical studies we examined were static and cross-sectional, essentially running counter to the essence of strategy. The static longitudinal cell is empty, since no one would undertake the expense of gathering longitudinal data to test a static model. The two dynamic-model cells are somewhat represented. However, the ideal for the field of strategy—the dynamic model with longitudinal data—is, as the critics would predict, now a very scant cell.

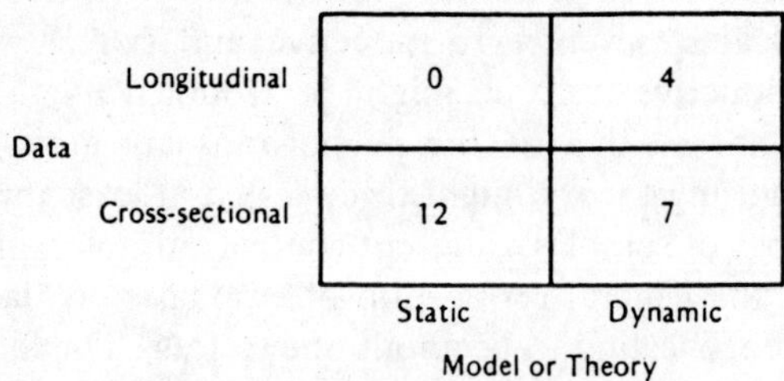


*Figure 2* Treatment of Time in Twenty-three Empirical Projects.

### *Naive assumptions?*

Dick Daft and Vicki Buenger, in their chapter, express concern with the field's assumptions about managerial work. Particularly to the extent that researchers assume managers to be rational maximizers, they are laboring under a very restrictive and naive view.

We explored the underlying assumptions about managerial work in the fifty early 1980s works, classifying the dominant assumption of each work as follows:

> *Strategic Rationality:* The general management task is to identify techno-economic opportunities and problems, systematically search for and weigh alternatives, and make choices that maximize organizational performance.
>
> *Bounded Rationality:* Organizations and individuals within them have bounded rationality. The management task is to accommodate these limitations or develop ways to minimize them (improved information flows, staffing, and so on).
>
> *Political:* The general management task is to maintain the organizational coalition by acquiring, using, allocating, and channeling power (both externally and internally).
>
> *Symbolic:* The general management task is to maintain the organizational coalition by creating and manipulating symbols (for both internal and external consumption).
>
> *Garbage Can:* Since organizations are "garbage cans" into which problems, solutions, and people are thrown together, the general management task is either (a) futile, (b) a matter of dealing with chaos, or (c) not amenable to coherent description and analysis.

This list is in order of the restrictiveness or naivete of the assumption, with strategic rationality being most restrictive and naive, and the garbage can assumption probably the least.

As table 2 indicates, and as Dick and Vicki speculate, the field is enamored with the underlying assumption of strategic rationality. Collectively, strategy researchers seem unwilling to cater to the humanly flawed

*Table 2* Dominant Underlying Assumptions About Managerial Work.

| | |
|---|---|
| Strategic Rationality | 26 |
| Bounded Rationality | 9 |
| Political | 5 |
| Symbolic | 2 |
| Garbage Can | 0 |
| No Single Dominant Assumption | 8 |

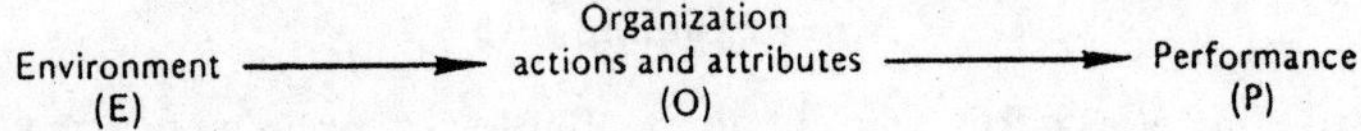


*Figure 3* Conceptual Elements in Strategy Research.

organization—the bundle of incomplete cognitions, cliques, biases, distorted sensors and informations channels, boredom, and distractions that typify the real firm. Unfortunately, if our assumptions outstrip and defy reality, our contributions to managerial practice are destined to be modest.

### *Too concerned with prescription?*

The final concern to be addressed—and here again, one that Dick and Vicki address in their chapter—is that the field of strategy is overly concerned with performance and prescription. My own view is that an emphasis on prescription is a central part of the mission and distinctive competence of the field of strategy. It is part of what sets us apart from, say, organization theory or economics. However, I agree it would be a mistake to focus solely on prescription without an understanding of the inner workings of the phenomena that lead to the prescriptions.

To examine the question of whether the field is overly prescriptive, we built a simple, concise framework for classifying all the conceptual elements that strategy researchers examine. As figure 3 portrays, there are three broad classes of conceptual elements: (E) environment, or phenomena existing outside the organization; (O) the organization's actions and attributes, including strategy, policies, people, information flows, and so on; and (P) performance, or effectiveness.

Using this three-element framework, the fifty works we examined can be classified according to whether they are prescriptive or not, where a prescriptive work is defined as having performance as a dependent construct. As table 3 reports, the primary emphases of the fifty works are about evenly divided between description and prescription.

We can start by looking at the tallies of descriptive studies—those that do not attempt to relate aspects of environment or organization to performance.

*Table 3* Dominant Conceptual Focus of Fifty Projects.

| *Descriptive* | | *Prescriptive* | |
|---|---|---|---|
| E | 1 | O,P | 5 |
| O | 7 | E,P | 1 |
| P | 1 | E,O,P | 16 |
| $O_1$,$O_2$ | 7 | | |
| E,O | 5 | | |

One work—my own on an empirical typology of industrial-product environments (Hambrick 1983)—examined only aspects of environments (E). There were seven works that focus on identifying and elaborating upon some single organizational phenomenon (O), be it slack, structure, executive behavior, or whatever. One—Ed Freeman's (1984) book on stakeholder analysis—focused exclusively on performance (P), asking such questions as: What constitutes performance? What do we need to know about performance? Seven works examined the associations or links between two or more different aspects of organizations ($O_1$,$O_2$). Five dwelt on relationships between environmental and organizational phenomena (E,O).

The remaining works (excluding seven that had no dominant assumption or discernible correspondence to our framework) were prescriptive. That is, they included performance as an explicit or implicit dependent construct. Five works focused on the links between certain organization characteristics and performance (O,P), usually implicitly arguing for universal prescriptions. One work—Scherer (1980)—focuses predominantly on the link between environmental (or industry) attributes and performance (E,P). Finally, a heartening sixteen—the largest number for any single category—took essentially contingency views, in which environment was posited as moderating the links between organizational characteristics or actions and performance (E,O,P).

This seems a very encouraging spread, highlighting that the field is not single-minded in its concern with prescription. A significant body of researchers have focused on the theoretical description of phenomena apart from their implications for performance. If I had one pet idea, however, it would be that we need more studies and theories that, like Ed Freeman's book, look strictly at performance. What constitutes performance? How should it change over time? What are the connections among various aspects of performance? Prescription should be our ultimate aim, but we must learn more about what really qualifies as an improved state for the organization.

## Needed directions: preparing for the nineties

This chapter has focused on where we have been as a field. It makes sense now to discuss where we ought to go from here. Some of my preferences already will have been apparent in the above analysis, but now I would like to discuss five specific hopes for future strategy research. These will not deal with topical areas of study or specific methodologies. Those choices depend on trends unfolding in the business environment around us, theoretical breakthroughs, and dead ends none of us can possibly foresee, as well as researcher tastes and repertoires. Instead, my emphasis will be on relatively broad themes that I hope will define the essential character of the strategy field in the 1990s.

### *Continuing commitment to generalism*

As a field matures, there is a natural tendency for specialization to occur. However, this trend is eventually destructive, leading to microscopic inquiries, lack of integration, and divisiveness. The field of strategy is falling victim to this trend, and we must somehow countervail it. Our researchers—particularly the younger researchers—are increasingly specialized, constrained in their theoretical and methodological range, and dogmatic about their preferred perspectives. At national meetings, I see more and more intolerant eye-rolling during paper presentations. As a member of several editorial review boards, I observe more and more fellow reviewers engaged in kneejerk criticisms, not of black-and-white matters but of matters on which no one really knows what perspective will eventually prove most informative.

Aggravating the problem is the increasing tendency for strategy departments at different schools to pursue "niche" strategies, some focusing on behavioral perspectives, others on industrial organization, institutional economics, or game theory. These specializations carry through to the doctoral programs of these schools, and the spiral of parochialism tightens all the more.

The phenomena with which we are concerned—issues facing general managers—inherently require a generalist perspective. The use of various frameworks, methods, and levels of analysis will provide us our best chance for moving knowledge forward.

As already noted, it is only realistic to expect researchers in a burgeoning field to specialize. However, the ideal is that they also will stay open-minded, engage in constructive give-and-take with those holding different interests, read widely, and be alert to deficiencies in their own approaches. We should promote these qualities in our professional societies and journals, in our schools and departments, and particularly in the training and socialization of our students.

### *Multiple methods*

After the above plea for diversity of perspective, it will not be surprising that I also hope to see diversity of research methods over the years ahead. Our field grew out of a clinical research tradition. This method took a great deal of abuse in the late seventies and early eighties; as our data showed above, the trend has been toward much heavier reliance on archival and survey data. Fortunately, the data also show a reasonable spread of methods used in our recent research. This diversity needs to continue, since every research question needs to be explored from different vantages. Some of those vantages incorporate great richness and texture; some provide tests of generalizability; some (lab experiments) provide stringent controls. Research will progress only with an interweaving of these methods. Researchers not only should be tolerant and encouraging of others in the use of various methods but should expand their own methodological repertoires in pursuit of their research questions.

### *Theory testing*

The strategy field has a tradition of idea generation with relatively little follow-up testing. It is, as the old wag goes, an area in which far more has been written than is known. In the recent past, as our data above show, researchers have done a somewhat higher number of deductive, theory-testing projects. This type of research is very important. Ironically, it often goes unsung and is even criticized as derivative or incremental.

In the academic business, ideas are a dime a dozen; in contrast, good ideas are exceedingly rare. However, in order to know whether an idea is good or not, it must be tested and retested. It may be the original theorist who earns the most eventual acclaim for a great idea. However, it is the testers—those who painstakingly design studies, operationalize complex constructs, and undertake the expense and frustrations of securing data—who ultimately inform us of the worth of different ideas. We need to keep the importance of theory testing squarely in front of us and bestow credit on those who do it well, each of us striving to do our fair share of testing—of both our own and others' ideas.

### *Dynamic models and data*

Strategy and all other aspects of top management work are dynamic—involving timing, sequencing, ebbs and flows, and responses and counter-responses. Yet, as our data above show, research in the field scarcely acknowledges the role of time. We must correct this problem. More of our models need to be dynamic, and our data need to be longitudinal.

Without necessarily embracing their assumptions about limits on managerial discretion, strategists stand to learn a great deal from population ecologists. They incorporate the flow of time into almost every model they build; similarly, they collect longitudinal data for all their empirical projects. These models and methods often require more ingenuity, money, and analytical sophistication than static models and cross-sectional data. However, adoption of these is essential to the future of strategy.

### *Realistic assumptions about managers and organizations*

Our data revealed that the vast preponderence of recent strategy research has labored under an assumption of strategic rationality in organizations. Top managers may intend to be rational maximizers (and they can be counted on to tell researchers of those intentions), but the reality is that they are finite individuals like the rest of us. When put together in a social context—complete with information distortions, division of labor, status seeking, and imprecise control systems—managers can be expected to deviate from techno-economic rationality all the more. The strategy field needs more models and methods that account for and examine departures from strategic rationality. This invariably will require more input from behavioral disciplines—particularly psychology, sociology, and political science—and proportionately less from economics and traditional management thought. Until our assumptions square with reality, we have little chance to influence managerial practice.

## Conclusion

I close by emphasizing that we, as a field of inquiry, must build into our efforts a capacity to be reflective and self-critical. We need the courage and patience to step back and see if we are on track and comfortable with where we are headed. Conversely, we must avoid yo-yoing around each time a critic claims the wisdom of a new path or perspective. We must be true to our charter: the study of general management problems from the point of view of the general manager. That is our distinctive competence, and it is a realm of great theoretical and practical promise.

## Note

Chandrasekaran Rajam, of Pennsylvania State University, deserves great credit for his help in several phases of this project.

## References

Allison, G. T. 1971. *Essence of Decision: Explaining the Cuban Missile Crisis*. Boston: Little, Brown and Company.

Andrews, K. R. 1971. *The Concept of Corporate Strategy*. Homewood, Ill.: Dow Jones-Irwin.

Ansoff, H. I. 1965. *Corporate Strategy*. New York: McGraw-Hill Book Company.

Boston Consulting Group. 1968. *Perspectives on Experience*. Boston: Boston Consulting Group.

Chandler, A. D., Jr. 1962. *Strategy and Structure: Chapters in the History of the American Enterprise*. Cambridge, Mass.: MIT Press.

Child, J. 1972. "Organizational Structure, Environment and Performance." *Sociology* 6: 1–22.

Daft, R. L. 1980. "The Evolution of Organizational Analysis in *ASQ*, 1959–1979." *Administrative Science Quarterly* 25, no. 3 (September): 623–636.

Evered, R. 1980. Review of *Strategic Management: A New View of Business Policy and Planning*, edited by D. E. Schendel and C. W. Hofer. *Administrative Science Quarterly* 25, no. 3 (September): 536–542.

Freeman, R. E. 1984. *Strategic Management: A Stakeholder Approach*. Marshfield, Mass.: Pitman.

Hambrick, D. C. 1983. "An Empirical Typology of Mature Industrial-Product Environment." *Academy of Management Journal* 26, no. 2: 213–230.

Harrigan, K. R. 1980. *Strategies for Declining Businesses*. Lexington, Mass.: D. C. Heath and Company.

Hofer, C. W. 1975. "Toward a Contingency Theory of Business Strategy." *Academy of Management Journal* 18: 784–810.

——. 1976. "Research on Strategic Planning: A Summary of Past Studies and Suggestions for Future Efforts." *Journal of Economics and Business* 28: 261–286.

Jauch, L. R. 1983. "An Inventory of Selected Academic Research in Strategic Management." In *Advances in Strategic Management*, edited by R. Lamb, pp. 141–175. Greenwich, Conn.: JAI Press.

Miles, R. E., and C. C Snow. 1978. *Organizational Strategy, Structure, and Process*. New York: McGraw-Hill Book Company.

Peters, T. J., and R. H. Waterman. 1982. *In Search of Excellence: Lessons from America's Best-Run Companies*. New York: Harper & Row.

Porter, M. E. 1980. *Competitive Strategy*. New York: Free Press.

Quinn, J. B. 1980. *Strategies for Change: Logical Incrementalism*. Homewood, Ill.: Richard D. Irwin.

Rumelt, R. P. 1974. *Strategy, Structure and Economic Performance*. Cambridge, Mass.: Harvard University Press.

Saunders, C. B., and J. C. Thompson. 1980. "A Survey of the Current State of Business Policy Research." *Strategic Management Journal* 1: 119–130.

Schendel, D. E., and C. W. Hofer, eds. 1979. *Strategic Management: A New View of Business Policy and Planning*. Boston: Little, Brown and Company.

Scherer, F. M. 1980. *Industrial Market Structure and Economic Performance*. Chicago: Rand McNally and Company.

Thompson, J. C. 1967. *Organizations in Actions*. New York: McGraw-Hill Book Company.

49

# THE THEORY AND PRACTICE OF STRATEGIC HRM AND PARTICIPATIVE MANAGEMENT

## Antecedents in early industrial relations

*Bruce E. Kaufman*

Source: *Human Resource Management Review* 11(4) (2001): 505–33.

**Abstract**

Two central concepts in contemporary management research are strategic human resource management (SHRM) and participative management (PM). Most writers on these subjects portray them as relatively recent (post-1970s) developments in the industry and, in turn, trace their origin in the academic literature to the post-World War II writings of scholars, such as Kurt Lewin, Douglas McGregor, Chris Argyris, H. Igor Ansoff, and Michael Porter. This chronology is largely correct if attention is restricted to the academic field of management, but it misses important antecedent contributions in both theory and practice made several decades earlier by industrial relations academics and management practitioners. This paper describes these early antecedents and demonstrates that both the concept and practice of SHRM and PM were explicitly articulated and implemented in the 1920s, albeit in a different idiom and context than today. 

### 1. Introduction

"Goodwill is a competitive advantage."

John R. Commons, 1919, p. 74

Two subjects extensively researched and discussed in the management literature are strategic human resource management (SHRM) and participative management (PM). As documented below, the conventional wisdom holds that both SHRM and PM are largely post-1970s business practices spawned by the need of American managers to substantially increase organizational performance in the face of growing domestic and international competition, new technologies, and changing social values. The intellectual roots of both SHRM and PM are, in turn, typically traced to the post-World War II writings of management, industrial organization and behavioral science scholars, such as H. Igor Ansoff and Michael Porter in the case of business strategy (from which SHRM gets much of its intellectual content) and Kurt Lewin, Chris Argyris, and Douglas McGregor in the case of PM.

A closer reading of the history of industrial relations (IR) and personnel management reveals, however, that both SHRM and PM had important antecedents in both theory and practice several decades earlier. In particular, both concepts first emerged in embryonic form out of a fundamental shift in HRM paradigms that took place roughly from 1915 to 1925. This new paradigm emphasized the importance of employees as organizational assets or *human resources*, was explicitly framed as an integrated set of HRM practices aimed at achieving competitive advantage in a *strategic* business sense, and made employee *participation* in the operation of the business a central part of the new style of management. Equally noteworthy is the fact that the major academic source of these new ideas is a group of IR scholars largely neglected in accounts of the rise of SHRM and PM — institutional labor economist John R. Commons and his colleagues of the Wisconsin School.

Each of these arguments is developed in more detail below. I begin by briefly summarizing and documenting the prevailing view in the management literature regarding the origins of SHRM and PM. Next, I describe the new HRM paradigm that emerged in the 1915–1925 period and the reasons behind its development. Then, I focus more specifically on, first, the strategic nature of this new HRM paradigm and, second, the key role played in it by the concept and practice of PM. Both concepts, I show, were explicitly discussed and described by Commons and other early IR scholars and soon made their way into the discourse and practice of employment management during the 1920s.

Although this paper is largely an essay in the history of thought, a number of insights and implications are generated that have current-day relevance for theory and policy. An example of the former is to call attention to Common's five models of employment management and their possible use as an alternative conceptual base for SHRM theory. An example of the latter is to highlight the deadening effect the combination of the Great Depression and National Labor Relations Act's ban on nonunion employee representation plans had on what was then (the 1930s) the most advanced corporate programs of participative management to be found anywhere in the world.

## 2. Review of the literature

SHRM and PM are independent concepts, although in the contemporary literature, the two are often linked together — typically in the context of high-performance work systems (Delaney & Godard, this issue; McMahan, Bell, & Virick, 1998). Definitions of SHRM vary, but most authors (e.g., Dulebohn, Ferris, & Stodd, 1995; Huselid, Jackson, & Schuler, 1997; Wright, 1998) suggest that the essence of the human resource perspective is that employees are viewed as valuable assets and SHRM, in turn, is the development and implementation of an overall plan that seeks to gain and sustain competitive advantage by managing these human assets through an integrated, synergistic set of HR practices that both complements and promotes the overall business strategy of the organization.

Definitions of PM also vary. Oftentimes, the term is also used more or less interchangeably with employee involvement (EI). Whatever the case, most authors agree that the essence of PM is conferring greater decision-making authority and responsibility to front-line employees so they, too, have some involvement (albeit often at a nonstrategic level) in the control and coordination of the basic activities and functions of the enterprise (Cotton, 1994). As Lawler, Albers, and Ledford (1992) emphasize, effective PM typically requires greater sharing of information, rewards, and power with front-line employees, as well as considerably greater investment in training.

Knowing what SHRM and PM are, the next question is where they originated both as intellectual constructs and in the real world of business practice. Although as noted above, SHRM and PM are distinct concepts, one reads in many places that both emerged at more or less the same time — the decade spanning from the mid-1960s to the mid-1970s — and have spread in popularity and influence in the years since due to such things as greater domestic and international competition and changing technology, workforce demographics, and social values.

Indicative of this point of view, for example, is this statement by Dyer and Holder (1988, p. 1): "The decade of the 1980s has brought another transformation in the practice and study of human resource management (HRM): The field has discovered, and indeed begun to embrace, a strategic perspective." In a similar vein, but with reference to PM, Dulebohn *et al.* (1995, p. 28) state that, "The famous General Motors Lordstown strike in 1970 demonstrated that when you have a highly educated work force being forced to work on very boring and monotonous jobs, dysfunctional behaviors will result . . . Part of these changing attitudes [of workers] was reflected in increased interest in having more input and involvement in workplace practices and decisions. We began to see evidence of such programs in many different forms . . . [and] while such efforts did not proceed without difficulty, they were nevertheless monumental and of historical significance in the evolution of the field."

Much the same conclusion is reached, albeit through a different route, by a number of prominent textbook authors in their discussion of the history of the field of personnel/HRM. Ivancevich (1995, p. 5), for example, states that, "The early history of personnel still obscures the importance of the HRM function to management. Until the 1960s, the personnel function was considered to be concerned only with blue-collar or operating employees. It was viewed as a record-keeping unit that handed out 25-year tenure pins and coordinated the company picnic." Similarly, Cascio (1992, p. 39) describes HRM up to the mid-1960s as in its "file-maintenance" stage of development — a description echoed by Noe, Hollenbeck, Gerhart, and Wright (1997, p. 4) when they say that, "From 1911 to 1930, human resource practices were conducted primarily by what was known as the 'personnel department.' The personnel department's major role was to keep track of employee records. . . ."

Lastly considered are the opinions of various management scholars who have taken a more in-depth look at the historical origins of SHRM and PM. These opinions should be given the greatest weight, since they reflect more in-depth research on the subject than is done by most textbook authors.

One oft-cited historical summary of the development of the personnel/HRM field is in an article by Carroll and Schuler (1983). There they present, starting in 1900, a summary of the major HRM innovations in each successive decade up to 1980. PM is listed as the major innovation in the decade of the 1960s, while SHRM is not listed at all. But in a more recent edition of his HRM textbook, Schuler (1995, p. 21) updates this summary to the 1990s and lists SHRM as one of the major innovations. Their historical schema is, thus, entirely consistent with the conclusions of the other authors cited above.

A second example, this time dealing only with SHRM, comes from an article by McMahan *et al.* (1998, p. 195). In a section entitled, "Brief Evolution of SHRM," they state that, "the study of strategic human resource management is a relatively new body of research. The area of strategic HR has its beginning in the late 1970s and early 1980s when the field was being influenced by the rapid emergence of the area of strategic management." In a similar vein, Wright and McMahan (1992, p. 295) state that the field of SHRM is in "its relative infancy." They go on to say that (pp. 297–298), "the field [HRM] has not evolved with great levels of integration across the various functions. Rather, each of the various HRM functions have evolved in relative isolation from one another . . . However, more recently, writers have begun to approach the area of HRM from a much more macroorientation — that is, what could more accurately be called SHRM." They cite a number of studies (e.g., Lengnick-Hall & Lengnick-Hall, 1988; Schuler & Jackson, 1987; Wright & Snell, 1991) and theoretical perspectives (e.g., resource based view of the firm, behavioral theory, transaction cost economics) that have made important contributions to the development of

SHRM, a common denominator of which is that they appeared only in recent years.

A number of management scholars have also written at more length on the origins and history of PM. One is struck, however, by the diversity of opinions on this subject. Consistent with Carroll and Schuler (1983), Lawler *et al.* (1992) also trace the origins of PM/EI to the early 1960s and, in particular, to the writings of behavioral scientists, such as Douglas McGregor, Chris Argyris, and Rensis Likert. Cotton (1994), on the other hand, traces PM back to the 1940s and the writings of social psychologist Kurt Lewin. A third opinion is offered by Stanton (1993), who attributes the origins of PM/EI to two behavioral scientists, Lester Coch and John French, who also wrote in the late 1940s but on the issue of organizational change.

## 3. Historical antecedents of modern SHRM and PM

The historical literature reveals that the origins of SHRM and PM predate all of the persons and "birth years" cited above. In point of fact, it was actually in the decade spanning the 1915–1925 period that SHRM and PM first emerged in embryonic form as both intellectual constructs and applied business practices, and if one year is to be picked as the birth year, it would be 1919. This was the year when institutional economist John R. Commons published *Industrial Goodwill*, the first major work by an American academic that: (a) developed the idea that employees are valuable organizational resources (including explicit use of the term "human resources"), (b) laid out a strategic choice framework with regard to alternative "bundles" of HRM practices, and (c) articulated the concept of PM, why it might improve organizational performance, and what particular model(s) of HRM it best fits.

### *3.1. Commons and the wisconsin school*

Although Commons' name is omitted entirely from many accounts of the early history of personal/HRM (e.g., Dulebohn *et al.*, 1995; Eilbert, 1959), and given only passing reference in others (e.g., Ling, 1965; Wren, 1994), it is demonstrably the case that at the time he was regarded as one of the nation's preeminent experts on labor issues and, as I have argued elsewhere (Kaufman, 1998, 1999), is legitimately viewed as a cofounder of the field of personnel/HRM (the other cofounders, I suggest, are Ordway Tead and Henry Metcalf). This claim will be surprising to many modern-day scholars, as Commons is most often associated with three distinct, nonmanagement subject areas: unions and labor history, as illustrated by the multivolume series *History of Labor in the United States* (Commons, 1918); labor legislation, such as workers' compensation, industrial safety, and unemployment insurance laws, which he helped draft and enact into law and wrote about in the most widely used labor law text of the day, *Principles of Labor Legislation*

(Commons & Andrews, 1916); and institutional economic theory (see Van de Ven, 1993), such as contained in his last major life's work, *Institutional Economics* (Commons, 1934a).

A fourth area of labor research and investigation pioneered by Commons, and the one in which his contributions are least recognized today, is personnel management. This phase of his research career and field investigation covers roughly the period 1915–1925 — the same period of time in which the field of personnel management was born and personnel departments were first established in industry.

The beginning point of his interest in personnel management was coterminous with his service as one of the nine members (and the only academic member) of the U.S. Commission on Industrial Relations, an investigative body created by President Taft in 1912 and which travelled throughout the United States during the next 2 years hearing testimony from employers, workers, unionists, and a wide range of other people on the causes of the numerous significant labor problems of that era, including widespread labor conflict, appalling levels of workplace injuries and fatalities, and glaring sources of inefficiency and waste in production (Harter, 1962). Through his service on the Commission, as well as earlier work with the National Civic Federation and the Industrial Commission of Wisconsin and a series of plant visits with Frederick Taylor and other experts on scientific management, Commons developed a keen interest and knowledge in the management side of IR [as used here and throughout, it is important to note that the term IR is defined broadly, in keeping with standard practice before WWII, to connote both the study of personnel/HRM and union–management relations; see Kaufman, 1993 and Kaufman, this issue].

The first of his publications to deal with personnel management was *Industrial Goodwill* (1919), a book that was described by the *Bulletin of the Taylor Society* (10/19:5) as in "a class of its own" with respect to the management of IR and a work, as I shall show below, that introduced for the first time the basic notions of SHRM and PM. Two years later, Commons (1921) published another major work on personnel management entitled, *Industrial Government*. This book was the product of personal visits by Commons and associates to 30 leading companies and details various aspects of their personnel/IR programs and methods of what was then called "industrial government" — a subject more often referred to today as "workforce governance" (see Kaufman, Lewin, & Adams, 1995). *Industrial Government* was, for that era, essentially the personnel/IR equivalent of Peters and Waterman's (1982) *In Search of Excellence*.

Commons' research and investigation from 1921 to 1925 or so then turned to methods by which government and business could stabilize employment and thereby provide greater job security for workers — a condition he considered to be the single most important prerequisite for improved production efficiency and employer–employee relations. This work culminated in another book, coauthored with two leading management practitioners, called *Can Business Prevent Unemployment?* (Commons, Lewisohn, Draper, & Lescohier, 1925). After this book, his research turned increasingly toward two nonlabor subjects, monetary policy and economic theory.

No other academic writer on labor issues was as widely cited in the literature of personnel management during the 1915–1925 period as John R. Commons (Kaufman, 1998). It is also noteworthy that three of his students at the University of Wisconsin — Sumner Slichter, William Leiserson, and Don Lescohier (members of what became known as the "Wisconsin School") — followed in Commons' footsteps and established reputations during the 1920s as leading academic experts on personnel management (Kaufman, 2000b). Indeed, the articles and book chapters written during the late 1910s-early 1930s by these three economists on the subject of personnel management (Leiserson, 1929; Lescohier, 1935; Slichter, 1919, 1920, 1929) rank as the most authoritative scholarly accounts available from that period on the early development, accomplishments, and shortcomings of the field.

### *3.2. Labor problems and their solution*

The germinal ideas behind the birth and development of personnel management as both a field of study and vocational practice in industry emerged in the 5–6 years preceding American entry into World War I (Jacoby, 1985). The first authoritative review of the origins and development of the field I am aware of was published in January 1920 by the Federal Board for Vocational Education under the title *Employment Management: Its Rise and Scope* (the term "employment management" was more frequently used than "personnel management" through most of the 1910s but in the 1920s came to be regarded as more narrow in conception than the latter). The report opens with this statement (p. 7):

> A great deal of thought is now being given by American business men to the subject of employment management. At one time, the labor problem seemed to be solely a matter of the policies of organized labor and the methods of industrial warfare. It now shows itself to be chiefly a question of the intelligent handling of the human relations, which result from the normal course of business day by day. It has to do with a study of the requirements of each occupation, the careful selection of men for their work, their adequate training, the fixing of just wages, the maintenance of proper working conditions, and the protection of men against undue fatigue, accidents, disease, and the demoralizing influences of a narrow and inadequate life, and the opening of a channel through which employees may reach the ear of the management for the expression of any dissatisfaction with its labor policies.

Several points about this quotation are noteworthy. First, it highlights the concept of "the labor problem," which was the anchoring idea around which all discussions of labor and employment issues revolved in the years up to the Great Depression (Kaufman, 1993). As initially conceived, the labor problem was a unitary construct and connoted the generalized struggle between labor and capital, and the conflict arising therefrom, over control of the twin processes of production and the distribution of income. After the turn of the century, the concept broadened into a plural form of "labor problems" in the recognition that labor problems take many distinct forms, such as high employee turnover, low work effort, poverty-level pay, strikes, and unsafe working conditions, and that these problems adversely affect both employers and employees (Leiserson, 1929). The object of the field of IR, as originally conceived in the late 1910s-early 1920s, was to devise theories and practices to ameliorate these labor problems, with the thought that in doing so both employers and employees could potentially gain (a win–win or "positive sum" game).

The next point concerns the progression of academic and practitioner thinking on the possible means by which to effect this solution to labor problems. By the late 1920s, it was widely agreed (e.g., Estey, 1928; Watkins, 1928) that there are three conceptually distinct "solutions" to labor problems, labelled at the time as the *workers*' solution (trade unionism and collective bargaining), the *employers*' solution (personnel management), and the *community's* solution (protective labor law and social insurance). As indicated in the above-cited quotation, the first of these proposed solutions to be extensively focused on was the workers' solution of trade unionism and collective bargaining. This line of research was begun in earnest in the 1880s with the publication of Ely's (1886) *The Labor Movement in America* and was carried on by a large number of scholars after the turn of the century, the most influential of these writers being Commons who was a student of Ely's and later a colleague of Ely's at Wisconsin.

Next in the order of development was the community's solution of protective labor legislation and social insurance. This second solution to labor problems was again pioneered by Ely and Commons, as illustrated by their role as founders and officers of a research and lobbying group created in 1906 called the American Association for Labor Legislation (AALL). The AALL was widely recognized for the next three decades as the most influential voice in America for protective labor legislation (Moss, 1996), such as laws on minimum wages, child labor, maximum hours, and industrial safety, and for social insurance programs, such as workers' compensation, unemployment insurance, national health insurance, and old age insurance (social security). Commons' leading role in this movement is also illustrated by his above-cited, nationally recognized text on labor law, *Principles of Labor Legislation* (Commons & Andrews, 1916).

The third solution to labor problems — the employers' solution of personnel management — was the last to be developed. It did not begin to take form until the early to mid-1910s. One of the principal precursors of personnel management — scientific management — had much earlier roots, however, in the writings on scientific management by Frederick Taylor (Jacoby, 1985; Lescohier, 1935). It is instructive to note that Taylor's (1895) first published paper on scientific management was entitled (emphasis added), "A Piece Rate System, Being a Step Toward a Partial *Solution of the Labour Problem.*" As is well known, Taylor sought to solve the labor problem by promoting cooperation between labor and capital and a win–win outcome of greater efficiency and higher profits and wages by discovering and implementing through scientific research the "one best way" to industrial management. The verdict of academic and practitioner writers (e.g., Bruere, 1929; Tead & Metcalf, 1920; Watkins, 1922) after the mid-1910s, however, was that Taylor's system had overemphasized the "physical" engineering aspects of industrial management and had neglected the "human" engineering side. As elaborated below, the field of personnel management that arose after 1915 was in essence a melding of Taylor's scientific management principles from engineering with consideration of the "human factor" from the then nascent fields of industrial psychology and industrial sociology (Wren, 1994). And, as indicated above and documented more thoroughly below, just as Commons played a leading role in the development of research and practice in the two other solutions to labor problems — collective bargaining and labor legislation/social insurance — so, too, did he play a leading role in the development of the third solution, personnel management.

Two other points from the above-cited quotation deserve brief mention. Note, for example, that the term *human relations* is explicitly used. Although conventional wisdom has it that the term "human relations" was a product of the Hawthorne experiments in the late 1920s–early 1930s, in actual fact, the term human relations was widely used a decade earlier in both academic and practitioner writings on personnel management (Kaufman, 1993, p. 205). More importantly, this early literature (including Commons' *Industrial Goodwill*) also grasped, albeit in a relatively heuristic, nontechnical way, many of the fundamental ideas advanced later by Mayo (1933) and Roethlisberger and Dickson (1939), such as the importance of informal work groups, the practice of output restriction by employees, and the nonlogical nature of many aspects of workplace behavior.

And, lastly, note that the present-day functional division of personnel/HRM into discrete activities of employee selection, training, compensation, employee relations, etc. was already clearly demarcated by the end of the 1910s. This immediately suggests that claims made in the contemporary HRM literature that pre-WWII personnel management was mainly a "record keeping" or "file maintenance" activity are exaggerations. But it does not address the other claim so often made in the contemporary literature, namely, that these different functional personnel activities were utilized in a piecemeal, ad hoc nature rather than as part of an integrated, strategic approach to the management of people and management of the business. This subject is now explicitly addressed.

### *3.3. Pre-WWI HRM practices: strategic or tactical?*

The issue is to determine at what historical point HRM practices and policies first passed from being "tactical" to "strategic." To answer this, in turn, requires clarity on what distinguishes strategic from tactical HRM. On this matter, Delery and Doty (1996, p. 802) state that, "The basic premise underlying SHRM is that organizations adopting a particular strategy require HR practices that are different from those required by organizations adopting alternative strategies." In a somewhat different formulation, Wright and McMahan (1992, p. 298) state that SHRM is, "the pattern of planned human resource deployments and activities intended to enable an organization to achieve its goals."

If these definitions of SHRM are accepted as a reasonable statement of the concept, considerable ambiguity arises as to whether personnel practices of American employers prior to WWI were strategic or nonstrategic (tactical). Consider this statement by Slichter (1929, p. 393) in an oft-cited review of the evolution of corporate personnel policies up to the late 1920s: "To the abundance of cheap immigrant labor are primarily attributable the two outstanding features of American labor policy before the war [WWI] — the tendency to adapt jobs to men rather than men to jobs, and the policy of obtaining output by driving the workers rather than by developing their good will and cooperation." He goes on to say that (p. 395), "With labor policies so crude and simple, industrial relations were not believed to require the attention of highly paid experts. The handling of men was largely left to the department foremen, who were free to hire, 'fire,' and promote as they saw fit, who set piece rates, and who often possessed considerable discretion in fixing hourly rates of pay."

If Slichter's assertions are accepted as factually correct, and given the above definitions of SHRM, one is led to conclude that employers prior to WWI were indeed practicing SHRM even though they had no formal personnel function or department in the organization (indeed, the absence of such was a strategic decision!). Note for example, that Slichter starts off using the phrase "American labor *policy*," where the term "policy" at that time and up until the 1980s had the clear connotation of a comprehensive business plan crafted to attain certain goals in light of external conditions and internal resources — in other words, a *strategy* (Yoder, 1970, p. 25, for example, uses the two terms interchangeably). Furthermore, note that according to Slichter, business firms consciously adopted this particular labor strategy because it had a good "fit" with the environment (a large supply of cheap labor) and competencies/characteristics of their human resources (largely unskilled and illiterate immigrants). And, finally, observe that the various personnel practices that made up the employers' labor policy ("drive" methods of work motivation, deskilling jobs to fit illiterate immigrants, low wages for unskilled labor) were mutually consistent with each other and supported the larger business goal of maximum profit.

A different perspective is provided by Dudley Kennedy (1919), a management consultant and frequent contributor of articles in the practitioner press. Writing in late 1919, he says (p. 354), "Only a few years ago, some of the more progressive large concerns began to consider the labor question as a problem. They began to sense the fact that they had been largely busied with the mechanical and financial side of the business, allowing the human side to drift where it would. This drifting policy was not conscious, but rather one of uninformed indifference and of a lack of appreciation of the growing complexity of the relations breeding . . . industrial unrest and general distrust." He goes on to say that (p. 355), "I have myself been almost dumbfounded to find how few large employers of workers have any definite constructive labor policy . . . ninety-nine times out of a hundred . . . he [the employer] will admit that he has only a negative policy or a policy of expediency."

If Kennedy's description of the situation is taken at face value, one is led to conclude that pre-WWI employers' did *not* typically practice SHRM. The sine qua non of SHRM, according to the above-cited definitions, is a conscious planning process in which managers devise HRM practices to best fit the environment and internal resources. But Kennedy states that employers largely "drifted" into the personnel practices then in use and that this drifting was not a conscious decision but one of neglect or expediency. He further states (p. 355) that many labor practices of that era were not the product of scientific thought but rather reflected a largely habitual allegiance to "the old idea of paying as little as possible" or unquestioned acquiescence to "the strict requirements of state law."

Given the conflicting evidence, it is not possible to say with assurance that personnel practices prior to WWI were indeed "strategic," at least in the sense cited above. It is quite evident, however, that the economic and political events surrounding World War I fundamentally changed both management consciousness and policy toward labor, leading to a pronounced *strategic* shift in personnel/HRM practices.

### *3.4. WWI and the birth of personnel management*

The personnel management movement antedated American involvement in World War I by several years. A major beginning point, for example, was the founding of the Employment Managers Association in Boston, MA in 1912 (Jacoby, 1985). But by all accounts, the political and economic events unleashed by the war gave a tremendous impetus to what was up to that point a slowly evolving and quite nascent movement. As Slichter explains, when labor is abundant and cheap, unions are weak, and public opinion demands little of management in the way of social responsibility toward labor, companies have scant incentive to avoid waste and spoilage of their human resources or to adopt more than "crude and simple" personnel practices.

However, with the entrance of the United States into the war, conditions changed radically, as did the incentives for a more liberal and strategically thought out labor policy. Indicative of this transformation are these comments of Water Matherly (1926). Of the prewar situation, he states (p. 256): "Personnel management, as it is understood in present-day industry, is of rather recent origin. While there are evidences of personnel work extending far back into industrial history, the attention devoted to it was incidental. It was not considered important enough to justify the establishment of a separate specialized department to handle the problems involved and to solve these problems in the light of scientific knowledge. Everything that was done was looked upon merely as a by-product of management as a whole." He goes to explain that interest in personnel administration began shortly before the war, and that (p. 257, emphasis added), "During the World War, the movement for the scientific handling of personnel received further impetus. From the very beginning of the war, personnel departments grew apace, since it was imperative to adjust the industrial machine to meet the wartime demands of the Allies for supplies and munitions. When the United States decided to enter the conflict, the improvement and conservation of *human resources* became all the more important."

As alluded to by Matherly, the production demands of the war soon created a labor shortage. Suddenly, the labor that had been so cheap and abundant was now scarce and dear, and the drive system of motivation that had effectively coaxed work effort out of a workforce fearful for their jobs now resulted instead in a wave of strikes, "soldiering" (loafing) on the job, and sky-high rates of labor turnover. These economic considerations, coupled with an emergent social movement during the war among all classes of American society for greater "industrial democracy," led most employers to fundamentally rethink their labor practices (Kaufman, 2000a).

Several points about this rethinking are important to note. First, for this rethinking to be "strategic" (per the definitions cited above), it must involve on the part of firms a deliberate, comprehensive consideration of alternative systems of labor management in light of both external conditions and internal resources and competencies. Prior to the war, prevailing management thought precluded effective strategizing because alternative "models" of labor management had not yet been articulated. On one hand, there was the traditional system of labor management that was largely unscientific and informal, and on the other, there was the new Taylor credo of scientific management. The problem with the latter, however, was that its emphasis on "the one best way" effectively precluded any role for management strategy per se, as the laws of science were presumptively deterministic as to the optimal structure and form of labor practices.

Into this lacuna stepped Commons and colleagues. Note first the following statement of Slichter (1920), for it clearly moves HRM away from Taylor's deterministic "one best way" and toward a contingency conceptualization. He says (p. 39), "Too often in discussions of systems and philosophies of management an absolutist point of view has been adopted and specific systems of management have been recommended as the only true 'scientific' systems of management. As a matter of fact, the desirability of managerial policies depends largely upon economic conditions. The drive system of management was fairly effective as long as labor was economically weak. But when capital lost its economic dominance, the drive system broke down and managers sought new methods of handling labor."

Slichter clearly implies here that management has a variety of alternative labor policies to choose from, and that this choice is shaped by, or contingent on, the external economic environment (but not deterministically so, for he later describes how management philosophy also shapes the choice of labor policy). Now, having recognized the contingent nature of HRM practices, the logical next step in formulating a strategic approach to labor policy is to identify alternative configurations or "bundles" of HRM practices that match different types of business and HRM strategies.

The first attempt at this I am aware of in the management literature (noting that in this period "management" was often considered a branch of "applied economics") is given by Commons in *Industrial Goodwill* (see also Leiserson, 1924). There he identifies five alternative theories or "models" of labor management. They are:

- *Commodity*. In this model, management treats labor as if it were a commodity. Labor is bought for as little as possible and used only as long as profitable. Supply and demand determine the terms and conditions of labor and labor practices are determined by and fluctuate with the market. This is the neoclassical economist's model.
- *Machine*. This model of labor management views workers as a machine, albeit a human one and, thus, uses principles of "human engineering" to determine optimal labor practices. Drawing its inspiration from Taylor's scientific management, this model attempts to discover through scientific investigation what "makes the worker tick" and then, using these insights, create an appropriate organizational structure, work process, and set of administrative practices to gain maximum production.
- *Public utility*. Rather than a commodity, in this model, labor is viewed as a valuable natural resource and asset for business firms. From this perspective, labor will be exploited and wasted, like other natural

resources, if labor practices are totally left to the forces of supply and demand. In what is one of the first uses of the term "human resources" in the literature, Commons states of workers (p. 130), "These human resources come to them [employers] after a heavy investment. The parents have invested something, The taxpayers and the schools have invested something." He then says (p. 129), "Somebody must pay for the conservation of the nation's human resources. If left to demand and supply, the most valuable resources are not conserved." Thus, to protect the nation's human resources labor should be treated as a "public utility" in the sense that its use in production is made compatible with the public interest through labor practices constrained and shaped by government legislation and regulation.

- *Good will.* This model of labor relations views the worker as a customer whose good will, or repeat business, the employer strives to attain and keep. Good will, in turn, is important because it creates the psychological conditions necessary for effective organizational performance — high employee morale, loyalty to the firm, and a willingness to cooperate and work hard toward a common end. Important determinants of good will are trust, fair dealing, and expectations of mutual gain and, thus, labor practices in this model are significantly shaped by these considerations.
- *Citizenship.* In all of the above models, the employer is, in effect, a dictator, albeit a potentially benevolent one, in that it is the employer who unilaterally determines the labor practices in the workplace. The employee's only option if dissatisfied is to quit and find a different job. In anticipation of the "exit-voice" model pioneered by Hirschman (1970) and popularized by Freeman and Medoff (1984), Commons posits a fifth model of labor management which treats the firm as a form of industrial government in which workers, like citizens in a democracy, are given a voice in the determination of the terms and conditions of employment and are protected from arbitrary and capricious actions of management (the "rulers") by a system of due process in the shop. Among the various labor practices necessary to implement this model (e.g., methods for dispute resolution), he states (p. 43) that effective voice (like the human resource term, his use of the word "voice" is one of the first in the literature) typically requires in all but the smallest firms a collective form of worker organization either in the form of a trade union or some type of employer-sponsored informal committee system or formal representation plan.

Having outlined Commons' five theories of labor management, two things should be noted. First, it is clear that each model suggests or emphasizes a different (although in some cases overlapping) set of HRM practices. A commodity approach to labor, for example, places emphasis on cost minimization, a short-term employment relationship, little in-house training, and no mechanisms for voice. The implications for personnel practices are obvious. If a good will approach is taken, however, security of employment is crucial to fostering labor's willingness to cooperate (Commons, 1919, pp. 65–73). So, too, are considerations of fairness in the payment of wages and dispensation of discipline. And, finally, with security of employment goes a long-term employer–employee relationship. All of these factors also have obvious implications for personnel practices, and the mix thereof, that best promotes overall organizational performance.

A second point to note is with regard to contingency. Commons quite clearly recognizes that there is no "one-size-fits-all" approach to HRM practices. He further observes that an important determinant of strategic choice is not only the objective external and internal conditions facing the decision maker but also the decision makers' philosophy toward business and labor. Both considerations are evident in these remarks (pp. 166–167), "If the . . . employment manager looks upon labor as a commodity, then he weighs the facts according to the theory of demand and supply. If he looks upon labor as a machine he gives weight to the facts that get maximum output from the individual. If he entertains the goodwill theory then the facts that promote goodwill are looked for and get a proper emphasis in mind. . . . Only the foolish, the ignorant, the biased, or the arbitrary man ties himself up to a single theory."

### *3.5. The rise of the welfare capitalism model*

Employers of that era did not, of course, have any of Commons' five labor management models in their head, but they nevertheless created in the late 1910s–early 1920s, and solidified over the course of the decade, a fundamentally new HRM paradigm that relied far less on the commodity concept of labor and far more on elements of the latter four concepts. This new HRM paradigm has since become known in the business and labor history literature as the "Welfare Capitalism" model (Cohen, 1990; Gitelman, 1992; Jacoby, 1985, 1997).

One test, per the previously cited definitions of SHRM, of whether a new set of HRM practices represents a "strategic" innovation is the extent to which it: (a) is formulated to complement and promote the organization's overall business strategy, and (b) contains individual HR practices that are mutually complementary and synergistic.

What was the business goal then driving companies? Reminiscent of contemporary writings that almost invariably call attention to the pressures of increased competition, Donald and Donald (1929, p. 147) describe the business environment of the 1920s, thus, "The end of the war marked the beginning of more severe competition due in part to excessive plant capacity. But the competitive struggle became intensified through increasing competition between lines of industry producing substitute commodities

. . . Improved transportation facilities [also] bring sources of supply in competition with each other, which formerly were serving noncompeting territories. The result has been a severe demand upon the manufacturing end of the business to bring costs of production down to even lower levels."

Faced with increased competitive pressure in product markets, one option for employers was to go back to prewar labor practices through intensified drive methods, production speedups, and a minimalist approach to pay, benefits, and working conditions. Particularly after the Depression of 1920–1921 ended the labor shortage spawned by the war and the threat of militant unionism, many employers did in fact revert back to some variation of the prewar model (Harris, 1982; Jacoby, 1985). As ruefully noted in management publications of that period (e.g., Matherly, 1926), one of the first actions taken by these firms was to abolish their newly formed personnel departments and lay-off the personnel manager and staff (another was to quickly cut wages, which precipitated much employee discontent). For these firms, then, their sudden conversion to progressive HRM during the war was much more of a stopgap tactic than a new long-term strategy.

On the other hand, other companies stuck with the new paradigm and strengthened and refined it over the decade. Slichter (1929, p. 401) explains the essence of this strategy, thus: "unwilling to try driving [and reluctant to cut wages], one course remained — to increase efficiency by developing a stable force and by winning the good will and cooperation of the men. This alternative was widely adopted." He goes on to say that (emphasis in original), "Possibly the most important determinant of post-war labor policies, at least during the last four or five years, has been the growing realization by managers of the close relationship between industrial morale and efficiency. When the severe drop in prices and in sales during 1920 and 1921 caused managers to search meticulously for methods of cutting costs and of increasing sales, many ways were found in which the workers could help *if they would*."

A significant segment of the employer community, therefore, sought to gain competitive advantage, not through prewar policies that treated labor as a commodity and a short-term cost to be minimized, but rather through a long-run policy that sought increased productivity and quality and reduced turnover and strike costs by emphasizing elements of Commons' four other labor management models. The manner and form in which this policy was implemented became known as the "Welfare Capitalism" model. It had four fundamental features (Kaufman, 1993):

- the introduction of science into HR management (e.g., employee selection tests, time and motion study, creation of a functional staff department with expertise in personnel management),

- the practice of human relations (e.g., foreman training in handling employees; positive methods of discipline),
- extensive employee welfare benefits (e.g., health insurance, old age pensions, job security, promotion from within),
- some form of industrial democracy (e.g., a shop committee or employee representation plan).

Was this model a new and distinct paradigm of people management? The answer is certainly "yes," and on two grounds. The first is the fundamental nature of the change in management's labor policy, a change so distinct and far-reaching that Slichter (1929, p. 432) was led to conclude that, "Modern personnel methods are one of the most ambitious social experiments of the age." A similar conclusion is reached by C. Canby Balderston, dean of the Wharton School at the University of Pennsylvania. In the early 1930s, he canvassed academics, business groups, and management consultants to identify those firms that were leaders in the nation in progressive employer–employee relations. After on-site visits, he selected 25, wrote mini-case studies of each, and then summarized the lessons to be learned in his book *Executive Guidance of Industrial Relations* (Balderston, 1935). In the concluding chapter, he proffers this statement (p. 255): "The changed attitude of the employers toward industrial relations seems to have been one of the striking developments of the decade. Whether it be the result of education or of the prosperity of the 1920s, once can scarcely deny the change in outlook."

One can also conclude that the HRM model implemented by Welfare Capitalist firms was a new and distinct model by examining its constituent parts. According to Lescohier (1935), in the decade prior to WWI, progressive HRM was characterized by two largely disconnected and narrow innovations: incentive forms of pay and various welfare benefits. By way of contrast, according to Balderston, the leading-edge personnel programs he examined at the start of the 1930s contained *13* distinct features covering all aspects of the employer–employee relation, such as provisions to insure fair wages, methods to regularize employment, clear policy guidelines on discipline and discharge, extensive training of foremen and supervisors, and some form of industrial democracy.

It must also be asked whether the new Welfare Capitalism model was indeed strategic in fact as well as in words. Four pieces of evidence suggest an affirmative answer.

The first is that the 13 personnel practices identified by Balderston were not adopted piecemeal or on some "mix and match" basis but, rather, represented, in his words (p. 290), an "integrated" approach and "composite program" for the purpose of gaining and sustaining competitive advantage.

One might suspect that this was a fortuitous development that "just happened," but the evidence is clear that even in the early 1920s businessmen were being counselled to think in strategic terms about HRM. In an address to the 1920 convention of the Industrial Relations Association of America (a group composed largely of personnel practitioners), for example, Leon Marshall (1920), dean of the University of Chicago School of Commerce, stated in his address to the group that the key to successful business is (p. 730), "getting men to work together effectively" and that in attaining this goal (p. 731), "personnel work ceases to be a congeries of uncoordinated, miscellaneous labor practices" and must "be administered as a coherent whole."

In a similar vein, Willard Hotchkiss (1923), an employer, consultant, and soon-to-be dean of the Stanford University School of Business, wrote in *The Harvard Business Review* that (p. 440, emphasis added), "When, however, we pass from *tactics to the question of major strategy*, industrial relations management . . . pervades all departments and crosses all department lines. Whether organized as a separate department or attached to central management, it must to succeed exercise an integrating, not a segregating, force on the business as a whole."

That this strategic vision was at least in part successfully implemented is then attested to by Leiserson (1929, pp. 139–140) who remarks that, "When completely developed, then, Personnel Management not only integrates under centralized control the movement of the personnel, through it employment policies, and provides proper conditions surrounding the working force, through its welfare or service policies, but also makes provision for something like a bill of rights, with a legislative organization to represent the workers from all parts of the plant, and some kind of judicial tribunal for the protection of the rights of both workers and management."

A second piece of evidence that the Welfare Capitalism model was a strategic choice is indicated by the very fact that only a minority of firms in the United States in the 1920s adopted something close to the full-fledged version. Writing in 1921, Commons spoke to the minority status of progressive HRM firms when he said (p. 263), "From 10 percent to 25 percent of American employers may be said to be so far ahead of the game that trade unions can not reach them. Conditions are better, wages are better, security is better, than unions can deliver to their members. The other 75 percent to 90 percent are backward." By the end of the decade, the number of progressive employers had grown in size and sophistication of management practices, but was still in the big picture of things a distinct minority. The number of workers covered by an employee representation plan, for example, tripled over the decade but yet, in 1929, less than 5% of all employees were covered, while only about one third of establishments with over 250 employees even had a personnel department (Lescohier, 1935). The point is that if everyone adopted the Welfare Capitalist model than the very notion of strategic choice would have doubtful utility in explaining the developments of the 1920s.

A third piece of evidence that the Welfare Capitalist model was strategic (i.e., long term in perspective) is that it led employers to adopt practices and policies that were clearly counter to their own short-run self-interests. A prime example is the "doctrine of high wages" embraced by the minority of progressive firms in the 1920s (Kaufman, 1996; Williams, 1927). The traditional "commodity" approach to labor was to "drive a hard bargain" and pay as low a wage as the market permitted. In the 1920s, however, a new theory gained credence that it was actually in the employer's interest to pay high (above-market) wages, since this augmented the purchasing power of employees who, in turn, then had the financial wherewithal to purchase the products of industry (other benefits, such as reduced turnover, were of course also an object). Despite the fact that such gains are clearly of a long-run nature and subject to "cheating" behavior on the part of individual firms (the "free rider" problem), the evidence is clear that many welfare capitalist firms did make high wages a central part of their personnel practices for the strategic reasons just outlined.

Finally, a fourth piece of evidence that the Welfare Capitalism model was indeed strategic comes from the strenuous attempt made by leading firms to keep it intact during the early Depression years even when great incentives and pressures built up to scrap it. As noted earlier, the Welfare Capitalism model was initially a response to tight labor markets, the rise of unions, and the need to cut cost through efficiency gains when wage cutting proved counterproductive. All of these factors disappeared as the economy plunged ever-lower during the early Depression years of 1930–1932.

With 25% of the workforce unemployed, employers certainly did not need to maintain the plethora of welfare benefits, an employee representation plan, or even an employment office in order to attract and keep workers, and suddenly the drive system, backed-up by a newly potent threat of discharge, became once again quite effective in getting the employees to work hard. And, also, the threat of unionization virtually collapsed as workers dared not go out on strike or so much as express interest in organizing for fear of being fired. Yet, despite the incentives to revert to a less progressive HRM policy, and the pressures of massive financial losses and the threat of bankruptcy (e.g., the steel industry was operating at less than 20% of capacity in 1932), most Welfare Capitalist employers maintained their personnel departments (albeit in reduced form), held the line on wages until the fall of 1931, provided extensive relief to their laid-off workers, and kept intact (if not always actively operating) their employee representation plans (Brody, 1980; Harris, 1982). The millions of dollars of extra cost incurred in this effort must be reckoned the price these firms were willing to pay to reap what they thought would be the long-run benefits from this new and socially progressive HRM strategy.

## 4. Antecedents of PM

Participative management, as noted above, is a separate and distinct concept from SHRM. An employer, for example, may make a strategic choice in favor of a commodity approach to labor and, as a result, will more than likely make little use of methods of PM.

The fact that PM is discussed in this paper along with SHRM is the result of a historical coincidence. The coincidence arises because employers, in thinking through the ramifications of nontraditional models of HRM in the late 1910s, realized once they made securing labor's good will a business objective that the autocracy inherent in the traditional "master–servant" relationship would have to be replaced by a measure of industrial democracy in the form of power sharing, joint consultation, and due process. Slichter (1920), thus, accurately describes the situation. Prior to WWI, he says (p. 37):

> By holding over labor the fear of discharge, capital was able to in considerable degree to control the speed of work, and to compel labor to produce what the management regarded as a fairly adequate day's work . . . altho aware of labor's lack of interest in production, and even of the deliberate efforts of workmen to limit it, [employers] did not regard the unsatisfactory state of industrial morale as an urgent or pressing problem. On the contrary, they . . . were inclined to regard attempts to develop labor's cooperation as not only unnecessary but useless.

Then, given the war time labor shortages and urgent demands on industry for production, he notes (p. 38):

> But with output dependent primarily upon labor's willingness to produce rather than upon capital's ability to compel production, labor's willingness to produce becomes of supreme consequence . . . The new conditions have created what may safely be termed the paramount managerial problem of the day — the problem of getting a satisfactory output when the control of production is largely in the hands of labor.

He further adds (pp. 38–39), "Nor is this problem a temporary one . . . it is likely in the long run to become steadily more acute."

As noted earlier, the first glimmerings of the new personnel management model that burst onto the industrial scene during and immediately after WWI actually appeared 5–6 years earlier. The same was true with respect to one of the important components of this new system-PM. Two seminal articles by practitioners, although viewed as utopian and even dangerously radical at the time, surfaced the concept for public discussion. The first was the memorial address delivered in 1915 upon the death of Frederick Taylor by future Supreme Court Justice Louis Brandeis, reprinted later in *Industrial Management* (Brandeis, 1918) under the title "Efficiency by Consent: to Secure Its Active Cooperation Labor Must be Consulted and Convinced in Regard to Changes." The second, and printed earlier in the November 1915 issue of the *Bulletin of the Taylor Society*, was a paper by management consultant Robert Valentine entitled, "The Progressive Relation of Efficiency to Consent." A quote from Brandeis' paper will convey the tenor of their thoughts.

> In the task of ascertaining whether proposed conditions of work do conform to these requirements [of scientific management], the laborer should take part. He is indeed a necessary witness . . . the participation of representatives of labor is indispensable for the inquiry which essentially involves the exercise of judgement . . . truth can only rule when accompanied by the consent of men.

These ideas suddenly gained widespread discussion and credibility upon American entry into the war. Partly, this new-found acceptance reflected an ideological shift in public opinion in favor of "industrial democracy," enunciated in these words by industrialist and convert to progressive HRM John D. Rockefeller Jr. (quoted in Selekman & Van Kleek, 1924, p. 32), "On the battlefield of France, this nation poured out its blood freely in order that democracy might be maintained at home and that its beneficent institutions might become available in other lands as well. Surely, it is not consistent for us as Americans to demand democracy in government and practice autocracy in industry." By "autocracy in industry," Rockefeller was referring to the legal doctrine of the time that the employment relationship is one of "master and servant."

As suggested by the above quote of Rockefeller, the idea of industrial democracy gained widespread acceptance in the business community in the late 1910s and was quickly translated into the more managerialist idiom of "PM." That the notion of PM is not a post-WWII concept is suggested, for example, by the title of a book by management consultant William Bassett (1919) and entitled, *When the Workmen Help You Manage*.

Bassett begins his book by striking this theme (p. 3), "Our big problem today is the fitting together of employer and employee upon a new basis of complete cooperation." Then, later, he argues that realizing this state of cooperation in industry requires (p. 24), "bringing in a measure of democracy to replace autocracy." And then democracy in industry gets translated into participative forms of management in these words (pp. 25–26, emphasis added),

> Directors of industry have two courses before them: they can fight the desires of the workingman for recognition and representation . . . , or they can combine to hitch their desires in double harness and put into the business the will and brain of every individual . . . [But] employers are apt to think of the participation of workers in the control of industry as taking something away . . . Yet it takes only a moment's thought to discover that profitable business is not built in such a fashion . . . Would not, then, the development of mutual work between employer and employee bring in so much talent now latent, *and get rid of so much supervision now thought necessary* as to insure profitable engagement for all the parties to industry?

Numerous other books and articles by management practitioners in the late 1910s-early 1920s articles struck much the same cord and, indeed, the term "participation in management" was widely used. Turning to academic writers, the concept of industrial democracy had been long-known and discussed, particularly after publication of the Webbs' (1897) highly influential book, *Industrial Democracy*. But the Webbs and later academic writers framed industrial democracy in terms of trade unionism and collective bargaining. The first academic to broaden the concept so that it included nonunion forms of EI and representation, and to recast it as a strategic element in the practice of personnel management, was Commons (1919) in *Industrial Goodwill*.

Commons notes, as did Brandeis, labor's hostility to scientific management. And he attributes this hostility to several factors (pp. 18–21): scientific management threatens to erode the worker's skills and autonomy on the job, is autocratic in nature ("government by experts"), and by fostering increased competition among individual workers it arouses a collective counter-response as workers use formal organization (unions) and informal sanctions (shunning, threats of violence) to protect their end of the wage–effort bargain. The end result is that scientific management defeats it purpose because the manner in which the program is developed and implemented loses labor's good will and, thus, leads to conflict and resistance.

Commons goes on to state that scientific management can work wonders in boosting efficiency and can be a boon, not a bane, to the workmen, but the key is winning labor's good will for then and only then will the employer gain the most crucial ingredients to success — labor's willing cooperation, interest, and commitment ("because it enlists his whole soul and all his energies in the thing the is doing"). The question, then, is how to accomplish this conversion from hostility to cooperation.

He states several preconditions on this matter. First, the employer must recognize that he has to deal with labor not only on an individual basis but also on a group basis for regardless whether the shop is unionized or not labor thinks and acts collectively. Second, the most fundamental precondition for successful development of good will is employment security — not a guarantee of a lifetime job but a reasonable expectation of continuity in employment given satisfactory job performance and company profits. Third, good will requires that shop governance be built on the rule of law and not the arbitrary decisions of men, meaning that either through collective bargaining or management policy, a system of "due process" must be developed that assures an impartial administration of justice. And, as a fourth factor, Commons identifies a need for some form of democratic governance mechanism, or as he puts it (p. 43, slightly paraphrased), "an organization for effective voice." Good will, he states, is built on giving employees an opportunity to affirmatively give consent, express opinions, and participate in decisions that affect them; and the result is (p. 109), "by admitting labor into the councils and authority of the company, they [employers] are winning industrial peace."

It is this fourth condition enumerated by Commons that is the root of the PM idea and that, as far as I am aware, had not been previously elaborated on by another American academic writer and made a linchpin component of a new HRM paradigm. And Commons does more than just identify the idea of PM, he goes further and describes what he sees as its limits and potentialities. In *Industrial Government* (Commons, 1921, p. 266), for example, he states two kinds of participation that labor does *not* desire: participation in executive-level business decisions and participation in the financial risks of running the organization Rather, workers are interested in participation at two levels.

One desired level of participation is in the performance of their job and the conditions surrounding it (pp. 113–114). As described in *Industrial Goodwill* (pp. 152–153), and later in his autobiography (Commons, 1934b), Commons was a leader in the industrial safety movement in the 1910s and discovered that involving employees in safety prevention was a far more effective device to reduce accidents than any safety program management could unilaterally devise. The same, he states, applies to other management HR programs, such as time and motion study (p. 124), as well as the performance of the job itself. With regard to the latter, the pay-off to participation, in his view, is that it helps elicit labor's interest in the work and having interest in the work leads to (p. 141) "overcoming obstacles that are not hopeless, means initiative, means thinking on the job."

The second level of participation he advocated is in the determination of shop rules, the terms and conditions of employment, and the administration of justice. This form of participation he framed in terms of the concept of industrial government. Much as political control of the state has evolved over hundreds of years from autocracy (divine right of kings) to representative democracy with an executive, legislative, and judicial branches, so, too, did Commons (1924) see a similar evolution taking place in the control of industry, albeit at a much less advanced stage. As indicated above, he did not think that workers wanted participation in the executive functions of management, but he did see a need and benefit of giving workers some voice and influence in the "legislative" and "judicial" branches of industrial government. In practice, this meant some form of collective organization of workers, either as a trade union or an employer-created shop committee, works council or more informal committee set-up. He states in this regard (p. 113), "There is no conclusive reason why constitutional democracy may not start with the employer as with the employees, It depends on his good faith and goodwill." Whatever the form of worker organization, its function is to allow employees to participate — not necessarily through a formal process of voting, but through discussion, problem-solving and involvement, in the making and implementing of all the rules and activities (i.e., the legislative process) that directly affect their work lives, be it the determination of wage levels, the scheduling of vacation days, or the planning of the annual company picnic. And, then, when disputes arise, the employee organization is there to make sure that due process is followed in the administration of justice and that all interests are represented in the process (the judicial function).

### *4.1. PM in the welfare capitalism era*

Commons' good will model of labor management and its governance perspective on employee participation in management were soon repeated and amplified upon in personnel textbooks (e.g., Tead & Metcalf, 1920; Watkins, 1928) and the journals and trade press Catering to management practitioners (e.g., Ching, 1928). More important than Commons' individual influence or perspective, however, was the widespread recognition and discussion of the general concept of PM during the entire decade of the 1920s and its growing adoption in practice.

Considerable favorable publicity and a strong public endorsement for PM came out of President Wilsons' two labor–management industrial conferences held in 1919. These conferences were convened as a national forum for discussion of ways to improve industrial efficiency and labor–management relations and were composed of leading business, labor, and public figures (the second conference contained only the latter group). The final report issued from the second conference states that the various forms of labor unrest and conflict (taken from extensive verbatim quotes in *Industrial Management*, 5/20:348–354, emphasis in original), "*reveal a desire on the part of workers to exert a larger and more organic influence upon the processes of industrial life.*" Toward that end, the report states that, "the strategic place to begin the battle with misunderstanding is within the industrial plant itself" and the appropriate organizational innovation is some type of structured employer–employee participation group, in the form of a decentralized system of joint committees or a plantwide works council in a nonunion setting and a joint union–management shop committee in a unionized setting, that can "provide for the joint action of managers and employees in dealing with their common interests."

Following on this was a continuous streams of articles in both academic and practitioner journals during the 1920s on PM. Illustrative of the former are the series of papers published in the *American Economic Review* (March Supplement, 1920: 103–125) on the subject of "Employees' Participation in Management" and the research monograph by Benjamin Selekman (1924) entitled, *Sharing Management with the Workers*. Illustrative of the latter is the lengthy article by Geoffrey Brown (1929) in the *Bulletin of the Taylor Society* entitled, "Workers' Participation in Management" and the section entitled, "Employees Demand a Voice in Those Affairs of Management Which Vitally Affect Them" in Eugene Benge's (1927) article on "Trends in Labor Management." The article by Brown is particularly interesting because in an appendix (pp. 19–21) he presents 25 mini-case studies on "Workers' Participation in Creative Production."

Just as is true today, the actual amount of genuine employee participation in management in the 1920s, and its record of accomplishment, fell considerably short of the hopes and pronouncements of its more ardent proponents. On the other hand, a comparison between 1915 and 1929 of the extent of PM in American industry reveals a pattern of remarkable change and innovation. The situation that existed prior to WWI is well described by Slichter (1920). He notes that the drive system then in widespread use depended for its effectiveness on instilling fear in the workmen. To accomplish this (p. 44),

> they [employers] maintained as a matter of policy a brusque, more or less harsh, distant and stern attitude toward their men. They resorted to discharge on fairly slight provocation. They discouraged the airing of grievances. The man with a complaint was told, "If you don't like things here, you can quit . . ." Above all, it was felt that the men must be made to feel that the management was strong and powerful, determined to have its way and not to be trifled with.

A decade later, a veritable revolution had occurred in "best practice" management thinking. The new philosophy was well stated by Swift & Company in its 1923 yearbook (quoted in Cohen, 1990, p. 161),

> The goal toward which Swift & Company is working in its relations with workers may be summed up as follows: To make employment more secure, to pay fair wages, and to make this possible by avoiding waste and by improving the whole economic machine; to lead, not drive men, by having well-trained and sympathetic executives and bosses; to provide for self-expression on the part of our workers,

> and to keep the way wide open for their education and advancement; to bring about a closer cooperation and a better understanding between the workers and management.

The watchwords in all of these types of statements were "cooperation," "loyalty," "esprit de corps," "genuine interest," "high morale," and so on. To obtain these, the consensus was that two things were required: that workers perceive they are getting a "square deal" and that they feel confidence and trust in management. Participative forms of management were regarded as only one, albeit quite possibly the most important, of the "bundle" of HRM practices required to develop these employee sentiments.

The breadth and depth of EI differed considerably among firms. The large majority of firms provided little to none. Others gave employees an opportunity to participate in management decision making on a narrowly defined, nonstrategic subject, say in the form of a joint employer–employee committee on safety or upkeep of the company housing. Once some success was enjoyed at his level, then EI spread to other subjects. Indicative of this trend is the statement (Benge, 1927, p. 125) that, "Committees are dotted throughout most industrial organizations, with varying degrees of responsibility and authority."

At the apex of the PM movement was a formal organizational structure for employee representation (Kaufman, 2000a; Nelson, 1993). In a union setting, the standard organizational structure was a local union or union shop committee affiliated with an independent national trade union. Until the 1920s, the notion of labor–management cooperation was a foreign concept to both sides, habituated as they were to life and death struggles. But by the middle of the decade, a few heavily publicized examples appeared of worker participation in management through local union committees. The shop committees on the B&O Railroad are the best known case (Brody, 1980; Jacoby, 1985).

The more extensive and developed efforts at PM occurred in progressive nonunion companies during the 1920s. These participative bodies were created by employers as part of their personnel programs and were typically called a shop committee, a works council, or employee representation plan (or "company union" by their critics). In 1919, 225 such plans existed covering 400,000 employees. A decade later, 400 plans were in operation covering 1.5 million workers (Kaufman, 2000a; Nelson, 1982). Typically, in these plans, employees voted in a secret ballot election for a certain number of worker delegates to serve on either a department committee or plant-wide council (large plants had several layers of committees) with a similar number of management representatives. Often, these councils or committees had written charters and the more progressive companies allowed the workers to help create the plans. Some representational committees served purely an advisory or communication function over a narrow range of personnel or production topics, but many others (and the proportion grew over time) allowed the councils to examine nearly any aspect of personnel policy, management treatment of the workforce, or production-related matters, and while management almost always maintained the final power of decision making many councils nevertheless exercised a meaningful degree of influence, including in some cases the right to obtain binding arbitration of unresolved differences. Written records from several representation plans show that employee proposals were approved and implemented in substantially more than one half of the cases (Burton, 1926).

Today, these nonunion representation plans of the 1920s are seldom mentioned in the management literature, and are almost totally ignored in the literature on PM and EI (see, e.g., Cotton, 1994; Lawler *et al.*, 1992. An exception is Wren, 1994). A reason, no doubt, is that in the 1930s, these plans fell into disrepute because many firms hastily erected them to serve as union avoidance devices during the wave of union organizing unleashed by the New Deal policies of the Roosevelt administration. As a result, in 1935 a Section 8(a)(2) was inserted into the National Labor Relations Act, which made illegal any form of nonunion representational committee created or financially supported by management (i.e., a "dominated" labor organization) and that engaged in discussions or dealings with management over a broad range of issues related to terms and conditions of employment (Kaufman, 2000a).

This unsavory reputation notwithstanding, up until the Depression in late 1929, the verdict of disinterested observers was that these nonunion representation committees were in a number of cases not only effective mechanisms for employee voice and participation but represented the crown jewel of the entire Welfare Capitalist HRM paradigm. Mary Parker Follett (1926), one of the keenest observers of the business scene in the 1920s, states, for example, that (p. 172), "One of the very encouraging things about business to-day is that in some instances workers are being given genuine participation in the control of industry," while Leiserson (1929, p. 154) observes that employee representation is, "perhaps the most significant contribution of personnel management."

## 5. Conclusion

A number of books and articles in the modern management literature explicitly or implicitly suggest that SHRM and PM are relatively recent concepts and practices. In an influential and oft-cited paper in the *Harvard Business Review* entitled, "From Control to Commitment in the Workplace," for example, Richard Walton (1985, p. 78) states that, "In the traditional approach [pre-1970s], there was generally little policy definition with regard to employee voice unless the work force was unionized, in which case damage control strategies predominated. With no union, management relied on an open-door policy, attitude surveys, and similar devices to learn about employees' concerns." He goes on to describe characteristics of the new "commitment" model of HRM, including (p. 79): "to inform employees about the business, to encourage participation by everyone," "growing concern for such questions of 'equity' as gain sharing, stock ownership, and profit sharing," and "Equally important to the commitment strategy is the challenge of giving employees some assurance of security."

The evidence provided in this paper suggests that this claim, and many others like it, lack sufficient historical perspective. SHRM and PM are not new ideas that suddenly burst forth in either theory or practice in the last two to three decades; rather, their roots go back more than a century and first appeared in visible form in the decade of 1915–1925. In the realm of theory, the concept of labor as a human resource, the strategic conception of HRM policy and practice, and the role of PM as an alternative to the traditional "command and control" system were all discussed and described by John R. Commons and other labor economists and IR scholars of that period. Likewise, leading progressive Welfare Capitalist employers of the 1920s consciously formulated and adopted an innovative package of HRM practices that represented a new strategic approach to the management of labor. This new system sought to move away from the adversarial, "zero sum" nature of the traditional commodity approach to managing labor and toward a new system that emphasized unity of interest, cooperation, and a mutual gains/"positive sum" outcome. Importantly, the leading practitioners of this new employment system explicitly recognized that it required an integrated, synergistic bundle of new HRM practices to be successful. Toward this end, progressive Welfare Capitalist employers created the first professionally staffed personnel departments, introduced employee handbooks and written policy guidelines, adopted scientifically based personnel practices, invested in supervisor training and other human relations practices, inaugurated a plethora of employee benefits and gain sharing programs, provided for greater job security and more equitable resolution of disputes, and created employee councils and committees to provide for greater voice and participation in management decision making.

Viewed over the long term, the writings of the early 20th century IR scholars and consultants clearly anticipated a number of themes found in the modern literature on SHRM and PM, just as the employment philosophy and practices developed in the 1920s by the leading Welfare Capitalist employers anticipated those found in modern-day "high-performance/high-commitment" workplaces. This being the case, the question emerges on why the contribution of both groups have been so widely unrecognized and neglected in modern times. In closing, I will provide brief thoughts and perspective on this matter.

The contribution of the early institutional labor economists to the development of management thought and practice has gone largely unrecognized for a variety of reasons. Today, for example, the discipline of economics is widely perceived to deal with markets, the determination of prices, and macroeconomic fluctuations — subjects which are largely orthogonal to the study of business organizations and the process of management. In the 1915–1925 period, however, the study of economics was construed more broadly to include all wealth-producing institutions, including both markets and business firms (Bossard & Dewhurst, 1931; Kaufman, 2000a, b). For this reason, economics was widely perceived at the time as the mother discipline of management and personnel management was frequently considered "applied labor economics" (Brissenden, 1926), making it natural and appropriate for economists such as Commons and colleagues to study not only labor markets, but also the newly emergent practice of personnel management in business firms. The fact that these labor economists were the most active and authoritative academic writers on personnel/HRM issues in that period was also abetted by the relatively underdeveloped state of other related disciplines circa the 1920s, such as industrial psychology, industrial sociology, and the administrative and organizational sciences. Since World War II, however, the latter range of disciplines has largely displaced economics as the center of research and writing on management and personnel/HRM subjects, making it natural that contemporary management writers — often having little training or interest in economics — would not be aware of the early contributions of Commons and colleagues.

Also important is the fact that Commons and fellow economists approached the subject of SHRM and PM from a different perspective than do most contemporary management researchers. As I argue in another paper in this symposium, management writers generally take a more "micro" and "internalist" perspective on employment issues while economists typically take a more "macro" and "externalist" perspective (i.e., the former seek explanations in individual and small group psychological processes and in firm-level management and organizational practices, while the latter look to broader factors external to individual firms, such as market forces, social class, labor movements, and government legislation). Thus, while Commons describes labor as a "human resource," develops five alternative models of labor management, and discusses the role of employee participation in management, he typically does it from the "macro/externalist" perspective of economists and, for this reason, it fails to resonate well or "fit" with much of modern-day management research which proceeds from an individual and behavioral/organizational science point of view. Likewise, the interest of the early labor economists in personnel/HRM was principally motivated by their desire to improve labor conditions and reform labor market institutions and policy, rather than in the theoretical or practical aspects of management per se — a perspective that also separates them from many contemporary management scholars.

Finally, mention should be made of the fact that even though Commons *et al.* were highly impressed by the contributions of personnel/HRM to improved employment conditions, they nonetheless continued to advocate the need for more extensive collective bargaining and labor legislation (Commons, 1920; Kaufman, 1997), a position that is also at odds with the implicit or explicit position of many writers in modern management. When the Depression discredited Welfare Capitalism and the New Deal gave birth to mass unionism, these labor economists largely abandoned the study of personnel/HRM and the younger generation — more schooled in economic theory and focused on the operation of markets — never became interested in it.

Perhaps more puzzling are the reasons modern-day management writers largely ignore the pioneering contributions made by the progressive Welfare Capitalist employers of the 1920s to a more strategic conception of personnel/HRM and the role of employee participation therein. It is undoubtedly correct that the large majority of employers during this period practiced only the most rudimentary form of personnel/HRM, seldom conceptualized or implemented personnel/HRM from an integrative/strategic perspective, and had zero interest in any form of employee participation in management (Jacoby, 1985, 1997). But the historical record is equally clear that a small but highly influential and visible elite of progressive employers in the 1920s set out to replace the traditional commodity/command and control system of people management with a different model that sought competitive advantage through unity of interest, cooperation, and investment in labor as a human resource (Hicks, 1941; Kaufman, 2000a). Although this new "high-commitment" HRM model of the 1920s probably entailed a larger element of paternalism, less opportunities for self-management by small-scale teams, and a more collective form of employee voice (formal plans of employee representation) than are found in modern-day high-performance enterprises, most of the personnel/HRM principles and practices discussed in leading management treatises of the late 20th century were articulated and practiced in embryonic form by leading employers in the early part of the century.

Why are these contributions not more extensively acknowledged? I surmise for several reasons. One, no doubt, is that many of these progressive experiments in SHRM and PM were wiped-out in the Depression and then submerged for several decades by the mass unionization of industry in the 1930s–1950s. Another is that the "crown jewel" of the Welfare Capitalist movement and the principle organizational vehicle for employee participation — the employee representation plan — has been portrayed in such a negative light that it has tarnished the entire experiment. Finally, there seems to be a natural inclination for the most recent vintage of management writers to systematically downgrade the accomplishments and ideas of former generations in order to increase the perceived novelty and importance of their own ideas — ideas that when examined more thoroughly often have been espoused and practiced in various guises for many years.

In sum, I hope to have demonstrated in this paper that both the theory and practice of SHRM and PM had important antecedents in the work of John R. Commons and other early IR scholars and in the new employment management paradigm established by progressive Welfare Capitalist firms of the 1920s. Both of these "roots" of modern management thought and practice were largely cut off and lost during the Depression decade of the 1930s. In the case of economists, their attention turned almost exclusively to labor markets and labor unions, leaving a void that was filled by behavioral scientists associated with the human relations movement and, later, the new field of organizational behavior (Kaufman, 1993). In the case of the nonunion Welfare Capitalist employers, most of these firms were unionized in the 1930s while the ones that remained unorganized took a more defensive, less visible posture, dropping employee representation plans and reorienting personnel/HRM more toward union avoidance (Harris, 1982; Jacoby, 1997). The interesting question that emerges from this scenario is what would both the theory and practice of personnel/HRM look like today if the Great Depression had never happened. My conjecture is that economists would have remained a larger presence in the field and that the Welfare Capitalist model of progressive personnel/HRM would have further developed and spread. In the last two decades, economists are again starting to explore organizational and personnel/HRM issues (see the Gunderson paper in this symposium), albeit from a neoclassical perspective rather than an institutional one, and the strategic and participative potentialities of personnel/HRM first grasped by the Welfare Capitalist employers have been rediscovered and popularized by modern management scholars and operationalized in what are now called high-performance workplaces. These are both positive developments but it is unfortunate that progress on both fronts was interrupted for three decades or more by the tumultuous events of the 1930s.

## References

Balderston, C. (1935). *Executive guidance of industrial relations*. Philadelphia, PA: University of Pennsylvania Press.

Basset, W. (1919). *When the workmen help you manage*. New York, NY: Century.

Benge, E. (1927). Trends in labor management. *Industrial Management, 73* (2), 124–125.

Bossard, J., & Dewhurst, J. (1931). *University education for business*. Philadelphia: University of Pennsylvania Press.

Brandeis, L. (1918). Efficiency by consent: to secure its active cooperation labor must be consulted and convinced in regard to changes. *Industrial Management, 2*, 108–109.

Brissenden, P. (1926). Labor economics. *American Economic Review*, *16*, 443–449 (September).

Brody, D. (1980). *Workers in industrial America: essays on the twentieth century struggle*. New York, NY: Oxford Univ. Press.

Brown, G. (1929). Workers' participation in management. *Bulletin of the Taylor Society*, *14* (1), 11–21.

Bruere, R. (1929). Industrial relations. In: H. Person (Ed.), *Scientific management in American industry* (pp. 455–472). New York, NY: Harper.

Burton, E. (1926). *Employee representation*. Baltimore, MD: Williams & Wilkins.

Carroll, S., & Schuler, R. (1983). Professional HRM: changing functions and problems. In: S. Carroll, & R. Schuler (Eds.), *Human resources management in the 1980s* (pp. 8/1–8/28). Washington: Bureau of National Affairs.

Cascio, W. (1992). *Managing human resources* (3rd ed.). New York, NY: McGraw-Hill.

Ching, C. (1928). Personnel work as a profit-maker. *Factory and Industrial Management*, *15*, 83–84 (January).

Cohen, L. (1990). *Making a new deal: industrial workers in Chicago, 1919–1939*. New York, NY: Columbia Univ. Press.

Commons, J. (1918). *History of labor in the United States* (vols. 1–2). New York, NY: MacMillan.

Commons, J. (1919). *Industrial goodwill*. New York, NY: McGraw-Hill.

Commons, J. (1920). Management and unionism. In: *Proceedings of the Industrial Relations Association of America* (pp. 125–130). Chicago, IL: IRAA.

Commons, J. (1921). *Industrial government*. New York, NY: MacMillan.

Commons, J. (1924). *Legal foundations of capitalism*. New York, NY: MacMillan.

Commons, J. (1934a). *Institutional economics*. New York, NY: MacMillan.

Commons, J. (1934b). *Myself*. Madison, WI: University of Wisconsin Press.

Commons, J., & Andrews, J. (1916). *Principles of labor legislation*. New York, NY: Harper.

Commons, J., Lewisohn, S., Draper, E., & Lescohier, D. (1925). *Can business prevent unemployment?* New York, NY: Alfred Knopf.

Cotton, J. (1994). *Employee involvement: methods for improving performance and work attitudes*. Newbury Park, CA: Sage.

Delery, J., & Doty, D. H. (1996). Modes of theorizing in strategic human resource management: tests of universalistic, contingency, and configurational performance predictions. *Academy of Management Journal*, *39* (4), 802–833.

Donald, W., & Donald, E. (1929). Trends in personnel management. *Harvard Business Review*, *7* (2), 143–155.

Dulebohn, J., Ferris, G., & Stodd, J. (1995). The history and evolution of human resource management. In: G. Ferris, S. Rosen, & D. Barnum (Eds.), *Handbook of human resource management* (pp. 19–41). Cambridge, MA: Blackwell.

Dyer, L., & Holder, G. (1988). A strategic perspective of human resource management. In: L. Dyer (Ed.), *Human resource management — evolving roles and responsibilities* (pp. 1.1–1.46). Washington: Bureau of National Affairs.

Eilbert, H. (1959). The development of personnel management in the United States. *Business History Review*, *33* (5), 345–364.

Ely, R. (1886). *The labor movement in America*. New York, NY: Crowell.

Estey, J. (1928). *The labor problem*. New York, NY: McGraw-Hill.

Follett, M. (1926). The influence of employee representation in remoulding of the accepted type of business manager. In: H. Metcalf, & L. Urwick (Eds.), *Dynamic administration: the collected papers of Mary Parker Follett* (pp. 167–182). New York, NY: Harper.

Freeman, R., & Medoff, J. (1984). *What do unions do?* New York, NY: Basic Books.

Gitelman, H. (1992). Welfare capitalism reconsidered. *Labor History, 13* (1), 5–31.

Harris, H. (1982). *The right to manage: industrial relations policies of American business in the 1940s*. Madison: University of Wisconsin Press.

Harter, L. (1962). *John R. Commons: his assault on Laissez Faire*. Corvalis, OR: Oregon Univ. Press.

Hicks, C. (1941). *My life in industrial relations*. New York: Harper & Bros.

Hirschman, A. (1970). *Exit, voice, and loyalty*. Cambridge, MA: Harvard Univ. Press.

Hotchkiss, W. (1923). Industrial relations management. *Harvard Business Review, 1*, 438–450 (July).

Huselid, M., Jackson, S., & Schuler, R. (1997). Technical and strategic human resource management effectiveness as determinants of firm performance. *Academy of Management Journal, 40* (1), 171–188.

Ivancevich, J. (1995). *Human resource management*. Chicago, IL: Irwin.

Jacoby, S. (1985). *Employing bureaucracy: managers, unions, and the transformation of work in American industry, 1900–1945*. New York, NY: Columbia Univ. Press.

Jacoby, S. (1997). *Modern manors: Welfare Capitalism since the new deal*. Princeton: Princeton Univ. Press.

Kaufman, B. (1993). *The origins and evolution of the field of industrial relations in the United States*. Ithaca, NY: ILR Press.

Kaufman, B. (1996). Why the Wagner Act: reestablishing contact with its original purpose. In: D. Lewin, B. Kaufman, & D. Sockell (Eds.), *Advances in industrial and labor relations* (vol. 7, pp. 15–68). Greenwich, CT: JAI Press.

Kaufman, B. (1997). Labor markets and employment regulation: the view of the 'Old Institutionalists'. In: B. Kaufman (Ed.), *Government regulation of the employment relationship* (pp. 11–55). Madison: Industrial Relations Research Association.

Kaufman, B. (1998). John R. Commons: his contributions to the founding and early development of the field of personnel/HRM. In: *Proceedings of the Fiftieth Annual Winter Meeting, Industrial Relations Research Association* (pp. 328–341). Madison, WI: Industrial Relations Research Association.

Kaufman, B. (1999). The evolution and current status of university HR programs. *Human Resource Management, 38*, 103–110.

Kaufman, B. (2000a). Accomplishments and shortcomings of nonunion employee representation in the Pre-Wagner Act years. In: B. Kaufman, & D. Taras (Eds.), *Nonunion employee representation: history, contemporary practice, and policy* (pp. 21–60). Armonk: M.E. Sharpe.

Kaufman, B. (2000b). Personnel/human resource management: its roots as applied economics. In: R. Backhouse, & J. Biddle (Eds.), *Toward a History of Applied Economics, Annual Supplement to History of Political Economy* (vol. 32, pp. 229–256). Durham, NC: Duke University Press.

Kaufman, B., Lewin, D., & Adams, R. (1995). Workforce governance. In: G. Ferris, S. Rosen, & D. Barnum (Eds.), *Handbook of human resource management* (pp. 404–424). Cambridge: Blackwell.

Kennedy, D. (1919). Employment management and industrial relations. *Industrial Management*, *58* (5), 353–358.

Lawler, E., Albers, S., & Ledford, G. (1992). *Employee involvement and total quality management: practices and results in fortune 1000 companies*. San Francisco, CA: Jossey-Bass.

Leiserson, W. (1924). The way to industrial peace. *The American Review*, *2*, 1–12 (May–June).

Leiserson, W. (1929). Contributions of personnel management to improved labor relations. In: *Wertheim lectures in industrial relations* (pp. 125–164). Cambridge, MA: Harvard Univ. Press.

Lengnick-Hall, C., & Lengnick-Hall, M. (1988). Strategic human resource management: a review of the literature and a proposed typology. *Academy of Management Review*, *13*, 454–470.

Lescohier, D. (1935). Personnel management. In: D. Lescohier, & E. Brandeis (Eds.), *History of labor in the United States, 1896–1932* (vols. 3–4, pp. 316–335). New York, NY: MacMillan.

Ling, C. (1965). *The management of personnel relations: history and origins*. Homewood, IL: Irwin.

Marshall, L. (1920). Incentive and output: a statement of the place of the personnel manager in modern industry. *Journal of Political Economy*, *28* (9), 713–734.

Matherly, W. (1926). The evolution of personnel management. *Industrial Management*, *72* (4), 256–257.

Mayo, E. (1933). *The human problems of an industrial civilization*. New York, NY: MacMillan.

Mc Mahan, G., Bell, M., & Virick, M. (1998). Strategic human resource management, employee involvement, diversity, and international issues. *Human Resource Management Review*, *8* (3), 193–214.

Moss, D. (1996). *Socializing security*. Cambridge, MA: Harvard Univ. Press.

Nelson, D. (1982). The company union movement, 1900–1937: a reexamination. *Business History Review*, *54*, 335–357 (Autumn).

Nelson, D. (1993). Employee representation in historical perspective. In: B. Kaufman, & M. Kleiner (Eds.), *Employee representation: alternatives and future directions* (pp. 371–390). Madison, WI: Industrial Relations Research Association.

Noe, R., Hollenbeck, J., Gerhart, B., & Wright, P. (1997). *Human resource management: getting a competitive advantage*. Chicago, IL: Irwin.

Peters, T., & Waterman, R. (1982). *In search of excellence*. New York, NY: Harper & Row.

Roethlisberger, F., & Dickson, W. (1939). *Management and the worker*. Cambridge, MA: Harvard Univ. Press.

Schuler, R. (1995). *Managing human resources*. Minneapolis, MN: West.

Schuler, R., & Jackson, S. (1987). Linking competitive strategies with human resource management practices. *Academy of Management Executive*, *1* (3), 207–219.

Selekman, B. (1924). *Sharing management with the workers*. New York, NY: Russell Sage Foundation.

Selekman, B., & Van Kleek, M. (1924). *Employees' representation in coal mines*. New York, NY: Russell Sage Foundation.

Slichter, S. (1919). The management of labor. *Journal of Political Economy*, *27* (10), 813–839.

Slichter, S. (1920). Industrial morale. *Quarterly Journal of Economics*, *35*, 36–60 (November).

Slichter, S. (1929). The current labor policies of American industries. *Quarterly Journal of Economics*, *43*, 393–435 (May).

Stanton, E. (1993). Employee participation: a critical evaluation and suggestions for management practice. *SAM Advanced Management Journal*, *58*, 18–23.

Taylor, F. (1895). A piece rate system, being a step toward a partial solution of the labor problem. *Transactions, 16*, 856–883.

Tead, O., & Metcalf, H. (1920). *Personnel administration: its principles and practice*. New York: McGraw-Hill.

Valentine, R. (1915). The progressive relation between efficiency and consent. *Bulletin of the Taylor Society*, *1*, 3–7 (November).

Van de Ven, A. (1993). "The institutional theory of John R. Commons" a review and commentary. *Academy of Management Review, 36*, 139–152 (January).

Walton, R. (1985). From control to commitment in the workplace. *Harvard Business Review*, *63* (2), 76–84.

Watkins, G. (1922). *An introduction to the study of labor problems*. New York, NY: Crowell.

Watkins, G. (1928). *Labor management*. New York, NY: McGraw-Hill.

Webb, S., & Webb, B. (1897). *Industrial democracy*. London: Longmans Green.

Williams, H. (1927). High wages and properity. *Industrial Management*, *33* (6), 325–327.

Wren, D. (1994). *The evolution of management thought* (4th ed.). New York, NY: Wiley.

Wright, P. (1998). Introduction: strategic human resource management research in the 21st century. *Human Resource Management Review*, *8* (3), 187–191.

Wright, P., & McMahan, G. (1992). Theoretical perspectives for strategic human resource management. *Journal of Management*, *18* (2), 295–320.

Wright, P., & Snell, S. (1991). Toward an integrative view of strategic human resource management. *Human Resource Management Review*, *1* (4), 203–225.

Yoder, D. (1970). *Personnel management and industrial relations*. Englewood Cliffs, NJ: Prentice-Hall.

# Part 7

# STRATEGIC MANAGEMENT: THE FUTURE CONSIDERED

# 50

# SOCIAL DEMANDS AS STRATEGIC ISSUES

## Some conceptual problems

*Francisco J. Arcelus and Norbert V. Schaefer*

Source: *Strategic Management Journal* 3(4) (1982): 347–57.

**Summary**

We argue that business firms are faced with new and changing social demands, and that it will be advantageous to the firm to treat the social demands as strategic issues. However, responding to these social demands strategically requires the application of new managerial concepts and techniques. In this paper we extend conceptually the lead–lag methodology of Ackerman and Bauer (1976), developed to deal with the evolutionary nature of social demands. Then we describe the problems of measurement, uncertainty and lack of common units of measures that have to be overcome before the responses to the social demands can be included in the strategic planning and budget process.

In the past the study of business and the demands society made upon it dealt mostly with the question of whether or not large private corporate institutions had a responsibility to society beyond the production of goods and services at a profit. The debate was generally moral and philosophic. The free market economists (e.g. Friedman, 1962; Manne and Wallich, 1972) stress that the responsibility of business is 'to use its resources and engage in activities designed to increase its profits, so long as it stays within the rules of the game, which is to say, engaged in open and free competition, without deception or fraud'. (Friedman, 1962: 133). In fact, Friedman (1962: 133) views the advocacy of social responsibility as 'a fundamentally subversive doctrine', subversive that is to a free economy.

Those that argue that businessmen have to take a larger view of their role within the economy and society (e.g. Votaw and Sethi, 1969; Committee for Economic Development, 1971) argue that their opponents' view rests on the assumptions of a perfect or near perfect market—perfect competition with either no externalities or the externalities left to government to deal with. The proponents of social responsibility stress that in practice there are and likely will always be some externalities to business activities, and government cannot (or should not) deal with all present and potential externalities. Further, there will be imperfections in the competitive environment which result in unequal distribution of power and resources. These imperfections give rise to a responsibility for competitors toward society to help deal with society's problem, particularly to mitigate the externalities of their own activities. Whatever the merit of these two philosophical or moral positions may be, companies are operating within a larger social system which makes demands on the organization beyond the production of goods and services. The increasing saliency of environmental issues, demands for greater product and workplace safety, minority hiring, improved product performance and the like have a direct effect on the operations of a company and thus on its economic performance.

Further, those that control the resources of the firm frequently will have certain commitments, based on their values, beyond the pursuit of some narrowly defined profit goal, and thus will want to direct part of the firm's resources to these commitments.

Managers operating in an environment in which social demands are being made, and to which they likely will have to respond sooner or later on top of their own social commitments, are confronted with the pragmatic problem of meeting these social demands, while at the same time succeeding in operating efficiently and successfully in a competitive economic environment.

While significant progress has been made in the techniques of social accounting and scanning, and a greater clarity about issues of social responsibility has been achieved through the conceptual models, only limited attention has been given to the decision problems facing the individual firm confronted by social demands. The only major work with a pragmatic managerial perspective on the decision process is by Ackerman and Bauer (1976). It is their contention that social demands have a life cycle like the product life cycle where, over time, public awareness and expectations and the enforcement of standards grow from a low point to a high point. At the high point, specific performance standards are forced upon the firm. During that time period the strategic options whether to lead or lag public expectations regarding a social demand are open to the firm. Ackerman and Bauer recommended that the response to lead or lag on any social demand be made on a strategic basis and be incorporated in the firm's strategy (1976:40).

It is the purpose of this paper to build upon the conception of social demands as strategic problems for the firm, first, by examining and presenting the strategic responses open to the firm in greater detail, and second, by exploring some of the problems of integrating the selection of a response to a social demand into the firm's strategic decision process.

## Social demands as part of the strategic decision process

### *Strategic responses*

The demands made by various groups within society upon business are many and varied, including the request to assist with most of the social problems facing society. The first task before the development of responses to social demands is the identification of those demands which should be included in the decision process. Chamberlain (1973) has convincingly argued that single companies are severely limited in their ability to deal with the many social demands made upon business. Preston and Post (1975), among others, have argued that only those social demands that are related to the primary operations of the firm, such as the production process, marketing, procurement and employment, should be part of the social purview of the firm. Based on such a narrowing of the social demands to be included in the set of a firm's social concerns, the literature (e.g. Post and Epstein, 1977) suggests the management should construct a map of social demands that affect the company's present and future operations. This mapping is based on a three step environmental scanning. First, the impact of present company activities on its social environment and the impact of the social environment on company activities should be identified. Second, through an overview approach of society as a whole, broad social trends, patterns of change, major value shifts, etc., should be monitored. Third, the impact of the monitored changes on present and future company activities, as identified in step one, should be established.

This map then represents the present and potential future social demands facing the firm. Because detailed proposals of the above or similar techniques have been presented elsewhere, we refer the reader to the literature (e.g. Fleming, 1981; also Ansoff, 1980).

As stated above, Ackerman and Bauer identified the option to lead or lag as the two strategic responses open to the firm. We suggest that conceptually the strategic responses can be divided into four categories:

1. *Status quo:* the firm decides to disregard the social demands at the present time. No changes in the firm's present operation or plans are undertaken, nor is any public stance taken by management.
2. *Pro-active adaptation:* a firm concludes that it is more advantageous to make an early response to a social demand even though it is not yet

required to do so by law. For example, a firm expects that even greater pollution control will be imposed on its operations in the future. Instead of waiting for the regulations to be imposed, the firm decides to respond now. Obviously, when responding early, various levels of pro-active responses are possible. The levels would range from what Ansoff terms 'internal readiness' (Ansoff, 1975:26) to an increased performance level that meets the social demand. Thus, the firm may decide only to investigate the various technologies available to greater control. Or, in a multiplant firm, it may install a new technology in one plant to establish the performance of a new technology. Or, when an older plant is renovated, it will be designed in such a manner that it will meet expected future required performance levels. Or, the firm may renovate all of its plants now to meet future performance levels.

3. *Public stance:* Under this response the firm decides to influence the evolution of the demand by entering the public policy process. Again, a wide variety of options and combinations are available, such as the regular public relations responses and institutional advertising to sway public opinion, trade and industry activities, lobbying, threats of plant closures, etc. Obviously the response will depend on the size of the firm and its potential to influence the evolution of the demand.
4. *Pro-active/public stance:* This response is a combination of the previous two. The firm decides to react to the social demand prior to legislative compulsion. At the same time the firms enter the public debate to influence the possible evolution of the demand.

### *Timing of responses*

However, besides the choice of strategic responses, the firm is also facing the strategic decision of when to respond to social demands. Ackerman and Bauer (1976) appear to imply that during the evolution of the demand the firm has the choice at one point in time to either lead or lag. It seems to us that the firm's reaction to a social demand is a sequential process that follows along the life cycle of the demand itself. The timelines of the reaction are a function of the 'relationship between the cumulative amplitude of the stimuli and an action threshold. The amplitude of each stimulus depends on a number of factors, including the influence of its source, the interest of the decision maker in it, the perceived payoff of taking action, the uncertainty associated with it, and the perceived probability of successful termination of the decision' (Mintzberg *et al.*, 1976:253). Thus, instead of a choice of lead or lag, the strategic decision facing the firm is to determine what response to make at any given point in time during the evolution of the demand.

Furthermore, the response strategy chosen at one point would be subject to review over time. This is needed in order to monitor its execution in light of perceived changes in the evolution of the demand or of changes in the firm's resources, overall strategy, or technology. In addition, strategic reviews of the responses chosen at an earlier time period are needed. This type of review is specially important in the case of social demands, because the amount and reliability of the available information increases as the demand evolves over time and since the responses to a given demand taken at different periods of time are not serially independent. In this way, the firm is able 'to determine whether the strategic issue has been well identified, whether it deserves the priority assigned to it, and whether the action strategy has been well chosen' (Ansoff, 1975:31).

Strategic reviews require the establishment of review periods. One alternative is to let the review periods coincide with the planning cycle. Because the speed of evolution may vary not only among social demands but during the evolutionary period, a major change may have occurred during review periods. When the change is discovered at the next review point, there may not be the desired or necessary response time (see Ansoff, 1980:143–145).

The other alternative is to view the evolution of a social demand as progress through a number of stages and to review the firm's response as the demand reaches a prespecified stage. Ansoff characterized the evolution of strategic issues by five successive stages of knowledge. The information available to the manager for planning defines the stage reached. Each successive stage makes more reliable planning possible. Sethi (1979), in his analysis of corporate responses to social demands according to social legitimacy and organizational philosophy, also describes four evolutionary stages: preproblem, identification, remedy and relief, and prevention. However, as with Ansoff's stages, the decision maker is not aware that a new stage has been reached till after he has undertaken an analysis at a time period of his choosing. The stage does not tell the manager that a review of the strategic response is necessary because of a further evolution of the demand. While conceptually enlightening and useful, these stages do not represent decision points for a mandatory review.

However, within the political process, social issues tend to evolve over time from emerging public awareness to legislation which legitimizes the former often controversial demand as an accepted norm of society. This life cycle can be broken down into distinct sequential stages (Eyestone, 1978) through which a demand will likely pass if it is to reach culmination in legislative form. Each stage can be defined in terms of society's actions in regard to a particular issue. These actions provide the information to which the firm can react. For analytical purposes, we have identified five stages, which in terms of their information content may be described as follows:

1. *Public awareness stage:* This stage represents an emergence of an awareness within society or segments of society that an undesirable state of affairs exists. This awareness is transformed into a demand for a change in that state of affairs. At this level, the demand is defined in very general terms and the high degree of uncertainty still present suggests rather imprecise information.
2. *Formation of pressure groups:* The demand is becoming more crystallized and certain either existing or newly formed groups will demand more specific action. At this point some preliminary estimates of costs and timing may be made because the information becomes more concrete. Based on the assessed strength of the pressure group, forecasts of the outcome of the process may become possible.
3. *Political debate stage:* The demand has evolved to such an extent that it is part of political debate reflected in media coverage, in platforms of political candidates, etc.; various options for the situation may be discussed. Calculation of costs and benefits of different options becomes more feasible.
4. *Legislative process stage:* This stage represents the movement of the demand from the drafting of a bill, to hearings, debate and final vote. Concrete proposals are being discussed and cost-effectiveness studies are feasible.
5. *Legislation stage:* The demand is crystallized in legislation, making it part of the legal environment of the firm. The impact on the firm's operations of the resulting regulations can be evaluated, but the flexibility in response selection is minimal.

The limitation of the life cycle to five stages is certainly arbitrary. The cycle can be described in greater detail by further subdividing the stages. Depending on the severity of the demand's impact on the firm and the strategy the firm intends to pursue, the legislation process, for example, can be easily subdivided into several separate stages: the introduction of the bill responding to the demand, the committee stage, the vote, etc. Several authors (e.g. Eyestone, 1978; Pross, 1975) have examined in greater detail one or more aspects of the life cycle. Nevertheless, for illustration here the five stages and their description are sufficient, since such a classification provides a general idea of the information content and thus of the degree of uncertainty likely to be encountered at each stage.

From the above, it can be seen that the firm's reaction to a social demand does not constitute a single stage decision process. Rather, it resembles a sequential process that follows along the life cycle of the demand itself. Each stage in the cycle represents a decision point, i.e. an opportunity for the company to respond to the demand placed upon it. Each successive stage contributes further information about the nature of the demand, thus providing management with additional inputs needed to re-evaluate responses taken at previous stages and to analyse and plan for future courses of action. Furthermore, the more advanced the stage, the lower the degree of environmental uncertainty and thus the more concrete the responses may be.

It should be noted that to disregard the evolving issue as it passes through some stage represents the implicit decision not to respond to the social demand, i.e. to exercise the status quo option.

## The selection of a response within the strategic decision process

Responding to social demands before required by law can have a number of distinct advantages for the firm. For one it provides time for the firm to make the development of an efficient response to the social demand possible. Once the law has been enacted the time limit set by government for compliance may be short. When the firm is forced to respond, a short response time limit may create a near crisis situation where a crash programme is required to arrive at a solution. The solutions to social demands, because of their 'newness' and frequent 'non-business' likeness, seldom are found readily apparent and available; rather, custom-made solutions have to be devised or, at best, ready-made solutions have to be modified to fit the particular situation. The decision process for such solutions would resemble the unstructured decision process described by Mintzberg *et al.* (1976:251) as a 'recursive, discontinuous process involving very difficult steps and a host of dynamic factors over a considerable period of time'. Because of the time pressure a more *ad hoc* crash response will likely be made with normal rules pushed into the background, where organizational lines are crossed, and the general criterion of efficiency is subordinated to that of getting results. Obviously it is unlikely that a response to a social demand under such a condition will approach the best one possible.

Another advantage may be the opportunity to gain a competitive edge. As Ansoff (1980) sees external threats to the firm being converted into opportunities by aggressive entrepreneurial management, so also do social demands present potential opportunities. Although all firms will be required to meet comparable standards by a set date, by responding early a firm may gain significantly competitive advantages. For example, foreseeing increased pollution control a firm could incorporate in their decision process regarding plant location, manufacturing processes and product design, the criterion for a cleaner environment. Subsequently, the firm may achieve cost advantages that are not available to firms which were forced by decree to rapidly modify or replace existing processes and products. Because of the rapid response required whole plants may have to be shut down by competing firms.

The firm's participation in the process of social decision-making by taking a public stance may result in a number of advantages. It is through the political-social decision-making process of society that not only the rules and regulations under which business operates are established, but, at times, even the methods to be used to achieve a required social performance are dictated. When a firm abdicates its role in the decision process it gives up its opportunity to influence the outcome of the process. A firm may have the managerial and technological expertise to provide information about the costs of various degrees of performance and about the effectiveness and availability of various technologies and techniques. Because of its expertise and/or its lobbying power the firm may be able to influence the level of performance, the techniques to be used, or the time frame in which change is to occur. The result of participation in the process will not only be in the firm's interest, but it can also better serve the public's interest because more complete information will be available to the social decision-making process.

Lastly, although legally the firm may be able to wait till social demands are included in law, various groups of society, such as consumer groups, churches, minorities and evironmentalists, can bring pressures to bear upon a firm. A single group or a number of groups acting together may through activities, such as the advocacy of consumer boycotts of a company's products, seriously threaten the sales and/or operation of the firm (e.g. Sethi, 1970). While the decision to disregard pressure groups prior to any law may be legally sound, the costs of not responding may far exceed the cost of an acceptable response. However, the potential benefits of an early response must weigh against the costs of making such a response. The selection of responses to social demands cannot be made in isolation from other strategic decisions facing the firm. The managerial and financial resources of any firm are limited and the firm will have to select among competing strategic threats and opportunities. An early response to a social demand is made due to the benefits expected by the firm or because of its social conscience. To each response and the potential resulting benefit, a cost is attached as to any other strategic alternative. Therefore, the decision of when and how to respond to a particular social demand has to be viewed as part of the strategic decision process in which the scarce resources are allocated to strategic options. The decision process referred to here does not comprise the unstructured strategic decisions described by Mintzberg *et al.* (1976) but is rather the on-going process by which a firm establishes its direction and priorities. Within that process the strategic responses to social demands will compete on the basis of some form of cost–benefit analysis against other regular strategic alternatives open to the firm, such as the addition of a new product or product lines, increased market penetration, improvement in plant and equipment for increased efficiency, etc. and other social commitments. Because of the limited resources available not all strategic alternatives and responses can be pursued and a selection will have to be made among them.

Before responses to social demands can be included with the other strategic alternatives in the selection process, a method of reliably evaluating the costs and benefits of responses must be found. Any evaluation methodology must: include techniques for measuring the costs and benefits of social responses; deal with the uncertainty inherent in social demands and the uncertainty of the impact of the responses to those demands on the firm; and, lastly, overcome the lack of common units of measures that makes difficult the selection of those strategic alternatives and responses that most advance the goals and objectives of the firm.

### *Measurement*

In the process of evaluating the various strategic responses to social demands, the firm must address the problems of measurement of costs and benefits of the available responses to social demands. The problem of measurement exists because of the infancy of social accounting and the cross-impact of the responses. Social accounting is still in its early stages. Not only is there no consensus about the techniques to be used, the indicators to be measured, or the overall reporting scheme, but even the various schemes offered suffer to some extent from theoretical and practical limitations (U.S. Department of Commerce, 1979). The often ill-defined nature of these costs makes the development of quantitative measures of performance difficult.

Further, in costing responses to social demands, two types of costs and benefits, the direct and indirect costs and benefits, must be taken into consideration. The direct costs are those associated with the external aspects of the possible responses (e.g. public relations, institutional advertising, lobbying) as well as those dealing with the implementation of the proposed response (e.g. the purchase and installation of pollution control equipment or the recruiting and training of minority personnel).

As there are direct costs, there are direct benefits. A direct benefit would be the saving in dollars on a total project by responding early rather than under the pressure of law. Returning to the example of pollution control, the costs of designing improved pollution control right into the construction or renovation of a new plant may be much cheaper than adding controls to an existing system later.

The indirect costs and benefits refer to the effects that the possible responses may have upon the various operations and objectives of the firm. For example, the installation of pollution control equipment may reduce operating efficiency, thus return on investment; it may require more highly skilled labour, which often is white and male, and therefore has a negative impact on minority hiring; it may reduce the production capability of the firm, with the corresponding decrease in market share. An indirect benefit may be an improvement in company image among its own employees and within the larger community. Such an improved image may increase the ability to retain and employ personnel, increase efficiency due to high morale, and may make relations with the firm's political environment easier due to the respect the firm has earned within the community.

While direct costs and benefits of social responses may at times be difficult to measure accurately, the indirect costs present an even greater challenge, because, in certain instances, the indirect costs and benefits are of such a magnitude that they must be taken into account in any evaluation of responses to social demands.

### *Uncertainty*

The uncertainty in regard to the evolution of social demands and the uncertainty as to the impact of responses to these demands represents a major challenge to the decision maker within the firm.

Once a social demand relevant to the firm and the demand's stage of evolution has been identified, the decision makers within the firm are dealing with uncertain future events. At each stage not only the future costs and benefits of each response must be ascertained but also the likelihood of each possible final outcome estimated. These estimates often have to be based not only on limited, but sometimes misleading information, particularly in the early stages of the demand. Further, a social demand may not necessarily reach the legislation stage. At any stage, due to a number of circumstances, it may lose support and drop from public awareness. The social environment is frequently volatile with social policies or social priorities being subject to sudden changes. Such an environment is likely to be far more turbulent than the more familiar economic environment, and the future less predictable. Also, the techniques developed for economic forecasting are not applicable to the volatile political/social environment. Decisions in such an environment are only, at best, decisions under uncertainty as defined in textbooks. The selection of a response, however, has to be based on the forecast of the evolution of the social demand and a likely final stage regardless of the reliability of the information available or the turbulence and uncertainty within the environment.

Obviously, the more stages the social demand evolves through, the more precise the information available, the more reliable the estimate of the final outcome, and the easier the selection of a response. At the same time, however, the possible advantages of responding early will diminish and at the end disappear.

The uncertainty about the evolution of the social demand is but one uncertainty facing the firm. Another is the need to predict the likelihood that the expected direct and indirect costs and benefits resulting from the potential responses to social demands will occur. Not only have the normal economic uncertainties that are part of dealing with future events to be taken into consideration, but also the likely magnitude of the indirect costs and benefits of responses estimated. In an earlier example we cited improved employee morale and greater respect for the firm within the political community as one possible benefit of an early response. In a thorough evaluation of the benefits of an early response not only would the magnitude of the improvement of morale and respect be estimated, but also the magnitude of the resulting likely tangible benefits to the firm such as increased output, less employee turnover, etc. be forecast. Empirical evidence so far appears not to have substantiated any direct relationship between improved image and tangible net benefits to a firm.

### *Common units of measure*

As previously stated, early responses to social demands represent another set of potential strategic options for the investment of the firm's resources. Owing to the limit of resources the firm must choose which of the various alternatives and responses it wishes to pursue. Such a choice requires an evaluation technique that takes into consideration the firm's multiple objectives (Ketty, 1979), for which common units of measures are generally lacking.

As Hofer and Schendel (1978) we differentiate between objectives and goals. We see goals as ultimate, open-ended, long run ends which reflect the purpose or mission of the organization. We define objectives as precise levels of performance which a firm attempts to achieve. Some objectives are set by the firm to serve as targets that measure the firm's progress toward its goals. These targets are desired levels of performance on a number of dimensions such as growth in sales, return on investment, market shares for its products.

Other objectives reflect the social constraints within which the firm has to operate. These objectives are at minimum levels of performance on a number of social dimensions which are to be exceeded (Hofer and Schendel, 1978). Levels of performance on social issues dictated by law, such as pollution emissions, are representative of these type of objectives.

Also, if those controlling the firm perceive it to be more than a pure economic entity, the firm may have a social goal of responding to social demands beyond the requirements of the law. This goal, to be managerially useful for planning purposes, must be translated into specific performance levels. These performance levels become another set of objectives to be met.

The different objectives discussed above are likely to have different units of measures. For example: pollution control objectives may be stated in terms of tons of sulphur emissions and the like; minority hiring efforts in numbers of blacks, chicanos, etc. hired and trained; safety programmes, in terms of accident frequency rates or similar standards; profitability may be expressed as earnings per share.

Responses to social demands will impact on several if not all of the objectives of the firm. While, at times, a response to a social demand will lead to an increase in performance for some objectives and not affect the others, frequently the impact will be positive on some and negative for the others. Further, the responses will have to be compared not only against the costs and benefits of the economic strategic alternatives but also against the present voluntary social objectives in order to select that combination of strategic responses and alternatives that will provide the greatest likely benefit, given the limited resources of the firm.

To arrive at a consistent evaluation of the strategic responses and economic alternatives, a priority structure for the goals and objectives of the firm must be established. Such a priority structure will make possible the calculation or, more likely, the estimation of the trade-offs between the various objectives to arrive at common units of measures. The careful ordering of priorities is of particular importance because different priority structures will lead to different evaluation results.

No generally acceptable procedures for the estimation of the trade-offs exist. However, a promising new approach has been suggested recently by Cooper and Ijiri (1979) using the goal programming formulation developed by Charnes and Cooper (1961) and extended by Ijiri (1965) and Lee (1972) among others. To illustrate the procedure, they consider the simple case of a firm with two products attempting to meet three objectives related to profits, pollution control and minority hiring. Given the operational, financial and social constraints within which the firm must operate, all three goals may not be achieved simultaneously. The objective is then to minimize the *deviation* from the achievement of these goals. Within this context the trade-offs measure the effect that the achievement of one objective (example: a prespecified minimum level of minority hiring) has on another (example: on profits). Obviously, these trade-offs have a value of zero if all three objectives are satisfied simultaneously.

## Concluding comments

If the support for a clean and healthy environment as measured by various recent public opinion polls—which show at times a near consensus on questions regarding support of the environmental issues—is any indication of the social priorities for the future, business will continue to be forced to respond to social demands in the years to come. Further, President Reagan's attempt to deal with social needs and demands through private and voluntary efforts will likely put still further demands on business.

Such a political-social environment will continue to challenge management to respond to social demands beyond the economic mission of their respective organizations. Given the necessity to respond to changes in markets, competition, and the rapidly changing technology, demands on the scarce resources will already be severe. The addition of claims on resources by social demands will require the integration of the decisions of when and how to respond into the strategic decision process.

While the problems of measurement, uncertainty and the absence of common measures create a major challenge to a manager attempting to respond strategically to social demands, there is no need to be overwhelmed. In regard to social accounting, efforts are under way in North America and Western Europe toward the formulation and development of better techniques and uniform standards as amply demonstrated by the growing body of literature on social accounting and social indicators, and its growing use in the corporate world (e.g., Estes, 1976; Committee for Economic Development, 1974; U.S. Department of Commerce, 1979; American Institute of Certified Public Accountants, 1977; Dierkes and Preston, 1977). But given the infancy of the art 'a firm may have no choice but to retreat to a description of management procedures and policy to estimate qualitatively the corporation's position or performance' (McAdam, 1973: 11, 14).

Although the problem of uncertainty will not be overcome by any one technique or any combination of forecasting techniques presently developed, there are, however, a number of techniques such as Delphi and scenario development (MacNulty, 1977) that can be of assistance. For a survey in social forecasting in U.S. corporations, we refer the reader to Newgren and Carroll (1979) and Fleming (1981). Also Martino (1980) suggests a methodology for technological forecasting designed to take into account different types of information input. The techniques for deciding whether to seed hurricanes (Howard, Matheson and North, 1972) and for the assessment of nuclear reactors (Lewis, 1980) deal with the problem of forecasting future events based on a high degree of uncertainty and limited information. In the end, however, management will have to rely on its own informed judgement in any decision.

For goal-programming and similar techniques to be effective a clear definition of priorities is necessary. Of particular importance is the development of procedures to quantify the priority structures. Mason and Mitroff (1979) report some efforts in that direction.

Overall, however, the techniques so far developed do not solve the problems of the selection and timing of responses to social demands and the associated problems of measurement, uncertainty and common measures. By extending the lead–lag methodology of Ackerman and Bauer (1976) and by exploring the problems of measurement, uncertainty and common measures, we hope to have provided a clearer understanding of the decision problems facing a manager attempting to deal with social demands strategically within the normal strategic decision process.

## References


Ackerman, W., and A. Bauer. *Corporate Social Responsiveness: The Modern Dilemma*, Reston, Reston, Virginia, 1976.

American Institute of Certified Public Accountants, Inc. *The Measurement of Corporate Social Performance*, New York, 1977.

Ansoff, H. 'Managing strategic surprise by response to weak signals', *California Management Review*, Winter 1975, pp. 21–23.

Ansoff, H. 'Strategic issue management', *Strategic Management Journal*, 1, 1980, pp. 131–148.

Chamberlain, N. W. *The Limits of Corporate Responsibility*, Basic Books, New York, 1973.

Charnes, A., and W. W. Cooper. *Management Models and Industrial Applications of Linear Programming*, Wiley, New York, 1961.

Committee for Economic Development. *Measuring Business, Social Performance: the Corporate Social Audit*, New York, 1974.

Committee for Economic Development. *Social Responsibilities of Business Corporations*, New York, 1971.

Cooper, W. W., and Yuri Ijiri. 'From accounting to accountability: steps to a corporate social report', in Kohler, E. I. *Accounting's Man of Principles*, Reston, Reston, Virginia, 1979.

Dierkes, M., and L. E. Preston. 'Corporate social accounting-reporting for the physical environment: a critical review and implementation proposal', *Accounting Organization and Society*, 2(1), 1977, pp. 3–22.

Estes, Ralph. *Corporate Social Accounting*, Wiley, New York, 1976.

Eyestone, R. *From Social Issues to Public Policy*, Wiley, New York, 1978.

Fleming, J. E. 'Public issue scanning', in Preston, L. E. *Research in Corporate Social Performance and Policy*, Vol. 3, JAI Press, Greenwich, Connecticut, 1981, pp. 155–173.

Frederic, William C. 'From $CSR_1$ to $CSR_2$: the maturing of business-and-society thought', Working Paper No. 279. Graduate School of Business, University of Pittsburgh, 1978.

Friedman, M. *Capitalism and Freedom*, University of Chicago Press, Chicago, 1962.

Hofer, Charles W., and Dan Schendel. *Strategy Formulation: Analytical Concepts*, West Publishing Co., St Paul, 1978.

Howard, R. A., J. E. Matheson and D. W. North. 'The decision to seed hurricanes', *Science*, 16 June, 1972, pp. 1191–1202.

Ijiri, Yuri. *Management Goals and Accounting for Control*, North-Holland, Amsterdam, 1965.

Ketty, Y. K. 'New look at corporate goals', *California Management Review*, Winter, 1979, pp. 71–79.

Lee, S. M. *Goal Programming for Decision Analysis*, Auerbach, Pennsauken, N.J., 1972.

Lewis, Harold W. 'The safety of fission reactors', *Scientific American*, March, 1980, pp. 53–65.

MacNulty, C. A. R. 'Scenario development for corporate planning', *Futures*, April 1977, pp. 128–138.

Manne, H., and H. C. Wallich. *The Modern Corporation and Social Responsibility*, American Enterprise Institute for Public Policy Research, Washington, D.C., 1972.

Martino, Joseph P. 'Technological forecasting—an overview', *Management Science*, January 1980, pp. 28–33.

Mason, Richard O., and Ian I. Mitroff. 'Assumptions of Majestic Metals: strategy through dialectics', *California Management Review*, Winter 1979, pp. 80–88.

McAdam, Terry W. 'How to put corporate responsibility into practice', *Business and Society Review*, Summer 1973, pp. 8–16.

Mintzberg, H., D. Raisinghani and A. Théorét. 'The structure of "unstructured" decision processes', *Administrative Science Quarterly*, June 1976, pp. 246–275.

Newgren, E., and B. Carroll. 'Social forecasting in U.S. corporations—a survey', *Long Range Planning*, 12(4), 1979, pp. 59–64.

Ostlund, Lyman E. 'Attitudes of managers toward corporate social responsibility', *California Management Review*, Summer 1977, pp. 35–49.

Post, J. E., and M. C. Epstein. 'Information systems for social reporting', *Academy of Management Review*, April 1977, pp. 81–87.

Preston, L. E., and J. E. Post. *Pricate Management and Public Purpose*, Prentice–Hall, Englewood Cliffs, N. J., 1975.

Pross, A. P. 'Pressure groups: adaptive instruments for political communication', in A. P. Pross (ed.), *Pressure Group Behaviour in Canadian Politics*, McGraw–Hill Ryerson, Toronto, 1975.

Richards, Max. *Organizational Goal Structures*, West Publishing Company, St Paul, 1978.

Sethi, S. P. *Business Corporations and the Black Man*, Chandler, Scranton, Penn., 1970.

Sethi, S. P. 'A conceptual framework for environmental analysis of social issues and evaluation of business response patterns', *Academy of Management Review*, January 1979, pp. 63–74.

U. S. Department of Commerce. *Corporate Social Reporting in the United States and Western Europe*, Report of the Task Force on Corporate Social Performance, Washington, July 1979.

Votaw, D., and S. P. Sethi. 'Do we need a new corporate response to a changing social environment?', *California Management Review*, Fall 1969, pp. 3–31.

51

# DIVERSIFICATION

## The growing confusion

*Richard Reed and George A. Luffman*

Source: *Strategic Management Journal* 7(1) (1986): 29–35.

**Summary**

Over the years the concepts of diversification have been simplified and a system of shorthand has developed for discussing the issues surrounding the strategy. Because of this a confusion in terminology has developed and sight of the fundamental principles involved has been lost within the vagaries of fashion. Selection of a particular strategy ought to be based on the clear identification of the benefits that the strategy will offer. Those benefits should be used to help solve specific problems. Only by returning to this type of thinking can the legitimacy of diversification be revived and the alternating acclamation and denunciation of the strategy be overcome.

There is an unmistakable ring of truth in the sentiment expressed by John A. Seeger (1984) when he states that for a concept to become part of our everyday language it must be both vivid and simple and yet contain terminology that is powerful, descriptive and concise. Seeger elucidates upon the intuitively appealing aspects of the BCG growth/share matrix by rightly criticizing the academics, writers and managers who have, over time, reduced the original concepts to the lowest common denominator. Such simplifications and generalizations have turned a useful tool of analysis into a lethal weapon when placed in untutored or unthinking hands.[1] Misuse and abuse have not been confined to growth/share matrices. Specific examples abound in every field. One prime example concerns the theory and practice of diversification, but this has the added debilitating factor of longevity.

## Simplicity and fashion

It has taken around a decade to reduce the Boston Consulting Group's idea to the demeaning illogicality of supporting the stars, milking the cows and kicking the dogs. In a period twice that long—since Chandler's work (1963)—we have seen, for diversification, at least two major sets of descriptive terminology devised which have been simplified and confused. We have also seen diversification become susceptible to the whims of strategic fashion which has dictated terms on how the strategy should be adopted, to what extent and in what form.

The point of adopting a strategy of diversification has always been, and always will be, to derive the particular benefits offered by having a broader product-market base. This truism is relevant not only to diversification but to all strategic options open to managers. Action is taken to achieve certain ends and the desired ends should be beneficial. The list of benefits offered by diversification is substantial. So too, is the list of problems. Different benefits appeal to different companies for different reasons. Problems which threaten deadly pitfalls to one organization will present no problem to another. The needs of companies are as individual as the needs of people and they should not, like people, be subjected to the vagaries of fashion.

As academics in the field of business policy we, the authors, are in the fortunate position of being in touch with the practising managers of today and students who, with a little help, will metamorphose into the managers of tomorrow. It is dismaying and alarming to witness the ease with which both groups are swayed by reported fashion in the business press.[2] We can only attribute this to the 'golden egg' syndrome—a desire to find one simple answer to all problems. In the absence of any such blinding apparition there is a continuing drive to generalize, simplify and to go with the crowd, perhaps in the hope of finding the goose that lays that golden egg.

Comments of company chairmen in interviews and in their statements in annual reports and accounts bear witness to the power of fashion. In the 1970s the chairman of one of Europe's leading confectionery makers boasted of the bold new diversification the company had made by successfully launching a new chocolate-covered wholemeal snack biscuit. It mattered not that the company drew a substantial portion of its income from an existing range of chocolate-covered snack biscuits, it simply mattered that diversification—the thing to do—should be linked with the company name. At about the same time the statement of the chairman of a respectable medium-sized printing concern boasted of a technological diversification. The diversification was a new way of printing existing products for the same customers. Had diversification not been fashionable would the same chairman have not simply stated that an improved printing process had been developed?

Examples of claims for diversification where arguably none exists are numerous. When fashions change an equal number of claims can be unearthed for companies decrying all association with diversification. For example, the chairman of a large British tobacco manufacturer vehemently denied that the company was becoming a conglomerate of unrelated activities when the company made decisive moves into food and brewing. This was about the time when the hastily thrown together conglomerates of the late 1960s and early 1970s started receiving a bad press as they divested poor acquisitions of a few years earlier. Again, it apparently mattered more how the actions were described than what they were, even though the moves had proved to be profitable.

## Confusion through terminology

The wheel of fashion has moved virtually full circle from the days of specialization through the heyday of conglomerates to the present advice of 'sticking to the knitting' (Price and Waterman, 1982). Established terminology for sticking to the knitting is essentially contained within the classification system used by R. P. Rumelt (1974). The major classifications would be Related or Dominant and sub-classifications would be Related-Constrained or Dominant-Constrained. The constrained elements describe the degree of diversification which, logically, is constrained to the core business of a firm. That is, there would be little movement away from the main established product-market. Sticking to the knitting has no directly comparable categorization within the other main system of descriptive terminology on diversification—the work of H. I. Ansoff (1965)—which is widely known and quoted by both managers and students.

In the mid 1960s when Ansoff published his timely book (*Corporate Strategy*) a genuine awareness of the benefits of strategic planning was gaining momentum in both our industry and our business schools. Of all the ideas he promulgated the one that was seized upon most avidly was the new products-new missions description for diversification. Horizontal diversification, concentric diversification and conglomerate diversification were terms grasped by an audience who were starved of the models which help mental digestion in other more established subject areas. These names have been taken and applied to all types of diversification regardless of the base reasons for adoption of the strategy. The late W. F. Glueck (1980) has pointed out, quite correctly, that diversification can be used not only for growth but also for a change of corporate direction. The point was obviously not missed by Ansoff. His matrices were clearly labelled 'Growth vectors in diversification' yet, over time, the relevance of that labelling has become clouded as emphasis on the complexities of diversification has increased at the expense of the end-results that may be achieved by diversifying. In many instances that end-result should be growth.

When companies who have been sticking to the knitting foresee disaster because of technological breakthrough which will render their products or services as obsolete as the proverbial buggy whip they will probably elect to diversify. Equally, companies whose growth expectations are stymied by life-cycle maturities may also seek new product-markets. Their reasons for taking the action are fundamentally different. In the first instance a major factor will be survival—a change of direction, company turnaround—and, unlike the second instance, growth objectives will be secondary. Where growth is sought the diversification strategy may be horizontal, vertical, concentric, or conglomerate. Where growth vectors are not implicit and a company is chasing other prime benefits use of the terminology can only be fallacious.

R. P. Rumelt (1974) recognized the importance of derived benefits through his escape paradigm for diversified companies. He suggested that whilst some of the companies in his research sample had poor levels of performance they may well have been worse had the companies not diversified at all. His work for the U.S.A., and the work of D. F. Channon (1973) for the U.K., overcame the main problems of dissociating diversification from the principal aims of any grand strategy in which it was incorporated. This was achieved by considering product-markets as being joint concerns which could only be distinguished by application of the discrete business activity concept. Considering diversification in this way is to some extent a subjective process but it makes the user think deeply about the business—are the activities discrete, are they really diversifications and (paradoxically) what is being achieved by the diversification? The end-result is a classification of companies into single, dominant, related and unrelated business categories.

## Mixing terminology

A muddied and confused picture of diversification emerges as cross-pollination occurs between Ansoff's growth vectors and the now accepted single, dominant related and unrelated categories. Both systems have their own merits and limitations. Users of either system are not hard to find[3] but fully initiated users of both systems are very rare indeed. This, we suspect, is partly because the initiated user is aware of the danger involved in cross-matching two essentially dissimilar systems. It is too easy to forget that Ansoff's system refers to growth by diversification whilst the alternative system encompasses all forms of diversification. However, the partly initiated student of strategy shows a remarkable penchant for attempting to mix the two. A single-product business offers no threat, it is not diversified. Any growth achieved cannot be attributed to activities in new or unrelated technologies or through sales to similar or new customers. At the other extreme of substantial diversification a very real threat of confusion exists. An unrelated type company operates in two or more distinct and disparate product-markets. According to Ansoff's matrix, growth by conglomerate diversification means moving into unrelated technologies to serve new customers.[4] To further complicate the issue, the term conglomerate serves to identify the fast-breeder type of company who employs a policy of growth by acquisition but whose acquisition need not necessarily be diversifications. Consequent and illogical conclusions can be thus derived; namely, all unrelated diversifications must be acquisitions, acquisition must be virtually synonymous with diversification and diversification by acquisition results in a conglomerate. Explained in this way the conclusions and therefore the thought processes that derive them appear positively asinine but the green student, mature students and some senior managers have been observed to stumble into the logic maze and to be trapped by the confusion of terms whilst misconceived ideas of fashion throw up a further debilitating smokescreen.

Equating horizontal, vertical and concentric growth with dominant and related diversification, be it constrained or otherwise, opens a Pandora's box of misunderstandings. For example, how should a company be classified if it diversifies through use of an offshoot to its existing technology and sells its new product or service to existing and new customers? Obviously, any serious attempt at judgement requires additional information—what are the changes in income due to the diversification and/or was growth the purpose of the diversification? An ability to ask such questions presupposes a comprehensive understanding of the theories from which the terminology is derived. At best, such apparent problems lead to a rejection of the complexities through a regression to simplistic notions of high and low levels of diversification. At worst, the means of achieving diversification and its eventual effects are ensnared and lost in a web of misconceived notions that arise from the preoccupation that accompanies attempts to resolve classification taxonomies within growth vector grids.

## Emphasizing the benefits

When confusion reigns the surest way of regaining confidence and understanding is to revert to the use of basic principles. The very fabric which makes up the maze of confusion has to be torn down and temporarily set aside until the foundations on which the logic is built have been excavated and exposed for inspection. One cornerstone of corporate philosophy is that strategies are adopted for the benefits that they offer. Logically the perceived benefits mirror corporate needs.

Continuing the theme of basic principles we feel it provident to dig a little deeper and explore the above statement which effectively states that corporate needs and selected strategies should be equal but opposite matched pairs. It contains implicit assumptions of enormous magnitude. It assumes that machinery exists for identifying threats so that they may be avoided. It assumes forecasting and monitoring so that opportunities may be identified, seized and exploited. It also assumes the organization has a full and accurate knowledge of its existing product-markets. If all these assumptions are fulfilled and opportunities in existing product-markets offer little promise then an organization would have justification for considering the risky business of diversification. As E. R. Biggadike (1979) points out, diversification is not a subject to be taken lightly. Any real alternative strategy requires serious consideration and its benefits should be counted and weighed against those obtained by taking the path to greater diversity.

If all the claimed benefits of diversification were genuine then no company could afford to remain in a single product-market. Lists of benefits are both extensive and numerous. Each writer over the past 20 years has added to, subtracted from and given special emphasis to individual attributes so that in culmination the strategy is engendered with a panacea-like quality—hence its rise to glory. As many firms have found out to their cost the prizes are never automatic and certainly never guaranteed—hence the disillusionment with broadbased diversification.

Rather than attempt to produce yet another definitive list of benefits we have brought together the most often cited (from innumerable sources) and linked them to reasons for adopting the strategy. Through the format shown in Figures 1 and 2 it is hoped that both the student and seasoned manager will consider the fundamentals rather than simply a possible pay-off from some minor benefit(s).

In emphasizing an approach via fundamental precepts we are not offering simplicity as an answer. Quite the reverse; we are advocating greater mental effort towards reaching a better decision on diversification. Basic strategic aims can only be decided after deliberate concentration on the company's present limitations and future needs. If those aims include survival, growth,

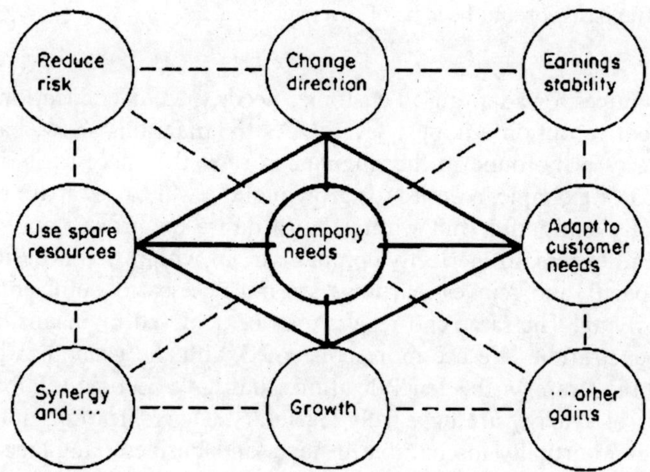


*Figure 1* Company needs and diversification payoffs.

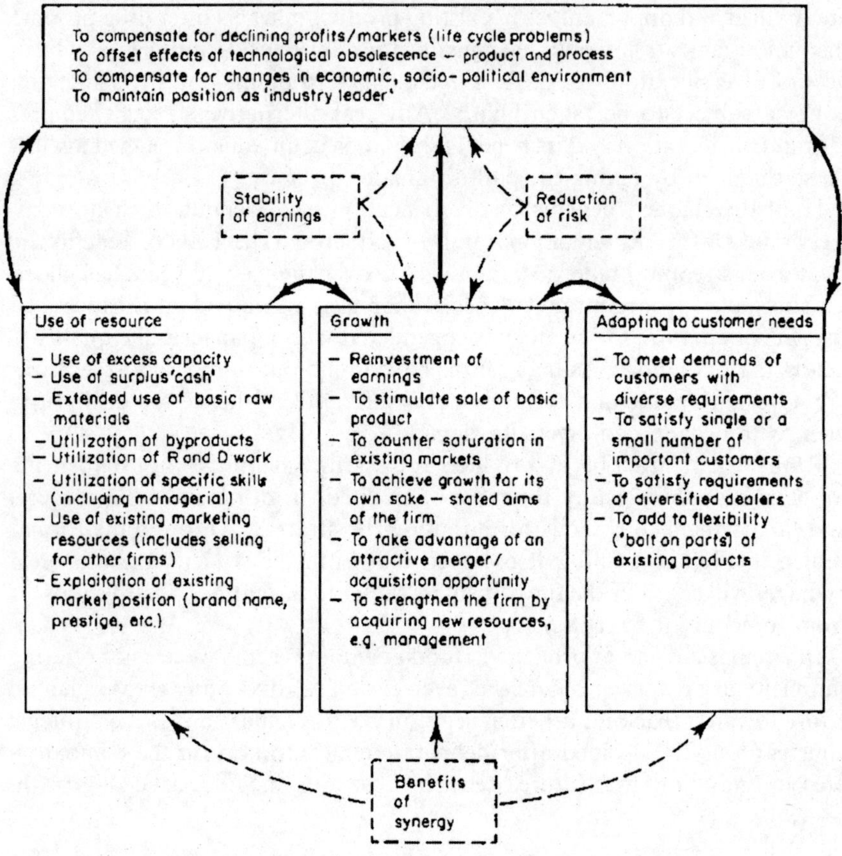


*Figure 2* The basis for and benefits of diversification.

use of resources, or adapting to customer needs then diversification may be one alternative option amongst several. As the diagrams show, basic aims are not necessarily found in the singular, nor are they necessarily mutually exclusive. For example, a desire for growth and a will to use spare resources are perfectly compatible but within that a desire for growth and a will to use spare resources are perfectly compatible but within that a desire to use excess capacity and reinvest earnings are not necessarily sufficient reasons for diversifying. The same end-results may be achieved by means of simple market penetration. We are more concerned with the generalizations surrounding the strategy; the generalizations that have become folklore.

Benefits of synergy are now truly legendary. Diversification and synergy have become virtually inseparable in texts and business language. Yet, as every student knows, those particular benefits show an almost unshakeable resolve not to appear when it becomes time for their release. To realize even part of the potential requires substantial effort on the part of the diversifying firm because the prizes are far from automatic. Stories of success invariably contain details of the great efforts needed to capitalize upon the potential benefits. Stories of failure to release the benefits never relate to the efforts expended after the diversification; they more usually contain general criticisms of the strategy in general.

Stability of earnings and reduction of risk do not have the same mystical properties as synergy; therefore, their legend is not as great. To gain these particular benefits the real work must be done before a diversification takes place. Analysis of markets, materials supplies, technological development and production processes are needed before the moves take place. If such benefits are not realized through a diversification then where the blame must lie is obvious—the conclusions drawn from the previous analysis were wrong. A healthy cynicism suggests this as being a powerful explanation for the lower levels of myth and mysticism connected to these benefits. Where pre-analysis is forced a natural conservatism is engendered and alternative strategies, which may offer fewer problems, are brought into the equation.

It is not the intention of this communication to go through all the detailed points of Figures 1 and 2 and offer arguments for or against. Such an activity would make us guilty of the very things we have been criticizing. Generalized points and simplified arguments are the staple diet of those looking for instant solutions. We are campaigning for better solutions through more thought and more strategic analysis.

## Conclusions

There are no easy answers available for solving the problems of confusion caused by misguided interpretation of the terminology used to describe the various forms of diversification. Similarly, there are no simple means of overcoming the cyclic euphoria and disenchantment with all or specific forms of the strategy. As with strategic management in general no golden egg solutions await hatching.

Throughout the preceding discussions all identified problems are seen to emanate from the way diversification is considered in our business schools, the fickle way in which its successes and failures are reported and in the way its (current) image is used for simple expedience. In short, guilty parties include academics, the business press and managers. It is up to those same parties to solve the problems. Specifically, we see a need for less emphasis on the shorthand methods of describing diversification and more emphasis on the potential of the strategy and under what circumstances the benefits can be of meaningful value. We see a need for integrity in the research and reporting of the facts surrounding diversifications within our industries; not all are good, not all are bad. Finally, we see a need for self-honesty and a realization of the fact that problems have no instant solutions in the form of fashionable actions. Most problems are specific and therefore relevant only to individual companies with their own individual expectations and requirements which, logically, require individual solutions.

## Notes

1 The McKinsey 7-S Framework (Peters and Waterman, 1982) offers, by the authors' own volition, a group of consciously tailored mnemonics that provide 'memory hooks'. How long will it be before simplification and generalization reduce strategy, structure, system, style, staff, skills and shared values to inane plug-in solutions to management problems?

2 The business press as defined here includes, in the main, the financial newspapers, business sections of daily newspapers and some popular management journals.

3 For example: for use of the Ansoff approach see Buckley (1981); for use of the Rumelt approach see Luffman and Reed (1982).

4 Note that the term 'unrelated' occurs within both descriptions, a source of some confusion in itself.

## References

Ansoff, H. I. *Corporate Strategy*, McGraw-Hill, New York, 1965.

Biggadike, E. R. 'The risky business of diversification', *Harvard Business Review*, **57**(3), 1979, pp. 103–111.

Buckley, P. J. 'The entry strategy of recent European direct investors in the USA', *Journal of Comparative Corporate Law and Securities Regulation*, **3**(3), 1981.

Chandler, A. D. *Strategy and Structure*, MIT Press, Cambridge, Massachusetts, 1963.

Channon, D. F. *The Strategy and Structure of British Enterprise*, Macmillan, London, 1973.

Glueck, W. F. *Business Policy and Strategic Management* 3rd edn, McGraw-Hill, New York, 1980.

Luffman, G. A. and R. Reed. 'Diversification in British industry in the 1970s', *Strategic Management Journal*, **3**(4), 1982, pp. 303–314.

Peters, T. J. and R. H. Waterman. *In Search of Excellence*, Harper & Row, New York, 1982.

Rumelt, R. P. *Strategy, Structure and Economic Performance*, Harvard Business School (Division of Research), Boston, Massachusetts, 1974.

Seeger, J. A. 'Research note and communication—reversing the images of BCG's growth share matrix', *Strategic Management Journal*, **5**(1), 1984, pp. 93–97.

52

# MEASURING AND MODELLING CHANGES IN STRATEGY

## Theoretical foundations and empirical directions

*Ari Ginsberg*

Source: *Strategic Management Journal* 9(6) (1988): 559–75.

Confronted by increasingly turbulent and complex environments, general managers have become more interested in understanding the conditions and forces that enable or disable successful changes in organizational strategies. Yet, largely because of their tendency to use fuzzy definitions and inadequate methodologies, empirical studies of changes in strategy have not provided practitioners with a set of well-tested theories. To provide a basis for circumscribing, evaluating, and directing future research, this paper begins by developing a framework for assessing and modelling changes in strategy. After discussing the forces that influence their occurrence and performance outcomes, the paper reviews a representative sample of empirical studies in terms of two major questions: (1) how are changes in strategy conceptualized and modelled? and (2) what methods of observation and analysis are employed? This review concludes with a report of important patterns and concerns followed by suggestions for future research.

Strategic management is fundamentally concerned with environmental changes and organizational adaptation (Ansoff, 1979; Hofer and Schendel, 1978). Accordingly, researchers describe strategy formulation as a discontinuous process (Hedberg and Jonnson, 1977); organizational strategies as patterns of resource allocations that are inherently involved with change (Mintzberg and Waters, 1982); and strategic managers as 'change-seekers' who 'must not only be adaptable to change, but must convince other people in the organization of the inevitability of change' (King and Cleland, 1978: 36).

Theories of strategic management increasingly reflect this focus on organizational change (Galbraith and Kazanjian, 1986; Lorange, Scott Morton and Ghoshal, 1986). Empirical research, however, appears to have become more and more preoccupied with cross-sectional designs that examine the synchronic, rather than the dynamic, aspects of organizational strategy (Galbraith and Schendel, 1983). The difficulties of conducting large-scale, hypothesis-testing longitudinal research, and the relative ease of access to 'static' data bases like PIMS, have exerted an important influence on this trend. Pendleton, Warren and Chang (1980) point out that measurements of change and formations of longitudinal designs have opened up a 'Pandora's Box' of dispute and controversy among social scientists. With regard to the measurement of strategic change, Snow and Hambrick (1980) raise a controversial question—at what point does an organizational response to environmental change represent a change rather than an adjustment in strategy? For example, if a firm enlarges or consolidates its domain, should this be considered a strategic adjustment rather than strategic change since its underlying orientation in relation to the environment remains the same?

Partly because of such conceptual and methodological issues, research findings on changes in strategy have not evolved into a coherent body of knowledge. Thus, it is not clear that widespread premises, such as the assumption that astute executives alter their firms' strategy to capitalize on environmental opportunities, are supported by empirical evidence. In attempting to provide a shared understanding of the scope and findings of research on changes in strategy, this paper begins by clarifying what we mean when we refer to such changes. After discussing key influences on, and outcomes of, changes in strategy, it reviews empirical studies in terms of conceptualization, modelling, and research methods. It then reports important patterns and concerns, and concludes by making suggestions for future research. In total, then, the aim of this paper is to provide a basis for circumscribing, evaluating, and directing empirical research on changes in strategy.

## Conceptualizing changes in strategy

### *The meaning of strategic change*

By definition, 'change' involves becoming different in some particular. However, the 'particular' that must become different for an organizational change to be defined as strategic is a subject of some controversy. The 'particulars' that become different when a strategic change occurs have been described both in terms of the *content* of strategy, i.e. the specifics of what was decided in terms of goals, scope, and/or competitive strategies, and in terms of the *process* of strategy-making, i.e. the enduring norms that reflect an organization's overall approach to managing its relationship with the environment. In contrast to the single-loop learning reflected by changes in *content*, changes in process reflect double-loop learning (Argyris, 1976). Not surprisingly, questions about whether or not such changes as the introduction of Egg McMuffin by McDonald's are strategic evoke heated debate when posed in MBA classes. As observed by Mintzberg (1987), proponents argue that the introduction of Egg McMuffin was a strategic change for the McDonald's fast food chain because it brought McDonald's into a new market, the breakfast one, extending the use of existing facilities. Opponents argue that it was not a strategic change because nothing really changed but a few ingredients: the Egg McMuffin was the same old McDonald's formula in a new package.

In discussing strategic change as a change in strategy content, authors have focused on shifts in both corporate and business-level strategy. Those focusing on changes in corporate-level strategy define strategic change as a realignment of a firm's selection of product/market domains and allocations among them (Ansoff, 1965). Those focusing on changes in business-level strategy define strategic changes as alterations in competitive decisions within particular product/market domains (e.g. alterations in price, or quality associated with a product) (Rumelt, 1974).

In discussing strategic change as a change in strategy-making process, researchers have focused on shifts in formal management systems and structures as well as transformations of organizational culture (Ansoff, 1979; Tushman and Romanelli, 1985). According to this view, unless the organization modifies its overall orientation to the environment in a way that substantially alters the strategy-making process, it has made a strategic *adjustment* rather than a strategic *change*. As argued by Snow and Hambrick, 'The distinction between change and adjustment may be subtle, but it is important to theory building. If most or all domain and structural changes are regarded as strategic changes, then theories can only be fragmented and ephemeral. But if these same modifications are viewed as adjustments, researchers can then look for consistencies in how an organization interacts with its environment' (1980: 529).

Although Snow and Hambrick's point is well taken, accepting a definition of strategic change that is more narrow than prevailing definitions of organizational strategy, which include both content and process approaches (Bourgeois, 1980; Chaffee, 1985; Ginsberg, 1984), seems unnecessarily restrictive. Moreover, fundamental shifts, or strategic reorientations, may occur incrementally as changes in strategy content (Quinn, 1978). Since they often result from the ordinary workings of day-to-day processes, such shifts are often not discovered to be fundamental until after they have taken place (Pondy and Huff, 1985). Hence, as Mintzberg (1987) has pointed out, whether an organizational change is defined as strategic or not depends not only *where* you sit', but '*when* you sit: what seems tactical today could prove strategic tomorrow'.

### *Classifying changes in strategy*

Since the term 'strategic change' evokes unresolvable controversy regarding the importance of the change that occurred, it may be less confusing and more useful to refer to 'changes in strategy' rather than strategic changes. Usage of this term directs us to classify changes in terms of the way we define strategy, and allows for the examination of consistencies within and across investigations of different types of change. By explicating and using the various definitions of strategy that can be found in the literature, we can eliminate much of the confusion in the field that stems from contradictory and ill-defined uses of this term (Mintzberg, 1987). Out next task then is to propose a conceptual framework that categorizes fundamental approaches for assessing changes in strategy.

Various definitions of the term 'change in strategy' can be better understood if they are classified along two fundamental dimensions. The first dimension distinguishes between conceptualizing strategy (1) in terms of a *position* that is reflected in the choices of product/market domains or competitive advantages through which firms define their relationship to the environment (Bourgeois, 1980), or (2) in terms of a *perspective* that is reflected in the integrated sets of ideas through which problems are spotted and interpreted and from which streams of decisions flow (Hedberg and Jonsson, 1977). While those who define strategy as a position look outward, seeking to locate the organization in its external environment, those who define strategy as a perspective look inside the organization, seeking to understand the 'collective mind' (often referred to as 'culture', 'ideology', or 'paradigm') that shapes the organization's enduring relationship with its environment (Mintzberg, 1987).

The second dimension distinguishes between conceptualizing changes as (1) changes in degree or *magnitude* (see, e.g., Miller and Friesen, 1983); or (2) changes in state or *pattern* (see, e.g., Galbraith and Schendel, 1983). According to the first definition, change in a nightmare would mean first-order change, such as more or less frightening nightmares; according to the second definition, change in a nightmare would mean second-order change, such as awakening from being asleep (Watzlawick, Weakland, and Fisch, 1974).

As illustrated in Table 1, together, these two dimensions result in four categories of change in strategy. Each category of change in position contains examples of both corporate-level (a) and business-level (b) positions. The two categories of change in perspective encompass both of these levels.

Now that we have clarified how two key dimensions can be used to operationally define changes in strategy, we next turn to the development of a

*Table 1* A framework for conceptualizing changes in strategy.

| | *Strategy as:* | |
|---|---|---|
| *Change in:* | *Position* | *Perspective* |
| Magnitude | (a) Change in the number of businesses in which a firm competes, or in the intensity of its business specialization.<br>(b) Change in the intensity of a firm's resource deployments to functional areas.<br>**1** | Change in the intensity of the norms and values that determine, and are reflected in, how and why a firm chooses its business domain, production processes, and administrative systems.<br>**2** |
| Pettern | (a) Change in the relatedness of the businesses in which a firm competes.<br>(b) Change in the configuration of a firm's resource deployments to functional areas.<br>**3** | Change in the configuration of the norms and values that determine, and are reflected in, how and why a firm chooses its business domain, production processes, and administrative systems.<br>**4** |

theoretical framework that can help us explain the occurrence and outcomes of different types of changes.

## *Modelling changes in strategy*

In modelling and analyzing changes in strategy, empirical research has focused on two fundamental questions: (1) what factors influence the occurrence of various types of change? and (2) what are the performance outcomes of these various types of change? This section discusses concepts that are pertinent to these questions.

### *Forces influencing the occurrence of change*

Like other kinds of organizational changes, shifts in strategy occur when forces creating pressure for change overcome forces that create resistance to change (Bigelow, 1982; Lundberg, 1984). However, changes in strategy primarily reflect the decisions of general managers to respond to changes in environmental threats and opportunities. These decisions may result either from intentional rationality and learning or from mimetic processes (Singh, House and Tucker, 1986).

The question of how often firms tend to undergo changes in strategy is rooted in a central debate in organizational theory regarding the relative influence of inertia forces, environmental feedback or feedforward, and strategic choice on activity patterns over time (Romanelli and Tushman, 1986). The predominance of inertial forces in organizations may explain the observation that periods of changes in magnitude tend to be interspersed with periods of discontinuous changes in pattern (Mintzberg and Waters, 1982; Tushman and Romanelli, 1985). Nevertheless, the frequency and duration of different types of changes may vary across different external and internal conditions or environmental changes. As Mintzberg and McHugh (1985) have obsetved, cycles of incremental and revolutionary changes in strategy appear to be of shorter duration in some organizations and more balanced between change in magnitude and change in configuration, while in others they are of longer duration with an emphasis on changes in magnitude that are interrupted by occasional, brief, and disruptive changes in direction or gestalt.

The relationship between pressures for, and resistance to, changes in strategy is a function of general managers' continual need to minimize two kinds of costs—those of being mismatched with the economic and sociopolitical environment, and those of changing to avoid the mismatch (Miller and Friesen, 1984). Hence, the appropriate nature of change can only be decided with reference to a particular set of internal and external conditions that determine the outcomes of decision-making processes (Friesen and Miller, 1986). Whether they encourage or block changes in strategy, external and internal forces provide answers to three fundamental questions: (1) Is something wrong with the current strategy? (2) Is there a need for a new strategy? and (3) Does the organization have the resources to implement a change in strategy? From the perspective of organizational adaptation theorists then, the central research question regarding changes in strategy is with identifying and explaining the key external and internal variables and associations which characterize the forces that signal disequilibrium in the firm's behavior, or those that stimulate movement toward more effective and efficient behavior.

As illustrated in Figure 1, changes in the firm's external and internal environment may increase both pressures for, and resistance to, change. Changes in the external environment (such as shifts in consumer values or competitive dynamics) and changes in the internal environment (such as shifts in organizational structure or managerial skills) may lead to pressure for change by providing feedback that a firm is misaligned with its *economic* environment. This misalignment in turn decreases the *effectiveness* of continuing with the current strategy (Leontiades, 1980) and increases the *efficiency* of engaging in multifaced and radical changes (Friesen and Miller, 1986). For example, the competitive forces unleashed by deregulation and the changing needs of clients have pressured a number of well-known investment banks into going public so as to be able to finance entry into new markets.

Changes in the external and internal environment that reflect shifts in the values and expectations of key organizational stakeholders may also

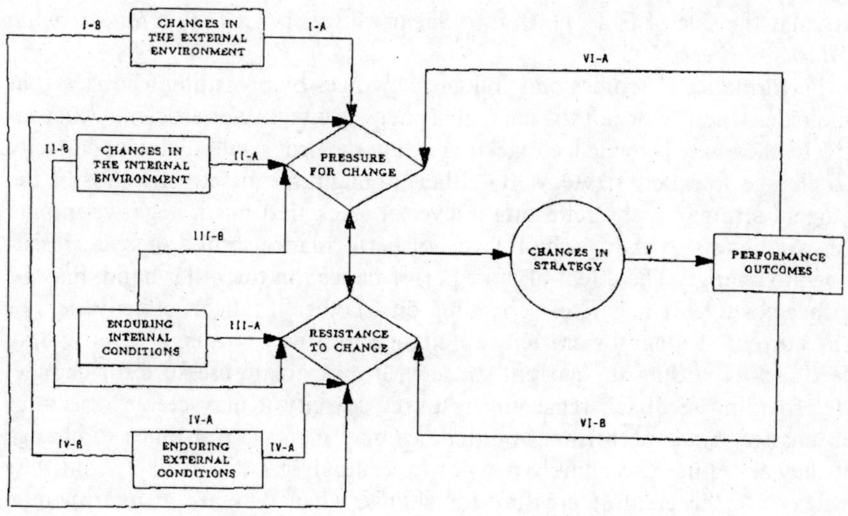


*Figure 1* A framework for modelling changes in strategy.

impair an organization's alignment with its *institutional* environment which in turn decreases the *legitimacy* of continuing with the previous strategy and encourages behaviors that are inconsistent with the previous strategy (Abrahamson, 1986). For example, the heightened fear of being 'ambushed' by the Justice Department or the Securities & Exchange Commission because of the insider-trading scandals that have occurred in the industry, and the shift in power from revenue-generating stars to professional managers, have helped investment banks to erode the legitimacy of previous strategies.

Alternatively, certain kinds of changes in the external or internal environment may also have a negative effect on a firm's willingness or ability to change to a new strategy, and may thereby serve to increase resistance to change (Lundberg, 1984). For example, Robert P. Rittereiser, brought into E. F. Hutton in 1985 to lead the firm out of its check-overdraft fiasco, was all set to announce sweeping strategic changes that included drastic reduction of the firm's regional offices, realignment of back-office systems, reduction of commissions, and the elimination of a number of business lines. However, soon after the market crash of 19 October 1987, Rittereiser realized that he would have to consider other options, including alliances that would allow for an injection of friendly capital. Meanwhile, his plans for change had been further undermined by the efforts of the previous CEO, Robert Fomon, who began to arrange the sale of E. F. Hutton soon after his departure by contacting a number of potential bidders and introducing them to the board of directors. Thus by the time Rittereiser went to the board meeting on 10 November with a modified version of his plan for change, the sale of E. F. Hutton to Shearson was practically a *fait accompli* (*Business Week*, 1987).

Performance outcomes may influence changes by providing feedback that indicates whether or not the current strategy is effective or efficient. Alternatively, they may provide feedback regarding the firm's willingness or capacity to change to a new strategy. By either highlighting the effectiveness of the current strategy or by reflecting a level of slack that has a negative impact on willingness to change, high levels of performance should increase resistance to change. The effect of poor performance, on the other hand, may be either positive or negative, depending on whether it reflects effectiveness of the current strategy or capacity to change to a new strategy. In providing feedback regarding the current strategy, it may create pressure for change; in providing feedback regarding resource scarcity it may create resistance to change. Since performance outcomes may increase resistance to change if they are either exceedingly poor or exceedingly good, it is likely that they will create the greatest pressure for change when they are at intermediate levels (Fombrun and Ginsberg, 1986).

By acting to stabilize and reinforce institutional behavior, enduring external conditions (reflected in environmental attributes, industry structure, and stakeholder values) and enduring internal conditions (reflected in the elaborate set of programs, goals and ideologies that have grown up around the organization) create incrtial forces that increase resistance to change (Hannan and Freeman, 1984; Meyer and Rowan, 1977). However, external and internal conditions that reflect high levels of uncertainty or munificence may also influence a firm to increase its experimenting behavior and may thereby serve to increase pressure for change (Dutton and Freedman, 1985; Lawrence and Dyer, 1983).

### *Forces influencing type of change*

Environmental changes influence the type of change as well as the way in which it occurs. For example, by creating misfits among the structural elements of a firm's configuration, certain kinds of changes may decrease the *efficiency* of piecemeal, first-order changes in strategy and may thereby increase pressures for quantum, second-order changes in strategy (Miller and Friesen, 1984). By dismantling institutional norms and power distributions, certain kinds of changes, such as executive succession, may also increase the *Legitimacy* of quantum changes in strategy (Ginsberg and Abrahamson, 1986).

External and internal conditions also influence the target and pace of change. For example, if a firm finds itself faced with the task of moving into a stable environment, it makes greater sense to engage in a quantum change in gestalt than a gradual change in magnitude. This is because the costs of moving into and out of an environment become relatively insignificant when the firm is entering an environment in which it will be able to capitalize on this change for a long time (Friesen and Miller, 1986). By the same token, in an environment which is unpredictable, but not to the extent where change is totally precluded, it will make sense to engage in an incremental change in magnitude rather than a quantum change in gestalt. Similarly, if a firm finds itself faced with tight internal coupling that can make change costly and disruptive, it will make sense to engage in a change that involves a dramatic shift in gestalt. By the same token, if the firm has a minimal degree of system coupling, it will make sense to engage in a shift in magnitude that involves a gradual change over time (Miller and Friesen, 1984).

Although formalized analytical methods may be quite useful for making decisions regarding changes whose consequences are well understood, they are of little use for making decisions regarding large-scale, complex changes (Braybrooke and Lindblom, 1963). Similarly, good *technical* management and competent *political* management may be quite useful for implementing changes in position when such changes are legitimized by the present strategy-making orientation, but they will be of little use for inducing changes in managerial perspectives or frames of reference (Shrivastava and Mitroff, 1984). Changes in the latter are much more difficult to trigger because managers have less direct control over the complex social processes through which symbols, meanings, and values are created (Allaire and Firsirotu, 1985). To reinforce, legitimize, and cognitively reorient the frames of reference organizational participants employ to construct strategic 'recipes' or 'formulae', top managers and other change agents may have to resort to political and symbolic actions, such as hiring a new figurehead or engaging external consultants (Ginsberg and Abrahamson, 1986; Johnson, 1986). An important research concern emerging from this perspective is thus with identifying and explaining the key associations which characterize the relationship between changes in strategy and the variety of change agents that modify organizational members' shared meanings, or serve to legitimize the strategic choices they make (Gray and Ariss, 1985).

### *Performance outcomes of changes in strategy*

Link V in Figure 1 is particularly important for translating descriptive studies of organizational adaptation into normative theories geared to improving organizational performance through changes in strategy. The option to move away from examining performance outcomes at some point is not a viable one for the strategy researcher, since performance improvement is at the heart of strategic management (Venkatraman and Ramanujam, 1986). However, rather than looking for the 'perfect' approach for assessing organizational performance, researchers should clarify the relevant frame of reference that is used, e.g. relative to a competitor, theoretical ideal, stated goal, past performance, or effective traits (Cameron, 1980). Hence, certain performance outcomes may be inappropriate for evaluating the success of certain types of changes in strategy. Thus, not surprisingly, Chakravarthy (1986) found that conventional referents of performance, which consist primarity of profitability measures, are unsatisfactory discriminants of excellent and non-excellent firms. More useful discriminants, his study indicated, were multifactor performance measures that focused on transformation as well as outcomes, and included the values of other stakeholders besides stockholders.

In evaluating the success of a change in strategy, the particular performance outcomes that are emphasized are likely to be a function of the theoretical perspective of the researcher. From an economic perspective the effect of such change on profitability or stockholders' wealth would be an important indicator of success; from an institutional perspective the achievement of environmental fit or longterm survival would constitute key indicators; and from an organizational development perspective the extent to which the members of interest groups involved in the organization perceive the change to be fair and just, as expressed in successful implementation, might constitute a key performance indicator (Carnall, 1986).

### *Summary*

To summarize, the basic assumptions of the model shown in Figure 1 are grounded in theories of organizational adaptation. Pressures for changes in strategy may be increased by external and internal changes or conditions (Links I-A, II-A, III-B, abd IV-B) and performance outcomes (Link VI-A) which create a recognizable 'misfit' with the present or future environment (Allaire and Firsirotu, 1985; Chakravarthy, 1982). The more strongly external and internal changes or performance outcomes highlight inadequacies of the current strategy and support the need for a new one, the greater will be the pressure for change. Nevertheless, awareness of the *need* to redress a misfit or gap will not generate changes in strategy if the organization lacks the capacity to do so. Conditions created by external and internal changes (Links I-B and II-B), performance outcomes (Link VI-B), or inertial forces (Links III-A and IV-A) that increase resistance to change must be countered so that the implementation of a change in strategy also becomes *feasible* (Dutton and Duncan, 1987).

In contrast to random organizational action theorists who view organizational change as having a strong component that precludes prediction of any relationship between changes in strategy and performance, organizational adaptation theorists seek to predict specific relationships between changes in strategy and performance. The nature of these relationships depends on the extent to which such changes restore or improve the organization's alignment with its economic and socio-political environment.

## A review of the empirical literature

Case studies that examine changes in strategy over long periods of time (e.g. Miles, 1982; Mintzberg and Waters, 1982; Mintzberg and McHugh, 1985) provide an important, indeed necessary, contribution to theory development. However, the remainder of this paper will concern itself with the contributions of studies that have employed statistical analysis to estimate and evaluate models of changes in strategy[1]. The sample of studies examined were drawn from a survey of articles and references on strategy-related topics that have appeared in management journals and proceedings during the past ten years.

### *Methodological tradeoffs*

Methods employed to investigate the constructs and theories discussed above reflect three fundamental tradeoffs surrounding research on organizational behavior over time (Miller and Friesen, 1982). The first of these involves the scope of the study: although selecting a small number of variables simplifies data gathering, model building, and statistical analysis, it increases the risk of specification error and the development of overly narrow perspectives. Selection of many variables, on the other hand, improves the chance of building more comprehensive and more accurate models and theories, but makes data gathering more difficult and increases the risk of ignoring changes in the gestalts and directions of these variables over time.

The second tradeoff involves the sample that is analyzed: although the selection of many firms in different industries may help to avoid the lack of generality inherent in single-firm and single-industry studies, it may be very expensive and time-consuming to obtain sufficient longitudinal data on each organization that captures shifts in perspective or changes in gestalt and direction. Moreover, as McKelvey (1978: 1438) notes, studying a diverse sample that is difficult to sort into homogenous components 'is akin to a biologist's wanting to make broad statements about heartbeat rates based on a sample of one elephant, one tiger, one rabbit and an alligator.'

The third tradeoff involves the precision reflected in data collection and analysis: by allowing for a broader inclusion of evidence, qualitative assessments can reveal deep insights into changes in perspective, as well as complex and dynamic interaction among organizational and environmental forces. However, they are also subject to errors of researcher bias, as well as reliability and replicability. Quantification of constructs, on the other hand, permits more objective, replicable, and reliable findings, but makes it difficult to examine important factors that are nonquantifiable and to build models that can deal adequately with a large number of interrelated variables.

After reviewing the empirical literature on changes in strategy in terms of key dimensions reflecting these three tradeoffs, the remainder of this section summarizes key patterns and discusses important concerns. In examining 'scope'-related choices the following questions will be addressed: (1) how were changes in strategy *conceptualized* (as classified in Table 1) and (2) how were changes in strategy *modelled?* (as classified in Figure 1)? In examining 'sample'-related choices, the following question will be examined: were firms in the *sample* from a single industry or from several industries? In examining 'precision'-related choices the following questions will be examined: (1) what *data source* was used to assess strategy (primary, i.e. retrospective data collected directly from members of the target organization, or secondary, i.e. historical data collected from sources external to the target organization)? (2) what approach was used to *measure change* (quantitative, e.g. difference in interval value at two points in time, or qualitative, e.g. the occurrence of an event? and (3) what type of *analysis* was used (i.e. cross-sectional approaches which do not examine causal relationships over time; panel approaches which examine the effect of variables in a previous period on variables in a current period; or event history approaches which examine the timing and sequence of events)?

## *Major findings*

### *The influence of environmental changes*

As shown in Table 2, findings regarding the influence of external environmental changes appear fragmented and somewhat contradictory. Changes in environmental attributes appeared to associate significantly with changes in the magnitude of strategy perspectives (Miller and Friesen, 1983). Moreover, some studies suggested that organizations tend to change their strategy configurations or directions in response to major environmental shifts brought about by such forces as deregulation or technological discontinuities, and that the impact of such shifts influences changes in strategy in a non-random way (Smith and Grimm, 1987; Tushman and Anderson, 1986). However, other studies found minimal support for the contention that common environmental challenges or conditions precipitated common changes in strategy perspective or position unless they were accompanied by external consultants (Ginsberg, 1986), new executives, or declining performance (Graham and Richards, 1979; Tushman, Virani and Romanelli, 1985).

### *The influence of performance outcomes*

The influence of poor or declining performance also received differential support. Schendel and Patton (1976) found that performance decline tended to spur firms to change strategy position only when it was severe. However,

*Table 2* A comparison of empirical studies of changes in strategy.

| | *Influence of changes in the external environment (Links I-A and I-B)* | *Influence of changes in the internal environment (Links II-A and II-B)* | *Influence of performance outcomes (Links VI-A and VI-B)* | *Influence of enduring external conditions (Links IV-A and IV-B)* | *Influence of enduring internal conditions (Links III-A and III-B)* | *Effects on performance outcomes (Link V)* |
|---|---|---|---|---|---|---|
| Change in the magnitude of a position (Quadrant 1) | Jauch *et al.* (1980) | | Schendel and Patton (1976)<br>Fombrun and Ginsberg (1986) | Cook (1975)<br>Fombrun and Ginsberg (1986) | Cook (1975)<br>Fombrun and Ginsberg (1986) | Schendel and Patton (1976)<br>Beattie (1980)<br>Singh *et al.* (1986) |
| Change in the magnitude of a perspective (Quadrant 2) | Miller and Friesen (1983)<br>Ginsberg (1986) | Ginsberg (1986) | | | | |
| Change in the pattern of a position (Quadrant 3) | Graham and Richards (1979)<br>Hambrick and Schecter (1983)<br>Smith and Grimm (1985)<br>Tushman *et al.* (1985)<br>Tushman and Anderson (1986) | Graham and Richards (1979)<br>Tushman *et al.* (1985) | Graham and Richards (1979)<br>Harrigan (1981)<br>Oster (1982)<br>Hambrick and Schecter (1983)<br>Tushman *et al.* (1985) | Harrigan (1981)<br>Oster (1982)<br>Tushman and Anderson (1986) | Harrigan (1981)<br>Oster (1982)<br>Hambrick and Schecter (1983) | Hambrick and Schecter (1983)<br>Smith and Grimm (1987)<br>Tushman and Anderson (1985) |
| Change in the pattern of a perspective (Quadrant 4) | Miller and Friesen (1980a, b) | Miller and Friesen (1980a, b). | | | | |

another study found that firms experiencing either very high or very low performance in a previous period were less likely to undergo change in strategy position than firms that experienced intermediate levels of performance (Fombrun and Ginsberg, 1986). Other studies found that poor or declining performance did not precipitate change in gestalt or direction unless it was accompanied by internal changes, such as executive succession (Tushman *et al.*, 1985), external changes, such as deregulation (Graham and Richards, 1979), or factors influencing resistance, such as industry characteristics (Harrigan, 1981; Oster, 1982).

### *The influence of enduring conditions*

A number of studies found that external conditions, such as industry barriers and market conditions, and internal conditions (as reflected in competitive posture and size) were important in constraining changes in magnitude, gestalt, and direction. These tended to focus on changes in strategy position, such as turnaround strategies (Hambrick and Schecter, 1983), divestiture (Harrigan, 1981), and stategic group entry (Oster, 1982), rather than strategy perspective. A study by Cook (1975) found managerial perspectives and behavior to be more important than organizational structure in differentiating strategic change tendencies. In general, few studies compared the relative effects or interrelationships of external and internal forces or changes creating pressure and conditions creating resistance to change.

### *Types of strategy change*

Although Cook (1975) found that organizational characteristics and environmental conditions differentiated modes of strategy change, his study is limited by its narrow sampling and operationalization of these modes. Using a taxonomic approach, Miller and Friesen (1980a) found fundamental transition patterns or archetypes that cropped up with impressive frequency in an extremely diverse set of firms. Nevertheless, because their research examines an extremely diverse sample of firms, and does not control for periodicity, it offers little insight into the relative influences of contextual origins, environmental changes, and managerial choice on the occurrence of different patterns.

Miller and Friesen (1980b) also examined the frequency of changes in strategy positions and perspectives over multiple periods and samples. Their results supported the observations of Mintzberg and Waters (1982) and Tushman and Romanelli (1985) that revolutionary changes in strategy perspective occur infrequently. Nevertheless, as they note, their focus is on significant general tendencies, not conditions that hold for all historical sequences, contexts, and types of change in strategy.

### *Effects on performance*

Less than half the reviewed studies examined the performance outcomes of changes in strategy. These defined success either in terms of turnaround (Hambrick and Schecter, 1983; Schendel and Patton, 1976), operating performance (Oster, 1982; Miller and Friesen, 1983; Smith and Grimm, 1987), risk, (Beattie, 1980), growth (Tushman and Anderson, 1986), or survival (Singh, House and Tucker, 1986).

The empirical literature does not appear to support any generalizable conclusions regarding the effects of changes in strategy on performance. Although theorists have argued that environmental conditions should moderate the performance outcomes of different types of changes (see, e.g., Friesen and Miller, 1986), results of reviewed studies do not seem to consistently support strategy–environment interaction as important. Miller and Firesen (1983) found only partial support for the influence of strategy–environmental change interactions in influencing operating performance. Moreover, Jauch *et al.* (1980) found no support for strategy content–environmental change interactions in influencing financial and managerial measures of performance.

The study conducted by Singh *et al.* (1986) suggests that the impact of changes in strategy on organizational survival may be a function of the type of change and the nature of internal conditions during the change. Their findings that core changes had no impact, or a negative impact, on organizational survival, while peripheral changes had a positive impact on organizational survival suggest that frequent changes in perspective, in contrast to frequent changes in position, may have a negative impact on organizational survival. Their findings that the impact of organizational changes depends on the stage of the organizational life cycle at the time of the change suggest that changes in strategy are more likely to influence organizational survival, whether positively or negatively, when they are made earlier in the organizational life cycle.

The fit between the pace of change and external or internal conditions may be critical for the prediction of success (Friesen and Miller, 1986). Yet none of the studies examined the effect of pace on performance outcomes. For example, a quantum change in strategy should be more profitable than an incremental one for a firm that is moving into a stable environment. This is because the costs of moving into and out of an environment become relatively insignificant when the firm is entering an environment in which it will be able to capitalize on this change for a long time (Friesen and Miller, 1986). By the same token, an incremental change in strategy should be more successful than a revolutionary one for a firm that is entering an environment which is unpredictable, but not to the extent where change is totally precluded. Similarly, a dramatic change in strategy should be more profitable than gradual change for a firm that is faced with tight internal coupling.

By the same token, a change in strategy that involves a gradual shift over time should be more profitable than a revolutionary change for a firm that has a minimal degree of system coupling (Miller and Friesen, 1984).

### *Patterns and concerns*

The fragmented nature of the empirical findings discussed above reflects a number of key shortcomings regarding the ways in which changes in strategy have been modelled. The studies reviewed generally fail to: (1) specify the complex nature of the effects of antecedent variables on change (e.g. linear vs curvilinear; mediating vs moderating; (2) specify performance outcomes; (3) control for the effects of different types of forces (e.g. inertial vs inductive; external vs internal; (4) control for the time ordering of factors influencing change; (5) control for the type of change (e.g. magnitude vs pattern; position vs perspective); and (6) control for the pace of change (incremental vs quantum).

Related to these modelling limitations are important patterns regarding sampling and analysis. Although Harrigan (1981) and Oster (1982) found that the effect of various forces on changes in strategy depended on industry context, studies generally negect to control for results due to sample heterogeneity. Furthermore, researchers generally employed quantitative measures of change in magnitude even though such measures tend to be based on observations of many organizations during relatively few periods, and are often inappropriate for capturing discontinuous changes that involve shifts in direction and gestalt. Finally, although studies generally gathered secondary historical, rather than primary, retrospective data, they tended to overwhelmingly employ cross-sectional analyses that are inadequate for examining causal relationships over time. In part this reflects the predominant concern of strategy researchers with developing variance, rather than process, theories. As described by Mohr (1982) the variance theory approach seeks to explain the variance in the dependent variable by treating independent variables as both necessary and sufficient, and their time ordering as immaterial; and the process approach treats independent variables as necessary conditions that are states rather than variables, and emphasizes the time ordering of the antecedents of the dependent variable, which is treated as a 'final cause'.

## Suggestions for future research

Two major reasons appear to account for the patterns discerned in the above review: (1) strategy researchers have tended to back away from the difficulties involved in using statistical methods to analyze complex causal models involving change; and (2) they have tended to be overly concerned with generalizabiity. The remainder of this section suggests directions that may help researchers deal with these difficulties and concerns.

### *Analyzing complex relationships involving change*

The difficulties involved in conducting research on changes in strategy are centered around four key concerns: (1) how to model the complex interaction of forces influencing changes in strategy in a way that simplifies data gathering and statistical analysis without necessarily increasing the risk of specification error; (2) what to consider in evaluating the success or failure of changes in strategy; (3) how to collect data that allow for the quantification of dynamic variables and are relatively inexpensive; and (4) how to statistically analyze causal relationships over time, despite the concern that common inferential assumptions regarding linearity, normality, and causal lags may be false.

#### *Modelling change*

It is clearly impractical to test for all possible combinations of factors influencing change. However, at a minimum, researchers should include constructs that adequately represent both inertial and inductive forces. As observed by Downs and Mohr (1976), the inability of innovation research to come cumulatively closer over time to some agreed-upon explanations is in part due to its skewed emphasis on variables reflecting inductive forces, at the expense of neglecting inertial forces. The typologies of changes in strategy and factors influencing these changes that were discussed earlier may be used to guide the development of parsimonious, yet theoretically meaningful, models.

The use of models developed to capture the complex nature of change may also provide a useful way to avoid serious specification errors. For example, a catastrophe theory model, which contains a number of qualitative properties, such as bimodality and hysteresis, may be quite helpful in capturing the divergent effects (catastrophic as well as continuous) of independent variables on changes in strategy.[2] ‘Cusp catastrophe’ models, which are tested inductively by attempting to fit empirical data to the model, are particularly useful for analyzing the influence of the relationship between pressure and resistance for change on the incidence and rapidity of organizational change (Bigelow, 1982).

#### *Examining performance outcomes*

Athough organizational changes are often difficult to evaluate, researchers investigating changes in strategy should pay more careful attention to relevant performance outcomes. Greater attention to indicators of success is particularly warranted because of the central role of changes in strategy in organizational adaptation. Singh *et al.* (1986) aptly observe that there is a strong need for studies that research the contextual factors which may have an impact on the adaptive or disruptive consequences of organizational change. For example, under what environmental conditions are certain types of changes in strategy adaptive, and when are they disruptive? Do changes in strategy in younger organizations have a different impact than change in older organizations?

Since the evaluation of organizational change depends on the evaluator's frame of reference (Carnall, 1986; Legge, 1984), researchers need to carefully develop constructs for evaluating changes in strategy. Some important questions that should be addressed include the following: How long after the change has occurred should evaluation of success take place (i.e. is the measurement interval long enough to detect underlying relationships obscured by short-term variation due to error, yet short enough to preclude fundamental changes in the causal system imposed from without)? What should be the appropriate focus of improvement or correction (e.g. profitability, growth, stakeholder satisfaction, etc.)? How does this vary for different types of changes or contexts?

### *Collecting data*

The use of published histories is particularly important for developing large sample, multivariate quantitative research designs for researching changes in strategy. As argued by Miller and Friesen (1982), studies which are considered longitudinal by virtue of the fact that they look at a series of static snapshots need to incorporate anecdotal histories which allow the researcher to capture more of a moving picture of the process of change that is occurring over time.

Content analysis of organizational documents, letters to shareholders, and corporate speeches, as well as published histories, provides an important way to quantify historical data. Hence, content analysis, which involves coding words, phrases, and sentences in terms of particular constructs, appears to hold much promise for researchers interested in going beyond anthropological types of field studies or questionnaire designs in the investigation of changes in strategy (Bowman, 1985). This methodology may be particularly useful to researchers interested in examining how changing norms and values (see, e.g., Dirsmith and Covaleski, 1983), or language and symbols (see, e.g., Huff 1985) are reflected in changes in strategy.

Although the use of published histories is a relatively inexpensive way of collecting objective information on dynamic relationships, such publicly available data are generally limited in terms of variables and populations of interest. As a result, researchers often have no alternative but to gather retrospective, survey data. Despite the evidence that retrospective or recall data can provide descriptions which are not substantially less accurate than those obtained for current data when certain precautions are taken (Moss and Goldstein, 1979; Huber and Power, 1985), there is also evidence testifying to the potential for bias (see, e.g., Schwenk, 1985). Hence, in addition to taking certain precautions (such as not asking respondents to describe events that have a strong emotional component regarding themselves) (Moss and Goldstein, 1979; Huber and Power, 1985), researchers utilizing retrospective data should try to monitor and adjust for those factors they believe might cause distortion. For example, a researcher who suspects that age and position of the respondent may distort recollection in a certain direction should look for supporting patterns in the data and then make commensurate adjustments.

The collection of primary data from multiple informants who are then cast as distinct methods in a structural equation methodological framework has been suggested as a fundamental approach for examining the reliability of single-informant data (Bagozzi and Phillips, 1982; Markus, 1984). Because of its explicit representation and testing of both measurement and latent construct linkages, the use of structural equation modelling, together with its widely used algorithm LISREL, enhances the integration of theory construction and theory testing (Hughes, Price and Marrs, 1986). Nevertheless, because of the complex nature of change in strategy, the use of LISREL to analyze multiple-informant data should be performed with caution, since it is not yet clear whether a lack of consistency between informants reflects poor interjudge reliability or the inherent complexity of these concepts perceived differently by various managers (Venkatraman and Grant, 1986). This caveat is particularly important in light of the difficulties involved in collecting sufficiently large samples of multiple informants per organization.

Finally, because of the inherent limitations of both published histories and retrospective surveys, as well as difficulties involved in collecting and interpreting multiple-informant data, researchers are urged to check the accuracy of their information by comparing the information derived from content-analyzed published accounts with information derived from questionnaires regarding changes that took place during the same period in the same organizations (see, e.g., Miller and Friesen, 1980a, b).

### *Statistical techniques*

Choices regarding time spans, number of sampling points, and statistical technique are a function of research scope and objectives and the rates of change being studied (Kimberly, 1976; Miller and Friesen, 1982). However, researchers using statistical analysis to examine panel data shoud be aware of important concerns such as ensuring that the appropriate causal lag period is examined.[3] Q-factor analysis, which clusters firms across variables, is an important method for dealing with the problem of discovering and interpreting nonlinearities that occur as the result of changes in relationships among many variables over time (Miller and Friesen, 1982). By clustering organizations along change scores of many variables, this method allows the researcher to detect structure in nonlinear data and to build a taxonomy of patterns of change. For a more detailed description of this technique and its application, see Miller and Friesen (1980a, 1982).

Finally, researchers interested in examining the timing and sequence of change should consider the use of event history regression techniques. Unlike the statistical techniques mentioned thus far, event history regression techniques are not confined to the analysis of relatively brief periods. These techniques have been expressly designed to address two important problems involved in studying the causes of events: (1) the 'censoring' of values of the dependent variable that are unknown for persons or collectivities that did not change during a given period; and (2) the exclusion of explanatory variables that may change in value over the observation period (Allison, 1984)[4]

### *How to avoid overgeneralizing*

A number of suggestions have been made to strategy researchers regarding the issue of overgeneralizing. Some of these pertain to the analysis of multiple-industry samples while others pertain to the sampling choices themselves. The researcher using a multiple-industry sample should consider supplementing the analysis with a random sample of organizations that are chosen as targets for field research (see, e.g., Miller and Friesen, 1982). Another way to control for various unspecified industry effects in statistical analysis of multiple-industry samples is to introduce dummy variables representing industry effects.

In choosing a sample design, researchers should consider employing carefully structured sample designs in which industries are stratified to ensure that sampling coincides with key factors in the hypothesized relationships (Harrigan, 1983). Quasi-experimental designs that collect data on population cohorts are particularly useful for controlling for the alternative hypothesized influences of contextual origins, environmental feedback, and strategic choice (Romanelli and Tushman, 1986). These cohort samples are identified 'on the basis of product class, which bounds the general set of resources that are critical to competition, and . . . on the basis of period of birth or entry, which attempts to insure that contextual conditions at the outset of the organization are constant' (p. 613).

A final suggestion regarding sampling pertains to the mission of strategic management as a field of study. Bower has argued that 'the charter of business policy is to focus on the life and death issues of central interest to the top managements of the firms' (1982: 632). To realize this mission, researchers interested in investigating changes in strategy should attempt to do so within a context that addresses contemporary issues of major concern. Firms in industries which have experienced transition as the result of technological or regulatory changes, e.g. telecommunications, banking, airlines, and many others, provide important as well as timely contexts for such research.

## Conclusions

Although there appears to be widespread agreement among strategic management researchers and practitioners that strategy needs to be conceptualized and modelled dynamically, most strategy research, like much of social science research, 'is characterized by synchronic data and diachronic interpretations of those data' (Kimberly, 1976: 322). Contradictory and ill-defined uses of terms such as strategic change have contributed to the fragmented nature of research examining dynamic models of strategy. To create a basis for integration with a view to developing greater insight into specific needs for improvement, this paper began by proposing a framework for conceptualizing and modelling changes in strategy, and then proceeded to review key findings and characteristics of the empirical literature.

The pervasiveness of cross-sectional analyses in strategy research and the dilemmas involved in trading-off model scope, sample scope, and measurement precision may indeed reflect formidable hurdles. Nevertheless, if we are to have a more cumulative and meaningful body of findings upon which practitioners as well as academics can draw, future research on the antecedents and outcomes of changes in strategy must be more strongly grounded in research designs that carefully measure, model, and analyze the complex and dynamic nature of such changes. Thus, while recognizing the inevitability of the research tradeoffs and difficulties involved in investigating changes in strategy, this paper challenges researchers to broaden and refine their approaches to construct development, model building, data collection, and analysis.

## Acknowledgements

This paper was supported in part by a grant from the Tenneco Fund Program at the Graduate School of Business Administration, New York University.

The author thanks Jane Dutton, Charles Fombrun, Richard Freedman, John Grant, Danny Miller, and N. Venkatraman for their helpful comments on an earlier draft.

## Notes

1 Readers interested in a more general overview of the literature on change in organizations at the individual, group, organization, and organization–environment interface levels are referred to Goodman (1982) and Legge (1984).

2 Readers interested in a detailed exposition of its properties or in reviewing an example of its application to changes in strategy are referred to Jiobu and Lundgren (1978) and Oliva and MacMillan (1985) respectively.
3 For a detailed treatment of such issues the interested reader is referred to Kimberly (1976), Pendeleton *et al.* (1980) and Markus (1984).
4 The reader interested in further detail should consult Allison (1984) or Tuma and Hannan (1984).

## References

Abrahamson, E. 'Organizational fashion: the evolution of technical, structural, and strategic norms'. Paper presented at the Academy of Management National Meeting, Chicago, 1986.

Allaire, Y. and M. Firsirotu. 'How to implement radical strategies in large organizations', *Sloan Management Review*, **26**(3), 1985, pp. 19–34.

Allison, P. D. *Event History Analysis*. Sage Publications, Beverly Hills, CA 1984.

Ansoff, H. I. *Corporate Strategy*. McGraw-Hill, New York, 1965.

Ansoff, H. I. *Strategic Management*. John Wiley and Sons, New York, 1979.

Argyris, C. 'Singe-loop and double-loop models in research on decision-making', *Administrative Science Quarterly*, **21**, 1976, pp. 363–375.

Bagozzi, R. P. and L. W. Phillips. 'Representing and testing organizational theories: a holistic construal', *Administrative Science Quarterly*, **27**, 1982, pp. 459–489.

Beattie, D.L. 'Conglomerate diversification and performance: a survey and time-series analysis', *Applied Economics*, **12**, 1980, pp. 251–273.

Bigelow, J. 'A catastrophe model of organizational change', *Behavioral Science*, **27**, 1982, pp. 26–42.

Bourgeois, L. J. 'Strategy and environment: a conceptual integration', *Academy of Management Review*, **5**, 1980, pp. 25–39.

Bower, J. L. 'Business policy in the 1980s', *Academy of Management Review*, **7**, 1982, pp. 630–638.

Bowman, E. H. 'Generalizing about strategic change: methodological pitfalls and promising solutions', in J. M. Pennings (ed.), *Organizational Strategy and Change*, pp. 319–335. Jossey-Bass, San Franscisco, 1985.

Braybrooke, D. and C. E. Lindblom. *A Strategy of Decision*. Free Press, New York, 1963.

*Business Week*. 'The fall of the house of Hutton', pp. 98–99, 102, 21 December 1987.

Cameron, K. 'Critical questions in assessing organizational effectiveness', *Organizational Dynamics*, Autumn, 1980, pp. 66–80.

Carnall, C. A. 'Toward a theory for the evaluation of organizational change', *Human Relations*, **39**, 1986, pp. 745–766.

Chaffee, E. E. 'Three models of strategy', *Academy of Management Review*, **10**, 1985, pp. 89–98.

Chakravarthy, B. S. 'Adaptation: a promising metaphor for strategic management', *Academy of Management Review*, **7**, 1982, pp. 35–44.

Chakravarthy, B. S. 'Measuring strategic performance', *Strategic Management Journal*, **7**, 1986, pp. 437–455.

Cook, C. W. 'Corporate strategy change contingencies', *Academy of Management Proceedings*, 1975, pp. 14–18.

Dirsmith, M. W. and M. A. Covaleski. 'Strategy, external communication, and environmental context', *Strategic Management Journal*, **4**, 1983, pp. 137–151.

Downs, G. W., Jr and L. B. Mohr. 'Conceptual issues in the study of innovation', *Administrative Science Quarterly*, **21**, 1976, pp. 700–714.

Dutton, J. E. and R. B. Duncan. 'The creation of momentum for change through the process of strategic issues diagnosis', *Strategic Management Journal*, **8**, 1987, pp. 279–298.

Dutton, J. M. and R. D. Freedman. 'External and internal strategies: calculating, experimenting, and imitating in organizations', in R. Lamb and P. Shrivastava (eds.), *Advances in Strategic Management*, Vol. 3, pp. 39–47. JAI Press, New York, 1985.

Ferber, M. A. and B. G. Birnbaum. 'Retrospective earnings data: some solutions for old problems', *Public Opinion Quarterly*, **43**(1), 1979, pp. 112–118.

Fombrun, C. J. and A. Ginsberg. 'Enabling and disabling forces on resource deployment', *Proceedings of the Decision Sciences Institute Annual Meeting*, Hawaii, pp. 1249–1251, 1986.

Friesen, P. H. and D. Miller. 'A mathematical model of the adaptive behavior of organizations,' *Journal of Management Studies*, **23**, 1986. pp. 1–25.

Galbraith, C. and D. Schendel. 'An empirical analysis of strategy types', *Strategic Management Journal*, **4**, 1983. pp. 153–173.

Galbraith, J. R. and R. K. Kazanjian. *Strategy Implementation: Structure, Systems, and Process*. West Publishing Company, St Paul, MN, 1986.

Ginsberg, A. 'Operationalizing organizational strategy: toward an integrative framework', *Academy of Management Review*, **9**, 1984, pp.. 548–557.

Ginsberg, A. 'Do external consultants influence strategic adaptation? An empirical investigation', *Consultation*, **5**(2), 1986, pp. 93–102.

Ginsberg, A. and E. Abrahamson. 'Legitimizing strategic change: the influence of executive succession and external consultants'. Paper presented at the Annual Academy of Management Meetings, Chicago, 1986.

Ginsberg, A. and N. Venkatraman. 'Contingency perspectives of organizational strategy: a critical review of the empirical literature', *Academy of Management Review*, **10**, 1985, pp. 421–434.

Goodman, P. S. and Associates. *Change in Organizations*. Jossey-Bass Inc., San Francisco, CA, 1982.

Graham, K. R. and M. D. Richards. 'Relative performance deterioration: management and strategic change in rail-based holding companies', *Academy of Management Proceedings*, 1979, pp. 108–112.

Gray, B. and S. S. Ariss. 'Politics and strategic change across organizational life cycles', *Academy of Management Review*, **10**, 1985, pp. 707–723.

Hambrick, D. C. and S. M. Schecter. 'Turnaround strategies for mature industrial-product business units', *Academy of Management Journal*, **26**, 1983, pp. 231–248.

Hannan, M. T. and J. Freeman. 'Structural inertia and organizational change', *American Sociological Review*, **49**, 1984, pp. 149–164.

Harrigan, K. R. 'Deterrents to divestiture', *Academy of Management Journal*, **21**, 1981, pp. 306–323.

Harrigan, K. R. 'Research methodologies for contingency approaches to business strategy', *Academy of Management Review*, **8**, 1983, pp. 398–405.

Hedberg, B. and S. Jonnson. 'Strategy formulation as a discontinuous process', *International Studies of Management and Organization*, **7**(2), 1977, pp. 88–109.

Hofer C. and D. E. Schendel. *Strategy Formulation: Analytical Concepts*. West Publishing, St Paul, MN, 1978.

Huber, G. P. and D. J. Power. 'Retrospective reports of strategic-level managers: guidelines for increasing their accuracy', *Strategic Management Journal*, **6**, 1985, pp. 171–180.

Huff, A. S. 'A rhetorical examination of strategic change', in L. R. Pondy, P. J. Frost, G. Morgan and T. C. Dandridge (eds), *Organizational Symbolism*, Vol. 1, pp. 167–183. JAI Press, Greenwich, CT, 1985.

Hughes, M. A., R. L. Price, and D. W. Marrs. 'Linking theory construction and theory testing: Models with multiple indicators of latent variables', *Academy of Management Review*, **11**, 1986, pp. 145–163.

Jauch, L. R., R. N. Osborn and W. F. Glueck. 'Short term financial success in large business organizations: the environment–strategy connection', *Strategic Management Journal*, **1**, 1980, pp. 49–63.

Jiobu, R. M. and T. D. Lundgren. 'Catastrophe theory; a quasi-quantitative methodology', *Sociological Methods and Research*, **7**, 1978, pp. 321–347.

Johnson, G. 'Managing strategic change: the role of strategic formulae', in J. G. McGee and H. Thomas (eds), *Strategic Management Research: A European Perspective*, pp. 71–91, John Wiley & Sons, London, 1986.

Kimberly, J. R. 'Issues in the design of longitudinal organizational research', *Sociological Methods and Research*, **4**, 1976, pp. 321–347.

King, W. R. and D. I. Cleland. *Strategic Planning and Policy*, Van Nostrand Reinhold, New York, 1978.

Lawrence, P. R. and D. Dyer. *Renewing American Industry*. Free Press, New York, 1983.

Legge, K. *Evaluating Planned Organizational Change*. Academic Press, London, 1984.

Leontiades, M. *Strategies for Diversification and Change*, Little, Brown, Boston, MA, 1980.

Lorange, P., M. F. Scott Morton and S. Ghoshal. *Strategic Control*. West Publishing, St. Paul, MN, 1986.

Lundberg, C. C. 'Strategies for organizational transitioning', in J. R. Kimberly and R. E. Quinn (eds), *Managing Organizational Transitions*. pp. 60–82, 1984.

Markus, G. B. *Analyzing Panel Data*. Sage Publications, Beverly Hills, CA, 1984.

McKelvey, B. 'Organizational systematics: taxonomic lessons from biology', *Management Science*, **24**, 1978, pp. 1428–1440.

Meyer, J. W. and B. Rowan. 'Institutionalized organizations: formal structure as myth and ceremony', *American Journal of Sociology*, **83**, 1977, pp. 341–363.

Miles, R. H. (In collaboration with K. S. Cameron). *Coffin Nails and Corporate Strategies*. Prentice Hall, Englewood Cliffs, NJ, 1982.

Miller, D. and P. H. Friesen. 'Archetypes of organizational transition', *Administrative Science Quarterly*, **25**, 1980a, pp. 268–299.

Miller, D. and P. H. Friesen. 'Momentum and revolution in organizational adaptation', *Academy of Management Journal*, **23**, 1980b, pp. 591–614.

Miller, D. and P. H. Friesen. 'The longitudinal analysis of organizations: a methodological perspective', *Management Science*, **28**, 1982, pp. 1013–1034.

Miller, D. and P. H. Friesen. 'Strategy-making and environment: the third link', *Strategic Management Journal*, **4**, 1983, pp. 221–235.

Miller, D. and P. H. Friesen. *Organizations: A Quantum View*. Prentice-Hall, Englewood Cliffs, NJ, 1984.

Mintzberg, H. 'Patterns in strategy formation', *Management Science*, **24**, 1978, pp. 934–948.

Mintzberg, H. 'Opening up the definition of strategy', in J. B. Quinn, H. Mintzberg, R. James (eds), *The Strategy Process: Concepts, Contexts, and Cases*. Prentice-Hall, Englewood Cliffs, NJ, 1987.

Mintzberg, H. and A. McHugh. 'Strategy formation in an adhocracy'. *Aministrative Science Quarterly*, **30**, 1985, pp. 160–197.

Mintzberg, H. and J. A. Waters. 'Tracking strategy in an entrepreneurial firm', *Academy of Management Journal*, **25**, 1982, pp. 465–499.

Mohr, L. B. *Explaining Organizational Behavior: The Limits and Possibilities of Theory and Research*. Jossey-Bass, San Francisco, CA, 1982.

Moss, L. and H. Goldstein. *The Recall Method in Social Surveys*. University of London Institute of Education, London, 1979.

Oliva, T. A. and I. C. MacMillan. 'A generic model of competitive dynamics'. Working Paper, Center for Entrepreneurial Studies, New York University, 1985.

Oster, S. 'Intraindustrial structure and the ease of strategic change', *Review of Economics and Statistics*, **64**, 1982, pp. 376–383.

Pendleton, B. F., R. D. Warren and H. C. Chang. 'Correlated denominators in multiple regression and change analyses', in E. F. Borgatta and D. J. Jackson (eds), *Aggregate Data: Analysis and Interpretation*, Sage Publications, Beverly Hills, CA, 1980.

Pondy, L. R. and A. S. Huff. 'Achieving routine in organizational change', *Journal of Management*, **11** 1985, pp. 103–116.

Quinn, J. B. 'Strategic change: logical incrementalism', *Sloan Management Review*, **20**, 1978, pp. 7–21.

Romanelli, E. and M. L. Tushman. 'Inertia, environments, and strategic choice: a quasi-experimental design for comparative-longitudinal research', *Management Science*, **32**, 1986, pp. 608–621.

Rumelt, R. *Strategy, Structure, and Economic Performance*. Boston: Graduate School of Business Administration, 1974.

Schendel, D. E. and G. R. Patton. 'Corporate turnaround strategies: a study of profit decline and recovery', *Journal of General Management*, Spring 1976, pp. 3–11.

Schwenk, C. 'The use of participant recollection in the modelling of organizational decision processes', *Academy of Management Review*, **10**, 1985, pp. 496–503.

Shrivastava, P. and I. I. Mitroff. 'Enhancing organizational research utilization: the role of decision makers' assumptions', *Academy of Management Review*, **9**, 1984, pp. 18–26.

Singh, J. V., R. J. House, and D. J. Tucker. 'Organizational change and organizational mortality', *Administrative Science Quarterly*, **31**, 1986, pp. 587–611.

Smith, K. G. and C. M. Grimm. 'Environmental variation, strategic change and firm performance: a study of railroad deregulation', *Strategic Management Journal*, **8**, 1987, pp. 363–376.

Snow, C. C. and D. C. Hambrick. 'Measuring organizational strategies: some theoretical and methodological problems', *Academy of Management Review*, **5**, 1980, pp. 527–538.

Thomas, K. W. and W. G. Tymon. 'Necessary properties of relevant research: lessons from recent criticisms of the organizational sciences', *Academy of Management Review*, **7**, 1982, pp. 345–352.

Tuma, N. B. and M. T. Hannan. *Social Dynamics: Models and Methods*. Academic Press, Orlando, FL, 1984.

Tushman, M. L. and P. Anderson. 'Technological discontinuities and organizational environments', *Administrative Science Quarterly*, **31**, 1986, pp. 439–465.

Tushman, M. L. and E. Romanelli. 'Organizational evolution: interactions between external and emergent processes and strategic choice', in B. M. Staw and L. L. Cummings (eds), *Research in Organizational Behavior*, vol. 8, pp. .... JAI Press, Greenwich, CT, 1985.

Tushman, M. L., B. Virany and E. Romanelli. 'Executive succession, strategic reorientations, and organizational evolution: the minicomputer industry as a case in point' *Technology in Society*, **7**, 1985, pp. 297–313.

Venkatraman, N. and J. H. Grant. 'Construct measurement in organizational strategy research: a critique and proposal', *Academy of Management Review*, **11**, 1986, pp. 71–87.

Venkatraman, N. and V. Ramanujam. 'Measurement of Business Performance in strategy research: a comparison of approaches', *Academy of Management Review*, **11**, 1986, pp. 801–814.

Watzlawick, P., J. H. Weakland and R. Fisch. *Change*. W. W. Norton, New York, 1974.

53

# STRATEGY AS MORAL PHILOSOPHY

*Alan E. Singer*

Source: *Strategic Management Journal* 15(3) (1994): 191–213.

A conceptual framework of 'Strategy as Moral Philosophy' is developed, with the corporation cast as a Moral Agent. This framework represents a counterpart, at the level of strategic management, to an emerging integration of economics with ethics at the aggregate level. Several implications are traced out for strategic management theories, practices, problems and pedagogy.

## Introduction

There is a growing body of opinion, previously expressed most forcefully within the business ethics discipline, that moral philosophy could inform strategic management and thereby complement or counterbalance the contribution from economics (e.g., Freeman, 1984; Goodpaster, 1985; Hosmer, 1991; to mention a few). At the level of management practice, there are many apparent similarities between strategic and ethical concerns. For example, both address the more uncertain, complex, important and longer-term problems of the firm in its environment (e.g., Hosmer, 1991). Within the business school curriculum, strategy and ethics courses both deal with similar topics, such as acquisitions, competitive intelligence, cultural differences, etc. Finally, while strategic management theory integrates the functional areas of management, together with their source disciplines (e.g., Jemison, 1981; Hitt and Tyler, 1991), moral philosophy now seems to be reemerging as the host discipline for an evolving reintegration of the social-sciences.

Despite these trends, ethical theories and concerns have not been widely accepted into the modern strategy portfolio. There are several possible explanations for this:

- *STRATEGY IS ABOUT SELF-INTEREST*: 'Strategy is how one goes about seeking personal gain' (Schendel, 1991:2). Put differently, ethical-*egoism* provides the definitive moral foundation for strategy, as a discipline. To the extent that moral philosophy then offers alternatives to egoism, or is critical of it, it becomes irrelevant.

- *STRATEGY TARGETS THE POWERFUL*: Strategy targets the upper echelons (e.g., Hambrick and Mason, 1990) or those seeking power. In contrast, ethical concerns are sometimes seen as 'an affliction of the weak' (e.g., Nietzsche, 1886).
- *STRATEGY IS PRACTICAL*: the discipline addresses the expressed concerns of practitioners, which are primarily commercial, legal and managerial; but not ethical.
- *STRATEGY IS MODERN*: Strategy addresses distinctively modern managerial problems; whereas moral philosophy is an ancient discipline.

Two decades of change have cast serious doubts on these explanations. First, stakeholder, environmental and other social issues have already entered mainstream strategic management (e.g., Andrews, 1980). These, in turn, represent a most significant extension of self-interest (e.g., Sen, 1977). Next, practicing CEOs have in fact expressed significant social, environmental and ethical concerns, in their words and actions (e.g., Jim Bere of Borg-Warner; Georges-Yves Kervern, of UAP). Moreover, a recent study of 12,000 senior corporate managers (Moss-Kanter, 1991) confirms that they are by no means alone. Finally, while moral philosophy may indeed be an ancient discipline, it also seems to have been forgotten, at least within the mainstream theory of strategic management.

Accordingly, it is the major purpose of this paper to redirect strategic thinking towards ethical concerns, not by an appeal, but by setting out a broad theoretical framework that potentially underpins such a redirection. The framework is located in the common ground now shared by concepts of strategy, rationality and ethics. It calls upon an emerging general theory of rational and moral behavior, that involves the identification and classification of multiple or *plural* behavioral prescriptions, together with a specification of their interrelationships, or *meta*relations (Figure 1). It has become increasingly apparent (e.g., Bryman, 1984; Freeman, 1984; Etzioni, 1988; Singer, 1991 *et seq.*) that this general theory could potentially inform strategy, particularly by augmenting its prescriptive dimensions.

While there are many paths to ethics in business, any road towards an integration of ethics with *strategic management* must, sooner or later encounter twin problems of corporate-rational-agency and corporate-moral-agency. Put simply, whereas strategy mainly concerns the behavior of, or on behalf of, the organization as a whole (e.g., Ansoff, 1987), ethics and rationality are often said to apply only to individuals. However, these problems of agency have, for some time, been described by philosophers and decision theorists (e.g., French, 1984; Levi, 1986) as mere roadblocks,

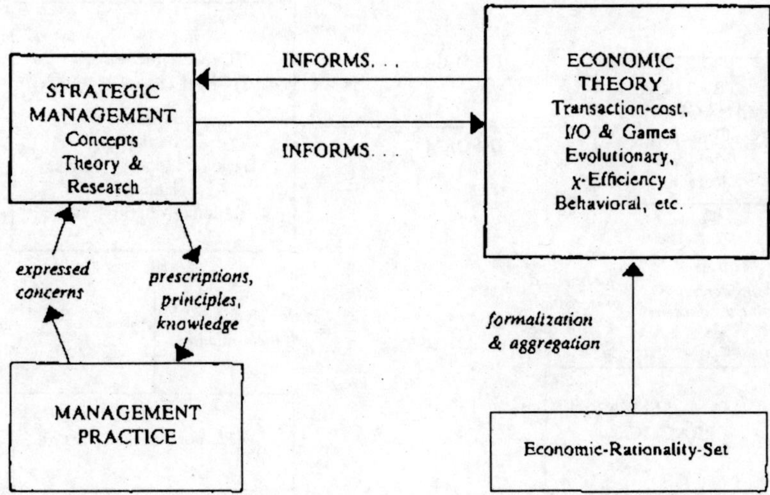


*Figure 1* Strategy, rationality and ethics.

that should be and can be negotiated, for the express purpose of building useful theories in the social and economic sciences.

Accordingly, in subsequent sections of the paper, the various roadblocks are systematically overcome, by invoking *plural* rationality and related ethical concepts. This, in turn, opens the way for a new and rather integrative conceptual framework that sees strategy and moral-philosophy as not only related, but essentially the same subject. Then, with the new framework in place, the concept of *prescription* in strategic management is reinterpreted. Strategy concepts and models are compared and evaluated with reference to their distinctive rational-moral assumptions and their associated *meta*rational and *meta*ethical relationships. Rational-ethical insights into such mysteries as competitiveness, sunk-costs and expressive actions are reintroduced to strategic management, via the new framework. In sum, the proposed framework provides a rather timely theoretical underpinning for the institutionalization of ethical concerns.

## Strategy-as-rationality

The role of *rationality* in strategic management theory is often identified with the contribution from economics, then contrasted with the perspective from administrative and organizational theories (e.g., Hitt and Tyler, 1991). When the strategy~rationality relationship is viewed via economics, its characteristics and limitations are well known (e.g., Rumelt, Schendel and Teece, 1991). On the positive side, economics has yielded strategy techniques and prescriptions, such as Porter's (1980) industrial attractiveness model, while

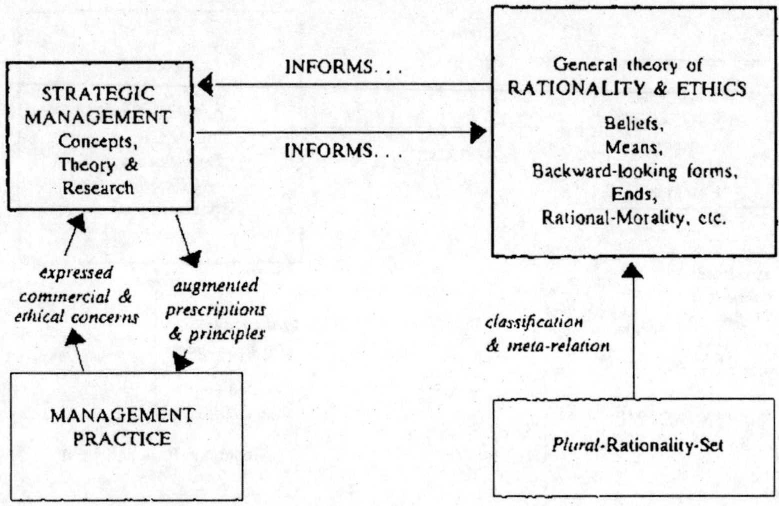


*Figure 2* Strategy, economics and rationalities.

empirical management studies have challenged some tenets of economic theory (Figure 2). More critically, formalization and aggregation have created a perceived gap between economic theory and business practice (e.g., Kay, 1991; Grubel and Boland, 1986; Rumelt *et al.*, 1991). Whereas economists seek and often find rationality-based understandings of industrial systems, strategic management as a discipline seeks to respond more directly to the expressed concerns of practicing corporate managers (Schendel, 1991).

In addition to the strategy~rationality linkages via economics, it is also rather productive to view the same relationship in a quite different way. As Table 1 (columns 2 and 3) indicates, the various distinctive forms of rationality (e.g., *bounded, systemic, selective*, etc.) in the main branches of economic theory, each captures a simple but rather important strategy prescription. Put differently, there is a set of *economic*-rationalities that informs strategy quite directly, without invoking the details of the associated formal, aggregate-level economic theory.

To the extent that the *economic*-rationality-set informs strategy in the way indicated in Table 1 and Figure 2, it must also now be asked whether or not *other* forms of rationality could do the same. Other forms have been defined in the wider spectrum of the cognitive and social sciences . . . and within a rapidly evolving ethical theory, or moral philosophy. Accordingly, the question of a wider and deeper association between strategy, rationality and ethics is explored in the remainder of the paper. First a framework of strategy-as-rationality is described, then the framework is extended towards a more complete integration of strategy with ethics.

*Table 1* Economics, rationalities and strategy-prescriptions.

| *Branch of economic theory* | *Form(s) of rationality* | *General prescription for management practice (i.e., managers should . . . )* |
|---|---|---|
| Transaction-cost e.g., Williamson, 1975; Teece, 1982 | bounded, weak | . . . take into account the costs of information search and processing (in decisions about strategy and structure). |
| I/O & Game Theoretic e.g., Porter, 1980; Saloner, 1991 | strategic | . . . consider the reactions of other entities to your moves and others' moves. Hence take into account reputations, beliefs, signals, etc. |
| Evolutionary Nelson and Winter, 1982 | systemic, adaptive | . . . learn from past mistakes. Discover rules in the environment. Utilize experience to continually refine beliefs. |
| $\chi$-efficiency Leibenstein, 1976 | selective, ratchet | . . . seek motivational devices that improve capabilities and develop the full potential of the firm. Allow for organizational inertia, or *status-quo* bias. |
| Behavioral Schwenk 1984. Hogarth and Makridakis, 1981 | cognitive, quasi | . . . take into account systematic biases, heuristic use, costs of search and processing for self (i.e., *meta*-cognition) and for others. |

### *An integrative framework*

The main elements of the conceptual framework that sees 'Strategy as Rationality' (Singer, 1992) are as follows: First, a family of more than 40 distinctive forms of rationality may now be identified within the source social sciences as a whole (Table 2). Collectively, these comprise a *plural*-rationality-set, **R**. Secondly, research in corporate strategy and planning has also revolved around a cluster of core concepts, like stakeholders, competitive positioning, identity preservation, incrementalism, forecast-use, strategic delay, to mention but a few. Collectively, these comprise a strategy-set, **S**. These two sets may be tied together with an explicit one-to-one correspondence.

Each distinctive form of rationality, in **R**, corresponds with a strategy concept, in **S**, whose meaning is either the same, or very, very similar. For example, Mintzberg's (1987) '5 P's of Strategy' each correspond to a distinctive form of rationality, as follows. (i) PLANS~*calculated* rationality (i.e., calculation of consequences), (ii) PERSPECTIVES~*substantive belief* rationalities (i.e., core mental constructs, attitudes), (iii) PLOYS~*strategic* rationality (i.e., gaming), (iv) POSITION~*expressive* rationality (communicative action, signaling), (v) PATTERN~*interactive* rationality ('in the eye of the beholder'). But that is just a start; the rationality-set, **R**, also contains

*Table 2* Strategy concepts and rationality concepts.

| *Strategy concept in **S*** | *Rationality concept in **R*** | *A source reference for rationality concept* |
|---|---|---|
| **1. Perspectives or expectations as beliefs:** | | |
| PERSPECTIVES | *belief, cognitive (substantive, epistemic)* | Simon (1987) |
| expectations | | |
| COMPETITOR-ANALYSIS | *strategic* | Elster (1979) |
| ploys | | Binmore (1987) |
| MYOPIC PLANS | *parametric* | Elster (1979) |
| EXTRAPOLATION | *extensive* | Walliser (1989) |
| historic data | | |
| MODEL-BASED EXPECTATIONS | *scientific, intensive* | Walliser (1989) |
| COMPLETE FORESIGHT | *perfect (omniscient, strong)* | Simon (1987) |
| | | Walliser (1989) |
| ASSUMPTIONS-SURFACING & TESTING | *minimal-belief* | Cherniak (1986) |
| (& brainstorming) | | |
| *ex post* STRATEGIC REVIEWS | *open* | Popper (1989) |
| **2. Strategic-decision as means-rationalities:** | | |
| MEANS-ENDS PLANNING LOGIC | *instrumental (zweickrationalitat)* | Weber (1947) |
| MAXIMIZATION & OPTIMIZATION | *perfect strong* | Simon (1987) |
| MODEL-BASED STRATEGY-SELECTION | *intensive* | Walliser (1989) |
| PROCESSES, RULES, ACCEPTABILITY | *imperfect procedural weak* | Hamlin (1986) |
| | | Simon (1987) |
| BOUNDED and *QUASI*-RAT (organization) | *bounded, quasi* | Simon (1987) |
| | | Thaler (1985) |
| ADAPTIVE-SEARCH PLANNING METHOD | *adaptive* | March (1978) |
| experiential-learning | | |
| DI-DA, COPE, etc. | *minimal-inference* | Cherniak (1986) |
| PROMISES, IRREVERSIBLE moves | *pre-commitment, weakness-of-will* | Elster (1979) |
| | | Thaler (1981) |
| DELIBERATE VS. EMERGENT STRATEGY | *excess-of-will* | Elster (1989) |
| STRATEGIC DELAY | *postponement* | Rawls (1972) |
| flexibility options-maintenance | | |
| $\chi$-efficiency CAPABILITIES, Potential | *selective* | Leibenstein (1976) |
| PATTERN (in stream of decisions) | *interactive (observer's perspective)* | Ackoff (1983) |

| | | |
|---|---|---|
| **3. Strategic-behavior as action-rationality:** | | |
| LOGICAL INCREMENTALISM | *action-rationality, practical-rationality* | Weber (1947)<br>Brunsson (1982) |
| SIGNALS, SYMBOLIC ACTS, (Position) | *expressive (2) communicative acts* | Hargreaves-Heap (1988) |
| **4. Historical-process as backward-looking-rationalities:** | | |
| FORWARD-IN-REVERSE planning logic | *systemic* | March (1978)<br>Hayes (1985) |
| EMERGENT VISION implicit goals | *posterior* | March (1978) |
| ORGANIZATIONAL-TRADITIONS (stability, coordination) | *contextual* | White (1988)<br>Habermas (1981) |
| STRATEGIC PERSISTENCE (completion of plans) | *resolute* | McLennen (1990) |
| SURVIVAL, ecological-models | *selected (by environment)* | Hannan & Freeman (1980) |
| *STATUS-QUO* bias | *ratchet (selective)* | Leibenstein (1976) |
| **5. Strategic-goals as ends-rationalities:** | | |
| OBJECTIVES, GOALS | *value, substantive, (wertrationalital)* | Hamlin (1986)<br>Weber (1947) |
| SHAREHOLDER-WEALTH with mgt. incentives | *self-interest egoism* | Rand (1964)<br>Sen (1977) |
| STAKEHOLDER APPROACH | *extended* | Simon (1964)<br>Sen (1977) |
| STAKEHOLDERS AS CONSTRAINTS | *sympathy, interdependent* | Sen (1977)<br>Etzioni (1986) |
| NOT-FOR PROFIT SERVICE ETHOS | *commitment, (altruism)* | Sen (1977) |
| VALUE-UNCERTAINTY IN PLANNING | *goal ambiguity in rational choice* | March (1978) |
| FORMULATING OBJECTIVES (process) | *deliberative, reflective* | Rawls (1972) |
| POLICY DIALOGUE As autonomous process, *Ringi* | *expressive (1), concern for autonomy* | Hargreaves-Heap (1989) |
| **6. Ethical reasoning as rational-morality:** | | |
| SOCIAL COST-BENEFIT-ANALYSIS | *utilitarianism* | Mill (1962) |
| FAIRNESS-GOALS RIGHTS-POLICIES | *contractarianism* | Rawls (1972) |
| STRATEGIC DUTY obligations | *deontology* | Kant (1956) |

such concepts as: *extensive*-rationality (Walliser, 1989), *open*-rationality (Popper, 1989), *minimal*-rationality, (Cherniak, 1986), and many forms of *ends*-rationality, concerning goals. These forms also correspond to core strategy concepts, respectively, as follows: the use of extrapolatory forecasts in planning; the use of *ex post* strategic reviews; techniques like dialectical inquiry, and the many roles and diversity of corporate objectives (Table 2).

Moreover, the notion that individual rationality has something to do with the choice of goals, as well as means to achieve them (e.g., Weber 1947, Rawls 1972) are now quite clearly echoed in modern strategic management theories, as follows:

1. RATIONAL-EGOISM~SHAREHOLDER-VALUE-CREATION. Egoism involves satisfying one's own preferences (i.e., utility maximization). If this is set in carefully specified market contexts, it formally yields Pareto-optimal outcomes. This result is at the heart of the normative theory of shareholder value-creation. Assuming appropriate managerial reward and incentive structures are in place, the two concepts, egoism for individuals and value-creation for firms, are then very similar in terms of their origin and their ethical justification (e.g., Hosmer, 1991).
2. RATIONAL-SYMPATHY~STAKE-HOLDERS-AS-CONSTRAINTS. Extended forms of ends-rationalities correspond with the general stakeholder approach in strategic management. Both flow from the idea that it is rational (right, good) to have other goals in addition to self-interest, or shareholder value-creation, respectively. The 'sympathy' form of extended individual rationality (Sen, 1977) corresponds precisely to Ansoff's (1965) stakeholders-as-constraints position. Both see that serving others' interests is prudential and pragmatically necessary, *en route* to achieving egoist goals in the longer term.
3. RATIONAL COMMITMENT~NOT-FOR-PROFIT. In contrast, Sen's rational commitments by the individual involve counter-preferential choice, genuine utility loss, or altruism. This corresponds to the special methods of a not-for-profit organization. In these cases, there is an over-riding (but rational) commitment to a nonfinancial cause (e.g., health provision, providing employment, aesthetics, etc.).

These forms of ends-rationality progressively increase in sophistication. The next level of complexity moves beyond attempts to specify rational goals, toward an emphasis on the processes of goal formulation. These more complex notions of ends-rationality recognize ambiguity (e.g., March, 1978) and the absence of universal ideals for rational choice. Doubt or ambiguity about goals is a central problem for individual rationality as it is for organizational strategy and planning (e.g., Friend and Hickling, 1987), accordingly we have:

4. DELIBERATIVE RATIONALITY~FOR-MULATING GOALS. The Rawlsian notion of a rational individual deliberating on goals corresponds to the concept of a policy dialogue, or the political and organizational process of goal formulation under ambiguity (e.g., Quinn, 1977).
5. EXPRESSIVE RATIONALITY~CONTINUOUS GOAL PROCESSES. In the absence of a definitive goal, the search for individuals' goals is continuous and important, or rational, in its own right. It underpins a person's sense of autonomy (self management) which is of ultimate value, beyond what is normally considered as economic wealth. This applies to the expressively rational individual (Hargreaves-Heap, 1989) as it does to 'rational' organizations (e.g., the *Ringi* process, that symbolizes organizational autonomy and identity).
6. SYSTEMIC (POSTERIOR) RATIONALITY~EMERGENT STRATEGIC VISION. In contrast with calculated meansends logic, systemic forms of individual rationality explicitly involve history. In particular, posterior rationality (e.g., March, 1978) refers to the emergence of individual goals, over time, as an historical process. This form of rationality corresponds to the ways-meansends recipe (or 'logic') for competitive organizational strategy, set out in a seminal article by Hayes (1985). Just as a rational person's goals emerge over time, as a function of historical experience and capabilities, so does the strategic vision of the firm.
7. ETHICAL REASONING CATEGORIES~STRATEGIC TYPOLOGY. Finally, each of the major approaches to *ethical* reasoning lends itself directly to a distinctive corporate policy. Utilitarianism in ethics corresponds to the use of social cost–benefit analysis in strategic choice; Contractarian or Rawlsian 'strategies' (Freeman, 1984) are ultimately driven by concerns of fairness and justice. Some organizations exist specifically to promote these ideals. Deontological or Kantian strategies recognize corporate duties, or simply doing what is right, even in situations where this runs counter to mainstream commercial considerations (Goodpaster, 1985; Singer and Van der Walt, 1987). The issue of politicized divestments by MNCs exemplifies this situation.

In sum, the language and conceptual foundations of strategic management theory very closely parallel those of the *plural* rationalities. This is surely no coincidence. It may be explained by the simple observation that both sets of concepts (**R** and **S**) are grappling with quite universal problems of action, decision and behavior, set in *socio*-economic contexts.

### *Isomorphism*

A more complete synthesis of strategy and rationality may be achieved by considering the 1:1 correspondence between **R** and **S**, set out in Table 2,

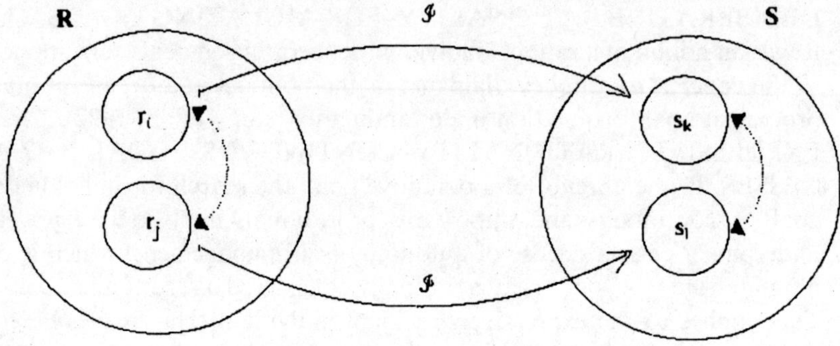


*Figure 3* The concept of isomorphism between **R** and **S**.

as an *isomorphism*, or structure-preserving map. A *quasi*-formal relational structure may be implanted in **R** (and hence in **S**) using two types of *meta*–rational relationship:

(i) '$r_i$ is a form of $r_j$'. For example, *sympathy* . . . is a form of . . . *extended-ends-rationality*.

(ii) '$r_k$ *has significant common properties with* $r_l$', for example, *expressive* rationality (which concerns communicative action like signaling) . . . *has significant common properties with* . . . Elster's (1979) *strategic-belief* rationality (which is concerned with gametheoretic interdependencies).

The relational structure in **S** is similar, and is preserved (or, in some cases implanted) using the structure-preserving **R** ~ **S** isomorphism. (Figure 3.)

Corresponding to (i) and (ii) in **R**, we have (i)* and (ii)*, in **S**, as relationships between their respective images, as follows:

(i)* *Stakeholders-as-constraints* (Ansoff, 1965) . . . is a form of . . . *organizational goal system.*

(ii)* *Positioning* is an ingredient of organizational strategy (e.g., Mintzberg, 1987). This strategy-concept . . . *has significant common properties with . . . signalling behavior*.

In these examples the relational structures in **R** and **S** are preserved. In other cases the mapping, considered as an isomorphism, uncovers or hints at relationships within **R** and **S** that have not yet received much attention in the respective literatures (Singer, 1991, 1992). The pattern of reasoning illustrated by these two examples may be made *quasi*-formal. Let ($r_i$, $r_j$) be any pairwise relationship in **R**, that is a *meta*–rational relationship like those described above. The mapping:

$$\mathscr{I}: \mathbf{R} \Rightarrow \mathrm{S} \text{ gives: } \mathscr{I}(r_i) = s_k \text{ and } \mathscr{I}(r_j) = s_l \text{ for some k, l.}$$

Then, for all i, j, we have:

$$\mathcal{I} \times \mathcal{I}(r_i, r_j) = [\mathcal{I}(r_i), \mathcal{I}(r_j)] = (s_k, s_l), \text{ for some k, l.}$$

The latter pairwise relationship, in **S**, is an interface relationship between a pair of strategy concepts. Expressed in words, 'all forms of rationality have their counterpart strategy concepts, while the strategy interface concepts reflect the *meta*–rational relationships.' That is, $\mathcal{I}$ is an isomorphism, or structure preserving map that identified **R** and **S** as essentially the same thing.

An isomorphism specified in this way effectively demonstrates that the concepts of strategic-management and plural-rationality are coextensive. 'Strategy' and 'Rationality' are, extensionally, all but equivalent, sharing almost all of their salient features. Put differently, inasmuch as the language and underlying concepts parallel one another, strategy is rationality. From this, it follows that the identity of the actor, or the agent, becomes the most salient differentiating factor (Figure 4). For rationality concepts, in **R**, the agent is normally an individual, or a cognitive system. For strategy concepts, in **S**, the organization as a whole is the primary candidate for the agent (Ansoff, 1987).

### *Corporate rational agency (CRA)*

Despite the correspondences set out above, organization theorists have, on the whole, tended to dismiss CRA. It has been condemned as a misleading concept, even 'irrational' (Brunsson, 1982). Specific *anti*-CRA arguments

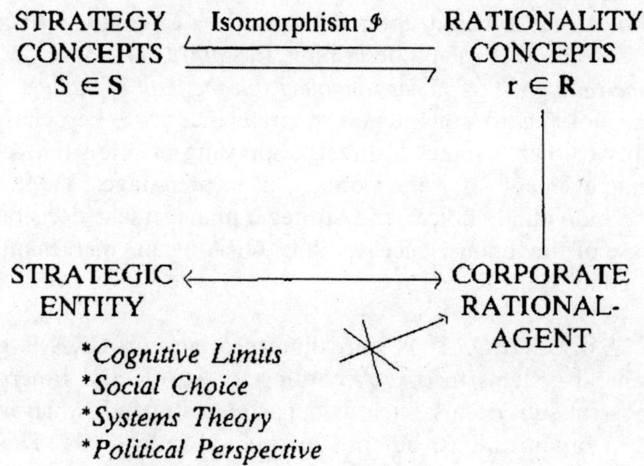


*Figure 4* Isomorphism and corporate-rational-agency.

have been offered, including (i) informational and cognitive limitations, (ii) social-choice theory, (iii) general systems theory, and (iv) political process perspectives. Each of these may now be confronted, using plural rationality concepts, as follows:

(i) *COGNITIVE LIMITS*: Neo-classical economists defined rationality in terms of consistent preferences, equivalent to utility maximization by the agent (e.g., firm). This has since been criticized because of the high level of knowledge needed about the objects-of-choice, or *omniscience*, that is needed to maximize.

However, the concept of *bounded* rationality directly responds to this critique, as it focuses on informational and cognitive limitations of the agent (Simon, 1987). Some sort of congruence between organizational planning concepts and the *bounded* rationality of individuals has been noted many times (e.g., Hogarth and Makridakis, 1981; Schwenk, 1984; Singer, 1991). Thus, the omniscience critique may be countered, simply by invoking an alternative interpretation of rationality, the 'R' in CRA.

(ii) *SOCIAL-CHOICE*: A second, related critique of CRA also flows from the neoclassical model. Arrow's (1963) theorem shows mathematically that it is impossible to combine individual values or preferences (for social outcomes) into a well-defined collective preference structure. If organizational actions are seen as determined by the votes of individual (rational) managers, the theorem undermines any idea of the group or firm as a unitary preference-satisfying rational agent.

To counter this, Levi (1986: 149) has constructed a formal theory of rational choice that is based upon unresolved value-conflicts (inconsistent preference) within the agent, describing the *anti*-CRA position as '*conceptual stonewalling which places roadblocks in the path of inquiry*.' The new theory does not regard consistency of preference as a key characteristic of rationality, rather, it takes a directly opposing position that places the effective management of value-conflict at center-stage. Value conflicts characterize individual choices and strategic management decisions. Thus, as in the case of the 'omniscience' critique, CRA again emerges intact, with a different concept of 'R.'

(iii) *SYSTEMS THEORY*: A third line of attack on CRA is grounded in general systems theory. According to Ackoff and Emergy (1972) purposeful subsystems, such as departments or individual managers, exist in organizations, but not in rational individuals. This distinction, they argue, drives a wedge between individuals (organisms) and organizations.

This purposeful-subsystems argument can now also be turned on its (metaphorical!) head, as newer theories claim that rational individuals do have autonomous psychological subsystems (e.g., Elster, 1986). New perspectives on rationality see the individual person as rather like a complex institution, with multiple departments, or multiple selves. Instead of treating the firm as a preference-satisfying individual (in economics) individuals are now being modelled as if they are like complex organizations (in psychological theories of the person). Once again, rationality and strategy concepts are converging.

(iv) *POLITICAL PERSPECTIVE*: Finally, power and authority have often been considered as alternatives to rationality and ethics as a basis for strategic action. For example, the political process perspective of Allison (1971) was proposed as an alternative, quite different way of viewing the process of governmental and organizational decision making.

Thanks to developments in the general theory of rationality, the idea that politics determine strategy no longer forces an outright rejection of CRA. Many concepts that were once considered *a*-rational, exclusive to psychology and politics, have now been developed into distinctive forms of rationality, elements of the *plural*-rationality-set **R**. Examples are: identity and the search for autonomy (Hargreaves-Heap, 1989), multiple-selves (Elster, 1986), access to knowledge (Cherniak, 1986), the realization of potential (Leibenstein, 1976), and the management of value-conflicts (Levi, 1986). As Table 2 makes quite explicit, rather similar concepts also now lie at the heart of modern strategic management theory. To summarize, one cannot simply dismiss a viewpoint that sees 'Strategy as Rationality,' simply by declaring that collectivities (firms, networks, etc.) are not rational agents. Like the *Hydra* of ancient Greece, whenever the idea of corporate-rational-agency is challenged, it reemerges, with multiple heads.

## Strategy as moral philosophy

If strategy and rationality are both broadly concerned with problems of action, decision and behavior set in socioeconomic contexts, then so too are ethics and the broad discipline of moral philosophy. Accordingly, the various rationalities $r \in \mathbf{R}$ are intertwined with almost all of the major approaches to ethical reasoning, such as teleology, deontology and contractarianism. In addition, recent developments in game-theory map out quite new pathways from the assumed rationality of players to their *de facto* morality.

Teleological, or consequentialist ethics are associated with instrumental rationality, or choosing means to achieve known goals. These include the pursuit of self-interest (*egoism*) and the greatest good for the greatest number (*utilitarianism*). The rationality–ethics linkages here are quite transparent. According to De George (1990: 44) 'A rationally operated company tries to maximize its good and minimize its bad.' (i.e., corporate-egoism) while utilitarianism 'describes what rational people do in making moral decisions.' It is also a description of what rational organizations do when they conduct a full socioeconomic cost–benefit analysis. Perhaps, then, the only distinction between rationality and ethics in these senses is that the former emphasizes means, while the latter emphasizes ends. Yet, in theory as in practice, means and ends are inextricably intertwined.

The role of rationality in an alternative, deontological ethics, is even more crucial. According to De George (1990: 66), the deontological tradition considers that '*being moral is the same as being rational.*' Also, 'by analyzing reason . . . we find the key to morality.' In this context 'reason' and 'rationality' incorporate conscious reflection and analysis, leading us to the categorical imperatives of the Kantian ethical tradition, (e.g., A moral agent should act according to universalizable principles.)

More recently, developments in game theory (*strategic belief* rationalities) have explained many aspects of apparently moral behavior. For example, Mackie (1978) has shown how game theory explains many principles of everyday morality, such as returning favors. In a similar spirit, Axelrod (1984) has used computers to explore the vast complexities of dynamic gaming, uncovering economically rational foundations for being nice, forgiving, provocative and clear. In Axelrod's analysis the players are disembodied, yet once again they have been honored elsewhere with a dual interpretation: as individuals (in Axelrod's own commentary) and as firms, in the strategy literature (e.g., Nielsen, 1988; Singer, 1988). Psychological games forge yet another pathway between rationality and ethics. In these games, players' pay-offs depend on the beliefs of the other players (as distinct from their strategy). This has allowed the effects of guilt and gratitude to be introduced to the calculus of game-playing (e.g., Geanakoplos and Pearce, 1989). In sum, as Williams (1985) has noted: '*It might turn out (that) we are committed to an ethical life . . . because we are rational agents.*' As new theoretical developments steadily unfold (e.g., McLennen, 1989) this remark becomes ever more salient. Moreover, it quite plainly applies with equal force to the 'ethical life' of the rational *corporation*. It is prompted, not by the definition of the agent, but by the many shared characteristics of rationality and morality.

The complete framework of Strategy as Moral Philosophy may now be set out (Figure 5). First, as outlined earlier, the structured set **S** of core strategic management concepts was considered as isomorphic to the set **R** of *plural*-rationalities. The implied concept of corporate-rational-agency was then defended against the major *anti*-CRA arguments by making a systematic appeal to broader and multiple concepts of rationality. Next, as indicated above, the overall fabric of the *plural* rationalities is quite sufficient

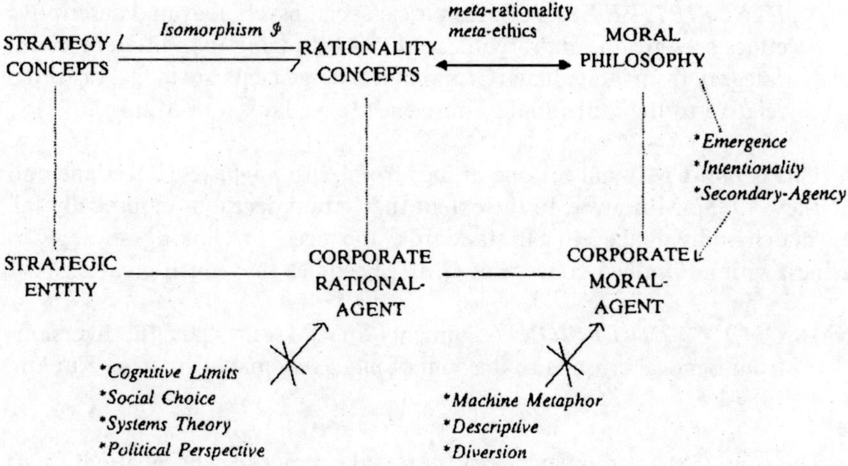


*Figure 5* A conceptual framework linking strategy with ethics.

to wrap up much of practical morality and a very large part of a wider ethical theory. Put differently, inasmuch as the language and underlying concepts parallel one another, rationality is morality. Together, these propositions lead to a framework of Strategy as Moral Philosophy, with the corporation now being cast as a moral agent.

### *Corporate moral agency (CMA)*

Like CRA in organization theory, CMA has also been repeatedly challenged in the business ethics literature. The tension between *pro-* and *anti-*CMA camps has at least equalled that between opposing camps on rational-agency, with the *anti-*CMA arguments including: (i) the machine metaphor, (ii) descriptive ethics, and (iii) CMA as a diversion. These independent challenges to CMA must now also be confronted. They are all quite vulnerable to the argument from *plural* rationality to ethics, as follows:

(i) *MACHINE METAPHOR*: The organization may be likened to a machine, controlled by *individuals* who must themselves accept moral responsibility (e.g., Danley, 1984).

This metaphor opposes CMA because it suggests that the individual managers are the only moral agents (i.e., blame drivers, not cars). However, the present identification of organizations as plurally rational agents, more akin to living systems than machines (in the Danley sense), completely undermines the metaphor, because such 'machines' are not rational agents.

(ii) *DESCRIPTIVE ETHICS*: Empirical social psychology and descriptive ethics sees groups and organizations as belonging to a different moral category from individuals. Group moral judgements are in fact distorted relative to the individual's conscience (e.g., Janis and Mann, 1977).

This is *anti*-CMA only if one argues from *is* to *ought* (e.g., Kadane and Larkey, 1983). Moreover, to the extent that group decisions empirically fail to match individual's ethical standards, the need for linking strategy to ethics, with an implied concept of CMA, becomes that much greater.

(iii) *CMA AS DIVERSION*: Arguments for CMA are harmful diversions from a moral crusade to the soul of *individual* managers (e.g., Rankin, 1987).

This *anti*-CMA argument does not make it clear whose attention is being diverted. In contrast, the new conceptual framework can be made operational as a technique for strategic analysis, that directs managerial attention to ethical concerns, alongside mainstream commercial issues (see next section). Finally, the case for CMA may be further reinforced by an appeal to some independent *pro*-CMA arguments from business ethics and moral philosophy as follows:

(i) *EMERGENCE*: This sees corporate conscience as an emergent property of complex, evolving, cognitive systems (e.g., Singer, 1984). Arguably, modem *corporations* are now at the critical stage of evolution where collective conscience is starting to emerge as a necessity of survival.
(ii) *INTENTIONALITY*: This analytic argument (French, 1984) sees the internal decision structure of the corporation as the key to a meaningful description of *corporate* acts as intentional and hence as carrying moral responsibility.
(iii) *SECONDARY AGENCY*: This argument (e.g., Werhane, 1983) likens the corporation to a hired-gun, with the *corporation* having the same moral standing as a hired individual who pulls the trigger.

In sum, denial of CMA has now become an extreme, barely tenable position. It could perhaps be sustained by insisting upon strictly *a*-rational foundations for ethics, like intuitionism or divine command theory. The only remaining tactic for denying CMA is radical indeed: a rejection of large tracts of existing prescriptive strategic management theory!

## Prescription in strategic management

The framework of Strategy as Moral Philosophy links the *plural* rationalities and ethics directly to prescriptive strategic management. In this section of the paper, it is first shown how, within the new framework, strategy concepts and models could be evaluated with reference to various *meta*-rational and *meta*-ethical criteria, i.e., criteria for choosing rationalities. Next, the framework is made operational as a strategic decision-aid, SCIO. Finally, it is suggested that several emerging themes in moral philosophy could now inform strategy, potentially illuminating some of the mysteries. Some broader implications for the theory, practice and teaching of strategy are then briefly considered in the concluding section of the paper.

### *Choosing rationalities*

When managers use particular concepts and models in their strategic thinking, they are at the same time making implicit choices between rational-moral principles. For example, a focus on such strategy concepts as competitive analysis, stakeholders-as-constraints, etc., also corresponds, within the framework, to a choice of rationalities, (*strategic, sympathy*), in **R**. This immediately invites the question:

'*Which rationalities and ethics should be used to prescribe strategy?*'

Moral philosophy has identified several *meta*-rational and *meta*-ethical criteria, for classifying and evaluating the $r \in \mathbf{R}$ (hence $s \in \mathbf{S}$) as follows:

#### *(a) Aggregate vs. agent orientation*

Some rationalities have served as foundations of formal aggregate-level economic theories, associated with public-policy prescriptions (e.g., Thaler and Sheffrin, 1981; Russell and Thaler, 1985). These are the economic rationalities, $r \in \mathbf{R}^{EC}$. In contrast, some other $r \in \overline{\mathbf{R}^{EC}} \subset \mathbf{R}$, e.g., *expressive, resolute, contextual*, are primarily oriented towards a localized decision-theory, more at the level of the individual (or corporate) agent. These forms emphasize some of the more subtle dimensions of rationality, involving identity and coordination. These 'agent-oriented' $r \in \overline{\mathbf{R}^{EC}}$ are, *prima facie*, at least as relevant as the elements of the *economic*-rationality-set, to problems of strategy at the level of the firm.

#### *(b) RUM-captured vs. elusive*

Some of the $r \in \mathbf{R}$ may be 'captured' by arguments that identify them, for at least some purposes, as special cases of *rational utility maximization (RUM)*, or formal rank-ordering of preferences (e.g., Hirshleifer, 1976). Sen's *sympathy* or Etzioni's (1986) *interdependent* utility are partly captured within this net, as is *bounded* rationality, after allowing for the costs of information and computation. In terms of the present framework, then, *RUM* (not itself listed in

Table 2) is simply an umbrella-term, covering, for some purposes, a subset $\mathbf{R}^{RUM} \subset \mathbf{R}$. Other r $\in$ **R** in contrast, are more 'elusive.' Examples include, *commitments, expressive, contextual* forms (Table 2). Within the present framework, the existence of these elusive forms implies that strategy should involve occasional (corporate) self-sacrifice; expression of (corporate) values; or the creation and maintenance of institutions and (corporate) traditions.

*(c) Temporal-orientation (forward-looking vs. backward-looking)*

Forward looking rationalities, $\mathbf{R}^{FOW} \subset \mathbf{R}$, are defined without reference to the past, while for r $\in \mathbf{R}^{BAK}$ there is at least some explicit historic reference. The set $\mathbf{R}^{BAK}$ includes: *posterior, adaptive, quasi, selected, resolute*, and *contextual forms*, amongst others (see subsection iii, below). The partition of $\mathbf{R} = \mathbf{R}^{BAK} \cup \mathbf{R}^{FOW}$ now underpins the broad strategy prescription of adapting to the past while, at the same time integrating with possible futures (Mintzberg, 1990; Ansoff, 1991; Kervern, 1990).

*(d) Meta-ethical scope*

Several other *meta* ethical criteria critically evaluate the scope of any given form of rationality, r $\in$ **R**, as follows:

*Globally vs Locally Optimal* (McLennen, 1990). A globally-optimizing r $\in$ **R** maximizes total lifetime utility for the agent, after taking into account the impact of current decisions on the agent's future preferences, learning, habit-formation and coordination with others (*resolute* is global, narrow *egoism* is local).

*Universalizable vs Exclusive* (Kant, 1956). A universalizable r $\in$ **R** is one that the agent prefers other agents to adopt (*Kantian* is universalizable, by definition, self-interest as *RUM* is not, in Prisoners' Dilemma Games.)

*Self-Supporting vs. Self-Defeating* (Gautier, 1990). A self-supporting r $\in$ **R** hypothetically chooses itself when used to select an r $\in$ **R**, as in Figure 6. While *Kantian* and *commitment* are self-supporting, in this sense, formal-*RUM* is self-defeating in the Prisoners' Dilemma.

Collectively, these and several other *meta*-criteria (perfect–imperfect; precision-of-definition, etc.) characterize a prescriptive gap that now separates the rationality assumptions of mainstream economic theory from several other normative principles of rationality and ethics. Put differently, while the axioms of *RUM* models in economics have a powerful normative appeal, so do various *meta*-criteria that *RUM* fails. Now, with Strategy as Moral Philosophy in place, these same *meta*-criteria could also be used to evaluate the corresponding strategy concepts, s $\in$ **S**.

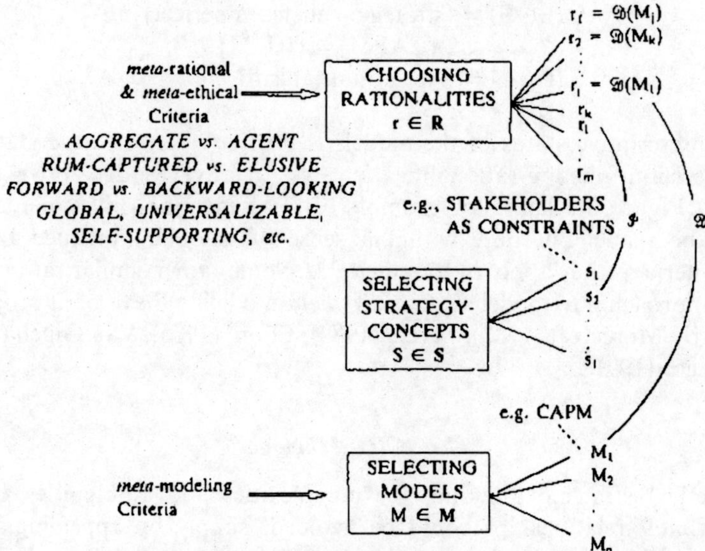


*Figure 6* Rationalities, strategy concepts and models.

For example, under the mapping $\mathcal{I}$, the concept of STAKEHOLDERS AS CONSTRAINTS, in **S**, corresponds to *rational sympathy* in **R**. As a form of rationality $r \in \mathbf{R}$ the latter is: *Agent-oriented, RUM-captured* (utility could be maximized after allowing for the impact on others), also *forward-looking, local, nonuniversalizable*, and *self-defeating*. 'STAKEHOLDERS AS CONSTRAINTS,' in **S**, is thus characterized as a component of a general prescriptive theory of strategy, in exactly the same way. Put differently, it makes sense to say that corporate strategy should be predicated on a view of stakeholders-as-constraints, but this sense of 'should' is explicitly qualified by the *meta*-criteria.

A rather similar approach also applies to evaluating and choosing formal strategy *models* (Singer, 1991). The decision-function-rationality, $\mathcal{D}(\mathbf{M})$ of a model $\text{M} \in \mathbf{M}$ (the set of models), is a mapping that associates any given model **M** with its underlying form(s) of rationality, $r_i^M \in \mathbf{R}$. More formally, for any given model, $\text{M} \in \mathbf{M}$, we have

$$\mathcal{D}(\text{M}) = \{r_1^M, r_2^M, \ldots r_k^M\} \subset \mathbf{R}$$

For example, strategy models such as the BCG growth-share-matrix (e.g., Day, 1986), the Capital Asset Pricing Model (e.g., Naylor and Tapon, 1982), Social Cost–Benefit Analysis (e.g., Prest and Turvey, 1965) are each mapped as follows:

$$\mathcal{D}(\text{BCG}) = \{\text{strategic-beliefs, imperfect}\}$$
$$\mathcal{D}(\text{CAPM}) = \{\text{RUM}\}$$
$$\mathcal{D}(\text{CBA}) = \{\text{Act-utilitarianism}\} \text{ etc.}$$

The prescriptive status of the models is then equated with the status of their decision-function-rationalities, $r \in \mathbf{R}$, relative to the above *meta*-criteria (Figure 6). Thus, for example, CAPM identifies investments that should be made, but only within a sense of 'should,' qualified by the *meta*-criteria as they apply to formal-*RUM*. Some rather similar rationality-based approaches to model evaluation (*meta*-modeling) have been proposed before, by Morecroft (1983), Myers (1984), Eilon, (1985), Van Gigch (1991) and Singer (1991).

### *The SCIO technique*

In practical strategic thinking, the complexities and ambiguities of the various *meta*-relationships could be avoided, simply by appealing to *all* of the principles of *plural* rationality and ethics. Rather similar appeals to multiple principles have been made before (e.g., Freeman, 1984; Hosmer, 1991, in the field of Business Ethics; with Mason and Mitroff, 1981, and Linstone, 1984, in the field of Management Science), yet, viewed historically, the wider appeal to rational-moral principles is a rather natural development. In the 1970s, there was a redirection of practical strategic thinking away from myopic profit planning (*parametric rationality*) towards competitive strategy (*strategic rationality*). In the 1980s *cognitive* forms of rationality, heuristics and biases, became the foundation for some new strategy prescriptions (e.g., Schwenk, 1984). Accordingly, it seems natural to ask whether managers could now reorient or expand their strategic, thinking to embrace the entire set, **R**. Put simply, attention should be paid to the fullest possible range of rational-moral principles.

If managers attend systematically to the plural rationalities, factors such as organizational histories and traditions, coordination with others, identities, rights and duties all take their place in strategic thinking alongside conventional economic considerations. To encourage this sort of integrative multidimensional approach, a new strategic decision model $M_R$ is needed, for which:

$$\mathcal{D}(M_R) = \mathbf{R}$$

Finding $M_R$ is quite simple: it is nothing other than Table 2, above! That table may itself be used as a checklist to structure a *plurally*-rational, hence ethical decision process. This has been called the SCIO technique (e.g., Singer 1992), or *I know* in Latin. 'SCIO' stands for: Specifying Canonical Issues and Options, with 'canonical' as most salient. It is an approach that could be used in a variety of strategic decision contexts, for example:

*POLITICAL DIVESTMENTS*: In politicized divestments by MNCs, the checklist directs attention to purely ethical issues as clean hands (the ethics of participation) and relativism (principles for different societies) that might otherwise be ignored. These may be considered relative to conventional commercial considerations, possibly expressed in terms of their impact on key performance parameters, like the effect of political pressure groups in the MNC home country (Singer and Van der Walt, 1987).

*ACQUISITIONS*: In acquisitions contexts, other elements of **R**, e.g., systemic, expressive, intensive forms, focus attention on such plurally-rational issues as traditions, identities, and formal-model-use within the target corporation, respectively.

*COMPETITIVE ANALYSIS*: SCIO may also be adapted for use in business competitor analysis (Singer, 1993b). In this context, a view of other organizations as plurally-rational-agents can enrich understanding of observed strategic behavior (see next subsection).

In yet other contexts, analysis of the firm's strategic position and prospects involves consideration of the sense of corporate autonomy, learning from mistakes, symbolic acts, fairness issues, etc. In sum, the SCIO technique forges quite practical linkages between strategic and ethical analysis.

### *Mysteries of strategy*

Further applications of Strategy as Moral Philosophy concern some of the more enduring mysteries, or paradoxes of strategy. Many of these may be recast as quite general rational-moral dilemmas. In this way, the theory potentially informs strategy, suggesting new directions and partial resolutions, as follows.

#### *Competitiveness and hyper-strategy*

'Competitiveness' has been defined in terms of the capabilities and potential of the firm (e.g., Hayes, 1985; Oral, Singer and Kettani, 1989), as well as the market. The organization-based theories (in **S**) could now be informed by some emerging rationality concepts (in **R**). Specifically, *hyper*-rationality, as defined by Ritzer and LeMoyne (1991), refers to possible synergies amongst *neo*-Weberian rationalities. In the Japanese industrial system, the *substantive-value*-rationality, groupism and harmony, tend to reinforce *scientific* or *theoretical-rationality* (R&D achievements). A corresponding concept of synergy, in **S**, now prescribes the implanting of such synergies in the organization (Singer, 1993c). This broad prescription is *universalizable*, side-stepping paradoxes sometimes associated with market competition, like the Prisoners' Dilemma.

*Strategy with sunk costs*

Investment decisions with sunk costs have been the focus of various strategy studies and models, $\mathbf{M}^{[SK]} \subset \mathbf{M}$, e.g., Staw, (1981), Bowen (1987), Schwenk and Tang (1989), to mention but a few. Further developments towards refining prescriptions could now be directly related to the entire set $\mathbf{R}^{BAK} \subset \mathbf{R}$, of *backward-looking* rationalities (e.g., McLennen, 1990). Specifically, there is a *non-empty* subset, $\mathbf{R}^{RAK*} \subset \mathbf{R}$, defined as:

$$\mathbf{R}^{BAK*} = \mathbf{R}^{BAK} - \left\{ \begin{array}{l} \mathrm{U}\{\mathscr{D}\mathbf{M}\} \\ \mathrm{M} \in \mathbf{M}^{[SK]} \end{array} \right.$$

The elements of $\mathbf{R}^{BAK*}$ include: *contextual, resolute, selected* forms of rationality, each of which could further inform the prescriptive theory of strategy, in situations involving sunk costs (Singer, 1993a).

*Strategic timing*

*Postponement* has recently been the focus of several strategy models, $\mathbf{M}_i \in \mathbf{M}^{[P]} \subset \mathbf{M}$ (Pindyck, 1991). These are all economic models with:

$$\mathscr{D}(\mathbf{M}_i) = \mathrm{RUM}, \text{ for all } \mathbf{M}_i \in \mathbf{M}^{[P]}$$

However, alternative rationality assumptions, particularly *precommitment* are also quite relevant to problems of corporate strategic timing. *Postponement vs. precommitment* is a paradox of rationality, as the former calls for delay, to obtain further information, but the latter prescribes immediate action before goals change. Thus, a framework of *plural*-rationality helps to make explicit some of the more subtle rationality-dimensions of strategic timing decisions.

*Autonomy and Identity*

Expressive rationality (in **R**) combines sociological with economic perspectives. It involves experimentation with preferences and is not *RUM*-captured (Hargreaves-Heap, 1989), It potentially yields a new theory of expressive strategy (in **S**), prescribing (corporate) acts as simple expressions of (corporate) identity, or autonomous corporate values, rather than the maximization of shareholder returns. In an environment of pervasive uncertainty, such strategies could be quite rational, but in a fundamentally different sense for means–ends plans.

In sum, several recent developments in the general theory of rationality and ethics are also, at the same time, contributing to a richer prescriptive theory of strategy. The present conceptual framework makes the contribution quite automatic. At the same time, modern strategy research has itself become relevant to descriptive and normative ethics. Empirical programs focusing on such issues as corporate competition and cooperation, organizational persistence and timing, divisional autonomy and identity, corporate social responsibility, etc. are at the same time tackling some enduring, even ancient, problems of moral philosophy.

## Conclusion

Social scientists investigating individuals' schemes of action have continued to develop categories of meaning that are shared by the strategic management discipline. The framework of Strategy as Moral Philosophy, with the corporation as a rational-moral agent, now makes this sharing much more direct and explicit. Some potential implications for prescription were set out in the preceding section. In addition, there are some wider implications for strategic management theory, business-school arrangements and managerial practices.

### *Implications for theory and research*

Further development of precriptive theories of strategy should more fully take into account corresponding progress in the general theory of rationality and ethics. There is a manifest symbiosis. Therefore, evolving principles of rational and moral behavior, with their associated *meta*-relations, should be considered as *prima facie* relevant to the strategic management discipline. Equally, empirical and conceptual progress in strategy should be carefully reviewed for its potential ability to advance descriptive and normative ethical theory. The examples offered in the preceding section are but an illustration of how this overall line of research could develop, in the future.

Earlier observations about strategy are also illuminated, using the new framework. These include the 'striking' congruence between administrative and ethical problems (Goodpaster, 1985), the 'uncanny' parallels between planning concepts and cognitive psychology (Hogarth and Makridakis. 1981), and the rather mysterious 'reverse logic' of planning, prescribed by Hayes (1985). More generally, Strategy as Moral Philosophy could complement the empirical programs of Hitt and Tyler (1991), or P. Marsh *et al.* (1988); the systems-theory programs of Zeleny (1980), or Van Gigch (1991); the philosophical approaches of Mason and Mitroff (1981), or Van Peursen (1989); and the artificial-intelligence approach of Sutherland (1989). Finally, the framework represents a counterpart, at the level of strategy, to the currently emerging synthesis of ethics with formal, aggregate-level economic theories (e.g., Etzioni, 1986, 1988; Hamlin, 1986; Sen, 1987; Gauthier, 1990, to mention but a few).

### *Implications for business schools*

For management education, there are some further implications commensurate with the new theoretical framework. These concern both the content of strategy courses and their institutional arrangements. At present, the subject of strategy is often taught separately from business ethics. Thus, students can attend traditional strategy courses that simply elaborate upon means for seeking personal gain, while other courses prescribe a different set of maxims, principles and values. Integration, or seeking balance, then becomes part of the hidden curriculum. Not surprisingly, some management students have sought to resolve the perceived conflict in the counselor's office, rather than academic libraries (e.g., Osiel, 1984). In contrast, the new framework offers one way of placing the conflict and its resolution directly onto the formal agenda of the business school. A corresponding reorientation in the teaching of economics has also been advocated, quite recently, by Etzioni (1988).

### *Implications for managers*

In practice, the SCIO technique (see preceding section) is but one of the potential spin-offs from the new framework. There are also implications for the design of management control systems and for the articulation of corporate missions.

Control and performance appraisal systems could be used to endow an organization, or its units, with distinctive moral characteristics, even a moral character (e.g., Goldman, 1980; Hosmer, 1991). In practical terms, decision methods like SCIO could be coupled to incentive systems that reward such collective behaviors as learning from past mistakes (*open, systemic*), preparedness for a crisis (*minimizing harm*), strong stakeholder relationships (*sympathy, commitments*), or the level of development of a unit's identity (*expressive*). Put differently, the framework licenses the use of control systems to institutionalize a much richer moral character than that prescribed by conventional economics and strategic management theory.

With regard to corporate mission statements and codes of ethics, references to environmental and social justice issues have, over the last two decades, become much more common. According to some economic and political theories, this trend could be a mistake, unless such mission statements really reflect nothing other than a public relations or marketing *ploy* (e.g., Friedman, 1970). Others, in contrast, have firmly rejected the associated prescription for *egoist* or cynical corporate actors (e.g., Sen, 1977, 1987; Goldman, 1980; Buchanan, 1985; Etzioni, 1988; Kuhn, 1992; to mention a few). These social scientists have all pointed to quite specific improvements in society and economy that could be expected to flow from corporate motivations that genuinely transcend profit maximization. Put differently, they have sought to justify, at the aggregate-level, in terms of a *meta*-theory of *economics*, the evolution of multiple corporate missions. The present framework now simply offers a corresponding justification, but it is within an extended theory of *strategic management*.

In sum, Strategy as Moral Philosophy now offers major corporate players a quite sustainable theoretical justification for their steps towards lifting the spirit of the competitive game. At least one CEO of a major corporation has publicly endorsed this *macro*-trend, describing a new synthesis of corporate strategy with *ethics* as: *Une therapeutique—la moins violente possible—des maladies de la societe*' (Kervern, 1990). Accordingly, the proposed framework is not only integrative, but it could also be practical and rather timely.

## Acknowledgements

The author acknowledges helpful comments from Professor LaRue T. Hosmer, University of Michigan, and from three anonymous referees.

## Appendix: Glossary of terms & symbols

| Form of Rationality (refer to Table 2) | Meaning(s) & Features |
|---|---|
| **1. Belief-rationalities** | |
| *belief, cognitive (Simon's 'substantive')* | The degree of objectivity, validity or veracity of the entity's beliefs and expectations. Integrity of the knowledge-base. |
| *strategic* | The entity's beliefs and expectations take into account the anticipated responses and interactions of other entities. 'The (entity) takes account of the fact that the environment is made up of other actors and that (it) is part of their environment, and that they know this, etc.' (Elster, 1979:18). |
| *parametric* | The entity treats its environment as a constant. Other entities are treated as parameters in a decision problem, as in myopic plans and adjusted cashflow-forecasts for capital budgeting calculations, etc. |
| *extensive* | The entity's expectations are formed by extrapolating historical data. |
| *scientific, intensive* | The entity creates models (symbolic representations) in the process of seeking the truth about the environment, then uses these models to shape expectations. |
| *perfect* | A hypothetical ideal. The entity has total knowledge of the world now and in the future. |
| *minimal (belief)* | One of several minimal requirements for a cognitive (thinking) entity. The entity can activate (access, use) some relevant beliefs and detect some inconsistencies in beliefs. |
| *open* | The entity takes corrective measures in response to all of its past mistakes, as identified by itself and others. |

**2. Means-rationalities**

| | |
|---|---|
| *Instrumental* | The entity selects the best means to achieve current known goals, given current beliefs. |
| *perfect, strong* | The entity calculates a hypothetical optimum, a course of action that is most preferred by the entity, under conditions of complete (or probabilistic) knowledge. |
| *intensive* | The entity selects a strategy (chooses the best action) as the output of a formal symbolic model. |
| *imperfect, procedural, weak* | The entity responds to recognized limits of its own knowledge, processing and inferential capabilities (cognitive simplification). |
| *bounded* | The entity allocates cognitive resources efficiently or optimally, attends selectively to information, satisfies with respect to goals and uses heuristics. |
| *quasi* | The entity makes choices that are consistent with empirically supported variants of SEU models, e.g., prospect theory, transaction utility theory. |
| *adaptive* | The entity uses decision rules and heuristics iteratively over time, as further information becomes available or as experience accumulates. |
| *minimal-inference* | The entity makes some appropriate inferences from some of its beliefs. |
| *precommitment* | The entity takes preemptive (and costly) action now to prevent its own possible future deviation from a longer term strategy or mission (weakness-of-will). |
| *excess-of-will* | Some outcomes desired or intended by the entity can *only* be achieved indirectly, as byproducts of intentions and actions directed elsewhere, e.g., achieving self-respect. (Compare Elster, 1989:19 with Mintzberg, 1987). |
| *rational-postponement* | For any proposed course of action by the entity, it is rational to also consider the value of waiting, delaying the action, or of keeping options open. |
| *selective (X-efficiency)* | The entity makes a trade-off of (i) a pressure to act in accordance with its capabilities and potential, against (ii) constraints perceived by the entity. |
| *interactive* | Rationality is 'in the eye of the beholder.' It is attributed by the observer to the observed pattern of an entity's behavior. |

**3. Action-rationalities**

| | |
|---|---|
| *action, practical* | Rational action to achieve a desired goal involves selective attention to content and process, within a responsive or reactive environment |
| *expressive, communicative* | In a social system, actions are primarily symbolic, (carrying meaning for others to interpret and respond to), rather than instrumental. Therefore a rational entity builds identity and reputation. |

**4. Backward-looking rationalities**

*systemic* Knowledge, goals, behavioral rules, and capabilities accumulate and must be developed by the entity, over time.

*posterior* The entity's goals (values, preferences) are products of its actions. Goals emerge and crystallize through processes of deliberation, reflection and dissonance.

*contextual* (i) An entity's actions should be oriented towards the creation and maintenance of institutions that symbolize a good life with others.
(ii) The social and historical context of a decision or problem directs and confines the entity's attention to particular problem attributes.

*resolute* An entity should persist with very long-standing missions or plans rather than abandon them in favor of a fleeting opportunity or preference. It is worthwhile to develop habits (or traditions) of task-completion.

*selected (environment)* Rationality, or rules of survival and growth, are located in the environment. Over time, the environment selects those entities that conform to the rules.

*ratchet* An entity's preferences are related to its past actions. Behavioral patterns 'run in a groove,' creating a *status quo* bias (cf. X-efficiency).

*adaptive & quasi* See 'means-rationalities,' above.

**5. Ends-rationalities**

*value substantive (Weber)* For any entity, some goals (values, preferences) are better, or more rational, than others.

*self-interest, egoism* An entity should make choices that satisfy its own consistent preferences, or maximize utility. In highly-specified ideal market contexts this criterion yields Pareto-optimality. This is the 'logic' of deliberate value-creation strategies (shareholder-wealth-maximization)

*extended* A rational entity has other goals, oriented towards the wider society or the interests of other entities, in additon to self-interest.

*sympathy, interdependent* Rational regard for others is simply prudential, it best serves the entities interests or enables it to maximize its utility in social or strategic contexts.

*commitment, altruism* A rational entity can make genuinely counterpreferential choices, sacrificing utility for the sake of other entities.

*deliberative* For a rational entity, the process of formulating or deciding upon goals (ambiguity reduction) must involve reflection, or deliberation.

*expressive* The process of ambiguity reduction is of great value in its own right. It yields an active sense of self-management, or autonomy, for the entity, as a byproduct.

**6. Rational-morality**

| | |
|---|---|
| *utilitarianism* | An entity should choose the action that will bring about the greatest good (variously defined as wealth, happiness, harmony, freedom, etc.) for the greatest number; as in social cost-benefit analysis. |
| *contractarianism* | An entity should act so as to promote fairness and justice. |
| *deontology* | Performance of duties and respect for rights is a paramount consideration in all behavior. |

**Symbols**

| | |
|---|---|
| $\sim$ | Corresponds to, is mapped to |
| $\mathcal{I} : \mathbf{R} \Rightarrow \mathbf{S}$ | $\mathcal{I}$ is a mapping (isomorphism) between the sets **R** and **S** |
| $\mathfrak{D}$ | is a mapping from **M** (the set of models) onto subsets of **R** |
| $r \in \mathbf{R}$ | r is a member (element) of **R** |
| $\mathbf{R}^{EC} \subset \mathbf{R}$ | The economic-rationality-set is a subset of **R** |
| $\overline{\mathbf{R}^{EC}}$ | The complement of $\mathbf{R}^{EC}$ in **R**. Other rationalities. |
| $\mathbf{R}^{RUM}$ | Forms of rationality that have been 'captured by **RUM**', i.e., it has been claimed that they are reducible to **RUM**, at least for some purposes. |
| $\mathbf{R}^{FOW}$ and $\mathbf{R}^{BAK}$ | Forward-looking and Backward-looking forms of rationality |
| $\mathbf{R}^{BAK*} \subset \mathbf{R}^{BAK}$ | The subset of $\mathbf{R}^{BAK}$ whose members are the various forms of rationality that are not implicit in existing models $\mathbf{M}^{[SK]}$ |
| $\mathbf{M}^{[SK]}$ | Models of strategy and decisions with *sunk costs*. (Superscript is an identifier). |
| $\mathbf{M}^{[P]}$ | Models of *postponement* and the value of waiting. |
| $r_i^M$ | A form of rationality implicit in a model **M**. Subscript is a counter; superscript is an identifier. |
| $M_R$ | Subscript is an identifier for a model $M \in \mathbf{M}$. |

## References


Ackoff, R. L. and F. E. Emery (1972). *On Purposeful Systems*. Tavistock, London.

Ackoff, R. L. (1983). 'An interactive view of rationality', *Journal of the Operational Research Society*, **34**(8), pp. 501–515.

Allison, G. (1971). *The Essence of Decision*. Little, Brown, Boston, MA.

Andrews, K. R. (1980). *The Concept of Corporate Strategy*. Irwin, Homewood IL.

Ansoff, H. I. (1965). *Corporate Strategy*. McGraw-Hill, New York.

Ansoff, H. I. (1987). 'The emerging paradigm of strategic behavior', *Strategic Management Journal*, **8**, pp. 505–515.

Ansoff, H. I. (1991). 'Critique of Henry Mintzberg's "The Design School: Reconsidering the basic premises of strategic management", *Strategic Management Journal* **12**, pp. 449–461.

Arrow, K. (1963). *Social Choice and Individual Values* (2nd ed). Wiley, New York.

Axelrod, R. (1984). *The Evolution of Cooperation*. Basic Books, New York.

Binmore, K. (1987). 'Modelling rational players', *Economics and Philosophy*, **3**, pp. 179–214.

Bowen, M. G. (1987). 'The escalation phenomenon reconsidered: Decision dilemmas or decision errors?', *Academy of Management Review*, **12**,(1), pp. 52–66.

Brunsson, N. (1982). 'The irrationality of action and action irrationality: Decisions, ideologies, and organizational actions', *Journal of Management Studies*, **19**, pp. 29–44.

Bryman, A. (1984). 'Organization studies and the concept of rationality', *Journal of Management Studies*, **21**, 4, pp. 391–408.

Buchanan, A. E. (1985). *Ethics, Efficiency and the Market*. Rowman and Allenheld, Totowa, NJ.

Cherniak, C. (1986). *Minimal Rationality*. MIT Press, Cambridge, MA.

Danley, J. R. (1984). 'Corporate moral agency: The case for anthropological bigotry'. In W. M. Hoffman and J. M. Moore (eds.), *Business Ethics: Readings and Cases in Corporate Morality*. McGraw-Hill, New York, pp. 172–179.

Day, G. S. (1986). *Analysis for Strategic Marketing Decisions*. West Publishing, St. Paul. MN.

DeGeorge, R. T. (1990). *Business Ethics* (3rd Ed). Macmillan, New York.

Eilon, S. (1985). 'Structuring unstructured decisions'. *OMEGA*, **13**,(5), pp. 369–377.

Elster, J. (1979). *Ulysses and the Sirens*. Cambridge University Press, Cambridge.

Elster, J. (1986). *The Multiple Self*. Cambridge University Press, Cambridge.

Elster, J. (1989). *Solomnic Judgements: Studies in the Limitations of Rationality*. Cambridge University Press, Cambridge.

Etzioni, A. (1986). 'The case for a multiple-utility conception', *Economics and Philosophy*, **2**, pp. 159–183.

Etzioni, A. (1988). *The Moral Dimension: Towards a New Economics*. Free Press, New York.

Freeman, R. E. (1984). *Strategic Management: A Stakeholder Approach*. Pitman, Boston, MA.

Friedman, M. (September 13, 1970). 'The social responsibility of business is to increase its profits'. *New York Times Magazine*.

Friend, J. A. and A. Hickling (1987). *Planning Under Pressure*. Pergamon, Oxford.

French, P. (1984). *Collective and Corporate Responsibility*. Columbia University Press, New York.

Gauthier, D. (1990). *Moral Dealing*. Cornell University Press, Ithaca, NY.

Geanakoplos, J. and D. Pearce (1989). 'Psychological games and sequential rationality', *Games and Economic Behavior* **1**, pp. 60–79.

Goldman, A. H. (1980). 'Business ethics: Profits, utilities and moral rights', *Philosophy and Public Affairs*, **9**(3), pp. 260–286.

Goodpaster, K. (1985). 'Ethical frameworks for management'. In J. B. Mathews, K. Goodpaster and L. Nash. (eds.), *Policies & Persons*, McGraw-Hill, New York, pp. 507–522.

Grubel, H. G. and L. A. Boland (1986). 'On the efficient use of mathematics in economics'. *Kyklos*, **39**, pp. 419–442.

Habermas, J. (1981). *Theorie des kommunikativen Handelns*. Suhrkamp*rankfurt* Frankfurt. (Translated by T McCarthy. *The Theory of Communicative Action*. Beacon Press, Boston, MA.)

Hambrick, D. C. and P. Mason (1984). 'Upper echelons: The organization as a reflection of its top managers', *Academy of Management Review*, **9**, pp. 195–206.

Hamlin, A. P. (1986). *Ethics, Economics and the State*. Wheatsheaf, Brighton.

Hannan, M. T. and J. Freeman (1980). 'The population ecology of organizations', *American Journal of Sociology*, **82**,(5), pp. 929–964.

Hargreaves-Heap, S. (1989). *Rationality in Economics*. Blackwell, Oxford.

Hayes, R. H. (November–December 1985). Strategic planning—Forward in reverse', *Harvard Business Review*, pp. 111–119.

Hirshleifer, J. (1976). *Price Theory and Application*. Prentice Hall, Englewood Cliffs, NJ.

Hitt, M. A. and B. B. Tyler (1991). 'Strategic decision models: Integrating different perspectives', *Strategic Management Journal*, **12**, pp. 327–351.

Hogarth, R. M. and S. Makridakis (1981). 'Forecasting and planning: An evaluation', *Management Science*, **27**(2), pp. 115–137.

Hosmer, LaRue T. (1991). *The Ethics of Management*. Irwin, Homewood, IL.

Janis I. L. and L. Mann (1977). *Decision Making: A Psychological Analysis of Conflict, Choice and Commitment*. Free Press, New York.

Jemison, D. B. (1981). 'The importance of an integrative approach to strategic management research', *Academy of Management Review*, **6**, pp. 601–608.

Kadane, J. B. and P. D. Larkey (1983). 'The confusion of is and ought in game theoretic contexts', *Management Science*, **29**, pp. 1365–1379.

Kant, I. (1956). *Critique of Practical Reason*. (Translated by L. W. Beck) Bobbs-Merrill, Indianapolis, IN.

Kay, J. (1991). 'Economics and business', *The Economic Journal*, **101**(401) pp. 57–63.

Kervern, G. Y. (1990). 'Au coeur des strategies', *Entreprise la Vague Ethique*. Assas Editions, Paris. pp. 49–54.

Kuhn, J. W. (1992). 'Ethics in business: What managers practice that economists ignore', *Business Ethics Quarterly*, **2**(3), pp. 305–315.

Leibenstein, H. (1976). *Beyond Economic Man: A New Foundation for Microeconomics*. Harvard University Press, Cambridge, MA.

Levi, I. (1986). *Hard Choices*. Cambridge University Press, Cambridge.

Linstone, H. A. (1984). *Multiple Perspectives for Decision Making*. Elsevier North Holland, New York.

Mackie J. L. (1978). The law of the jungle, moral alternatives and the principles of evolution. *Philosophy*, **53**, pp. 455–464.

March, J. G. (1978). 'Bounded rationality, ambiguity and the engineering of choice', *Bell Journal of Economics*, **9**, pp. 587–608.

Marsh, P., P. Barwise, K. Thomas and R. Wensley (1988). 'Managing strategic investment decisions'. In J. McGee and H. Thomas (eds.), *Strategic Management Research: A European Perspective*. Wiley, Chichester, pp. 86–136.

Mason, R. O. and I. I. Mitroff (1981). *Challenging Strategic Planning Assumptions*. Wiley Interscience, New York.

McLennen, E. (1990). *Rationality and Dynamic Choice: Foundational Explorations*. Cambridge University Press, Cambridge.

Mill, J. S. (1962). *Utilitarianism (1861)*. Collins, London.

Mintzberg, H. (1987). 'The strategy concept. 1: Five P's of strategy', *California Management Review* **30**(1), pp. 11–24.

Mintzberg, H. (1990). 'The Design School: Reconsidering the basic premises of strategic management', *Strategic Management Journal*, **11**, pp. 171–195.

Morecroft, J. D. W. (1983). 'Rationality and structure in behavioral models of business systems', *Proceedings of the 1983 International Systems Dynamics Conference*, Massachusetts Institute of Technology, Cambridge, MA.

Moss-Kanter, R. (May–June 1991). 'Transcending business boundaries: 12,000 World managers view change', *Harvard Business Review*, pp. 151–164.

Myers, S. C. (1984). 'Finance theory and financial strategy', *Interfaces*, **14**, pp. 126–137.

Naylor, T. H. and F. Tapon (1982). 'The capital asset pricing model: An evaluation of its potential as a strategic planning tool', *Management Science*, **28**(10), pp. 1166–1173.

Nielsen, R. P. (1988). 'Cooperative strategy', *Strategic Management Journal*, **9**, pp. 475–492.

Nietzsche, F. (1886). *Beyond Good and Evil*. Nauman, Leipzig.

Nelson, R. R. and S. G. Winter (1982). *An Evolutionary Theory of Economic Change*. Harvard University Press, Cambridge, MA.

Oral, M., A. E. Singer and O. Kettani (1989). 'The level of international competitiveness and its strategic implications', *International Journal of Research in Marketing*, **6**, pp. 267–282.

Osiel, M. (Summer 1984). 'The politics of professional ethics', *Social Policy*. pp. 43–48.

Pindyck, R. S. (1991). 'Irreversibility, uncertainty and investment', *Journal of Economic Literature*, **29**, pp. 1110–1148.

Popper, K. (1989). 'The critical approach versus the mystique of leadership', *Human Systems Management*, **8**, pp. 259–265.

Porter, M. E. (1980). *Competitive Strategy*. Free Press, New York.

Prest, A. R. and R. Turvey (1965). 'Cost benefit analysis: A survey', *Economic Journal*, **75**, pp. 685–705.

Quinn, J. B. (Fall 1977). 'Strategic goals: Process and politics', *Sloan Management Review*, pp. 21–37.

Rand, A. (1964). *The Virtue of Selfishness*. New American Library, New York.

Rankin, N. L. (1987). 'Corporations as persons: Objections to Goodpaster's "Principle of Moral Projection"', *Journal of Business Ethics*, **6**, pp. 633–637.

Rawls, J. (1972). *A Theory of Justice*. Clarendon Press, Oxford.

Ritzer G. and T. LeMoyne (1991). 'Hyperrationality: An extension of Weberian and *Neo*-Weberian theory. In G. Ritzer, *Metatheorising in Sociology*, Lexington Books, Lexington, MA, pp. 93–115.

Rumelt, R. P., D. Schendel and D. J. Teece (1991). 'Strategic management and economics', *Strategic Management Journal*, **12**, Winter Special Issue, pp. 5–29.

Russell, T. and R. Thaler (1985). 'The relevance of *quasi*-rationality in competitive markets', *American Economic Review*. **75** pp. 1071–1082.

Saloner, G. (1991). 'Modeling, game theory, and strategic management', *Strategic Management Journal*, **12**, Winter Special Issue, pp. 119–136.

Schendel, D. (1991). 'Editor's comments on the winter special issue', *Strategic Management Journal*, **12**, Winter Special Issue, pp. 1–3.

Schwenk, C. R. (1984). 'Cognitive simplification processes in strategic decision making', *Strategic Management Journal*, **5**, pp. 111–128.

Schwenk, C. R. and M. J. Tang (1989). 'Economic and psychological explanations for strategic persistence, *OMEGA*, **17**(6), pp. 559–570.

Sen, A. K. (1977). 'Rational fools: A critique of the behavioural foundations of economic theory'. *Philosophy and Public Affairs*, **6**, pp. 317–344.

Sen, A. K. (1987). *On Ethics and Economics*. Blackwell, Oxford.

Simon, H. A. (1964). 'On the concept of organizational goal', *Administrative Science Quarterly*, **9**(1), pp. 1–22.

Simon, H. A. (1987). 'Rationality in psychology and economics'. In R. M. Hogarth and M. W. Reder (eds.), *Rational Choice*. University of Chicago Press, Chicago, IL, pp. 25–40.

Singer, A. E. (1984). 'Planning, consciousness and conscience', *Journal of Business Ethics*, **3**, pp. 113–117.

Singer, A. E. and N. T. van der Walt (1987). 'Corporate conscience and foreign divestment decisions', *Journal of Business Ethics*, **6**, pp. 543–552.

Singer, A. E. (1988). 'Book review of 'The evolution of cooperation' by R. Axelrod', *Journal of Macro Marketing*, **8**,(1), pp. 59–61.

Singer, A. E. (1991). 'Meta-rationality and strategy', *OMEGA*, **19**(2), pp. 101–110.

Singer, A. E. (1992). 'Strategy as rationality', *Human Systems Management*, **11**(1), pp. 7–22.

Singer, A. E. (1993a). 'Strategy with sunk costs', *Human Systems Management*, **12**,(2), pp. 97–114.

Singer, A. E. (1993b). 'Plural rationality and strategic intelligence'. In J. E. Prescott and P. T. Gibbons (eds.), *Global Perspectives on Competitive Intelligence*. Published by the Society of Competitive Intelligence Professionals, Alexandra, VA, August 1993, pp. 351–366.

Singer, A. E. (1993c). 'Competitiveness as *hyper*-strategy'. Paper presented at the Fifth Asia-Pacific Research in Organizational Studies (APROS) colloquium, East-West Center, Hawaii, December 1993.

Staw, B. M. (1981). 'The escalation of commitment to a course of action', *Academy of Management Review*, **6** (4), pp. 577–587.

Sutherland, J. W. (1989). *Towards a Strategic Management and Decision Technology*. Theory & Decision Library. Kluver, Boston, MA.

Teece, D. J. (1982). 'Towards an economic theory of the multiproduct firm', *Journal of Economic Behavior and Organization*, **3**, pp. 39–63.

Thajer, R. (1985). 'Mental accounting and consumer choice', *Marketing Science*, **4**, pp. 199–214.

Thaler, R. and H. Sheffrin (1981). 'An economic theory of self-control', *Journal of Political Economy*, **89**, pp. 392–406.

Van Gigch, J. P. (1991). *System Design Modelling and Metamodelling*. Plenum, New York.

Van Peursen, C. A. (1989). 'Philosophy and management', *Human Systems Management*, **8**, pp. 267–272.

Walliser, B. (1989). 'Instrumental rationality and cognitive rationality', *Theory and Decision*, **27**, pp. 7–36.

Weber, M. (1947). *The Theory of Social and Economic Organisation*. Oxford University Press, Oxford.

Werhane, P. H. (1983). 'Corporations, collective action, and institutional moral agency'. In W. M. Hoffman, J. M. Moore, D. A. Fedo (eds.), *Corporate Governance and Institutionalizing Ethics*. Lexington Books, Lexington, MA, pp. 163–171.

White, S. K. (1988). *The Recent Work of Jurgen Habermas: Reason, Justice and Modernity*. Cambridge University Press, Cambridge.

Williams, B. (1985). *Ethics and the Limits of Philosophy*. Cambridge University Press, Cambridge.

Williamson, O. E. (1975). *markets and Hierarchies: Analysis and Antitrust Implications*. Free Press, New York.

Zejeny, M. (1980). 'Strategic management within human systems management', *Human Systems Management*, **1**, pp. 179–180.

# 54

# STRATEGY AS REVOLUTION

*Gary Hamel*

Source: *Harvard Business Review* 74(4) (1996): 69–82.

Let's admit it. Corporations around the world are reaching the limits of incrementalism. Squeezing another penny out of costs, getting a product to market a few weeks earlier, responding to customers' inquiries a little bit faster, ratcheting quality up one more notch, capturing another point of market share–those are the obsessions of managers today. But pursuing incremental improvements while rivals reinvent the industry is like fiddling while Rome burns.

Look at any industry and you will see three kinds of companies. First are the rule makers, the incumbents that built the industry. IBM, CBS, United Airlines, Merrill Lynch, Sears, Coca-Cola, and the like are the creators and protectors of industrial orthodoxy. They are the oligarchy. Next are the rule takers, the companies that pay homage to the industrial "lords." Fujitsu, ABC, U.S. Air, Smith Barney, J. C. Penney, and numerous others are those peasants. Their life is hard. Imagine working at Fujitsu for 30 years trying to catch IBM in the mainframe business, or being McDonnell Douglas to Boeing, or Avis to Hertz. We Try Harder may be a great advertising slogan, but it's depressingly futile as a strategy. What good will it do to work harder to follow the rules when some companies are rewriting them? IKEA, the Body Shop, Charles Schwab, Dell Computer, Swatch, Southwest Airlines, and many more are the rule breakers. Shackled neither by convention nor by respect for precedent, these companies are intent on overturning the industrial order. They are the malcontents, the radicals, the industry revolutionaries.

Never has the world been more hospitable to industry revolutionaries and more hostile to industry incumbents. The fortifications that protected the industrial oligarchy are crumbling under the weight of deregulation, technological upheaval, globalization, and social change. But it's not just the forces of change that are overturning old industrial structures – it's the actions of companies that harness those forces for the cause of revolution. (See the insert "Nine Routes to Industry Revolution.")

What if your company is more ruling class than revolutionary? You can either surrender the future to revolutionary challengers or revolutionize the way your company creates strategy. What is required is not a little tweak to the traditional planning process but a new philosophical foundation: strategy *is* revolution; everything else is tactics.

The following ten principles can help a company liberate its revolutionary spirit and dramatically increase its chances of discovering truly revolutionary strategies. Companies in industries as diverse as personal care products, information services, food processing, insurance, and telecommunications have internalized and acted on these principles. Every organization, however, must interpret and apply them in its own way. These are not a set of step-by-step instructions but a way of thinking about the challenge of creating strategy – the challenge of becoming an industry revolutionary.

## Principle 1: Strategic planning isn't strategic

Consider your company's planning process. Which describes it best – column A, on the left, or column B, on the right?

Unless your company is truly exceptional, you've probably admitted that the words in column A are more fitting than those in column B. In the vast majority of companies, strategic planning is a calendar-driven ritual, not an exploration of the potential for revolution. The strategy-making process tends to be reductionist, based on simple rules and heuristics. It works from today forward, not from the future back, implicitly assuming, whatever the evidence to the contrary, that the future will be more or less like the present. Only a tiny percentage of an industry's conventions are ever challenged, rendering strategy making largely extrapolative. An industry's boundaries are taken as a given; thus the question is how to position products and services within those boundaries rather than how to invent new, uncontested competitive space. Further, the planning process is generally elitist, harnessing only a small proportion of an organization's creative potential.

Perhaps most disturbing, strategy making is often assumed to be easy, especially in comparison with implementing strategy. But of course strategy making is easy when the process limits the scope of discovery, the breadth of involvement, and the amount of intellectual effort expended. Of course the process is easy when its goal is something far short of revolution. How often has strategic planning produced true strategic innovation? No wonder that in many organizations, corporate planning departments are being disbanded. No wonder that consulting firms are doing less and less "strategy" work and more and more "implementation" work.

The essential problem in organizations today is a failure to distinguish *planning* from *strategizing*.[1] Planning is about programming, not discovering. Planning is for technocrats, not dreamers. Giving planners responsibility for creating strategy is like asking a bricklayer to create Michelangelo's *Pietà*.

Most executives know a strategy when they see one. Wal-Mart has a clear strategy; so does Federal Express. But recognizing a strategy that already exists is not enough. Where do strategies come from? How are they created? Strategizing is not a rote procedure – it is a quest. Any company that believes that planning can yield strategy will find itself under the curse of incrementalism while freethinking newcomers lead successful insurrections.

## Principle 2: Strategy making must be subversive

Galileo challenged the centrality of Earth and man in the cosmos. The American colonists challenged the feudal dependencies and inherited privileges of European society. Picasso and other modernists challenged representational art. Einstein challenged Newtonian physics. Revolutionaries are subversive, but their goal is not subversion. What the defenders of orthodoxy see as subversiveness, the champions of new thinking see as enlightenment.

If there is to be any hope of industry revolution, the creators of strategy must cast off industrial conventions. For instance, Anita Roddick, the founder of the Body Shop, turned Charles Revson's hope-in-a-bottle formula on its head. Instead of assuming, as the cosmetics industry always had, that women lack self-confidence and will pay inflated prices for simple formulations if they believe that they will make them more attractive, Roddick assumed that women have self-esteem and just want lighthearted, environmentally responsible products. Roddick wasn't kidding when she said, "I watch where the cosmetics industry is going and then walk in the opposite direction."

Identify the 10 or 20 most fundamental beliefs that incumbents in your industry share. What new opportunities present themselves when you relax those beliefs? Consider the hotel industry's definition of a day, which begins when you check in and ends at noon, when you must check out. But if you check in at 1 A.M. after a grueling journey, why should you have to check out at the same time or pay the same amount as the person who arrived at 5 the previous afternoon? If a rental-car company can manage a fleet of cars on a rotating 24-hour basis, why can't a hotel do exactly the same with a fleet of rooms?

Rule makers and rule takers are the industry. Rule breakers set out to redefine the industry, to invent the new by challenging the old. Ask yourself, What are the fundamental conventions we have examined and abandoned in our company? Can you think of more than one or two? Can you think of any at all? If not, why not? As a senior executive, are you willing to embrace a subversive strategy-making process?

**Nine routes to industry revolution**

Unless you are an industry leader with an unassailable position – a status that, given the lessons of history, not even Microsoft would be wise to claim – you probably have a greater stake in staging a revolution than in preserving the status quo: The opportunities for revolution are many and mostly unexplored. How should a would-be revolutionary begin? By looking for ways to redefine products and services, market space, and even the entire structure of an industry.

**Reconceiving a product or service**

**1. Radically Improving the Value Equation**. In every industry, there is a ratio that relates price to performance: X units of cash buy Y units of value. The challenge is to improve that value ratio and to do so radically – 500% or 1,000%, not 10% or 20%. Such a fundamental redefinition of the value equation forces a reconception of the product or service.

Fidelity Investments, for instance, wondered why a person couldn't invest in foreign equity markets for tens or hundreds of dollars rather than thousands. On a recent flight, I heard one flight attendant say to another, "I just moved some of my investments from the Europe Fund to the Pacific Basin Fund." Such a comment would have been inconceivable a decade or two ago, but Fidelity and other mutual-fund revolutionaries have redefined the industry's value equation. Hewlett-Packard's printer business and IKEA are other value revolutionaries.

**2. Separating Function and Form**. Another way to challenge the existing concept of a product or service is to separate core benefits (function) from the ways in which those benefits are currently embodied in a product or service (form). Any organization that is able to distinguish form from function and then reconceive one or both has the opportunity to create an industry revolution.

Consider credit cards, which perform two functions. First, a credit card inspires a merchant to trust that you are who the card says you are: your name is embossed on the front, your signature appears on the back, and your photo may even appear in the corner. Nevertheless, credit card fraud is a rapidly escalating problem. In what form will "trust" be delivered in the future? Probably through biometric data: a handprint, voiceprint, or retinal scan. Any credit card maker that is not investing in those technologies today may be surprised by interlopers. Second, a credit card gives you permission to charge up to your credit limit. What new opportunities appear if you distinguish permission as a general function from the particular case of permission to charge? In many hotels, a card with a magnetic stripe gives guests "permission" to enter their rooms. Did credit card makers see the opportunity to use the cards in this way? No, the card security market is owned largely by newcomers.

**3. Achieving Joy of Use**. We live in a world that takes ease of use for granted. The new goal is joy of use. We want our products and services to be whimsical, tactile, informative, and just plain fun. Any company that can wrap those attributes around a mundane product or service has the chance to be an industry revolutionary.

What's the most profitable food retailer per square foot in the United States? Probably Trader Joe's, a cross between a gourmet deli and a discount warehouse, which its CEO, John Shields, calls a "fashion food retailer." Essentially without competition, its 74 stores were averaging annual sales of $1,000 per square foot in 1995 – twice the rate of conventional supermarkets and more than three times that of most specialty food shops. Customers shop Trader Joe's as much for entertainment as for sustenance. The store stocks dozens of offbeat foods – jasmine fried rice, salmon burgers, and raspberry salsa – as well as carefully selected, competitively priced staples. By turning shopping from a chore into a culinary treasure hunt, Trader Joe's has more than doubled its sales over the last five years to $605 million.

**Redefining market space**

**4. Pushing the Bounds of Universality**. Every company has an implicit notion of its served market: the types of individuals and institutions that are – and are not – customers. Revolutionary companies, however, focus not just on their served market but on the total imaginable market.

A few years back, who would have considered children a likely market for 35-millimeter film? Would you have given your $500 Nikon to an eight-year-old? Probably not. Parents today, however, think nothing of giving a disposable camera to a child for a day at the beach, a birthday party, or the family's vacation. The single-use camera has made access to photography virtually universal. In 1995, the single-use-camera market reached 50 million units, worth close to $1 billion at retail. From class to mass, adult to child, professional to consumer, and national to global, the traditional boundaries of market space are being redefined by revolutionary companies.

**5. Striving for Individuality**. No one wants to be part of a mass market. We'll all buy the same things – but only if we have to. Deep in our need to be ourselves, to be unique, are the seeds of industry revolution.

A woman who wants a perfect-fitting pair of jeans, for example, can now get measured at one of Levi Strauss's Personal Pair outlets, and a computer will pick out exactly the right size. The woman's specifications are sent to Levi's by computer, and her made-to-order jeans arrive a few days later. The price? Just about $10 more than an off-the-shelf pair. Levi's plans to introduce, the Personal Pair system to nearly 200 stores in the United States by the end of the decade. The company is counting on its revolutionary approach to put a considerable dent in the growing market for private-label jeans.

**6. Increasing Accessibility**. Most market spaces have temporal and geographic bounds: customers must go to a specific store at a specific location between certain hours. But market space is becoming cyberspace, and every day industry revolutionaries are resetting consumers' expectations about accessibility.

Consider First Direct, a bank that can be reached only by telephone. The fastest-growing bank in Great Britain, First Direct was opening 10,000 new accounts per month in mid-1995-the equivalent of two or three branches. The professionals and workaholics who make up First Direct's half million customers carry, on average, a balance that's ten times higher than the average balance at Midland Bank, First Direct's parent, while overall costs per client are 61% less. One of the first U.S. banks to experiment with so-called direct banking estimates that it will ultimately be able to close at least half of its branches.

**Redrawing industry boundaries**

**7. Rescaling Industries**. As industry revolutionaries seek out and exploit new national and global economies of scale, industries around the world-even office cleaning and haircutting – are consolidating at a fearsome pace. Any industry that was local, such as consumer banking, is becoming national. Any industry that was national, such as the airline business, is becoming global.

Every minute and a half, Service Corporation International buries or cremates someone, somewhere in the world. Performing 320,000 funerals per year, SCI has become the world's largest funeral operator in an industry that traditionally has been very fragmented. Most funeral operators have been family businesses. By buying up small operators, SCI has reaped economies of scale in purchasing, capital urilization (sharing hearses among operators, for example), marketing, and administration.

Of course, an industry can be scaled down as well as up. Bed-and-breakfast inns, microbreweries, local bakeries, and specialty retailers are the result of industries that have scaled down to serve narrow or local customers segments more effectively.

**8. Compressing the Supply Chain**. The cognoscenti use the word *disintermediation* in its literal sense; the removal of intermediaries.

Wal-Mart, for instance, essentially turned the warehouse into a store, thus disintermediating the traditional small-scale retailer. And Xerox hopes to reinvent the way companies distribute printed documents by disintermediating trucking companies from the printing business. Why, Xerox asks, should annual reports, user manuals, catalogs, employee handbooks, and other printed matter be hauled across the country in trucks? Why not send the information digitally and print it close to where it is needed? Xerox is working with a variety of partners to stage this revolution.

**9. Driving Convergence**. Revolutionaries not only radically change the value-added structure within industries but also blur the boundaries between industries. Deregulation, the ubiquity of information, and new customer demands give revolutionaties the chance to transcend an industry's boundaries.

For example, a consumer can now get a credit card from General Motors, a mortgage from Prudential or GE Capital, a retirement account at Fidelity Investments, and a checkbook from Charles Schwab. Innovative hospitals "capitate" lives, guaranteeing to provide an individual with a full range of health services for a fixed sum per year. Insurance companies, such as Aetna, respond by refashioning themselves into health care providers. Boston Market offers hot family-style meals for takeout, and supermarkets respond by offering an ever wider selection of prepared foods, further blurring the boundary between the grocery and fast-food industries.

Industry revolutionaries don't ask what industry they are in. They know that an industry's boundaries today are about as meaningful as borders in the Balkans.

### Principle 3: The bottleneck is at the top of the bottle

In most companies, strategic orthodoxy has some very powerful defenders: senior managers. Imagine an organizational pyramid with senior managers at the apex. (It has become fashionable to draw the pyramid with customers at the top and senior managers at the bottom. But as long as senior managers retain their privileges – corporate aircraft, spacious suites, and so on – I prefer to leave the pointy end at the top.) Where are you likely to find people with the least diversity of experience, the largest investment in the past, and the greatest reverence for industrial dogma? At the top. And where will you find the people responsible for creating strategy? Again, at the top.

The organizational pyramid is a pyramid of experience. But experience is valuable only to the extent that the future is like the past. In industry after industry, the terrain is changing so fast that experience is becoming irrelevant and even dangerous. Unless the strategy-making process is freed from the tyranny of experience, there is little chance of industry revolution. If you're a senior executive, ask yourself these questions: Has a decade or two of experience made me more willing or less willing to challenge my industry's conventions? Have I become more curious or less curious about what is happening beyond the traditional boundaries of my industry? Be honest. As Ralph Waldo Emerson wrote, "There are always two parties, the party of the past and the party of the future; the establishment and the movement." To which party do you belong?

## Principle 4: Revolutionaries exist in every company

It is often said that you cannot find a pro-change constituency in a successful company. I disagree. It is more accurate to say that in a successful company you are unlikely to find a pro-change constituency among the top dozen or so officers.

Make no mistake: there are revolutionaries in your company. If you go down and out into your organization – out into the ranks of much maligned middle managers, for instance – you will find people straining against the bit of industrial orthodoxy. All too often, however, there is no process that lets those revolutionaries be heard. Their voices are muffled by the layers of cautious bureaucrats who separate them from senior managers. They are isolated and impotent, disconnected from others who share their passions. So, like economic refugees seeking greater opportunity in new lands, industry revolutionaries often abandon their employers to find more imaginative sponsors.

No one doubts that Jack Welch of General Electric, Percy Barnevik of ABB Asea Brown Boveri, and Ray Smith of Bell Atlantic are pro-change leaders. But rather than celebrating the exceptions – the few truly transformational executives who populate every tome on leadership – isn't the greater challenge to help the pro-change constituency that exists in every company find its voice? Sure, there are some radical corporate leaders out there. But weren't they always revolutionaries at heart? Why couldn't they have had a much greater impact on their companies earlier in their careers? Perhaps they, too, found it difficult to challenge the combined forces of precedence, position, and power. It would be sad to conclude that a company can fully exploit the emotional and intellectual energy of a revolutionary only if he or she succeeds in navigating the tortuous route to the top. How many revolutionaries will wait patiently for such a chance?

As a corporate leader, do you know where the revolutionaries are in your own organization? Have you given them a say in the strategy-making process? One thing is certain: if you don't let the revolutionaries challenge you from within, they will eventually challenge you from without in the marketplace.

## Principle 5: Change is not the problem; engagement is

Senior executives assume two things about change that squelch revolutionary strategies. The first assumption is that "people" – that is, middle managers and all the rest – are against change. The second assumption follows from the first: only a hero-leader can force a timid and backward-looking organization into the future. All too often, change epics portray the chief executive dragging the organization kicking and screaming into the twenty-first century. Enough of top-management grandstanding. Humankind would not have accomplished what it has over the past millennium if it was ambivalent about change or if the responsibility for change was vested in the socially or politically elite.

Imagine that I coax a flatlander to the top of a snow-covered mountain. After strapping two well-waxed skis onto the flatlander's feet, I give the nervous and unprepared nonskier a mighty push. He or she goes screaming over a precipice; I'm booked for murder. One could well understand how the novice might not appreciate the "change" I sought to engineer. Now imagine that the nonskier takes lessons for a few days. The now fledgling skier may ascend the same mountain and, though full of caution, voluntarily point the skis downhill. What has changed? Even with a bit of training, skiing is not without risks. But in the second scenario, the skier has been given a modicum of control – an ability to influence speed and direction.

All too often, when senior managers talk about change, they are talking about fear-inducing change, which they plan to impose on unprepared and unsuspecting employees. All too often, *change* is simply a code word for something nasty: a wrenching restructuring or reorganization. This sort of change is not about opening up new opportunities but about paying for the past mistakes of corporate leaders.

The objective is not to get people to support change but to give them responsibility for engendering change, some control over their destiny. You must engage the revolutionaries, wherever they are in your company, in a dialogue about the future. Does your strategy-making process do this? Do you secretly believe that change is better served by a more compliant organization than by a more vociferous one? When senior managers engage their organization in a quest for revolutionary strategies, they are invariably surprised to find out just how big the pro-change constituency actually is.

## Principle 6: Strategy making must be democratic

Despite years of imploring people to bring their brains to work, to get involved in quality circles, process reengineering, and the like, senior managers have seldom urged them to participate in the process of strategy creation. But if senior managers can't address the challenge of operational improvements by themselves – witness their reliance on quality circles, suggestion systems, and process-improvement task forces – why would they be able to take on the challenge of industry revolution? After all, what do a company's top 40 or 50 executives have to learn from one another? They've been talking at one another for years. Their positions are well rehearsed, and they can finish one another's sentences. In fact, there is often a kind of intellectual incest among the top officers of a large company.

The capacity to think creatively about strategy is distributed widely in an enterprise. It is impossible to predict exactly where a revolutionary idea is forming; thus the net must be cast wide. In many of the companies I work with, hundreds and sometimes thousands of people get involved in crafting strategy. They are asked to look deeply into potential discontinuities, help define and elaborate the company's core competencies, ferret out corporate orthodoxies, and search for unconventional strategic options. In one company, the idea for a multimillion-dollar opportunity came from a twenty-something secretary. In another company, some of the best ideas about the organization's core competencies came from a forklift operator.

To help revolutionary strategies emerge, senior managers must supplement the hierarchy of experience with a hierarchy of imagination. This can be done by dramatically extending the strategy franchise. Three constituencies that are usually underrepresented in the strategy-making process must have a disproportionate say. The first constituency is young people – or, more accurately, people with a youthful perspective. Of course, some 30-year-olds are "young fogies," but most young people live closer to the future than people with gray hair. It is ironic that the group with the biggest stake in the future is the most disenfranchised from the process of strategy creation.

My definition of success in a strategy-creation process is exemplified by an executive committee spending half a day learning something new from a 25-year-old. Recently, a young technical employee in an accounting company explained the implications of virtual reality to the senior partners. His pitch went like this: "Think about a complex set of corporate accounts. How easily and quickly can you uncover the subtle relationships among the numbers that might point to a problem or opportunity? Virtual reality will allow you to 'fly' over a topography of corporate accounts. That big black hole over there is a revenue shortfall, and that red mountain is unsold inventory. A few small companies are already working on applying virtual reality to financial accounts. Are we going to get on board or risk getting left behind?" The partners actually learned something new that day. When was the last time a Generation-X employee in your company exchanged ideas with the executive committee?

The people at an organization's geographic periphery are the second constituency that deserves a larger say in strategy making. The capacity for strategic innovation increases proportionately with each mile you move away from headquarters. For a U.S. company, the periphery might be India, Singapore, Brazil, or even the West Coast. For a Japanese company, it might be Indonesia or the United States. At the periphery of an organization, people are forced to be more creative because they usually have fewer resources, and they are exposed to ideas and developments that do not conform to the company's orthodoxies. Remember the old Chinese defense of local exceptions to central rule: The emperor is far away and the hills are high. But again, in many companies the periphery has little say in the strategy-making process. If a company aims to generate 40% or 50% of its revenues in international markets, international voices should have a say in the strategy-making process to match.

The third constituency that deserves a disproportionate say is newcomers, people who have not yet been co-opted by an industry's dogma. Perhaps you've looked outside your company or industry for senior executives with fresh perspectives. But how systematically have you sought the advice of newcomers at all levels who have not yet succumbed to the dead hand of orthodoxy? Think about last year's strategic-planning process. How many new voices were heard? How hard did you work to create the opportunity to be surprised?

Inviting new voices into the strategy-making process, however, is not enough. Senior executives must ensure that they don't drown out people who are overly inclined to deference. In one company, the young representative of a strategy-creation team presented the group's findings to the management committee. When the anxious young employee showed up at the appointed place and hour, he was confronted by a daunting spectacle: 12 executives, most with more than 20 years of seniority, ensconced in high-backed leather chairs arranged around an enormous boardroom table. The brave young manager never stood a chance. Less than five minutes into the four-hour talk, he was being pelted with disbelief and skepticism. The management committee demonstrated its capacity for (unwitting) intimidation and learned little.

After this fiasco, the people attempting to facilitate the dialogue saw to it that the setting for the next meeting was very different. First, it was held off-site on neutral territory. Second, all 25 members of the strategy-creation team were invited; thus they out-numbered the executives. Third, the management committee sat in ordinary chairs arranged in a semicircle – they had no table behind which to hide. Finally, the management committee was asked to hold all comments during the presentation. Afterward, each member of the management committee was assigned two members of the team for a four-hour discussion that focused on how the team had arrived at its conclusions. The next morning, the executives were willing to admit that they had learned a lot, and they were able to give helpful advice to the team members about where they should deepen and expand their work.

That is strategy making as a democratic process. People should have a say in their destiny, a chance to influence the direction of the enterprise to which they devote their energy. The idea of democracy has become so enervated, and the individual's sense of responsibility to the community so feeble, that they can both be summarized in the slogan One Person, One Vote. That notion represents not the full ideal of democracy but its minimal precondition. If one exercises the rights of citizenship only once every 1,461 days, can one claim to be a citizen in any meaningful sense? In the corporate sphere, suggestion schemes and town hall meetings are but the tender shoots of a pluralistic process. Democracy is not simply about the right to be heard; it is about the opportunity to influence opinion and action. It is about being impatient and impassioned, informed and involved. The real power of democracy is that not only the elite can shape the agenda. One's voice can be bigger than one's vote. Susan B. Anthony, Martin Luther King, Jr., Ralph Nader, Rush Limbaugh, and Jesse Jackson have all had an influence on political thought and action that has gone far beyond a single vote.

What percentage of the employees in your company have ever seen a copy of the corporate strategy, much less participated in its creation? No wonder that what passes for strategy is usually sterile and uninspiring. Saul Alinsky, one of the most effective social revolutionaries in the United States this century, wrote this about the output of top-down, elitist planning: "It is not a democratic program but a monumental testament to lack of faith in the ability and intelligence of the masses of people to think their way through to the successful solution of their problems. . . . the people will have little to do with it." That which is imposed is seldom embraced. An elitist approach to strategy creation engenders little more than compliance.

## Principle 7: Anyone can be a strategy activist

Perhaps senior managers are reluctant to give up their monopoly on the creation of strategy. After all, how often has the monarch led the uprising? What can so-called ordinary employees do to ensure that their company becomes or remains the author of industry revolution? Plenty. They can become strategy activists. Today frontline employees and middle managers are inclined to regard themselves more as victims than as activists. They have lost confidence in their ability to shape the future of their organizations. They have forgotten that from Gandhi to Mandela, from the American patriots to the Polish shipbuilders, the makers of revolutions have not come from the top. Notwithstanding all the somber incantations that change must start at the top, is it realistic to expect that, in any reasonable percentage of cases, senior managers will start an industry revolution? No.

In one large company, a small group of middle managers who were convinced that their company was in danger of forfeiting the future to less conventional rivals established what they called a "delta team." The managers, none of whom was a corporate officer, had no mandate to change the company and asked no one for permission to do so. Over several months, they worked quietly and persistently to convince their peers that it was time to rethink the company's basic beliefs. This conviction gradually took root among a cross section of managers, who started asking senior executives difficult questions about whether the company was actually in control of its destiny. Did the company have a unique and compelling view of its future? Was the company ahead of or behind the industry's change curve? Was it at the center or on the periphery of the coalitions that were reshaping the industry? Ultimately, senior managers conceded that they could not answer those questions. The result was a concerted effort, spanning several months and hundreds of employees, to find opportunities to create industry revolution. Out of this effort came a fundamental change in the company's concept of its mission, a score of new and unconventional business opportunities, and a doubling of revenues over the next five years.

Activists are not anarchists. Their goal is not to tear down but to reform. They know that an uninvolved citizenry deserves whatever fate befalls it, as do cautious and cringing middle managers. People who care about their country – or their organization – don't wait for permission to act. Activists don't shape their opinions to fit the prejudices of those they serve. They are patriots intent on protecting the enterprise from mediocrity, self-interest, and mindless veneration of the past. Not every activist ends up a hero. Shortly after he became president of the Supreme Soviet, Nikita Khrushchev gave a speech to a large group of Communist Party leaders in which he denounced the excesses of Stalin. During a pause, a voice rang out from the back of the hall, "You were there. Why didn't you stop him?" Taken aback by such impertinence, Khrushchev thundered, "Who said that?" The questioner slunk low in his seat and was silent. After a long, uncomfortable minute in which his eyes raked the audience, Khrushchev replied, "Now you know why." It is often safer to be silent. The corporate equivalent of Lubyanka is an office without a telephone or a window. Dissenters aren't shot for treason; they're asked to take a "lateral career move."

Listen to Thomas Paine: "Let them call me rebel and welcome, I feel no concern from it; but I should suffer the misery of devils, were I to make a whore of my soul." In a corporate context, this sounds like hyperbole. But think of the great companies that have fallen hopelessly behind the change curve because middle managers and first-level employees lacked the courage to speak up. To be an activist, one must care more for one's community than for one's position in the hierarchy. The goal is not to leave senior executives behind. The goal is not to stage a palace coup. But when senior managers are distracted, when planning has supplanted strategizing, and when more energy is being devoted to protecting the past than to creating the future, activists must step forward.

## Principle 8: Perspective is worth 50 IQ points[2]

Without enlightenment, there can be no revolution. To discover opportunities for industry revolution, one must look at the world in a new way, through a new lens. It is impossible to make people smarter, but you can help them see with new eyes. Remember when you took your first economics course? I do. It didn't make me any smarter, but it gave me a new lens through which to look at the world. Much that had been invisible – the link between savings and investment, between interest rates and exchange rates, and between supply and demand – suddenly became visible.

A view of the corporation as a bundle of core competencies rather than a collection of business units is a new perspective. A view of discontinuities as levers for change rather than threats to the status quo is a new perspective. A view that imagination rather than investment determines an organization's capacity to be strategic is a new perspective.

Any company intent on creating industry revolution has four tasks. First, the company must identify the unshakable beliefs that cut across the industry – the industry's conventions. Second, the company must search for discontinuities in technology, life-styles, working habits, or geopolitics that might create opportunities to rewrite the industry's rules. Third, the company must achieve a deep understanding of its core competencies. Fourth, the company must use all this knowledge to identify the revolutionary ideas, the unconventional strategic options, that could be put to work in its competitive domain. What one sees from the mountaintop is quite different from what one sees from the plain. There can be no innovation in the creation of strategy without a change in perspective.

## Principle 9: Top-down and bottom-up are not the alternatives

The creation of strategy is usually characterized as either a top-down or bottom-up process. Strategy either emerges as a grand design at the top – think of Jack Welch's famous "three circles," which defined GE's future business focus–or bubbles up from lone entrepreneurs, such as the man who invented Post-It Notes at 3M. But all too often, top-down strategies are dirigiste rather than visionary. And in all too many companies, the entrepreneurial spark is more likely to be doused by a flood of corporate orthodoxy than fanned by resources and the support of senior executives. In my experience, new-venture divisions, skunk works, and the musings of research fellows are no more likely to engender an industry revolution than is an annual planning process.

Just as a political activist who fails to influence those with legislative authority will make little lasting difference, a strategy activist who fails to win senior managers' confidence will achieve nothing. Senior managers may not have a monopoly on imagination, but they do have a board-sanctioned monopoly on the allocation of resources. To bankroll the revolution, senior executives must believe, both intellectually and emotionally, in its aims. So although the revolution doesn't need to start at the top, it must ultimately be understood and endorsed by the top. In the traditional model of strategy creation, the thinkers are assumed to be at the top and the doers down below. In reality, the thinkers often lie deep in the organization, and senior managers simply control the means of doing.

To achieve diversity of perspective and unity of purpose, the strategy-making process must involve a deep diagonal slice of the organization. A top-down process often achieves unity of purpose: the few who are involved come to share a conviction about the appropriate course of action and can secure some degree of compliance from those below. A bottom-up process can achieve diversity of perspective: many voices are heard and many options are explored. But unity without diversity leads to dogma, and diversity without unity results in competing strategy agendas and the fragmentation of resources. Only a strategy-making process that is deep and wide can achieve both diversity and unity.

Bringing the top and bottom together in the creation of strategy will help bypass the usually painful and laborious process whereby a lowly employee champions an idea up the chain of command. Managers, many of whom may be more intent on protecting their reputations for prudence than on joining the ranks of the lunatic fringe, are likely to shoot down any revolutionary idea that reaches them. There are many ways of linking those on the bottom with those in the officer corps. Senior executives can sponsor a process of deep thinking about discontinuities, core competencies, and new rules that involves a cross section of the organization. Senior managers can participate as team members–together with secretaries, sales-people, and first-level engineers – in the search for revolutionary opportunities. An executive committee can devote one week per month to keeping up to speed with the revolutionary ideas that are gestating deep in the organization.

What senior executives must not do is ask a small, elite group or the "substitute brains" of a traditional strategy-consulting firm to go away and plot the company's future. With neither senior managers nor a substantial cross section of the organization involved, the output will likely be considered a bastard by all except those who created it.

Of course, senior managers must ultimately make hard choices about which revolutionary strategies to support and what resources to commit, but they must avoid the temptation to judge prematurely. In the quest for revolutionary strategies, a senior executive must be more student than magistrate. In one company, the CEO believed that the strategy-making team was responsible for convincing him that it had come up with the right answers. That is the wrong attitude. It is the CEO's responsibility to stay close enough to the organization's learning process that he or she can share employees' insights and understand their emerging convictions. In the traditional planning process, outcomes are likely to cluster closely around senior managers' prejudices; the gap between recommendations and pre-existing predilections is likely to be low. But that is not the case in a more open-ended process of strategic discovery. If the goal is to ensure that the resource holders and the revolutionaries end up at the same place at the same time, senior executives must engage in a learning process alongside those at the vanguard of industry revolution.

## Principle 10: You can't see the end from the beginning

A strategy-making process that involves a broad cross section of the company, delves deeply into discontinuities and competencies, and encourages employees to escape an industry's conventions will almost inevitably reach surprising conclusions. At EDS, such a process convinced many in the organization that it was not enough to be a business-to-business company. As the dividing line between professional life and personal life was blurring, EDS realized that it had to become capable of serving individuals as well as businesses. After an open and creative strategy-making process, EDS installed automated teller machines in many 7-Eleven stores. Months earlier, few would have anticipated, much less credited, such a move.

Not everyone enjoys surprises. Senior managers cannot predict where an open-ended strategy-making process will lead, but they cannot go only part of the way to industry revolution. If nervous executives open up a dialogue and then ignore the outcome, they will poison the well. In one company, senior managers articulated their reluctance to staff a strategy-making team with a cohort of young, out-of-the-box employees. The CEO was convinced that he needed to set clear boundaries on the work of the eager revolutionaries. Defending his desire to impose prior restraint on the strategy-creation process, he asked, "What if the team comes back with dumb ideas?" The response: "If that is the case, you have a bigger problem – dumb managers." Senior managers should be less worried about getting off-the-wall suggestions and more concerned about failing to unearth the ideas that will allow their company to escape the curse of incrementalism.

Though it is impossible to see the end from the beginning, an open-ended and inclusive process of strategy creation substantially lessens the challenge of implementation. Implementation is often more difficult than it need be because only a handful of people have been involved in the creation of strategy and only a few key executives share a conviction about the way forward. Too often, the planning process ends with the challenge of getting "buy-in," of getting what is in the heads of the bosses into the heads of the worker bees. But when several hundred employees share the task of identifying and synthesizing a set of unconventional strategic options, the conclusions take on an air of inevitability. In such a process, senior managers' task is less to "sell" the strategy than to ensure that the organization acts on the convictions that emerge. How often does the planning process start with senior executives asking what the rest of the organization can teach them about the future? Not often enough.

To invite new voices into the strategy-making process, to encourage new perspectives, to start new conversations that span organizational boundaries, and then to help synthesize unconventional options into a point of view about corporate direction – those are the challenges for senior executives who believe that strategy must be revolution.

## Notes

1 Thanks to James Scholes, my colleague at Strategos, for suggesting this distinction.

2 I owe this aphorism to Alan Kay, a research fellow at Apple Computer. Kay's point that new thinking depends more on perspective than on raw intelligence is as apropos to strategy innovation as it is to new-product innovation.

# 55

# MUSINGS ON MANAGEMENT

*Henry Mintzberg*

Source: *Harvard Business Review* 74(4) (1996): 61–7.

Management is a curious phenomenon. It is generously paid, enormously influential, and significantly devoid of common sense. At least, the hype about management lacks common sense, as does too much of the practice. I should really say impractice, because the problems grow out of the disconnection between management and the managed. The disconnection occurs when management is treated as an end in itself instead of as a service to organizations and their customers.

These concerns had been building in my mind for years when a particular event caused them to gel. I had been asked to give a speech at the World Economic Forum in Davos, Switzerland, in 1995; so I visited managing director Maria Cattaui in her office near Geneva to discuss possible topics. I first proposed a presentation on government and suggested she allot me the better part of an hour to cover the topic properly. "I would really prefer you do something on management," she replied. "And besides, many chief executives tend to have an attention span of about 15 minutes."

I went home, thought about this, and decided to respond in kind. It was a perfect opportunity. I listed ten points on one sheet of paper under the label "Musings on Management" and faxed it to Maria Cattaui. Fortunately, she was open-minded — indeed, enthusiastic. So that was what I presented at Davos: ten points, by then reduced to ten minutes, one musing on management per minute.

The *Harvard Business Review* being even more open-minded, I can now develop my musings at somewhat greater length. Readers should be warned, however, that I will insult almost everyone in one way or another. I must apologize to those I miss, for the object of my exercise is to shake us all out of the complacency that surrounds too much of the practice of management today, a practice that I believe is undermining many of our organizations and hence our society. We had better take a good look at what is wrong with this hype called management.

## 1. Organizations don't have tops and bottoms

These are just misguided metaphors. What organizations really have are the *outer* people, connected to the world, and the *inner* ones, disconnected from it, as well as many so-called *middle* managers, who are desperately trying to connect the inner and outer people to each other.

The sooner we stop talking about top management (nobody dares to say *bottom* management), the better off we shall be. The metaphor distorts reality. After all, organizations are spread out geographically, so that even if the chief executive sits 100 stories up in New York, he is not nearly as high as a lowly clerk on the ground floor in Denver.

The only thing a chief executive sits atop is an organization chart. And all that silly document does is demonstrate how mesmerized we are with the abstraction called management. The next time you look at one of these charts, cover the name of the organization and try to figure out what it actually does for a living. This most prominent of all corporate artifacts never gets down to real products and real services, let alone the people who deal with them every day. It's as if the organization exists for the management.

Try this metaphor. Picture the organization as a circle. In the middle is the *central* management. And around the outer edges are those people who develop, produce, and deliver the products and services — the people with the knowledge of the daily operations. The latter see with complete clarity because they are closest to the action. But they do so only narrowly, for all they can see are their own little segments. The managers at the center see widely — all around the circle — but they don't see clearly because they are distant from the operations. The trick, therefore, is to connect the two groups. And for that, most organizations need informed managers in between, people who can see the outer edge and then swing around and talk about it to those at the center. You know — the people we used to call middle managers, the ones who are mostly gone.

## 2. It is time to delayer the delayerers

As organizations remove layers from their operations, they add them to the so-called top of their hierarchies — new levels that do nothing but exercise financial control and so drive everyone else crazy.

I used to write books for an independent publishing company called Prentice-Hall. It was big — very big — but well organized and absolutely dedicated to its craft. Then it was bought by Simon & Schuster, which was bought by Paramount. Good old Prentice-Hall became a "Paramount Communications Company." It was at about this time that one of my editors quoted her new boss as saying, "We're in the business of filling the O.I. [operating income] bucket." Strange, because my editor and I both had thought the company was in the business of publishing books and enlightening readers. Next, publisher Robert Maxwell got involved, and not long ago the whole thing was bought yet again, so that now Prentice-Hall has become a "Viacom Company." After all this, will publishing books remain as important as satisfying bosses?

Take the metaphor of the circular organization and plunk a financial boss on top of the chief in the center. Then pile on another and perhaps another. The weight can become crushing. To use a favorite management expression, the new layers don't "add value" at all. By focusing on the numbers, they depreciate true value and reduce the richness of a business to the poverty of its financial performance. Listen to what *Fortune* wrote a few years ago: "What's truly amazing about P&G's historic restructuring is that it is a response to the consumer market, not the stock market" (November 6, 1989). What's truly amazing about this statement is the use of the phrase "truly amazing."

Nowhere does the harshness of such attitudes appear more starkly than in the delayering of all those middle managers. Delayering can be defined as the process by which people who barely know what's going on get rid of those who do. Delayering is done in the name of the "empowerment" of those who remain. But too many of them, at the outer edges, become disconnected instead, while the real database of the organization, the key to what was its future, lines up at the unemployment office. Isn't it time that we began to delayer the delayerers?

### 3. Lean *is* mean and doesn't even improve long-term profits

There is nothing wonderful about firing people. True, stock market analysts seem to love companies that fire frontline workers and middle managers (while increasing the salaries of senior executives). Implicitly, employees are blamed for having been hired in the first place and are sentenced to suffer the consequences while the corporations cash in. Listen to this sample of contemporary management wisdom: "In the face of the dismaying results that began in 1985, just after John Akers became CEO, and that persisted, IBM failed to accept the reality that its so-called full-employment practice, in which it forswore layoffs, was no longer workable. A retired IBM manager who worked closely for years with IBM's top executives recalls the mystique that grew up around this practice: 'It was a religion. Every personnel director who came in lived and died on defending that practice. I tell you, this was like virginity.' Just recently, a day late and a dollar short, IBM at last gave it up" (*Fortune*, May 3, 1993).

You can almost feel the writer gloating and thinking, Isn't this wonderful — finally IBM has joined the club. The magazine article, about big companies in decline, was entitled "Dinosaurs?" But everyone knows that dinosaurs lasted a couple of hundred million years and, even then, probably succumbed to natural forces. With mass firings and other callous behaviors toward one another, we could well be getting rid of ourselves after barely a few hundred thousand years.

I did some work recently for a large U.S. insurance company, with no market analysts to worry about because it is a mutual. I was told a story about a woman there who was working energetically to convert a paper database to an electronic one. Someone said to her, "Don't you know you are working yourself out of a job?" "Sure," she retorted. "But I know they'll find something else for me. If I didn't, I'd sabotage the process." Imagine how much her feeling of security is worth to that company. Or imagine the case of no job security. A few years ago, some middle managers at one of the major Canadian banks formed what they called their 50/50 club. They were more than 50 years old and earning more than $50,000 per year, and it was clear to them that many members of the group were systematically being fired just before they qualified for their pensions. How much sabotage was going on at that bank?

Lean *is* mean. So why do we keep treating people in these ways? Presumably because we are not competitive. And just why aren't we competitive? To a large extent because we have been unable to meet Japanese competition. So how do we respond? By managing in exactly the opposite way from the Japanese. Will we never learn?

## 4. The trouble with most strategies are chief executives who believe themselves to be strategists

Great strategists are either creative or generous. We have too few of either type. We call the creative ones visionaries – they see a world that others have been blind to. They are often difficult people, but they break new ground in their own ways. The generous ones, in contrast, bring strategy out in other people. They build organizations that foster thoughtful inquiry and creative action. (You can recognize these people by the huge salaries they don't pay themselves. Their salaries signal their people, We're all in this together. Salaries are not used to impress fellow CEOs.) The creative strategists reach out from the center of that circular organization to touch the edges, while the generous ones strengthen the whole circle by turning strategic thinking into a collective learning process.

Most so-called strategists, however, just sit on top and pretend to strategize. They formulate ever so clever strategies for everyone else to implement. They issue glossy strategic plans that look wonderful and take their organizations nowhere with great fanfare. Strategy becomes a game of chess in which the pieces–great blocks of businesses and companies – get moved around with a ferocity that dazzles the market analysts. All the pieces look like they fit neatly together – at least on the board. It's all very impressive, except that the pieces themselves, ignored as every eye focuses on the great moves, disintegrate. Imagine if we took all this energy spent on shuffling and used it instead to improve *real* businesses. I don't mean "financial services" or "communications," I mean banking or book publishing.

Consider how we train strategists in the M.B.A. classrooms. We take young people with little business experience – hardly selected for their creativity, let alone their generosity – and drill them in case after case in which they play the great strategists sitting atop institutions they know nothing about. An hour or two the night before to read 20 pithy pages on Gargantuan Industries and its nuclear reactors and then off to 80 supercharged minutes in the classroom to decide what Gargantuan must do with itself into the next millennium. Is it any wonder that we end up with case studies in the executive suites – disguised as strategic thinking?

## 5. Decentralization centralizes, empowerment disempowers, and measurement doesn't measure up

The buzzwords are the problem, not the solution. The hot techniques dazzle us. Then they fizzle. *Total quality management* takes over and no one even remembers *quality of work life* – same word, similar idea, no less the craze, not very long ago. How come quality of work life died? Will TQM die a similar death? Will we learn anything? Will anyone even care?

The TQM concept has now magically metamorphosed into empowerment. What empowerment really means is stopping the disempowering of people. But that just brings us back to hierarchy, because hierarchy is precisely what empowerment reinforces. People don't get power because it is logically and intrinsically built into their jobs; they get it as a gift from the gods who sit atop those charts. Noblesse oblige. If you doubt this, then contrast empowerment with a situation in which the workers really do have control. Imagine a hospital director empowering the doctors. They are perfectly well empowered already, with no thanks to any hospital managers. Their power is built into their work. (Indeed, if anything, doctors could stand a little disempowering – but by nurses, not by managers.)

Better still, consider a truly advanced social system: the beehive. Queen bees don't empower worker bees. The worker bees are adults, so to speak, who know exactly what they have to do. Indeed, the queen bee has no role in the genuinely strategic decisions of the hive, such as the one to move to a new location. The bees decide collectively, responding to the informative dances of the scouts and then swarming off to the place they like best. The queen simply follows. How many of our organizations have attained that level of sophistication? What the queen bee does is exude a chemical substance that holds the system together. She is responsible for what has been called the "spirit of the hive." What a wonderful metaphor for good managers – not the managers on top but those in the center.

If empowering is about disempowerment, then is decentralization about centralizing? We have confounded our use of these words, too, ever since Alfred P. Sloan, Jr., centralized General Motors in the 1920s in the name of what came to be called decentralization. Recall that Sloan had to rein in a set of businesses that were out of control. There was no decentralization in that.

Part and parcel of this so-called decentralization effort has been the imposition of financial measures – control by the numbers. If division managers met their targets, they were ostensibly free to manage their businesses as they pleased. But the real effect of this decentralization *to* the division head has often been centralization *of* the division: the concentration of power at the level of the division chief, who is held personally responsible for the impersonal performance. No wonder that now, in reaction, we have all this fuss about the need for empowerment and innovation.

Division chiefs – and headquarters controllers looking over their shoulders – get very fidgety about surprises and impatient for numerical results. And the best way to ensure quick, expected results is never to do anything interesting; always cut, never create. That is how the rationalization of costs has become to today's manager what bloodletting was to the medieval physician: the cure for every illness.

As a consequence of all this (de)centralizing and (de)layering, measurement has emerged as the religion of management. But how much sensible business behavior has been distorted as people have been pushed to meet the numbers instead of the customers?

"After all you've done for your customers, why are they still not happy?" asked the title of a recent article (*Fortune*, December 11, 1995). The answer: because business "has not yet figured out how to define customer satisfaction in a way that links it to financial results." Be quite clear what this means: customers will be satisfied and happy only when companies can put a dollar sign on them.

To explain its point, *Fortune* included a box labeled "What's a Loyal Customer Worth?" It offered several steps to answering that question: first, "decide on a meaningful period of time over which to do the calculations"; next "calculate the profit . . . customers generate each year"; after that, "it's simple to calculate net present value . . . The sum of years one through *n* is how much your customer is worth . . ."

Just a few easy steps to a happier customer. Because no article on management today can be without its list of easy steps, here come my "Five Easy Steps to Destroying Real Value" (any step will do):

- *Step 1.* Manage the bottom line (as if companies make money by managing money).
- *Step 2.* Make a plan for every action. (No spontaneity please, definitely no learning.)

- *Step 3*. Move managers around to be certain they never get to know anything but management well, and let the boss kick himself upstairs so that he can manage a portfolio instead of a real business. (For *herself*, see Musing 9, below.)
- *Step 4*. When in trouble, rationalize, fire, and divest; when out of trouble, expand, acquire, and still fire (it keeps employees on their toes); above all, never create or invent anything (it takes too long).
- *Step 5*. Be sure to do everything in five easy steps.

If this sort of thing sounds familiar, it's because the analytical mentality has taken over the field of management. We march to the tune of the technocrat. Everything has to be calculated, explicated, and categorized. The trouble is that technocrats never get much beyond the present. They lack the wisdom to appreciate the past and the imagination to see the future. Everything is centered on what's "in," what's "hot." To plan, supposedly to take care of the future, they forecast, which really means they extrapolate current quantifiable trends. (The optimists extrapolate positive trends; the pessimists, negative ones.) And then, when an unexpected "discontinuity" occurs (meaning, most likely, that a creative competitor has invented something new), the technocrats run around like so many Chicken Littles, crying, "The environment's turbulent! The environment's turbulent!"

Measurement is fine for figuring out when to flip a hamburger or how to fill the O.I. bucket at that "communications" company. But when used to estimate the market for a brand new product or to assess the worth of a complicated professional service, measurement often goes awry. Measurement mesmerizes no less than management. We had better start asking ourselves about the real costs of counting.

## 6. Great organizations, once created, don't need great leaders

Organizations that need to be turned around by such leaders will soon turn back again. Go to the popular business press and read just about any article on any company. The whole organization almost always gets reduced to a single individual, the chief at the "top." ABB exists in the persona of Percy Barnevik. And General Motors is not an incredibly complex web of three quarters of a million people. It's just one single hero: "CEO Jack Smith didn't just stop the bleeding. With a boost from rising auto sales, he made GM healthy again" (*Fortune*, October 17, 1994). All by himself!

Switzerland is an organization that really works. Yet hardly anybody even knows who's in charge, because seven people rotate in and out of the job of head of state on an annual basis. We may need great visionaries to create great organizations. But after the organizations are created, we don't need heroes, just competent, devoted, and generous leaders who know what's going on and exude that spirit of the hive. Heroes – or, more to the point, our hero worship – reflect nothing more than our own inadequacies. Such worship stops us from thinking for ourselves as adult human beings. Leadership becomes the great solution. Whatever is wrong, the great one will make it right.

Bill Agee was the great hero at Bendix. Out he went. Jim Robinson played the same role at American Express. Suddenly that flipped over, too. And on it goes. Who's next? The popular business press is amazing for its ability to turn on a dime. Every magazine issue is a whole new ball game – no responsibility for what was written just a few weeks earlier. Too bad the press has developed the technocrat's blindness to the past.

Part of this cult of leadership involves an emphasis on the "turning around" of old, sick companies. Just look what we invest in that! Think of all those consulting firms specializing in geriatrics, ready to help – hardly a pediatric, let alone an obstetric, practice to be found. Why don't we recognize when it's time for an old, sick organization to die? Would we say that it was one of the great wrongs of this century to have let a talent like Winston Churchill die? Of course not; it was a natural event, part of the life cycle. But when it comes to the great old companies, we feel compelled to keep them alive – even if it means we must resort to interventionist life-support systems.

What we really need, therefore, is a kind of Dr. Kevorkian for the world of business – someone to help with pulling the plug. Then young, vibrant companies would get the chance to replace the old, spent ones. Letting more big companies die – celebrating their contributions at grand funerals – would make our societies a lot healthier.

## 7. Great organizations have souls; any word with a *de* or a *re* in front of it is likely to destroy those souls

Well, there are still some healthy big organizations out there. You can tell them by their individuality. They stay off the bandwagon, away from the empty fads. Did you ever wonder why so many really interesting ones headquarter themselves far from the chic centers of New York and London, preferring places like Bentonville, Arkansas (Wal-Mart Stores), and Littlehampton, West Sussex (The Body Shop)?

If you really want to adopt a new technique, don't use its usual name, especially with a *de* or *re*. Call it something completely different. Then you will have to explain it, which means you will have to think about it. You see, techniques are not the problem; just the mindless application of them. Wouldn't it be wonderful if the editors of HBR printed a skull and cross-bones next to the title of every article, like those on medicine bottles: an example might be "Warning! For high-technology companies only; not to be taken by mass-production manufacturers or government agencies."

Consider the mindless application of reengineering. I opened the popular book on the topic and at first thought, This is not a bad idea. But when

I saw the claim on page 2 that the technique "is to the next revolution of business what specialization of labor was to the last," namely, the Industrial Revolution, I should have closed the book right there. Hype is the problem in management; the medium destroys the message. But I read on. Wasn't this what the Ford Motor Company did to automobile production at the turn of the century, what McDonald's did to fast food 30 years ago? Every once in a while, a smart operator comes along and improves a process. Companies like Ford and McDonald's did not need the book; quite the contrary. They needed imagination applied to an intimate knowledge of a business.

In other words, there is no reengineering in the idea of reengineering. Just reification, just the same old notion that the new system will do the job. But because of the hype that goes with any new management fad, everyone has to run around reengineering everything. We are supposed to get superinnovation on demand just because it is deemed necessary by a manager in some distant office who has read a book. Why don't we just stop reengineering and delayering and restructuring and decentralizing and instead start thinking?

## 8. It is time to close down conventional M.B.A. programs

We should be developing real managers, not pretending to create them in the classroom.

I have been doing a survey. I ask people who know a lot about U.S. business to name a few of the really good U.S. chief executives, the leaders who really made, or are making, a major *sustained* difference. I am not talking about the turnaround doctors but the real builders. (Stop here and make your own list.)

You know what? Almost never has anyone been named who has an M.B.A. No one ever seems to mention Bill Agee or measurement maven Robert McNamara, two of Harvard's best-known graduates. Many do name Jack Welch, Andy Grove, Bob Galvin, and Bill Gates. This is rather interesting because all these people have been either seriously educated (Welch and Grove both have doctorates in chemical engineering) or hardly formally educated at all (Galvin and Gates never finished bachelor's degrees).

Years ago, when things were going better in U.S. business, I used to think that the brilliance of the country's management lay in its action orientation. Managers didn't think a lot; they just got things done. But now I find that the best managers are very thoughtful people (whether or not they have Ph.D.s) who are also highly action oriented. Unfortunately, too many others have stopped thinking. They want quick, easy answers. There is an overwhelming need to be in the middle of whatever is popular. Getting an M.B.A. may be just another example of that need.

It is plain silly to take people who have never been managers–many of whom have not even worked full-time for more than a few years–and pretend to be turning them into managers in a classroom. The whole exercise is too detached from context. We need to stop dumping management theories and cases on people who have no basis even to judge the relevance.

Let's begin by recognizing today's M.B.A. for what it is: technical training for specialized jobs, such as marketing research and financial analysis. (And these are *not* management.) Then maybe we can recognize good management for what *it* is: not some technical profession, certainly not a science or even an applied science (although sometimes the application of science) but a practice, a craft. We have some good things to teach in management schools; let's teach them to people who know what's going on.

It used to be that the M.B.A. was a license to parachute into the middle of an organization, there to climb the proverbial ladder without ever having developed an intimate understanding of what lies below–in order to boss around the people who have.

That was bad enough. But now we have a new and more insidious track to the executive suite. After the M.B.A., you work as a consultant with some prestigious firm for a time, skipping from one client organization to another. And then you leap straight into the chief executive chair of some company, making judicious moves to others in the hope that you may one day end up running a company like IBM. That system might work on occasion. But it is no way to build a strong corporate sector in society.

I think of that approach as a cookie model of management because it was born in what might be called generic consumer-products companies – the ones that sell consumer goods that come out identically, like cookies, one after another. Certain critical skills in these businesses reside in marketing and can be carried from one company to another, but only within this narrow consumer-goods sphere. Cookie management just doesn't work for running nuclear reactors or conducting liver transplants. So there has to be a better way to select and develop managers. Maybe the Groves, Galvins, Gateses, and Welches of this world–who, incidentally, have devoted their careers to single companies – know of one.

## 9. Organizations need continuous care, not interventionist cures

That is why nursing is a better model for management than medicine and why women may ultimately make better managers than men. The French term for a medical operation is "intervention." Intervening is what all surgeons and too many managers do. Managers keep operating on their systems, radically altering them in the hope of fixing them, usually by cutting things out. Then they leave the consequences of their messy business to the nurses of the corporate world.

Maybe we should try nursing as a model for management. Organizations need to be nurtured – looked after and cared for, steadily and consistently. They don't need to be violated by some dramatic new strategic plan or some gross new re-organization every time a new chief executive happens to parachute in.

In a sense, caring is a more feminine approach to managing, although I have seen it practiced by some excellent male chief executive officers. Still, women do have an advantage, in which case the corporate world is wasting a great deal of talent. Let us, therefore, welcome more women into the executive suites as perhaps our greatest hope for coming to our senses.

A few years ago, I spent a day following around the head nurse of a surgical ward in a hospital. I say "following around" because she spent almost no time in her office; she was continually on the floor. (Bear in mind that, long ago, the partners of Morgan Stanley operated on the floor, too: their desks were right on the trading floor.)

But being on the floor has not been the favored style of management, in nursing or elsewhere. Two other styles have been preferred. One can be called the *boss* style, in which the manager knows and controls everything personally, like Nurse Ratched in *One Flew Over the Cuckoo's Nest*. This style has gradually been replaced by the currently popular *professional* style, in which whoever knows management can manage anything, regardless of experience. Here credentials are what matter, and these, together with the absence of firsthand experience, help to keep managers in their offices reading performance reports and supposedly empowering their subordinates. Professional management is management by remote control.

At the first sign of trouble, empowerment becomes encroachment by senior managers, who, because they don't know what is going on, have no choice but to intervene. And so the organization gets turned into a patient to be cured, even if it was not really sick in the first place. It finds itself alternating between short bouts of radical surgery and long doses of studied inattention.

There is a third style, not nearly common enough but practiced by that head nurse I followed around and by other effective managers. Let's call it the *craft* style of managing. It is about inspiring, not empowering, about leadership based on mutual respect rooted in common experience and deep understanding. Craft managers get involved deeply enough to know when not to get involved. In contrast to professional managers who claim "hands off, brain on," the craft manager believes that if there is no laying on of hands (to extend our metaphor), the brain remains shut off.

Women complain about glass ceilings. They can see what goes on up there, at the so-called top; they just cannot easily get through. Well, glass ceilings apply to all sorts of people in all sorts of situations, and that includes the people above who cannot touch what is below, who cannot even be heard when they shout. But worse still may be the concrete floors.

Too many managers can't even see what is going on at the ground level of their organizations, where the products are made and the customers served (presumably). This suggests that we need more than *transparency* in management. We need to smash up the ceilings and bust down the floors as well as break through the walls so that people can work together in that one big circle.

In her book, *Female Advantage: Women's Ways of Leadership* (Doubleday, 1990), Sally Helgesen found that women managers "usually referred to themselves as being in the middle of things. Not at the top, but in the center; not reaching down, but reaching out." Does that sound like our metaphor of the circle? I guess we have now come full circle, so it is time to conclude with our last musing–about which I will add nothing.

**10. The trouble with today's management is the trouble with this article: everything has to come in short, superficial doses**

# 56

# THINGS FALL APART?

## Discourses on agency and change in organizations

*Raymond Caldwell*

Source: *Human Relations* 58(1) (2005): 83–114.

**Abstract**

The history of the concept of 'agency' in organizational theory over the last 50 years makes dismal reading. From a position of unbounded optimism that organizational change could be managed as a rational or planned process with a transparent agenda, we now confront restructured workplaces characterized by new forms of flexibility, hyper-complexity and chaos in which the nature, sources and consequences of change interventions have become fundamentally problematic. How did this occur and what implications does it have for our understanding of agency and change in organizations? Should we assume that rationalist concepts of centred agency are no longer viable, or should we welcome the plural and promising new forms of decentred agency emerging within organizations? This article presents a selective interdisciplinary history of competing disciplinary discourses on agency and change in organizations, classified into *rationalist, contextualist, dispersalist* and *constructionist* discourses. Although the four discourses clarify the meta-theoretical terrain of agency in relation to organizational change theories, the growing plurality of discourses challenges the social scientific ambitions of the research field to be objective, cumulative or unified. It is concluded that the future for research on agency and change in organizations is characterized by new opportunities for empirical investigation and intervention, but also by mounting threats to the epistemological rationale of objective knowledge and the efficacy of practice.

What should the unit of analysis of 'agency' be in organizational change theory? Is it possible to integrate competing concepts of agency into a coherent theory of organizational change? Can we have theories of organizational change without purposeful or intentional concepts of agency? Fifty years ago these perplexing questions were often answered positively. Archetypes of agency were identified with models of rational action, and organizational change was conceived of as a process that could be effectively planned and managed to achieve instrumental outcomes. A classic exemplification of this rationalist view is Lewin's concept of the 'change agent' as an expert facilitator of group processes of planned change although his original concept has gone through many reformulations within various traditions of organization development theory and consultancy practice (Armenakis & Bedeian, 1999; Tichy, 1974). Outside the organizational development tradition, however, over-rationalized models of agency have been challenged from their very inception, both theoretically and practically. Simon's (1947) persuasive critique of decision-making processes in complex organizations is still a classic starting point for 'contextualist' attacks on the rationalism propounded by corporate planners, functional specialists and other experts (Mintzberg, 1994; Pettigrew, 1997). His work also anticipated later ideas on 'logical incrementalism' and 'emergent' concepts of strategy and organizational change, although this has rarely been acknowledged (Quinn, 1980).

Challenges to rationalism, planned organizational change and expertise have also emerged from far-reaching transformations of the workplace over the last two decades. During the 1980s, post-Fordist models of organizational flexibility and new modes of information technology radically undermined the idea that organizational success depended on traditional bureaucratic modes of workplace authority, stability and control. Managerial agency and leadership was no longer identified primarily with the traditional roles of instructing, directing and controlling work processes. Instead, managers and leaders were now expected to encourage 'commitment' and 'empower' employees to be receptive to culture change, technological innovation and enterprise. The new vehicles for this 'dispersal' or distribution of agency were new self-managed teams, quality circles and task groups, which acted as internal agents of transformation and change, as well as sources of distributive knowledge and expertise (Nonaka, 1994).

This overall picture of a gradual shift or dispersal of agency in organizations towards decentred groups or teams, has been popularized in concepts of the 'learning organization' and, more recently, in the idea of 'communities of practice' (Senge, 1990; Wenger, 1998). Theses concepts broadly conceive of organizations not as top-down structures of rational control, but as loosely coupled systems, networks or processes of 'enactment' and collective knowledge creation that devolve autonomy to agency at all levels. These ideas are, of course, partly a recognition of the fact that central hierarchical control has declined in many organizations and that large-scale organizational change is simply too complex and high-risk for any one group or individual to lead. It is in these terms, that proponents of the learning organization have rejected the bureaucratic and mechanistic idea that organizations 'need "change agents" and leaders who can "drive change"' (Senge, 1999). Instead, leadership and agency become identified with systemic forms of learning by broadening leadership theory to encompass potentially participative models of learning across the whole organization (Stacey, 2001).

Although this history of the growing diversity and plurality of forms of agency in organizations can be plotted in relation to transformations of the workplace, it can also be delineated in terms of an overall transition from rationalist epistemologies of agency to the increasing fragmented discourses of 'social constructionism' (Gergin, 2001). Rationalist epistemologies of agency have, of course, a long and complex intellectual genealogy in philosophy, but they are broadly characterized by a belief in human beings as rational subjects or autonomous actors who can act in an intentional, predictable and responsible manner towards predetermined goals or planned outcomes. These assumptions are essential in creating 'objective' ideals of rational scientific knowledge and its application to human action and practice, including universal ideals of ethical behaviour. Rationalist epistemologies are therefore scientific, prescriptive and interventionist. In contrast, the multivarious forms of social constructionism invariably undermine science and rationalism and with it ideals of agency and organizational change centred on rationality. Not only does knowledge of the natural world not have a predetermined structure or laws discoverable by rational investigation, but also ideas of 'human action', 'personality', 'intentionality' and 'agency' are equally problematic. For social constructionists, all forms of knowledge, understanding and action are culturally and historically relative and must therefore be situated within competing discourses (Foucault, 1992).

This brief historical and epistemological overview of the nature of agency and change in organizations charts a profound and increasingly disconcerting transformation. From a position of great optimism regarding the practical efficacy and potential emancipatory role of rational action, expert knowledge and 'change agency', we now confront a plurality of conflicting ideals, paradigms and disciplinary self-images that are increasingly difficult to meld in any coherent manner. We must ask how this fragmentation occurred, and what epistemological implications it has for understanding the future prospects for new forms of agency and change in organizations. Should we give up the search for an 'integrated paradigm' or interdisciplinary ideal of change agency that goes beyond the Babel of increasingly competing discourses and the disparate contingencies of practice? Or, should we accept the plurality of discourses and the eclecticism of practice as itself a positive affirmation of new and more positive ideals of decentred agency?

This article presents a selective, synthetic and critical historical review of some of the literature and empirical research on agency and change in organizations. The review, however, is not strictly chronological and takes the form of a heuristic classification of four 'discourses' on agency and organizational change: *rationalist, contextualist, disperalist* and *constructionist*. Rationalist discourses tend to give priority to centred agency, concepts of planned change and the possibilities of strategic action. Contextualist discourses focus on processes of 'emergent' change and the bounded nature of centred agency in organizations. Dispersalist discourses focus predominantly on systemic or self-organizing processes of learning in organizations, while giving autonomy to new forms 'conjoint agency', 'sensemaking', 'distributed leadership' and 'communities of practice' (Gronn, 2002; Weick, 2001; Wenger, 1998). Constructionist discourses decentre human agency within discursive practices over which human actors appear to have little rational or intentional control. Overall, these four discourses can be defined as forms of language, meaning and interpretation representing and shaping relatively coherent social, cultural or disciplinary fields of knowledge and practice that embody contextual rules about what can be said, by whom, where, how and why.

Although the review of the four discourses is deliberately interdisciplinary, it cannot hope to encompass all the various paradigms and traditions of research and practice within each set of discourses (Alvesson & Karreman, 2000). Despite these limitations, the classification of the four discourses provides an overarching meta-theoretical framework for exploring the nature of agency that straddles different and competing *disciplinary discourses* about organizational change. The meta-theoretical task is therefore conceived of as an overall attempt to: (i) gain a better understanding of competing disciplinary discourses and the diversity of theories; (ii) develop an overall perspective on the nature of agency and change in organizations; (iii) explore the difficulties in developing multidisciplinary theories or models of organizational change (Van de Ven & Poole, 1995); and (iv) indicate, where appropriate, future avenues for empirical research.

Although the four discourses provide a way to map the metatheoretical terrain of agency and change in organizations, they do not offer the prospect of a 'grand theory', meta-narrative or a new paradigm. A parallel search for synthesis has constantly been reinvented in sociological explorations of agency and structure, but without any success in achieving theoretical integration; and there are lessons here for other disciplines (Archer, 2003; Bourdieu, 1990; Giddens, 1984). Nor is there any remote prospect of a synthetic 'recontextualization' of an overall 'order of discourse' that would somehow link micro-discourses on agency to more grandiose macro-level structural analysis of social order or social change: a move from discourses to *Discourse*. In this respect, the oppositions and relationships between the concepts and dichotomies explored within a cultural or disciplinary field of discourse cannot be stated universally. Instead, the formulation and reformulation of concepts of agency and change depend on the specific theoretical discourses or practices within which they occur (Bourdieu, 1990; Foucault, 2000). Moreover, social 'scientific' knowledge of agency is itself a socially constructed discourse and practice that may simply reproduce old dichotomies in the conceptual language of an apparently new paradigm (Abbott, 2000; Hacking, 1999). This epistemological dilemma presents a challenge not only to rationalism, but also to many versions of social constructionism which appear to affirm the nominalism of discourse analysis while somehow claiming to 'critically' transcend the dichotomies that underpin their often debilitating theorization of agency. In this respect, discourse analysis is always in danger of sliding from nominalism to reductionism.

The article begins by selectively discussing the four discourses. This leads to a discussion of possible research agendas within each of the discourses. The theoretical implications of a temporal, fragmented and noncumulative understanding of knowledge and action for the future analysis of agency and organizational change are then discussed. Finally, it is concluded that organizational theories of change are in danger of falling apart because they cannot reconstruct a coherent epistemological or moral idea of agency as a basis of knowledge, human action or change management practice.

## Rationalist discourses: in search of change agency

There is a vast range of rational concepts of agency in the social sciences, from rational choice models of economic action to cognitive theories of instrumental behaviour. In the field of organization change theory, however, the most influential models of rationalist discourses of change agency have their origins in the influential work of Kurt Lewin (1947, 1997, 1999), although his ideas have gone through many reformulations within the various traditions of organizational development ('OD') research and practice (Armenakis & Bedeian, 1999). It is impossible to examine all these reformulations while doing justice to the scope of Lewin's work. Instead, the primary focus here is on the four key attributes of rationalist discourses of centred agency that are invariably synonymous with the Lewinian legacy and the OD tradition: *rationality, expertise, autonomy* and *reflexivity*.

### *Rationality*

Lewin's work created a framework for a profoundly rationalist approach to change agency and organizational change. All three of his core concepts of 'force field analysis', 'group dynamics', and 'action research' involved an overriding search for a rational and participative methodology of behavioural change (Lewin, 1997, 1999). Force field analysis was based on the assumption that group behaviour is held in a 'state of quasi-stationary equilibrium' by a constellation of equal and opposite forces that can be measured in terms of their strength and direction (Lewin, 1999: 34). These relatively stable structures of group behaviour form homeostatic systems that can be subject to planned change by processes of rational interventions operating through *negative* or compensating feedback mechanisms. This model both allows Lewin to conceive of 'change and constancy as relative concepts', and also to conceive of feedback as a way of indirectly pushing a fluid and changeable system towards a rational or predetermined goal. At its most schematic, negative feedback entails comparing the current state of a behavioural system to a desired functional state, and then moving the system in a direction that minimizes the differences between the two. This is the decisive idea that informs Lewin's three-stage process of 'unfreezing, moving and refreezing' behaviour into a new quasi-stationary state: 'by adding forces in the desired direction or by diminishing opposing forces' (1999:280). It also underpins his idea of 'resistance' to change as a dynamic within a system of forces: 'Only by relating the actual degree of constancy to the strength of forces toward or away from the present state of affairs can one speak of degrees of resistance or stability of group life in a given respect' (Lewin, 1947: 13–14). Essentially, resistance is a systems concept that allows Lewin to conceive patterns of continuity and discontinuity within relatively static structures of group behaviour. In this respect, behavioural change is not conceived of as intrinsically emergent or processual, but rather as a planned process requiring the intervention of a 'change agent'. Ultimately, Lewin's rational systems model is expert-centred in that the change agent or action researcher acts as a feedback mechanism ensuring transitions between states of stability while helping to diffuse or dissipate resistance.

### *Expertise*

Although the concept of the change agent as expert (or action researcher) offering rational persuasion has its origins in Lewin's work, it has gradually been differentiated and broadened within the OD tradition to cover a whole array of expert interventions involving 'technical, specialist or consulting assistance in the management of a change effort' (Beckhard, 1969: 101). This assistance may take a variety of forms. Some situations call for an advisor role, whereas others may emphasize the role of the consultant as educator, analyst or councillor. The paradigmatic OD consultancy role is, however, that of the 'process consultant' as defined by Schein: 'The process consultant seeks to give the client insight into what is going on around him, within him and between him and other people' (1988: 27). In this expert-centred role the consultant seeks to act as an 'unbiased' facilitator positively involved in consultative or consensus-seeking interventions based on feedback and group ownership (Tichy, 1974). The attributes required in this role are, therefore, broadly synonymous with 'process consultation': listening, providing feedback, counselling, coaching, and intergroup dynamics (Schein, 1988). However, given that this is partly an expert-consultancy or diagnostic role, the organizational development practitioner must also be able to demonstrate general consultancy skills and an instrumental knowledge of OD tools and techniques (Worley & Feyerherm, 2003). Essentially, the process consultant offers expert knowledge both in the objective-neutral manner of the interventions and the diagnostic tools applied.

### *Autonomy*

Within the OD tradition, 'autonomy' or the possibility of choice appears to be invested primarily in the change agent and the practice-oriented model of action research. As a consequence, there is virtually no discussion of the ability of individuals to freely choose rational ends. This curious absence can be traced back to Lewin (1999) in which the rationality of the group takes precedence over the individual as an explanatory framework; and choice is reduced to participative methods of group learning towards a predetermined end. It is also evident in the various stands of the OD tradition, which appear to suggest that autonomous individuals and groups operating within learning organizations freely choose functional goals in relation to holistic ideals or transcendent ends (Senge, 1990). But if individuals have limited autonomy to choose ends and organizations or groups are not systems with pre-given goals (e.g. adapativeness), then the neutral benevolence of action research as a participative methodology of behavioural change becomes fundamentally problematic.

This issue raises a central question: what, precisely, is the goal of action research as an experimental science of practice, *persuasion or empowerment?* If it is only rational persuasion, then action research is in danger of becoming purely an instrumental technique of control with agendas set by others: leaders, managers or consultants. This self-abnegation would also leave it with very little to say on the vast range of moral issues raised by its expert ideal of scientific practice. For the continuum of persuasion can lead from rationality to coercion, and all sorts of congeries in between. Alternatively, if action research is identified with empowerment then it becomes a mechanism for 'joint consultations' within an agreed ethical framework. This would appear to partly concur with Lewin's vague notion of action research as a microcosm of a free and democratic society, a sort of mini-theory of participation and consensus in operation. 'The only hope . . . for a permanent foundation of successful social management, and particularly for a permanent democratic society of the common man, is a social management based to a high degree on a scientific insight which is to be accessible to the many' (Lewin, 1999: 334). But this liberal ambition remains oblique and it appears unrealistic without a definition of autonomy and its link to rationality (Habermas, 1984). Only in the most idealized form can action research amount to a rational consensus-seeking intervention free of manipulation, power or coercion (Gergin, 2003).

Faced with this dilemma, some OD practitioners have fallen back on a conflation of instrumental expertise and power: 'The OD consultant strives to use power that is based on rationality, valid knowledge, and collaboration and to discount power based on and channelled by fear, irrationality and coercion' (Bennis, 1969: 79). Other practitioners have, however, sought to stretch the participative ethos into a new world of decentred agency defined by participative self-organization processes of communicative interaction between equal partners in an open dialogue. Neither of these approaches stands up to critical security, precisely because they do not propose a credible concept of autonomy defined by the possibility of choice.

### *Reflexivity*

The concept of reflexivity in the OD tradition has assumed many forms, but it tends to be fundamentally Janus-faced: pointing in opposite directions towards epistemologies of knowledge and epistemologies of practice. If the link between knowledge and action, theory and practice is defined by scientific presuppositions, then the nature of reflection on change processes tends to follow the logic of 'instrumental problem solving made rigorous by the application of scientific theory and technique' (Schon, 1983: 22). The change agent is essentially an expert providing reflexivity in the form of feedback (Weick, 2001). If, however, the main focus is on practice or 'reflection in action', as in models of action research, then change interventions follow an experimental methodology, iteratively moving back and forth between theory and practice. In this formulation the change agent is essentially a reflexive practical theorist committed to the service of theory to practice.

Most OD practitioners tend to vacillate between these two positions, although some have sought a fusion between science and practice in the notion of 'action science' that yields causal propositions and highly formalized techniques of reflexive practice – a hard position that harks back to Lewin (Argyris, 1982). But even the apparently weaker or softer intervention techniques of the 'reflective practitioner' (Schon, 1983) and 'process consultant' (Schein, 1987) tend to involve a strongly rationalistic bias in that the practitioner is the scientist in action involved in and yet detached from both his subject and the diagnostics of practice: 'The process of relating to others have decisive influences on outcomes and must themselves become objects of diagnosis and intervention if any organization improvement is to occur' (Schein, 1988: 17). Moreover, the central goal of reflexivity is to reveal the causal nature of action and harness the capacity of human agents to make conscious rational choices to change their behaviour. This amounts to a partial attempt to create a bridge between the epistemological asymmetry of the individual or group as an object of investigation set apart from the investigator. But again, this linkage is based on a participant-observer concept of reflexivity as feedback that is fundamentally rationalistic in its understanding of the 'logic of practice' (Bourdieu, 1990). Ultimately, the only way out of this epistemological dilemma is to contextualize the temporal and embedded meanings within practice by decentring them from a subject-object episteme of knowledge creation, thereby extending the possibilities of reflexivity beyond rationalism (Foucault, 1992). This is precisely what occurs in constructionist discourses and to a lesser extent in more moderate 'sensemaking' concepts of agency (Gergin, 2001; Weick, 2001).

Although organizational development theory and practice has provided some important insights into the nature of organization change, it faces increasing challenges to its agency-centred concepts of *rationality, expertise, autonomy* and *reflexivity*. These challenges first emerged from moderating explorations of bounded rationality and the examination of organizational contingencies, but they gradually broadened into more wide-ranging critiques coming from contextualist and constructionist discourses. Here, the persistent criticisms are that the model of change envisaged by OD appears more suited to *planned change*, conceived as a rational and linear process within relatively stable organizational systems that have the resources and time to implement incremental change (Dumphy & Stace, 1993). Attacks on expertise have also reinforced this questioning of rationalism, and these attacks have perhaps been even more corrosive of the OD tradition (Weick, 2001). Certainly, the normative assumption that the change agent can facilitate consensus or agreement on change and that this apparently participative mode of change is 'best', tends to underplay the expert rhetoric and vested interests that underpin consultancy interventions, as well as the manipulative dynamics at work in group processes and the broader coercive and political aspect of power relations in processes of organizational change.

Organizational development practitioners have partly addressed some of these issues by broadening the scope of practice to embrace larger issues of power and culture. However, this has only highlighted the intrinsic ambiguities and oblique concept of 'autonomy' that partly sustain the apparently unbiased neutrality of the change agent role, both as an expert intervention or a mode of reflexive practice.

This is a critical issue that will not go away. As originally conceived, the change agent role mixed rhetoric and reality, power and expertise (Lewin, 1999). It was an expression of the core democratic mission of the OD movement to further equality, empowerment and consensus-building within the workplace, as well as a practical action-centred mechanism for successfully implementing change. However, the increasing shift of OD practitioners towards management-driven interventions that can deliver 'value' or 'performance' has led to a greater emphasis on more instrumental, mechanistic and product models of consultancy that place the change agent primarily in the role of expert selling change tools or solutions. Given this convergence, it is increasingly difficult to differentiate the collaborative process role of the change agent as a facilitator of autonomy from other managerialist conceptions of agency (Worley & Feyerherm, 2003). The history of organizational development theory and practice is one of repeated failures to come to terms with the ambiguities and paradoxical nature of change agency as both an expert intervention and a self-empowering or democratic form of group involvement. In these circumstances, the OD concept of reflexivity looks increasingly problematic; not only because its prescriptive claims to rationalism fail to address issues of interest or power, but also because it appears outmoded in the face of competing discourses on the temporal and embedded nature of agency as a form of enacted practice (Weick, 2001: 399).

## Contextualist discourses: embedding agency and change

Contextualist discourses have a long and distinguished academic lineage, crossing a range of disciplinary fields and assuming many sub-varieties. Simon's (1947) critique of 'objective rationality' in complex organizations, Lindblom (1959) on 'the science of muddling through', Cyert and March (1963) on 'bonded rationality', and Quinn (1980) on the 'logical incrementalism' of the strategy process are all forerunners or proponents of contextualist ideas, as is the more recent work of Mintzberg (1994) on 'strategy as craft'. However, the most influential recent exponent of a contextualist approach within the change management field is undoubtedly Pettigrew (1987, 1997, 2003). His programmatic intent is to create 'theoretically sound and practically useful research on change', that explores the 'contexts, content, and processes of change together with their interconnectedness through time' (Pettigrew, 1987: 268). This was conceived as a direct challenge to 'ahistorical, aprocessual and acontextual' approaches to organizational change; especially planned change approaches, instrumental ideals of managerial agency, and the variable-centred paradigms of organizational contingency theories (Pettigrew, 2003). Moreover, Pettigrew appeared to create a new variant of contextual analysis: *incrementalism with transitions*; an approach that sought to pragmatically accommodate both continuity and discontinuity in the organizational change process by 'embedding' agency in context.

Although Pettigrew's position is complex and has evolved (and is still evolving) in various directions, it can be summed-up in four core propositions:

1. the iterative, non-linear or processual nature of change over time: 'an organization or any social system may profitably be explored as a continuing system, with a past, a present and a future' (Pettigrew, 1985: 36);
2. the multiplicity of internal and external 'levels of analysis', including those within organizations and their external environments;

3 the central influence of micro-politics and conflicts between organizational actors over the direction, rationality and outcomes of change (Pettigrew, 2003); and
4 the unintended consequences, unpredictability and paradoxical nature of all rational action, management planning and strategic decision making.

Although none of these ideas is new, Pettigrew's original contribution was to transform case histories into context-rich case studies of strategic change and strategic choice that embedded agency in organizational change processes.

Although Pettigrew's contextual analysis of the embeddedness of agency and organizational change is often powerful and illuminating, it also has four main weaknesses.

### *Processual change*

Pettigrew claims that: 'Change and continuity, process and structure, are inextricably linked' (1985: 1). However, his historical and contextual location of organizational change within 'processual dynamics of changing' undermines the analytical clarification of *structure* as a 'continuing system' with enduring macro properties. Instead, structure or 'structuring' are diffused within the holistic and processual dynamics of 'outer and inner contexts', and this is compounded by the absence of any clear definitions or classifications of contexts. For Pettigrew, context appears to form the ontological presupposition of processes of 'becoming' that are always temporal and indeterminate: 'Human conduct is perpetually in a process of becoming. The overriding aim of processual analysis therefore is to catch this reality in flight' (1997: 338).

This implicit affirmation of temporality and choice is, however, somewhat contradictory. Organizational change as an apparent contextual counterpoint to systemic ideas of order, stability or structure is conflated with *processual change*, rather than both continuities and discontinuities that may be predetermined or open-ended. As a result, processual change becomes synonymous with incrementalism or its sub-variant, emergent transitions, rather than structural, environmental trajectories or other 'path-dependent processes'. Processual change is, therefore, by definition unintended, unplanned, unstructured and indeterminate and this allows the affirmation of agency as choice (Giddens, 1984). While these ideas erode the theoretical edifice of rationalist discourses of agency as a mode of planned intervention, they also undermine its substantive counterpoints: the possibility of continuity as order, and stability and discontinuity as radical transformational change. Ultimately, Pettigrew wants organization change defined by the perpetual transcendent temporality of processual contexts, rather than organizational change that is a temporal interplay of continuity and discontinuity, systems and processes, determinism *and* choice.

### *Levels of analysis*

If Pettigrew's analysis of the processual dynamics of change is truncated, so too is his multi-level analysis of internal and external environmental contexts. He warns that it is not sufficient to treat the macro 'context' as 'either just a descriptive background, or an electric list of antecedents' (1985: 36–7). Yet this is precisely what occurs in his work. No systemic, functional or network concept of the interrelationships of organizational levels is offered, and the environment is contextualized as a realm of agency *with* choice rather than an arena of possible structural determinism. Pettigrew has, therefore, no adequate concepts that theorize the boundaries of organizations or the possible efficacy of organizational processes; correspondingly, in most of his work he has little or no interest in the possible causality of structure or environment. Instead, the narrative interpretation of the uniqueness of historical contexts performs an explanatory role, replacing any structural or variable-centred analysis of organizational transformation and change (Pettigrew, 1997, 2003).

### *Organizational politics*

The central importance Pettigrew places on organizational politics or competing interests has two key functions, it clarifies modes of 'bonded rationality' in decision making while affirming the possibility of agency and choice. In this respect, contextual analysis is anti-deterministic and antidualist, while retaining a strong affinity to the virtues of liberal individualism (Giddens, 1984; Pettigrew, 1987). Yet paradoxically, by emphasizing the rich narrative of context as a dynamic of partial closure and bounded choice, agency appears to lose any decisiveness in defining goals or bringing about outcomes; it is simply a micro-manifestation of competing interest group behaviours. Pettigrew has, therefore, no overarching need for a contextual theory of leadership or agency (Osborn *et al.*, 2002). Moreover, processual analysis as a narrative of interests and power sidelines a systematic exploration of organizations as broader economic, cultural or institutional entities involved in larger patterns of resource allocation, social reproduction, normative regulation or the mediation of professional expertise (DiMaggio & Powell, 1991). In this respect, clashes of interests and power and the politics of choice, replace any systematic, structural or institutional analysis of the normative, symbolic or cultural bases of power, authority or legitimacy (Castells, 2000; Habermas, 1984; Parsons, 1951).

### *Theory and practice*

Finally, Pettigrew has insisted that his work is designed to be practically useful. However, his focus on unintended consequences and the lack of predictability of change processes allows few possibilities to define the directionality of strategic change and therefore to prescribe any practical advice on how change can be managed (Dawson, 1994). In particular, leadership as a mode of agency and change becomes peripheral to the holistic ambitions of contextual analysis (Osborn *et al.*, 2002). In this respect, contextualist discourses appear to reject the apparent reductionism of 'contingency' and prescriptive perspectives on strategic change, which still retain instrumental models of expertise and archetypes of strategic agency that partly bridge the gaps between theory and practice (Ansoff, 1991). Naturally, this antipathy towards strategic action has led some contextualists to stray back towards the rationalism of practice as an escape from 'highly abstract and largely impenetrable explanations which have no practical value' (Dawson, 1994: 41). But a radically alternative approach would be, of course, to embrace a fundamental critique of the 'logic of practice' by contextualizing contextualism (Bourdieu, 1990).

Pettigrew and his colleagues have continued to develop their contextual discourse as processual analysis, while addressing many of its familiar weaknesses: the overemphasis on description and the historical particularity of each case, and the corresponding avoidance of casual propositions or generalizations. In addition, the intrinsic difficulty of Pettigrew's form of contextualism is that it places too much emphasis on choice and liberal individualism, while failing to theorize the nature of decentred agency. But perhaps the most important overall problem remains the ambivalence of contextual analysis towards theory. 'While a contextualist methodology perhaps naturally points towards the adoption of an intensive, longitudinal, case study based form of analysis, it does not by itself supply an adequate theoretical underpinning' (Pettigrew *et al.*, 1992: 23). The reasons for this theoretical deficit are intrinsic to the particularity of case-based analysis, but they also derive from what it excludes from analysis. Contextualist discourses are constructed as a series of counterpoints against rationality, order, planned change, deliberate strategies, managerial agency and systems thinking. But as a series of competing methodological contentions, contextualist discourses have been unable to develop ideas that can really challenge or replace the theoretical edifice of rationalist discourses. Paradoxically, by emphasizing difference, contextualism is in danger of becoming simply anti-system, anti-structure, anti-planning and, therefore, the antithesis of both systematic theoretical analysis and strategic change interventions.

## Dispersalist discourses: decentring agency and change

At the heart of dispersalist discourses is the idea of leadership and managerial agency as decentred or distributed team process. This is certainly not a new idea, but its significance has grown enormously over the last decade (Gronn, 2002). There are a number of factors that partly explain this development.

The reduction of central hierarchical control in organizations has resulted in a growing emphasis on project and cross-functional teams as mechanisms to achieve greater horizontal coordination across organizational divisions, units and work processes. This is also associated with a shift towards information-intensive and network organizations with 'distributed intelligence', creating new opportunities for knowledge creation and innovation at multiple levels (Castells, 2000; Nonaka, 1994). In addition, the emergence of flexible forms of manufacturing and supply chain management founded on flexible 'economies of scope', rather than Fordist economies of scale has allowed greater potential for decentralized decision making.

Dispersalist discourses on agency have grown naturally out of these changes in the workplace. Agential dispersal is the process of distributing agency throughout organizations. In principle, it is a form of empowerment and 'distributed leadership' designed to create or institutionalize a wider organizational base or network of support for change. This is reinforced by the idea that large-scale organizational changes are simply too complex and high-risk for a few individuals to lead or direct, even when there is a strong sense of vision and direction.

Although there are an enormous and growing variety of dispersalist discourses, only four are outlined here: (i) the learning organization, (ii) communities of practice, (iii) distributed leadership, and (iv) chaos or complexity theories. All of these discourses have a variety of sources, involve different assumptions and are sometimes contradictory in their implications. They do, however, share some common features in their emphasis on decentred agency and systemic self-organization.

### *The learning organization*

This concept is currently the most influential model of a team approach to change agency and organizational change, certainly among many practitioners. The concept of the learning organization conceives of organizations not as hierarchical structures, but as macro- and micro-processes of 'enactment' and knowledge creation that give primacy to leadership and change agency at all levels. Everyone throughout the organization is therefore expected to work collaboratively by harnessing their knowledge, skills and insights to constantly renew and improve organizational success. This amounts to an extension of leadership theory by identifying decentred agency with a distributed yet unified striving to realize collective or systemic goals (Senge, 1990). In this respect, the learning organization concept overlaps with rationalist discourses.

### *Communities of practice*

The concept of 'communities of practice' enriches and reformulates the idea of learning organizations by moving towards a 'social theory of learning' founded on practice. Wenger (1998, 2000) argues that organizations are both designed 'institutions' and emergent 'constellations of practice'. This is a theoretical arbitration of traditional action and structure dichotomies in that practice becomes a mediated realm of mutual engagement and shared meaning. But the *duality of meaning* is retained in that 'agency' and 'structure' are conceived as both designed and emergent: products and processes of 'participation' and 'reification' that occur within communities of practices (Wenger, 1998). Because communities of practice are relatively autonomous, this allows for the creative reshaping of organizations by participation and mutual engagement: 'The point of design is to make organizations ready for the emergent by serving the inventiveness of practice and the potential for innovation inherent in its emergent structure' (Wenger, 1998:245). Organizational change and redesign are therefore conceptualized as an emergent and iterative process of self-organization within communities of practice, rather than the outcome of a predetermined strategy or the top-down design interventions of experts.

### *Distributed leadership*

The concept of 'distributed leadership' challenges many of the theoretical and prescriptive assumptions underlying conventional leadership paradigms: especially the leader-centrism implied in most leadership-followership dichotomies. Instead, the empirical focus shifts towards structural changes within the workplace that have allowed the increasing emergence of autonomous and devolved forms of 'concertive action' and 'conjoint agency' (Gronn, 2002). In this respect, the concept of distributed leadership has strong affinities with the idea of 'sensemaking' agency and the associated exploration of 'loosely coupled systems' as the structural referent of organizational change (Weick, 2001).

### *Complexity theories*

Complexity and chaos theories, with their origins in physics, computer science and mathematical biology, have often been transposed into discussions of organizational change as well as broader ideas of 'hyper-complexity', network organizations and societies, and the growing challenges of 'informational capitalism' (Anderson, 1999; Castells, 2000; Flake, 1998; Maguire & McKelvey, 1999). In all these discourses the central idea is that dynamic systems are in a constant state of self-organizing dis-equilibrium, which allows them to change. This occurs through 'dissipative structures' of energy or devolved networks of information interchange that allow order and chaos, continuity and transformation to occur simultaneously, and without the hidden hand of purposiveness or teleology. Effectively, 'order is free' because it appears to emerge from simple bottom-up processes or rules that create non-linear dynamics of bounded instability (Kauffman, 1993). Applied to organizational change theory these ideas have encouraged a rejection of conventional rationalist subject-object dichotomies of knowledge creation, concepts of centred agency and a reinterpretation of organizational change as an emergent, self-organizing and temporal process of communication and learning (Stacey, 2001).

Despite the increasing significance of dispersalist discourses for understanding agency and change in organizations they have been notably weak in exploring the implications of their analysis for 'practice' in at least four overlapping areas. The systemic and 'unitarist' ideal of organizational learning as a collective process raises fundamental issues of how learning, formal and 'tacit', can be dispersed throughout an organization; who is involved in learning, where does it take place, what is being learnt, how does it accumulate, and how can it be applied (Easterby-Smith *et al.*, 2000; Hendry, 1996)? Until these questions are answered, the learning organization remains more rhetorical prescription than realistic practice. Similarly, Wenger's (1998) idea that communities of practice are sustained through the ongoing 'negotiation of meaning' is often confusing because it operates through reciprocal processes of 'participation' and 'reification' that lack analytical clarity. Participation appears to depend on an idealized notion of mutual meaning creation in practice, whereas reification is an amorphous concept covering virtually every form of signification and objectification of human activity (Wenger, 1998). Thus, although the duality of participation-reification opens up classical organizational issues of autonomy and control, no systemic, structural or institutional categories are offered to explain how workplace control or power is produced and reproduced. Instead, Wenger claims that: 'External forces have no direct power over this production because, in the last analysis (i.e. in the doing through mutual engagement in practice), it is the community that negotiates its enterprise' (1998: 80). In this respect, Wenger is in danger of an old-style idealization of community while failing to explore the limits of communities of practice as a form of decentred agency. In a parallel manner, concepts of distributed leadership often have similar difficulties; they tend to ignore the opposite ends of their bipolar continua: 'focused' or leader-centred agency and how it fits within new modes of organizational autonomy and control within the workplace (Gronn, 2002). Finally, complexity theories challenge the mythology of management development professionals who perpetuate the rationalist illusion of objective knowledge and change agent expertise, but their concepts of 'participative self-organizing learning' diffuse any sense of how decentred agency can be managed, controlled or developed in organizations (Stacey, 2001). All of these issues are implicit in constructionist discourses, but they take on much more radical and disconcerting implications.

## Constructionist discourses: change without agency?

Constructionist discourses are enormously diverse, partly because they embrace epistemological 'perspectivism' and have multiple points of intersection with the various intellectual movements of 'poststructuralism' and 'postmodernism'. This makes it almost impossible to disentangle the various strands of constructionist discourses (Gergin, 2001; Parker, 1998). There are, however, at least four concerns that help define the programmatic intent of constructionism.

### *Anti-rationalism*

Most forms of social constructionism are hostile to the claims of reason and rationalism, both as a foundation for knowledge of the world of things and as a guide to human conduct. Constructionism argues that rationalism is neither a foundation of truth nor a basis for self-knowledge, moral conduct or political emancipation; it is simply one discourse among many.

### *Anti-scientism*

Constructionism holds that the 'laws' or 'facts' of the natural and human sciences are constructions within discourse that could be otherwise. Science is not a cumulative or progressive understanding of 'how the world is', nor does its knowledge of laws or facts predetermine how the natural or human science will evolve (Hacking, 1999).

### *Anti-essentialism*

Constructionists hold that there are no essences or inherent structures inside objects or people. Just as nature is not immutably fixed by entities designated as 'atoms', 'cells', or 'molecules', so human subjects are not predetermined objects with discoverable properties such as 'human nature', 'intentionality', 'free will' or 'personality'. These entities do not have an existence outside socially constructed discourses.

### *Anti-realism*

Constructionists deny that the world has a fixed or predetermined reality discoverable by empirical observation, theoretical analysis or experimental hypothesis. There can be no truly objectivist or realist epistemologies founded on the subject-object and appearance-reality dichotomies that have characterized the history of western rationalist thought (Foucault, 2000).

These are very broad meta-theoretical statements of constructionist positions and their implications will vary enormously in relation to the disciplinary fields, research traditions or theoretical perspectives within which they are developed. Even within the apparently singular field of Foucauldian-inspired constructionist organizational theory there is enormous plurality (McKinlay & Starkey, 1998). Nevertheless, these statements broadly indicate that most constructionist discourses are compatible with the long tradition of relativism and nominalism in western philosophy (Hacking, 1999).

Until recently, there have been few serious attempts to explore the farreaching implications of constructionist discourses for the understanding of agency and change in organizations, although this is beginning to be addressed in a more systematic and critical manner (Newton, 1998). Interestingly, some of the most challenging sociological explorations in this area have come not from within organizational theory, but from feminist theorists (McNay, 2000).

There are at least four key areas in which constructionist discourses have had an impact on the understanding agency and change in organizations.

### *Dualism*

Constructionist discourses offer a relentless challenge to conventional static dichotomies within theoretical systems. Binary oppositions invariably lead to polar extremes: the idea that one side of a dichotomy has greater validity or more explanatory power over the other. Constructionists, therefore, reject the either/or logic of individual-society and agency-structure dichotomies and propose a simultaneous both/and analysis that is fundamentally temporal. But it is often unclear how this unification or temporal fusion occurs. If it occurs within new nominalist discourses we are never sure of what 'agency' or 'structure' actually refers to or explains, unless of course, discourses embrace 'realism' or some form of analysis that partly solidifies its categories (Parker, 1998). Most constructionists have, therefore, been unable to escape the epistemological problems of nomimalism, although some have partly done so by replacing old dichotomies with new and apparently more integrated ones.

### *Boundaries*

Constructionist discourses challenge the 'reality' of organizations as entities with enduring functional, structural or systemic properties by calling into question the ontological status of the temporal boundaries that define units and levels of analysis (e.g. individual, dyad, group, organization). As boundaries are constantly defined and redefined over time within human discursive practices, so what exists within and outside organizations is always a shifting or temporal creation rather than a static given (Linstead, 2004). Some constructionists therefore reject any realist account of 'structure' or 'system' as an analytical or explanatory category and offer instead an emergent or processual view of reality which focuses on how the *differences* that define entities are produced and reproduced within discursive practices. However, to explain the endurance, stability or continuity of 'boundaries' requires systemic concepts that bridge or overcome the explanatory gaps left by the 'deconstruction' of structure (Hassard & Parker, 1993). Correspondingly, there is also a need for analytical concepts that explore the interrelationships between units and levels of analysis. Many constructionist discourses have been unable to fill these apparent gaps without importing some form of surrogate determinism to explain the routine reproduction of 'objective' or collective orders of meaning within discursive practices (Foucault, 1991).

### *Power*

The most influential exponent of a constructionist reading of power is undoubtedly Foucault (1991, 2000). Unlike mainstream theories of power, which focus on how power is concentrated in the hands of the few or is distributed through a plurality of institutions and collective agents, Foucault's innovation was to focus primarily on the micro-dynamics of 'disciplinary power'. The multi-various forms of disciplinary power arise within discourses of knowledge which create insidious modes of subjugation by expertise (e.g. the regulation and surveillance of behaviour) and self-subjugation through self-discipline. But, these discourses of 'power/knowledge' are intrinsically disparate and diffuse. They are not only organizationally decentralized, but also decentred from any ontological or epistemological concept of the human subject as an autonomous or rational agent with 'causal powers'. Foucault decouples centred agency and power. The subject is, therefore, a diffused historically constituted entity, a shifting analytical fiction within discourse, always subsumed or determined by power and unable to step outside itself to unmask or deface this power (Hayward, 2000).

With no centre of ontological or epistemological gravity outside of constructed discourses, power appears everywhere and nowhere, and Foucault's (2000) use of the term is notoriously infinite and indiscriminate. Unsurprisingly, when he does address the 'infinitesimal mechanisms' of disciplinary power, they are dispersed through 'discursive formations' of expertise and 'archipelagos' of localized practices that envelop all areas of society and human behaviour. Within these disciplinary networks, human agents are the conduits through which 'embodied' interpersonal power circulates to discipline the body, regulate the mind and control the emotions (McNay, 2000). Paradoxically, disciplinary power is therefore more invisible and yet more effective than the repressive face of macro-power exercised from above because it occupies a realm of mutual culpability and constraint in which ideas of rational autonomy and freedom are problematic. Even deciding who has power over others is never clear, although Foucault (2000) argued, in a characteristically self-contradictory manner, that there was an analytical dividing line separating the powerful from the marginalized, dispossessed and powerless. Although these ideas critically 'deconstruct' notions of hierarchy and leadership, power and control in both society and organizations, they also undermine a belief in the possibility that individuals or groups can affect social or organizational change. Only in Foucault's later work (1986) is there the tentative possibility of re-engaging with the conceptual opposite of decentred agency: an active, politically engaged and potentially autonomous epistemological subject.

### *Change*

Most constructionist discourses reject the idea of grand meta-narratives of historical or societal change. They are also deeply hostile to all rational, teleological or directional models of organizational development and change (Van de Ven & Poole, 1995). The sources of this antipathy are complex. Constructionist discourses place agency and change within the processual temporality of discourses about the present. These apparently circular or self-referential discourses reject any centre of gravity in a rationalist ontology or epistemology of agency, thereby eliminating historical causality, teleology or any idea of a prescriptive endpoint or outcome. Why offer prescriptions if all we have are ever-changing orders of discourse that enact 'games of truth and error' (Foucault, 2000)?

This apparent dissolution of narratives of the past and future has, however, some serious analytical implications. Agency and structure are dissolved or synthesized into the processual dynamics and practices of discourse about the present. This appears to neatly remove the conventional 'structuralist' and functionalist understanding of change as the opposite of stasis: external determinism or evolutionary adaptiveness. Instead, change is always emergent, always temporal — there is no structural stasis.

Is this the end of directionality? Not completely. It simply reappears in constructionist discourses in other guises, precisely because change cannot be explained or analysed in purely processual terms. For example, many Foucauldian constructionists appear to eliminate or submerge 'agency' in discursive practices, yet they hold out the self-reflexive hope of thinking new possibilities of ethical action, resistance and change that will transform the rationalist discourses of liberal individualism. By default, they create a problematic of change without agency. Similarly, even those constructionists, who openly embrace postmodernity as a world of perpetual change characterized by fragmentation and chaos, reintroduce some implicit teleology in the very dichotomy of 'modernity' versus 'postmodernity'. Despite these paradoxes, constructionist discourses often fail to seriously address issues of theorizing agency and change, beyond the standard references to the rejection of grand meta-narratives or the affirmation of ontologies of becoming.

## Discussion

### *Future research*

The four discourses on agency and organizational change clearly underscore the growing fragmentation and complexity of the research field. We now confront an enormous diversity of competing discourses on 'agency', both individual and team focused, autonomous and decentred, that no longer fit within the conventional rationalist ideals of organizational change theory and practice. The widespread espousal of the search for learning organizations, ideas of distributed leadership, theories of organizational complexity and contructionist discourses on decentred agency have finally crystallized this shift towards potentially more inclusive and team-based models of leadership, agency and change in organizations.

This new plurality is in some respects a positive development. All too often the variety of forms of agency in organizations have been identified with one-dimensional rationalist theories of leadership, managerial models of control or exclusive concepts of change agent expertise (Caldwell, forth-coming). These formulations of singular ideals have both exaggerated the autonomous role of leaders and managers in organizational change and undermined the various practical roles other human actors can actually play in processes of organizational change. There are, however, new dangers lurking in the breakdown of rationalist discourses and the growing ascendancy of contextualist, dispersalist and social constructionist ideas. Some of these dangers can be briefly explored by examining both the different research agendas within each of the four discourses and the possibilities for establishing a future direction for interdisciplinary research within an intrinsically multidisciplinary field.

A central research issue for rationalist discourses is likely to be the growing challenges to expertise. As knowledge becomes more specialized, differentiated and distributed within organizational settings that are less hierarchical and more decentralized the strategic issues of how to manage, develop and exercise 'expertise' becomes increasingly central. This is an enormously difficult challenge in the face of changing forms of knowledge creation, new measures of professional 'competence', competing modes of expertise and reflexivity, and the external scrutiny of publics, 'overloaded' or disillusioned with competing expert discourses and practices (Beck, 2000; Willard, 1998). Moreover, challenges to regimes of 'disciplinary power' are likely to intensify within the workplace, especially under the assault of constructionist discourses. In this respect, the forces that lead to dependence on expertise can lead to its disintegration as it is devalued in the eyes of its users or rejected by its subalterns.

The problematic role of professions and consultants in the creation, diffusion and institutionalization of new expert discourses about knowledge, power and agency clearly present major possibilities for future research. As key carrier groups and 'knowledge entrepreneurs' they are often crucial in developing new instrumental product ideas, or the hard and soft technologies of 'managing change' or 'facilitating change' that can be engineered or programmed into organizations as quick-fix solutions. How these interventions are managed is particularly relevant to organizational development practitioners and other change management consultants, who often use a curious mix of uncodified knowledge, instrumental expertise, project management techniques, practical know-how and political skills to effect change. But the turnover of ideas and the legacy of re-engineering and change programme failures suggest a need to explore why certain ideas and process succeed or fail — and how they are rhetorically reinvented. It is also important to research the dislocation of managers as change agents by consultants. Moreover, exploration of the ethics of professional conduct and consultancy practice are increasingly required in the face of the recurrent convergence of technocratic expertise and managerial interests and the countervailing need to include broader constituencies of employees and other stakeholders in achieving successful organizational change.

If rationalist discourses suggest generalizing research agendas around issues of intervention, consultancy practice and professional expertise, then contextualism appears to point in the opposite direction: towards an awareness of the empirical embeddedness and historical particularity of change processes as revealed through the contextual exploration of small numbers of discrete and highly intensive case studies (Pettigrew, 1997). This focus presents enormous scope for a wide-ranging case research on the context, content and processes of change, although there have been few case studies that have emulated the richness of Pettigrew's early work. More research on linking processes to a comparative analysis of organizational outcomes is also likely, and this holds out greater possibilities for combining processual analysis with larger scale statistical mapping techniques and an exploration of macro-micro issues (Pettigrew, 2003). But the overriding 'contextual realism' of processual analysis, its emphasis on the temporal interconnectedness of past, present and future, will mean that it is unlikely to overcome its deep ambivalence towards rationality, systematic theory, causality and the directionality of change. Moreover, the continued focus on the all-enveloping complexity of context poses a research challenge in developing a theory of practice. So far, contextualist discourses simply repeat their opposition to instrumental tools, prescriptive recipes of practice or programmatic action, without providing alternative conceptions of practice. Finally, although a concept of embedded agency as socially bounded action in dynamically complex and shifting contexts is likely to remain a vital research topic, the full implications of 'leading change' as a distributed or dispersed process have yet to be fully explored within contextual research. In this sense, perhaps the greatest weakness of contextualism is that it never developed a theory of agency to complement its processual explorations of the nature of strategic choice and organizational change.

It is within dispersalist discourses that issues of change leadership and decentred agency have been theorized, although it is difficult to speculate on where research in this area will lead given its growing plurality. Concepts of self-organizing complexity and the learning organization open up myriad research possibilities for exploring the micro-dynamics of decentralized order and control. However, it is likely that the concepts of distributed leadership and 'conjoint agency' provide probably the most immediately fruitful avenues for future research on team-based forms of leadership and agency. As the tensions between differentiation and integration in organizations intensify, concertive actions by groups provide new ways of accommodating new forms of role interdependence and work coordination (Gronn, 2002). This insight applies equally to organizational change interventions, which involve both a need for synergy between goals and a reciprocal sharing of influence among change agents. But this will require much more research work on multiple levels and micro-units of analysis of conjoint change agency, while not losing sight of the macro or structural dimensions of organizations, including the ubiquitous counterforces of control. It is often forgotten that moves towards increased autonomy, decentred agency and 'concertive action' are partly sustained by the creation of new systemic logics of electronic surveillance and 'concertive control' within the workplace (Baker, 1999). Complexity theories have also been slow to address these issues, focusing instead on the possibilities that *order without control* will emerge from simple rules of behaviour or interaction — a highly problematic idea. Nor can future research rule out the ever present danger that conjoint agency may not be able to cope with the imperatives of organizational integration or act as an effective substitute for leadership and transformation from above.

Fundamentally different research agendas of power and control are central to the *Change-without-agency problematic* that threatens to envelop discussions of organizational change within constructionist discourses. Constructionist discourses are, by definition, diffuse because they argue for a perspectivial image of knowledge, a decentring of the epistemological and moral subject of science, rationalism and humanism, and an accompanying fragmentation of social and organizational life. Constructionism, therefore, appears to remove human agents from centre stage by placing them within a multiplicity of discourses and practices they do not control, they are simply the conduits and bearers of discourses of knowledge and power. Yet this decentring of agency allows an illumination of the nature of power as discourse, especially the multiple forms and shifting boundaries of micropower. This power forms an insidious basis of social control that 'produces the agent', effectively robbing human actors of their ability to choose their ends. But this 'defacing of power' or its decoupling from autonomous rational agents with free will or unconstrained choices can be viewed as a means of creating an opening for resistance and marginalized discourses that give voice to the disempowered (Hayward, 2000; Parker, 1998). This suggests potentially wide-ranging, but intrinsically fractured research agendas. For, paradoxically, the contructionist defacing of power may be unsustainable without an escape from the debilitating nominalism of discourse analysis. In this respect, constructionist research may have to rebuild an epistemological island of knowledge with a concept of critical realism, or at least a viable methodological distinction between 'knowledge' and 'power'. Only in this way can the decoupling of autonomous agency from power be reconstituted as a connection between decentred agency and change.

Finally, the challenges of creating any coherent research pathways that link or intersect the four discourses should not be underestimated. The idea that change can be managed as a planned or linear process is central to the action-research concept of the individual change agent as both a rational and 'objective' actor who can create change (Lewin, 1947). This is central to the OD tradition and many models of leadership, managerial control and strategic planning which assume the neutral interventions of rationality or expertise in the face of competing interests (Ansoff, 1991). Contextualists also hold on to an ideal of intentionality, despite their emergent and processual perspectives: they attack rationalism as a foundation of action, but not the self-assertion of agency in the face of uncertainty (Pettigrew, 1997). Even some constructionists have embraced a linkage between rationalism and realism as a form of change intervention: 'We can intervene directly in clarifying consequences of discursive frameworks with speakers (as in training or action research, for example), as well as commenting on the discursive-political consequences of discursive clashes and frameworks' (Parker & Burman, 1993: 170). However, in transformed organizational contexts where changes are emergent, processual, political or the outcome of competing rhetorical discourses, neutral or expert-centred ideals of rationality and agency are deeply problematic (Finstad, 1998). Such ideals invariably depend on a corresponding concept of agency as intentional action by individuals or groups towards a pre-determined ends or rational outcomes. Without this concept, human actors, both individually and collectively, may be perceived as the bearers, filters or puppets of change processes over which they have little or no control. Worse still, change interventions may be conceived as a political mechanism of macro-power and disciplinary power, rather than a means of realizing the broader possibilities of shared knowledge or insight.

## *Things fall apart?*

Is there really any prospect of finding a way out of the Babel of competing discourses? Or should we even look for one? While the four sets of discourses offer possibilities for clarifying the future theoretical and empirical research agendas essential for the exploration of agency and change in organizations they do not hold out the possibility of a convergence of research pathways and certainly no synthetic 'theory' or unified model. There are at least four major reasons for this.

### *The limits of knowledge*

Most of the knowledge articulated within the competing and diffuse disciplinary paradigms and discourses relevant to agency and change in organizations lack a *cumulative* logic. After decades of empirical research and theoretical discussion on organizational change, innovation and leadership, we are no nearer to a widely agreed body of knowledge in any of these specialist areas. Nor is there currently any prospect of 'universal' or more modest interdisciplinary paradigms emerging. If anything, the opposite may be occurring, as social contructionist, postmodernist or cultural and historically relativist approaches to epistemology and knowledge creation intensify disciplinary insecurity and the territorial warfare between opposing paradigms (Abbott, 2000; Hacking, 1999). This does not, of course, rule out the legitimate middle range theoretical task of classifying the plurality of newly emerging forms of agency within organizations. One could argue that this is, in fact, the most important future empirical research goal, given the retrospective insight into the fragmented nature of specialist research and the equally diverse nature of centred–decentred agency as modes of practice. Certainly, middle range theory has always been a way of avoiding the vortex of 'bottomless empiricism', although it is a poor defence against both paradigm incommensurability and the corrosive logic of nominalism within constructionist discourses.

### *The failure of synthesis*

There has always been only one practical guiding principle for the exploration of agency and structure: *agency without structure is blind, structure without agency is empty*. Yet, there have been no successful attempts to link the micro-level understanding of agency to macro-level structural, institutional or 'causal' models of organizational change. Instead, there has been a persistent tendency to over-emphasize or privilege one side of the dichotomy.

For example, Van de Ven and Poole's (1995) fourfold typology of organizational change (life cycle, teleology, dialectics, and evolution) gives ontological priority to causal and structural models of change as 'process', while offering no serious exploration of agency; it therefore drifts inexorably towards mechanistic formulations and determinism. One way out of this dilemma would be to argue that the micro versus macro problem is a delusion or dualisms to be overcome. This makes ontological sense, but epistemologically it comes at the price of analytical clarity, in that most forms of constructionism dissolve agency into discourses of power and knowledge and are unable to connect agency with change. This analytical cul-de-sac highlights an equally intractable problem. Without some kind of systemic, institutional or even larger scale 'structural' concept of organizational change and development, teleological, causal or otherwise, it is very difficult to have any really coherent models of agency that escape the unresolved problematics of the micro–macro dichotomy. Parsons' (1951) classic structural–functional theorizing could not find a way out of these problematics half a century ago and Giddens's (1984) alternative 'structuration' theory has ended in an equally dismal theory of 'agency' that moderates rationalism while lacking analytical specificity or practical efficacy. Perhaps we still need both the classic delusions of synthesis *and* dualism, for without the striving for unity or identity we cannot appreciate diversity and difference?

### *The eclipse of the subject*

Concepts of agency cannot be formally grounded in a purely 'rational' or intentional ideal of human action, knowledge or communication, despite the heroic efforts of rationalists to achieve such an ideal (Habermas, 1971, 1984). Because the nature and options for action are always externally constrained and internally context dependent, human actors are, by definition, multi-various creators of discourses and rhetorics of knowledge and expertise that both legitimize and symbolize a belief that change can be achieved, even if the goals, rationalities and outcomes of the process are often unpredictable. This predicament can engender a debilitating embrace of nominalism and a corresponding rejection of rationalism. This is the uncompromising message of radical constructionist discourses in which the subject is potentially subsumed in the contingencies of self-referential discourses of power/knowledge (Foucault, 2000). If these arguments are taken to their logical conclusion there is really no need for teleological explanations of actions and moral conduct: all action is not chosen, there is no need for a subject at all. But is this destruction of choice the end of agency directed towards rational goals or 'discursive ethics'? Certainly, agency and organizational change become precarious without a self-fulfilling belief that intention, knowledge and rational actions have efficacy in a world enveloped by complexity, uncertainty and risk, even if the goals and outcomes of our actions are unpredictable. Paradoxically, theories of change agency may be able to live with the challenges of decentred agency, but they cannot live without a belief in choice. Even Foucault (1986) never really gave up on the possibility of an ideal of autonomy founded on choice.

### *The paradoxes of practice*

Almost all forms of agency, whether centred or decentred, are modes of enactment in practice that mix intentionality and moral action, power and knowledge. This is why all apparently expert or rational interventions in human affairs are subject to ethical scrutiny and self-questioning, in their formulation, planned outcomes and unintended consequences. This also explains why the ideal of the 'change agent' as an 'unbiased' facilitator of planned change has always been an intellectual and moral illusion, an illusion that has rarely been confronted within the soft scientism of action research or the instrumentalism of managerial agency and consultancy practice (Schein, 1990; Schon, 1983). It is not simply claims to expertise that have given the change agent concept a degree of theoretical coherence, but also the evaluative positions it denotes. Implicitly, change management interventions are invariably linked to some assumptions or evaluations about the direction of change in organizations and society. These reflexive evaluations may be supported by the search for 'value-relevant' objective knowledge, but they are rarely inseparable from 'value judgements' in the everyday world of action and involvement (Weber, 1949). Without such judgements, the rational intent or moral purpose of knowledge and the role of agency in organizations is deeply problematic. Yet we can rarely have the complacent assurance that our actions are ethical rather than another face of power. Ultimately, it is only through practice that these ethical paradoxes are both partly resolved and recreated in new forms.

These four issues clearly create profound difficulties in defining the scope and role of agency in organizational change, both as a form of practical involvement and as an empirical research subject. Taken together, they threaten to achieve the empirical and theoretical equivalent of the constructionist loss of the 'subject', the prospect that both the disciplinary object and subject of organizational change theory and practice may fall apart. Confronted with these dilemmas and their implications, the hybrid and eclectic interdisciplinary legacy of organizational change theories and change agency practices must affirm the possibility of a positive middle way between competing and increasingly fragmented discourses and paradigms for managing change. For without this belief in the mediation of knowledge to inform fragile ideals of 'rational' dialogue, practice and moral action in the face of organizational complexity, risk and uncertainty, all our human aspirations for change may lose their vital centre of gravity: *the hope that we can make a difference.*

## References

Abbott, A. *Chaos of disciplines*. Chicago: University of Chicago Press, 2000.

Alvesson, M. & Karreman, D. Varieties of discourse: On the study of organizations through discourse. *Human Relations*, 2000, 53, 1125–49.

Anderson, P. Complexity theory and organizational science. *Organizational Science*, 1999, 10, 233–6.

Ansoff, H. The design school: Reconsidering the basic premises of strategic planning. *Strategic Management Journal*, 1991, 12, 449–61.

Archer, M. S. *Structure, agency and the internal conversation*. Cambridge: Cambridge University Press, 2003.

Argyris, C. *Reasoning, learning and action*. San Francisco: Jossey Bass, 1982.

Armenakis, A. & Bedeian, A. Organizational change: A review of theory and research in the 1990's. *Journal of Management*, 1999, 25, 293–315.

Baker, J. R. *The discipline of teamwork*. London: Sage, 1999.

Beck, U. *The brave new world of work*. Cambridge: Polity Press, 2000.

Beckhard, R. *Organizational development: Strategies and models*. Reading, MA: Addison-Wesley, 1969.

Bennis, W. *Organizational development*. Reading, MA: Addison-Wesley, 1969.

Bourdieu, P. *The logic of practice*. Cambridge: Polity Press, 1990.

Caldwell, R. *Agency and change: Rethinking change agency in organizations*. London: Routledge, forthcoming.

Castells, M. *The rise of the network society*, Vol. 1, 2nd edn. Oxford: Blackwell, 2000.

Cyert, R. M. & March, J. G. *A behavioural theory of the firm*. Englewood Cliffs, NJ: Prentice Hall, 1963.

Dawson, P. *Organizational change: A processual approach*. London: Chapman, 1994.

DiMaggio, P. J. & Powell, W. W. (Eds). *The new institutionalism in organizational analysis*. Chicago: University of Chicago Press, 1991.

Dumphy, D. & Stace, D. The strategic management of corporate change. *Human Relations*, 1993, 46, 905–18.

Easterby-Smith, M., Crossan, M. & Nicolini, D. Organizational learning: Debates past, present and future. *Journal of Management Studies*, 2000, 37, 783–96.

Finstad, N. The rhetoric of organizational change. *Human Relations*, 1998, 51, 717–40.

Flake, G. W. *The computational beauty of nature: Computer explorations of fractals, chaos, complex systems, and adaptation*. Cambridge, MA: MIT Press, 1998.

Foucault, M. *The care of the self*. New York: Pantheon, 1986.

Foucault, M. *Discipline and punish: The birth of the prison*. London: Penguin, 1991.

Foucault, M. The subject and power. In H. Dreyfus & P. Rabinow (Eds), *Michael Foucault: Beyond structuralism and hermeneutics*. Brighton: Harvester, 1992, pp. 208–26.

Foucault, M. *Essential writings of Foucault 1954–1984, Power*, Vol. 3. (J. D. Faubion, Ed.). New York: Free Press, 2000.

Gergin, K. J. *Social constructionism in context*. London: Sage, 2001.

Gergin, K. J. Action research and orders of democracy. *Action Research*, 2003, 1, 39–56.

Giddens, A. *The constitution of society*. Cambridge: Polity Press, 1984.

Gronn, P. Distributed leadership as a unit of analysis. *Leadership Quarterly*, 2002, 13, 423–51.

Habermas, J. *Knowledge and human interests*. Boston: Beacon Press, 1971.

Habermas, J. *The theory of communicative action*, Vol. 1. London: Heinemann, 1984.

Hacking, I. *The social construction of what?* Cambridge, MA: Harvard University Press, 1999.

Hassard, J. H. & Parker, M. (Ed.). *Postmodernism and organizations*. London: Sage, 1993.

Hayward, C. *De-facing power*. Cambridge: Cambridge University Press, 2000.

Hendry, C. Understanding and creating whole organizational change through learning theory. *Human Relations*, 1996, 48, 621–41.

Kauffman, S. A. *The origins of order*, New York: Oxford University Press, 1993.

Lewin, K. Frontiers in group dynamics. *Human Relations, 1947, 1*, 5–41.

Lewin, K. *Resolving social conflicts and field theory in social science* [Reissue of two previous anthologies]. New York: American Psychological Society Press, 1997.

Lewin, K. *The complete social scientist: A Kurt Lewin reader* (M. Gold, Ed.). New York: American Psychological Society Press, 1999.

Lindblom, C. E. The science of muddling through. *Public Administration Review*, 1959, 19, 79–88.

Linstead, S. (E.d.). *Organization theory and postmodern thought*. London: Sage, 2004.

Maguire, S. & McKelvey, B. (1999) Complexity and management: Moving from fad to firm foundations. *Emergence: Complexity and Organization, 1999, 1*, 5–49.

McKinlay, A. & Starkey, K. *Foucault, management and organization theory: From panopticon to technologies of self*. London: Sage, 1998.

McNay, L. *Gender and agency: Reconfiguring the subject in feminist social theory*. Cambridge: Polity Press, 2000.

Mintzberg, H. *The rise and fall of strategic planning*. London: Prentice Hall, 1994.

Newton, T. J. Theorizing subjectivity in organizations: The failure of Foucauldian studies. *Organization Studies, 1998, 19*, 415–47.

Nonaka, I. A dynamic theory of organizational knowledge creation. *Organizational Science, 1994, 5*, 14–37.

Osborn, R. N., Hunt, J. G. & Jauch, L. R. Toward a contextual theory of leadership. *Leadership Quarterly, 2002, 13*, 797–837.

Parker, I. (Ed.). *Social constructionism, discourse and realism*. London: Sage, 1998.

Parker, I. & Burman, E. (Eds). *Discourse analytic research*. London: Routledge, 1993.

Parsons, T. *The social system*. Glencoe, IL: Free Press, 1951.

Pettigrew, A. M. *The awakening giant: Continuity and change in ICI*. Oxford: Blackwell, 1985.

Pettigrew, A. M. Context and action in the transformation of the firm. *Journal of Management Studies, 1987, 24*, 649–70.

Pettigrew, A. M. What is processual analysis? *Scandinavian Journal of Management, 1997, 13*, 337–48.

Pettigrew, A. M. Innovative forms of organizing: Progress, performance and process. In A. Pettigrew, H. Thomas & R. Whittington (Eds), *Innovative forms of organizing*. London: Sage, 2003, pp. 331–51.

Pettigrew, A., Ferlie, E. & McKee, L. *Shaping strategic change*. London: Sage, 1992.

Quinn, J. B. *Strategies for change: Logical incrementalism*. Homewood, IL: Irwin, 1980.

Schein, E. H. *Process consultation, Volume 2. Lessons for managers and consultants*. Reading, MA: Addison Wesley, 1987.

Schein, E. H. *Process consultation, Volume 1. Its role in organizational development*, 2nd edn. Reading, MA: Addison Wesley, 1988.

Schein, E. H. Back to the future: Recapturing the OD vision. In F. Massarik (Ed.), *Advances in organizational development*, Volume 1. Norwood, NJ: Ablex, 1990.

Schon, D. *The reflective practitioner*. London: Temple Smith, 1983.

Senge, P. *The fifth dimension: The art and practice of the learning organization*. London: Century Business, 1990.

Senge, P. Learning for a change. *Fast Company, 1999, 24*(May), 178–85.

Simon, H. *Administrative behaviour*. New York: Macmillan, 1947.

Stacey, R. D. *Complex responsive processes in organizations: Learning and knowledge creation*. London: Routledge, 2001.

Tichy, N. Agents of planned change: Congruence of values, cognition's and actions. *Administrative Science Quarterly, 1974, 19*, 164–82.

Van de Ven, A. H. & Poole S. P. Explaining development and change in organizations. *Academy of Management Review*, 1995, 20, 510–40.

Weber, M. *The methodology of the social sciences*. New York: Free Press, 1949.

Weick, K. *Making sense of the organization*. Oxford: Blackwell, 2001.

Wenger, E. *Communities of practice: Learning, meaning and identity*. Cambridge: Cambridge University Press, 1998.

Wenger, E. Communities of practice and social learning systems. *Organization*, 2000, 7, 225–46.

Willard, C. A. *Expert knowledge: Liberalism and the problem of knowledge*. Chicago: University of Chicago Press, 1998.

Worley, C. G. & Feyerherm, A. E. Reflections on the future of organizational development. *Journal of Applied Behavioural Science*, 2003, 39, 97–115.

# INDEX